THE WESTERN CASE FOR MONOGAMY OVER POLYGAMY

For more than 2,500 years, the Western tradition has embraced monogamous marriage as an essential institution for the flourishing of men and women, parents and children, society and the state. At the same time, polygamy has been considered a serious crime that harms wives and children, correlates with sundry other crimes and abuses, and threatens good citizenship and political stability. The West has thus long punished all manner of plural marriages and denounced the polygamous teachings of selected Jews, Muslims, Anabaptists, Mormons, and others.

John Witte, Jr., carefully documents the Western case for monogamy over polygamy from antiquity until today. He analyzes the historical claims that polygamy is biblical, natural, and useful alongside modern claims that anti-polygamy laws violate personal and religious freedom. While giving the arguments pro and con a full hearing, Witte concludes that the Western historical case against polygamy remains compelling and urges Western nations to hold the line on monogamy.

John Witte, Jr., is Robert W. Woodruff University Professor, McDonald Distinguished Professor, and Director of the Center for the Study of Law and Religion at Emory University. A world authority in legal history, he has directed twelve major international projects on democracy, human rights, religious liberty, marriage, family, and children. He has lectured throughout the world and published twenty-seven books, including *Christianity and Human Rights: An Introduction* (Cambridge, 2010) and *The Sins of the Fathers: The Law and Theology of Illegitimacy Reconsidered* (Cambridge, 2009).

CAMBRIDGE STUDIES IN LAW AND CHRISTIANITY

Series Editor

John Witte, Jr., *Emory University*

Editorial Board

Nigel Biggar, *University of Oxford*
Marta Cartabia, *Italian Constitutional Court / University of Milano-Bicocca*
Sarah Coakley, *University of Cambridge*
Norman Doe, *Cardiff University*
Brian Ferme, *Marcianum, Venice*
Richard W. Garnett, *University of Notre Dame*
Robert P. George, *Princeton University*
Mary Ann Glendon, *Harvard University*
Kent Greenawalt, *Columbia University*
Robin Griffith-Jones, *the Temple, the Inns of Court*
R. H. Helmholz, *University of Chicago*
Mark Hill, *Q. C., Cardiff University / University of Pretoria*
Wolfgang Huber, Bishop Emeritus, *United Protestant Church of Germany /
Universities of Heidelberg, Berlin, and Stellenbosch*
Michael W. McConnell, *Stanford University*
John McGuckin, *Columbia University / Union Theological Seminary*
Mark A. Noll, *University of Notre Dame*
Jeremy Waldron, *New York University / University of Oxford*
Michael Welker, *University of Heidelberg*

The Cambridge Studies in Law and Christianity series publishes cutting-edge work on Catholic, Protestant, and Orthodox Christian contributions to public, private, penal, and procedural law and legal theory. The series aims to promote deep Christian reflection by leading scholars on the fundamentals of law and politics, to build further ecumenical legal understanding across Christian denominations, and to link and amplify the diverse and sometimes isolated Christian legal voices and visions at work in the academy. Works collected by the series include groundbreaking monographs, historical and thematic anthologies, and translations by leading scholars around the globe.

Volumes in the Series:

The Western Case for Monogamy Over Polygamy John Witte, Jr. (2015)
Pope Benedict XVI's Legal Thought Marta Cartabia and Andrea Simoncini (2015)
The Distinctiveness of Religion in American Law Kathleen A. Brady (2015)

The Western Case for Monogamy Over Polygamy

JOHN WITTE, JR.

Emory University

CAMBRIDGE
UNIVERSITY PRESS

CAMBRIDGE
UNIVERSITY PRESS

32 Avenue of the Americas, New York, NY 10013-2473, USA

Cambridge University Press is part of the University of Cambridge.

It furthers the University's mission by disseminating knowledge in the pursuit of education, learning, and research at the highest international levels of excellence.

www.cambridge.org
Information on this title: www.cambridge.org/9781107499171

First published 2015

Printed in the United States of America

A catalog record for this publication is available from the British Library.

Library of Congress Cataloging in Publication Data
Witte, John, 1959– author.
The western case for monogamy over polygamy / John Witte, Jr.
    pages   cm
ISBN 978-1-107-10159-3 (hardback) – ISBN 978-1-107-49917-1 (paperback)
1. Polygamy – Law and legislation.   2. Polygamy – Religious aspects.   I. Title.
K686.W58   2015
346.01′6–dc23   2014047363

ISBN 978-1-107-10159-3 Hardback
ISBN 978-1-107-49917-1 Paperback

For

Hope and Justin, Baylor and Alina

Contents

Illustrations

Preface

This book began as an expert opinion prepared for the attorney general of Canada. A group of Fundamentalist Mormons in the town of Bountiful, British Columbia, had challenged the constitutionality of Canada's traditional criminal prohibition on polygamy. The attorney general sought to uphold the law. Various religious liberty and human rights groups wanted it struck down. My task was to document the Western legal tradition's arguments in favor of monogamy and against polygamy, from classical and biblical times until today.

It was not an easy task, in part because I am a strong advocate of human rights and usually counsel the protection of religious freedom, even for religious communities that depart from the cultural mainstream. It was also not an easy task because the Western legal tradition has not been clear or consistent in its arguments against polygamy, despite making polygamy a serious crime since the third century. My task for the attorney general was to sketch some of these shifting teachings of the tradition and report on them. The challenge in writing this book was to fill in and filigree the historical picture only crudely sketched in my opinion. Much of this book takes up that task, filling an ample and surprising gap in the historical literature (at least in a Romance language). The further challenge was to determine whether the various traditional Western arguments for monogamy and against polygamy, once fully retrieved and reconstructed, are still cogent in our day. I believe they are, and the last part of this book presses that case, albeit more briefly as it is the historical arguments against polygamy, not the modern policy implications of this history, that are my main concern.

I have incurred a number of debts in preparing this volume. I wish to thank the crack legal team in the attorney general of Canada office in Vancouver – Craig Cameron, Keith Reimer, and B.J. Wray – for many stimulating conversations about this topic. I wish to thank Professors Thomas C. Arthur, Rafael Domingo, Judith Evans-Grubbs, David Heith-Stade, R.H. Helmholz, David G. Hunter, Thomas J. Kuehn, Sara McDougall, Michael J. Perry, Philip L. Reynolds, and

Mathias Schmoeckel for their expert counsel in guiding me to and through various specialized historical materials. I wish to thank Dr. James Billington, Librarian of Congress, and Dr. Carolyn Brown, Director of the John Kluge Center of the Library of Congress, who were kind enough to invite me to sit in the Cary and Ann Maguire Chair in Ethics and American History for a semester and finish the research on this project. I am grateful for the excellent research assistance of Zachary Eyster, Elliott Foote, Mark Goldfeder, Caleb Holzaepfel, Christopher Huslak, Brian Kaufman, Justin Latterell, Andy Mayo, Tobias C. Tatum, and Katie Elizabeth Beam Pimentel Toste – all fine students associated with the Center for the Study of Law and Religion at Emory University. I wish to thank Amy Wheeler and Anita Mann in the Center for their excellent administrative work on this and related projects. I wish to thank Elizabeth Christian and Kelly Parker Cobb in the Emory Law Library for their extraordinary efforts in finding many obscure sources and helping me negotiate the new virtual world of scholarly research. I remain deeply grateful for the generous support of my work provided by Dr. Craig Dykstra and his colleagues at the Lilly Endowment, Inc., and by Ambassador Alonzo L. McDonald and his colleagues in the McDonald Agape Foundation. And heartfelt thanks to my wife, Eliza, for enduring many dinner conversations about this book in the making and providing her keen editorial insights.

This book is dedicated to our daughter Hope and her husband Justin and to their children Baylor and Alina. Their (monogamous!) marriage and family life have added great joy to our lives, as Eliza and I have taken on the new privilege and pleasure of being grandparents.

Introduction

FIGURE 1. "Marriage Certificate," from the American School (nineteenth century). Used by permission of Library Company of Philadelphia, PA, USA / Bridgeman Images.

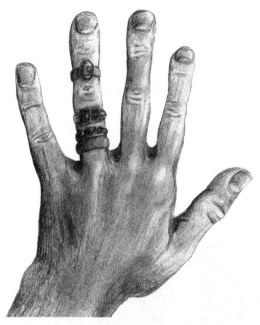

FIGURE 2. "Polygamy," by Amy Spencer.
Used by permission of the artist.

What is the Western tradition's case for monogamy over polygamy, and is that case still convincing in a post-modern and globalizing world? Are there sufficiently compelling reasons to relax Western laws against polygamy, and is this a desirable policy given the global trends away from polygamy and given the social, economic, and psychological conditions that often attend its practice? Or, are there sufficiently compelling reasons, reconstructed in part from the tradition, to maintain and even strengthen these anti-polygamy measures, in part as an effort to hasten the global demise of this practice? This book lays out the historical sources that should help inform the debates about these hard questions.

Questions about polygamy are likely to dominate Western family law in the next generation. Two generations ago, contraception, abortion, and women's rights were the hot topics of Western family law and the culture wars. This past generation, it has been children's rights and same-sex rights that have dominated public deliberation and litigation. On the frontier of modern Western family law are hard questions about extending the forms of valid marriage to include polygamy, and extending the forums of marital governance to include religious and cultural legal systems that countenance polygamy. This book aims to put those looming questions in larger and longer context.

THE AMERICAN CONTEXT

A century and a half ago, Mormons made international headlines by claiming the religious right to practice polygamy, despite federal criminal laws against it.[1] In four main cases from 1879 to 1890, the United States Supreme Court firmly rejected their claims, and threatened to dissolve the Mormon Church if they persisted. Part of the Court's argument was historical: the common law has always defined marriage as monogamous, and to change those rules "would be a return to barbarism." Part of the argument was prudential: religious liberty can never become a license to violate general criminal laws lest chaos ensue. And part of the argument was sociological: monogamous marriage "is the cornerstone of civilization," and it cannot be moved without upending our whole Western culture.[2] Contemporaneous European courts and legislatures were equally dismissive of Mormon and other polygamists' claims.[3] These old cases remain the law of the West. Most Mormons renounced polygamy in 1890, and in 1906, Mormon Church leaders made polygamy a ground for excommunication from their church.[4]

The question of religious polygamy is back in the headlines, now involving a Fundamentalist Mormon group that has retained the church's traditional polygamist practices. The Fundamentalist Latter Day Saints (FLDS) are a Mormon splinter group, created in 1890, and operating continuously in various subgroups since then. Their early founders rejected the mainline Mormon Church's departure from its traditional polygamous teachings and practices. The FLDS regarded polygamy as a central religious practice, critical to their own salvation. Seeking to escape social stigma and criminal prosecution, the church members withdrew into small, isolated, and often religiously controlled communities scattered throughout the thinly populated American west, as well as in western Canada and Mexico. The largest

[1] On early Mormon polygamy, see George D. Smith, *Nauvoo Polygamy* (Salt Lake City, UT: Signature Books, 2011); Brian G. Hales, *Joseph Smith's Polygamy*, 3 vols. (Salt Lake City, UT: Greg Kofford Books, 2013).

[2] *Reynolds v. United States*, 98 U.S. 145 (1879); *Murphy v. Ramsey*, 114 U.S. 15, 45 (1885); *Davis v. Beason*, 133 U.S. 333 (1890); *Church of Jesus Christ of Latter Day Saints v. United States* together with *Romney v. United States*, 136 U.S. 1 (1890). For context and case analysis, see Sarah Barringer Gordon, *The Mormon Question: Polygamy and Constitutional Conflict in Nineteenth Century America* (Chapel Hill: University of North Carolina Press, 2002).

[3] For England, see, e.g., *Hyde v. Hyde* (1866) L.R. 1 P & D. 130; *In re Bethel* (1887), 38 Ch.D. 220. For Scotland, see F.P. Walton, *Scot Marriages: Regular and Irregular* (Edinburgh: W. Green & Sons, 1893); *Polygamous Marriages: Capacity to Contract a Polygamous Marriage and the Concept of the Potentially Polygamous Marriage* (London: Her Majesty's Stationery Office, 1982). For Ireland, see 10 Geo. 4, c. 31, s. 26. For the Continent, see discussions later in this chapter.

[4] See R.S. van Wagoner, *Mormon Polygamy: A History*, 2nd ed. (Salt Lake City, UT: Signature Books, 1989), 168; Irwin Altman and Joseph Ginat, *Polygamous Families in Contemporary Society* (Cambridge: Cambridge University Press, 1996), 37–38.

such community today, under the leadership of Warren Jeffs, has 8,000 to 10,000 members. Total FLDS membership in America today is roughly 60,000, although exact numbers are elusive.[5] These FLDS communities are now coming into the public eye. *The New York Times Magazine* had a major exposé on them in 1999.[6] *National Geographic* carried a cover story and national television feature on them in 2010.[7] Popular television shows like *Sister Wives* and *Big Love*, popular magazines like *People* and *Time*, and a spate of tell-all biographies and television appearances are making the polygamous lifestyle look mainstream, even edgy and glamorous.[8]

But for all this new experimentation, the legal reality is that polygamy is still a crime in every state in the United States, and those who practice it risk criminal punishment.[9] This is precisely what happened on April 3, 2008, when state authorities raided an FLDS community in Eldorado, Texas, called the Yearning for Zion Ranch. The authorities were acting on preliminary evidence that under-aged girls were being forced into sex and spiritual marriages with men two or three times their age. They eventually removed some 129 mothers and 439 children from the ranch, and put them into state protective custody. They found twelve girls, aged 12 to 15, who had been forced into marriages, seven of them already with child. They found 262 other children – in 91 of the 146 families on the Ranch – who were themselves victims of child abuse, statutory rape, or neglect, or had witnessed or been exposed to the sexual abuse, assault, or rape of another child within their

[5] See Cardell K. Jacobson and Lara Burton, eds., *Modern Polygamy in the United States: Historical, Cultural, and Legal Issues* (Oxford/New York: Oxford University Press, 2011), esp. xvi (map of FLDS communities), 163–184. See also *Polygamy in Canada: Legal and Social Implications for Women and Children – A Collection of Policy Research Reports* (Ottawa: Status of Women Canada, 2005); Martha Bailey and Amy J. Kaufman, *Polygamy in the Monogamous World: Multicultural Challenges for Western Law and Policy* (Santa Barbara, CA: Praeger, 2010), esp. 69–132; Janet Bennion, *Polygamy in Primetime: Media, Gender, and Politics in Modern Fundamentalism* (Waltham, MA: Brandeis University Press, 2012).

[6] Timothy Egan, "The Persistence of Polygamy," *New York Times Magazine* (February 28, 1999): 51.

[7] "The Polygamists," *National Geographic Magazine* (February, 2010), with a show on the National Geographic Channel (February 10, 2010).

[8] Alex Tresniowski, "This is Home," *People Magazine* (March 23, 2009); Belinda Luscombe, "I Do, I Do, I Do, I Do: Polygamy Raises Its Profile in America", TIME: HEALTH & FAMILY July 26, 2012, http://healthland.time.com/2012/07/26/i-do-i-do-i-do-i-do-polygamy-raises-its-profile-in-america. See, additionally, Bennion, *Polygamy in Primetime*; Bailey and Kaufman, *Polygamy*, 69–70.

[9] See, e.g., *State v. Green*, 99 P.3d 820 (UT S. Ct., 2004); *Utah v. Holm*, 137 P. 2d. 726 (UT S. Ct., 2006); *Arizona v. Fischer*, 199 P.3d. 663 (AZ Ct. App., 2008). But see *Brown v. Herbert*, 2012 Bloomberg Law 27041 (D. Utah, February 3, 2012), where the federal district court held that Kody Brown and his sister wives faced a credible threat of prosecution for bigamy from Utah authorities, and thus had standing to press a federal constitutional case against the county attorney for chilling their First Amendment free speech rights in airing their show, and advocating their polygamous lifestyle. See also *Brown v. Buhman* (D.C. Utah, December 13, 2013) (granting summary judgment for the Browns that Utah's prohibition on polygamy is unconstitutional).

household.[10] Eleven men were eventually charged with polygamy, sexual assault, and child abuse. All eleven have been convicted – with punishments ranging from seven to seventy-five years. Warren Jeffs, the prophet of this FLDS community, was also convicted and sentenced to life imprisonment plus twenty years for forcing two under-aged girls into spiritual marriages with others, and for forcing a 15-year-old girl to join his harem and bear his child.[11] He faces additional accomplice bigamy charges both in Utah and Texas for presiding over other spiritual marriages of minors in other FLDS communities.[12]

Many of the legal questions raised by the Texas ranch case are easy. Coerced marriages, statutory rape, sexual assault, and other abuses of children are all serious crimes. The adults on the ranch who committed these crimes, or were complicit in them, are criminals. They have no claim of religious freedom that will excuse them, and no claim of privacy that will protect them from prosecution. Dealing with the children, ensuring proper procedures, and sorting out the evidence are all practically messy and emotionally trying questions, but they are not legally difficult. The order of the Texas courts to return most of the children who had been seized from their homes during the raid underscores an additional elementary legal principle – that decisions about child custody and about criminal liability must be done on an individual basis as much as possible.[13]

The harder legal question is whether criminalizing polygamy is still constitutional. Texas criminal law makes marriage to two or more persons at once a felony – a first degree felony if one of the parties is younger than 16 years of age.[14] Every other American state has comparable criminal prohibitions on the books against

[10] See *Eldorado Investigation: A Report from the Texas Department of the Family and Protection Services* (December 22, 2008), at http://www.dfps.state.tx.us/documents/about/pdf/2008-12-22_Eldorado.pdf (June 29, 2012). For an earlier study of marriage demographics in FLDS communities, see Altman and Ginat, *Polygamous Families*, 460–478.

[11] *Jeffs v. State*, 2012 WL 1068797 (Texas App, March 29, 2012) No. 03–11–00568–CR, at *1.

[12] Linda F. Smith, "Child Protection Law and the FLDS Raid in Texas," in Jacobsen and Burton, eds., *Modern Polygamy*, 301–330; Bailey and Kaufman, *Polygamy*, 116–120. In a separate case in Utah, Jeffs was convicted as an accessory to two counts of statutory rape for presiding over a compelled spiritual marriage of a 14-year-old girl to her cousin in another FLDS community. The case was reversed, however, and remanded for a new trial because of erroneous jury instructions. See *State v. Jeffs*, 243 P. 3d 1250 (Utah, 2010). See also Stephen Singular, *When Men Became Gods: Mormon Polygamist Warren Jeffs, His Cult of Fear, and the Women Who Fought Back* (New York: St. Martin's Press, 2013).

[13] In re Steed, 2008 WL 2132014 (Tex. Court of Appeals, 2008), affirmed in In re Texas Department of Family and Protective Services, 255 S.W. 3d 613 (Sup. Ct. Texas 2008).

[14] Texas Penal Code 25.01 (Bigamy). Texas – and other states like Utah and Colorado with FLDS polygamists – extends the definition of bigamy to include parties who cohabit with, purport to marry, or maintain the appearance of being married to a second spouse, while still married to a first. Ibid. This provision was designed to preclude bigamists like Tom Green, who divorced each of his wives before marrying the next one, yet kept all of them in his harem. Utah sent him to prison. See *State v. Green*, 99 P.3d 820 (UT S. Ct., 2004) and discussion in Joanna Grossman and Lawrence M.

polygamy or bigamy.[15] These criminal prohibitions have been in place in America since its earliest colonial days and have been part of Western criminal law since the third century; polygamy was, in fact, a capital crime in the West from the ninth to the nineteenth centuries. Can these 1,750-year-old criminal laws against polygamy withstand a challenge that they violate an individual's constitutional rights to privacy and sexual liberty, to marriage and domestic autonomy, and to equal protection and non-discrimination – in addition to the rights to religious liberty?[16]

In the nineteenth century, when the first Mormon cases reached the federal courts on religious liberty grounds alone, none of these additional constitutional rights claims was yet available to pro-polygamy litigants. Now they are, and the Supreme Court has used them to uphold every adult citizen's rights to consensual sex, cohabitation, marriage, divorce, contraception, abortion, sodomy, and same-sex relations, if not marriage.[17] Do Texas and other states have strong enough reasons to uphold their traditional criminal prohibitions of polygamy against such constitutional claims, especially if made by a party with deep religious convictions? May a religious polygamist at least get a religious liberty exemption from compliance with these laws? That would make polygamy a tolerated practice for these religious parties – a "de facto" form of marriage, as lawyers call it. The state would not prosecute them for polygamy. But the state would also not enforce their polygamous marriage contracts, provide them with family services or protections, or accord the spouses any of the thousands of rights and privileges available to state-recognized families. No state burdens, no state benefits: polygamous families and their religious communities under this arrangement would become "a law unto themselves."

That raises a still harder legal question – whether a state legislature could or should go further, by not only decriminalizing polygamy, but legalizing it as a valid marriage option for its citizens. In one sense, this move from toleration to recognition, from "de facto" to "de jure" polygamy, seems like a small step. After all, American states today, viewed together, already offer several models of state-sanctioned domestic life for their citizens: straight and same-sex marriage, contract and covenant marriage, civil union and domestic partnership.[18] Each of these off-the-rack models of domestic life has built-in rights and duties that the parties have to each other and to their children

Friedman, *Inside the Castle: Law and the Family in 20th Century America* (Princeton, NJ: Princeton University Press, 2011), 28–32.

[15] See discussion on terminology later in this chapter, pp. 27–33.

[16] A qualified "no" is the answer of a federal district court in *Brown v. Buhman* (D.C. Utah, December 13, 2013).

[17] See esp. *Griswold v. Connecticut*, 381 U.S. 479 (1965); *Roe v. Wade*, 410 U.S. 113 (1973); *Eisenstadt v. Baird*, 405 U.S. 438 (1972); *Carey v. Population Services International*, 431 U.S. 678 (1977); *Planned Parenthood v. Casey*, 505 U.S. 833 (1992); *Roemer v. Evans*, 517 U.S. 620 (1996); *Lawrence v. Texas*, 539 U.S. 558 (2003); *U.S. v. Windsor*, 570 U.S. __ (2013); *Hollingsworth v. Perry*, 570 U.S. _ (2013).

[18] See Joel A. Nichols, ed., *Marriage and Divorce in a Multicultural Context: Multi-Tiered Marriage and the Boundaries of Civil Law and Religion* (Cambridge/New York: Cambridge University Press, 2012).

and other dependents. And the parties can further tailor these built-in rights and duties through private prenuptial contracts.[19] With so much marital pluralism and private ordering already available, why not add a further option – that of polygamous marriage? Why not give to polygamous families the same rights and duties, privileges and protections that are afforded to other domestic unions recognized by state law? Would that not be better than consigning polygamists to a shadow marriage world controlled by religious authorities, who have none of the due process constraints that the constitution imposes on governmental authorities?

Once we contemplate decriminalizing, or even legalizing polygamous marriage, that raises a still harder question – whether polygamy should be reserved to religious parties alone. If we leave religious liberty claims aside, are the other constitutional claims of privacy, autonomy, equality, and the like strong enough on their own to grant any consenting adult the right to enter a polygamous marriage, regardless of religious conviction? Indeed, won't a policy of restricting polygamy to religious parties alone inevitably trigger a claim of discrimination by the nonreligious? Why should religious polygamists alone get special treatment? After all, the argument goes, what is at issue are the fundamental rights to marriage and its attendant constitutional protections and statutory benefits. Should these rights and benefits not be available to all citizens regardless of their religious status?

These questions are not unique to the FLDS Church. In the United States, various Muslim, Vietnamese Hmong, and Native Americans, as well as various émigrés from Africa, Asia, and the Middle East have been quietly practicing polygamy under the supervision of religious and cultural leaders, and in defiance of state criminal laws.[20] Various "poly communities" have also emerged in America – from sundry free love polyamorists and "pantagamists" on the left[21] to conservative Muslims in the inner cities who see polygamous households as the only way to deal with the massive numbers of single mothers and non-marital children in their communities who need male support.[22] It is only a matter of time before these groups press for state recognition of their plural marriages, especially if they are targeted for

---

[19] See Brian Bix, "Private Ordering and Family Law," *Journal of the American Academy of Matrimonial Lawyers* 23 (2010): 249–285.

[20] See, e.g., Nina Bernstein, "In Secret: Polygamy Follows Africans to New York," *New York Times* (March 23, 2007); Ann Lacquer Estin, "Unofficial Family Law," in Nichols, ed., *Marriage and Divorce*, 92–119; Katharine Charlsley and Anika Liversage, "Transforming Polygamy: Migration, Transnationalism and Multiple Marriages Among Muslim Minorities," *Global Networks* 13 (2013): 60–78; Miriam Koktvedgaard Zeiten, *Polygamy: A Cross-Cultural Analysis* (Oxford/New York: Berg, 2008), 165–184.

[21] See examples of their literature at http://groups.yahoo.com/neo/groups/PolyResearchers/info. See also Philip L. Kilbrie and Douglas R. Page, *Plural Marriage for Our Times: A Reinvented Option?* 2nd ed. (Santa Barbara, CA: Praeger, 2012), esp. 77–88; Mark Goldfeder, "Chains of Love in Law: Revisiting Plural Marriage" (SJD Thesis, Emory, 2013), Pt. I, ch. 3; Maureen I. Strassberg, "The Challenges of Post-Modern Polygamy: Considering Polyamory," *Capital Law Review* 31 (2003): 439.

[22] See, e.g., Barbara Bradley Hagerty, "Philly's Black Muslims Increasingly Turn to Polygamy, NPR (March 28, 2008), http://www.npr.org/templates/story/story.php?storyId=90886407; Patricia Dixon-Spears, *We*

prosecution – and there are plenty of academics who are now pushing their case in the literature.[23] It is also only a matter of time before litigants press for reform of America's immigration ban on polygamists in place since 1875 that bars polygamists from naturalization, and even entry into the country.[24]

Even if these anti-polygamy laws are not openly challenged on federal or state constitutional grounds, they may well slowly become dead letters on the books. The status of being in a polygamous marriage itself, while formally prohibited by criminal law in every state, now rarely moves law enforcement authorities to action. Most state prosecutors today will move on polygamous individuals or groups only if they engage in other criminal activities, like coerced marriages or sex involving children, or if they seek to engage in social welfare, social security, or tax fraud to support their multiple wives and children. Indeed, the state attorney general in Utah recently issued a formal declaration, condoned by the governor, that his office would not prosecute even brazen public polygamy per se.[25] This declaration comes despite the fact that Utah has one of the few American state constitutions to prohibit polygamy, a vestige of its early experiments with Mormon polygamy.[26] Utah today, like other American states, treats polygamy mostly as an aggravant to other crimes. It is a point of leverage for prosecutors to pursue attendant sexual or social welfare crimes, and it gives judges power to impose heavier punishments on the duly convicted.

THE BROADER WESTERN AND GLOBAL CONTEXT

Most of America's common law cousins[27] have comparable criminal prohibitions against polygamy and face comparable pressure to remove these prohibitions or at

Want for Our Sisters What We Want for Ourselves: African-American Women Who Practice Polygyny by Consent (Baltimore, MD: Imprint Editions, 2009).
[23] See Concluding Reflections, pp. 442–447.
[24] See Kerry Abrams, "Polygamy, Prostitution, and the Federalization of Immigration Law," *Columbia Law Review* 105 (2005): 641–716; Claire A. Smearman, "Second Wives' Club: Mapping the Impact of Polygamy in U.S. Immigration Law," *Berkeley Journal of International Law* 27 (2009): 382–447.
[25] See Jennifer Weissman, "Killing Anti-Bigamy Laws Softly: Not to Prosecute Polygamy Must be Abandoned" (forthcoming). This policy was already being discussed in 1998. See James Brooke, "Utah Struggles with a Revival of Polgamy," *New York Times* (August 23, 1998): sec. 1, at 12.
[26] Utah Const. Art. III, sec. 1; see also Ariz. Const. Art. XX, par. 2; Idaho Const. Art. I, sec. 44; N.M. Const. Art XXI, sec. 1; Okla. Const. Art I., sec. 2.
[27] South Africa, which blends common law with Roman-Dutch law, recognizes "customary African polygamy" but not Muslim polygamy. See Recognition of Customary Marriages Act 120 (1998), and discussion of the act and case law in Johan D. Van der Vyver, "Multi-Tiered Marriages in South Africa," in Nichols, ed., *Marriage and Divorce*, 200–219, at 203–207; Tracy E. Higgins, Jeanmarie Fenrich, and Ziona Tanzer, "Gender Equality and Customary Marriage: Bargaining in the Shadows of Post-Apartheid Legal Pluralism," *Fordham International Law Review* (2007): 1653–1708, 1684ff. Likewise, India, which draws in part on the common law, recognizes Muslim polygamous marriages.

least grant exemptions from them for religious and cultural minorities.[28] In Canada, for example, an FLDS group in Bountiful, British Columbia, supported by a wide spectrum of pro-polygamy supporters, pressed for the repeal of Canada's traditional criminal law against polygamy on grounds of liberty, privacy, autonomy, equality, nondiscrimination, self-determination, freedom of religion, freedom of association, and other rights set out in Canada's Charter of Rights and Freedoms, and in various international human rights instruments to which Canada is a signatory. In a closely watched 2012 case, the British Columbia Supreme Court came down resolutely in support of Canada's traditional criminal law against polygamy.[29] Drawing on empirical, historical, and comparative arguments and data, the court held that legalizing polygamy would visit inevitable and disproportionate harms on women, children, and society and that granting religious exemptions to practice polygamy privately would give untoward power to religious authorities who are not bound by due process or other rule of law constraints in the treatment of their members.[30] The constitutionality of polygamy will likely come before the Supreme Court of Canada in due course. The outcome before this high court, famous for its avant-garde opinions, is by no means clear.[31]

See detailed discussions in Tahir Mahmood, *Statute-Law Relating to Muslims in India* (New Delhi: Institute of Objective Studies, 1995); Werner Menski, *Modern Indian Family Law* (Richmond, Surrey: Curzon Press, 2001).

[28] Bailey and Kaufman, *Polygamy*, 69–132.

[29] *Criminal Code*, R.S.C. 1985, c. C-46 s. 293: "Everyone who (a) practises or enters into or in any manner agrees or consents to practise or enter into (i) any form of polygamy, or (ii) any kind of conjugal union with more than one person at the same time, whether or not it is by law recognized as a binding form of marriage, or (b) celebrates, assists or is a party to a rite, ceremony, contract or consent that purports to sanction a relationship mentioned in subparagraph (a)(i) or (ii), is guilty of an indictable offence and liable to imprisonment for a term not exceeding five years." This law builds on *An Act Respecting Offences Relating to the Law of Marriage*, R.S.C. 1886, c. 161, as amended by *An Act further to amend the Criminal Law*, S.C. 1890, c. 37, s. 11, as well as *Criminal Code*, S.C. 1953–54, c. 51, s. 243. See analysis of the statutory history and context in Martha Bailey, "Polygamy and Unmarried Cohabitation," in Bill Atkin, ed., *The International Survey of Family Law, 2011 Edition* (Bristol: Jordan Publishing, 2011), 123–146.

[30] Reference re: Section 293 of the *Criminal Code of Canada*, 2011 BCSC 1588. See careful case analysis in Thomas H.W. Buck, "From Big Love to the Big House: Justifying Anti-Polygamy Laws in an Age of Expanding Rights," *Emory International Law Review* 26 (2012): 939–996; and more critical readings in Lori G. Beaman and Gillian Calder, eds., *Polygamy's Rights and Wrongs; Perspectives on Harm, Family, and Law* (Vancouver: University of British Columbia Press, 2013); Angela Campbell, "Bountiful Voices," *Osgoode Hall Law Journal* 47 (2009): 183–234; id., "Bountiful's Plural Marriages," *International Journal of Law in Context* 6 (2010): 343–361.

[31] For contrary arguments, see, e.g., Nicholas Bala, "Why Canada's Prohibition of Polygamy is Constitutionally Valid and Sound Policy," *Canadian Journal of Family Law* 25 (2009): 165–221; Angela Campbell, *Sister Wives, Surrogates, and Sex Workers: Outlaws by Choice?* (Farnham, Surrey: Ashgate, 2013). For additional historical context, see Sara Carter, *The Importance of Being Monogamous; Marriage and Nation Building in Western Canada to 1915* (Edmonton: University of Alberta Press, 2008).

A decade before the British Columbia case, the Canadian provinces of Ontario and Quebec faced a strong push by Muslims and other groups to establish Shari'a arbitration tribunals for governance of Muslim marriages, as a part and product of Canada's firm commitment to multiculturalism. That proposal was thoroughly debated, but ultimately defeated.[32] But the stated concern was not so much about the legalization of polygamy as about giving religious authorities and religious laws a role in the governance of the family lives of Canadian citizens. Since then, Canadian multicultural theorists have pushed hard to develop nonreligious arguments in favor of a "multi-conjugal" society that would include state-recognized polygamy and other forms of polyamory subject to private ordering norms.[33]

Australia and New Zealand likewise face challenges from various Aboriginal groups as well as Asian, African, and Middle Eastern immigrants who have been pressing for the right to practice polygamy under the governance of their own religious customs and courts.[34] Both countries have had firm criminal prohibitions against polygamy since colonial days, and these laws have been confirmed in recent criminal law and family law statutes and cases.[35] Neither country recognizes Aboriginal polygamous unions as valid marriages,[36] nor do they accept second marriages that were contracted abroad, although they grant some social welfare benefits to known polygamists. In Australia, the human rights case for polygamy is harder to press because the country lacks a national bill of rights,[37] and the international human rights norms to which Australia is a signatory have not been interpreted to support a right to practice polygamy.

[32] Marion Boyd, Office of Canadian Attorney General, *Dispute Resolution in Family Law, Protecting Choice, Promoting Inclusion* (2004), http://www.attorneygeneral.jus.gov.on.ca/english/about/pubs/body/fullreport.pdf. See different perspectives in Jean-François Gaudreault-Desbiens, "Religious Courts, Personal Federalism, and Legal Transplants," in Rex Ahdar and Nicholas Aroney, eds., *Sharia in the West* (Oxford: Oxford University Press, 2010), 59–70, and Ayelet Schachar, "Faith in Law? Diffusing Tensions Between Diversity and Equality," in Nichols, ed., *Marriage and Divorce*, 357–378.

[33] See various perspectives in Daniel Cere, "Canada's Conjugal Mosaic: From Multiculturalism to Multi-Conjugalism?" in Nichols, ed., *Marriage and Divorce*, 284–308; Mohammed H. Fadel, "Political Liberalism, Islamic Family Law, and Family Law Pluralism," in ibid., 164–199; see also earlier analysis in Lisa M. Kelly, "Bringing International Human Rights Law Home: An Evaluation of Canada's Family Law Treatment of Polygamy," *University of Toronto Faculty of Law Review* 65 (2007): 1–38.

[34] See, e.g., Law Reform Commission (Australia), *Multiculturalism and the Law*, Report No. 57, 1.15–18 (2002); id., *The Recognition of Aboriginal Customary Laws*, Report No. 31, 95–124 (1986); Abdullah Saaed, "Reflections on the Establishment of Shari'a Courts in Australia," in Rex Ahdar and Nicholas Aroney, eds., *Sharia in the West* (Oxford: Oxford University Press, 2010), 223–239; Ann Black, "In the Shadow of our Legal System," in ibid., 239–254.

[35] See New Zealand Crimes Act 1961, sec. 205–206 with discussion in *R v. Clinton*, CA177/99 (June 29, 1999); Australia Marriage Act 1961, sec. 94 with discussion in *Dohm v. Acton FamCA* 482 (2008); *Wold v. Kleppir FamCA* 178 (2009).

[36] For New Zealand, see *Rangai Kerehoma v. Public Trustee* [1918], CLR 483 (SC).

[37] See Paul Babie and Neville Rochow, eds., *Freedom of Religion Under Bills of Rights* (Adelaide: University of Adelaide Press, 2012).

These Canadian, Australian, and New Zealand criminal prohibitions on polygamy were all modeled in part on traditional English criminal laws against polygamy that go back to Anglo-Saxon days and remain in place in the 1861 Offenses Against the Person Act and its ample modern statutory echoes.[38] These English laws on polygamy also continue to influence the laws of many of the fifty-three sovereign nations that are part of the British Commonwealth today and share a common law heritage. Although England rarely prosecutes polygamists today,[39] it does not recognize polygamous marriages; only the first marriage counts as valid.[40] A 2004 English statute empowers immigration officers to arrest without warrant any person seeking to enter the United Kingdom who is suspected of bigamy or polygamy.[41] Polygamy remains an issue especially in contested inheritance and marital property cases, where the first wife and her children almost always get priority.[42] Nonetheless, England, like some other common law countries, does sometimes provide public assistance and social welfare benefits to the wives, children, and dependents of polygamous families.[43] While England's 1998 Human Rights Act provides protection for the fundamental rights to marriage and association, to privacy and family life, and to thought, conscience, and belief, so far these provisions have not been used successfully to challenge England's traditional prohibitions on polygamy.[44] Comparable laws and restrictions are in place in Scotland, Wales, Ireland,[45] and Northern Ireland,[46] although some courts and commentators are pressing for the relaxation if not rejection of traditional criminal laws against polygamy.[47]

[38] UK Stat. 1861, c. 100, s. 57; UK Stat. 1972, c. 38, s.2–3; U.K. Stat. 1995, c. 42, Pt. 2, ss. 5, 7. See also Chapter 7 in this book.
[39] For earlier prosecutions for polygamy under the 1861 statute (more than 1,500 in the Old Bailey alone before 1913), see sources in Chapter 7, pp. 305–320.
[40] For a recent polygamy conviction, see *Regina v. Trigger Alan Mike Seed Philip Stark*, [2007] EWCA 254.
[41] UK ST 2004 c. 19, s. 14.
[42] See, e.g., *Whiston v. Whiston*, 1 All E.R. 423, 431 [1995]; *Rampal v. Rampal* [2001] EWCA Civ 989.
[43] See, e.g., *Imam Din v. National Assistance Board*, [1967] 2 QB 213 (granting a polygamist assistance) and *Fuljan Bibi v. Chief Adjudication Officer*, [1997] EWCA Civ. 1967 (denying the same). See additional sources in Bailey and Kaufman, *Polygamy*, 150–158, 181–183.
[44] 1998 Human Rights Act, sec. 42, sch. 1, arts. 8–9, 11–12.
[45] The Polygamous Marriages Order 1995 No. 3211 (NI. 20).
[46] See, e.g., Northern Ireland Law Reform Advisory Committee, Discussion Paper No. 6: Marriage Law (2000), [2000] NILRAC 6; The Law Commission Working Paper No. 83, and the Scottish Law Commission Consultative Memorandum 56, "Polygamous Marriages: Capacity to Contract a Polygamous Marriage and the Concept of the Potentially Polygamous Marriage (London: Her Majesty's Stationery Office, 1982); Draft Criminal Code for Scotland [2003], SLC (CP) 2.
[47] Russell Sandberg et al., "Britain's Religious Tribunals: 'Joint Governance' in Practice," *Oxford Journal of Legal Studies* 33 (2013): 263–291; Robin Griffith-Jones, ed., *Islam and English Law: Rights, Responsibilities and The Place of Shari'a* (Cambridge: Cambridge University Press, 2013).

Anglican Archbishop Rowan Williams set off a firestorm on February 7, 2008 by suggesting that some "accommodation" of Muslim family law was "unavoidable" in the United Kingdom. His speech was nuanced and qualified, carefully discussing the "growing challenge" of "communities which, while no less 'law-abiding' than the rest of the population, relate to something other than the British legal system alone." But he was strongly denounced for his open queries about "what degree of accommodation the law of the land can and should give to minority communities with their own strongly entrenched legal and moral codes."[48] England, the Archbishop's critics charged, will be beset by "licensed polygamy," barbaric punishments, and brutal violence against women encased in suffocating burkas if official sanction is given to Shari'a courts and Muslim family law.[49] None of this has come to pass in the United Kingdom. Anti-polygamy laws remain firmly in place, and Muslim mediators and arbitrators are forbidden from knowingly presiding over polygamous unions for fear of losing their licenses or being charged as accomplices to the crime of polygamy.[50]

Like Western common law countries, Western civil law countries forbid polygamy.[51] Every Latin and Central American country has criminal prohibitions of polygamy on the books, which are sometimes also echoed in their family laws.[52] Statutory punishments for convicted polygamists range from fines or three months in prison (Cuba)[53] to seven years of prison (Belize[54] and Guyana[55]) or hard labor (Haiti[56] and

---

[48] Dr. Rowan Williams, "Archbishop's Lecture – Civil and Religious Law in England: A Religious Perspective," (February 7, 2008), available at http://www.archbishopofcanterbury.org/1575# and reproduced with excellent commentaries in Griffith-Jones, ed., *Islam and English Law*. See also Dominic McGoldrick, "Accommodating Muslims in Europe: From Adopting Sharia Law to Religiously Based Opt Outs from Generally Applicable Laws," *Human Rights Law Review* 9 (2009): 603–645.

[49] See, e.g., Catherine Bennett, "It's one Sharia Law for Men and Quite Another for Women," *The Observer (The Guardian (U.K.))*, February 10, 2008, available at http://www.guardian.co.uk/commentisfree/2008/feb/10/religion.law.

[50] See, e.g., *O'B. v. R.* [1999] IEHC 186.

[51] See, e.g., José Aguilar Saldaña, *El delito de bigamia y su responsabilidad penal* (Mexico City: n.p., 1955); Elvira Coralia Esparza Torres, *El delito de bigamia* (Mexico, 1961); Paulino Campbell Carvallo, *El delito de bigamia ante la jurisprudencia de los tribunales chilenos* (Santiago, 1948); Alberto Arteaga Sánchez, *De los delitos contra las buenas costumbres y buen orden de la familias* (Caracas: Editorial Juridica Alva, 1989), 167–190; Claudia Ramirez Pizarro, *Implicaciones civiles de la bigamia* (Bogota: Pontificia Universidad Javeriana, 1990), 172–184; José Iureta Goyena, *Delitos de aborto, bigamia y abandon de niños y de ostras personas incapaces* (Montevideo: Casa A. Barreiro y Ramos, 1932), 95–153. I am grateful to Elliott Foote for helping me with these Spanish and Portuguese sources and statutes.

[52] Columbia punishes polygamy as a form of perjury or "falsifying public documents" with punishments ranging from four to nine years in prison. Penal Code, bk. 1, title 9, chapter 3, art. 287. See also Pizarro, *Implicaciones civiles de la bigamia*, 172–184.

[53] Penal Code, bk. 2, title 9, chap. 2, sec. 3, art. 306.

[54] Penal Code, pt. 2, title 17, art. 313.

[55] Penal Code, title 8, art. 83.

[56] Penal Code, title 2, chap. 1, sec. 4, art. 288.

Jamaica[57]). A few countries allow judges to take account of indigenous customs or cultural ignorance of the law of monogamy in their sentencing.[58] But no Latin or Central American country gives an outright exemption to indigenous polygamy in its penal code, and a few countries – including the influential country of Brazil – explicitly prohibit accommodation of indigenous or religiously based polygamy.[59] Intentional or fraudulently induced polygamy is more severely punished. But even negligently or mistakenly entered polygamy is still liable to criminal sanction. A number of countries also hold liable accomplices and government officials who knowingly issue marriage licenses to polygamists. The Penal Code of Honduras is typical:

> Article 171. The person who contracts a second or subsequent marriage without having legitimately dissolved the previous, will be punished with a punishment of two to five years of imprisonment. The law imposes an equal punishment on a single person who knowingly contracts marriage with a married person.
>
> Article 173. The civil servants who authorize marriages prohibited by law, with full knowledge, or without the concurrence of any of the requisites of existence or of validity of the same, will be sanctioned with a fine of 50,000–100,000 lempiras and disqualification for four to six years.[60]

These prohibitions have been in place in Latin and Central America since colonial days, and they reflect the penal laws of the European mother countries that originally colonized them – Spain, Portugal, France, Germany, and the Netherlands, especially. All these Continental European mother countries share the civil law tradition, rooted in Roman laws that criminalized polygamy since the third century CE. These ancient criminal prohibitions on polygamy were consistently maintained in civil law lands throughout the medieval and early modern periods, and were renewed during the modern legal codification movements. Both the influential 1794 Prussian Civil Code and the 1810 Napoleonic Penal Code, for example, expressly prohibited polygamy. "Whoever, being engaged in the bond of wedlock, shall contract a second marriage before the dissolution of the preceding one shall be punished with hard labour for a time," reads the Napoleonic Penal Code, which was duplicated in a number of European lands.[61] Likewise, the Bavarian Penal Code of

---

[57] Offenses Against the Person Act, sec. 71.

[58] See, e.g., Bolivia, book I, title III, chapter II, article 39, sec. 4; El Salvador Penal Code, book I, title II, chapter III, section I, article 29, sec. 5; Mexico, Penal Code – book I, title III, chapter I, article 52; Peru Penal Code, book I, title II, chapter II, article 15.

[59] Penal Code, title 7, article 235.

[60] Penal Code, bk. 2, title 4, chap. 2, art. 171.

[61] French Penal Code (1810), bk. 3, title 2, chap. 1, sect. 4, art. 340. See also the Allgemeines Landrecht für die Preußischen Staaten (1794), part 2, title 1, art. 16.

1813, "the first modern, rational, and liberal penal code,"[62] although it removed many traditional crimes, still prohibited polygamy for all parties. As the Code's principal author, Paul Johann Anselm von Feuerbach, put it, "Since the state recognizes as valid only a simple marriage, everyone is subject to the laws of bigamy in the state, even if the principles of his religion might allow him to practice polygamy."[63] The 1871 Criminal Code of the German Empire similarly punished all intentional polygamists with "penal servitude up to five years."[64] The Spanish Penal Code of 1848 also prohibited all citizens from practicing polygamy, including its many Muslim citizens; this continued a Spanish tradition of anti-polygamy legislation going back to seventh-century Visigothic laws and several important medieval Spanish legal codes.[65] These criminal prohibitions remain on the books in the revised criminal statutes and codes of most European lands today, although countries like Belgium,[66] Luxembourg, and Switzerland now treat polygamy mainly as an impediment to valid marriage that can lead to divorce or annulment, and private suits for fraud.[67]

Debates about the legal status of polygamy are sharpening on the Continent, however, with the rapid rise of new polygamous immigrants.[68] "In a lot of European countries, marriage is not just an aspect of the immigration problem; it *is* the immigration problem."[69] For example, France is said to be home to more than

[62] Arnd Koch et al., eds., *Feuerbachs Bayerisches Strafgesetzbuch Die Geburt liberalen, modernen und rationalen Strafrechts* (Tübingen: Mohr Siebeck, 2014).

[63] Paul Johann Anselm von Feuerbach, *Lehrbuch des gemeinen in Deutschland geltenden peinlichen Rechts* (Giessen: G.F. Heyer, 1801), sec. 426 (http://www.deutschestextarchiv.de/book/view/feuerbach_recht_1801/?hl=Polygamie&p=371). I am grateful to my colleague Professor Rafael Domingo for alerting me to this source.

[64] Strafgesetzbuch (1871), Part II, ch. 13, sec. 171.

[65] El Código penal de 1848, art. 385. On the long history of anti-polygamy statutes in Spain, see http://noticias.juridicas.com/articulos/45-Derecho%20Civil/200504-3655132531051141.html.

[66] Belgium and the Netherlands are said to have had the first open polygamous marriage with a man and two wives, although it is not clear whether both marriages have been licensed by the state. See Robin Fretwell Wilson, "Introduction," to Robin Fretwell Wilson, ed., *Reconceiving the Family: Critique of the American Law Institute's Principles of the Law of Family Dissolution* (Cambridge: Cambridge University Press, 2006), 1; Paul Belien, "First Trio 'Married' in the Netherlands," *Brussels Journal* (September 27, 2005) (http://www.brusselsjournal.com/node/301).

[67] On Germany, France, the Netherlands, and Denmark, see Katharina Boele-Woekli et al., *De Juridische Status van Polygame Huwelijken in Rechtsvergleichend Perpsectief* (The Hague: Boom Jurdische Uitgevers, 2010), esp. 11–12, 49–50, 77–78, 137, 152–157, 161–163. See also the older studies: Stefano Riccio, *La Bigamia* (Naples: Jovene, 1934); Marino Aldo Colecci, *Il delitto di bigamia* (Naples: Jovene, 1958). I am grateful to my doctoral student, Rinaldo Cristofori, for helping me with these Italian sources.

[68] A comprehensive European study of contemporary polygamy laws and their enforcement evidently remains a desideratum. For a partial study see Boele-Welki et al., *De Juridische Status van Polygame*.

[69] Christopher Caldwell, *Reflections on the Revolution in Europe: Immigration, Islam, and the West* (New York: Doubleday, 2009), 228, quoted and discussed in Bailey and Kaufman, *Polygamy in the Monogamous World*, 147.

20,000 polygamous families, comprising more than 200,000 persons, despite firm new immigration and legal enforcement reforms enacted in 1993.[70] Smaller numbers of polygamists are scattered throughout the rest of the European Union – nearly a million persons all told, according to some estimates, although exact numbers are not known. Many of these polygamous families hail from Africa, the Middle East, and Asia, and most of them are Muslims of various schools of thought and law. European nations, as a matter of course and comity, recognize marriages contracted abroad even in countries that formally recognize polygamy. But they routinely deny visas and bar entry to known polygamists, as well as to second wives and their children who are seeking to unite with a husband or father who has moved to Europe. Even though Continental lands rarely prosecute known polygamists, only the first marriage of a polygamous household is usually recognized as valid, especially in disputes about marital property and inheritance. Like common law countries, civil law countries in Europe differ widely in their treatment of polygamous household members in the delivery of education, charity, social welfare, health care, and other state benefits that turn on marital status. Tensions over these domestic issues have heightened between European Muslims and non-Muslims in recent years – in part as a broader nativist reaction to new immigrants in Europe, in part as a broader cultural backlash against Muslims occasioned by 9/11, Fort Hood, the English and Spanish train station bombings, and ongoing battles with jihadists at home and abroad.[71]

At the time of this writing, no major constitutional case in a European land has yet tested the constitutionality of Europe's anti-polygamy laws and regulations. The European Court of Human Rights has resisted arguments for the state recognition of polygamy, even if pressed on religious freedom, family rights, privacy, equality and nondiscrimination, and other human rights grounds set out in the 1953 European Convention of Human Rights (and echoed in the 2000 Charter of the Fundamental Rights of the European Union). In the signature 2010 case of *Şerífe Yiğit v. Turkey*, for example, the European Court upheld Turkey's law that required couples to marry monogamously in a civil ceremony before a state official. Turkish law does not recognize a religious marriage ceremony to be sufficient to create a valid marriage at state law, and it threatened prison to any religious official who presided over a marriage without a prior civil registration of the marriage. The stated purpose of the

[70] Institut Montaigne, "La polygamie en France: une fatalité"? (November 20, 2009), available at http://www.institutmontaigne.org/medias/documents/polygamie_en_france.pdf. See also Giovanni Camparia and Olivia Salimbeni, *Marriage as Immigration Gate: The Situation of Female Marriage Migrants from Third Countries to EU Member States* (Berlin: Berlin Institute for Comparative Social Research, 2004).
[71] See, e.g., Marie-Claire Foblets et al., eds., *Islam & Europe: Crises are Challenges* (Leuven: UPL in Context, 2010).

Turkish law, as the European Court saw it, "was to protect women against polygamy. If religious marriages were to be considered lawful all the attendant religious consequences would have to be recognized, for instance the fact that a [Muslim] man could marry four women." "Turkey aimed to put an end to a marriage tradition which places women at a clear disadvantage, not to say in a situation of dependence and inferiority, compared to men." This Turkish prohibition of polygamy was thus not a violation of the European Convention's stated right to marriage and a family, the European Court concluded, nor a form of religious or gender discrimination.[72]

In a similar move, the European Council has made clear that "the right to family reunification should be exercised in proper compliance with … the rights of women and children." "In the event of a polygamous marriage, where the sponsor already has a spouse living with him in the territory of a Member State, the Member State concerned shall not authorize the family reunification of an additional spouse."[73] The Council has condemned polygamy as an offense against the rights of women and the demands for gender equality – a position also taken by the United Nations Committee on the Elimination of Discrimination Against Women. The European Council has further grouped polygamy with "slavery and other crimes in the name of honour or tradition, of violence, trafficking, female genital mutilation, forced marriage, polygamy, or deprivation of identity (for example, when women are forced to wear the burka, the nigab, or a mask)." Member States, the Council declared, must have "zero tolerance" for such offenses against the "indispensable" rights of individual women and children.[74]

Outside the West, several other large and populous nations have also prohibited polygamy: Japan (1880),[75] the Soviet Union (1920s),[76] Thailand (1935),[77]

[72] *Şerife Yiğit v. Turkey* (App. 3976/05) (2 November 2010), para. 62 and 82.
[73] Council Directive 2003/86/EC (September 22, 2003), preamble 11; art. 4.4, in *Official Journal of the European Union* L 251/12 (3.10.2003). Some scholars are concerned that this prescription against reunification of polygamous families may ultimately hurt the rights of women and children by leaving them in foreign lands without the support of their husband and father. See Clare McGlynn, *Families and the European Union: Law, Politics, and Pluralism* (Cambridge: Cambridge University Press, 2006), 134–135.
[74] European Parliament Resolution of March 13, 2007 on a Roadmap for Equality Between Women and Men, 2006/2131 (INI), *Official Journal of the European Union* C 301 E/56 (13.12.2007). See also United Nations Committee on the Elimination of Discrimination against Women General Recommendation no. 21: "Polygamous marriage contravenes a woman's right to equality with men, and can have such serious emotional and financial consequences for her and her dependents that such marriages ought to be discouraged and prohibited."
[75] See esp. Japanese Penal Code (1907), art. 184 http://www.cas.go.jp/jp/seisaku/hourei/data/PC.pdf.; see also Hirishi Oda, *Japanese Law*, 3rd ed. (Oxford: Oxford University Press, 2009), 430–435, 457–458.
[76] See detailed sources in Harold J. Berman, "Soviet Family Law in the Light of Russian History and Marxist Theory," *Yale Law Journal* 56 (1946): 26–57. Today, the Russian Parliament (the Duma) is facing pressure to permit polygamy not only for its ample Muslim communities, but as a remedy for its low birth rate and high rate of lonely singles. See Maria Katbamna, "Half a Good Man is Better than None," *The Guardian* (October 26, 2009).
[77] Civil and Commercial Code §1452.

China (1950),[78] India for all but Muslims (1955),[79] and Nepal (1963).[80] Taken together, the 120-plus Western and non-Western countries that today formally ban or do not recognize polygamy represent the vast majority of the world's population. Nonetheless, they represent only 15–20 percent of the world's known cultures.[81] Anthropologists estimate that of the ca. 1,200 known cultures in the world, 75–85 percent of them (depending on who is counting and what domestic forms are being counted) recognize polygamy as a valid form of marriage.[82] Many of these polygamous cultures, anthropologists tell us, are found in smaller tribal groups often living in "traditional, isolated, low technology cultures" under the governance of customary laws. Many have traditions of arranged marriages in which women in particular have little control over their choice of husband, although some women choose polygamy to gain access to the resources and protection of powerful men. Many of the women who enter polygamous unions voluntarily or involuntarily are rural, poor, and uneducated; they and their children provide vital labor for the agricultural and other low-technology, labor-intensive household economies that are common in these polygamous communities.[83] In addition to these groups, a number of Aboriginal or Indigenous Peoples in the Americas, Australia, New Zealand, and Oceania recognize polygamy, and very occasionally polyandry (one wife with multiple husbands).[84] Most often, anthropologists report, the polygamous practices of all these groups fade when their

[78] *The Marriage Law of the People's Republic of China* (1950; rev. 1980 and 2001), art. 27, chaps. 1–2: "Article 1: The feudal marriage system that allowed arranged or forced marriage, that admit man's superiority to woman and woman's inferiority to man, and that neglect children's interests shall be abolished. A new democratic marriage system based on marriage freedom for man and woman, monogamy, equality between man and woman, and protection of women and children's lawful rights shall be implemented. Article 2: Bigamy and concubinage shall be prohibited. Child bride shall be prohibited. Any interference with a widow's freedom of marriage be prohibited." My thanks to Professor Ruihua Zhong of Beijing for translating this text for me.
[79] Hindu Marriage Act § 5(i) (1955).
[80] Nepal Marriage Registration Act 2028, §4(a) (1971).
[81] See Human Relations Area Files (http://www.yale.edu/hraf/), Area File 595, built on the work of George P. Murdock, *Atlas of World Cultures* (Pittsburgh, PA: University of Pittsburgh Press, 1981).
[82] See various studies summarized in Walter Scheidel, "A Peculiar Institution? Greco-Roman Monogamy in Global Context," *The History of the Family* 14 (2009): 280–291, at 281–282; G. Clark, "Human Monogamy," *Science* 282 (1998): 1047–1048; P. Gray, "Ethnographic Atlas Codebook," *World Cultures* 10 (1998): 86–136, at 89–90.
[83] Altman and Ganit, *Polygamous Families*, 40–41, citing Human Relations Area Files; Alean Al-Krenawi and Vered Slonim-Nevo, "Polygyny and its Impact on the Psychosocial Well-Being of Husbands," *Journal of Comparative Law* 37 (2006): 174; Laksham Marasignhe, "Conversion, Polygamy, and Bigamy: Some Comparative Perspectives," *Asia Pacific Law Journal* 4 (1995): 72; Satoshi Kanazawa and Mary C. Still, "Why Monogamy?" *Social Forces* 78 (1999): 25–50, and summary of more recent anthropological literature in Scheidel, "A Peculiar Institution," 284–289.
[84] See H.R.H. Prince Peter, *A Study of Polyandry* (The Hague: Mouton & Co., 1963); Nancy E. Levine and Walter H. Sangree, "Women with Many Husbands: Polyandrous Alliance and Marital Flexibility in Africa and Asia," *Journal of Comparative Family Studies* 11(3) (1980): 283–410.

members are exposed to urbanization, technology, and mass media or when members leave the community.[85]

A good number of these polygamous cultures are found within the fifty-five Muslim majority countries in Africa, the Middle East, and Asia whose state laws recognize polygamy as a valid form of marriage, albeit with Turkey (since 1926) and Tunisia (since 1956) excepted.[86] But official recognition of polygamy by state, customary, and/or Islamic law hardly means that all families in these countries are polygamous. In a comprehensive survey of polygamous practices in these lands as of 2010, Canadian jurists Martha Bailey and Amy Kaufman have shown that polygamy is a controversial and shrinking practice among many modern day Muslims in these regions, particularly among younger, educated, and urbanized Muslims who typically reject the practice.[87] To be sure, in the African "polygyny belt"[88] from Senegal to Tanzania, where customary laws and older traditions often combine with Islamic teachings, 30–40 percent of all married men are thought to practice polygamy.[89] But in Muslim-majority Arab countries of northern Africa, like Egypt, Algeria, Libya, and Morocco, polygamy is practiced in less than 3 percent of all households. In the Middle East, countries such as Jordan and Lebanon have comparably low rates, whereas in others (including Saudi Arabia, Yemen, and some of the Gulf states) polygamy prevails in 10–20 percent of all households – some of them elite and powerful families, most of them poor, rural, and tribal. In Eurasia and South Asia, where more than 60 percent of Muslims of the world now live, most countries (including Indonesia, the largest Muslim country in the world), have polygamy rates of less than 10 percent. Even in Asian countries such as Pakistan and Bangladesh, where polygamy is more common, state laws insist, on pain of fine and imprisonment, that a Muslim man may marry up to four wives only if the first wife consents and only if he can support his wives and children equally and fully.[90]

---

[85] Miriam Koktvedgaard Zeitzen, *Polygamy: A Cross-Cultural Analysis* (Oxford/New York: Berg, 2008); Peter Bretschneider, *Polygyny: A Cross Cultural Study* (Uppsala: Almquist and Wiksell International, 1995); and the older classic study of Remi Clignet, *Many Wives, Many Powers: Authority and Power in Polygynous Families* (Evanston, IL: Northwestern University Press, 1970).

[86] See detailed country and regional studies and perspectives in Abdullahi A. An-Na'im, ed., *Islamic Family in a Changing World: A Global Resource Book* (London/New York: Zed Books, 2002); Pearl and Menksi, *Muslim Family Law*; Lynn Welchman, ed., *Women's Rights and Islamic Family Law* (London/New York: Zed Books, 2004).

[87] Bailey and Kaufman, *Polygamy*, 7–68, with detailed sources in ibid., 190–216.

[88] Scheidel, "A Peculiar Institution," 284.

[89] See studies in R.J. Lesthaege, ed., *Reproduction and Social Organization in sub-Saharan Africa* (Berkeley: University of California Press, 1989) and various statistics on polygyny in these countries at www.statcompiler.com.

[90] Bailey and Kaufman, *Polygamy*, 7–68, with detailed sources in ibid., 190–216. See also the close studies and updated bibliography in An-Na'im, *Islamic Family Law*, esp. 34, 73–74, 101, 160–161, 195–196, 210, 256–257, 289–290.

These latter restrictions on the practice of polygamy reflect common Muslim teachings, rooted ultimately in the sacred texts of Islam. Scholars of Islamic theology make clear that Islam regards marriage as an essential institution, and it encourages all faithful fit adults to marry. Marriage, the Qur'an teaches, builds alliances among groups and families, produces and nurtures legitimate children, protects and supports orphaned or abandoned women, and most importantly provides an essential means for husband and wife to provide material, physical, emotional, and spiritual support for each other.[91] The strong assumption and preference of the Qur'an is for monogamy not polygamy.[92]

Polygamy is only an option – not an obligation – for Muslims. The only two Qur'anic verses on point aim to restrict rather than encourage polygamy – which most (although not all) scholars believe was a common practice in seventh-century Arabia where the Prophet Mohammed lived. One Qur'anic verse allows polygamy but only in the narrow context of protecting female orphans from the abuses of their guardians: "If you fear that you shall not be able to deal justly with the orphans, marry women of your choice, two, three, or four; but if you fear that you shall not be able to deal justly (with them) then only one."[93] The second verse, however, questions whether justice can in fact be done to all women in a polygamous marriage: "You are never able to be fair and just as between women, even if it is your ardent desire. But turn not away (from a woman) altogether, so as to leave her (as it were) hanging (in the air). If you come to a friendly understanding, and practice self-restraint, God is Oft-forgiving, Most Merciful."[94] In the Hadith, the second most important sacred Muslim text after the Qur'an, the Prophet refused to allow his cousin Ali, who had married the Prophet's daughter Fatimah, to take a second wife for fear of harming or hurting her. "Fatimah is part of me," the Prophet said; "whatever hurts her hurts me, and whatever harms her harms me."[95]

More conservative schools of Islamic jurisprudence, particularly the Wahhabi and Hanbali schools, have long read these sacred texts together to allow for a limited right to practice polygamy for men of ample means, and this has persisted in some Islamic communities to this day, both in Muslim-majority lands and in dispersed Muslim communities throughout the world, including in the West. In Muslim lands and communities that follow the more liberal teachings of the Malaki and

---

[91] See, e.g., Qur'an 4.1, 3, 127; 7.189; 16.72; 17.24; 24.32; 30.21; and other texts gathered in Azizah Y. Al-Hibri, and Raja' M. El Habti, "Islam," in *Sex, Marriage, and Family in World Religions*, ed. Don S. Browning, M. Christian Green, and John Witte, Jr. (New York: Columbia University Press, 2006), 150–225. See also Harald Motzki, "Marriage and Divorce," in Jane McAuliffe, ed., *Encyclopedia of the Qur'an* (BrillOnline Reference Works).
[92] Al-Hibri and El Habti, "Islam," 186.
[93] Qur'an 4.3 (Al Nisa', The Women), using translation in ibid., 186.
[94] Qur'an 4.129, in ibid., 187.
[95] Hadith, bk. 62, no. 157, in ibid., 187.

Shafi'i schools of jurisprudence, however, polygamy is an unpopular and shrinking domestic practice, particularly for families in urban settings and more developed cultures. A number of Muslim jurists within these schools have been openly critical of the practice, because of concern for the treatment of women and children.[96]

Nobody knows the exact number of practicing polygamists around the world. In the nations where it is legal, polygamy tends to be either the prerogative of wealthy and powerful families, or the practice of rural and undeveloped communities that follow customary law – although in some Muslim-majority countries, polygamy appeals to a wider cross section of the population. In the nations where is it not legal, polygamy tends to be the practice of smaller Indigenous, tribal, and religious communities, and the experimental practice of small and sometimes edgy countercultural groups on the far right and the far left. "Most of the world has abandoned polygamy" over the past century, a trend hastened by colonization, globalization, urbanization, feminization, industrialization, Westernization, and Christianization.[97] But polygamy remains in place in parts of the world, and in a few places the practice is growing.[98] Martha Bailey and Amy Kaufman summarize the vast anthropological literature that seeks to explain why:

> Because polygamy is often a deeply entrenched sociocultural practice, endorsed by Islam and traditional religions, law and policy makers find it difficult to eliminate or restrict the practice. Apart from any religious underpinnings, social conditions provide a climate within which polygamy can thrive.... Often a relatively small number of men control a disproportionate share of resources. These high-status males mate more often and leave more offspring. In these conditions, women may actually seek out polygamous marriages. A polygamous marriage may be an economic advantage for a woman with few options. Rural women with little or no education and low socioeconomic status are more likely to be in a polygamous marriage. Educated women of higher socioeconomic status have more options and are far less likely to be in a polygamous marriage....
>
> Men in some areas desire large families to expand their alliances and bolster their standing in the society. As well, children may be needed to increase the labor supply within a kinship network. And in many polygamous regions there is a strong preference for male children. Men may seek out additional wives if their first wives give birth to female children only or are barren. Men may also take additional wives for sexual satisfaction, particularly in societies with lengthy post-partum sexual taboos. In communities where families commonly arrange first marriages, men

---

[96] See, e.g., critique of 'Abduh, *Al-A'mal al-Kamilah*, 2:84–95 (nineteenth century CE), in ibid. 187–188.

[97] Bailey and Kaufman, *Polygamy*, 7.

[98] For a good distillation of current anthropological teaching about the causes and conditions of polygamy, see Kevin MacDonald, "The Establishment and Maintenance of Socially Imposed Monogamy in Western Europe," *Politics and the Life Sciences* 14 (1995): 3–23.

may seek out additional wives to satisfy their desire for a love match or to exercise their own choice. Polygamy is also found in closed cultures, where open displays of courtship and affection are shunned. In addition, polygamy has historically been used in place of divorce, particularly in countries that stigmatized divorce or that have limited grounds for divorce, and high thresholds for proving these grounds.[99]

THE WESTERN CASE AGAINST POLYGAMY DISTILLED

What, therefore, is the Western case for monogamy over polygamy, and is that case still convincing today? In the chapters that follow I show that, for more than 2,500 years, the Western legal tradition has defined marriage as the union of one man and one woman with the fitness, capacity, and freedom to marry each other. This has been the consistent normative teaching of ancient Greeks and Romans, first millennium Jews and Christians, medieval Catholics and early modern Protestants, modern Enlightenment philosophers and liberals, common law and civil law jurists alike. Although monogamous marriage is neither good for everyone, nor always good, these writers have argued, in general and in most cases, that monogamous marriage brings both essential private goods to the married couple and their children and vital public goods to society and the state.[100]

The historical sources commend monogamy on various grounds. The most common argument is that exclusive and enduring monogamous marriages are the best way to ensure paternal certainty and joint parental investment in children who are born vulnerable and utterly dependent on their parents' mutual care and remain so for many years. Exclusive and enduring monogamous marriages, furthermore, are the best way to ensure that men and women are treated with equal dignity and respect within the domestic sphere, and that husbands and wives and parents and children provide each other with mutual support, protection, and edification throughout their lifetimes, adjusted to each person's needs at different stages in the life cycle. This latter logic also applies to dyadic same-sex couples, who have gained increasing rights in the West in recent years, including the right to marry and to parent in some places.

For more than 1,750 years, in turn, the Western legal tradition has declared polygamy to be a serious crime – a capital crime from the ninth to the nineteenth centuries. Although some Western writers and rulers have allowed polygamy in rare individual cases of urgent personal, political, or social need, virtually all Western writers and legal systems have denounced polygamy as an alternative form

---

[99] Ibid., 7–8.
[100] See, e.g., a sampling of the historical and modern social science literature in John Wall et al., eds., *Marriage, Health and the Professions* (Grand Rapids, MI: Wm. B. Eerdmans, 2002).

of marriage and have denounced the occasional polygamous experiments of early Jews, medieval Muslims, early modern Anabaptists, nineteenth-century Mormons, and current day immigrants to the West.

The historical sources condemn polygamy on a number of grounds. The most common argument is that polygamy is unnatural, unfair, and unjust to wives and children – that is, a violation of their fundamental rights. Polygamy, moreover, is also too often the cause or consequence of sundry other harms, crimes, and abuses. And polygamy, according to more recent writers, is a threat to good citizenship, social order, and political stability, even an impediment to the advancement of civilizations toward liberty, equality, and democratic government. For nearly two millennia, therefore, the West has thus declared polygamy to be a crime, and has had little patience with occasional arguments raised in its defense.

Both historical social observers of polygamy and modern social scientists have emphasized the serious harms too often associated with polygamy. Young women are harmed because they are often coerced into early marriages with older men. Once pushed aside for a rival co-wife, women are reduced to rival servants or slaves within the household. They are then exploited periodically for sex and procreation by detached husbands. They are forced to make do for themselves and their children with dwindling resources as still other women and children are added to the household against their wishes. If they protest their plight, if they resort to self-help, if they lose their youthful figure and vigor, they are often cast out of their homes – impoverished, undereducated, and often incapable of survival without serious help from others.

Children are harmed, these same historical and modern observers continue, because they are often set in perennial rivalry with other children and mothers for the affection and attention of the family patriarch. They are deprived of healthy models of authority and liberty, equality and charity, marital love and fidelity, which are essential to their development as future spouses, citizens, and community leaders. And they are harmed by having too few resources to support their nurture, education, care, and preparation for a full and healthy life as an adult.

Men are harmed by polygamy, too. Polygamy promotes marriage by the richest men, not necessarily the fittest men in body, mind, or virtue. In isolated communities, polygamy often leads to ostracism of rival younger men, the "lost boys" who have fewer marital opportunities and are often consigned to seduction, prostitution, and other untoward sexual behavior. Polygamy inflames a man's lust, for once he adds a second wife, he will inevitably desire more, even the wife of another. And polygamy deprives men of that essential organic bond of exclusive marital companionship and friendship, which ancients and moderns alike say is critical to most men's physical, psychological, moral, and even spiritual health.

The Western legal tradition reminds us that even the biblical titans of the faith who practiced polygamy did not fare well. Think of the endless family discord of Abraham with Sarah and Hagar, or Jacob with Rachel and Leah. Think of King David who murdered Uriah the Hittite to add the shapely Bathsheba to his already ample harem. Think of King Solomon with his "thousand wives," whose children ended up raping, abducting, and killing each other, precipitating civil war in ancient Israel. Anthropologists point to similar problems in modern polygamous households and communities.[101] "Whether it is practiced in a Western democracy or sub-Saharan Africa, polygamy produces harmful effects that ripple throughout a society," Rose McDermott concludes after a thorough cross-cultural study of polygamy in 170 countries. All these polygamous communities "suffer from increased levels of physical and sexual abuse against women, increased rates of maternal mortality, shortened female life expectancy, lower levels of education for girls and boys, lower levels of equality for women, higher levels of discrimination against women, increased rates of female genital mutilation, increased rates of trafficking in women and decreased levels of civil and political liberties for all citizens."[102]

The Western legal tradition has thus long regarded polygamy as a *malum in se* offense – something "bad in itself." Other *malum in se* offenses today include slavery, sex trafficking, prostitution, indentured servitude, obscenity, bestiality, incest, sex with children, self-mutilation, organ-selling, cannibalism, and more. Most Western legal systems still consider all of these activities to be inherently wrong – or too often the cause or consequence of other wrongdoing. That someone wants to engage in these activities voluntarily for reasons of religion, bravery, custom, or autonomy makes no difference. That other cultures past and present allow such activities makes no difference. That these activities do not necessarily cause harm in every case also makes no difference. For nearly two millennia, the Western legal tradition has included polygamy among the crimes that are inherently wrong because polygamy routinizes patriarchy, jeopardizes consent, fractures fidelity, divides loyalty, dilutes devotion, fosters inequity, promotes rivalry, foments lust, condones adultery, confuses children, and more. Not in every case, to be sure, but in enough cases to make the practice of polygamy too risky to condone as a viable legal option.

---

[101] See analysis and recent literature on polygamy and poverty in Michèle Tertilt, "Polygny, Fertility, and Savings," *Journal of Political Economy* 113 (2005): 1341–1371; id., "Polygyny, Women's Rights, and Development," *Journal of the European Economic Association* 4 (2006): 523–530.

[102] Rose McDermott and Jonathan Cowden, "Polygyny and its Effect on Violence Against Women, Children, and Within the State," (forthcoming). See also L.D. Shepherd, "The Impact of Polygamy on Women's Mental Health: A Systematic Review," *Epidemiology and Psychiatric Sciences* 22 (2013): 47–62; Maura Strassberg, "The Crime of Polygamy," *Temple Political and Civil Rights Law Review* 12 (2003): 353.

Furthermore, allowing religious polygamy as an exception to the rules is even more dangerous, the Western legal tradition has held, because it will make religious communities a law unto themselves, and a potential rival to the state. Again, some religious communities and their members might well thrive with the freedom to practice polygamy quietly among their voluntary faithful. But, inevitably, closed repressive regimes will also emerge, as can be seen in the Yearning for Zion Ranch case that we started with and in many earlier communities that we shall explore in the course of this book.

These and many other arguments against polygamy, which I analyze at length in the pages that follow, are not just about how to maintain Christian traditions in "a secular age."[103] The reality is that the West's arguments against polygamy are both pre-Christian in origin and post-Christian in operation: "pre-Christian" in that the Bible has no clear prohibition against polygamy, and includes more than two dozen polygamists among the leaders of the faith; pre-Christian, furthermore, because the Christian Church was rather slow to ban polygamy, even though it quickly condemned many other sexual practices of the Roman Empire in which the church was born. It was the "pagan" Roman emperors who criminalized polygamy in 258 CE, more than a century before they established Christianity – and nearly a millennium before church authorities finally issued comparably firm prohibitions. The medieval Catholic Church and early modern Protestant churches, too, eventually made these anti-polygamous sentiments a part of their theology, ethics, and religious norms, and added their own deep arguments that became important to the Western case against polygamy. But Christianity was as much a carrier as an inventor of the West's aversion to polygamy. And its normative stands against polygamy were as much philosophical and prudential in argument as they were theological and biblical.

Because of this, the Western tradition's aversion to polygamy also eventually became decidedly "post-Christian" as well. Long after they disestablished Christianity and granted religious freedom to all peaceable faiths, Western nations in Europe and North America remained firmly opposed to polygamy. Indeed, some of the strongest Western arguments against polygamy came from eighteenth- and nineteenth-century Enlightenment liberals and common lawyers who firmly rejected Christianity but also firmly rejected polygamy as a betrayal of reason, nature, utility, fairness, liberty, and common sense. Additionally, they marshaled their strongest anti-polygamy arguments not so much against secular sexual libertines but against several avant-garde Christians who were pressing the case for polygamy on natural and utilitarian grounds – that is, as a cure-all for all manner of sexual, social, and psychological ills both at home and abroad on the new colonial and foreign mission fields of Africa and Asia.

---

[103] Charles Taylor, *A Secular Age* (Cambridge, MA: Belknap Press, 2007).

These arguments against polygamy are also not simply about how to maintain traditional morality in a new age of sexual liberty. To be sure, polygamy has long been included on a long roll of traditional sex crimes. That roll also included adultery, fornication, abortion, contraception, and sodomy which have all now been eclipsed by modern constitutional and cultural norms of sexual liberty. Therefore, it is easy to think that the crime of polygamy is vulnerable to the same generic logic of sexual liberty that undercuts so many other traditional sexual norms. Anti-polygamists often trade in this simple morality-versus-liberty dialectic in warning against the dangers of the slippery slope. A good example is Justice Scalia's dissent in *Lawrence v. Texas* (2003), the case that struck down traditional sodomy laws. "State laws against bigamy, same-sex marriage, adult incest, prostitution, masturbation, adultery, fornication, bestiality, and obscenity are all now called into question," Justice Scalia wrote in an ominous warning that clatters loudly in the literature of conservative family groups to this day.[104] Pro-polygamists do the same thing by painting their opposition with the same broad brush of bigotry. The anti-polygamists of today, they argue, are just like the slaveholders, chauvinists, and homophobes of the past, clutching to their traditional morality at the cost of true liberty for African-Americans, women, and same-sex parties.[105]

But traditional morality versus modern liberty is too blunt a dialectic to sort out the modern cases for and against polygamy. It is too blunt, in part, because the modern logic of liberty and human rights was founded, in no small part, on traditional morality. Much of our modern Western rights structure was created by "traditional" Catholics and Protestants from 1200 to 1700, long before liberal Enlightenment philosophers and jurists set out to work. Indeed, by 1650, Christians of various types had already defined, defended, and died for every right that would appear a century and a half later in the United States Bill of Rights or in the French Declaration of the Rights of Man and of the Citizen.[106] And a good case has been made that modern human rights norms still need religious and moral sources and sanctions

---

[104] *Lawrence v. Texas*, 539 U.S. at 590 (Scalia, J., dissenting). See also *Romer v. Evans*, 517 U.S. 620, 648–650 (Scalia, J., dissenting).

[105] See, e.g., Margaret Denike, "The Racialization of White Man's Polygamy," *Hypatia* 25 (2010): 852–874; Marta Ertman, "Race Treason: The Untold Story of America's Ban on Polygamy," *Columbia Journal of Gender and Law* 19 (2010): 287–366.

[106] See, e.g., Brian Tierney, *The Idea of Natural Rights: Studies on Natural Rights, Natural Law, and Church Law, 1150–1625* (Grand Rapids, MI: Wm. B. Eerdmans, 1997); Brian Tierney, *Liberty and Law: The Idea of Permissible Natural Law, 1100–1800* (Washington, DC: Catholic University Press of America, 2014); John Witte, Jr., *The Reformation of Rights: Law, Religion, and Human Rights in Early Modern Calvinism* (Cambridge: Cambridge University Press, 2007); John Witte, Jr. and Frank S. Alexander, eds., *Christianity and Human Rights: An Introduction* (Cambridge: Cambridge University Press, 2010).

to be fully cogent and effective even in our post-establishment and post-modern secular polities.[107]

The dialectic of morality versus liberty is also too blunt because proponents of modern liberty have their own morality, grounding their arguments in deep moral beliefs, values, ideals, and metaphors – not least the foundational moral concept of human dignity on which the modern human rights revolution has been built since 1948.[108] The notion that modern liberals press only neutral, objective, and value-free arguments in favor of liberty and equality while Christians and other faith traditions trade only in prejudicial, subjective, and judgmental moral values now faces very strong epistemological headwinds.[109] Every serious school of legal, political, and social thought today rests ultimately on a foundation of fundamental beliefs and values.[110] Indeed, some versions of modern secular liberalism at work in parts of the modern Western academy and elite media are becoming as fundamentalist about the cogency and correctness of their ideas, methods, and arguments as Christian and other religious fundamentalists of the past.

We need to get beyond easy caricatures and simple dialectics to think through the Western case for monogamy over polygamy and its continued utility and validity today. And that is the main aim of this book. In the chapters that follow, I analyze this case as it emerges variously in biblical, Talmudic, and medieval Jewish sources, in early Greek, Roman, and Germanic laws, in first millennium and medieval canon law texts, in parallel patristic and scholastic writings, in the legal and theological tracts of the sixteenth-century Protestant and Catholic Reformations, in early modern England, in Enlightenment liberal philosophies, and in the Anglo-American common law tradition. To be sure, that still leaves ample parts and periods of the Western tradition untouched, but it provides a strong and representative tour of the archives. In each chapter, I work through the theoretical and legal discussions about monogamy and polygamy that have survived, focusing on the seminal texts that shaped the Western legal tradition's case for monogamy over polygamy. I present

---

[107] See sources and discussion in John Witte, Jr. and M. Christian Green, eds., *Religion and Human Rights* (Oxford/New York: Oxford University Press, 2012); W. Cole Durham, Jr. and Brett G. Scharffs, *Law and Religion: National, International, and Comparative Perspectives* (New York: Aspen Publishers, 2010).

[108] See, e.g., Louis Henkin et al., *Human Rights* (New York, Foundation Press, 1999), 80; and more fully Michael J. Perry, *The Political Morality of Liberal Democracy* (Cambridge: Cambridge University Press, 2010).

[109] See a good summary of recent criticisms from various quarters in John Perry, *The Pretenses of Loyalty: Locke, Liberal Theory, and American Political Theology* (New York: Oxford University Press, 2011); Chris Eberle, *Religious Conviction in Liberal Politics* (Cambridge/New York: Cambridge University Press, 2002); Michael J. Perry, *Love and Power: The Role of Religion and Morality in American Politics* (New York: Oxford University Press, 1991).

[110] See sources and discussion in John Witte, Jr., "Law, Religion, and Metaphor Theory" (forthcoming).

the strongest arguments for polygamy that emerged intermittently in the Western legal tradition, and the strongest rejoinders that emerged, often immediately and loudly, to denounce these pro-polygamy arguments. And, as reported case law becomes available in later medieval and early modern sources, I also present a few illustrative case studies to show how some of these arguments applied in practice. In the concluding chapter, I offer a reconstruction of these historical arguments for monogamy over polygamy, and weigh them against the constitutional and human rights arguments for polygamy, which I took up at the beginning of this Introduction.

THE SHIFTING TERMINOLOGY OF PLURAL MARRIAGES

Before moving into the long historical analysis that comprises the bulk of this book, we need to be aware of the shifting and slippery terminology that attaches to our subject. The term "polygamy" usually brings to mind either the oft-prurient thought of sharing a bed with two or more spouses, or the troubling thought of subjugated women forced to endure life in the harem of a wealthy, powerful, and older man. Some might also think of the traveling cad who keeps secret wives in multiple cities, or the malicious deserter who abandons his wife and children, and marries another woman down the road without bothering to end the prior marriage.[111] Movie and literature lovers might also think of the tragic stories of a long deserted spouse who finally gives up hope and gets married to another, only to have the first spouse reappear after heroic struggle on the high seas or the battlefield, or after overcoming dire illness or long captivity. Think of Lord Tennyson's *Enoch Arden* or Tom Hanks's *Cast Away* or *The Return of Martin Guerre*. All these are core cases of polygamy in the Western legal tradition.

But historically the term "polygamy" covered a number of other forms of plural union as well, and the term was combined with a number of other shifting and confusing terms. Table 1 sets out the forms and names of plural marriage that have been discussed in the Western legal tradition since biblical and classical times, and which have been subject to restrictions and sanctions by the state, and sometimes the church, too. All of them were considered to be forms of the generic category of "polygamy," and the rationales for their respective punishment were often intertwined.

Real Polygamy

As Table 1 shows, the core and clearest case of polygamy in the Western tradition involves a man or woman with two or more spouses at the same time. Historically,

---

[111] See, e.g., Lawrence M. Friedman, "Crimes of Mobility," *Stanford Law Review* 43 (1991): 637–658.

TABLE 1. *The Historical field of polygamy*

Name of offense	Relationships covered by the offense
Real Polygamy/Bigamy (also called Polygyny and Polyandry)	a husband with 2 or more wives; a wife with 2 or more husbands
Constructive Polygamy (also called Interpretive Polygamy or Quasi-Polygamy)	a man or woman with 2 or more fiancées a man or woman with 1 or more fiancé(e)s and 1 or more spouses a husband with a wife and 1 or more concubines a man with 2 or more concubines a husband who married or had sex with 2 or more sisters sequentially a man or woman who took both a spiritual vow and a marital vow

Clerical Bigamy (also called Digamy; later called Irregularity)	an ordained priest or avowed monk who had, before taking vows
	• married 2 or more wives in a row
	• married a woman who had already taken a spiritual vow
	• married a non-virginal wife who was
	  ◦ widowed
	  ◦ a former concubine
	  ◦ a former prostitute
	  ◦ a former fornicator
	  ◦ a former actress
	  ◦ an earlier victim of rape or abduction by another
	  a deaconess/avowed nun who had married 2 or more husbands

Successive Polygamy (also called Bigamy, Digamy, Sequential Polygamy)	a divorcee who married before the death of the former spouse a widow(er) who remarried too soon or too often

the term "bigamy" was sometimes used if a person had only two spouses at the same time; "trigamy" for three spouses, "quadragamy," for four spouses and so on. But "polygamy" was the more common generic word describing the act of having two or more spouses at the same time. Technically, the term "polygyny" (from the Greek *poly* for many and *gyne* for wife or woman) describes a man having two or more wives. "Polyandry" (combining *poly* with the Greek term *anēr* for man) describes the quite rare instance of a woman having two or more husbands. And the term "polyamory" is the generic term often used to describe all manner of plural spousal and sexual arrangements. These technical terms were occasionally used in historical texts, and are used more frequently in the social science literature today. But again "polygamy" was and is the more common generic word for having two or more spouses at the same time.

Writing in the thirteenth century, the leading jurist of his day, Hostiensis (c. 1200 – c. 1271), called this core case of having two or more spouses at the same time to be "real" or "proper" bigamy or polygamy (*polygamia vera, bigamia propria*) as opposed to various forms of what he called "constructive polygamy" or "successive polygamy" that we will describe in a moment.[112] Three centuries later, the great English jurist, Sir Edward Coke (1552–1634) echoed this view, calling his fellow common lawyers to use the term "polygamy" to describe only the crime of having two or more spouses at the same time.[113] William Blackstone (1723–1780) echoed this view in eighteenth-century England as did James Kent (1763–1847) in nineteenth-century America.[114] But other jurists, judges, and legislators throughout Western history still sometimes used the terms "bigamy," "polygyny," "polyandry," and "polyamory," as well as "digamy" (double marriage) to describe a case of "real polygamy" even though these terms sometimes had other meanings, too.[115]

Writing alongside Hostiensis and Coke, other medieval and early modern jurists began to call for a greater differentiation of types or degrees of "real polygamy" – a hierarchy of offenses from more serious to less serious. Various soft taxonomies of "real polygamy" slowly began to emerge in early modern times with different punishments attached to each level of offense. Some distinctions were based on the defendant's state of mind: intentionally or knowingly having two spouses was considered more serious than innocently or negligently taking a second spouse (thinking, wrongly, that the first spouse was dead or that the first marriage had properly ended). Some distinctions were based on the defendant's actions and the harm he caused: keeping two or more spouses in the same house or bed was considered more

---

[112] Hostiensis, *Summa Aurea in titulos decretalium* [1537 Lyon ed.], ed. and ann. Nicolas Superantii, repr. ed. (Aalen: Scientia Verlag, 1962), fol. 40v. This "real versus constructive" formulation is oft repeated in later medieval and early modern sources. See, e.g., Ludovici Engel, *Universi juris canonici*, 4th ed. (Venice: Jacob Hertz, 1593), I.21.2–3.

[113] Sir Edward Coke, *The First Part of the Institutes of the Law of England*, 1st American ed. (Philadelphia, PA: Robert H. Small, 1853), 80a–80b, n.1. Continental writers were pressing the same argument. See, e.g., Lucius Ferrarius Prompta, *Bibliotheca canonica, juridica, morali, theologice*, 7 vols. (Venice: Gaspar Storti, 1782), vol. 6, s.v. "polygamia."

[114] William Blackstone, *Commentaries on the Laws of England*, 4 vols. (Oxford: Oxford University Press, 1765), 4.13.2 ("what some have corruptly called *bigamy*, which properly signifies being twice married, but is more justly denominated *polygamy*, or having a plurality of wives at once"); James Kent, *Commentaries on American Law*, 4 vols. (New York: O. Halsted, 1826–1830), 2:45. See also Leonard Shelford, *A Practical Treatise on the Law of Marriage and Divorce* (London: S. Sweet, 1841), sec. 224.

[115] See, e.g., Leo Miller, *John Milton Among the Polygamophiles* (New York: Loewenthal Press, 1974), 239–241; George Elliott Howard, *A History of Matrimonial Institutions*, 3 vols. (Chicago, IL: University of Chicago Press, 1904), 1:83ff.; Anne McLaren, "Monogamy, Polygamy, and the True State: James I's Rhetoric of Empire," *History of Political Thought* 25 (2004): 446–480, 473–476.

serious than secretly having two or more spouses in different locales, each unknown to the other. Some distinctions were based on the number of victims drawn into the polygamy. Having three spouses at the same time was worse than having two; having four was worse than having three. Forcing, inducing, or inviting one or more of the spouses to accept the polygamy was worse because it made them accomplices in the defendant's crime, if not criminals themselves. Drawing parents, priests, peers, and others knowingly into blessing or supporting an illegal second or third marriage was also more serious than keeping it secret.

By the seventeenth century, various jurists used these many forms of real polygamy to set out more refined taxonomies of types or degrees of real polygamy, and these slowly began to penetrate the law books and statutes of Western lands.[116] The real payoff for these distinctions came during the sentencing of convicted polygamists. Even though polygamy was a capital offense in the West from the ninth to the nineteenth centuries, execution orders were reserved only for intentional and unrepentant polygamists, especially those who openly kept multiple spouses at the same time or systematically married several women and then abandoned them and their minor children leaving them destitute. Most polygamists were convicted of lower grades of polygamy and faced lighter punishments – shame punishments, public confessions, fines, prison, whipping, indentured servitude, enslavement, banishment, or a term of rowing in the galleys.

From the time of the early Roman Empire until today, it has always been the state that has punished "real polygamy" as a crime, and a rather serious crime at that. Only in the later Middle Ages did "real polygamy" also become a serious spiritual offense, eventually punished simultaneously by the church courts and the Inquisition – and with no sympathy for claims of double jeopardy. By the seventeenth century, however, both Catholic and Protestant churches dropped their involvement in the criminal prosecution of polygamy. But they continued to impose spiritual discipline on real polygamists among their faithful, barring them from the church or at least from church offices.

Constructive Polygamy

Once various degrees of real polygamy came to be classified, it became easier to talk about what Hostiensis called "constructive polgamy" or "quasi-polygamy"

---

[116] The most extensive arguments for the *ius commune* on the Continent are in Diego Garzia de Trasmiera, *De Polygamia et Polyviria libri tres* (Palermo: Apud Decium Cyrillum, 1638); Ioannis Montaigne, *Tractatus de utraque bigamia*, in *Tractatus Universi Juris*, 16 vols. (Venice, 1584), vol. 9, folios 121v-132r. On common law differentiation, see G.W. Bartholomew, "Polygamous Marriages and English Criminal Law," *Modern Law Review* 17 (1954): 344–359; J.H.C. Morris, "The Recognition of Polygamous Marriages in English Law," *Harvard Law Review* 66 (1953): 961–1012.

(*polygamia interpretativa*). This was a form of plural union that approximated, emulated, or was a step on the way toward committing real polygamy. The classic form of constructive polygamy was being doubly engaged, or being married to one spouse and then getting engaged to a second, or vice versa. Another was having a wife as well as a regular live-in concubine (which pre-Christian Roman law had already prohibited). Another was having made religious vows to be a cleric or a monastic (and thus becoming "married" to Christ and the church) but then getting engaged or married to a person. Several other more attenuated forms of quasi-polygamy were recognized as well.

For much of Western legal history, these forms of "constructive polygamy" or "quasi-polygamy" were viewed as spiritual offenses punishable by the church, more than as criminal offenses punishable by the state. But occasionally, these offenses were viewed as both sins and crimes, and subject to the spiritual sanctions of the church and the criminal penalties of the state. For example, in both Germanic law and early modern Protestant law when engagement contracts were taken more seriously and not so easily broken, double engagements or being engaged to one and married to another was punished by both church and state. Similarly, in Catholic lands, monastics or clerics who abandoned their religious vows and got married to another person were not only disciplined by the church but, having lost their privilege of benefit of clergy, were subject to state criminal punishment as well. In these and other instances, the boundary between "real" and "constructive" polygamy was much blurrier. And again, in these cases, claims by some parties of double jeopardy were routinely rebuffed.

Successive Polygamy

A distinct Christian contribution to the Western case for monogamy over polygamy was the concept of "successive polygamy" – improperly being married to two or more spouses in a row rather than at the same time. In several passages, the New Testament strongly discouraged if not outright prohibited the divorced and the widowed from getting remarried. Neither Roman law nor Jewish law recognized these as forms of polygamy before the advent of Christianity, and state laws eventually dropped this category of polygamy after the sixteenth century. But "successive polygamy" of remarried divorcees and widow(er)s was a major part of the Western legal tradition's concerns about polygamy from the fourth to the sixteenth centuries. It dominated a good deal of the theoretical discussion of monogamy versus polygamy in the West, and was sometimes conflated with the discussion of "real polygamy." Some of the arguments that eventually came to justify the prohibitions against successive polygamy also had a bearing on the criminalization of "real polygamy." Some were simple a fortiori arguments: If marriage to two wives in a row is prohibited, then marriage to two at the same time is even more obviously wrong. But more serious were the arguments that focused on the powerful symbolism and social goods of a single monogamous marriage which called both real and successive polygamy into question.

The introduction of this new distinctly Christian form of "polygamy" complicated the Western case for monogamy over polygamy and also complicated the terminology. Later advocates for and against polygamy liked to quote selected passages from some of these earlier sources that seemed to be endorsements or condemnations of "real polygamy" not realizing that many of the passages concerned "successive polygamy" instead of "real polygamy."

Clerical Polygamy or Bigamy

A final distinctive form of plural marriage, also largely introduced by Christianity, was the concept of "clerical bigamy" or "clerical polygamy." This was not a religious official who practiced "real polygamy," as some later commentators mistakenly assumed. It was instead the special offense of a candidate for clerical ordination who had been married to two or more wives in a row (the preceding marriage ending by death, divorce, or annulment) or a candidate who had married only once but his wife was not a virgin at the time of their marriage. Both the Hebrew Bible and early Roman laws governing the pontiffs and temple officials had laws concerned with priestly purity, virginity, and monogamy. But it was again Christianity that made concerns for "clerical bigamy" prominent in the fourth to sixteenth centuries. The basis for these rules was the repeated New Testament statements that a bishop or deacon had to be "the husband of one wife" and a deaconess the "wife of one husband." The emerging rationale for these rules, rooted in the symbolic power of a single monogamous marriage, provided further indirect support for the Western legal tradition's case for monogamy over polygamy.

Those clergy who wittingly or unwittingly had taken two or more wives or a single non-virginal wife before their ordination, were charged with clerical bigamy or clerical polygamy. They were removed from clerical office, and severely sanctioned if they had been intentionally fraudulent in hiding prior multiple marriages or the non-virginity of their one wife. Particularly in the High Middle Ages, church and state officials worked together to root out clerical bigamists, and this prohibition became an important part of the state's criminal law as well as an impediment to a number of civil and political benefits and offices. After the sixteenth century, the category of "clerical bigamy" largely faded from state law, though it remained an important part of Catholic canon law and of early Anglican ecclesiastical law as well.

With this conceptual and linguistic field now before us, let us move into the historical texts, beginning with early Judaism, where "real polygamy" was the only real concern. In the chapters thereafter, we turn to early Christianity, where all these forms of plural union were discussed separately and together – "real," "constructive," "successive," and "clerical" polygamy alike.

1

From Polygamy to Monogamy in Judaism

FIGURE 3. "The Harem," from Thomas Rowlandson, Private Collection.
Used by permission of the Bridgeman Art Library.

FIGURE 4. "The Idolatry of Solomon," from Frans Francken II, Private Collection. Used by permission of the Bridgeman Art Library.

INTRODUCTION

The Hebrew word for a co-wife (*tzarah*) literally means "trouble."[1] Taking a second wife was not viewed as wrong, sinful, unnatural, or evil in ancient Judaism as it was in ancient Greek, Roman, and Christian cultures of the West. But polygamy was, nonetheless, "trouble," and by the eleventh century CE it became more trouble than it was worth and was banned by the Jewish communities of the West.

The original warrant for Jewish polygamy was the Hebrew Bible. To be sure, monogamy was the paradigmatic form of marriage in the Bible. God called the first man and the first woman to "cleave" together as "two in one flesh" and commanded them to be "fruitful and multiply." God modeled this monogamous marriage in his own metaphorical "covenant marriage" with his one chosen bride, Israel. And God set forth his rules for monogamous marriage and family life both in the natural law and in the Mosaic law. Nonetheless, God allowed his ancient chosen people of

---

[1] Michael J. Broyde, "Jewish Law and the Abandonment of Marriage: Diverse Models of Sexuality and Reproduction in the Jewish View, and the Return to Monogamy in the Modern Era," in Michael J. Broyde and Michael Ausubel, eds., *Marriage, Sex, and Family in Judaism* (Lanham, MD: Rowman & Littlefield, 2005), 88–115, at 89.

Israel to practice polygamy. More than two dozen polygamists appear in the Hebrew Bible – almost all of them kings, judges, or members of aristocratic families. Many of these were good men who were faithful to God; two of the kings, in fact, were given their multiple wives directly by God's prophets. None of these men was punished for practicing polygamy. And not a single commandment against – or for – polygamy appeared in the Hebrew Bible.

But a good number of the polygamous patriarchs of the Hebrew Bible had ample "trouble" in their households – bitter rivalry between their wives, bitter disputes among their children over inheritance and political succession, and deadly competition among the half-siblings that ultimately escalated to rape, incest, adultery, kidnapping, enslavement, banishment, murder, and even civil war. The Mosaic law accommodated polygamy, but also set limits on the practice as a safeguard against rivalry and abuse. These limits were also reflected in some of the surviving marriage contracts and instructions from later biblical times.

Throughout the first millennium of the common era, the Rabbis read these Mosaic laws and biblical stories to allow for polygamy, even while Roman and later Germanic laws prohibited the practice with growing severity. Polygamy was never a common practice among the Jews, either in biblical times or after the diaspora in 70 CE. But a few Jewish aristocrats kept multiple wives and concubines throughout the first millennium, following the examples of the biblical patriarchs. While polygamy could and often did spell "trouble," the Rabbis argued, it also could bring ample rewards and benefits: more protection for the man from sexual temptation; more children and laborers for the family business and farm; more power and prestige for the family in the community; more heirs to continue the family name and property; more alliances across family lines; more opportunities for women to marry and have children, especially when men, food, housing, and protection were scarce or when a first husband died prematurely.

By the end of the first millennium of the common era, culminating in the decrees of Rabbi Gershom in ca. 1030, however, much of the Jewish community banned the practice of polygamy and curbed the husband's right of unilateral divorce. The driving concern for these reforms was the "trouble" polygamy caused to wives and children within the household and the trouble that polygamy occasioned for Jewish communities in a Christian culture that was ever more insistent on monogamy. Not all Jews followed this prescribed new path of monogamy thereafter, particularly the Sephardic and Karaite Jews who lived in Muslim and other lands where polygamy was permissible. But the dominant normative position and practice of Jewish law after 1100 was for monogamous marriage as God had created it – a "two in one flesh" union between male and female.

This chapter analyzes briefly the long and complex Jewish pilgrimage over two millennia from polygamy to monogamy – from a legal culture that permitted polygamy as a minority practice alongside monogamy to a legal culture that countenanced monogamy alone.[2]

MONOGAMY VERSUS POLYGAMY IN THE HEBREW BIBLE

The Creation of Monogamy

The two stories of the creation of the world in Genesis 1 and 2 were an essential source for the idea of monogamy in the Jewish tradition – and in the broader Western legal tradition as well. Biblical scholars now believe that these two chapters, written several hundred years apart, first appeared together in the Second Temple period in the sixth century BCE. This was the time when a remnant of the Jews returned to the land of Israel from Babylonian exile, rebuilt the temple in Jerusalem, and reissued the Torah (the Jewish law), now with these creation narratives at its head.[3] These creation narratives became both a celebration of the divine origins of marriage and, for some later interpreters, the starting point for a natural law governing men and women, husbands and wives.[4]

The older account of the creation of man and woman – written some 3,000 years ago, in the tenth or early ninth century BCE – appears in Genesis 2:18–24. The first verses of Genesis 2 recount how God created the heavens and the earth and placed the first man in a paradise, called the Garden of Eden. But this paradise was not complete without the creation of the first woman:

> Then the Lord said, "It is not good that the man should be alone. I will make him a helper as his partner." So out of the ground the Lord formed every animal of the field and every bird of the air, and brought them to the man to see what he would call them; and whatever the man called every living creature, that was its name. The man gave names to all cattle, and to the birds of the air, and to every animal of the field; but for the man there was not found a helper as his partner. So the Lord God caused a deep sleep to fall upon him, and he slept; then he took one of his ribs and closed up the place with flesh. And the rib that the Lord God had taken from the man he made into a woman and brought her to the man. Then the man

[2] This chapter draws heavily on a detailed research memorandum commissioned from my former student, now colleague, Mark Goldfeder. His original research memorandum was so excellent that I encouraged him to publish it as a freestanding article, which he has now done. See Mark A. Goldfeder, "The Story of Jewish Polygamy," *Columbia Journal of Law and Gender* 26 (2014): 234–315. With his kind permission, I have drawn on his sources and translations throughout; where I have used his writing directly I have quoted him.

[3] See John J. Collins, "Marriage, Divorce, and Family in Second Temple Judaism," in Leo G. Perdue et al., eds., *Families in Ancient Israel* (Louisville, KY: Westminster John Knox Press, 1997), 104–162, at 127–128.

[4] See David Novak, *Natural Law in Judaism* (Cambridge: Cambridge University Press, 1998).

said, "This at last is bone of my bones and flesh of my flesh; this one shall be called Woman, for out of Man this one was taken." Therefore a man leaves his father and his mother and clings to his wife, and they become one flesh.[5]

"One-flesh" union meant more than just the sexual coupling between a man and a woman. The Hebrew word for "flesh" (*basar*) is better translated as "human substance" or "real human life."[6] To be joined in one flesh signifies "the personal community of man and woman in the broadest sense – bodily and spiritual community, mutual help and understanding, joy and contentment in each other."[7] Especially when read in the context of Adam's searching for a proper mate, the passage underscores that it was only in the woman, and not in any other creature, that the man found someone like him, someone with whom to compare and complete himself. To be fully human thereafter, Adam and Eve needed each other.[8] That was what Adam was celebrating when he said of Eve, "This at last is bone of my bones and flesh of my flesh." And that is the fundamental human good that the institution of marriage serves to confirm, channel, and celebrate. The Talmudic Rabbis taught that it is "only after marriage and the union of man and woman into one person that the image of God may be discerned in them. An unmarried man, in their eyes, is not a whole man."[9] The later Book of Ecclesiastes (ca. 400 BCE) also underscored this: "Two are better than one, because they have a good reward for their toil. For if they fall, one will lift up the other.... Again, if two lie together, they keep warm; but how can one keep warm alone?"[10]

A later account of creation recorded in Genesis 1 emphasized that the man and the woman were created as image-bearers of God and are commanded to become two in one flesh in order to produce children and to continue to populate the earth with God's image-bearers.

> Then God said, "Let us make humankind in our image, according to our likeness; and let them have dominion over the fish of the sea, and over the birds of the air, and over the cattle, and over all the wild animals of the earth, and over every creeping thing that creeps upon the earth." So God created human kind in his image, in the image of God he created them, male and female he created them.

[5] Genesis 2:18–24 (NRSV). All biblical quotations herein are from the Revised Standard Version (RSV) unless (as here) otherwise indicated.

[6] Michael G. Lawler, *Secular Marriage, Christian Sacrament* (New York: Twenty-Third Publications, 1985), 6–8.

[7] Claus Westerman, *Genesis 1–11: A Commentary*, trans. J.J. Scullion, S.J. (Minneapolis, MN: Augsburg Publishing House, 1984), 232.

[8] John E. Coons and Patrick M. Brennan, *By Nature Equal: The Anatomy of a Western Insight* (Princeton, NJ: Princeton University Press, 1999), 55–62.

[9] Lawler, *Secular Marriage, Christian Sacrament*, 7–8. See BT Yevamot 62b; Genesis Rabbi 17:2 on Gen. 2:18 and further discussion in Judith R. Baskin, "Bolsters to Their Husbands: Women as Wives in Rabbinic Literature," *European Judaism* 37(2) (2004): 88–102.

[10] Ecclesiastes 4:9–11.

God blessed them, and God said to them, "Be fruitful and multiply, and fill the earth and subdue it."[11]

Genesis 5:1–2 repeated this creation account more cryptically: "When God created humankind, he made them in the likeness of God. Male and female he created them, and he blessed them and named them 'humankind' [*adam*] when they were created." But the story went on to describe how the perfect order of creation was destroyed by the fall of Adam and Eve into sin. The first sins recorded in the Bible thereafter were Cain's murder of his brother Abel, and then his son Lamech's act of taking "two wives" instead of one, and also committing murder.[12] An angry God thus destroyed the creation with the Flood. He saved only Noah and his family and notably "two of every sort of animal … male and female."[13] After the Flood, God restored the world and repeated his command "to be fruitful and multiply, bring forth abundantly on the earth and multiply in it."[14]

These creation narratives, the Talmudic Rabbis later made clear, were not about marriage per se, save the oblique reference to a man "clinging" to his "wife" rather than just any woman. But these narratives were a primal source of the natural institution of marriage, whose rules, procedures, and aspirations were laid out more fully in the rest of the Hebrew Bible, not least the Mosaic law. The Hebrew Bible later treated God's ceremonial presentation of Eve to Adam as a celebration of the first wedding feast. The Book of Tobit, from the fourth or third century BCE, celebrates this in the wedding prayer that Tobias offered to his new wife Sarah:

> Blessed are you, O God of our ancestors. And blessed is your name in all generations forever. Let the heavens and the whole creation bless you forever. You made Adam, and for him you made his wife Eve as a helper and support. From the two of them the human race has sprung. You said, "It is not good that the man should be alone; let us make a helper for him like himself." I am now taking this kinswoman of mine, not because of lust, but with sincerity. Grant that she and I may find mercy and that we may grow old together.[15]

All these creation narratives and celebrations privileged monogamy, the union of one man and one woman. That monogamous ideal was repeated several times in later passages in the Hebrew Bible that enjoined a man to "cling" to his wife

---

[11] Genesis 1:26–31 (NRSV).

[12] Genesis 4:19–24.

[13] Genesis 7:9. But see Genesis 7:2–3, where seven pairs of some animals are taken.

[14] Genesis 9:1–7.

[15] Tobit 8:5–7 (NRSV). Mark Goldfeder makes clear that Tobit is not generally considered part of the Hebrew Bible canon, although it makes an appearance in truncated form in the Midrash *Bereishit Rabbah*. For other Jewish wedding feasts, he cites Midrash *Tehillim* [ed. Buber] 68:4, Geneses Rabbah 18:1 Midrash *Tanhuma* [ed. Buber], Hayei Sarah 2. In BT Berakhot 61a, God even acted as the "best man" of sorts at a wedding feast.

exclusively, forgoing all others.[16] "Drink waters from your own cistern, flowing water from your own well," the ancient Proverb declared metaphorically. "Let your fountain be blessed and rejoice in the wife of your youth. Let her affection fill you at all times with delight, be infatuated always with her love."[17] "Enjoy life with the wife whom you love, all the days of your life."[18] The Prophet Malachi rebuked a man for betraying his wife in defiance of God's own created order of monogamous marriage and his own faithful covenant marriage to his single metaphorical bride, Israel. "[T]he Lord was witness to the covenant between you and the wife of your youth, to whom you have been faithless, though she is your companion and your wife by covenant. Has not the one God made and sustained for us the spirit of life? And what does he desire? Godly offspring. So take heed to yourselves, and let none be faithless to the wife of his youth."[19]

Polygamy for Procreation

But this biblical ideal of faithful monogamy sometimes stood in tension with the biblical command to procreate. What must a man do if his wife would not or could not conceive? He must "marry another woman to procreate through her," the Rabbis said[20] – either divorcing his first wife as Deuteronomy 24:1–4 allowed him to do or retaining his first wife while adding another. "No man may abstain from keeping the law 'Be fruitful and multiply' (Gen. 1:28), unless he already has children," the Rabbis declared. "If he married a woman and lived with her ten years and she bore no child, it is not permitted him to abstain" from fulfilling his legal obligation to procreate.[21]

The second woman brought into the marital bed to produce children could be either a wife or a concubine. A concubine (*pilegesh*) in the Hebrew Bible was generally viewed as a secondary wife, and the man was called her "husband."[22] Unlike a prostitute, a concubine in ancient Israel lived within the man's household, and she and her children received daily support, special gifts, and inheritance from her husband. She was also expected to remain faithful to the man and could be charged

---

[16] See, e.g., Proverbs 2:17; Ezekiel 16:8.
[17] Proverbs 5:18–19.
[18] Ecclesiastes 9:9.
[19] Malachi 2:13–16.
[20] Mishnah Sotah, 4:3.
[21] See also Tosefta Yevamot 8:5. But see the Midrash *Pesikt de-Rav Kahana* 22:2, quoted and discussed in Baskin, "Bolsters to Their Husbands," 99, offering alternative Midrashic texts on this obligation to take a second wife or divorce the first.
[22] See, e.g., Judges 19:3.

with adultery if she slept with someone else; any child born of that adulterine union would be deemed a bastard (*mamzer*).[23]

The Rabbis pointed to the story of Abraham, Sarah, and Hagar, recorded in Genesis 15–16, as the exemplary biblical case of practicing polygamy for the sake of procreation.[24] God had promised Abraham that he would have a son as his heir, who would yield countless descendants – as many "as the stars of the heavens and the sand on the seashore."[25] But for ten years thereafter Abraham and his wife Sarah had no children. Concerned that time was running out, Sarah urged Abraham to take her maidservant Hagar and have children by her following the custom of the day for childless couples. Abraham obliged. Hagar conceived and bore Abraham a son named Ishmael.

But the Rabbis also pointed to the story of Abraham as a warning that a second wife brought "trouble" to the household, even for a faithful man of God like Abraham. For the Genesis story went on to report that, already when she was pregnant, Hagar "looked with contempt" upon Sarah, her barren mistress.[26] Sarah was livid. She dealt harshly with Hagar who fled into the wilderness until an angel enjoined Hagar to return. Ishmael was born and raised in Abraham's household. Abraham embraced him as his firstborn son and circumcised him to signify him as one of God's own. Fifteen years later, however, Abraham and Sarah were miraculously blessed with the birth of their own son Isaac, as God had promised. Sarah grew jealous of the adolescent Ishmael "playing with" her newly weaned son Isaac.[27] She grew concerned about Isaac's claims to Abraham's vast wealth. "Cast out this slave woman with her son," she enjoined Abraham, "for the son of this slave woman will not be heir with my son Isaac."[28] Abraham sent Hagar and Ishmael away into the desert. An angel again saved them, and Ishmael grew up to be a skilled huntsman and warrior. He became the father of twelve sons who became princes of the tribes of the ancient Middle East.[29] After his wife Sarah died, Abraham remarried, and he also took more concubines. He gave Ishmael and other unnamed "sons of his concubines" various gifts but no inheritance; his estate went to Isaac.[30]

---

[23] See Michael L. Satlow, *Jewish Marriage in Antiquity* (Princeton, NJ: Princeton University Press, 2001), 192–195.

[24] BT Yevamot 64a.

[25] Genesis 15:2–6; 22:17.

[26] Genesis 16:4.

[27] "*Tzad chet hoof*," the Hebrew words for "playing," often have a sexual overtone in the Hebrew Bible. See, e.g., Genesis 17:17, 18:12–15, 19:14, 21:6–9, 26:8, 39:14–17. I am grateful to my colleague Michael J. Broyde for alerting me to this reading.

[28] Genesis 21:8–10.

[29] Genesis 25:9–18.

[30] Genesis 25:1–6.

Abraham was not the only early biblical patriarch to take other women to bear him children. His brother Nahor had a wife and a concubine, too, who produced a dozen children for him.[31] His grandsons Esau and Jacob were also polygamists, but like Abraham they had trouble. Esau's multiple wives, some of them foreigners, the Bible reports, "made life bitter" for Esau's parents, Isaac and Rebekah, and this greatly "displeased" them.[32] Esau's brother Jacob had even more trouble. Their uncle Laban had tricked Jacob into marrying his elder daughter, the "weak-eyed" Leah, instead of her sister, the beautiful Rachel whom Jacob loved. Jacob, after working for seven years to get this privilege, had reluctantly retained Leah. A week later, he got permission to marry Rachel as well but only in exchange for seven more years of labor and a later warning from Laban: "If you ill-treat my daughters, or take other wives besides my daughters, though no one else be about, remember, God Himself will be witness between you and me."[33] Jacob "hated" Leah, Genesis reports, but she produced many sons for him. Jacob loved Rachel, but she produced no children. This put Rachel and Leah in bitter conflict. Escalating the hostility, Rachel gave Jacob her maidservant Bilhah who produced two sons for Jacob. Leah countered by giving Jacob her maidservant Zilpah who produced yet another son. All the while, Jacob continued to sleep with Rachel, who finally conceived and had a son Joseph. This only escalated the feud between Rachel and Leah. The sins of these parents were visited on their children, too. Joseph's half-brothers sold him into slavery in Egypt, and only miraculously were they reconciled.[34] Reuben, the eldest son of Jacob, later slept with his step-mother and was disinherited.[35] Judah impregnated his daughter-in-law, whom he had mistaken for a prostitute.[36]

A third biblical story of polygamy and procreation in 1 Samuel 1 also featured bitter rivalry between two wives. A man of God named Elkanah had taken two wives, Hannah and Peninnah. He loved them both, but Hannah produced no children, while Peninnah produced many, so Elkanah gave Peninnah the lion share of the food and sacrificial offering. This produced "rivalry" between the wives "year after year," the Bible reports: Peninnah would "provoke [Hannah] sorely to irritate her, because the Lord had closed her womb." Hannah "was deeply distressed and wept bitterly" and stopped eating. Only after she prayed fervently for many days in the temple was she finally able to produce a son for Elkanah, the later prophet Samuel.[37] It was stories like this that prompted Ben Sirach later to say: "It is a heartache and

[31] Genesis 22:20–24.
[32] Genesis 26:34–35; 28:6–9.
[33] Genesis 31:50.
[34] Genesis 37:1–28.
[35] Genesis 35:22; 49:2–3; 1 Chronicles 5:1.
[36] Genesis 38.
[37] 1 Samuel 1:1–20.

sorrow when one wife is the rival to another."[38] "Happy is the man who has [one] good wife, the number of his days is doubled. A noble wife gladdens her husband, and he lives out his years in peace. A good wife is good fortune; she falls to the lot of those who fear the Lord. Whether rich or poor, he has a stout heart, and always a cheerful face."[39]

Polygamy for Power and Prestige

The patriarchs of the Hebrew Bible practiced polygamy not only to produce children but also to demonstrate their wealth and power. Several judges and kings of later Israel, most of them faithful men of God, were polygamists. The good Judge Gideon, the Bible reports, had "many wives" who produced for him "seventy sons."[40] King Saul had an unspecified number of wives as well as a concubine.[41] His rival and successor, the great King David had seven wives before he reigned in Jerusalem,[42] and added more wives and concubines when he left Hebron.[43] The Bible reports that some of these wives were, in fact, King Saul's widows whom God had given to David when he took over the throne: "I gave you your master's house, and your master's wives into your bosom ... and if this were too little I would add to you as much more."[44] King Solomon had a harem of 700 wives and 300 concubines.[45] King Jehoiachin had an unspecified numbers of "wives."[46] King Manasseh had a wife and at least one concubine.[47] King Rehoboam of the House of Judah had eighteen wives and sixty concubines; they produced for him twenty-eight sons for whom he sought multiple wives as well.[48] King Abijah of Judah had fourteen wives who produced twenty-two sons and sixteen daughters.[49] King Ahab of Israel was said to have the "fairest wives" of unspecified number.[50] King Joash, the Bible reports, "did what was right in the eyes of the Lord all the days of Jehoiada the priest. Jehoiada got for him two wives, and he had sons and daughters."[51] The chronicles and genealogies in the

---

[38] Ecclesiasticus 26:6.
[39] Ecclesiasticus 26:1–4.
[40] Judges 8:30.
[41] 2 Samuel 3:7; 12:8.
[42] 2 Samuel 3:2–5, 14.
[43] 2 Samuel 5:13.
[44] 2 Samuel 12:8.
[45] 1 Kings 11:3.
[46] 2 Kings 24:15.
[47] 1 Chronicles 7:14.
[48] 2 Chronicles 11:21, 23.
[49] 2 Chronicles 13:21.
[50] 1 Kings 20:3.
[51] 2 Chronicles 24:3.

Hebrew Bible also name a dozen other minor judges or men of leading families who were said to have more than one wife or who had so many children that they had to have had multiple wives and concubines.[52]

These royal and aristocratic polygamous households of ancient Israel had fewer reported troubles than those of Abraham, Esau, and Jacob. But some of these polygamous families were plagued with trouble, too. Gideon's son, Abilemech, born of a concubine, killed seventy of his half-brothers in order to succeed to their father; only one half-brother named Jotham escaped, and he stoked up insurrection against Abilemech that plagued his reign as Judge of Israel.[53] King David, despite having an ample harem already, lusted after the beautiful Bathsheba, wife of Uriah. He committed adultery with her, leading to her pregnancy. David then had Bathsheba's husband killed, and married her.[54] God's prophet condemned him. David ultimately repented of his sin, and he and Bathsheba were rewarded with the birth of the later King Solomon. But David's polygamous household was rife with conflict thereafter. His son Amnon lusted after his half-sister Tamar for a long time. She befriended and cared for him. But when she refused his sexual advances, Amnon raped Tamar to her great shame and grief. Tamar's full brother Absalom was outraged and had Amnon murdered. This set off a bitter feud within King David's household, made worse by Absalom sleeping with one of his father's wives while he rebelled against his father; he was eventually killed, much to David's grief.[55] King Solomon, despite his special divine gift of wisdom, was ultimately misled by his many wives to worship false gods, and had to forfeit most of his kingdom, save Judah, under pressure of his competing half-sons and other kin who were fomenting civil war.[56]

Polygamy of Necessity

The Hebrew Bible also countenanced polygamy in cases of necessity. Even a polygamous marriage was considered better for a woman in that ancient world

---

[52] In alphabetical order: Judge Abon with forty sons (Judges 12:14); Ashur, the father of Tekoa in the family of Judah with two wives (1 Chronicles 4:5); Caleb of the House of Judah with five wives and a concubine (1 Chronicles 2:18–19, 46–48); Esau's son Eliphaz had a wife and a concubine (Genesis 36:10–12); Ezra with two wives, perhaps concurrent (1 Chronicles. 4:17–18); Judge Ibzan with thirty sons and thirty daughters (Judges 12:9); Judge Jair who had thirty sons (Judges 10:4); Judge Jerahmeel had two wives and six sons (1 Chronicles 2:25–26); Machir of the family of Naphthali had two wives (1 Chronicles 15–16); Mered of the house of Judah had four wives (1 Chronicles 4:17–19); Shaharaim of the house of Benjamin had three wives and nine sons (1 Chronicles 8:8–10); Jacob's son Simeon with two wives and six sons (Genesis 46:10; Exodus 6:15). The Web site biblicalpolygamy.com includes ten more biblical figures, but their polygamy is not so clear.

[53] Judges 9:1–6.

[54] 2 Samuel 11:1–27.

[55] 2 Samuel 13–19:8; 1 Kings 1–2.

[56] 1 Kings 11.

than spinsterhood or widowhood, or being consigned to her father's or brother's house after reaching maturity.[57] The Prophet Isaiah, for example, pointed out that in times of war, famine, or pestilence, when "men were more rare than fine gold," a proverbial "seven women" – that is, a complete number – would be happy to marry one husband rather than be endangered by living alone, or disgraced by not having a marital home and children: "And seven women shall take hold of one man in that day, saying, 'We will eat our own bread and wear our own clothes, only let us be called by your name; take away our reproach.'"[58]

This same principle of necessity was at work in the early biblical practice of "levirate marriage." This was the ancient custom that a brother (a *levir*) was to marry his dead brother's widow, evidently even if that surviving brother was already married. Genesis 38 reports that Judah's first son Er was married to a woman named Tamar. When he died, Judah ordered his next son Onan to take Tamar as his wife "to raise up offspring for your brother." Onan slept with Tamar but "spilled his seed on the ground" for which sin God "slew him." Tamar was sent back to her father's house to wait until Judah's third son Shelah was of age to marry her.[59]

A variation of this practice of levirate marriage is described in the touching early biblical story of a widow named Naomi and her daughter-in-law Ruth. Naomi's husband Elimelech owned land in Israel, but he lived in Moab with his two sons, one of whom, Mahlon, was married to Ruth. Elimelech and his two sons died in a famine. Naomi and Ruth decided to return to Israel. On arrival, Ruth gleaned the fields of one of Naomi's kinsmen, Boaz, who befriended her and gave her and Naomi food. Boaz then sought to have Naomi's family's land sold to her next of kin, which came with the customary obligation to take care of Naomi and Ruth, the widow of the heritable son Mahlon. If that kinsman would not buy the land, Boaz said, he himself would buy it and take up the obligation of care for Ruth and Naomi. The Book of Ruth chapter 4 reports this exchange between Boaz and his kinsman:

> Then Boaz said, "The day you buy the field from the hand of Naomi, you are also buying Ruth the Moabitess, the widow of the dead, in order to restore the name of the dead to his inheritance." The next of kin said: "I cannot redeem it for myself, lest I impair my own inheritance. Take my right of redemption yourself, for I cannot redeem it."[60]

The story goes on to report that Boaz then purchased the land, and married Ruth. They had a son Obed whom Naomi nursed and through whom the family name was

57 See Claire Gottlieb, "Varieties of Marriage in the Bible and Their Analogues in the Ancient World" (Ph.D. Diss. New York University, 1989), 86.
58 Isaiah 4:1; 13:12.
59 Genesis 38:1–11.
60 Ruth 4:5–6.

preserved.[61] These rules of levirate marriage, made necessary by the early death of a husband, became a rule of the Mosaic law, and one of the most important sources of polygamy in later Jewish law.

The Mosaic Law

Some of these early practices of polygamy reported in the Hebrew Bible were reflected in the Mosaic law. Monogamy was presupposed in the many detailed Mosaic laws on marital formation, maintenance, and dissolution; on proper sexual behavior by men and women before, within, and after marriage; on the special roles and duties of boy and girl, man and woman, fiancé and fiancée, husband and wife, parent and child, master and servant, brother and sister-in-law, householder and patriarch; and on dowries, marital property, child support, and family inheritance, including primogeniture (the testamentary privileging of the eldest male).

Although monogamy was presupposed, the Mosaic law both contemplated and regulated the practice of polygamy. The Mosaic laws of levirate marriage, which we just encountered in the early stories of Tamar and Ruth, presupposed a world of polygamy. Deuteronomy 25 reads:

> "If brethren dwell together, and one of them dies, and has no child, the wife of the dead shall not be married outside the family to a stranger; her husband's brother shall go in to her, and take her as his wife, and perform the duty of a husband's brother to her." And the first son whom she bears shall succeed to the name of his brother who is dead, that his name may not be blotted out of Israel. And if the man does not wish to take his brother's wife, then his brother's wife shall go up to the gate to the elders, and say, "My husband's brother refuses to perpetuate his brother's name in Israel; he will not perform the duty of a husband's brother to me." Then the elders of his city shall call him, and speak to him, and if he persists, saying "I do not wish to take her," then his brother's wife shall go up to him in the presence of the elders, and pull his sandal off his foot, and spit in his face; and she shall answer and say, "So shall it be done to the man who does not build up his brother's house." And the name of his house shall be called in Israel, The house of him that had his sandal pulled off.[62]

The Mosaic law of incest prohibited a man from any sexual encounter with his brother's wife; this was serious incest.[63] But the duty of levirate marriage was the exception to this rule. Breaching this duty brought shame on the man and his

---

[61]   Ruth 4:13–21.
[62]   Deuteronomy 25:5–10.
[63]   Leviticus 18:16 and 20:21.

household. Many later Rabbis made clear that it was no excuse for a man to refuse this levirate marriage duty because he was already married.[64]

Polygamy was implicit in another law of incest set out in Leviticus 18:18: "And you shall not take a woman as a rival wife to her sister, uncovering her nakedness while her sister is yet alive." The implication of this passage is that a man could take another unrelated woman as a second wife, but not a sister to his first wife, lest there be rivalry akin to that between Jacob's sister wives, Leah and Rachel. Some later interpreters would read this passage the opposite way as an a fortiori argument against polygamy: If even two sisters, who are more inclined to love and forgive each other, cannot get along in a polygamous household, then surely two unrelated women, who do not have that natural affection, cannot forced to compete for the same husband and his resources in a polygamous household. But the Talmudic Rabbis read this passage to say a man can take two or more wives, so long as they are not sisters.

Polygamy was also implicit in the law of seduction. The Mosaic law prohibited an engaged or married woman from having sex with any other man. A woman who did so was charged with adultery, and she was to be stoned to death along with her lover – unless she could prove that the man raped her despite her resistance.[65] It was not considered adultery, however, for a single or married man to have sex with prostitutes, maidservants, or single slaves.[66] Even so, the Mosaic law provided: "If a man seduces a virgin, who is not betrothed, and lies with her, he shall give the marriage present for her, and make her his wife. If her father utterly refuses to give her to him, he shall pay money equivalent to the marriage present for virgins."[67] In the event of marriage, "because he has violated her, he may not put her away [by divorce] all his days."[68] This duty of a seducer to marry his lover without divorce was a protection for a despoiled virgin. The duty applied to him, whether he was married or unmarried at the time of the seduction, the Rabbis later said. If a married man seduced a virgin, he had to pay her father the bride price and marry her, too, if the father consented.

The Mosaic law of slavery also presupposed the practice of polygamy. Exodus 21 reads:

> When you buy a Hebrew slave, he shall serve six years, and in the seventh he shall go out free, for nothing. If he comes in single, he shall go out single; if he comes in married, then his wife shall go out with him. If the master gives him a wife and she

[64] Mishnah Yevamot 4:11.
[65] Deuteronomy 22:22–27; Leviticus 20:10.
[66] Leviticus 20:20–22.
[67] Exodus 22:16–17; Deuteronomy 22:28–29.
[68] Deuteronomy 22:29.

bears him sons or daughters, the wife and her children will be her master's and he shall go out alone. But if the slave plainly says, "I love my master, my wife, and my children: I will not go out free," then his master will bring him to God, and he shall bring him to the door or the doorpost; and his master shall bore his ear through with an awl; and he shall serve him for life.[69]

This was not an explicit endorsement of polygamy, but it presupposed that a master could simply add his slave's wife and children to his household even if that master was already married. If her husband left her upon his emancipation from slavery, the slave woman could remain unmarried, but she could just as well be added to the master's harem.

A more explicit endorsement for polygamy came through in the related rules of arranged marriages, which, given the presupposition of dower payments to the father for the hand of the bride, were sometimes tantamount to slavery with the daughter called a "slave." Exodus 21 continued:

When a man sells his daughter as a slave, she shall not go out as the male slaves do. If she does not please her master, who has designated her for himself [as a wife], then he shall let her be redeemed; he has no right to sell her to a foreign people, since he has dealt faithlessly with her. If he designates her for his son [to marry], he shall deal with her as with a daughter. If he takes another wife to himself, he shall not diminish her food, her clothing, or her marital rights.[70]

This passage placed clear limits on the authority of the husband respecting his first wife. He was allowed to "take another wife," but he had to give equal treatment to his first wife.

Another passage, in Deuteronomy 21, ordered a polygamous man to give equal treatment to the children of his two wives as well when it came to inheritance, even if there was conflict in the household:

If a man has two wives, the one loved and the other disliked, and they have borne him children, both the loved and the disliked, and if the first-born son is hers that is disliked, then on the day when he assigns his possessions as an inheritance to his sons, he may not treat the son of the loved as the first-born in preference to the son of the disliked who is the first-born.[71]

Finally, the Mosaic law explicitly warned the kings of Israel not to have too many wives: "And he shall not multiply wives for himself, lest his heart turn away; nor shall he multiply for himself silver and gold."[72] And, in elaboration of the Mosaic law of

---

[69] Exodus 21:1–6.
[70] Exodus 21:7–12.
[71] Deuteronomy 21:15–16.
[72] Deuteronomy 17:17. See also 1 Kings 11:4.

priestly purity, "the High Priests of Jerusalem were expressly commanded to marry but one wife."[73]

Not much evidence survives of these early Mosaic laws in action. But a few surviving marital contracts from the fifth century BCE make clear that the spouses could agree that the husband give up the right to add more wives. Laban had extracted this promise from his nephew Jacob, as we saw. This no-polygamy provision was included in a Jewish marriage contract found in Elephantine, a Jewish colony in Egypt, and dated around 441 BCE. Here the husband (Ashor) promises the wife (Miphtahiah) as follows:

> And I shall have no right to say I have another wife besides Miphtahiah and other children than the children whom Miphtahiah shall bear to me. If I say I have children and wife other than Miphtahiah and her children, I will pay to Miphtahiah the sum of 20 kerashin, royal weight, and I shall have no right to take away my goods and chattels from Miphtahiah; and if I remove them from her (erasure) I will pay to Miphtahiah the sum of 20 kerashin, royal weight.[74]

And at least one ancient Jewish community, living in Qumran near the Dead Sea, rejected polygamy as an option for their members. The Dead Sea Scrolls that have survived from this community condemn marriage to one's niece, divorce, and polygamy, calling all of them forms of fornication (*zenut*), even though the Mosaic law had allowed all three of these practices.[75] One first century BCE scroll from the Qumran, named the "Damascus Document," provided as follows:

> They are caught by fornication, taking two wives in their lives, while the foundation of creation is "male and female he created them." And those who entered [Noah's] ark went two by two into the ark. And of the prince it is written "Let him not multiply wives for himself."[76]

---

73 Ze'ev W. Falk, *Jewish Matrimonial Law in the Middle Ages* (Oxford: Oxford University Press, 1966), 5–6, citing BT Yoma 13a; M Yoma 2a. See Leviticus 16:9–11 and 21:1–24 for the laws of priestly purity and M Yoma 2a. Falk says that this rule of priestly monogamy, while not explicit in the Hebrew Bible, was "a rule established while the Temple was still standing." Ibid., 6. n.1. Priestly monogamy was also the rule in ancient Egypt. See sources in Louis M. Epstein, *Marriage Laws in the Bible and the Talmud* (Cambridge, MA: Harvard University Press, 1942), 10.

74 Arthur E. Cowley, ed., *Aramaic Papyri of the Fifth Century, B.C.* (Osnabruck: Otto Zeller, 1967), 45–46. See parallel agreements in Babylonian and Assyrian documents described in *Encyclopedia Judaica*,12:259; Falk, *Jewish Matrimonial Law*, 5.

75 See Robert Eisenman, *James the Brother of Jesus: The Key to Unlocking the Secrets of Early Christianity and the Dead Sea Scrolls* (New York: Viking Books, 1997), 40, 81, 104.

76 Damascus Document 4:20–5:5 in James H. Charlesworth et al., eds., *The Dead Sea Scrolls; Hebrew, Aramaic, and Greek Texts, with English Translations*, 4 vols. (Tübingen: Mohr Siebeck/Louisville, KY: Westminster John Knox Press, 1997), 2:19–21 (quoting Genesis 1:26; Deuteronomy 17:17).

MONOGAMY VERSUS POLYGAMY
IN THE MISHNAH AND TALMUD

While the Qumran community may have prohibited polygamy, most other Jewish communities permitted the practice, before and after the destruction of the Temple and the diaspora of the Jews in 70 CE. Jewish historian Josephus (37–ca. 100 CE), for example, said that "it is our ancestral custom that a man have several wives at the same time."[77] Early Church Father, Justin Martyr (d. 165 CE), included in his diatribe against Judaism a complaint that the "blind and stupid sages" of his day permitted Jewish men to "marry four or five wives at a time"[78] Justin Martyr went on derisively:

> If any of you [Jews] see a beautiful woman, and desire to have her, they [the rabbis] cite the example of Jacob, who was Israel, and other Patriarchs to prove that there is no evil in such practices. How wretched and ignorant they are even in this respect! ... [Y]our teachers never considered the more divine in the purpose for which each thing was done, but rather what concerned base and corruptible passions.[79]

But the Rabbis who discussed polygamy were not exercising "base and corruptible passions" so much as discerning the purpose of "the divine" in giving them the Mosaic laws that included polygamy. Although monogamy was the norm, polygamy had been allowed by the Mosaic law. The practice thus persisted in first millennium CE Judaism "in a small number of noble families side by side with monogamy among the people at large," writes Jewish family law historian, Ze'ev Falk. "The vast majority of Jews [practiced] monogamy, yet no general prohibition against polygamy was laid down" by the Rabbis either in the Mishnah of the late second century CE or in the Jerusalem and Babylonian Talmuds of the fifth and sixth centuries CE.[80] Instead, the Rabbis followed the Mosaic law in favoring monogamy but in permitting polygamy and regulating its use in accordance with the moral lessons of the Hebrew Bible.

[77] Flavius Josephus, *The Wars of the Jews*, 1.24.2, in *Josephus in Nine Volumes*, Louis H. Feldman et al., trans. and eds. (Cambridge, MA: Harvard University Press, 1934–1965), volume 2; Flavius Josephus, *Jewish Antiquities*, 17.1–3, 14, in ibid., volume 8. See also BT Sukah 27a.

[78] Justin Martyr, *Dialogue with Trypho*, c. 134, in *The Fathers of the Church: Saint Justin Martyr*, Thomas B. Falls, trans. and ed. (Washington, DC: Catholic University Press of America, 1965).

[79] Ibid.

[80] Falk, *Jewish Matrimonial Law*, 2–6. See also Satlow, *Jewish Marriage in Antiquity*, 189–192; Epstein, *Marriage Laws*, 12–33; Adiel Schremer, "How Much Jewish Polygny in Roman Palestine?" *Proceedings of the American Academy for Jewish Research* 63 (1997–2001): 181–223.

Monogamous Teachings

The Rabbis reminded their readers that God had created the marriage of Adam and Eve as "two in one flesh" and had declared his creation to be "very good."[81] As Rabbi Yehuda ben Beteira put it: "If Adam was intended to have ten wives, they would have been given to him. But he was intended to marry only one wife. So, too, my wife is enough for me. My portion is enough."[82] A Midrash on Genesis criticized the first biblical polygamist, Lamech, for taking two wives – the first wife LaAddah for procreation, the second Zilla for sexual pleasure. By having two wives, the Midrash said, Lamech's first wife was reduced to "a widow" while his second wife was treated "like a harlot."[83] This same concern about stigmatizing multiple wives made Rabbi Judah hesitant to allow his long absent son either to divorce his now barren wife who had waited for him while he was away studying or to add a second wife for procreation since others would likely call her "his mistress."[84] Judah's grandson Hillel was more acerbic: "He who multiplies wives multiplies witchcraft."[85] The Rabbis practiced what they preached: "Among the numerous rabbis whose biographies are recounted in the Talmudic sources not one was a bigamist."[86]

The Rabbis made clear that polygamy was not always good for the man either. The Babylonian Talmud included an account of Rabbi Isaac who told a parable about a man who had two wives, one young and one old: "The young one used to pluck out his white hair, and the old one used to pluck out his black hair. Finally, he was bald on both sides."[87] Elsewhere, the Talmud warned a man: "Do not marry two women. But if you do marry two [women], then marry a third."[88] The worry, later commentators explained, was that two wives may conspire against the husband, but a third would check the first two and provide insurance for her husband.[89]

The Rabbis also warned about the problems of inheritance among rival wives and their children. When Rabbi Tarfon was asked about the status of the children of rival wives,[90] he replied:

---

[81] Midrash Genesis Rabbah, 9:7.
[82] Quoted by Solomon Schechter, ed., *Avot D'Rabbi Nathan*, Version B (Vienna: Chaim David Lippe, 1887), ch. 2, 9. See also BT Sanhedrin 97a.
[83] Genesis Rabbah 23:2. See also JT Yevamot 7d.
[84] BT Ketubot 62a.
[85] BT Ab 2,5, translated by Epstein, *Marriage Laws*, 19.
[86] Falk, *Jewish Matrimonial Law*, 6. But see Goldfeder, "The Story of Jewish Polygamy," 261–262, who references JT Yevamot 4:12 and BT Yevamot 37b, cryptically referencing a few Jewish sages being at least nominally polygamous.
[87] BT Bava Kamma 60b.
[88] BT Pesachim 113a.
[89] Ibid.
[90] A disagreement between the Houses of Shammai and Hillel recorded in M Yevamot 1:4.

"Why do you put my head between two great mountains, between the House of Shammai and the House of Hillel? They will destroy my head! However I testify that the family of the House of Alubai from Beit Sevaim and the family of the House of Kufai from Beit Mekoshish are the descendants of rival wives. And high priests have come from them that have presided over sacrifices at the temple." Rabbi Tarfon said, "I want a daughter of a rival-wife to come before me so that I can marry her into the priesthood."[91]

The worry about children also extended to the problems of unintentional incest that could result. Intentional incest was evident already in the polygamous household of King David, where numerous half-siblings lived side by side and had sex with each other. It could also occur when a man secretly kept wives in different places, and so the Rabbis declared in elaboration of this biblical warning: "A man shall not marry one woman in one place and then marry another in another place, lest the children (unknown to each other) meet and a brother marry a sister."[92]

Polygamous Practices

Nonetheless, both the Mishnah and the Talmud make regular references to polygamy in their rulings and in their discussion of Mosaic laws on point. The Mishnah, for example, reports a case of a man who betrothed five women simultaneously, with one woman accepting him on behalf of them all.[93] The Talmudic Rabbis later drew the lesson from this case that one man could be engaged to multiple women and at the same time, and that a woman may accept a token of betrothal for herself and for her co-wives.[94] The Rabbis also reported on other occasional polygamists among the dispersed Jews.[95] And the Babylonian Talmud quotes Raba who said famously: "A man may marry wives in addition to his [first] wife, so long as he has the means to maintain them."[96] In summarizing the prevailing Jewish law of this early day Moses Maimonides (1135–1204) included numerous biblical and Talmudic references to polygamy.[97] The upshot of all these early texts, he concluded was that:

A man may marry several wives, even one hundred, either at the same time or one after the other, and his wife may not prevent him, provided he can supply each one

---

[91] Tosefta in Yevamot 1:10.
[92] BT Yoma 18b.
[93] BT Kiddushin 2:6.
[94] JT Yevamot 1:1, 1:6, 2:1, 3:3, 3:5, 3:10, 4:1, and 5:3.
[95] BT Sukkah 27a.; BT Yevamot 15a; Tos. Yeb. 1.10; Yeb. 15b; JT Yeb. 3a.
[96] BT Yevamot 65a.
[97] See, e.g., Mishne Torah, Hilchot Ishut, 6:14, 6:15, 17:1, in Moses Maimonides, *Mishne Torah Yad Hachzakah from The Book of Utterances, The Book of Agriculture, The Book of Purity, The Book of Damages, The Book of Acquisitions, The Book of Judgements, and The Book of Judges*, trans. Avraham Yaakov Finkel, 7 vols. (Scranton, PA: Yeshivath Beth Moshe, 2001).

with the food, clothing, and conjugal rights that are due to her. But he may not compel them to dwell in one courtyard, but rather each one by herself.[98]

The Rabbis recognized that the law of levirate marriage set out in Deuteronomy 25 was the strongest warrant for polygamy in the Mosaic law.[99] The Mishnah stated clearly that if a man has four married brothers who all died, he may perform levirate marriage with all four widows at the same time. In the Bible, after all, a later sage wrote, only the king is ordered "not to multiply wives to himself" lest he be distracted from his royal duties or levy too heavy a tax to support his burgeoning household. "But an ordinary man who has nothing to say to the public need not restrict himself, as long as he can support each one in food and clothing."[100] Other Rabbis added this same disclaimer that the man must be able to support all of his wives – suggesting that four wives were enough, leaving him free to visit each one at least once a month.[101]

But four wives was not an absolute limit in cases of levirate marriage or related cases of necessity. The Jerusalem Talmud, for example, included a story of thirteen brothers, all but one of whom died childless. The widows of the deceased brothers requested Rabbi Judah HaNasi to order the one surviving brother who was already married to perform his duty of levirate marriage with all twelve of his surviving sisters-in-law. The Rabbi is reported to have said to the man:

"Go initiate levirate marriage." He said to him, "I can't." Each one of the wives said, "I will pay maintenance for my month." The brother-in-law said, "Who will pay maintenance for the intercalated [thirteenth] month?" Rabbi said, "I will pay maintenance for the intercalated month." And he prayed for them, and they left him. Three years later, they came carrying thirty-six children. They came and stood themselves before Rabbi's courtyard. [Some people] went up and told him, "There is a crowd of children below that want to greet you." Rabbi looked out from the window and saw them. He said to them, "What is your business?" They said to him, "We want you to pay the intercalated month." And he paid the intercalated month.[102]

This case combined both levirate marriage and necessity, and it was unusual in that both the wives and Rabbi Judah volunteered to pay for maintenance in all

---

[98] Ibid., Hilchot Ishut, 14:3. A contemporaneous Midrash on Exodus Rabbah 1:14–16, deriding Pharaoh's decree to kill all the male Hebrew infants before the Exodus, stated similarly that: "Whoever gave you [Pharaoh] this counsel is a fool. You should have killed the females. If there are no females, from where will the men marry wives? A woman cannot marry two men, but one man can take ten wives, or a hundred. So, 'the princes of Zoan are idiots, the wisest of Pharaoh's counselors is a poor counsel,' [Is. 19:11] because they gave him this counsel."
[99] M. Yevamot 1.
[100] Lewin, Osar HaGe'onim Yebamot, p. 134, using translation in Falk, *Jewish Matrimonial Law*, 10–11.
[101] BT Yevamot 44a.
[102] JT Yevamot 4:12.

thirteen months of the Jewish lunar-based calendar. Another case of pure necessity is reported in the Jerusalem Talmud, and again it was used to condone polygamy, now well beyond the presumed limit of four wives. The case involved one Rabbi Tarfon, a prominent JT Tanna who was also a priest. In a year of severe drought, the Rabbi is said to have married 300 women at once, so that they could, as his wives, eat from a portion of the special heave offering (the *terumah*) which was given for the priests and their families.[103]

Both the Mishnah and the Talmud made clear, however, that the laws of levirate marriage made polygamy only an option, not an obligation for a surviving brother. The Mosaic law had already provided that a man could refuse to marry his brother's widow, albeit at the risk of being censured by the ritual (called *chalitzah*) of having his sandal pulled off. And the Mishnah had already said that a man should not take a second wife if he could not afford to support her. Elsewhere the tradition said that a man could refuse levirate marriage if he was already married and did not want to become a polygamist. This latter refinement emerged in the Targum's discussion of semi-levirate marriage in the Book of Ruth. In the biblical account, as we saw, Boaz's next of kin "redeemer" refused to buy land for fear that the attendant obligation to care for Ruth and Naomi would dilute his estate and leave his son too small an inheritance. In the Targumist's account, however, the man is reported to have refused to buy the land because he was already married, and did not want to take Ruth as a second wife and bring trouble to his household. Here's how the biblical passage is rendered in the Aramaic Bible: "The redeemer said, 'In such circumstances I am not able to redeem myself. Because I have a wife I have no right to marry another in addition to her, lest there be contention in my house and I destroy my inheritance. You, redeem my inheritance for yourself, for you have no wife, for I am not able to redeem.'"[104]

Even earlier on, the Mishnah had already recognized that a married man was sometimes "at liberty to remain monogamous" and to refuse the duty of levirate marriage for that reason.[105] The old Mosaic rule, the Mishnah provided, was that "the commandment of levirate [marriage] takes precedence over the commandment of unshoeing" the brother who refuses to marry his dead brother's widow. The intention of the levirate marriage command was to induce a man to practice this "meritorious need" for the sake of preserving his dead brother's name and family. "But nowadays, when such is no longer the intention, it is held that the commandment of unshoeing takes precedence over the commandment of levirate" marriage. Even a well-heeled

[103] Tosefta Ketubot 5:1; JT Yevamot 4:12. The Jerusalem text, however, makes it clear that the marriages were only nominal.
[104] Targum to Ruth 4:5–6 in R.G. Beatie, trans. *The Aramaic Bible*, vol. 19 *Targum of Ruth*, ed. D.R.G. Beattie (Collegeville, MN: The Liturgical Press, 1987), 11.
[105] Falk, *Jewish Matrimonial Law*, 9.

man, whether single or married, could now refuse levirate marriage, albeit at the risk of losing his shoes.[106]

RESTRICTIONS ON JEWISH POLYGAMY

External Legal Restrictions

After the sixth century CE, the dispersed Jewish communities gradually restricted the use of polygamy until Rabbi Gershom and his colleagues finally banned the practice in the eleventh century. Some of these restrictions were externally induced. Already in 258 CE, as we see in Chapter 3, pre-Christian Roman emperors made polygamy a crime of infamy in the Roman Empire, and these laws were later confirmed by the Christian emperors from Constantine onward. After the fifth century, Byzantine Emperors of the East and the Germanic kings of the West gradually escalated the punishments for polygamy, before making it a capital crime in the ninth century.[107]

In implementing these anti-polygamy laws in the West, both the Roman emperors and Germanic kings after them took special aim at Jewish polygamists living in Palestine and elsewhere. In 393 CE, Emperor Theodosius and others announced: "None of the Jews shall … enter into several marriages at the same time."[108] In 535 CE, Emperor Justinian repeated this prohibition, calling polygamy "contrary to nature," declaring that all children born of the second wife to be illegitimate and non-heritable, and ordering the seizure of one quarter of the property of any practicing polygamists.[109] Two years later, however, Justinian granted a narrow exemption for a few Jews living in the town of Syndios and in the region of Tyre to continue to practice polygamy. Justinian made clear that this was an "indulgence and remission of the penalties" only for a few older and wealthy Jewish men who were "begging, in tears, not to be compelled to be separated from their wives" or deprived of "lawful successors." He made clear that he was "granting this favor to them alone" and it was "not a precedent for others"; indeed, he threatened "exile for life" to any who tried to exploit this narrow exemption from the general criminal laws against polygamy. Justinian also exacted a high price for this exemption: "each of them shall pay ten pounds of gold," and the exemption would die with these parties.[110]

---

[106] M. Bechorot, 1:7, using translation in Falk, *Jewish Matrimonial Law*, 9. See also BT Yebamot 39b.
[107] See Chapter 3 in this book, pp. 107–114.
[108] *Code of Justinian*, 1.9.7, in Paul Krüger, ed., *Corpus Iuris Civilis* (Berlin: Weidmann, 1928–1929).
[109] *The Novels of Justinian*, Nov. 12; Nov. 89.5.12, in S. P. Scott, ed., *The Civil Law* 7 vols., repr. ed. (New York: AMS Press, 1973), vol. 7.
[110] Justinian, Novel 139.1.

This one narrow exemption aside, general criminal prohibitions against polygamy persisted in later Byzantine and Germanic laws of the sixth to tenth centuries. Some of these Germanic laws, like the Visigothic Code (ca. 642 CE), took sharp aim at what they called the "perfidies" and "iniquities of the Jews." The Visigothic Code aimed "to put an end to ancient errors" of the Jews, so "that others may not arise in future eras." Polygamy was among these "ancient errors" that needed to be "expurgated." "Jews shall not marry according to their custom ... nor desire or practice any other nuptial ceremony than that customary among Christians," the Visigothic Code declared. Those Jews who defied this law by practicing polygamy were to be stoned, burned, or sold into slavery with all their property confiscated.[111]

Most scholars assume that such strong secular prohibitions on polygamy had to have had a substantial effect on the Jewish community – especially given that polygamy was only an option not an obligation for Jews, and given that Roman and Germanic laws still permitted divorce and remarriage.[112] As prolific Jewish historian Salo Baron put it: "No matter how little Jews were inclined to obey Roman legislation when it differed from their own, public violation of imperial criminal law throughout a lifetime, open to denunciation from any quarter, necessarily became unusual."[113] Nonetheless, Baron continued, the Rabbis still insisted on the theoretical possibility of polygamy, however unrealistic it had become in practice, and however much trouble it may cause within the household. This was a form of scholarly resistance to mandatory Greco-Roman ideas of monogamy, and an effort to maintain an ancestral heritage against the influx of foreign ideas and institutions.[114] It was also an effort to reject Jewish sectarians, like the authors of the Damascus Document, who had treated polygamy as a form of adultery or fornication. As S. Lowy wrote:

> [T]the Rabbis clung rigidly to an ancient legal freedom as expressed in the law, even if it was out of keeping with their own ethical feeling. It seems that, although they were opposed to polygamy on grounds principally moral, because the sectarians had proscribed polygamy on the basis of an alleged Biblical injunction, they could not themselves openly and explicitly condemn it. Social conditions did not warrant such radical preaching, since in reality the Jewish family life was, as a rule, monogamous. They were thus in the happy position of being able to afford to retain in their legal doctrine the traditional right of polygamy, and this academic

---

[111] *The Visigothic Code (Forum Judicum)*, bk. 2, title 12.1–6, 12, trans. S.P. Scott, Library of Iberian Sources Online (http://libro.uca.edu/vcode/visigoths.htm).

[112] See Chapter 3 in this book, pp. 107–114.

[113] S.W. Baron, *A Social and Religious History of the Jews*, 18 vols. (New York: Columbia University Press, 1952–1983), 2:226.

[114] Ibid., 2:227–228.

tendency was emphasized, so as "to lend no support to the words of them that say that monogamy was a biblical commandment."[115]

Internal Restrictions

It was easier to practice polygamy for the Babylonian Jews living in Persia, whose surrounding Zoroastrian culture permitted polygamy. It was also easier for the Sephardic and Karaite Jews who lived in Muslim lands in southern Spain, north Africa, and the Middle East, which permitted polygamy, too. But even in these Jewish communities, the practice of polygamy evidently was still restricted to only a few elites. The sixth-century CE Babylonian Talmud quotes Raba's famous endorsement of polygamy: "A man may marry wives in addition to his [first] wife, so long as he has the means to maintain them."[116] But this passage sits right next to a statement by Rabbi Ami who declared that if a husband whose wife has not borne him children wants to take another wife: "He must in this case pay her [his present wife] the amount of her marriage contract (*ketubah*)" – that is, the dowry price stipulated in the marital contract which was due to the wife in case of his death or their divorce.[117]

Rabbi Ami's declaration extended traditional Mosaic laws and earlier rabbinic rulings, by making polygamy more expensive for a rich man and by providing greater protection for the first wife. Deuteronomy 24:1–4 gave a man an unlimited right to unilateral no-fault divorce of his wife if she no longer pleased him, and made no provision for her postmarital support. Exodus 21:10 provided that if, in lieu of divorcing his first wife, the man "takes another wife to himself, he shall not diminish her [the first wife's] food, her clothing, or her marital rights." And Deuteronomy 21:15–17 insisted that "if a man has two wives, the one loved and the other disliked, and they have both borne him children," he must give both sets of children their proper inheritance. The Mishnah had already extended these rules to say that if a man takes a second wife and divorces his first wife, he must pay his first wife a dowry rather than dismiss her empty-handed.[118] Rabbi Ami extended this principle further to say that if a man retains his first wife and takes a second, he must give his first wife her dowry immediately.[119]

[115] S. Lowy, "The Extent of Jewish Polygamy in Talmudic Times," *Journal of Jewish Studies* 9 (1958): 115–138, at 130–131.
[116] BT Yevamot 65a.
[117] Ibid.
[118] Ibid.
[119] Falk, *Jewish Matrimonial Law*, 8.

Later Rabbis pressed on this principle of protection for the first wife. In the ninth-century, Hilai Gaon of Sura wrote: "When a man marries a second wife while the first one is still alive, and the latter is in agreement – well and good, but when she disagrees she may demand her marriage portion. The man is to be compelled to divorce her, even against his will" and to pay her dowry before he can take another wife and share whatever remaining property he has with her.[120] Although Hilai did not prohibit polygamy entirely, he ruled that a widow could refuse levirate marriage if her brother-in-law was already married.[121]

Similar provisions appeared in Jewish marital contracts found among the many documents discovered in the Cairo *Geniza*, which date from the eighth century CE forward. In an exhaustive study of these documents, Mordechai Friedman has found some thirty cases of polygamy among the "wealthy, upper class Jews" living in Cairo from the tenth to the thirteenth centuries. But he has also found a number of contractual "no-polygamy" provisions, akin to what we saw in the marital contract from the Jewish community in Elephantine, Egypt more than a millennium earlier.[122] One such *Geniza* contract includes this warranty by the husband: "And he undertakes further not to marry a second wife within her lifetime and not to keep in his house a serving woman whom she abhors; and if he should take a second wife or keep such a servant in his house, he undertakes to pay the marriage portion in full" – presumably then divorcing her and leaving her free to marry another man.[123] Contractual provisions like this were sometimes combined with a wedding oath by the husband, swearing to his bride, before their families and community, that "he shall not marry another while he is married to the present bride."[124]

Such contractual provisions, Louis Epstein reports, have "survived to this day in the sephardic ketubah" or marriage contract. Sephardic Jews, who often lived in Muslim lands, did not recognize the "prohibition of R. Gershom against polygamy, and this ketubah clause was the only safeguard this bride could have. By the popularity of this clause, which in the last few centuries has become practically standard, it becomes evident how much resistance the Jewish community, even in the Orient where polygamy is not offensive, has offered to polygamy."[125] Although there are some references to cases of polygamy in the responsa of Sephardic rabbis

[120] Lewin, Osar Ha'Ge'nomin, *Yebamot*, 134, using translation in Falk, *Jewish Matrimonial Law*, 11.
[121] Ibid.
[122] See Mordechai A. Friedman, "Polygyny in Jewish Tradition and Practice: New Sources from the Cairo Geniza," *Proceedings of the American Academy for Jewish Research* 49 (1982): 33–68; id., "The Monogamy Clause in Jewish Marriage Contracts," *Perspectives in Jewish Learning* 4 (1972): 20–40; Mordechai Friedman, ed., *Jewish Marriage in Palestine*, 2 vols. (New York: Jewish Theological Seminary, 1980).
[123] Maimonides *Responsa*, p. 197, using translation in Falk, *Jewish Matrimonial Law*, 10.
[124] Epstein, *Marriage Laws*, 24–25.
[125] Ibid., 24.

in medieval Spain, polygamy was not widely practiced there. And when it was practiced, men were required to pay their first wife, sometimes even without an express contractual provision. The prominent eleventh-century Rabbi Alfasi, for example, reported a case in which a first wife forced her husband to pay her the "customary fine" of 200 dinars as a condition for his taking a second wife.[126]

The small sect of Karaite Jews that first emerged in the eighth and ninth centuries in Muslim lands of the Middle East, were more permissive about polygamy but they also sought to protect the wives in polygamous households. The Karaites followed both biblical law (without the Talmud) and Islamic law in allowing polygamy for men with sufficient wealth to support more than one wife. And they made polygamy mandatory if a man's first wife did not produce children after ten years. But, regardless of whether the marital contracts included a no-polygamy provision, the Karaites prohibited polygamy if it caused the co-wives to be "rivals" or "vexed" (*lizeror*), drawing this lesson from the stories of polygamy in the Hebrew Bible. As Louis Epstein reports the Karaite rules:

> By vexing they understand not a state of unhappiness arising out of jealousy, but primarily neglect of sexual satisfaction, and secondarily curtailment of food, clothing, and house comforts. To the Karaites, where one wife is neglected, polygamy is practically equal to incest, for it derives its prohibition from the levitical section on incest [a man cannot marry two sisters]; therefore a polygamous marriage of the prohibited kind is altogether invalid, as is the rule for all incestuous marriages. Even divorcing one wife on account of another is equal to a violation of incest. Where there is no neglect of one wife for the other, polygamy is permitted and legally unrestricted. Ethically, however, the Karaites follow the precepts of the Babylonian amora, supported by the teaching of Mohammedism, that a man shall not marry more than four wives.[127]

If the first wife could not produce a child after ten years of marriage, the Karaites permitted her husband to marry a second wife even if it "vexed" the first wife. But in such a case, the man had to set up his first wife in a separate home so she would not be humiliated "by witnessing the armours between her husband and her rival."[128]

THE POLYGAMY BAN OF RABBI GERSHOM

While Sephardic and Karaite Jews continued to regulate polygamy by contractual provisions and communal policies, the Ashkenazi of Western Christendom officially prohibited polygamy and banned from the community any Jew who continued the

[126] See sources and discussion in Goldfeder, "The Story of Jewish Polygamy," 285–286.
[127] Epstein, *Marriage Laws*, 23.
[128] Ibid., 23–24.

practice. Unlike the "no-polygamy" clauses in Jewish marital contracts, this new ban prohibited polygamy even if the wife consented to it, and even if the man was willing to pay her dowry. A second ban also prohibited unilateral no-fault divorce by the husband, regardless of whether his wife could have children. Divorce was now permitted only on proof of mutual consent of the parties or on proof of hard fault by either party such as adultery, desertion, cruelty, or crime. The ban effectively mandated faithful monogamy as the new ideal of Jewish law – "male and female cleaving as two in one flesh."

The ban (or *herem* in Hebrew) is attributed to Rabbi Gershom ben Judah of Mayence (960–ca. 1040), and is commonly referred to as "the ban of our teacher, Gershom." Most scholars think the ban was issued around 1030, at a council of Jewish scholars gathered near the city of Worms under the presidency of Rabbi Gershom – although some question whether Rabbi Gershom was its author or Worms the venue.[129] Most scholars think that the ban was originally only temporary (set to expire in 1240 CE / 5000 on the Jewish calendar), but it quickly became a permanent part of Jewish law thereafter, and students were encouraged to study and maintain it as if it were biblical command.[130] Some scholars think that the ban was simply rendering official what had long been customary among Ashkenazic Jewry – to practice faithful monogamy alone.[131] Even so, the ban was a major shift, because it explicitly prohibited practices that the Torah and Talmud had long permitted – polygamy and unilateral male divorce.

The original text of the ban has not survived, but its teachings were widely recognized in succeeding centuries. In the early twelfth century, for example, Rabbi Eliezer ben Nathan made clear that polygamy "was the rule in former generations, when a man married a second wife.... But in our generation, one cannot marry a second wife."[132] For today "a communal ordinance prohibits polygamy."[133] Another twelfth-century responsum from Rabbi Eliezer ben Joel HaLevi posed a case in which a man with a demented wife wished to marry a second wife – both to have a sexual outlet and to produce and raise children by her. A Jewish council refused his request to practice polygamy on grounds of necessity. As Rabbi Eliezer reported, the council thought it was "preferable that one soul should be lost than that an enormity

[129] For sources of competing interpretations, see Louis Finkelstein, *Jewish Self-Government In the Middle Ages* (Westport, CT: Greenwood Press, 1972), 25ff. Falk, *Jewish Matrimonial Law*, 24–34.

[130] *Resp. HaRosh*, 43:8, quoted in Goldfeder, "The Story of Jewish Polygamy," 286–288.

[131] In the chronicles of first crusade of 1095, for example, the entire list of martyrs does not contain a single Jewish polygamist. See Avraham Grossman, *Pious and Rebellious: Jewish Women in Medieval Europe*, Jonathan Chipman, trans. (Waltham, MA: Brandeis University Press, 2004), 73.

[132] *Even Ha'Ezer, Ketubot* 5, quoted by Falk, *Jewish Matrimonial Law*, 16.

[133] *Even Ha'Ezer*, p.121c, quoted by ibid., 16.

be carried out as precedent for generations to come."[134] Monogamy was now the norm, and the ban on polygamy was not subject to exception.[135]

The Talmud had ordered a man to marry a second wife if his first wife had not produced any children within ten years of their marriage, but many medieval scholars believed that the new ban prohibited this. It was now viewed as better for the couple to die childless than for the man to add a wife. The Torah and Talmud had also encouraged a brother to marry his dead brothers' widows, even if he was already married. Some medieval rabbis thought "that the ordinance laid down by Gershom was not intended to nullify this biblical commandment"[136] of levirate marriage, especially when the Jewish community faced massive losses of men during the pogroms and needed to make provision for the many widowed women and children. But, "in the course of time legal opinion has become crystallized in favor of enforcing the herem even where the levirate duty is involved."[137]

The no-polygamy and no-unilateral-divorce rules together did pose occasional cases that led to the introduction of dispensations from the ban in cases of urgent necessity. Both the Torah and Talmud had permitted a man to divorce his wife if she no longer "pleased" him.[138] Now divorce required mutual consent or proof of hard fault. What was a man to do in cases of domestic trouble but not hard fault – say, when his wife converted to Christianity, became heretical or disloyal to her family or community, became insane or frigid, or engaged in suspicious or dangerous activities – but she would not or could not consent to a divorce? Eventually the Jewish community provided a procedure for exemption in such emergency situations. One hundred rabbis, from three different countries, had to agree that an exemption was warranted in such a case. If they agreed, the husband had to file a divorce bill and deposit a full dowry payment with the Jewish court. The first wife could collect this bill and dowry at her leisure, but the man could marry a second wife even before she had done so. These dispensations were evidently quite rare, but they provided an equitable release valve when it was really needed.

Rabbi Gershom's ban on polygamy drew to itself a variety of rationales. It could not have been a coincidence that this ban emerged in Western Christian lands that were sharpening their own marital ideas of faithful monogamy and enforcing them with growing severity in both state and church courts. These same Christian rulers were sharpening their attacks on Muslim polygamy at the same time and including that practice among the many rationales for their bloody crusades against

[134] Solomon Luria, *Responsa* 65, quoted by ibid.
[135] Epstein, *Marriage Laws*, 27.
[136] Eliezer ben Joel HaLevi, quoted by Falk, *Jewish Matrimonial Laws*, 17.
[137] Epstein, *Marriage Laws*, 27, citing various medieval sources.
[138] For Talmudic interpretations of various divorce rules in Jewish law, see Broyde, "Jewish Law and the Abandonment of Marriage."

Muslim "infidels" in the Middle East.[139] Although direct evidence is scant, Jewish communities had to have faced pressure to bring their marital laws in line with prevailing Christian norms if they wished to remain socially and economically active in Western Christendom. Allowing a few elites the luxury to practice polygamy at the risk of censure and repression of the whole Jewish community became more trouble than it was worth.[140] Rabbi Jacob Emden later said this explicitly: Gershom's ban was necessary to relieve the growing Christian pressure on the Jewish community to conform.[141]

But the Jewish community also had strong engines for reform within its own teachings and traditions, going back to biblical times. Various medieval sages and later commentators cited internal factors that led the Jewish community to move from polygamy to monogamy.[142] A major concern of medieval Rabbis was to prevent husbands from betraying the trust and hard work of their first wives when they grew older, less attractive, or incapable of having more children and were then pushed aside for a younger rival wife.[143] Particularly when read alongside his prohibition on unilateral no-fault male divorce, Rabbi Asheri declared, Gershom had effectively "legislated to equate the power of the woman with that of the man."[144] Another repeated concern of the medieval Rabbis was to avoid potential vexation, rivalry, and infighting among the co-wives,[145] which could lead to other violations of the Mosaic and Jewish law – perjury, stealing, adultery, inheritance problems, and worse, as the stories of the biblical patriarchs already revealed.[146] Another concern was that even a rich man could not be sure he could support his wives and children in the vulnerable socioeconomic climate of Western Christendom, where Jews were restricted in their livings, businesses, and occupations, and were intermittently persecuted, subject to property confiscations or pogroms.[147] As one sixteenth-century Italian sage put it: "Since we are in Exile, we should not take many wives, nor beget many children, since we would not be able to fend for them properly."[148]

---

[139] See Chapter 4 in this book, pp. 158–163.
[140] Sheilat Yaavetz II:15, quoted by Goldfeder, "The Story of Jewish Polygamy," 297.
[141] Ibid.
[142] See a good overview in Michael S. Berger, "Two Models of Medieval Jewish Marriage: A Preliminary Study," in Broyde and Ausubel, eds., *Marriage, Sex, and Family*, 116–148, at 128–132.
[143] See detailed sources in Goldfeder, "The Story of Jewish Polygamy," 296–298; see also Finkelstein, *Jewish Self-Government*, 29, 142–143.
[144] Rabbi Asheri, Responsum 42:1, quoted by Menachem Elon, *Jewish Law: History, Sources, Principles*, trans. Bernard Auerbach and Melvin J. Skyes, 4 vols. (Philadelphia/Jerusalem: The Jewish Publication Society, 1994), 2:786. See also Broyde, "Jewish Law and the Abandonment of Marriage," 102–107 on the significance of Rabbi Gershom's decrees.
[145] Mordechai (Germany), Ketuvot #291, quoted by Goldfeder, "The Story of Jewish Law," 296.
[146] Rabbi Moshe Shick, *Even Ha'Ezer* 4, quoted by Goldfeder, "The Story of Jewish Law," 297.
[147] See sources quoted by ibid., 297–299.
[148] Meir Katzenellenbogen from Padua, Responsa 14, quoted by Falk, *Jewish Matrimonial Law*, 26–27.

Avraham Grossman believes that the main motivation and impetus for the ban was the economic activity of Jewish men during Rabbi Gershom's lifetime. Many were engaged in international trade and took lengthy trips to remote lands, including to predominantly Muslim countries where polygamy remained permissible. These shifty businessmen would take second wives while they were gone, and then either abandon or divorce them when they returned to their first homes.[149] Rabbi Gershom and his student, Judah HaKohen, referred to these cases frequently and with some alarm.[150] A later edict of Rabbi Jacob ben Meir prohibited Western Jewish traders from being away from home for more than a year and a half, and required them to stay home for at least half a year on return.[151] A parallel edict of Maimonides prohibited Jewish women living in Egypt from marrying Western Jewish men:

> Maimonides enacted edicts on behalf of the welfare of Jewish women; namely; that no woman be married to a foreign Jew, who is not from the community of Egypt, unless he brings proof that he is not married, or takes an oath to this effect on a Pentateuch. And any foreign man who married a woman here and wished to go out to another country is not allowed to leave, even if his wife agrees to this, until he writes her a divorce and gives it to her.[152]

SUMMARY AND CONCLUSIONS

Judaism provided the Western tradition with its first laboratory to test the case of monogamy over polygamy. In the Jewish tradition, "polygamy" meant one man with multiple wives (polygyny), not one woman with multiple husbands (polyandry). While the Mosaic law provided clearly: "Thou shalt not commit adultery,"[153] Jewish law regarded as adultery only sexual intercourse between a married woman and a man who was not her husband. It was not adultery for a married man to have sexual intercourse with another woman – whether a slave, prostitute, concubine, or second wife. Polyandry was thus by definition adultery; polygyny was not adultery at all – as it would become in early Christianity.

---

[149] See Avraham Grossman, "Ashkenazim to 1300," in N.S. Hecht et al., eds., *An Introduction to the History and Sources of Jewish Law* (Oxford: Clarendon Press, 1996), 317–319 and more generally Irving S. Agus, *The Heroic Age of Franko-German Jewry* (New York: Yeshiva University Press, 1969), 23–77.

[150] See sources in Avraham Grossman, *The Historical Background to the Ordinances on Family Affairs Attributed to Rabbenu Gershom Me'or ha-Golah ("The Light of the Exile")*," in Ada Rapoport-Albert and Steven J. Zipperstein eds., *Jewish History: Essays in Honour of Chimen Abramsky* (London: P. Halbam, 1988), 7–8. See additional sources in Goldfeder, "The Story of Jewish Polygamy," 299–301.

[151] Quoted in Finkelstein, *Jewish Self Government*, 140–141; see also Elliott A. Dorff and Arthur Rosett, *A Living Tree: The Roots and Growth of Jewish Law* (Albany: State University of New York Press, 1988), 418–419.

[152] Teshuvot HaRambam 2:347, quoted by Goldfeder, "The Story of Jewish Polygamy," 300.

[153] Exodus 20:13; Deuteronomy 5:17.

The Hebrew Bible made clear that while polygamy was an optional form of family life, sometimes it was a necessity. In cases of seduction, enslavement, poverty, famine, or premature death of one's brother, the Bible provided that even a married man could be called to marry a second woman to protect and support her and her children. The Rabbis of the Mishnah and Talmud added that a married man whose wife was barren had to marry a second wife after ten years in order to "be fruitful and multiply." Some men, particularly kings and aristocrats, also took wives and concubines to demonstrate their power and prestige, to enhance their opportunities for licit sex, to increase their family alliances and heirs, and to provide additional domestic labor for their homes and businesses. Despite firm new Roman laws against polygamy after the third century CE, and even firmer Germanic laws, the practice continued throughout the first millennium of the common era among some wealthy Jewish men who were capable of supporting their multiple wives and children. The first millennium Rabbis recommended no more than four wives even for a wealthy man, but this was not an absolute limit in cases of necessity.

Although polygamy was licit throughout the biblical period and into the first millennium, it nonetheless often spelled "trouble." Several of the biblical patriarchs who practiced polygamy faced rivalries among their wives, children, and parents; dissipated wealth, support, and protection for dependents; increased lust among husbands and decreased sexual satisfaction among their wives; bitter disputes between their half-children over paternal support, inheritance, and succession, and more; and growing hostility against the Jewish community by secular rulers. The Mosaic laws and Talmudic Rabbis commanded polygamists to treat their wives equally and to bequeath their estates properly among the children of all their wives. The first millennium Rabbis additionally provided that men who divorced their first wives, or added a second wife while retaining the first, had to pay the first wife her dowry. They also allowed Jewish couples to negotiate for "no polygamy" clauses in their marriage contracts and "no polygamy" vows in their wedding liturgies.

These latter provisions eventually became steps along the way to the outright ban on polygamy and no-fault divorce in the famous decree ascribed to Rabbi Gershom in 1030. This decree, which expressly changed the rules of the Torah and Talmud, brought the Ashkenazi Jewish communities in conformity with prevailing monogamous ideals of Western Christendom. But it also lifted to new normative prominence earlier biblical and rabbinic ideals of marriage as a "two in one flesh" union between "male and female." Monogamy, medieval sages argued in echoing the Bible, was the form of marriage created by God in Paradise and exemplified by Yahweh in his faithful covenant relationship with his chosen bride, Israel. Monogamy allowed the husband and wife alike to enjoy wholesome equality in and with the other, and to bear and raise children in the ways of the Lord.

2

The Case for Monogamy Over Polygamy in the Church Fathers

FIGURE 5. "Lamech and His Two Wives," from William Blake (1795). Used by permission of the Granger Collection, New York City.

Die Hochzeit zu Cana.

Jesus spricht zu ihnen: füllet die Wasserkrüge mit Wasser, und sie fülleten sie bis oben an. Und er spricht zu ihnen: schöpfet nun, und bringets dem Speisemeister, und sie brachtens.
Ev. Johannis. Cap. 2. v. 7. 8.

FIGURE 6. "Wedding at Cana," from Julius Schnorr von Carolsfeld, *Die Bibel in Bildern.* Courtesy of the Pitts Theology Library, Candler School of Theology, Emory University.

While the Jewish tradition treated polygamy as "trouble," the Christian tradition treated it as "adultery" – a serious moral offense on the part of both men and women, and a ground for their excommunication from the church. The Christian tradition, however, had ample trouble trying to contain and explain the many Hebrew Bible texts that countenanced the polygamy of God's chosen people of Israel. Eventually, these texts were treated as divine dispensations for a practice that could no longer be countenanced in the Christian church or community.

The Jewish practice of polygamy eventually became a source of intense Christian antipathy. Jews "have four or five wives" at a time, complained Justin Martyr already in 150 CE in his dialogue with a Jewish philosopher named Typho,[1] and the laws of

---

[1] Some scholars claim that Typho may have been the Tanna Rabbi Tarfon, a priest who married 300 women during a drought so they could receive a portion of the heave offering given to priests. See

their "blind and stupid teachers" allow them to marry "as many as they wish."[2] But in allowing polygamy, Justin continued, "your teachers" have put their "base and corruptible passions" above "the more divine purpose" and natural law of marriage.[3] "All who, by human laws, are twice married are sinners in the eyes of our Master."[4] This would become a standard line in later Christian attacks on Judaism. True Christians are faithful monogamists, the "rhetorical hardball"[5] argument went; Jews are adulterous polygamists.[6]

This chapter takes up the early Christian case for monogamy over polygamy set out by the Church Fathers in the first six centuries CE. The Bible was the starting point for their teachings, and the chapter thus begins by laying out the relevant New Testament texts on marriage. It then turns to the writings of the Church Fathers on monogamy versus "real polygamy" (one man with two or more wives). The Church Fathers, as we see, soon expanded the offense of polygamy to include "successive polygamy" (remarriage of divorcees and widow(er)s) as well as "clerical polygamy" (clergy who had been married more than once before ordination).[7] In the first four centuries CE – before Christianity became the established religion of the Roman Empire – these writings were quite widely scattered and often inconsistent. In the fifth century CE, St. Augustine of Hippo emerged as the leading Western Christian authority of sex, marriage, and family life, and his integrative views became the most prominent for the emerging Western tradition, although they enjoyed no monopoly.

Chapter 1 in this book, p. 54; and J.D. Gereboff, *Rabbi Tarfon: The Tradition, the Man, and Early Judaism* (Missoula, MT: Scholars Press for Brown University, 1979).

2   Justin Martyr, *Dialogue with Typho the Jew*, c. 151, in *The Ante-Nicene Fathers: The Writings of the Fathers Down to A.D. 325*, Alexander Roberts, et al. trans. and ed., 10 vols., repr. ed. (Peabody, MA: Hendrickson Publishers, 1995), 1:270 [hereafter ANF]. See also Louis M. Epstein, *Marriage Laws in the Bible and the Talmud* (Cambridge, MA: Harvard University Press, 1942), 17–19.

3   *Dialogue*, c. 134. In ibid., c. 141, Justin reiterates that the purpose of the patriarchs' polygamy was "not to commit adultery, but that certain mysteries might thus be indicated by them."

4   Justin Martyr, "The First Apology," ch. 15, in ANF 1:167. It is not clear from this passage whether Justin's reference to "double marriage" is against real or successive bigamy.

5   Luke Timothy Johnson, "Religious Rights and Christian Texts," in *Religious Human Rights in Global Perspective: Religious Perspectives*, ed. John Witte, Jr. and Johan D. van der Vyver (The Hague: Martinus Nijhoff, 1996), 65–96, at 76.

6   On the long history of Christian anti-Semitism, see Marvin M. Perry and Frederick M. Schweitzer, eds., *Jewish-Christian Encounters Over the Centuries* (New York: Peter Lang, 1984); Jeremy Cohen, ed., *Essential Papers on Judaism and Christianity in Conflict: From Late Antiquity to the Reformation* (New York: New York University Press, 1991); Solomon Grayzel, *The Church and the Jews in the XIIIth Century*, 2 vols., repr. ed. (New York: Jewish Theological Seminary, 1989); Heiko A. Obermann, *The Roots of Anti-Semitism in the Age of Renaissance and Reformation* (Philadelphia: Fortress Press, 1984).

7   On this terminology, see the Introduction, pp. 30–33.

NEW TESTAMENT TEXTS

Monogamous Ideals

The early church started with the same Hebrew Bible passages on marriage and polygamy that occupied the Rabbis, now read together with several important New Testament passages. The New Testament did not explicitly command monogamy or explicitly prohibit polygamy, but the monogamous ideal of marriage came through repeatedly.[8] Jesus condoned the created structure of marriage as a "two in one flesh union" between a man and a woman, designed for the mutual affection of husband and wife and their mutual procreation of children. He used this image to rebuke the Pharisees of his day who allowed for easy unilateral divorce by a husband: "[H]e who made them from the beginning made them male and female, and said, 'For this reason a man shall leave his father and mother and be joined to his wife, and the two shall become one flesh'" (Matt. 19:4–6).[9] St. Paul later repeated this same "two in one flesh" image to condemn sexual immorality, in particular sex with a prostitute.

> Do you not know that your bodies are members of Christ? Shall I, therefore, take the members of Christ and make them members of a prostitute? Never! Do you not know that he who joins himself to a prostitute becomes one body with her? For, as it is written, "The two shall become one flesh." But he who is united to the Lord becomes one spirit with him. Shun immorality. Every other sin which a man commits is outside the body; but the immoral man sins against his own body. Do you know that your body is a temple of the Holy Spirit within you, which you have from God? You are not your own; you were bought with a price. So glorify God in your own body. (1 Cor. 6:15–20)

Paul emphasized the need for bodily purity and faithful sexual union with one's spouse alone. To be sure, he followed both Jesus and various Greek and Roman philosophers of his day in teaching that marriage is not for everyone: "It is well for a man not to touch a woman," he wrote. "I wish that all were [celibate] as I myself am" (1 Cor. 7:1, 7). But Paul condoned marriage for those tempted by sexual sin, saying it was "better to marry than to burn" with lust (1 Cor. 7:9, KJV). And within marriage, he instructed the husband and wife alike to have equal regard for the conjugal rights and sexual needs of the other:

---

[8] For a recent introduction with detailed bibliography, see William Loader, *The New Testament on Sexuality* (Grand Rapids, MI: Wm. B. Eerdmans, 2012); see also Richard Hays, *The Moral Vision of the New Testament: A Contemporary Introduction to New Testament Ethics* (San Francisco: HarperSanFrancisco, 1996), esp. 347–378.

[9] See David Instone Brewer, "Jesus's Old Testament Basis for Monogamy," in Steve Moyise and J.L. North, eds., *The Old Testament in the New Testament* (Sheffield: Sheffield Academic Press, 2000), 75–105.

[B]ecause of the temptation to immorality, each man should have his own wife, and each woman her own husband. The husband should give to the wife her conjugal rights, and likewise the wife to her husband. For the wife does not rule over her own body, but the husband does; likewise the husband does not rule over his own body, but the wife does. Do not refuse one another except perhaps by agreement for a season, that you may devote yourselves to prayer; but then come together again, lest Satan tempt you with lack of self-control. I say this by way of concession, not of command. (1 Cor. 7:2–7)

This important passage echoed the Hebrew Bible in commending sex to marital couples, but also went beyond this traditional teaching in pressing this ethic in more exclusive and egalitarian terms. It underscored the mutual rights of both the wife and the husband to sexual bonding, the mutual sacrifice expected for the body of the other, and the mutual need for husband and wife to agree together to abstain from sex, but then only for a season, lest the unused marital bed tempt either of them to test their neighbor's bed.

This egalitarian language of mutuality and equality of a monogamous couple was even more pronounced in Ephesians 5, a passage written either by St. Paul or by one of his disciples in the later first century CE. The full passage bears quotation:

Be subject to one another out of reverence for Christ. Wives, be subject to your husbands as you are to the Lord. For the husband is the head of the wife just as Christ is the head of the church, the body of which he is the Saviour. Just as the church is subject to Christ, so also wives ought to be, in everything, to their husbands.

Husbands, love your wives, just as Christ loved the church and gave himself up for her, in order to make her holy by cleansing her with the washing of water by the word, so as to present the church to himself in splendor, without a spot or wrinkle or anything of the kind – yes, so that she may be holy and without blemish. In the same way, husbands should love their wives as they do their own bodies. He who loves his wife loves himself. For no one ever hates his own body, but he nourishes and tenderly cares for it, just as Christ does for the church, because we are members of his body. "For this reason a man will leave his father and mother and be joined to his wife, and the two will become one flesh." This is a great mystery and I am applying it to Christ and the church. (Eph. 5:21–32)

The final verse of this passage would become the biblical source for the later Christian idea that marriage is a sacrament, modeled on the enduring and exclusive monogamous union of Christ the bridegroom and the Church his chosen bride.[10] In his famous translation of this passage from Greek into Latin, St. Jerome (ca. 347–420) translated the Greek word for "mystery" (*mysterion*) into the Latin

---

[10]   See also Matthew 22:1–14, 25:1–13.

word for "sacrament" (*sacramentum*). This rendered Ephesians 5:32 as: "This is a great sacrament [*mysterion; sacramentum*], and I am applying it to Christ and the church." Contemporaneous Church Fathers like St. Augustine, we shall see in a moment, experimented with the idea of marriage as a sacrament, although he did not regard marriage as a sacrament on the order of baptism or the eucharist. In the twelfth century, however, French theologian, Peter Lombard (ca. 1100–ca. 1164), made this move, treating marriage as one of the seven sacraments of the church. Various Catholic theologians and local church councils in the Middle Ages echoed and elaborated this view. This view also shaped the canon law of the medieval church, which treated sacramental marriage as an enduring and exclusive monogamous union that could be formed only between baptized Christians in good standing who were governed by the church. The Council of Trent in 1563 made these sacramental teachings part of official Catholic dogma, and they remain at the heart of the Catholic theology and canon law of marriage to this day. The sacramental image of marriage as a union modeled on the exclusive and enduring relationship of Christ and his church would become an important part of the Western case for monogamy over polygamy as we shall see in later chapters.

Successive Polygamy

The New Testament said nothing directly against "real polygamy" (having two or more spouses at the same time), even though it set out long lists of other sexual sins. The New Testament also said nothing about the polygamous practices of several Old Testament patriarchs and occasional first-century Jews, even though Jesus attributed the permissive rules of divorce in Jewish law to the "hardness of heart" of God's people (Matt. 19:8). Jesus and St. Paul both condemned the desires and actions of adultery (sex with a second party while being married to a first). St. Paul further condemned prostitution, sodomy, incest, seduction, immoderate dress and grooming, and other forms of sexual "immorality" and "perversion."[11] But the New Testament was silent on "real polygamy."

Instead, the New Testament dealt with two cases of "successive polygamy" – having another spouse either after divorce or after death of the first spouse.[12] Remarriage after divorce was more closely restricted. In Matthew 5:31–32, Jesus said that "everyone who divorces his wife, except on the ground of unchastity, makes her an adulteress; and whoever marries a divorced woman commits adultery." In Matthew 19:9,

---

[11] Romans 1:24–27; 1 Corinthians 5:1; 6:9, 15–20; Ephesians 5:3–4; Colossians 3:5–6; 1 Timothy 2:9–10; 3:2; 1 Thessalonians 4:3–8. See also Hebrews 13:4: "Let marriage be held in honor among all, and let the marriage bed be held undefiled; for God will judge the immoral and the adulterous."

[12] 1 Corinthians 7:1, 7, 25–35. 39–40; 1 Timothy 3:2, 12; Titus 1:6; 1 Timothy 5:9–16.

Jesus restricted husbands somewhat, too: "[W]hoever divorces his wife, except for unchastity, and marries another commits adultery." St. Paul mitigated the plight of the divorced woman in providing that once "her husband dies, she is free from the law, and if she marries another man she is not an adulteress."[13] But the bottom line of the New Testament was pretty clear: divorced men should not remarry, divorced women could not remarry until their first husband had died.

This was a very different teaching than first-century Roman law and Jewish law. Roman law allowed both men and women and their families to initiate a divorce, and left both parties free to remarry thereafter.[14] Jewish law, building on Deuteronomy 24, gave men the exclusive right to divorce, but gave both parties freedom to remarry thereafter, except they could not remarry each other.[15] The New Testament not only restricted the right to divorce but also raised the moral stakes on these rules by charging improperly remarried parties with adultery – a mortal sin for Christians with serious consequences for a person's place both in the church and in the afterlife.

These New Testament passages on remarriage after divorce would become a major preoccupation and point of controversy for the Christian tradition thereafter, beginning already with the early Church Fathers, as we shall see in a moment. Eventually, Catholics and traditional Anglicans banned all remarriages of divorced men or women alike until the death of their first spouse. Those divorcees who did marry were considered to be successive polygamists or "digamists" ("doubly married"), and they were subject to spiritual discipline. Orthodox Christians and non-Anglican Protestants allowed for remarriage after divorce, at least for the innocent party, and after a time of healing (and of assurance of no pregnancy from the prior marriage). Protestants, in particular, explicitly rejected the theology and law of "digamy" or "successive polygamy" in these cases.

The New Testament discouraged the remarriage not only of divorcees, but also of widow(er)s. In 1 Corinthians 7, St. Paul urged widows "to remain single" but said that "if they cannot exercise self-control, they should marry."[16] "A wife is bound to her husband as long as he lives," Paul continued. "If the husband dies, she is free to be married to whom she wishes, only in the Lord. But in my judgment she is happier if she remains as she is."[17] Paul returned to this topic in a letter to Timothy. He now distinguished between younger widows with children and older "real widows" who were "left all alone." "Real widows," he said, should remain single, and come under the special care of the church community. If able, they should serve as deaconesses

13 1 Corinthians 7:39; Romans 7:2–3.
14 See Chapter 3 in this book.
15 See Chapter 1 in this book.
16 1 Corinthians 7:8–9.
17 1 Corinthians 7:39–40.

in the church or as teachers or mentors of younger women. But younger widows will inevitably "desire to remarry," said Paul. So: "I would have younger widows marry, bear children, rule their households, and give the enemy no occasion to revile us." It is better to allow them to remarry than force them into celibacy and have them and the church "incur condemnation for having violated their first pledge."[18]

These passages, too, would become major subjects of commentary and controversy in the Christian tradition. The Catholic tradition discouraged, but ultimately allowed, widows and widowers to remarry, but not too often and not too soon after the death of the first spouse. The Orthodox Christian tradition eventually prohibited all widows and widowers to remarry, even though they allowed divorcees to remarry. Both Catholics and Orthodox again treated improperly remarried widow(er)s as successive polygamists, or "digamists," and subjected them to spiritual discipline. Protestants generally allowed the widowed to remarry after a time of healing, and they again explicitly rejected the theology and law of successive polygamy in these cases.

Clerical Polygamy or Bigamy

A final set of New Testament passages that informed the Christian tradition's treatment of polygamy concerned the multiple marriages of bishops, deacons, and deaconesses who served the church. The fullest discussion is in Paul's first letter to Timothy:

> Now a bishop must be above reproach, the husband of one wife, temperate, sensible, dignified, hospitable, an apt teacher, no drunkard, not violent but gentle, not quarrelsome, and no lover of money. He must manage his own household well [for] if a man does not know how to manage his own household, how can he care for God's church?[19]

Paul similarly commanded a deacon to be "the husband of one wife"[20] and a deaconess be "the wife of one husband."[21] These restrictions on clerical marriage echoed the Mosaic laws of priestly holiness and their prophetic echoes.[22]

These passages, too, became contested in the Christian tradition. Pro-polygamy advocates would repeatedly use these passages to argue that, while the New Testament clergy had to be monogamous, the laity were left free to be polygamous. Why otherwise single out clergy for a special command to be monogamous? But

---

[18] 1 Timothy 5:3–15.
[19] 1 Timothy 3:2–5.
[20] 1 Timothy 3:12.
[21] 1 Timothy 5:9.
[22] Leviticus 21:1–24; Ezekiel 44:22.

the main focus of the tradition was on the marriages of clergy before and after their ordination. The early church canons encouraged clergy to remain single and celibate, but allowed them to retain their one wife even after ordination. Those candidates for ordination who had more than one wife in a row, however, say after the first wife's death, were no longer eligible for ordination. Furthermore, those who married or remarried while in clerical office were removed from office. All these clerical candidates or officers with more than one wife came to be called "clerical bigamists" or "clerical polygamists." Catholics after 1123 prohibited all ordained clergy from having a wife after ordination, and prohibited anyone who had been married more than once from seeking clerical ordination or taking monastic vows. Orthodox Christians retained the rule that an ordained priest or deacon could have one wife even while in office, but an Orthodox bishop could not be married. Protestants allowed both clerical candidates and sitting clergy to have a wife, and put no special restriction on their remarriages after the divorce or death of the first wife either before or after their ordination. Protestants explicitly rejected the theology and law of "clerical bigamy" or "clerical polygamy."

The balance of this chapter and the next chapter analyze the theology and the law of "polygamy" in all its variations in the first millennium. This chapter focuses on the Church Fathers' theological writings from the second to the sixth centuries. The next chapter focuses on the emerging Roman and Germanic secular laws against real polygamy, as well as the treatment of various types of polygamy in the emerging canon laws and penitential rules of the early church both before and after the Christianization of the Roman Empire. Successive chapters thereafter take up the medieval and early modern Protestant cases against polygamy.

TERTULLIAN'S OPENING ARGUMENTS AGAINST POLYGAMY

Tertullian of Carthage (ca. 160–ca. 225), an apologist and theologian with knowledge of Roman law and Greek philosophy, offered the first sustained Christian discussion of monogamy versus polygamy that has survived. Tertullian would become a problematic figure among some of the later Church Fathers; Augustine, in fact, charged him with heresy because of his views about marriage and remarriage. But, in his day, Tertullian was quite influential, and for centuries thereafter his views had to be taken into account, even if they could be accepted only with heavily qualifications.

Marriage, Tertullian wrote in an early letter to his wife, is a "natural" estate created by God. It is "designed" as "the union of man and woman, blest by God as the seminary of the human race, and devised for replenishment of the earth, and the furnishing of the world" with people. But marriage must be pursued "singly," Tertullian insisted. "For Adam was the one husband of Eve, and Eve his one wife – one woman, one rib." "There were more ribs in Adam, and hands that knew no weariness in God; but not more wives in the eye of God. And accordingly the man of God, Adam, and the woman of God, Eve, discharging mutually the duties of one marriage, sanctioned for mankind ... one prescriptive rule of monogamy."[23] Tertullian returned to these themes in his tract, *On Monogamy*, now rooting the dyadic structure of marriage in the biblical injunction that "two shall become one flesh":

> The rule of monogamy is neither novel nor strange.... One female did God fashion for the male, [for] in the introductory speech which preceded the work itself, He said, "It is not good for man to be alone; let us make an help-meet for him." He would have said "helpers" if He had destined him to have more wives. He added, too, a law concerning the future: "And two shall be made into one flesh" – not three or four.[24]

Polygamy is a crime that is "second place only to homicide," Tertullian went on. He based this judgment on the biblical story of Lamech, the first polygamist recorded in the Bible, who was descendant of the first murderer, Cain. Lamech was himself both a polygamist and a murderer, and the two crimes were connected in Tertullian's view. The Bible's account reads:

> Lamech said to his wives: "Adah and Zillah, hear my voice; you wives of Lamech, hearken to me when I say: I have slain a man for wounding me, a young man for striking me. If Cain is avenged sevenfold, truly Lamech seventy-seven fold."[25]

For Tertullian, this was the first clear biblical indication that polygamy was often the cause and consequence of many other serious crimes. In this case, it was the assault by the young man against Lamech – perhaps out of envy or pursuit of his second wife, Tertullian's commentators added.[26] Lamech retaliated disproportionately by murdering his young attacker and another man, too. His polygamy, in turn, set a bad example for his descendants, for even "the sons of God" among them "took to wife such of them as they chose,"[27] without regard for God's monogamous design of marriage. It was the polygamy, murder, envy, adultery, violence, and other sins

[23] Tertullian, *To His Wife*, I.2, in ANF 4:39; id., *An Exhortation to Chastity*, c. 5, in ANF, 3:53.
[24] Tertullian, *On Monogamy*, c. 4, in ANF, 3:61–62.
[25] Genesis 4:23–24.
[26] Tertullian's student, Arnobius, associated polygamy with murder, sodomy, adultery, and holding wives in common. Arnobius, *Against the Heathens*, ANF 6:432. See also Justin Martyr, *The First Apology* c. 15, in ANF, 1:167 who associated polygamy with lust, fornication, and adultery. Ephrem the Syrian argued that Lamech's murder was designed to allow for new marriages between the descendants of Seth (the good) and Cain (the evil). Thomas Oden, ed., *Ancient Christian Commentary on Scripture I: Genesis 1–11* (Downers Grove, IL: InterVarsity Press, 2002), 113.
[27] Genesis 6:2.

of the earliest people on earth, Tertullian wrote, that prompted God to destroy the world with the Flood and to start again.[28]

With Noah, the earth was restored, again "with monogamy as its mother." Noah and his sons each had one wife, following the natural order of "two in one flesh." "Even in the very animals monogamy is recognized, for fear that even beasts should be born of adultery. 'Out of all the beasts,' said God, 'out of all flesh, two shalt thou lead into the ark, that they live with thee, male and female'.... Even unclean birds were not allowed to enter with two females each." Although many animals reverted to polygamy after the Flood, a number of others like nesting birds remained monogamous, and humans should, too, following the design of human creation.[29]

Tertullian recognized that, after the Flood, a few of the ancient patriarchs and kings of Israel did practice polygamy and concubinage – causing "three or more to be joined in one flesh" as he put it. He treated this as God's temporary dispensation from the law of monogamy for a case of natural necessity. Much like a farmer allows young trees to grow indiscriminately before he prunes them, Tertullian argued, so God allowed the first humans on earth to operate with "ample laxity." Despite God's natural laws against incest, the first humans after Adam and Noah took blood relatives as their spouses, because those were the only mates at hand. Despite "the prescriptive rule" of monogamy, they took multiple wives and concubines in order to fulfill God's mandate to "be fruitful and multiply and fill the earth." But all this was a temporary dispensation from the natural law and design of marriage. Now that the earth is filled with people, and roughly divided between male and female, God has "recalled the indulgence" and repeated his command that male and female should unite as "two in one flesh." St. Paul gave "additional reinforcement" to this "law of unity in marriage" by connecting the "two in one flesh" image to the "mysterious union of Christ and the Church." But, even before this Christian connection had been made, the "heathen" Greeks and Romans grasped clearly the natural structure of marriage, for they "hold monogamy in highest honor" and have devised their laws of marriage to give "glory to monogamy."[30]

Tertullian also recognized that St. Paul commanded a bishop, presbyter, or deacon of the church to be "the husband of one wife" and a deaconess "the wife of one husband." Those texts had led some in Tertullian's day to argue that, while a cleric could have only one wife, a layperson could have two or more wives. Because Paul had to make a special law against the polygamy of clerics, the argument went, that must mean that the Old Testament toleration of polygamy remains in place in

---

[28] Tertullian, *On Monogamy*, c. 4
[29] Ibid.
[30] Ibid., c. 6; id., *On Chastity*, cc. 5–6, 13.

the New Testament church. Why else would the church need a special prohibition on polygamy for its clerics? Nonsense, said Tertullian. In the first place, the New Testament makes clear elsewhere that all believers are really priests to each other, and thus must behave as such – an early statement of the "priesthood of all believers" doctrine.[31] But, even if we distinguish between clergy and laity, we must recognize that we all have "the right of a priest in our own person." We should thus have the "discipline of a priest" as well, especially in case we are later called into priestly service or holy orders, or pressed to perform a priestly function like an emergency baptism.[32]

But more to the point, Tertullian continued, these "husband of one wife" passages are not about the simultaneous marriages but about the successive marriages of clerics prior to their ordination. Ideally, all clerics should be lifelong bachelors, in imitation of Christ and St. Paul. And, while in office, they must be single and celibate so that they are not distracted from their spiritual duties by wives and children, "wombs and breasts," and various household chores. But the reality is that many come to the priesthood after having already been married earlier in life. They had once been tempted by their "carnal" appetites, and had availed themselves of "God's indulgence" that "it is better to marry than to burn." Fair enough, wrote Tertullian; after all, he, too, had married once. But what Paul means is that aspiring priests and deaconesses have to be strong enough in spirit to forgo "God's carnal indulgence" a second time, let alone a third or fourth. It was bad enough that these aspiring servants of the church could not make "the highest grade of immaculate virginity." It was bad enough that they had allowed for a "dulling of their spiritual faculties ... in a first marriage." It would be even worse if these aspiring priests had been so spiritually weak that they had married two or more times. Therefore, Paul just set a "prudent limit" of one prior marriage for any aspiring priest or deaconess, protecting the priest and the priesthood from spiritual weakness and sinful temptation. Upon entry into divine service, priests (and other "men and women in ecclesiastical orders") become permanently "wedded to God" who will "restore the honor of their flesh" damaged by their first marriage and "slay any concupiscence of lust" that remains within them.[33]

Although the Bible explicitly prohibited clergy from having more than one spouse, Tertullian knew that it was more ambiguous about the second marriages of the laity after divorce. Tertullian quoted the relevant biblical passages about the

---

[31] An early statement of the priesthood of all believers that would become prominent in later Protestant circles. See C. Cyrill Eastwood, *The Royal Priesthood of the Faithful: An Investigation of the Doctrine from Biblical Times to the Reformation* (Minneapolis: Augsburg Press, 1963).

[32] Ibid., cc. 7–8; id., *On Monogamy*, ch. 7, 12; id., *On Baptism*, c. 6, in ANF 3:672.

[33] Id., *On Chastity*, cc. 9–12; id., *On Monogamy*, c. 3, 12.

remarriage of divorcees. He also noted that the New Testament granted divorced men more freedom to remarry than divorced women.[34] Tertullian removed this disparity of treatment by saying that divorced men could not remarry either, at least while their ex-wives were still alive. He came to this by a novel reading of Jesus's gloss on the law: "Thou shalt not commit adultery." Jesus had singled out married men, not women, in saying that "to look lustfully after a second woman was to commit adultery with her."[35] Now, Tertullian reasoned, "a man, divorced from his first wife in body, is still married to her in spirit," at least while she is alive. And it is impossible for a man to marry a second wife without looking at her with lust, because he would not want to remarry unless he "burned with lust." Therefore, a divorced man, too, effectively commits adultery by entering a second marriage. Divorced men and women alike, therefore, should avoid remarriage, and those who do so, should be spiritually disciplined.[36]

Tertullian was initially more ambivalent about the remarriage of widows and widowers. He knew that Paul prohibited older "real widows" from remarriage, but specifically allowed "young widows" with children to remarry given their sexual needs and practical difficulties of living on their own. And he also knew that the New Testament said nothing at all about the remarriage of widowed men. Given his inventive arguments to achieve equal treatment of divorced men and women, we might expect Tertullian to do the same for widowed men and women. But he did just the opposite. He treated Paul's practical reasons for remarriage as more pertinent for widowed men than for widowed women. And he allowed remarriage only for older widows beyond childbearing years ("real widows" whom Paul said should remain celibate), but not for younger widows (whom Paul said should remarry).

Here's how he came to this counterintuitive reading: Tertullian accepted the reality that some widowed men might wish to remarry. After all, they had a "house to be managed; a family to be governed; chests and keys to be guarded; the wool-spinning to be dispensed; food to be attended to; cares to be generally lessened." Tertullian thought these purported "needs" of widowers were really "excuses for their indiscipline," but he conceded that they might be grounds enough for remarriage. Just as the Old Testament allowed a man to divorce because of "the hardness of his heart," he wrote grudgingly, so the New Testament allowed a man to remarry because of "the infirmity of the flesh." A widowed man in that circumstance could marry an older widow who is "fair in faith, dowered with poverty, and sealed with age" and thus not capable of producing more children. "A plurality of *such* wives is pleasing to God," Tertullian wrote, in a strange rhetorical slip from his usual pro-monogamy stance.[37]

[34] Ibid., c. 9–13.
[35] Matthew 5:27–28.
[36] Id., *On Chastity*, cc. 9–10.
[37] Ibid., c. 12; id., *On Monogamy*, c. 15.

Tertullian would not, however, allow a widowed man to remarry simply because he had pressing sexual needs or wanted to have children and heirs. To lose your wife is to regain your soul, Tertullian told widowers, for you can now focus on the things of the spirit and not of the flesh. "You have ceased to be a debtor," a slave to sexual desire and carnal pleasure. "Happy man!" You are now free to focus on "matters of conscience and continence," to "savor spirituality," to "bend over the Scriptures" without distraction or domestic anxiety. You can now do what St. Paul had always encouraged Christian men to do: "give your undivided attention to the Lord."[38] Tertullian was equally dismissive of the widowed man who wanted to remarry in order to produce children and heirs. The church and society get more than enough children from other couples, he countered, and children are a distraction from the spiritual life. "Let the well-known burden of children – especially in our case – be sufficient to counsel widowhood." Moreover, to worry about one's legacy and heirs is to ignore the reality that our true reward lies in heaven, not on earth. All this was rather vague and pious talk after Tertullian's realistic and prudential take on the material concerns of daily life that might counsel a widowed man to remarry. And it ignored altogether St. Paul's counsel to single persons, including notably the widowed, "that is better to marry than to burn with lust."[39]

Tertullian also ignored St. Paul's explicit counsel that a younger widow should be allowed to remarry and to tend to her new husband, children, and household. Tertullian named such a remarriage "a species of adultery." He came to this by extending the Bible's treatment of the divorced woman as an adulteress. A wife is bound to her first husband in body and soul, Tertullian wrote. A divorced woman "has been separated from her husband in soul as well as body, through discord, anger, hatred, and causes of complaint." Yet, even if she was not at fault, the Bible calls her an adulteress if she gets remarried. Now, by comparison, a widowed woman is separated from her husband only in body. She remains bound to him in soul. "She prays for his soul, and requests refreshment for him meanwhile, and fellowship with him in the first resurrection; and she offers her sacrifice on the anniversaries of his falling asleep." Although he is "disjoined from her in flesh, he remains in her heart, [and] is to this hour her husband." For a wife to abandon her "helpless" husband in these circumstances and to remarry another, "would be a crime ... even worse than adultery and divorce" – a betrayal of the soul, not just the body.[40]

Tertullian realized that this argument might seem hard to mesh with Jesus's explicit statement that in heaven "they will neither marry, nor be given in marriage."[41] But,

---

[38] 1 Corinthians 7:35.
[39] Id., *On Chastity*, cc. 9–12; see also id., *On Monogamy*, c. 9–11.
[40] Ibid., c. 10.
[41] Matthew 22:30.

he countered, Jesus was talking about new marriages made in heaven, not existing marriages on earth, whose faithful maintenance was essential to get to heaven in the first place. He also realized that this argument could apply just as well to widowed men, who were bound to pray for the souls of their departed wives. Now contradicting his earlier statements that had allowed remarriage for younger men with ample households to manage, he said that the remarriage of a widowed man would have to be viewed as adultery, too. "We speak to each sex:" it "is incumbent on both" to remain "two in one flesh" alone and not to remarry.[42]

Perhaps it was these anomalies that persuaded Tertullian in later life to call for the prohibition of second marriages altogether for anyone – clerical or lay, man or woman, divorced or widowed. This was part and product of his increasingly negative attitude toward sex, marriage, and family life altogether, which was a feature of the Montanist sect that he joined in his last years. Tertullian had never been robust in his embrace of sex and marriage; indeed, he wrote to his wife that he wanted to have a sexless spiritual marriage as much as possible. But in his last years, as a Montanist and a widower, he moved to a rigid sexual asceticism that discouraged first marriages and prohibited all second marriages. Instead, he extolled virginity, chastity, and celibacy as the higher spiritual good for Christians who were called to emulate the purity of Jesus and the virginity of Mary, his mother.[43]

MONOGAMY VERSUS POLYGAMY IN THE LATER CHURCH FATHERS

Despite his austere rejection of all remarriage – a move that would later earn him charges of heresy[44] – Tertullian set many of the terms for the debate about polygamy in the early church. He also lifted up most of the relevant biblical passages that would become axiomatic for the Western legal tradition until early modern times. Like Tertullian, a number of Church Fathers treated monogamy as the only natural form of human marriage, and denounced real polygamy as something "unnatural," "beastly," "evil," "criminal," and "heretical."[45] Like Tertullian, they viewed the "two in one flesh" image of the Bible as a divine commandment about the structure

---

[42] Ibid., cc. 10–11.

[43] See Philip L. Reynolds, *Marriage in the Western Church* (Leiden: Brill, 1994), 189–200.

[44] Augustine regarded the absolute prohibition of second marriages unnecessary, and one of the heretical marks of the Montanists among others. See Augustine, *De Haeresibus*, cc. 26, 38; Augustine, "The Excellence of Widowhood," c. 4 in Augustine, *Treatises on Various Subjects*, ed. Roy J. Deferrari (Washington, DC: Catholic University of America Press, 1952), 283–284.

[45] See *The Canons of Basil of Caesarea* (c. 370), canon 80, in Philip Schaff and Henry Wace, eds., *A Select Library of Nicene and Post-Nicene Fathers of the Christian Church*, Second Series, repr. ed. (Grand Rapids, MI: Eerdmans, 1952), 14:609 [hereafter NPNF 2d]; St. John Chrysostom, *Homilies on Genesis*, Homily 56.12, trans Robert C. Hill, 3 vols. (Washington, DC: The Catholic University of America Press, 1992), 3:124; Athanasius, *History of the Arians*, c. 73, in NPNF 2d, 4:297.

of marriage that confirmed and extended the natural law that had already been understood by Greeks, Romans, and others. Like Tertullian, they viewed the polygamy of the Old Testament patriarchs as a temporary case of natural necessity made possible by divine dispensation from the natural law.

Also like Tertullian, many Church Fathers became increasingly focused not so much on "real polygamy" but on "successive polygamy." Rather than simply rejecting remarriage, however, as Tertullian eventually did, the later Fathers placed remarriage in a hierarchy of sexual virtues and vices. On the top of the scale of virtue, they placed virginity, chastity, and celibacy. Next came faithful single marriage and single widow(er)hood. At the bottom of the scale of virtue was remarriage of widow(er)s and divorced men, with each remarriage less virtuous than the last, but nonetheless a "virtue," rather than "a species of adultery," as Tertullian had put it.[46]

On the top of the scale of sexual vice, in turn, they put adultery, incest, and sodomy, all of which the Bible explicitly outlawed as unnatural sexual interactions for humans. Next came various other forms of fornication and sexual interaction between single parties, as well as spurning one's spouse for no reason. Least sinful was concubinage, which in Roman law was an exclusive relationship between a single man and a single woman. These hierarchies of sexual vice came to explicit expression in the emerging canon laws and penitential books of the first millennium church that assigned different spiritual punishments based on the gravity of the sin. We review those early canon laws in the next chapter.

Exactly where real polygamy fit on this hierarchy of sexual vice, however, was not clearly resolved by the Church Fathers. On one end of the spectrum of opinion was Tertullian who regarded real polygamy as the most serious crime: an "unnatural act," "second only to murder," and often associated with other serious crimes and sexual deviations. This view was accepted by a few other Fathers,[47] and it would echo intermittently in the later tradition. But that view left Abraham, Jacob, Solomon, and other great polygamous leaders of the faith vulnerable to charges of grave sin and unnatural acts, with an overindulgent God evidently looking on. It also did not explain why some humans and why so many animals had polygamous tendencies. That gave some later Fathers, notably St. John Chrysostom and St. Augustine of Hippo, ample enough pause for them to treat polygamy not so much as unnatural,

[46] In his *City of God*, ch. 15.26, Augustine saw this hierarchy already allegorically prefigured in the construction of Noah's ark, with "chaste marriage dwelling in the ground floor, chaste widowhood in the upper, and chaste virginity in the top storey." St. Augustine, *City of God*, trans. Gerald G. Walsh et al., eds., Vernon J. Bourke (Garden City, NY: Image Books, 1958).

[47] See, especially, the heated controversy over Jovinian's views of virginity versus marriage versus remarriage, recounted with detailed citations in David G. Hunter, *Marriage, Celibacy, and Heresy in Ancient Christianity: The Jovinianist Controversy* (Oxford: Oxford University Press, 2007).

but as an unspiritual relation that undercut the distinctly Christian goods and goals of marriage.

An important early figure in this discussion was Tertullian's contemporary, Clement of Alexandria (ca. 150–ca. 215), a distinguished Christian philosopher familiar with Platonism. Clement pressed a natural law argument for monogamous and exclusive marriage, and viewed real polygamy as an "unnatural" form of marriage and a dangerous species of adultery. "Nature has adapted us for marriage, as is evident from the structure of our bodies, which are male and female," wrote Clement. And "nature urges us to have children." We are born with a physical capacity to unite with the opposite sex. We are born with a natural desire to have sex and to produce a child in our own "likeness," who "attains to our same nature," and who eventually becomes "a proper successor in our place."[48]

While nature calls us to have sex and to produce children, Clement continued, natural law forbids humans from "random, illicit, or irrational scattering of seed" through masturbation, fornication, prostitution, adultery, sodomy, and more.[49] Our sexual and marital lives are more structured than this, and must be more disciplined. Jews, Greeks, and Christians alike understand these natural limits, and reflect them in their laws: "[T]hose who indulge in excess violate the laws of nature and harm themselves in illegitimate unions," Clement wrote. Like Plato and Moses, "[o]ur Lord wanted humanity to *multiply*, but he did not say that people should engage in licentious behavior, nor did he intend for them to give them over to pleasure as if they were born for rutting." "Even irrational animals have a proper time for sowing seed." Rational humans, capable of understanding the law of nature, should know even better. "Our entire life will be spent observing the law of nature, if we control our desires from the start."[50]

This law of nature, Clement continued, is particularly important for men whose perennial inclination to sexual roving can make them "more licentious than the irrational creatures" unless they are constrained. Both the natural law and the positive laws that are built upon it thus press men to be monogamous and to be faithful to their wives.

When the noble Plato [in his *Laws*] recommended that "you shall abstain from every female field that is not your own, he derived this from his reading of the biblical injunction: "*You must not lie with your neighbor's wife or defile yourself with*

48 Clement of Alexandria, *Stromata, or Miscellanies* 2.23; 3.6, ANF, 2:377–379, 389–391; see also Clement of Alexandria, *Stromateis, Books One to Three*, trans. John Ferguson (Washington, DC: Catholic University of America Press, 1991), 249–255, 284–291.
49 Clement, *Stromata*, 2.10.95.
50 Ibid., 2.10.83, 90–95 (quoting Plato, Laws, 8.838E, 839A, 841; Genesis 1:28, Leviticus 18:20, 22; Ezekiel 43:9), using translation in David G. Hunter, *Marriage in the Early Church* (Minneapolis, MN: Fortress Press, 1992), 41–42.

her." "There should be no sowing of sterile, bastard seed with concubines," [Plato says]. Do not sow "where you do not wish your seed to grow." "Do not touch anyone except your wedded wife." Only with a wife are you permitted to enjoy physical pleasure for the purpose of producing descendants, for all this the Logos allows.[51]

The Bible reflects this same natural law, said Clement, with its repeated commands that "two shall join in one flesh" in order to "be fruitful and multiply," and that both husband and wife must "not commit adultery." These biblical passages "established monogamy" for God's people, just as the natural law established the same rule for the rest of the world. God did allow certain Old Testament patriarchs temporarily to practice "polygamy because of the need for increased numbers" of people in the world. But now, with the earth fully populated, "He no longer approves of polygamy" but has reestablished "monogamy for the production of children and the need to look after the home. Woman was introduced as a 'partner' in this" – a single and exclusive partner until her death or that of her husband.[52]

Writing a century after Clement, Lactantius (ca. 260–ca. 340), a philosopher and tutor of the first Christian emperor, Constantine, also began with a Christian defense of the natural law of monogamous marriage – now combining biblical teachings with Stoic philosophy and Roman law. Lactantius defined natural law, in typical Stoic fashion, as a rule of "true, right reason, agreeing with nature, diffused among all" people. The source of this natural law is "the one common Master and Ruler of all, even God, the framer, arbitrator, and proposer of this law." Using their "right reason," Lactantius argued, Stoics and Christians alike have understood and applied this law of nature, and developed overlapping teachings on what is commanded for marriage and what is "contrary both to nature and to the institution which God has created."[53]

Like the Stoics, Christians condone marriage between a fit man and a fit woman of the age of consent, and they form unions with the consent of their parents and the participation of their families. Like the Stoics, Christians condemn incest, adultery, prostitution, concubinage, homosexuality, sodomy, pederasty, and other such "lustful furies" and "libidinous excesses," which are "nefarious," "abominable," "execrable," even "insane." And like the Stoics, Christians do not kill their wives in order to seize their dowries, nor do they engage in random sexual coupling outside of marriage.[54]

---

[51] Clement, *Stromata*, 2.23.137; Clement, *The Instructor*, 2.10.90–91, using translation in Hunter, *Marriage in the Early Church*, 41–42.

[52] Clement, *Stromata*, 3.47, 80, 82, using translation by John Ferguson, in *Fathers of the Church Series* (Washington, DC: The Catholic University of America Press, 1991), vol. 85.

[53] Lactantius, *Divine Institutes*, 6.8, 6.23, in ANF 7, quoting in part from Cicero, *De Republica*, 3.22.16.

[54] Ibid., 3.21.5–8; 6.18–19.

In particular, Christians like Stoics reject the idea of open sex and anonymous parentage set out in Plato's *Republic* (although, evidently unknown to Lactantius, Plato had rejected this idea in his later *Laws*, the text which Clement had celebrated in expounding his natural law of marriage). In the *Republic*, as Lactantius reported it, Plato said that "the state will be in harmony and bound together with the bonds of mutual love if all should be the husbands, and fathers, and wives, and children of all." This scheme of free and open sex, said Lactantius, encouraged "many men to flock together like dogs to the same woman." It ensured that men "superior in strength shall succeed in obtaining her" or that other men superior in cunning will set up a brothel or barter system for sex. To Lactantius, such libertinism with multiple sexual partners and "no fixed marriage" could only lead to rampant "adulteries, lusts [and] promiscuous pleasures." It could only breed animosity and violence among men and women who compete for prized mates. The lack of stability and commitment provided by monogamous marriage would not be good for adults or children. "What man would love a woman, or what woman a man, unless they always lived together, unless a devoted mind and fidelity mutually preserved has made *caritas* [charity] inseparable." What incentive, moreover, would either party have to care for their children or vice versa. "Only if a man truly knows that his children are really his, will he be able to love them," Lactantius argued. And only if a child knows who his father and mother are will that child be able to love, honor, and obey them, and tend to them when they grow old and decrepit. "Nature herself cries out against" this Platonic system, Lactantius concluded. Even the birds know better. "For almost all birds make marriages, and equals join together, and they make their own nests like nuptial beds with harmonious mind; and they love their own offspring, since they are certainly their own; and if you should substitute someone's children, they drive them off."[55]

While nature and the natural law have taught Stoics and Christians a great deal in common about marriage and family life, Lactantius continued, "it is divine instruction only which bestows wisdom." Indeed, without the wisdom of God revealed in the Bible and the Christian tradition, a person can be "overpowered by nature" and natural philosophy and bewildered by its immense variety. Indeed, on the question of polygamy versus monogamy, why are pair-bonded birds taken to be natural models for human marriages? Why not a pride of lions under one dominant male, or a herd of does bound to one prize buck? The "precepts of God, because of their simplicity and truth," Lactantius wrote, help us sort through the teachings of nature and philosophy, and thereby exert "the best influence on the minds of men."[56]

---

[55] Ibid., 3.21–22; 6.23, using, in part, the translation in Judith Evans Grubbs, *Law and Family in Late Antiquity: The Emperor Constantine's Marriage Legislation* (Oxford: Clarendon Press, 1995), 89.

[56] Lactantius, *Divine Institutes*, 3.26.

One such simple biblical truth, said Lactantius, is that we must not commit adultery, for that violates the Bible's command that only "two shall become one flesh," not three or four. That should lead Christians to denounce the prevailing double standard of sexual morality that punishes an adulterous woman severely but often winks at the straying husband who sleeps with prostitutes, slaves, and maidservants. God's command against adultery applies equally to husband and wife, said Lactantius, and it should be equally enforced "in public law" and "within private walls." A Christian man "who has a wife should not wish to have, in addition, either a slave or a free woman, but should keep faith with his marriage. Indeed, it is not as the reasoning of public law has it, that only the woman who has another man is an adulteress, but the husband, even if he has many women, has been absolved from the crime of adultery. But divine law so joins the two in marriage, that is in one body," each with an equal duty of fidelity to the other, each with an equal right of care from the other. That is what the creation story meant in calling a man and a woman to remain "two in one flesh." That is what Christ meant when he called all persons to abide by the Golden Rule: "[D]o unto others as you would have done to you." That is what St. Paul meant when he called Christian spouses to love and sacrifice for each other in this same mysterious way that Christ loved and sacrificed for his church. "Let the behavior of the two spouses begin to influence one another, let them bear the yoke with equal commitment. Let us imagine ourselves in the other's place. For this is virtually the summit of justice; not to do to another what you yourself do not wish to suffer from another."[57]

Lactantius had put his finger on a central question for the later Church Fathers – and indeed for the Western legal tradition altogether: how cogent was a natural law argument for monogamy alone, without the further wisdom of the Bible and the Christian tradition, without the further support of practical, prudential, or philosophical arguments, or without adverting to the common practices, customs, and experiences of diverse peoples – the "common law of the nations" (*ius gentium*) as the jurists called it? Clement evidently thought that his natural law theory of marriage was sufficient to prove the superiority of faithful monogamous marriage, and he was content to show the parallel teachings of Moses, Plato, and Jesus to drive home his point. Lactantius was not so sure. After all, it was Plato who had experimented with the idea of open sex and anonymous parentage. It was the Roman jurists who had countenanced a sexual double standard for husbands. And it was Moses who had tolerated polygamy, despite God's primal command at creation that "two shall become one flesh." Something more than a simple argument from nature was evidently needed to support faithful and exclusive monogamous marriage.

[57] Ibid., 6.23.23–30, using translation in Grubbs, *Law and Family*, 90–91.

Many later Church Fathers agreed with Lactantius, and they returned to the biblical story of creation, but now with an emphasis on the New Testament glosses of Jesus and St. Paul. The "two in one flesh" model of marriage, they argued, was grounded not only in the creation story of Adam and Eve, but more fully and finally in the mysterious union of Christ and the Church. St. Jerome, for example, wrote:

> One rib was in the beginning formed into one wife. "They shall be two," He said, "in one flesh." Not three or four; for were there more, there would not be two. Lamech, a man of blood and a murderer, was the first to divide one flesh between two wives. For his fratricide and his polygamy, he paid one and the same penalty, the Flood.[58]

But Jerome added to this creation story the critical gloss of St. Paul that tied the natural union of male and female to the supernatural union of Christ and the church:

> The creation of the first man should teach us to reject more marriages than one. There was but one Adam and but one Eve; in fact, the woman was fashioned from the rib of man. Thus divided they were subsequently joined together in marriage; in the words of scripture, "the twain shall be one flesh," not three or four. "Therefore a man shall leave his father and his mother, and cleave unto his wife." Certainly it is not said "to his wives." Paul in explaining the passage refers it to Christ and the church; making the first Adam a monogamist in the flesh, and the second [Christ] a monogamist in the spirit.[59]

"If there were two Christs," St. Gregory Nazianus (ca. 329–ca. 390) added, "there would be two husbands, or two wives; since Christ is one – the one head of the church – there is one flesh also." To take multiple wives is "swine-like."[60]

From Old Testament Polygamy to New Testament Monogamy

Jerome, Gregory, and other later Church Fathers, presented this move from flesh to spirit, from Adam to Christ, as a narrative of progress. They described a progression of virtue from the permissible polygamy of the Old Testament, to the permissible monogamy of the New Testament, to the eventual abolition of marriage altogether in heaven – a state already anticipated by those spiritual elites who were able to practice celibacy, virginity, and chastity in this life.[61] For example, St. Methodius

---

[58] Jerome, *Contra Jovinian*, 1. c. 14, PL 23:233.
[59] Jerome, Letter 123, ANF 6:230–232.
[60] Or. 37, 8, *Patrologiae Graecae* 36:292B, using translation in John Meyendorff, "Christian Marriage in Byzantium," *Dumbarton Oaks Papers* 44 (1990): 99–107, at 100–101. Gregory went on to condemn multiple remarriages: "The first is legal, the second is condoned, the third is illegitimate, and that which is beyond is swine-like." Ibid.
[61] Jerome, *Contra Jovinian*, cc. 5–15. See also Justin Martyr, *Dialogue with Typho*, c. 134 and discussion in Sara McDougall, *Bigamy and Christian Identity in Late Medieval Champagne*

(d. 311), a distinguished bishop and theologian on whom Jerome in part relied, depicted biblical history as moving to an ever greater realization of sexual virtue. Abraham, Methodius said, was the first to abandon incest,[62] but he retained and practiced polygamy and concubinage, as did his descendants. "From the time of the prophets, however, the contracting of marriage with several wives was done away with" – with the last Prophet Malachi driving home the lesson that each man was to remain content with "the wife of your youth," who "is your companion and your wife by covenant" (Mal. 2:14–15). In the New Testament, Methodius continued, "chastity has succeeded to the marriage of one wife, taking away by degrees the lusts of the flesh until it removed entirely the inclination for sexual intercourse" in the saintly lives of the celibate and chaste.[63]

St. John Chrysostom (ca. 345–407), the leading Greek Church Father, used this narrative of progress to nuance Tertullian's account of polygamy in the Old Testament and to underscore the powerful religious symbolism of monogamy for Christians. Chrysostom preached at length on Jacob's polygamous (and incestuous[64]) marriages to Leah and her younger sister Rachel. While polygamy and incest are certainly "evil" in our day, and these acts predictably occasioned much strife even in the household of faithful Jacob, Chrysostom insisted, we cannot simply "judge happenings in those times by present conditions."

> In those times, you see, since it was the very beginning, people were allowed to live with two or more wives so as to increase the race; now, on the contrary, because through God's grace the human race has expanded into a vast number, the practice of virtue has also increased. I mean, Christ by his coming has sown the seeds of virtue among human beings and turned them into angels, so to say, thus rooting out all that former

(Philadelphia: University of Pennsylvania Press, 2012), 20–21. The fullest narrative of progress comes through in Augustine's *City of God*, bks. 14–21. See also discussion of his views later in this chapter, pp. 88–93.

[62] Not really, because Abraham married either his sister or niece. See Gen. 11:29; 20:12.

[63] Methodius, *The Banquet of the Ten Virgins*, cc. 3–5, in ANF 6:312–314. See also Origen, *Commentary on Matthew*, cc. 16–20, in ANF 10: 505–510.

[64] Although Chrysostom evidently did not address the "necessity" for the first humans to practice incest, other Church Fathers did. Augustine, *City of God*, bk. 15.16, defended the incest of Adam and Eve's children. Justin Martyr, *Dialogue with Typho*, ch. 134, called Jacob's incestuous marriage to Leah and Rachel "unlawful." Origen, *Homilies on Genesis and Exodus*, trans. Ronald E. Heine (Washington, DC: The Catholic University of America Press, 1982), 116–117, defended the incestuous polygamy of Lot's daughters as well. As Genesis reports the story, God had destroyed Sodom and Gomorrah by fire and brimstone, allowing Lot and his two daughters to escape. His daughters feared that they were the only ones left on earth. "Our father is old, and there is not a man on earth to come to us." So they agreed to get their father drunk and on successive nights slept with him "so that we may preserve offspring through our father." They each got pregnant and had children (Gen. 19:30–38). Origen thought this an apt case of "necessity of restoring the human race." "What they did was sinful, but excusable since it would have been more sinful to allow the extinction of humans. They had sex not for their own pleasure but out of concern for preserving the human race." Ibid.

practice. Do you see how we should not be proposing that practice [of polygamy] but seek out everywhere what is useful? Take note: since the practice itself was evil, see how it has been rooted out and no one is free now to propose it.[65]

For Chrysostom, the move from polygamy to monogamy was part and product of the growth of spiritual virtue and moral discernment among God's people. It was considered virtuous and useful among the Old Testament patriarchs to practice polygamy and concubinage. That lifestyle filled the earth more quickly, and it was more "just" and "dignified" than the "open and promiscuous sexual communes" maintained by other ancient pagans, contemplated in Plato's *Republic*, and still practiced by some heretics in the early church.[66] But now, among New Testament Christians, it is considered virtuous and useful to practice faithful monogamy. For Christians, that lifestyle has replaced polygamy, concubinage, and fornication, even if it is better yet to practice celibacy and virginity for those so gifted.[67]

The New Testament teaches that monogamous marriage is not just a form of "fleshly passion" or "bodily union" naturally designed for procreation, Chrysostom went on in a series of sermons. For Christians, marriage is also a type of "spiritual birth" or "spiritual union," a distinct way of participating in the life and body of Christ which is the church. That is what St. Paul meant in Ephesians 5:32 when he called the "two in one flesh" model of marriage "a great mystery," a reflection and expression of the union of Christ and the church. Among us Christians, Chrysostom proclaimed, "the household is a little church." If your marriage imitates the loving and sacrificial relationship of Christ and his church, "your perfection will rival the holiness of monks."[68]

The "great mystery" of a monogamous Christian marriage goes beyond the symbolic analogy between husband and wife, Christ and the church, Chrysostom insisted. Marriage is also a symbolic bridge between flesh and spirit, between the creation of God and the incarnation of Christ. Indeed, "when husband and wife are united in marriage, they are no longer seen as something earthly, but as the image of

[65] Chrysostom, *Homilies on Genesis*, Homily 56.12. His discussion of this story comprises Homilies 55–57.
[66] See, e.g., sources and analysis in Kathy L. Gaca, "The Pentateuch or Plato: Two Competing Paradigms of Christian Sexual Morality in the Second Century CE," in Amy J. Levine and Maria Mayo Robbins, eds., *A Feminist Companion to Patristic Literature* (Edinburgh: T & T Clark, 2008), 125–136; Stephen Benko, *Pagan Rome and Early Christians* (Bloomington: Indiana University Press, 1984), 54–78; id., "The Libertine Gnostic Sect of the Phibonites According to Epiphanius," *Vigiliae Christianae* 21 (1967): 103–119.
[67] For his treatment of celibacy and monasticism, see John Chrysostom, *On Virginity. Against Remarriage*, trans. Sally R. Shore (Lewiston, NY: Edwin Mellen Press, 1982); id., *A Comparison Between a King and a Monk/Against the Opponents of the Monastic Life: Two Treatises by John Chrysostom*, trans. David G. Hunter (Lewiston, NY: Edwin Mellen Press, 1988).
[68] *St. John Chrysostom On Marriage and Family Life*, trans. Catherine P. Roth and David Anderson (Crestwood, NY: St. Vladimir's Seminary Press, 1986), 57, 61–62, 85.

God himself." The union of a Christian couple in marriage reflects and celebrates the mysterious work of God the Father at creation, his "ingenuity in the beginning of dividing one flesh into two" by creating "Eve from the rib of Adam." Yet God wanted our male and female nature "to remain one even after its division, so He made it impossible for either half to procreate without the other." Christian marriage is thus the mirror image of our creation as male and female. It is a reunion of what God divided at creation yet wanted reunited in order for men and women to "be fruitful and multiply." As such, a monogamous Christian marriage symbolizes the mystery of the creation.[69]

Christian marriage also symbolizes the mystery of the incarnation, Chrysostom insisted. The union of a Christian couple in "one flesh" and "one spirit" reflects and participates in the mysterious dual nature of Christ himself. Christ is a God who became a man, a spirit who took upon himself human flesh. Christian marriage is a mirror image, an inverse reflection of this miracle of the incarnation. It elevates the life of the flesh into the life of the spirit. "Paul does well here to talk of flesh and bones" in comparing our marriages with the incarnation of Christ, Chrysostom declared. "For the Lord has exalted our material substance by partaking of it Himself," by "loving, redeeming, and elevating" our human nature, by showing us how the life of the flesh can be united with the life of the spirit. That is what a loving Christian marriage helps a man and woman to achieve and experience. It is a great and gracious mystery that Christ "left the Father and came down to us, and married His bride the Church, and became one spirit with her." It is likewise "a great mystery that a man should leave him who gave life to him and brought him up and her who suffered in labor and childbirth ... and be united to one whom he has not always known and who often has nothing in common with him, and should honor her above all others." "This is not a human accomplishment," Chrysostom wrote. "It is God who sows love in men and women. He causes both those who give in marriage and those who are married to do this with joy. Therefore Paul said, 'This is a great mystery.'"[70]

St. Augustine (354–430), the leading Latin Father, drew an even sharper contrast between the natural utility of polygamy in the Old Testament world and the spiritual efficacy of monogamy in the New Testament world. "When polygamy was a common custom, it was not a crime," Augustine wrote; "it now ranks as a crime because it is no longer a custom." Rebuffing the arguments of some critics of Old Testament patriarchy, Augustine insisted that Abraham, Jacob, David, and other patriarchs who practiced polygamy committed no offense "either against nature, or against common custom, or against positive law." Their polygamy was

---

[69] Ibid., 75.
[70] Ibid., 50–53, 95.

no offense against nature, for they took many wives and concubines "in order to have offspring." Having children is what the "hidden law of nature" inclines all humans to pursue. Humans, like animals, can naturally reproduce by pair-bonding, but they can just as naturally reproduce in groups of one male with several females – though the converse is not naturally possible. Thus, Augustine wrote, for "one man to have had several wives … is not against the nature of marriage. Many women can conceive children by one man, but one woman cannot do so by many men." The Old Testament patriarchs' polygamy was also not an offense "against custom," Augustine continued, for "it was a general practice at that time and in those parts" for a man to take several wives and concubines in order to have as many children as possible, which the Bible repeatedly said were a blessing from God. Nor was their polygamy an offense against "positive law, for there was none that prohibited it." Indeed, even the Mosaic law, the positive law of the ancient Jews, made some provision for polygamy.[71]

Before Christ, Augustine continued, it was "a custom free from all blame that one man should have several wives in order that children should be born to him."[72] What made it "blameless" in the case of Old Testament patriarchs like Abraham and Jacob was that these men took multiple wives not out of lust or lack of self-control but out of desire to fulfill God's command "to be fruitful and multiply." Indeed, these ancient men accepted circumcision, which was a symbolic – and, for a time, a painful physical – decision to cut off the lusts of the flesh.[73] (Contrast that to King David, "whose adulterous and murderous pursuit" of Bathsheba betrayed both "unbounded lust" and indiscriminate selfishness.) And what made the ancient patriarchs' polygamy exemplary, even in that ancient day, was that they took other women with their first wife's permission – indeed in Abraham's case, on his wife Sarah's insistence.[74]

[71] Augustine, *Contra Faustum*, bk. 21, c. 47. See similar language in Augustine, *On the Good of Marriage*, cc. 17, 25, 26, in NPNF 1, 3:397–413, and in *St. Augustine: Treatises on Marriage and Other Subjects*, trans. Charles T. Wilcox, ed. Roy J. Deferrari (Washington, DC: Catholic University of America Press, 1969), 9–54. Augustine was writing against the Manichaeans of his day who had used the polygamy of the Old Testament patriarchs to criticize their morality and undermine the validity of the Old Testament altogether. Augustine was no friend of polygamy, ultimately, but defended the patriarchs' use of polygamy in that cultural context. See discussion in David G. Hunter, "Reclaiming Biblical Morality: Sex and Salvation History in Augustine's Treatment of the Hebrew Saints," in *In Domino Eloquio/In Lordly Eloquence: Studies in Patristic Biblical Interpretation in Honor of Robert L. Wilken*, eds. Paul M. Blowers et al. (Grand Rapids, MI: Wm. B. Eerdmans, 2002), 317–335.

[72] Augustine, *De Doctrina Christiana*, bk. 3, c. 12, n. 20, PL 34:73, using translation in G.H. Joyce, S.J., *Christian Marriage: An Historical and Doctrinal Study*, 2nd ed. (London: Sheed and Ward, 1948), 575. See also Augustine, *City of God*, c. 16, c. 38.

[73] Augustine, *Quaestiones in Heptateuchum*, bk. 5, q. 27, quoted in Lombard, bk. 4, dist. 33., ch 4. This last point concerning circumcision as a deterrent to lust was set out in Origen, *Sermons on Genesis* 3.6, PG 12:180–181.

[74] Augustine, *Good of Marriage*, cc. 15, 17; see also Ambrose, *On Abraham*, c. 4., n. 23, trans. Theodosia Tomkinson (Etna, CA: Traditionalist Orthodox Studies, 2000 [1919]). See also Augustine, *City of God*,

Since the coming of Christ, however, Augustine continued, "polygamy is no longer permissible."

> There is no need for procreation like there was before. Back then it was permissible for husbands who were capable to take other women in order to have many children. But now that certainly is not lawful. The mysterious difference of our time provides us with a greater opportunity to rethink what actions or inactions are just. Today, it is better for a man not to marry even one wife, unless he cannot control himself. Back then, it was no fault for him to have several wives, even if he could have easily restrained himself, for piety in that time demanded something else [namely, as many children as possible].[75]

Augustine repeated this argument several times. In his famous work *On Christian Doctrine*, for example, he wrote:

> Righteous men of long ago visualized the kingdom of heaven as an earthly kingdom.... In the interests of creating offspring there was a perfectly blameless practice for one man to have several wives. For the same reason it was not honorable for one woman to have several husbands; that does not make a woman more fertile, and it is indeed a form of immoral prostitution to seek profit or children through promiscuity. Given such social conventions, things that the saints of those days could do without any lust – although they were doing something which cannot be done without lust nowadays – are not censured by Scripture....

> For if one man according to the custom of his time could be chaste with many wives, another today can be lustful with a single wife. I approve the man who exploits the fertility of many women for a purpose other than sex more highly than one who enjoys one woman's flesh for its own sake. In one case, there is the motive of self-interest, in accordance with the conditions of the time; in the other, the satisfaction of a lust caught up in the pleasure of the world. In God's eyes the men to whom the apostle allowed sexual intercourse with their individual wives because of lack of self-control, are at a lower stage than those who each had several wives but looked only to the procreation of children in the sexual act (just as in eating and drinking a wise man looks only to physical health).[76]

This was a different argument about Old Testament polygamy than Tertullian's earlier argument from divine dispensation and natural necessity, which Clement, Lactantius, and Jerome all echoed. Tertullian saw monogamy as an enduring rule

---

c. 15.23, and detailed discussion of Abraham, Sarah, and Hagar in John Witte, Jr., *The Sins of the Fathers: The Law and Theology of Illegitimacy Reconsidered* (Cambridge: Cambridge University Press, 2009), 11–13, 39–42.

[75] Augustine, *Good of Marriage*, c. 15 in Augustine, *De bono coniugali, De sancta uirginitate*, ed. P.G. Walsh (Oxford: Clarendon Press, 2001), 30–31 (my translation).

[76] Augustine, *De Doctrina Christiana*, R.P.H. Green, ed. and trans. (Oxford: Clarendon Press, 1995), bk. 3.46–47, 3.61.

of natural law, which was confirmed in the biblical admonition of "two in one flesh." The patriarchs' polygamy was in application of God's temporary equitable dispensation from the natural law of monogamy. God had granted this dispensation because the world needed more people, and polygamy would fill the world faster than monogamy. The world is full now, and therefore polygamy is again outlawed. All must live by God's natural law of "two in one flesh." That rule will continue unless and until another case of real natural necessity arises. This argument from natural necessity would recur many times in the tradition, with both religious and political leaders claiming the power to grant dispensations for polygamy on God's behalf in individual cases of pressing need.

Augustine, by contrast, saw polygamy as consistent with the natural law viewed alone. Procreation, not monogamy, was the enduring rule of natural law, he said. That rule was confirmed in the biblical command to "be fruitful and multiply." It has always been perfectly natural for one male to have several females and to have children by each of them in fulfillment of the natural law. This natural law has not changed. What has changed is the function of sex and marriage, and their place in the hierarchy of Christian virtues. Before Christ, marriage was all about procreation, which men could pursue with one or more wives, and with concubines, too. Since Christ, marriage is also about enduring fidelity to one's spouse in imitation of the mysterious union of Christ and his church. That is what the repeated "two in one flesh" passages in the Bible were projecting. In the Old Testament these passages were a description of the marital perfection of Paradise, which could not be maintained after humanity's fall into sin. In the New Testament, however, these passages are a "prophesy" about what Christian marriage should be. That's why Ephesians 5 treated the mutual love and sacrifice of husband and wife as a reflection and imitation of the mysterious union of Christ and his bride, the church.[77]

Christians thus embrace marriage not only for the natural good of children (*proles*), countenanced by the natural law. They also embrace marriage for the

---

[77] St. Augustine, "Two Books on Genesis Against the Manichees," bk. 2, c. 13.19, c. 24.37, in *St. Augustine on Genesis*, trans. Ronald J. Teske, S.J. (Washington, DC: The Catholic University of America Press, 1991), 115. See also *City of God*, c. 14.10–14, on the perfection of marriage in Paradise. In *The Good of Marriage*, c. 18, Augustine made the polygamy of the patriarchs a form of prophesy, too. "[T]he many wives of the ancient fathers signified our future churches of all races subject to one man-Christ.... Therefore just as the multiple marriages of that time symbolically signified the future multitude subject to God in all peoples of the earth, so the single marriages of our time symbolically signify the unity of all of us subject to God which is to be in one heavenly city." See also Justin Martyr, *Dialogue with Typho*, c. 134 on Jacob, Rachel, and Leah: "The marriages of Jacob were of two types of that which Christ was about to accomplish. For it was not lawful for Jacob to marry two sisters at once.... Now Leah is your people and synagogue; but Rachel is our Church. And for these, and for the servants of both, Christ even now serves."

spiritual goods of fidelity between husband and wife (*fides*), and sacramental stability within the City of God (*sacramentum*).[78] The natural law and the natural good of children allow polygamy. But the Gospel and the spiritual goods of fidelity and stability require monogamy.

Augustine expanded on these themes in his famous tract on *The Good of Marriage*. For Christians, he wrote, marriage is a good institution not "solely because of the procreation of children," but also because of the "companionship," friendship, "charity," and "mutual sacrifice between husbands and wives" – in sickness and in health, in youth and in old age. In a Christian marriage, each spouse "observes that promise of respect and of services due to each other." Augustine focused especially on the need for sexual fidelity between husband and wife and the teaching of St. Paul that marriage gives husband and wife an equal power over the other's body, an equal right to demand that the other spouse avoid adultery, and an equal claim to the "service, in a certain measure, of sustaining each other's weakness, for the avoidance of illicit intercourse" with third parties. Marriage is "a contract of sexual fidelity," said Augustine, and couples may and should maintain active sexual lives for "the larger good of continence," even if they cannot have children, at all or any longer.[79]

For Christians, Augustine went on, marriage also offers the good of a "sacrament." Augustine treated the mysterious union of Christ, the bridegroom, with the church, his bride, as the very paradigm of marriage, the marriage *par excellence*, which every Christian marriage should seek to imitate. He treated each marriage between Christian believers as a miniature version of this great divine marriage, a visible expression of this invisible mystery, this *sacramentum*. "It was said in Paradise before sin: 'A man shall leave his father and mother and be joined to his wife and they will be two in one flesh,' which the Apostle says is a 'great sacrament in Christ and in the Church.' Therefore what is great in Christ and in the Church is very small in individual husbands and wives, but is nevertheless a sacrament of an inseparable union."[80]

The sacramental good of marriage confirms the marital goods that the natural law provides, Augustine argued, but also curbs the sexual sins that the natural law permits. The natural law urges males and females to join together in one flesh for the good of procreation. That countenanced polygamy both among the patriarchs

[78] Augustine, *Good of Marriage*, c. 32; id, *On Marriage and Concupiscence*, I.11, 19, in *Early Church Fathers: Nicene and Post-Nicene Fathers, First Series*, Philip Schaff, trans. and ed., 14 vols. [1886–1889], repr. ed. (Peabody, MA: Hendrickson Publishers, 1994), 5:258–309 [hereafter NPNF 1].

[79] Augustine, *Good of Marriage*, cc. 3, 6–11; id., *On Marriage and Concupiscence*, I.15–18; id., *On Adulterous Marriages*, I.2, II.12–17, all in Augustine, *Treatises on Marriage*, 61–134.

[80] Augustine, *On Adulterous Marriages*, I.23, using translation in Reynolds, *Marriage in the Western Church*, 292. See also Augustine, *On the Gospel of St. John*, Tract 44, 9.2, in NPNF 1, 7:245.

of old, and among many animals still today who gather in large herds of one male with several females and their offspring. The sacrament of marriage, as a symbol of Christ's union with his one true church, calls Christians to accept a higher law of monogamy and to spurn polygamy, concubinage, and sexual unions with anyone but one's spouse. The natural law teaches couples to remain faithful to each other for the sake of their children who need them, but allows for separation when there are no children. The ancient patriarchs, operating under both the natural law and the Mosaic law, thus practiced divorce and remarriage, particularly when their wives proved barren. So do many animals today who drive out those mates who cannot produce offspring. The sacrament of marriage, in imitation of God's eternal faithfulness to his elect, calls Christians to remain faithful to their spouses to the end, regardless of their procreative capacity. "For this is what is preserved 'in Christ and in the Church': that . . . even when women marry or men take wives 'for the sake of procreating children', a man is not allowed to put away a barren wife in order to take another, fruitful one."[81]

SUCCESSIVE AND CLERICAL POLYGAMY IN THE LATER CHURCH FATHERS

Following New Testament leads, the Church Fathers also addressed whether second marriages were a form of successive polygamy. The question they raised was the one already lifted up by Tertullian: is there really much difference between having two spouses at the same time, or having two spouses in a row? A few Western Fathers – mostly the sectarian groups called Montanists, Manichaeans, and Encratites – followed Tertullian in banning all remarriages for widows, divorcees, and clergy alike, and they used the same arguments he had pressed for perpetual and exclusive monogamy. Under this logic, all those who remarried were both adulterers and polygamists. These Fathers sometimes called the clergy to refrain from blessing or presiding over second or third marriages, baptizing or legitimating children born of such unions, or offering these families any pastoral services or poor relief. This firm stance appears in a few church canons in the West, too, as we shall see in the next chapter, and it became the settled canonical position of the later Eastern Orthodox churches.[82]

The later Western Fathers and church councils, however, eventually treated this absolute rule of no remarriage as heretical, and insisted that those who had been

---

[81] Augustine, *Good of Marriage*, cc.17, 21; id., *Adulterous Marriage*, I.21; id., Sermon 1: On the Agreement of the Evangelists, 23–26; id., *On Marriage and Concupiscence*, I.10–11; id., *De Genesi ad Litteram*, IX.7, PL 34:397.

[82] See Meyendorff, "Christian Marriage in Byzantium"; David Heith-Stade, "Marriage in the Canons of Trullo," *Studia Theologica* 64(2) (2010): 4–21.

properly remarried could not be scorned or disciplined by fellow church members.[83] The Latin Fathers defended this right to remarriage with different logics and limits, however.[84] St. Jerome pushed for a more permissive understanding of remarriage – despite his strong preference for chastity over marriage. "I do not condemn digamists, or even trigamists, or if such a thing can be said, octagamists."[85] It is "insulting" both to God, the author of marriage, and to Christians who choose remarriage to "place them on a level with whoremongers and the most licentious persons." Marriage, after all, is in part God's remedy for sin. St. Paul made clear that "it is better to marry than to burn" with lust (1 Cor. 7:9).

> For on account of the dangers of fornication he allows virgins to marry, and makes that excusable which in itself is not desirable, so to avoid this same fornication, he allows second marriages to widows. For it is better to know a single husband, though he be a second or third, than to have many paramours.

Jerome further chided the churchmen of his day who withheld alms and other charitable services from widows who had remarried. How can you say that "she who has had two husbands, even though she be a widow, decrepit and in want, is not a worthy recipient of the church's funds? But if she be deprived of the bread of charity, how much more is she deprived of the bread which comes down from heaven."[86]

For the remarriage of widows, Jerome had St. Paul on his side. And, unlike Tertullian and his followers, he applied 1 Corinthians 7 and 1 Timothy 5 directly to support the remarriage of widowed women. He extended this right of remarriage to widowed men as well, with a simple *a fortiori* argument. Because the New Testament permits innocent divorced men to remarry, and because it generally gives men more marital freedom than women, innocent widowers should be allowed to remarry, too. In fact, Jerome pressed further by arguing that twice married men should be eligible for clerical ordination, too. Are we not "straining out a gnat and swallowing camels" with too punctilious a reading of the "husband of one wife" passages, Jerome asked earnestly. After all, there are plenty of bishops and priests now serving who had been married once, and are now living with concubines, visiting prostitutes, or worse. Would it not be better to have an honest cleric who "withdrew into the privacy of his own chamber" a second time with a lawfully married second wife than a cleric who "outrages public decency in the hot eagerness of [his] lust?"[87] Moreover, Jerome

[83] See the Council of Laodecia, Canon I, and The Captions of the Arabic Canons Attributed to the Council of Nicea, Canon LXVI, in NPNF 2, 14:50, 125, but more likely sixth-century Byzantine canons. On these, see Chapter 3, pp. 123–125.
[84] See detailed sources and discussion in Henri Crouzel, *L'eglise primitive face au divorce; du premier au cinquieme siècles* (Paris: Beauchesne, 1971).
[85] Quoted in editorial notes in NPNF 2, 14:72.
[86] Jerome, *Against Jovinianus* (393), in NPNF 2, 6:348, 358–359.
[87] Jerome, Letter 69, 2, 5–8, 10 in NPNF 2, 6:142–148, at 142–144.

argued, the Bible's "husband of one wife" requirement is not absolute. Read what Paul says in 1 Timothy 3: "Now a bishop must be above reproach, the husband of one wife, temperate, sensible, dignified, hospitable, an apt teacher, no drunkard, not violent but gentle, not quarrelsome, and no lover of money. He must manage his own household well [for] if a man does not know how to manage his own household, how can he care for God's church?" This is not a mandatory checklist for ordination, Jerome argued, but a set of criteria for judging who is worthy of the clerical office. And one way of judging the morality of an aspiring priest is to see if he was faithful to "one wife at a time" – not if he had one wife in a lifetime.[88]

Jerome had a harder time with the New Testament's repeated instruction that a divorced woman had to wait until the death of her first husband before she could remarry, lest she become an adulteress. In one letter, Jerome addressed a question whether a woman could divorce and remarry when her first husband had been convicted of particularly flagrant adultery and sodomy. Jerome applied this biblical instruction literally:

> As long as the husband lives, though he be an adulterer, though he practice unnatural vice, though he be steeped in every kind of profligacy, and forsaken by his wife because of these enormities, he is still accounted her husband, and it is forbidden her to take another partner.

If she does remarry, both she and her purported new husband are adulterers, he concluded, and they must be spiritually disciplined.[89]

But in a later letter, Jerome returned to his more permissive stance. A young woman had divorced her first adulterous and abusive husband and remarried another man before her first husband had died. Should she be spiritually punished? No, Jerome now said. A young divorcee sometimes can be in the same position as a young widow – "burning with lust" through no fault of her own. It makes no sense to withhold from her God's soothing remedy of marriage. For her, a second marriage is "necessary," too, he concluded, using the language of equitable dispensation that animated the discussions of Old Testament polygamy.

> I freely admit her guilt, but I appeal on the ground of necessity. "It is better to marry," the Apostle says, "than to burn." She was still very young and unable to persevere in widowhood. She experienced a law in her members struggling against the law in her mind, and she found herself being overcome and dragged as a captive to sexual intercourse. Therefore, she thought it was better to confess her weakness openly and submit to the shadow, as it were, of an unworthy marriage than to

present the appearance of an univira [a once-married woman] while leading the life of a courtesan.[90]

Only a few Church Fathers were as permissive as Jerome about second marriages of priests and divorcees.[91] Most stuck to the literal teachings of Jesus and St. Paul, and saw remarriages of widows and innocent divorced husbands as the only acceptable option for Christians, albeit not an ideal one. As Ambrosiaster put it:

> First marriages are celebrated in heaven with God's blessing, whereas second marriages, even in the present world, lack glory. They are permitted because some people have no self-control and because women often claim the privileges of widowhood at too young an age. For these reasons, Paul makes allowance for second marriages, but because it is better for a woman to remain continent in order to have greater merit in the future, he gives the advice which in spiritual terms is most important, that she should exercise self-control.[92]

Augustine wrote similarly that just as it is better to be celibate than married, so it is better to remain widowed than to remarry. But Christians should not chide those who lawfully remarry, Augustine counseled a worried mother who had sought his advice. Second marriages "are not condemned, but simply less honored. For just as the holy virginity which your daughter has chosen does not condemn your single marriage, so your widowhood does not condemn the second marriage of another."[93]

Although widows and widowers could remarry, Augustine continued, divorcees could not. He based this different treatment not only on the Bible but also on his emerging sacramental understanding of marriage. A Christian sacramental marriage, Augustine argued, creates "an enduring sacred bond" between the couple, like the eternal bond between Christ and his church. Even if the Christian couple does not produce children, even if they separate and divorce, even if one of them purports to marry another, "there remains between the partners as long as they live some conjugal thing [*quiddam coniugale*] that neither separation nor remarriage can remove." "So enduring, in fact, are the rights of marriage between those [Christians] who have contracted them, that they remain husband and wife" even if they divorce and purport to marry others. The sacrament of marriage ends only when one spouse dies – for, as Jesus said, in heaven "they neither marry, nor are given in marriage" (Matt. 22:30).[94]

---

[90] Quoted in ibid., 202.

[91] See, e.g., Origen, *Commentary on Matthew*, c. 22, in ANF 10:510; see also Theodoret of Syria, Letter 110, NPNF 2, 3:290.

[92] Ambrosiaster, *Commentaries on Romans and 1–2 Corinthians*, trans. Gerald L. Bray (Downers Grove, IL: InterVarsity Press Academic, 2009), Comm. 1 Cor. 7:40, p. 158.

[93] Augustine, *De Bono Viduitatis*, n. 6, *Patrilogia Latina* 40:433, using translation in Joyce, *Christian Marriage*, 585.

[94] Augustine, *On Marriage and Concupiscence*, I.11; id., *Good of Marriage*; cc. 6, 7, 15, 17, 32; id., *Adulterous Marriage*, I.12, II.9–11.

In his substantial tract, *On Adulterous Marriages* (419), Augustine argued that a Christian operating under divine law was still permitted to divorce an adulterous or spiritually deserting spouse, but divorce for him now meant only separation from bed and board. A Christian could not remarry another spouse until their first spouse died. For, despite their divorce at law, the couple remained married in fact, and to marry another would be to commit adultery and polygamy in violation of the indissoluble marital bond that still remained. Augustine thereby preserved the indissolubility of marriage, even if the actual relationship between husband and wife was now broken. He preserved the right to divorce, but now in the form of what later came to be called separation from bed and board. And he preserved the right to remarriage, but now only if and when one's spouse had died.[95]

Augustine, moreover, treated these limited rights of divorce for adultery and remarriage after death as concessions to human frailty that pious Christians should strive to forgo. It was best for a Christian not to divorce on any grounds and not to remarry at any time. Such rights "are lawful, but not necessarily expedient," Augustine wrote, adducing St. Paul's counsel of Christian prudence (1 Cor. 10:23). While the teaching of Christ allows for divorce in the case of adultery, it is better for an innocent spouse to forgive and reconcile with the other, just as God forgives mortal sinners. Although the counsels of Paul permit a pious believer to "let a faithless spouse depart" (1 Cor. 7:15), it is better to remain joined in marriage, so that the unbelieving spouse is "sanctified by the faith" of the other, and their children are brought up in the Lord. Augustine presented this "good/better" balance as a dialectic between justice and charity, rule and mercy, law and Gospel, command and counsel, precept and prudence, the law of the state and the law of Christ. And while his strong preference was for no divorce and no remarriage in the church, he also recognized that "it is difficult to draw with some universal dividing line the distinction between what is unlawful, and therefore inexpedient, and what is lawful, although inexpedient."[96]

SUMMARY AND CONCLUSIONS

The New Testament complicated the emerging Western case of monogamy over polygamy. The Old Testament had several texts and examples of real polygamy that stood juxtaposed to the monogamous marital ideals of the creation story in Genesis and of the covenant marriage metaphor in the Prophets. This dialectic between monogamy and polygamy would occupy the Rabbis for the next millennium before the Jewish tradition settled on monogamy alone by the start of the second millennium CE, with only a few dissenters. However, the Old Testament and the Talmudic

---

[95] Augustine, *Adulterous Marriage*, I.6–12, II.4–5, 13.
[96] Ibid., I.13–15; II.8, 10, 17, 19, 22.

Rabbis treated priestly marriage and the remarriage of divorcees and widow(er)s as normal and expected. The New Testament repeated the monogamous ideals of the Old Testament creation story, but said nothing about "real polygamy" and nothing against its practice among several leading men of faith in the Old Testament. Instead it focused on the successive polygamy of divorcees and widow(er)s and the clerical polygamy of bishops, deacons, and deaconesses.

The Church Fathers of the second through sixth centuries focused on two main questions in their discussions of polygamy. The first question was why so many Old Testament patriarchs practiced polygamy with seeming impunity. One answer, introduced by Tertullian, was *historical*: this was God's temporary dispensation in early times to fill an empty world more efficiently. A second answer, introduced by Jerome, was *prudential*: in cases of dire natural necessity, even natural laws against polygamy (and incest) may be equitably dispensed. A third answer, pressed by Chrysostom, was *developmental*: polygamy was virtuous in earlier, simpler civilizations, but monogamy is now the marital norm of Greek, Roman, and Christian communities, a virtue which Christians ground in the mysterious union of Christ and the church. A fourth answer, introduced by Augustine, was *structural*: marriage is a multidimensional institution, and while polygamy serves its natural goods of producing children, only monogamy serves its spiritual goods of fostering the mutual fidelity and sacramental stability that uniquely become a Christian marriage. All four of these arguments about polygamy – the historical, the prudential, the developmental, and the structural – would regularly echo, separately and together, in the Western legal tradition.

A second question concerned the definition and limits of polygamy, and how it related to other sexual offenses. All the Fathers who wrote on the topic agreed that the core case of polygamy was the act of being married to two or more spouses at the same time. It was worse to live that way openly, knowingly, or against the wishes of the first wife, for that exacerbated the harm done to self, spouse, and society. It was also worse if the marital parties shared the same bed in "open sexual congress," as the Fathers politely called orgies, for that was simply lust writ large. A few Fathers, notably Augustine, treated polygamy as something natural but contrary to current custom and Christian teachings. A few other Fathers, notably Lactantius, treated polygamy as something dangerous, and too often associated with household rivalries, internecine conflict, violence, sibling rape, and even murder. The sternest Fathers, starting with Tertullian and Clement, thought that polygamy was "perpetual adultery," an ongoing betrayal of the first spouse and first marriage. Others called it "grave fornication," "an abomination" of marriage, "an unnatural act," "a beastly thing," "an evil thing." Such language overlapped with later Roman laws that, we see in the next chapter, grouped polygamy with adultery and incest as serious crimes that were "infamous," "abominable," "nefarious," "wicked," "unnatural," and "execrable" offenses against the laws of God and the state.

But that said, it must also be said that the Church Fathers did not analyze polygamy at nearly the length they treated many other theological and legal questions. They were largely content to say that polygamy was contrary to the natural design of marriage as "two in one flesh" or the supernatural model of marriage as the mysterious bond between Christ and the church. But that begged the question, as Augustine already pointed out. Why is "two in one flesh" taken to be the natural design of marriage when nature has so many other polygamous forms? And why, to put the same question back to Augustine, is the mysterious union of Christ and the church a model for monogamy, given that many different Christians and churches in the world are bonded to the one same Christ, the metaphorical husband? The Fathers did not address these questions – in part because no one pressed them to say more. The pressure they faced was not to defend monogamy against polygamy, but to defend marriage against those who preferred chastity and celibacy and others who permitted extramarital sex especially with slaves, servants, and prostitutes.

Following the New Testament, the Church Fathers extended the category of polygamy to include unauthorized second marriages. They regarded this as a form of successive polygamy or "double marriage" ("digamy"). Most Fathers grudgingly tolerated remarriage after the death of one's spouse. A few allowed divorcees with pressing sexual or household needs to remarry even before the death of their first spouse. Most Fathers prohibited second marriages to any aspiring cleric or deaconess in direct application of St. Paul's rule that they be "the husband of one wife" or "the wife of one husband."

The Church Fathers wrote a great deal more about successive polygamy than real polygamy. This was, in part, because the New Testament, while silent on real polygamy, addressed second marriages half a dozen times, setting out a very different Christian ethic from prevailing Roman law and Jewish law that both encouraged remarriages. Such novel teaching required explication and defense, within the church and without. The Fathers' preoccupation with successive polygamy was also driven, in part, because Jesus had raised the moral stakes by charging improperly remarried parties with adultery – a mortal sin for Christians with serious consequences for a person's place in the church and in heaven thereafter. Drawing the lines between permissible and impermissible marital unions was thus critical.

Tertullian eventually drew the line at first marriage: Because husbands and wives are united in body and soul, even death does not break the soul bond between them, and thus divorcees and widows can never remarry. Augustine drew the line at the death of the first spouse: The sacramental bond between husband and wife remains intact only while both parties are still living, leaving widow(er)s free to remarry. Jerome drew the line at necessity. Marriage is a remedy for sin, and it is better for a divorcee or widow(er) to remarry than to burn with lust or to commit other sins like fornication.

Where to draw the line was not just an abstract theological question, however, but also an intensely practical question for Christians as they navigated the edges of real and successive polygamy. Was it polygamy to have a wife and a concubine, or two concubines, or two fiancé(e)s? Was it polygamy to betroth one party and then marry another, or vice versa, and which woman (and children) stood to inherit if the man died? Was it polygamy to marry another when one's first spouse had intentionally deserted the home? Or inexplicably disappeared for a long time? Or left the church and renounced the faith? Was it polygamy for a new convert to the faith to leave his or her former non-Christian spouse, and remarry another Christian? Could a Christian convert, who had two or more spouses before baptism, retain both? What happens when a first spouse returns to find the other once deserted party remarried? Some of these questions still face church and state authorities today as they sort out prima facie cases of polygamy and as they set the boundary lines separating the offenses of polygamy, adultery, and fornication. The early church leadership – individual theologians, bishops, and popes, and eventually church councils and synods, too – began to issue rules and rulings to deal with these questions, drawing in part on Roman law precedents. These became part of the emerging canon law of the church. This is the subject of the next chapter.

3

Polygamy in the Laws of State and Church
in the First Millennium

FIGURE 7. "Goddess Vesta Blesses a Roman Wedding Ceremony," Roman (second century AD).
Used by permission of Unknown Ancient Art and Architecture Collection Ltd. / Bridgeman Images.

FIGURE 8. "Alcibiades amongst the Hetaerae," from Cosroe Dusi, Museo Civico Revoltella, Trieste, Italy.
Used by permission of Museo Civico Revoltella, Trieste, Italy / Bridgeman Images.

Distinguished family scholar, Don S. Browning, once called the early Christian family the "Graeco-Roman family with a twist."[1] Christianity emerged in a Graeco-Roman legal culture that had already defined "lawful marriage" as "the union of a man and a woman, a partnership for the whole of life, involving divine as well as human law."[2] The "ancient law" of Rome required monogamy.[3] The pre-Christian Roman emperors prohibited polygamy. "[A] woman cannot marry two men, nor can a man have two wives," wrote the Roman jurist, Gaius, in ca. 170 CE, summarizing the Roman law of his day. Polygamy is "nefarious," and a man who enters such a union "is considered to have neither a wife nor children." His

---

[1] Don S. Browning, "The Family and Christian Jurisprudence," in *Christianity and Law: An Introduction*, ed. John Witte, Jr. and Frank S. Alexander (Cambridge: Cambridge University Press, 2010), 163–184, at 163–164.

[2] *The Digest of Justinian*, 23.2.1, ed. Theodor Mommsen and Paul Krueger, trans. Alan Watson, 4 vols. (Philadelphia: University of Pennsylvania Press, 1985) (hereafter "Dig.").

[3] The language is from *The Code of Justinian*, 7.15.3.2, in Paul Krüger, ed., *Corpus Iuris Civilis* (Berlin: Weidmann, 1928–1929) (hereafter "CJ"). See also note 31 in this chapter.

purported wives are nothing more than "harlots," and his children are no better than "spurious bastards conceived through promiscuous intercourse."[4]

Christianity adopted these basic Roman law teachings on monogamy and polygamy. But Christianity also added to them, pressing for a monogamous union that was more egalitarian, more exclusive, and more enduring. Roman law forced parties to choose between a concubine and a wife; they could not have both. Christianity denounced concubinage altogether, requiring Christians either to marry or to remain single. Roman law maintained a sexual double standard, forbidding wives to commit adultery but allowing husbands to indulge with impunity in sex with prostitutes and slaves. Christianity denounced extramarital sex altogether, and called Christian husbands and wives alike to remain faithful to each other exclusively. Roman law forced a man to divorce his wife or dismiss his concubine before marrying another woman. Christianity sharply restricted divorce and denounced the second marriages of divorcees. Roman law encouraged widows and widowers to remarry after a year. Christianity discouraged such remarriages, especially if repeated.

What emerged in the first centuries of the common era were two normative systems that were both for monogamy and against polygamy. They both agreed on the core case of monogamy – marriage between one man and one woman. They both agreed on the core case of real polygamy – marriage between one man and two or more wives at the same time. Roman law extended the range of valid monogamy to include the quasi-marital relationship of concubinage. Christianity extended the range of polygamy to include the remarriages of divorcees and widow(er)s and the double marriages of ordained clergy. But in basic outline, these normative systems were parallel. They slowly began to converge after the Christianization of Rome in the fourth and fifth centuries CE, yet they remained separate. Not only was Christianity only partly successful in converting Roman law and later Germanic law to its norms of sex, marriage, and family life.[5] But the church also did not simply become a ward of the state and its law. "Christians live in two cities," Augustine wrote famously in ca. 420 CE, the City of God and the City of Man, and they must

---

4   Institutes of Gaius, 1.63–64, in T. Lambert Mears, ed., *The Institutes of Gaius and Justinian: the Twelve Tables, and the CXVIIIth and CXXVIIth Novels* (Clark, NJ: Lawbook Exchange, 2004 [1882]). See also ibid., 4.182. The language recurs in *Justinian's Institutes*, 1.1.10, ed. Paul Krüger, trans. Peter Birks and Grant McLeod (Ithaca, NY: Cornell University Press, 1987) [hereafter "Inst."]. See also Jos. Zhishman, *Das Eherecht der orientalischen Recht* (Vienna: Wilhelm Braumüller, 1864), 373–174; Riccardo Astolfi, *Studi sul matrimonio nel diritto romano postclassico e giustinianeo* (Naples: Jovene Editori, 2012), 124–125.

5   See various views discussed in Philip L. Reynolds, *Marriage in the Western Church: The Christianization of Marriage During the Patristic and Early Modern Periods* (Leiden: Brill, 1994); Judith Evans Grubbs, "Christianization of Marriage? Christianity, Marriage, and Law in Late Antiquity," in *Ehe-Familie-Verwandtschaft: Vergellschaftung in Religion und sozialer Lebeswelt* (Paderborn: Ferdinand Schönigh, 2008), 105–124.

"honor the authorities" in each.[6] "Two powers there are," Pope Gelasius added in 494: "the sacred power" of the pope who is "in charge of spiritual things" and the secular power of the emperor who governs the secular matters "of the human race."[7] Marriage and family life are both spiritual and secular in character, and thus come within the jurisdiction, the law-making power, of both church and state.

This chapter analyzes the treatment of polygamy in the first millennium canon law texts, viewed in the context of evolving Greek, Roman, and Germanic laws on monogamy and against polygamy.

GRAECO-ROMAN AND GERMANIC LAWS ON
MONOGAMY AND POLYGAMY

Monogamous Ideals

Already half a millennium before the time of Jesus, ancient Greece and ancient Rome had chosen monogamy as the only valid form of marriage that could produce legitimate and heritable widows and children. Sixth- and fifth-century BCE laws of various Greek city-states made clear that valid marriages had to be monogamous, and this norm also became commonplace in the first Roman law collections that have survived from the mid-fifth century BCE.[8] Monogamy was a "quintessentially Greek" institution of the ancient world, Stanford ancient historian Walter Scheidel has shown, and the Thracian Greeks and the Romans after them regarded polygamy as "a barbarian custom or a mark of tyranny."[9]

By the fourth century BCE, Greek philosophers were extolling the private and public goods of monogamous marriage. Plato (ca. 428–ca. 347 BCE), for example, said that a "just republic ... must arrange [for] marriages, sacr[ed] so far as may be. And the most sacred marriages would be those that were most beneficial."[10] The most beneficial, Plato later said, were monogamous marriages that met the natural

---

[6] St. Augustine, *City of God*, trans. Gerald G. Walsh et al., ed. Vernon J. Bourke (Garden City, NY: Image Books, 1958).

[7] Sidney Z. Ehler and John B. Morrall, *Church and State through the Centuries: A Collection of Historic Documents with Commentaries* (Westminster, MD: Newman Press, 1954), 10–11.

[8] Susan Lape, "Solon and the Institution of the 'Democratic' Family Form," *Classical Journal* 98 (2002–03): 117–139.

[9] Walter Scheidel, "A Peculiar Institution; Greco-Roman Monogamy in Global Context," *History of the Family* 14 (2009): 280–291, at 283. See more fully Walter Erdman, *Die Ehe im alten Griechenland*, repr. ed. (New York: Arno Press, 1979 [1934]), 87–103; Cynthia B. Patterson, *The Family in Greek History* (Cambridge, MA: Harvard University Press, 1998).

[10] Plato, *Republic* V 458E, in *The Collected Dialogues of Plato, Including the Letters*, trans. and eds. Edith Hamilton and Huntingdon Cairns (New York: Pantheon Books, 1961), 575, 698. My colleague Philip Reynolds has pointed out that Greek term *"hieros"* that appears back-to-back in this quotation is better translated as "sacred" both times rather than as "sacrament" the first time, and "sacred" the second as the translators have done.

human need for dyadic love as a way for humans to complete themselves. "This then is the source of our desire to love each other. Love is born into every human being; it calls back the halves of our original nature together; it tries to make one out of two and heal the wound of human nature." "Why should this be so? It's because ... we used to be complete wholes in our human nature, and now 'Love' is the name for our pursuit of wholeness, for our desire to be complete."[11]

An early Greek handbook offering instructions on wedding liturgies echoed Plato's emphasis on the natural and social goods of dyadic pairing of husband and wife:

> After the proemia there should follow a sort of thematic passage on the god of marriage, including the general consideration of the proposition that marriage is a good thing. You should begin far back, telling how Marriage was created by Nature immediately after the dispersal of Chaos, and perhaps also how Love too was created then.... You should go on to say that the ordering of the universe ... took place because of Marriage.... [Marriage] also made ready to create man, and contrived to make him virtually immortal, furnishing successive generations to accompany the passage of time.... Marriage gives us immortality ... it is due to Marriage that the sea is sailed, the land is farmed, philosophy and knowledge of heavenly things exist, as well as laws and civil governments – in brief, all human things.[12]

Plato's student Aristotle (384–321 BCE) viewed monogamous marriage as the foundation of the polis. He envisioned humans as political or communal animals who form states and other associations "for the purpose of attaining some good."[13] "[E]very state is composed of households," Aristotle wrote famously in his *Politics*.[14] Every household, in turn, is composed of a "pairing of those who cannot exist without one another. A male and female must unite for the reproduction of the species – not from deliberate intention, but from the natural impulse ... to leave behind them something of the same nature as themselves."[15] Aristotle extended this view in his *Ethics*, now emphasizing the natural inclinations and goods of dyadic marriage beyond its political and social expediency:

> The love between husband and wife is evidently a natural feeling, for nature has made man even more of a pairing than a political animal in so far as the family is an older and more fundamental thing than the state, and the instinct to form communities is less widespread among animals than the habit of procreation. Among the generality of animals male and female come together for this sole

[11] Plato, *Symposium*, trans. Alexander Nehmans and Paul Woodruff (Indianapolis: Hackett Publishers, 1989), 25–31.
[12] *Menander Rhetor*, trans. and eds. D.A. Russell and N.G. Wilson (Oxford: Oxford University Press, 1981), 136–139.
[13] Aristotle, Politica, 1.1.1, in *The Politics of Aristotle*, trans. and ed. Ernest Barker (New York: Oxford University Press, 1962).
[14] Ibid., 1.3.1.
[15] Ibid., 1.2.2.

purpose [of procreation]. But human beings cohabit not only to get children but to provide whatever is necessary to a fully lived life. From the outset the partners perform distinct duties, the man having one set, the woman another. So by pooling their individual contributions [into a common stock] they help each other out. Accordingly there is general agreement that conjugal affection combines the useful with the pleasant. But it may also embody a moral ideal, when husband and wife are virtuous persons. For man and woman have each their own special excellence, and this may be a source of pleasure to both. Children too, it is agreed, are a bond between the parents – which explains why childless unions are more likely to be dissolved. The children do not belong to one parent more than the other, and it is the joint ownership of something valuable that keeps people from separating.[16]

In the centuries after Plato and Aristotle, the Roman Stoics repeated and glossed these classical Greek views about monogamous marriage, even while many of them celebrated celibacy as the higher ideal for philosophers seeking quiet contemplation. For example, Musonius Rufus (b. ca. 30 CE) described marriage in robust companionate terms that prefigured the familiar language of the Western marriage liturgy:

The husband and wife ... should come together for the purpose of making a life in common and of procreating children, and furthermore of regarding all things in common between them, and nothing peculiar or private to one or the other, not even their own bodies. The birth of a human being which results from such a union is to be sure something marvelous, but it is not yet enough for the relation of husband and wife, inasmuch as quite apart from marriage it could result from any other sexual union, just as in the case of animals. But in marriage there must be above all perfect companionship and mutual love of husband and wife, both in health and in sickness and under all conditions, since it was with desire for this as well as for having children that both entered upon marriage.[17]

Musonius's student, Hierocles (early second century CE), argued that it was incumbent upon all men, even philosophers seeking quiet contemplation, to marry and to maintain a household. For "the married couple is the basis of the household, and the household is essential for civilization," he wrote, echoing Aristotle.[18] While procreation remained the ultimate ideal of marriage, in Hierocles's view, the consistent companionship and mutual care of husband and wife was no less important, even in the absence of children:

---

[16] Aristotle, *The Nicomachean Ethics*, 8.12, in *The Ethics of Aristotle*, trans. and ed. J.A.K. Thomson, repr. ed. (New York: Penguin Books, 1965). The interpolation "into a common stock" is an alternative translation that appears in several other translations of this passage.

[17] *Musonius Rufus: The Roman Socrates*, trans. and ed. Cora E. Lutz (New Haven, CT: Yale University Press, 1947), 89.

[18] Grubbs, *Law and Family*, 59.

[T]he beauty of a household consists in the yoking together of a husband and wife who are united to each other by fate, are consecrated to the gods who preside over weddings, births, and houses, agree with each other and have all things in common, including their bodies, or rather their souls, and who exercise appropriate rule over their household and servants, take care in rearing their children, and pay attention to the necessities of life which is neither intense nor slack, but moderate and fitting.[19]

The prolific Roman historian and moralist, Plutarch (46–120 CE) extolled the pleasures of marital love, intimacy, and friendship between husband and wife. The ideal marriage, he wrote, is "a union for life between a man and a woman for the delights of love and the getting of children." "In the case of lawful wives, physical union is the beginning of friendship, a sharing, as it were, in great mysteries. The pleasure [of sexual intercourse] is short; but the respect and kindness and mutual affection and loyalty that daily spring from it ... [renders] such a [marital] union a 'friendship.'" And again: "[N]o greater pleasures derived from others, nor more continuous services are conferred on others than those found in marriage, nor can the beauty of another friendship be so highly esteemed or so enviable as when a man and wife keep house in perfect harmony.'"[20]

The Gradual Criminalization of Polygamy

Even though monogamy was the marital ideal of this classical Western world, both Greek and Roman laws did allow a married man to have sex with his slaves and prostitutes with impunity. These laws also allowed a married man to retain a longstanding concubine so long as she did not live in the marital home and did not inherit anything from the man.[21] Roman law later banned this latter practice; a man could have a wife or a concubine, but not both.[22]

---

[19] Ibid., 59–60 (quoting Hierocles).
[20] Plutarch, *Life of Solon*, 20.4, in *Plutarch's Lives*, trans. Bernadotte Perrin (London: William Heinemann, 1928); Plutarch, *The Dialogue of Love*, §769–770, in *Plutarch's Moralia*, trans. L. Pearson (London: W. Heinemann, 1960). See analysis in Sarah B. Pomeroy, ed., *Plutarch's Advice to the Bride and Groom and a Consolation to his Wife* (New York: Oxford University Press, 1999).
[21] On the complex Greek and Roman laws of concubinage, see Ernst Hruza, *Polygamie und Pellikat nach Griechischem Rechte* (Erlangen/Leipzig: A. Deichert'sche Verlagsbuch, 1894); Paul Meyer, *Der römischen Konkubinat nach den Rechtsquellen und den Inschriften* (Leipzig: G.B. Teubner, 1895); Raimund Friedl, *Der Konkubinat im kaiserlichen Rom: von Augustus bis Septimus Severus* (Stuttgart: F. Steiner, 1996).
[22] CJ 5.26.1 (quoting Constantine in 326); see Grubbs, *Law and Family*, 294–304, on the pre-Constantian sources of this prohibition. See also Walter Scheidel, "Monogamy and Polygyny," in Beryl Rawson, ed., *A Companion to Families in the Greek and Roman Worlds* (Malden, MA: Blackwell, 2011), 108–115, at 111.

Both Greek and Roman law also made occasional allowances for polygamy in individual cases of necessity. For example, Athens in the late-fifth century BCE, temporarily allowed polygamy after the Peloponnesian War had killed most of the men in the city, leaving women desperate for husbands and the now vulnerable city desperate for rapid repopulation.[23] A few Aegean kings and Macedonian rulers also claimed the privilege to practice polygamy.[24] But, as Daniel Ogden reports after a thorough study, these royal Greek polygamists had the same bitter experience with polygamy that befell the Old Testament polygamists whom we encountered two chapters ago: "Their various wives were in fierce competition with each other to ensure both their own status and the succession of their sons.... Rival wives hated each other; the various groups of paternal half-siblings hated each other; but the most intense hatred of all was reserved for the relationship between the children and their stepmothers."[25] This royal polygamous experiment accordingly soon imploded. In Rome, at the end of the Republic, Julius Caesar (100–44 BCE) – famous for his military prowess, but infamous for his philandering – ordered that a special law be passed "allowing him, with the hope of leaving issue, to take any wife he chose, and as many of them as he pleased." His contemporaries, however, charged him with "unnatural lewdness and adultery," and little evidently came of his efforts.[26] Julius Caesar's successor, the first Roman emperor, Caesar Augustus (63 BCE–14 CE) enacted sweeping reforms of Roman law, including the laws of marriage and family life, with monogamy again at the foundation.[27]

Until the third century CE, Roman law did not criminalize polygamy. If a man claimed to have two or more wives, the law simply recognized as valid only the first properly married wife. It was considered "legally impossible" to have more than one wife or marriage at the same time.[28] Writing around 55 BCE, for example, the leading Roman jurist and philosopher, Marcus Tullius Cicero (106–43 BCE), described the case of a Roman citizen who left his wife with child in Spain, and moved to Rome. Without bothering to send the first wife a bill of divorce, he married a second woman in Rome and produced a child with her, too, but then died intestate. Both wives and

---

[23] See sources in Daniel Ogden, *Greek Bastardy in the Classical and Hellenistic Periods* (Oxford: Oxford University Press, 1996), 72–75.

[24] See Hruza, *Polygamie und Pellikat*; Daniel Ogden, "The Royal Families of Argead Macedon," in Rawson, ed., *Blackwell Companion*, 92–107, summarizing his longer account in id., *Polygamy, Prostitutes, and Death: The Hellenistic Dynasties* (Swansea: Duckworth with the Classical Press of Wales, 1999).

[25] Ibid., ix–x.

[26] C. Seutonius Tranquillus, *The Lives of the Twelve Caesars*, ch. 1, 52, trans. Alexander Thomson, rev. ed. T. Forester (London: George and Sons, 1890), 34.

[27] See Susan Treggiari, *Roman Marriage: Iusti coniuges From the Time of Cicero to the Time of Ulpian* (Oxford: Oxford University Press, 1991), 229–319.

[28] Joanna Misztal-Konecka, *Bigamia w prawie rzymskim* (Lublin: Wydawnictwo Kul, 2011), 331–332. I am grateful to my doctoral student, Claudia Sarti, for her help in analyzing this important Polish study.

their children evidently claimed the estate. This second woman in Rome, Cicero concluded, was only a concubine and her child was a bastard. Neither of them, in fact, could have inherited from the man, even if he had left a last will and testament making them his beneficiaries. It was "scandalous impertinence," said Cicero, that the man did not know the law well enough to divorce his first wife and to cut her off from the inheritance.[29] Writing two centuries later, in ca. 170 CE, Gaius, as we saw, treated the purported second wife as a concubine or prostitute and the children as bastards, neither of whom could inherit.[30] Gaius's contemporary Aulus Gellius (ca. 125–ca. 180) wrote similarly that "a woman was called an infamous concubine (*pellex*) if she was connected and lived with a man who had a wife legally married to him." The prohibition on a married man living with or marrying his concubine in addition to his wife, "appears to be a very old law," Gellius went on; "it is said to be King Numa's" – that is, Numa Pompilius, the second king of Rome (ca. 716–673 BCE).[31]

The only "lawful marriage" that could produce heritable widows and children is the union of one man and one woman who have the freedom, fitness, and capacity to marry each other, wrote several Roman jurists in the second and third centuries CE.[32] Once "voluntarily contracted" and "consensually formed," such a monogamous marriage was viewed as a presumptively "inseparable communion," "a sacred and enduring union" contracted for the sake of "marital affection" and the "propagation of offspring."[33] Only the death of one's spouse or a formal divorce could break the marital union and leave the now-single party free to remarry another spouse properly.

In an imperial edict of 258 CE, Rome for the first time criminalized polygamy, and began to impose criminal punishments on intentional polygamists and their accomplices, while continuing to foreclose second spouses and their children from inheritance.[34] The first imperial edict on point provided as follows:

There is no doubt that he who has two wives at the same time must be branded with infamy. Such cases must take into consideration not only the law that forbids a

[29] Cicero, *De Oratore*, 1.40.183, trans. E.M.P. Moor, 2nd ed. (London: Methuen and Company, 1904), 70–71. For the Roman law of inheritance, see Alan Watson, *The Law of Succession in the Later Roman Republic* (Oxford: Clarendon Press, 1991).

[30] Institutes of Gaius, 1.63–64.

[31] *The Attic Nights of Aulus Gellius* (Cambridge, MA: Harvard University Press/Loeb Classical Library, 1961), 4.3.3. See also Sextus Pompeius Festus, *De verborum significatu quae supersunt cum Pauli epitome*, ed. Wallace Martin Lindsay (Leipzig: Teubner, 1913), 248, who writes of this ancient law: "a concubine (*pellex*) shall not touch the altar of Juno" – that is, get married before Juno, the goddess of marriage. "If she touches it, she shall sacrifice, with her hair unbound, a female lamb to Juno." I am grateful to Professor Rafael Domingo for bringing these ancient texts to my attention.

[32] Dig. 23.2.1 (Modestinus); Dig. 48.5.12.12 (Papinian).

[33] Dig. 23.2.1 (Ulpian); see also Dig. 24.1.32; 25.1; 35.1; Inst. 1.9–10.

[34] On the evolving Roman laws against polygamy, see esp. Astolfi, *Studi sul matrimonio*, 123–134.

citizen to contract more than one marriage at the same time, but also the intention of the citizen [in forming the second marriage]. So, he who pretended to be single, but already had another wife living in the province can lawfully be accused of the crime of fornication *(stuprum)*. But you [the innocent second wife] are not liable because you thought that you were his wife. You can get back from the provincial governor all the property that you deplorably lost on account of the fraudulent marriage and which must be returned to you without delay.[35]

Another imperial rescript of 285 CE repeated the charge that "anyone under Roman rule who has two wives will be branded with infamy."[36]

A series of other edicts and juridical commentaries over the next century rounded out the Roman criminal law of polygamy, and began increasing the punishment for those convicted of polygamy.[37] These laws underscored that parties who knowingly or intentionally entered into an engagement or marriage contract, while already engaged or married to another, would be charged with a special form of "fornication" *(stuprum)* or "adultery" *(adulterium)* for which they would incur the sentence of "infamy" *(infamia)*.[38] Infamy in classical Roman law was not only a source of social stigma; it was also a legal black mark that precluded a party from holding public office or other positions of trust or authority, from appearing or testifying to press a number of private claims, and from exercising a number of private and public rights, even if they were citizens.[39] A party could be branded with infamy, even if the second marriage he intended to enter would have been invalid (say, because the parties were not of the same class or were too closely related by blood). "Since the deed is blacklisted," wrote the leading jurist, Ulpian (ca. 170–228), "even if someone only arranges for a marriage or betrothal with a woman he either cannot or should not take as his wife, he will be on the blacklist."[40] It was the intent to enter the second contract that triggered the charge of polygamy and the punishment of infamy for those convicted.

These punishments and deprivations were also extended to knowing accomplices to the polygamy. A father or guardian could incur infamy if he knowingly ordered those under his authority to enter into a polygamous union: such an accomplice in polygamy, "can be considered in a way to have done so himself," said Ulpian.[41] No engagement or marriage could proceed without a formal and final breaking of the

---

[35] CJ 9.9.18.

[36] CJ 5.5.2.

[37] See the careful analysis of the evolving texts in Mistzal-Konecka, *Bigamia*, 127–248, and Luigi Sandirocco, "Binae Nupitae et Bina Sponsalia," *Studia et Documenta Historiae et Iuris* 70 (2004): 165–216.

[38] CJ 6.57.5.1. See also CJ 5.27.2; *Codex Theodosianus*, Paul Krüger ed. (Berlin: Weidmann, 1923–1926), 4.4.6 [hereafter "C Th"].

[39] Dig. 3.2.1; Dig. 3.2.13.1–4; CJ 9.9.18; CJ 5.3.5; Grubbs, *Law and Family in Late Antiquity*, 167–169; A.H.J. Greenidge, *Infamia in Roman Public and Private Law* (Oxford: Clarendon Press, 1894).

[40] Dig. 3.2.13.4 (Ulpian).

[41] Dig. 3.2.1 (Julian) and Dig. 3.2.13.1–4 (Ulpian).

prior engagement or a successful divorce from the prior marriage. Until that time, a woman or her family to a second contract could not keep or claim property from her purported new fiancé or husband. The man, in turn, could reclaim any property from his purported fiancée or wife and her family if she proved to be married or engaged already.[42] Both the man and the woman could be punished for attempting or practicing polygamy if they knew of the other's prior engagement or marriage contract – although an innocent single woman who had been coerced or tricked into joining a polygamous relationship would be spared.[43] In turn, if a woman was engaged for two years but the man failed to marry her within that period, she was free to break the engagement and leave him for another man. In such a case, the first man and his father or guardian could be charged for negligence or laziness in neither marrying the woman nor breaking the engagement.[44]

After the Christianization of the Roman Empire in the fourth and fifth centuries, the Christian emperors repeated and extended these existing prohibitions against polygamy. They eventually put bigamy or polygamy as a separate felony (*crimen extraordinarium*) alongside adultery and incest, which were all "wicked," "unnatural," and "treacherous" "violations of morality."[45] Christian Emperor Justinian's massive *Corpus Iuris Civilis* (529–534 CE) collected these earlier laws against polygamy, which he repeated and extended in his own "new laws" (*Novellae*) thereafter. "When a man is married to a lawful wife, he cannot contract any other marriage during the existence of that first marriage, nor produce legitimate children from it," reads one of his Novels. This is an "act of licentiousness."[46]

The Christian emperors also repeated and extended traditional prohibitions on sexual relationships that could border on or encourage polygamy. First, men were again forbidden from having both a wife and a concubine at the same time.[47] Second, convicted adulterers, both men and women, were forbidden from ever marrying their former adulterous paramours, even after divorce from or death of their innocent first spouse.[48] Third, consecrated virgins, widows, and nuns, who had made vows of chastity could not thereafter marry since they were now "married to Christ." A man who engaged or married such an already consecrated woman was guilty of a serious crime; his goods were to be confiscated, and he was either to be exiled or executed.[49]

---

[42] CJ 9.9.18; CJ 5.3.5.

[43] Ibid.; Treggiari, *Roman Marriage*, 279.

[44] C Th 3.5.8.4.

[45] CJ 5.9.1; 5.27.2; 6.57.5; C Th 4.4.6; Nov. 12.1.

[46] Nov. 89.12.5.

[47] CJ 5.26.1.

[48] C Th 9.7.8; see earlier formulation in Dig. 23.2.24 (Modestinus).

[49] C Th 9.25.1–3; CJ 1.3.5; Nov. 123.43. A few later Roman laws also mentioned with little detail that deacons and priests could not have more than one wife, and if "they marry a second time they shall not be eligible for the high office of the priesthood." CJ 1.3.19. These were small echoes of more elaborate canon law rules on clerical bigamy discussed later in this chapter and in Chapter 4.

Fourth, a new widow was forbidden to remarry until after a suitable one-year period of mourning for her late husband – and of waiting to ensure she was not carrying his child. A widow who "hastens to contract a second marriage without having properly mourned for her first husband, becomes infamous," both pre- and post-Christian laws provided. Such a woman risked losing all or a substantial portion of her legacy from her late husband's estate and having any child born of another man during this mourning period declared illegitimate. Moreover, any man who knowingly marries a woman during her one-year mourning period likewise risked the charge of infamy.[50]

Later Roman emperors, as we saw in Chapter 1, took special aim at Jewish polygamists. In 393, Emperor Theodosius and others announced: "None of the Jews shall … enter into several marriages at the same time."[51] In 535, Emperor Justinian repeated this prohibition, calling polygamy "contrary to nature" and declaring again that all children born of the second wife to be illegitimate, and ordering the seizure of one quarter of the property of any practicing polygamists.[52] Justinian did grant a narrow exemption for a few polygamous Jews in the region of Tyre, but he made clear that he was "granting this favor to them alone" on their "payment of ten pounds of gold" and that the exemption would die with these parties.[53]

This one narrow exemption aside, general criminal prohibitions against polygamy persisted in later Roman legislation in the Eastern Byzantine Empire. By the ninth century, Byzantine Emperor Theophilus declared real polygamy by anyone to be a capital crime.[54] These capital laws against polygamy slowly multiplied in both the East and the West after the year 900, particularly as university jurists in the West began glossing the Roman law prohibitions on polygamy collected in the newly discovered books of Roman law.[55]

---

[50] CJ 5.9.1–3; Dig. 3.2.1; C Th 3.8.1. See Judith Evans Grubbs, "Promoting Pietas in Roman Law," in Rawson, ed., *Companion*, 377–392.

[51] CJ I.9.7.

[52] Nov. 12; Nov. 89.5.12.

[53] Nov. 139.1. See Chapter 1, p. 55 for a more detailed discussion of this special exemption for selected Jews in the Roman Empire to practice polygamy. Later Western writers would reject religious liberty exemptions from criminal law prohibitions on polygamy. See discussion by John Locke in Chapter 9, pp. 366–367 by Paul Johann Anselm von Feuerbach in the Introduction, p. 14 and by nineteenth-century common law jurists and the Supreme Court in Chapter 10, pp. 434–436.

[54] *Institutionum graeca paraphrasis Theophilo antecessori vulgo tributa ad fidem librorum manu*, ed. Cantadori Ferrini (Berolini: S. Calvary, 1884), 1.10.6.i

[55] Some of these early glosses and commentaries by civilians and canonists are collected and sifted in an early sixteenth-century tract: Ioannis Montaigne, *De Bigamia*, in *Tractatus Universi Juris* (Venice, 1584), 9:242–261. See, e.g., the Statute of Bologna, 4.33, in Gina Fasoli and Pietro Sella, *Statuti di Bologna dell'anno 1288* (Vatican City: Biblioteca apostolica vaticana, 1937–1939), 1:197 and 1287 Statute of Ferrara, 4.55, in William Montorsi, ed., *Statuta Ferrari, Anno MCCLXXXVII*, 4.55 (Ferrara: Casa di risparmio di Ferrra, 1955), 271, with discussion in James A. Brundage, *Law, Sex, and Christian Society in Medieval Europe* (Chicago, IL: University of Chicago Press, 1987), 478. See also ibid., 539–540, discussing later Italian statutes prohibiting polygamy, including making it a capital offense

After the fall of the Western Roman Empire in the fifth century CE, a few Germanic law codes followed suit. The Visigothic Code (ca. 642), for example, which operated in much of modern-day Spain, required that if a woman knowingly married an already married man, she was to be turned over to the first wife or her heirs, and could be enslaved or "disposed of" as the first wife saw fit, "death alone being excepted." Similarly, a man who knowingly married the fiancée of another would be compelled to become that other man's slave.[56] Engagement contracts were serious business for many Germanic peoples both before and after their Christianization. The breach of an engagement contract by sexual contact or by contracting a second engagement was punishable as adultery. The Visigothic Code was particularly severe:

> If a marriage contract has been entered into between an intended husband and the parents of an intended wife; or with the woman herself, if she has the right to make the contract; the dowry being duly given, and an agreement made in writing, before witnesses, according to custom, and as is prescribed by law; and, afterwards the girl or the woman is convicted of having committed adultery, or of having betrothed herself to another man, or of having married, she, along with her unlawful husband, or adulterer, or betrothed to whom she has given herself contrary to her solemn agreement, shall be delivered up as slaves, with all their property, to the person to whom she was first betrothed.[57]

Other Germanic laws, although not inflicting slavery, still saddled the guilty party with heavy fines and damages payable to the king and to the fiancée's family. They also ordered a doubly contracted man to wait at least three years before entering into any other engagement contract.[58] To avoid such problems, a few Germanic laws (following Roman law precedents) required a man to marry his fiancée within two years, or he would forfeit his bride price and pay other damages to the first woman's family, leaving the woman free to marry another. If he broke off his engagement before the two years in order to marry another woman, the law required him to make an elaborate declaration that the first woman's virtue and virginity remained intact even though he had fallen in love with another woman. He could break the

in Reggio Emilia. For later medieval statutes in Italy and beyond, see Anna Esposito, "Adulterio, concubinato, bigamia: testimonianze della normativa statuturia della Stato pontificio (secoli XIII-XVI), in *Trasgessioni: Seduzione, concubinato, adulterio, bigamia (XIV-XVIII secolo* (Bologna: Il Mulino, 2004), 21–42; Stefano Riccio, *La Bigamia* (Naples: Dott. Eugenio Jovene, 1934), 23–24.

56 Visigothic Code, bk. 3, title 6.2–3, in *The Visigothic Code (Forum Iudicum)*, trans. S.P. Scott (Boston: The Boston Book Company, 1910), 114–116. See Suzanne Fonay Wemple, *Women in Frankish Society: Marriage and the Cloister 500–900* (Philadelphia: University of Pennsylvania Press, 1981), 39–40, on their enforcement.

57 Visigothic Code, bk. 3, title 4, law 2, using translation in the Library of Iberian Sources: http://libro.uca.edu/vcode/visigoths.htm.

58 Bavarian Code, 7.16.

engagement without damages or declarations only if his fiancée had committed premarital adultery or if she had become inflicted with leprosy, madness, blindness, or a comparable serious condition.[59]

Later Anglo-Saxon rulers put polygamy alongside adultery and incest as serious crimes and sins deserving of "hell-fire." The laws of King Ethelred (ca. 994) and of King Canute (1027), for example, both provided that a man shall "have no more wives than one, and that shall be his wedded wife, and he who seeks to observe God's law aright and to save his soul from hell-fire shall remain with the one [wife] as long as she lives."[60]

POLYGAMY IN THE EARLY CANON LAW OF THE CHURCH: THE CANONS OF BASIL THE GREAT

In its first three centuries, the Christian Church had a testy and sometimes tempestuous relationship with the sophisticated Graeco-Roman law and culture in which it was born. Early Christian leaders did adopt a number of Roman legal institutions and practices, including a number of their marriage and family norms. They also taught the faithful to pay their taxes, to register their properties, and to obey the Roman rulers up to the limits of Christian conscience and commandment. But Christians could not accept the Roman imperial cult nor readily partake of the pagan rituals required for participation in public life. They further urged the Roman rulers to reform the law in accordance with basic Christian teachings – to protect religious freedom, to outlaw infanticide and easy divorce, to expand charity and education, to curb military violence and criminal punishments, to emancipate slaves, and more. In response, the Roman emperors at the end of the first century condemned Christianity as an "illicit religion" exposing Christians to intermittent waves of brutal persecution until the fourth century.

Emulating the sophisticated legal communities of Judaism, the early churches organized themselves into separate legal communities bound together by the teachings and morality of Jesus and his followers. By the turn of the second century CE, church leaders began to issue laws – after the third century called "canons" – to

---

[59] Ibid., 7.15. See detailed analysis and literature on Germanic betrothals in Reynolds, *Marriage in the Western Church*, 74–99.

[60] Laws of Etherlred, ch. 6.12, in Benjamin Thorpe, ed., *Ancient Laws and Institutes of England*, repr. ed. (Clark, NJ: The Lawbook Exchange, 2003 [1840]), 135–136; Laws of Canute, 7.3, in A.J. Robertson, ed., *The Laws of the Kings of England from Edmund to Henry I* (Cambridge: Cambridge University Press, 1925), 163. See also a Northumbrian law (ca. 950), item 61: "We prohibit, with God's prohibition, that any man have more wives than one." "The Law of Northumbrian Priests," *in Ancient Laws and Institutes*, 2:301. This prohibition seems to be about real polygamy, not successive polygamy, as item 64 provides separately that "if anyone forsake his lawful wife, as long as she lives, and unlawfully wed another woman, let him not have God's mercy."

govern the conduct of the clergy and laity in the church.[61] In the first three centuries, when Christianity remained "illicit" and often persecuted, these canon laws were largely scattered letters of advice by Christian bishops, theologians, hermits, and spiritual sages as well as occasional decrees by local synods and councils.[62] In the fourth through sixth centuries, when Christianity became the established religion of the Roman Empire, these canons became much more elaborate and detailed, as strong popes and other bishops emerged to govern the Western Church, and as various regional synods as well as ecumenical councils of the church issued more expansive decrees for the integration of the church's teachings and practices.

From the sixth to the tenth century, after the Western Empire had fallen, high clergy and church councils continued to issue occasional new canons, along with letters of advice and discipline. These were supplemented by provisions in the penitential books that guided the moral life of the faithful, at least locally where those books were being used.[63] Later first millennium scholars, councils, and kings prepared occasional collections of the church canons, which proved critical to their survival into the next millennium.[64] But the canon law of the first millennium remained incomplete and inconsistent. Moreover, without a regular system of courts,

[61] Ludwig Buisson, "Die Entstehung des Kirchenrechts," *Zeitschrift der Savigny-Stiftung für Rechtsgeschichte (Kanonistische Abteilung)* 52 (1966): 1–175.

[62] See sources and discussion in Hamilton Hess, *The Early Development of Canon Law and the Council of Serdica* (Oxford: Oxford University Press, 2002), esp. 5–35.

[63] See a good collection in John T. McNeill and Helena M. Gamer, *Medieval Handbooks of Penance: A Translation of the Principal libri poenitentiales and Selections from Related Documents* (New York: Columbia University Press, 1990 [1938]). See also Hugo Connolly, *The Irish Penitentials and Their Significance for the Sacrament of Penance Today* (Dublin: Four Courts Press, 1995); John T. McNeill, *The Celtic Penitentials and their Influence on Continental Christianity* (Paris: Librairie ancienne honoré champion, 1923); Brundage, *Law, Sex, and Christian Society*, 153–169 and a tabular summary of sources and their main teachings in ibid., 597–601, and in Rob Meens, "The Frequency and Nature of Early Modern Penance," in *Handling Sin: Confession in the Middle Ages*, eds. Peter Biller and A.J. Minnis (York: The Medieval Press, 1998), 36–61. On the importance of monastic and penitential rules as forms and forums for law, see David D'Avray, *Medieval Religious Rationalities: A Weberian Analysis* (Cambridge: Cambridge University Press, 2010).

[64] Many of the Latin texts are available in searchable format at http://ccl.rch.uky.edu/search-latin-corpus. For a good sampling of important conciliar texts in English translation, see *The Seven Ecumenical Councils*, Philip Schaff and Henry Wace, trans. and eds. (New York: Charles Scribner's Sons, 1900), and reprinted in NPNF 2, vol. 14. See also a good English translation of the *Diversorum sententiae Patrum* (ca. 1048–1054) in *The Collection in Seventy-Four Titles: A Canon Law Manual of the Gregorian Reform* (Toronto: Pontifical Institute of Medieval Studies, 1980). For a good bibliographic overview, see Lotte Kéry, *Canonical Collections of the Early Middle Ages (ca. 400–1400)* (Washington, DC: Catholic University of America Press, 2000), with brisk summaries in Kenneth Pennington, "The Growth of Church Law," in Augustine Casiday and Frederick W. Norris, eds., *The Cambridge History of Christianity, Vol. 2: Constantine to c. 600* (Cambridge: Cambridge University Press, 2008), 386–402; R.H. Helmholz, "Western Canon Law," in John Witte, Jr. and Frank S. Alexander, eds., *Christianity and Law: An Introduction* (Cambridge: Cambridge University Press, 2008), 71–88; Brundage, *Law, Sex, and Christian Society*, 159–163.

the church as a whole could only sporadically enforce these rules, although strong popes and bishops did enforce these rules in individual cases. (In the late first and early second millennia, a series of canonical collections, culminating in Gratian's *Decretum* (ca. 1140) and Gregory IX's *Decretales* (1234), yielded a new "concordance of discordant canons," which the medieval church enforced with a hierarchy of church courts that eventually governed throughout Western Christendom. Those collections are the subject of the next chapters.)

Sex, marriage, and family life were an integral part of the church's canon laws from the very start. Already in the second and third centuries, various rules prohibited the sins of adultery, fornication, and sodomy, and also commended chastity, modesty of dress, and separation of the sexes during bathing and education. Third- and fourth-century canons ordered bishops, priests, deacons, and other leaders of the church to be chaste, heterosexual, and "the husband of one wife" (and deaconesses to be "the wife of one husband"). Fourth- and fifth-century canons ordered clerics to be single or at least sexually continent after their ordination, and also ordered all clerics to avoid prostitution, concubinage, and other sexual activities on pain of losing their clerical offices. For the laity, the early canons repeated the New Testament's long lists of sexual sins to be avoided: incest, sodomy, prostitution, seduction, and other forms of sexual "immorality" and "perversion."[65] In the fourth and fifth centuries, the canons added new rules against bestiality, abortion, infanticide, child prostitution, pedophilia, pederasty, and abuse of wives, children, and servants. Lay Christians were forbidden from marrying Jews, heretics, heathens, and their adulterous lovers who later became single. And, most importantly for our purposes, lay Christians were discouraged from real, successive, and constructive polygamy.[66]

The church's laws governing sex, marriage, and family life stood alongside the family laws of the Roman and later Germanic authorities. These parallel spiritual and secular legal systems had overlapping, sometimes converging, provisions on a number of legal questions. But, particularly after the fourth-century Christianization of Rome, the church deferred to and ordered its members to follow many of the state's laws governing the more technical aspects of engagements and marital formation, maintenance, and dissolution; spousal roles, rights, and responsibilities; child care, custody, and control; marital property, gifts, dowries, inheritance, guardianship, and more.[67]

[65] Romans 1:24–27; 1 Corinthians 5:1; 6:9, 15–20; Ephesians 5:3–4; Colossians 3:5–6; 1 Timothy 2:9–10; 3:2; 1 Thessalonians 4:3–8.

[66] See illustrative provisions in NPNF 2, 14:11, 46–51, 70, 73, 79, 81–82, 92, 95, 98, 129, 149, 156, 157, 279, 280, 452, 460–462, 569–570, 604–613.

[67] See generally Judith Evans Grubbs, *Women and the Law in the Roman Empire: A Sourcebook on Marriage, Divorce and Widowhood* (London: Routledge, 2002).

The Canons of Basil the Great (ca. 329–ca. 379), issued around 374–375 CE, offer a good distillation and illustration of the early canon laws of the church.[68] Basil's Canons are important for our story, because they are among the few surviving early canons to focus closely on various types of polygamy banned by the early church. They also offer a rare glimpse into the relative gravity of these offenses compared to other sexual and nonsexual offenses. Basil inserted these Canons into longer letters that helped contextualize and explicate them. And several of his Canons were echoed by later ecumenical church councils and in the collections of canons and penitentials.[69] So, let us linger over this collection for a few pages to see how polygamy was treated.

More than half of Basil's Canons – forty-nine out of ninety-three – addressed issues of sexuality and marriage. Of these, seventeen Canons touched on polygamy of various sorts:

Canon 4. They that marry a second time, used to be under penance a year or two. They that marry a third time, three or four years. But we have a custom, that he who marries a third time be under penance five years, not by canon, but tradition. Half of this time they are to be hearers, afterwards co-standers; but to abstain from the communion of the Good Thing, [until] when they have shewed some fruit of repentance.[70]

---

[68] These canons are duplicated in NPNF 2, 14:604–611 (listing ninety-three canons), most of them excerpted from Basil's Letters to Bishop Amphilocus of Iconium, in NPNF 2, 8:223ff. as well as in Basil's Letters Nos. 178, 199, and 217 in *Saint Basil: The Letters*, 4 vols., trans. Roy J. Deferrari (New York: G.P. Putnam, 1930), 5–48, 103–134, 241–266. For a recent study, see Juana Torres, "De epístolas privadas a cánones privadas a cánones disciplinarios: las 'cartas canónicas' de Basilio de Cesarea," *Lex et religio. Studia Ephemeridis Augustinianum* (Rome: Istituto Augustiniano, 2013), 437–446.

[69] See, e.g, George Nedungatt and Michael Feathersone, eds., *The Council in Trullo Revisited* (Rome: Pontificio Istituto Orientale, 1995), canon 87, pp. 166–168; *The Penitential of Theodore*, bk. 2, c. 14.3 in McNeill and Gamer, *Medieval Handbooks of Penance*, 196.

[70] My colleague Philip L. Reynolds tells me that these categories in the Byzantine tradition are both (1) standard phases of reentry from penance (as here) and (2) levels of penitential exclusion, which could be applied separately. "One needs to keep in mind that penitents and the possessed, like the catechumens, could not participate in the Eucharist; that the catechumens were expelled from the church after the readings and homily; and that the mystery itself was conducted in the Holy of Holies, which no one could enter except the priest and deacons, but others could watch from the nave, which was still sacred space. So: (1) the weepers or mourners had to remain outside, fully excluded; (2) the hearers could stand at the entrance and watch and hear the Scriptures and homily, but they were then dismissed with the catechumens; (3) the kneelers or prostrators could come into the church and prostrate themselves before the lectern during the 'word' part of the service, but again would then have to leave with the catechumens; and (4) the co-standers could remain with the congregation 'throughout the service,' but could not receive the bread and wine. The next step after being a co-stander was full communion." See, additionally, Andrew Skotnicki, *Criminal Justice and the Catholic Church* (Lanham, MD: Rowman Littlefield, 2008), 78. Comparable penitential steps are retained in the Canons of Trullo (692), which drew in part on Basil's Canons.

Canon 9. Our Lord is equal, to the man and woman forbidding divorce, save in cases of fornication; but custom requires women to retain their husbands, though they be guilty of fornication. The man deserted by his wife may take another, and though he were deserted for adultery, yet St. Basil will be positive, that the other woman who afterward takes him is guilty of adultery; but the wife is not allowed this liberty. And the man who deserts an innocent wife is not allowed to remarry.

Canon 12. The canon excludes from ministry those who are guilty of digamy.

Canon 18. That the ancients received a professed virgin that had married, as one guilty of digamy, viz., upon one year's penance; but they ought to be dealt with more severely than widows professing continency, and even as adulterers....

Canon 23. That a man ought not to marry two sisters, nor a women two brothers. That he who marries his brother's wife, be not admitted till he dismiss her.[71]

Canon 24. A widow put into the catalogue of widows, that is, a deaconess being sixty years old, and marrying, is not to be admitted to communion of the Good Thing, till she cease from her uncleanness; but to a widower that marries no penance is appointed, but that of digamy. If the widow is less than sixty years, it is the bishop's fault who admitted her deaconess, not the woman's.

Canon 31. She whose husband is absent from home, if she co-habits with another man, before she is persuaded of his death, commits adultery.

Canon 36. A soldier's wife marrying after the long absence of her husband, but before she is certified of his death, is more pardonable than another woman, because it is more credible that he may be dead.

Canon 37. That he, having another man's wife or spouse taken away from him is guilty of adultery with the first, not with the second.

Canon 41. A widow being at her own discretion, may marry to whom she will.

Canon 46. She that marries a man who was deserted for a while by his wife, but is afterward dismissed upon the return of the man's former wife, commits fornication, but ignorantly: she shall not be prohibited marriage, but it is better that she not marry.

Canon 48. A woman dismissed from her husband, ought to remain unmarried, in my judgment.

Canon 50. We look on third marriages as disgraceful to the Church, but do not absolutely condemn them, as being better than a vague fornication.

---

[71] It is not clear whether this prohibition applies to "two sisters" or "two brothers" as the same time (as in the story of Jacob, Leah, and Rachel), or sequentially (rendering this an incest impediment). It is clear that Basil's Canons, like other early canons, was outlawing "levirate" marriage – the Mosaic requirement that a brother marry his dead brother's widow, which was one ground on which Jewish law allowed for polygamy. See Leviticus 18:16, 20:21; Deuteronomy 25:5 and discussion in Chapter 1. See additional discussion on the canon law prohibitions on marriage to "two sisters" later in this chapter, p. 127.

Canon 53. A widow slave desiring to be married a second time, has, perhaps, been guilty of no great crime in pretending that she was ravished; not her pretence, but voluntary choice is to be condemned; but it is clear, that the punishment of digamy is due to her.

Canon 77. He that divorces his wife, and marries another, is an adulterer; and according to the canons of the Fathers, he shall be a mourner, a hearer two years, a prostrator, three years, a co-stander one year, if they repent with tears.

Canon 78. So shall he who successively marries two sisters.

Canon 80. The Fathers say nothing of polygamy as being beastly, and a thing unagreeable to human nature. To us it appears a greater sin than fornication. Let therefore such [as are guilty of it] be liable to the canons, viz., after they have been mourners one year – let them be hearers three years – and then be received.[72]

Real Polygamy

Basil's very last Canon in this quotation, number 80, is the first clear canonical prohibition against real polygamy (having two or more spouses at the same time) that I have found from the first millennium. Basil assigned four years of penance to known polygamists – one year of mourning outside the church, three years of lying prostrate during the service of the Eucharist before being readmitted to communion.[73] Harsh as this might sound to modern ears, this was rather light punishment in Basil's broader scheme of spiritual discipline. His Canons assigned far longer penance to other sexual offenses: brother-sister incest and infanticide (twenty years); adultery, sodomy, bestiality, other incest, and breach of vows of chastity (fifteen years); abortion (ten years); fornication, "madly loving" one's sister or mother-in-law, or illegal divorce and remarriage (seven years). The Canons described polygamy as "worse than fornication," but they assigned fornicators seven years of penance, polygamists only four years. This was even less than the five years of penance assigned to a widow(er) who remarried twice (a "trigamist").[74]

To be sure, not all penance was equal in Basil's system of discipline. The "mourning" and "prostrating" steps of penance that polygamists had to bear were among the more arduous and publicly shaming steps of spiritual discipline in the day. And, to be sure, Basil may have thought it wise not to assign so severe a punishment for what was evidently a new sexual offense in the canon law. But theologians and homilists had been discussing polygamy for more than two centuries before him, and the sterner Fathers had called polygamy an act of perpetual "adultery" which

---

[72] Canons of Basil, reprinted in NPNF 2, 14:604–609.
[73] Ibid., Canons 3, 80.
[74] Ibid., Canons 2, 4, 21, 23, 33, 37, 52, 58, 59, 60, 62, 63, 67, 68, 75, 76, 77, 78, 79.

was "second only to murder"[75] – offenses to which Basil assigned fifteen and twenty years of penance, respectively. Moreover, Roman law had treated polygamy as a crime of *infamia* for more than a century before Basil. It could be that Basil thought it better to have the state's criminal law, rather than the church's canon law, root out polygamy. But his Canons included many other serious crimes against persons and properties, listing them as sins that required penance in the church in addition to whatever criminal punishment the state imposed.[76]

The reality was that real polygamy was a relatively light offense for Basil, at the bottom of his hierarchy of sexual crimes and sins. At the top of this hierarchy were adultery, incest, sodomy, bestiality, infanticide, and breach of vows. These serious sexual offenses were punished with the same penitential severity as willful murder, poisoning, sorcery, idolatry, and wizardry. In the middle came fornication, abortion, illegal divorce and remarriage, incest with a half-sister, marrying two sisters in a row, or "madly loving" a sister or mother-in-law. These were still relatively serious sexual offenses, punished at roughly the same level as involuntary homicide, perjury, assault, and grave robbing. At the bottom were polygamy and digamy, punished just a bit more than confessed petty theft (which got two years).

While they were unusual, if not unique, in addressing real polygamy so directly, Basil's Canons were typical in their careful attention to other types of polygamy recognized by the early church – that of priests (called clerical bigamy) and of divorcees and widow(er)s (called successive polygamy). For these offenses, Basil followed New Testament teachings directly and then added provisions to reach cases not addressed in the Bible.

Successive Polygamy

Following St. Paul, Basil made clear that widows were free to remarry (save those who had become deaconesses). But widows who did remarry were assigned a year or two of penance, five years if this was their second remarriage. This penance was owed even by slave women or rape victims who had been forced to marry their first husbands. It was the morality of the second marriage that was the issue, not the quality of the first marriage. Basil extended this right of remarriage to widowers, too, and assigned them comparable penance for their second and third marriages. But, a third marriage ("trigamy"), he said, was "disgraceful to the Church." Indeed, it

[75] See discussion earlier on p. 74.
[76] Ibid., Canons 7, 8, 11, 13, 14, 30, 56, 57, 61, 64, 66, 82. In ibid., Canon 3, Basil showed that he was concerned with double jeopardy: "A deacon guilty of fornication is deposed, not excommunicated; for the ancient canon forbids a single crime to be twice punished." But for him, double jeopardy meant two punishments by the church or the state, not separate punishments by the church and the state for one offense. See also ibid., Canon 51.

is no longer described as marriage at all, but as polygamy, nay rather as limited fornication. It is for this reason that the Lord said to the woman of Samaria, who had had five husbands, "he whom thou now hast is not thy husband." He does not reckon those who had exceeded the limits of second marriage as worthy of the title of husband or wife. In cases of trigamy, we have accepted a seclusion of five years.[77]

Finally, Basil followed the letter and spirit of the New Testament rules on divorce and remarriage.[78] A man who "divorces his wife and marries another is an adulterer," Canon 77 declared flatly, staking out a firmer position than the Bible's – although if the man was repentant he got only seven of the usual fifteen years of penance for adultery. A man who separates from his wife for no cause, and lives with another woman, with or without marriage, is also a presumptive adulterer. But in other Canons and letters, Basil allowed an innocent man to divorce an adulterous wife, and thereafter marry another single and unrelated woman, as Matthew 19 provided. He also allowed a man to break an engagement and remarry another woman if his fiancée was kidnapped or abducted and returned, presumably no longer as a virgin.[79]

Both Scripture and "custom" impose stricter rules on wives, Basil continued matter-of-factly, despite his earlier complaints about the sexual double standards of Roman law:

> The decree of our Lord, that it is forbidden to withdraw from marriage except in the case of fornication applies equally to men and to women, at least according to the logic of the idea. But the custom is different, and we find much stricter prescriptions for women [who must] keep their husbands, even if the husbands commit adultery and fornication.[80]

Wives must also keep their husbands if they become abusive, criminal, wastrel, or heretical:

> If she was being beaten and would endure the blows, it would have been better for her to tolerate her husband than to separate from him. If she would endure the loss of money, that is not an acceptable reason. But if her motivation was the man's living in fornication, that is not the customary observance of the church. Rather, a wife is instructed not to separate from an unbelieving husband, but to remain, because it is uncertain what will result.[81]

---

[77] Ibid., Canon 24, 30, 41, 50, 53; Letter 188, in NPNF 2, 8:225–226. See also Letter 155, sect. 4, in NPNF 2, 8:214.

[78] "Second marriage is a remedy against fornication," he wrote in a letter, "not a means of lasciviousness. 'If they cannot contain themselves,' it is said, 'let them marry.' But if they marry [again], they must not break the law." See Letter 155, sect. 4, in NPNF 2, 8:214.

[79] Canons of Basil, Canons 9 and 22, using translation in Hunter, *Marriage in the Early Church*, 143–144.

[80] Canon 9, using translation in ibid., 143–144. See also Canons of Basil, Canon 24.

[81] NPNF 2, 14:604–609, Canons of Basil, Canon 9.

The New Testament did not address the plight of a spouse who was physically deserted or abandoned by the other. Basil's Canons filled in the rules, and again were harder on wives than on husbands. A long deserted wife could not remarry or cohabit with another man "before she is persuaded of the death of her husband." If she does remarry, and her first husband proves to be alive, she is guilty of adultery, with its rule of fifteen years of penance. Basil made only one modest concession: "a soldier's wife marrying after the long absence of her husband, but before she is certified of his death, is more pardonable than another woman, because it is more certifiable that he may be dead." Basil went considerably easier on a husband whose wife had deserted him, for whatever reason. The deserted husband, "unable to contain himself," could marry another woman with impunity. But if his wife returned, he would have to take her back, and dismiss his second wife. The second wife, in that case, was not guilty of adultery, and could remarry, although Basil (following St. Paul) recommended that she remain single.[82]

Clerical Bigamy

Also following St. Paul, Basil insisted that ordained clergy could be "the husband of one wife" alone, and that a "deaconess" could be the "wife of one husband." Those guilty of clerical bigamy "are excluded from the ministry," Canon 12 declared flatly. The letter of this New Testament law, as Basil saw it, was that any aspiring priest, deacon, or deaconess could have had only one marriage before taking their vows or office, and if they had more than one, they could not hold spiritual office. The spirit of this law was to protect the priest and priestly office from sexual misconduct, and Basil drew out the implications of this in some of his other Canons. A priest who had innocently and mistakenly entered an "unlawful" single marriage before his ordination could no longer administer the sacraments, although he was not defrocked. A lector or priest who had premarital sex with his fiancée before his ordination was suspended from office for a year; he was banned from office altogether if the woman with whom he had fornicated proved not to be his fiancée but a second woman. Priests, deacons, and deaconesses who lapsed into adultery or remarriage after taking their vows were deposed from spiritual office for good. A deaconess guilty of having sexual contact or committing "lewd acts" with a pagan was deposed and assigned seven years of penance before being readmitted to communion. Professed monks or nuns who gave up their vows and returned to secular life were treated as adulterers, and assigned fifteen years of penance. A professed virgin, who proved to have been married before, was charged with adultery – unless she had been married before she had converted to or been confirmed in the faith.[83]

---

[82] Ibid., Canons 31, 35, 36, 37, 39, 44, 48 and Letter 188 in Hunter, *Marriage in the Early Church*, 141–142.

[83] Ibid., Canons 3, 12, 18, 19, 20, 24, 27, 32, 44, 51.

REAL POLYGAMY IN LATER FIRST MILLENNIUM CANON
LAW AND PRACTICE

Basil's Canons were (proto)typical of other canon laws and penitential rules that treated various forms of polygamy in the first millennium church. These sources generally started with biblical rules where they existed, and then extended their letter and spirit to reach new questions not addressed by the Bible. Some canons and penitential rules were stricter than Basil's, some more lenient, but most worked similarly.

After the canons of Basil, the first millennium canon law sources fell largely silent on real polygamy. One collection of canons, likely issued in the later fifth or sixth centuries, did include a couple of fragmentary canons on real polygamy. These canons, written in Arabic, were not discovered until the sixteenth century, and it is thought that they operated only in the Eastern Byzantine Empire if at all. There is no mention or record of them in the Western collections of canons from the late first millennium or in the great syntheses of canon law of the High Middle Ages.[84] Nonetheless, given the rarity of canons on real polygamy from the first millennium, it is worth studying them.

The first canon addresses real polygamy explicitly, but then breaks off after dealing with the punishment of a priest:

Of him who has married two wives at the same time, or who through lust has added another woman to his wife, and of his punishment.

If he be a priest he is forbidden to sacrifice and is cut off from the communion of the faithful until he turns out of the house the second woman, and he ought to retain the first [wife]....[85]

The second canon also addresses the real polygamy of a priest or deacon, and then mentions the real polygamy of a layman, too:

Of taking a second wife, after the former one has been disowned for any cause, or even not put away....

---

[84] On the provenance of these canons, see "Excursus on the Number of the Nicene Canons," in NPNF 2, 14:44–45 and Karl Joseph von Hefele, *A History of the Councils of the Church, From the Original Documents*, 5 vols., repr. ed. (New York: AMS Press, 1972), 1:355–375.

[85] This is listed as Council of Nicaea, Canon 24 in NPNF 2, 14:47; although the editors make clear that until the sixteenth century, this canon and the ones cited in the next note were not included among the original twenty Nicene canons. This is now standard lore. See, e.g., Giusepee Alberigo, ed., *Conciliorum Oecumenicorum Generaliumque Decreta Editio Critica* (Turnhout: Brepols Publishers, 2006), volume 1: The Oecumenical Councils From Nicaea I to Nicaea II (325–387), who excludes these from the collection of authentic Nicene canons.

If any priest or deacon shall put away his wife on account of her fornication, or for other cause, as aforesaid, or cast her out of doors for any external cause, or that he may change her for another more beautiful, or better, or richer, or does so out of lust which is displeasing to God [and thereafter] he shall contract another marriage with another, or without having first put her away shall take another, whether free or bond; and shall have both equally, they living separately and he sleeping every night with one or other of them, or else keeping them both in the same house and bed, let him be deposed. If he were a layman, let him be deprived of communion.[86]

Like Basil's Canons, these canons treat real polygamy rather lightly – even more lightly than Basil's. These canons simply deposed priests who practiced polygamy and then reinstated them if they banished their second wife from the home. Basil's Canons deposed priests for far less serious offenses like simple fornication, with no right of reinstatement. These canons simply deprived a lay polygamist of the Eucharist without being clear about what, if any, steps of penance were owed thereafter. Basil's Canons assigned four years of rather arduous penance before a real polygamist could return to the Eucharist.

These two canons and Basil's single canon are all the canon law provisions on real polygamy that I have found from the first millennium. The penitential books, designed to help guide the moral lives of Christians, were silent on real polygamy as well, although they treated in ever greater detail all manner of other sexual misconduct – homosexuality, lesbianism, sodomy, bestiality, incest, adultery, fornication, prostitution, lustful thoughts, illicit sexual touching of self and others, nocturnal emissions, sexual timing and positions, and more.[87] It could be that Basil's canon prohibiting real polygamy, given its eminent authorship, was taken to be the church's clear and final word on the subject. But so many other subjects on sex, marriage, and family life – which Basil had also addressed definitively – came in for endless discussion, applications, and extensions in later canonical and penitential books. The reality was that real polygamy was simply not a major topic of the canon law of the church. Instead, the first millennium church looked to the state and its criminal laws to continue to prohibit and punish real polygamy as it had since antiquity.

While these state laws may have deterred commoners, a number of Germanic kings and nobles practiced real polygamy or at least formal concubinage with

---

[86] This is listed as Council of Nicaea, Canon 56 in NPNF 2, 14:49–50. Canon 57, in ibid., 14:50 is another suggestive fragment which, too, breaks off: "Of having two wives at the same time, and of a woman who is one of the faithful marrying an infidel; and one of the form of receiving her to penance."

[87] See Pierre J. Payer, *Sex and the Penitentials: The Development of a Sexual Code 550–1150* (Toronto: University of Toronto Press, 1984).

multiple women, as well as informal and incestuous concubinage with their slaves and servants and their daughters. Many of these were pious Christian men who dined with bishops, abbots, and missionaries and who patronized the church. Gregory of Tours, for example, reports that the Merovingian Christian King Dagobert (ca. 603–639), "like Solomon," enjoyed three wives, two of them sisters, as well as numerous concubines. He reports further on the multiple wives, concubines, and incest of Frankish kings Guntram, Charibert, and Sigibert.[88] Adam of Bremen, commenting on the northern German and Swedish monarchs wrote: "Each one has according to the extent of his powers two or three wives or more at the same time; the rich and the nobles have uncounted numbers."[89] Even the redoubtable Frankish king, Charlemagne (742–814) – who was later sainted for his promotion of Christianity and his promulgation of laws that restated and strengthened many traditional canon laws on marriage and the family – had some eleven wives and concubines and produced some twenty children, at least ten of them illegitimate. To be sure, Charlemagne was not a "real polygamist"; he evidently took his wives in succession, but his sexual conduct fell far short of the ideals of Christian sexual morality.[90]

It was not just Germanic kings who practiced polygamy, however – evidently thinking themselves above their own criminal laws. Some powerful lords and land barons of the last half of the first millennium – including a few enterprising clerics[91] – also kept harems of wives, concubines, female slaves, and servant girls. This was a classic case of what anthropologists call "resource polygyny."[92] Rich and powerful men in small isolated communities kept for themselves most of the available women, but inevitably at the cost of rivalry within their households and within the community at large. Harvard family historian David Herlihy and others have

---

[88] Gregory of Tours, *History of the Franks*, Louis Thorpe, trans. (Harmondsworth: Penguin, 1974), iv.3. See also *Scriptorum rerum Merovingicarum*, ed. Bruno Krusch, 2:146–147, 315, 408, and discussion in Brundage, *Law, Sex, and Christian Society*, 146 and David Herlihy, *Medieval Households* (Cambridge, MA: Harvard University Press, 1985), 49.

[89] Adam of Bremen, *History of the Archbishops of Hamburg-Bremen*, trans. F.J. Tschan (New York: Columbia University Press, 1959), 203.

[90] See this and other examples in Wemple, *Women in Frankish Society*, 38–40, 75–96. See also Mathias Becher, *Charlemagne*, trans. David S. Bachrach (New Haven, CT: Yale University Press, 2003), 131–132; Paul Fouracre, "The Long Shadow of the Merovingians," in Joanna Story, ed., *Charlemagne: Empire and Society* (Manchester: Manchester University Press, 2003), 5–20, at 16.

[91] Brundage, *Law, Sex, and Christian Society*, 150–152. In a telling anecdote, St. Boniface complained to Pope Zacharias (741–752) that some priests and deacons slept with four or five concubines at the same time, with no cost to their promotion, even to bishoprics. Boniface, *Die Briefe des heiligen Bonifatius et Lullus*, ed. M. Tangl, 2nd ed. (Berlin: Weidmannsche Verlagsbuchhandlung, 1955), Letter 50, p. 82.

[92] See the detailed study in Peter Bretschneider, *Polygyny: A Cross-Cultural Study* (Uppsala: Acta Universitatis Upsaliensis, 1995).

documented several such pockets of polygamy in early medieval lands: "The rich man cohabiting with several women seeks to guard them from all other men, but the task is difficult. Men without sex partners will seek to overcome their deprivation through the purchase of a concubine, if they have money; through abduction, if they have the power; or through seduction, if they have the charm. Moreover, the woman … may resent the fact that she shares her husband's attention and looks for satisfaction, or even retribution, in her own extramarital affairs. And the disgruntled wife will have no trouble finding willing paramours."[93] "The high prestige which the Church accorded to the life of virginity probably also contributed to the shortage of women willing to marry." "The dearth of women assured them favorable marriage terms, but had as counterpart frequent abduction [and] considerable promiscuity."[94]

It was only toward the end of the first millennium, Herlihy shows, that the church's teachings on monogamy and the parallel state laws against polygamy came to be "slowly adopted and enforced" in the West. This resulted in more even distribution of men and women, "reduced abductions and rapes of women and probably calmed the endemic violence of early medieval life." These norms of church and state together, "prevented men of the elites from accumulating or retaining many women in their houses and gave non-elite males a better chance of gaining a mate." For "the same rules of sexual and domestic conduct" in favor of monogamy and against polygamy now governed rich and poor alike. "The king in his palace, the peasant in his hovel; neither was exempt."[95]

CONSTRUCTIVE POLYGAMY IN LATER FIRST MILLENNIUM CANON LAW

While the early medieval church looked to the state to prohibit and punish real polygamy, it focused its canon law on illicit relationships that bordered on polygamy – cases of double sisters, double engagements, double vows, double sex partners, and other forms of what came to be called "constructive polygamy" or "quasi-polygamy."[96] Before the eleventh century, the canon law treated all these cases of constructive polygamy as forms of adultery or fornication, offenses which were much more severely punished offenses than real polygamy. This yielded the irony that a real polygamist was only lightly punished at canon law (up to four years of penance), while a constructive polygamist was heavily sanctioned (up to fifteen years of penance). But the converse was true at secular law: real polygamists risked

---

[93] Herlihy, *Medieval Households*, 39–40.
[94] Ibid. 55. On abduction in Germanic law, see Reynolds, *Marriage in the Western Church*, 101–117.
[95] Herlihy, *Medieval Households*, 78, 157. See also David Herlihy, "The Family and Religious Ideologies in Medieval Europe," *Journal of Family History* 12 (1987): 3–17.
[96] On this terminology, see the Introduction of this book.

serious criminal punishment by the state, even execution by the ninth century, whereas most constructive polygamists were not viewed as criminals at all.

One form of constructive polygamy prohibited by the canon law was marriage to two sisters in a row.[97] Marrying two sisters at the same time was the most famous case of real polygamy in the Bible – with Jacob marrying Leah and Rachel and bringing ample discord and rivalry to his home and children as a consequence.[98] Jacob's double marriage would clearly have been a crime at first millennium state law. But the church's canon law went further and prohibited a man from marrying his sister-in-law even after the first sister (his wife) had died and the man was now a single widower. The risk of intra-family discord, rivalry, and seduction within the extended family was simply too high if successive marriages to sisters remained possible.[99] Other canons not only repeated these prohibitions, but also imposed special rules for cases when a man and his wife's sister succumbed to temptation and had an affair. An eighth-century law put it thus: "He who has slept with two sisters, and one of them was his wife, is to have neither of them; nor are the adulterers ever to be joined in marriage."[100] Prohibiting adulterers from marrying each other, even after they had become single, was a commonplace of the canon law as well as the Roman law. Any other rule would incentivize adulterous couples to divorce or kill the first spouse(s) in order to be together. But forcing the adulterer to separate and abstain from his own wife after his adultery, regardless of the couple's wishes, was unusual. Reconciliation after adultery was the norm; in fact, wives could not dismiss or divorce their adulterous husbands. The canon law made special provision for the wife in these cases in which her husband slept with her sister: if she had been "unaware of the crime, and cannot contain herself, she may marry whomever she wishes in the name of the Lord."[101]

A second form of constructive polygamy prohibited by the early canon law was maintaining a wife and a concubine at the same time. Some Old Testament patriarchs had kept multiple concubines in addition to multiple wives – often slaves

---

[97] The Council of Neo-Caesarea (c. 315), c. 2 prohibited a woman from marrying two brothers as well, on pain of permanent excommunication. NPNF 2d, 14:79. The Council of Ancyra (314), c. 25 deals with a case where a man betrothed a woman, then seduced her sister. He then married the first woman, and the second woman, now pregnant, killed herself. The man and his accomplices were each given ten years of penance.

[98] See Genesis 29–31. Also somewhat implicated was the Mosaic law of levirate marriage that commanded a brother (a "levir") to marry his sister-in-law if his brother passed away. See Chapter 1, pp. 44–47. It was again the intra-familial rivalries which could ensue that concerned the early church leadership.

[99] See discussion on pp. 42–43.

[100] Capitulare Vermeriense (753), using translation in Peter Lombard, *The Sentences*, bk. 4, dist. 34.5.1, trans. Giulio Silano (Toronto: Pontifical Institute of Medieval Studies, 2007). See earlier rules against marrying two sisters, even after widowerhood, in Council of Elvira, c. 61; Apostolic Canons, c. 19.

[101] In a ruling by Pope Zacharias (741–752), quoted in *Decretum*, c. 32, q. 7, c. 23.

or servant girls. Some of these concubines were taken for sexual pleasure or as tokens of wealth and power. Some of them were used as surrogate mothers to produce heritable children: Think of Abraham with Hagar (the handmaid of Sarah), or Jacob with Bilhah and Zilpah (the servant girls of Rachel and Leah). The pre-Christian Roman emperors had already prohibited all such double unions, and the Christian emperors repeated these provisions: A man could have one concubine, or one wife, but not both. Moreover, the later Christian Roman emperors made it easier for a man to legitimate his concubine's children and to leave them an inheritance.[102] Several Church Fathers, notably Augustine and Jerome, had denounced not only Old-Testament-style multiple concubinage but also Roman-style single concubinage as a betrayal of true Christian marriage. But their efforts to expunge Roman-style single concubinage as a legitimate alternative to marriage largely failed.[103] The early canon law and penitential books thus just largely fell in line with the Roman law during the first millennium, threatening excommunication for a man who tried to retain both a wife and a concubine, or who failed to provide for the latter's children.[104]

This form of constructive polygamy came up in a few cases put to the early popes. Pope Leo the Great (440–461), for example, addressed the question whether a woman could marry a man who already had a concubine and a child by her. Leo permitted the marriage, but on two conditions. First, the first woman must truly be a concubine, and not a de facto wife, a "woman who should appear to have become free, to have been legitimately dowered, and to have been honored by public nuptials." Moreover, before marrying the second woman, the man would have to banish his concubine and her child just as Abraham had done with Hagar and Ishmael in response to Sarah's order: "Cast out the bondwoman and her son" (Gen. 21:10). If both these conditions were met, said Leo, the marriage to the second woman was "not bigamy but an honorable proceeding."[105]

The converse situation was whether a lawfully married wife had any relief if her husband took a concubine – or resumed relations with a previous concubine – over the wife's protests. This was at issue in a famous and protracted battle between Pope Nicholas I (r. 858–867) and King Lothar II (ca. 835–869). Several complicit churchmen and church councils supported Lothar's defamatory accusations against

---

[102] See sources in John Witte, Jr. *The Sins of the Fathers: The Law and Theology of Illegitimacy Reconsidered* (Cambridge: Cambridge University Press, 2009), 58–64.

[103] See Brundage, *Law, Sex, and Christian Society*, 98–103; Reynolds, *Marriage in the Western Church*, 38–40.

[104] See, e.g., See Council of Toledo (c. 397), c. 17, in José Vives, *Concilios visigóticus e hispano-romanos* (Barcelona: Consejo Superiod de Investigaciones Científicas, Instituto Enrique Flórez, 1963), 23; The Welsh Canons (ca. 550–650), c. 68, in McNeill and Gamer, *Medieval Handbooks on Penance*, 381; The Penitential of Finnian (ca. 525–550), cc. 27, 39, 41, in ibid., 92, 95.

[105] Letter 164 to Niceatus, the Bishop of Aquieia, in NPNF 2, 12:102, 110.

his first wife, designed to drive her away and allow him to marry his longstanding concubine. But Pope Nicholas used the grave threat of excommunication to compel Lothar to dismiss the concubine and maintain his first marriage.[106] A ninth-century Byzantine canon gave the first wife in such a situation the right to divorce her husband and seek another, a provision which became a staple of later Eastern Orthodox canon law.[107] The closest Western equivalent was a seventh-century Germanic law that gave a wife's parents the right to take back their daughter, allowing her to divorce her polygamous husband if she wished.[108] The medieval canon law rejected this solution as an end-run on its strict rules against divorce. But these early canons of allowing a wife to divorce her polygamous husband became part of the civil law and common law after the sixteenth-century Protestant Reformation.[109]

A third type of constructive polygamy was when a person took both marital and spiritual vows. The early canons, following St. Paul, considered avowed monks, nuns, and clerics to be "married to Christ" and the church (1 Tim. 5:11). It was considered adulterous for such a person to return to secular life – like "a dog who returned to its vomit" – even if he or she remained without any sexual or marital contact.[110] So, if that person had taken their spiritual vows first, a subsequent engagement or marriage vow constituted serious adultery. Indeed, such a "spiritual adulterer" could not do penance to reconcile themselves to their first "spouse," the church, until after the death of their second spouse. As Pope Innocent I (402–417) put it:

> Those who marry Christ spiritually, if afterwards they marry [a spouse] publicly, are not to be admitted to penance, unless the ones to whom they had joined have departed from this world. If this rule is kept in the case of human beings – that whoever has married another while her husband is alive is considered an adulteress, nor is she allowed to do penance, unless one of the two has died – how much more is it to be kept of her who had previously joined herself to the immortal Bridegroom and later chose to pass to human marriage![111]

It was a harder question if the engagement or marital vow came first, and now the person wanted to pursue an avowed religious life. It was easy enough if the couple was only engaged, had not exchanged marital property, had not had sex, and both

---

[106] See Mathias Schmoeckel, "Fall 6: Der lotharische Ehestreit: Seine Protaganisten und ihre Perspektiven," in U. Falk, M. Luminati, and M. Schmoeckel, eds., *Fälle aus der Rechtsgeschichte* (Munich: Beck, 2008), 77–95; Karl J. Heidecker, *The Divorce of Lothar II: Christian Marriage and Political Power in the Carolingian World* (Ithaca, NY: Cornell University Press, 2010), and more briefly Wemple, *Women in Frankish Society*, 84–88.

[107] Basilica, 27.7, and discussion of other sources in Zhishman, *Das Eherecht*, 750–753.

[108] Lex Langobardorum, Grimoald 6, in MGH Leges, 4:94.

[109] See discussion in Chapters 6, 7, and 10.

[110] The Burgundian Penitential, c. 30, in McNeill and Gamer, *Medieval Handbooks on Penance*, 276.

[111] Innocent I, *Epistola* 2, c. 13, n. 16 using translation in Lombard, *Sentences*, bk. 4, dist. 38.2.9. See also Nedungatt and Featherstone, eds., *The Council of Trullo*, Canon 44, p. 126.

now consented to the breakup. In those cases, the early canons allowed the parties to break their engagement with impunity, leaving the now single lay party free to marry another person while the other pursued religious life.[112] It got progressively harder to break the engagement or marital contract if the couple had publicly celebrated their union, had exchanged property, had consummated their union, and/or if the other partner objected to the breakup. The growing weight of canonical authority was to allow clerical and monastic vows to break engagement contracts but not consummated marriage contracts, and certainly not when the other party objected. Pope Gregory the Great (590–604) put this position definitively:

> Some say that marriages ought to be dissolved for the sake of religion. But it should be known that, even though human law has granted this, divine law has forbidden it. But if it should suit both to lead a continent life, who would dare denounce this? For we know of many saints who have both previously led continent lives with their marriage partners, and afterwards transferred themselves to the rules of the holy Church. But if the wife does not seek to attain the continence which the husband desires, or the husband refuses what the wife desires, it is not possible to dissolve their wedlock, because it is written: *The wife has no power over her own body, but her husband does; similarly, the husband has no power over his own body, but the wife does.*[113]

A fourth type of constructive polygamy recognized by canon law was back-to-back engagements, or a simultaneous engagement to one party and marriage to another. Roman law, in fact, had treated these double contracts as forms of polygamy, and blacklisted as "infamous" those who knowingly entered the second contract and punished their accomplices as well. A man could dissolve his engagement contract, but he had to make this clear to his fiancée, and to do so without defaming her or her family, or impugning her integrity.[114] A few later church canons and penitential rules held similarly. But the canon law charged the doubly contracted party not with polygamy but with adultery, and ordered him or her to dismiss the second fiancé(e) and return to the first.[115]

Dissolving an engagement contract because of sickness is what may have been at issue in an otherwise startling ruling by Pope Gregory II (r. 715–731). In a letter

---

[112] See, e.g., The Penitential of Theodore, 1.14.5, 7; 2.12.4–16, in McNeill and Gamer, *Medieval Handbooks of Penance*, 196.

[113] Gregory the Great, *Registrum epistolarum*, bk. 11, letter 45 (27), using translation in Lombard, *Sentences*, bk. 4, dist. 27.1. See similar ruling by Eugenius II in the Roman Synod (826), c. 36, quoted in McNeill and Gamer, *Medieval Handbooks of Penance*, 165.

[114] See Greenidge, *Infamia in Roman Law*, 128.

[115] See, e.g., Nedungatt and Featherstone, eds., *The Council of Trullo*, Canon 98, p. 179; The Penitential of Theodore, bk. 2, tit.12.34–35, in McNeill and Gamer, *Medieval Handbooks of Penance*, 211.

of 726, Gregory addressed a question put to him by St. Boniface, a missionary to England. Boniface's question does not survive, but Gregory's answer does:

> As regards your question what a husband is to do, if his wife has been attacked by illness, so that she is incapable of conjugal intercourse, it were best if he could continue as he is, and practise self-restraint. But since this demands exceptional virtue, the man who cannot live in continence, had better marry. But let him not fail to furnish her with support, since she is kept from married life by sickness, not debarred from it by some abominable offence.[116]

Four centuries later, in attempting to harmonize the first millennium canons, the great canonist Gratian professed shock at Gregory's permissiveness, and declared this ruling to be "without authority" or precedent, and without any value or validity for the medieval church.[117] One of Gratian's commentators, named Rolandus, thought that Gregory's ruling was infelicitously stated but not necessarily wrong. The purported "wife" in question, Rolandus argued, may well have been only a "fiancée" – because the early canon law used the same Latin term "*uxor*" for a wife or a fiancée. Before their marriage had been consummated, the woman had contracted a disease that precluded intercourse, Rolandus reasoned. This was now viewed as an impediment to marriage that allowed the man to dissolve his engagement contract and pursue another woman with impunity. Gregory, Rolandus concluded, was simply encouraging the man to be humane to his sick first fiancée – now doubtless destined to be a spinster – even if he married another woman instead of "burning with lust."[118]

Rolandus's reading became standard in later canon law circles, and it was bolstered by the reality that Gregory II was so utterly conventional on other issues of marriage and family life.[119] This was not a pope given to making waves. But Gregory may have simply been riding a wave already started by the earlier Church Fathers. Several Fathers, we saw in the previous chapter, had viewed polygamy as a natural institution designed both to produce children and to channel natural sex drives.

[116] Pope Gregory II, "Replies to Questions Put by Boniface" (November 22, 726), in *The Anglo-Saxon Missionaries in Germany*, trans. and ed. C.H. Talbot (London: Sheed and Ward, 1954), 80–81. Pro-polygamists have naturally highlighted this passage. See, e.g., Eugene Hillman, *Polygamy Reconsidered: African Plural Marriage and the Christian Churches* (Maryknoll, NY: Orbis Books, 1975), 23. See also discussion of this letter by Philip Melanchthon and Bernard Ochino in Chapter 5, pp. 208–209, 237.

[117] D. 32.7.18.

[118] Friedrich Thaner, ed., *Die Summa Magistri Rolandi nachmals Papst Alexander III*, c. 32.5; 32.7 (Innsbruck: Verlag von Wagner'schen Universitäts-Buchhandlung, 1874), 181–182, 187–188. See also John T. Noonan, Jr., "Who Was Rolandus?" in Kenneth Pennington and Robert Somerville, eds., *Law, Church, and Christian Society* (Philadelphia: University of Pennsylvania Press, 1977), 21–48.

[119] G.H. Joyce, SJ, *Christian Marriage: An Historical and Doctrinal Study*, 2nd ed. (London: Sheed and Ward, 1948), 333.

Others had said that polygamy might become necessary in a case of "urgent natural necessity."[120] Here, a married man, whose wife was too sick to have sex, was seeking an equitable dispensation from the law to pursue the lesser sin of polygamy, rather than fall into the graver sin of adultery. Perhaps this was a classic case of "double effect" – equitably choosing the lesser of two evils. And who better to judge the equities of the situation and to grant a dispensation than the vicar of Christ on earth, the pope? Gregory II's letter would come up for repeated discussion again, both in medieval writings and in discussions of the infamous early modern cases of Henry VIII of England and Philip of Hesse. We revisit these cases and Gregory's letter in later chapters.[121]

SUCCESSIVE POLYGAMY IN LATER FIRST MILLENNIUM CANON LAWS

Remarriage of Divorcees

Basil's Canons had followed New Testament rules on the remarriage of divorcees. They prohibited divorced women from remarrying until their husbands had died, regardless of their innocence or their first husband's fault.[122] But they allowed innocent divorced men to marry single, non-divorced women if they had dismissed their first wives for adultery. Basil's position was reflected in other early canons. The Canons of Elvira (c. 300–309), for example, targeted divorced women only: "A baptized woman who leaves an adulterous husband who has been baptized, for another man, may not marry him. If she does, she may not receive communion until her former husband dies, unless she is seriously ill."[123] Moreover, "if a Christian woman marries a man in the knowledge that he deserted his former wife without cause, she may receive communion only at the time of her death."[124]

---

[120] See discussion in Chapter 2, pp. 75–76, 82–92.

[121] See discussion in Chapter 5, pp. 208–209; see Joyce, *Christian Marriage*, 574–584 and Eugene Hillman, "Polygamy and the Council of Trent," *The Jurist* 33 (1973): 358–376, at 365–371, on various theological approaches to this letter and broader issue in the Middle Ages.

[122] See detailed sources and discussion in Henri Crouzel, *L'Église primitive face au divorce* (Paris: Beauchesne, 1971).

[123] Council of Elvira, c. 9, in Samuel Laeuchli, *Power and Sexuality: The Emergence of Canon Law at the Synod of Elvira* (Philadelphia: Temple University Press, 1972), with translation of the canons by Kenneth Pennington, posted at http://faculty.cua.edu/pennington/Canon%20Law/ElviraCanons.htm.

[124] Ibid., c. 10. The Council of Arles (314) addressed cuckolded men: "As regards those who find their wives to be guilty of adultery, and who being Christians are, though young men, forbidden to marry, we decree that, so far as may be, counsel be given them not to take other wives, while their own, though guilty of adultery, are still living." C. 1.10, using translation in Joyce, *Christian Marriage*, 310. See other examples in Jo-Ann McNamara and Suzanne F. Wemple, "Marriage and Divorce in the Frankish

After the fourth century, however, the canons moved in two opposing directions. One minor trajectory of canons, inspired by Jerome's more permissive teachings,[125] permitted both wives and husbands to remarry after their divorce. Marriage is a remedy for sin, the argument went, and divorced men and women alike do better to marry than to burn with lust. This teaching converged with the permissive Roman laws on divorce and remarriage that mainline Christianity tried to reform, but to modest avail. Roman law had allowed divorced men to remarry immediately; divorced women had to wait for one year to avoid any issues of disputed paternity and heritability of any children born to her. But the legal norm and the cultural expectation was for both divorced parties to remarry. These Roman law views influenced Germanic law, which also permitted remarriage at least for innocent divorcees, and usually, after a period of penance, for the guilty party as well.[126] Similar permissive views came into the penitential books, giving both parties at least a second chance. The late seventh-century *Penitential of Theodore* offers a good example:

[I]f a man puts away his wife on account of [her] fornication, if she was his first, he is permitted to take another; but if she wishes to do penance for her sins, she may take another husband after five years....

If a husband makes himself a slave through theft or fornication or any sin, the wife, if she has not been married before, has the right to take another husband after a year. This is not permitted to one who has been twice married.[127]

Several seventh- and eighth-century councils in the Frankish Empire experimented with comparable remarriage rules for divorcees, too, and remarriage after divorce became a standard in Eastern Orthodox canon law.[128]

A second trajectory of canons, inspired by Augustine's more restrictive teachings,[129] prohibited men and women alike to remarry until the death of the first spouse. Marriage was an enduring sacramental bond between husband and wife for life, the argument went. Even if separated from each other or divorced by civil decree, a husband and wife remained spiritually bonded to each other. Neither of them could marry another spouse before their first spouse had died and the spiritual bond between them had finally dissolved. The first surviving canon to state this explicitly was issued by the Council

Kingdom," in *Women in Medieval Society*, ed. Susan Mosher Stuard (Philadelphia: University of Pennsylvania Press, 1976), 95–124.
[125] See Jerome's discussion in Chapter 2, pp. 94–95.
[126] Ostrogoths followed Roman law and permitted remarriage after divorce if prevailing local laws allowed. Visigoths allowed remarriage of divorcees who were innocent parties. Bavarians and Lombards permitted husbands to put away their wives for cause, and even for pleasure if he paid a fine, and could remarry another. See Long. ii.13.1; Leg. Rip. tit. 35.
[127] The Penitential of Theodore, bk. 2, 12.5, 9 in McNeill and Gamer, *Medieval Handbooks of Penance*, 208–209.
[128] See the detailed discussion in Joyce, *Christian Marriage*, 304–379.
[129] See Augustine's discussion in Chapter 2, pp. 96–97.

of Carthage in ca. 407: "In accordance with evangelical and apostolic discipline, neither a man dismissed by his wife, nor a woman dismissed by her husband may marry another. Rather they should remain as they are or be reconciled to each other. Those who con[d]emn this law should be subjected to penitence."[130] The later fifth-century *Apostolic Canons* were firmer: "If any layman put away his wife and marry another, or one who has been divorced by another man, let him be excommunicated."[131] "The union with the second woman can have no claim to legality," Pope Innocent I added. She and any children are to be cut off from the man's estate, and the children rendered permanent bastards.[132]

After ample digression and experimentation with more permissive regimes, several later canons and penitential rules echoed this view.[133] Charlemagne's *Capitularies* (789) was one of the most famous: "[N]either shall a wife who has been put away by her husband take another husband, during the lifetime of her own, nor should a man take another wife while his former wife lives."[134] Later penitential rules called such an illicit remarriage a form of adultery, and assigned harsh penance. One penitential book of ca. 750 provided: "If anyone puts away his legal wife and marries another, he shall be excommunicated, even if the former wife consents."[135] This rule of no remarriage for divorcees until the death of the first spouse would become the canonical position of the medieval church, with men and women alike charged with adultery if they remarried prematurely.

Remarriage after Desertion

Basil's Canons had allowed a deserted husband to remarry but withheld that right from a deserted wife, unless she was certain of her husband's death. A few canons throughout the first millennium maintained this position. But most canons tightened the rules of remarriage for husbands, and relaxed them for wives, in order to achieve a more gender-balanced norm of remarriage after desertion.

The most authoritative pronouncement came from Pope Leo I in 458, a time of perilous warfare as the Roman Empire was collapsing under Germanic invasion.[136] As Leo described it, some husbands who marched to war did not return, and their wives had remarried "under stress of loneliness" or fear of

---

[130] Council of Carthage, XI, c. 8, using translation in Reynolds, *Marriage in the Western Church*, 152.
[131] Canon 48, in NPNF 2, 14:597.
[132] Letter to Probum, in PL 20:602, using translation in Joyce, *Christian Marriage*, 320.
[133] See the detailed treatment in ibid., 304–379, with selected canons reprinted in ibid., 609ff.
[134] Canon 43, in MGH Leges, 1:99. See other examples in McNeill and Gamer, *Medieval Handbooks of Penance*, 133.
[135] The Judgment of Clement, c. 14, in ibid., 272.
[136] Letter 159 to Nicaetus, secs. 2–5, in NPNF 2d 12:102–113.

ravishment. Some wives, in turn, were captured and carried off as spoils of war, and their husbands, after failing to rescue them, had remarried. What happened if, against all odds, the first husband or wife returned? The first marriage was to be restored, Leo ruled, but all parties were to be considered innocent. To underscore the priority of the first marriage, Leo quoted Proverbs 19:15 ("a woman is joined to a man by God") and Matthew 19:6 ("what God hath joined let no man separate"). These verses, he said, make clear that "we are bound to hold that the compact of the lawful marriage must be renewed . . . and take every pain that each should recover what is his own." If a man wants his wife back, she must go, and if she refuses to return, she must be excommunicated. If the husband, however, does not want his wife back, later canons made clear, she could retain her second husband, and he could, after a time, pursue a second wife. Later canons also added that children born of the second marriages of deserted spouses were legitimate, even if those second marriages were later dissolved on the return of the first spouse.[137]

The penitential books took up these questions as well, addressing not only cases of involuntary desertion but also intentional or malicious desertion of a spouse. One set of late seventh-century rules reads thus:

> If a woman leaves her husband, despising him, and is unwilling to return and be reconciled to her husband, after five years, and with the bishop's consent, he shall be permitted to take another wife.
>
> If she has been taken in captivity by force and cannot be redeemed, [he may] take another after a year.
>
> Again, if she has been taken into captivity her husband shall wait five years; so also shall the woman do if such things have happened to the man.
>
> If, therefore, a man has taken another wife, he shall receive the former wife when she returns from captivity and put away the later one; so also shall she do, as we have said above, if such things have happened to her husband.
>
> If an enemy carries away any man's wife, and he cannot get her again, he may take another. To do this is better than acts of fornication.
>
> If after this the former wife comes again to him, she ought not to be received by him, if he has another [wife], but she may take to herself another husband, if she had [only] one before. The same ruling stands in the case of slaves from over the sea.[138]

[137] See X.17.14.

[138] The Penitential of Theodore, bk. 2, chap. 12, cc. 18–25, in McNeill and Gamer, *Medieval Handbooks of Penance*, 210. The Penitential of Cummean, II.29 in ibid., 105 required a man to take back his deserting wife if she returned, and to do penance for a year for marrying the second wife. See also Nedungatt and Featherstone, eds., *The Council of Trullo*, canon 93, pp. 172–173: "If a woman, whose husband has gone away and disappeared, cohabits with another man before being certain

Desertion was sometimes not only physical, but also spiritual. Sometimes a new Christian convert, who was already married, wanted to abandon a pagan spouse and marry a believer. Sometimes, a Christian husband or wife lapsed from the faith, or even worse was excommunicated. Could the Christian spouse in those instances get remarried? No, said the early canons. In 1 Corinthians 7:12–16, St. Paul's had said that a believer should retain an unbelieving spouse in hopes of (re)converting them to the faith. If the unbeliever deserted the home, the believing spouse had no duty to pursue them, but also no right to remarry another spouse. Ambrosiaster already put this rule firmly: "if you join with others, you are adulterers; and your children born of this union are both unclean, that is, they are bastards."[139] "If anyone had a virgin wife before baptism, while she lives," a ninth-century canon added, "he cannot have another [wife] after baptism. For it is crimes that are dissolved in baptism, not marriages."[140]

Remarriage of Widow(er)s

In accord with Basil's Canons, a number of early canons permitted widows and widowers to remarry, and ordered that they not be shunned or criticized by fellow believers.[141] Some canons assigned a period of fasting and mourning after the death of the first spouse, especially for widows, before remarriage was licit.[142] Other canons ordered priests to desist from blessing or presiding over the remarriages, or joining the subsequent wedding feasts of the faithful even after their penance.[143] Others discouraged too many remarriages if a person was so unfortunate as to be widowed several times.[144] But remarriage of widow(er)s was allowed, and no stigma could be attached to those who exercised this right to remarry. In fact, some later penitential

---

of her husband's death, she commits adultery. Likewise soldiers' wives who have married after the disappearance of their husbands shall be liable on the same grounds as those who in the absence of their husbands did not await their return, except that in this case there is a certain excuse, the suspicion of death being more probable. As for a woman who in ignorance has married a man whose wife has left him for a time, and is then left by him on account of the return of his former wife, she has committed adultery, though in ignorance. She shall not, therefore, be forbidden to marry; but it is better if she remain as she is. And if a soldier should ever return, whose wife in his long absence has married another man, the soldier, if he chooses, shall take again his own wife, pardon being granted to her, because of her ignorance, and also to the man who took her in second marriage."

[139] Ambrosiaster, Comm. 1 Cor. 7:14.

[140] Council of Tribur (895), c. 39, using translation in Lombard, *Sentences*, bk. 4, dist. 39.5.2. Gratian, *Decretum*, c. 28.2.1 cites this as the Council of Meaux, c. 1. See other authorities gathered in ibid., c. 28.1 to 28.3.

[141] Council of Nicaea (325), c. 8, in NPNF 2, 14:192.

[142] Council of Laodicaea (ca. 343–381), c. 1, in NPNF 2, 14:126 and other texts in Gratian, *Decretum*, c. 27.1.33, 27.2.13; 31.1.11–12; 32.3.6; X.4.21.

[143] Council of Neo-Caeserea (315), c. 3, in NPNF 2, 14:80; St. Hubert Penitential, c. 55, in McNeill and Gamer, *Medieval Handbooks of Penance*, 294; The Roman Penitential, c. 94, in ibid., 312.

[144] Council of Neo-Caeserea (315), c. 3, in NPNF 2, 14:80.

books, following 1 Timothy 5, encouraged younger widow(er)s to remarry, especially if they had children or were still capable of having them. Additional remarriages were permitted to those who lost several spouses, but they were never encouraged.[145]

The Eastern Orthodox churches of the first millennium eventually prohibited remarriage to widow(er)s, and labeled those who did remarry as "bigamists," "digamists," or "polygamists."[146] This language occasionally seeped into Western writings and canons as well prior to the sixth century. But the Western canons eventually branded this position as heretical, and allowed surviving spouses to remarry after their prior spouse had died. The canons added that a surviving spouse could not remarry if they had killed their prior spouse, nor could they marry their former adulterous lover.

CLERICAL POLYGAMY IN LATER FIRST MILLENNIUM CANON LAWS

Basil's Canons had made clear that an aspiring priest, deacon, or deaconess could have (had) only one spouse. Later canon law rules repeated this rule frequently.[147] "He who has taken a second wife can in no way be a cleric," declared Pope Innocent I; "because it is written [in the Bible] 'a husband of one wife'. And again, 'Let my priests be married once.'"[148] Pope Leo the Great concurred: "Where husbands of widows or those having several wives have been promoted to the priesthood, we order them by the authority of the apostolic see to be cut off from all ecclesiastical offices and from the name of the priesthood."[149]

Several canons called these doubly married candidates for the priesthood "bigamists," "digamists," or "polygamists" – even if they had properly taken a second spouse only after the death of the first. Remarriage of widow(er)s was acceptable for the laity, but not for the clergy. The canons listed such clerical bigamists or polygamists alongside sundry other "infamous" persons who were ineligible for the church's holy orders – thieves, sacrilegists, grave robbers, the incestuous, murderers, perjurers, rapists, poisoners, and others "who are not sound in body or do not have a sound mind or intellect, or who stand disobedient to the decrees of the saints or who manifest madness: all these, I say, ought not to be promoted to sacred orders."[150]

---

[145] See James A. Brundage, "The Merry Widow's Serious Sister: Remarriage in Classical Canon Law," in Robert R. Edwards and Vickie Ziegler, eds., *Matrons and Marginal Women in Medieval Society* (Woodbridge, Suffolk: The Boydell Press, 1995), 33–48.

[146] See John Meyendorff, "Christian Marriage in Byzantium," *Dumbarton Oaks Papers* 44 (1990): 99–107; David Heith-Stade, *Marriage as the Arena of Salvation: An Ecclesiological Study of the Marital Regulation in Canons of the Council of Trullo* (Rollinsford, NH: Orthodox Research Institute, 2011).

[147] See, e.g, *The Collection in Seventy-Four Titles*, titles 5.51; 15.118; 16.144–145, 150, 151, 155.

[148] Ibid., title 16.145.

[149] Ibid., title 16.151.

[150] Ibid., title 5.51. See also the "The Dialogue of Egbert (ca. 750)," in McNeill and Gamer, *Medieval Handbooks of Penance*, 329–340.

A few later canons and penitential rules extended this "husband of one wife" rule to ban a clerical candidate who had lived with a concubine or a long-standing lover as well, even if he was single at the time of his ordination. The spirit of the Bible's "husband of one wife" rule was that a priest could have only one prior relationship with a woman, the argument went. A man who had entered more than one prior sexual relationship was thus still a bigamist ineligible for clerical office.[151] Indeed "a virginal priest" – a life-long bachelor free from any sexual contact at any time in his life – was the ideal.[152] Part of the argument for this ideal was that even a once-married candidate for ordination was still effectively remarrying: first he had a carnal marriage with a woman, and now he sought a spiritual marriage to Christ and the church. While a second marriage was acceptable, a single marriage was better. And while a single carnal marriage was acceptable, a single spiritual marriage to Christ and the church alone was better still. A further argument for the ideal of a life-long "virginal priest" was that any slippage on a matter so fundamental as sex and marriage would open the clerical office to all manner of unseemly candidates: "yesterday a catechumen, today a bishop; yesterday in the theatre, today in the church; at night at the track, in the morning at the altar; not long ago a patron of the arts, now a consecrator of virgins."[153]

Several canons focused on the purity and virginity not just of the priest, but of his one permitted wife as well. She, too, had to be, in effect, "the wife of one husband." On her wedding day with her future priest husband, she had to have been a virgin not "a widow, or a divorced person, or a harlot, or a servant, or an actress," or even an innocent victim of rape, kidnapping, or abduction.[154] Both the dignity of the sacrament of priestly ordination and the reputation of the ordained cleric and his office required purity on the part of husband and wife alike. As Pope Leo I wrote in a lengthy letter in 466:

Who then would dare to allow this injury to be perpetuated upon so great a sacrament, seeing that this great and venerable mystery is not without the support of the statutes of God's law as well, whereby it is clearly laid down that a priest is

[151] See, e.g., The Canons of the Holy and Altogether August Apostles, c. 19, in NPNF 2, 14:595; Council of Orleans (538), c. 10.9, in Corpus Christianum, Latina (Turnhout: Brépols, 1953-), 148A, 119.
[152] See, e.g., the early Irish laws recounted in McNeill and Gamer, Medieval Handbooks of Penance, 372.
[153] The Collection in Seventy-Four Titles, title 15.137.10. This last quotation from Jerome – although used by later writers to warn against the slippery slope of promoting the wrong candidates – is more about clerical bigamy and morality than about clerical virginity. See David G. Hunter, "The Raven Replies: Ambrose, Letter to the Church at Vercelli (ep. ex. coll. 14) and the Criticisms of Jerome," in Jerome of Stridon: His Life, Writings and Legacy, ed. Andrew Cain and Josef Lössl (London: Ashgate, 2009), 175–189.
[154] The earliest known laws are from the Gallic Council of Valentium in 374 and from Pope Siricus in ca. 385. Nedungatt and Featherstone, eds., The Council of Trullo, Canon 3, pp. 69–74. See also The Collection in Seventy-Four Titles, title 16.150.

to marry a virgin and that she who is be the wife of a priest is not to know another husband? [Lev. 21.13; see also Ezek. 44:22].... If then even in the Old Testament this kind of marriage among priests is adhered to, how much more ought we who are placed under the grace of the Gospel to conform to the Apostle's precepts; so that though a man be found endowed with good character, and furnished with holy works, he may nevertheless in no wise ascend to the grade of deacon, or the dignity of the presbytery, or to the highest rank of the bishopric, if it has been spread abroad either that he himself is not the husband of one wife, or that his wife is not the wife of one husband.[155]

The emerging concern in these early church canons was to protect the purity and dignity of the sacraments of ordination and marriage. This would become a critical argument in support of the church's new prohibitions on clerical and lay polygamy in the latter Middle Ages.

Later first millennium canons strove to set a rule of even more "exact perfection" by encouraging a priest who still had his wife upon ordination to abstain from sexual intercourse with her – at least on the days he performed the Eucharist (in protection of the dignity of this sacrament, too), but ideally at all times.[156] The ideal for a married priest was that his marriage would become "spiritual instead of carnal ... whereby both the affection of their wives may be retained and the marriage functions cease."[157] A few canons and later penitential books went further and declared it adultery for a bishop or priest to have sex with his wife at any time after ordination.[158] As the so-called Roman Penitential (ca. 830) put it: "If after his conversion or advancement any cleric of superior rank who has a wife has relations with her again, let him know that he has committed adultery," and will be subject to twelve years of penance, "five on bread and water."[159]

To remove all such sexual temptations, several canons, penitential rules, and Germanic laws prohibited clergy from having any other women in their households besides their wives and their mothers or blood sisters.[160] "To be always with a woman and not have sexual relations with her is more difficult than to raise the dead," a popular adage went.[161] Some of the penitential rules worked hard to protect the

[155] Leo the Great, Letter 12, in NPNF 2, 12:13.
[156] The rules were stricter in Western churches than Eastern churches. See David G. Hunter, "Clerical Marriage East and West," in *Brill Companion to Priesthood in the Middle Ages* (forthcoming).
[157] Canons of Trullo, Canon 3; see also *The Collection in Seventy-Four Titles*, title 16.150; Council of Africa Code (419), c 3, in NPNF 2, 14:444–445.
[158] Council of Carthage II (390), n. 1, quoted in Lombard, *Sentences*, bk. 4, dist. 37.1.2.
[159] "The So-Called Roman Penitential of Halitgar (ca. 830), Prescriptions of Penance," items 7–8, in McNeill and Gamer, *Medieval Handbooks of Penance*, 302.
[160] See, e.g., Canons of Trullo, Canon 5.
[161] Bernard of Clairvaux, quoted by Caroline Walker Bynum, *Jesus as Mother: Studies in the Spirituality of the High Middle Ages* (Berkeley/Los Angeles: University of California Press, 1982), 145.

clergy and the clerical office from any sex contact and compromise. Included among the *Penitentials of Theodore* (ca. 668–690), for example, were the following rules:

> If a priest is polluted in touching or in kissing a woman he shall do penance for forty days.
>
> If a presbyter kisses a woman from desire, he shall do penance for forty days.
>
> Likewise if a presbyter is polluted through imagination, he shall do penance for a week.
>
> For masturbation, he shall fast for a week....
>
> A monk or holy virgin who commits fornication shall do penance for seven years.
>
> He who often pollutes himself through the violence of his imagination shall do penance for twenty days....
>
> For masturbation, the first time he shall do penance for twenty days, on repetition, forty days; for further offenses fasts shall be added....
>
> Basil gave the judgment that a boy should be permitted to marry before the age of sixteen if he could not abstain; but that if he is already a monk, [and marries], he is both [classified] among bigamists and shall do penance for one year.[162]

These emerging first millennium rules proved to be steps along the way to banning clerical sex and marriage altogether, which the Second and Third Lateran Councils finally and formally pronounced for all clerics (bishops, priests, deacons, and subdeacons) in 1123 and 1139. Thereafter, the church issued a series of increasingly stern canon law prohibitions on clerical concubinage, fornication, prostitution, and other sexual associations that inevitably spiked after clerical marriages were banned. The life-long "virginal priest" remained the ideal; the single, unmarried priest became the norm. An aspiring priest, who was married only once to a properly virginal wife, could now seek ordination only after his marriage had ended.[163]

SUMMARY AND CONCLUSIONS

The first millennium church's canon laws on sex, marriage, and family life followed the Bible, both in content and in accent, and then adapted these biblical norms to new situations, sometimes absorbing secular laws and customs in so doing. The Bible had no explicit prohibition on real polygamy, and the canon law did not prohibit it outright until the fourth century. Even then, the few canon laws on point treated real polygamy rather lightly. Adultery was punished nearly four times more severely;

---

[162] The Penitential of Theodore, bk. 1, tit. 8.1–4, 6, 14 in McNeill and Gamer, *Medieval Handbooks of Penance*, 191–192. See comparable provisions in other penitentials in ibid., 92, 104, 253, 274–275, 302–303, 368.

[163] Brundage, *Law, Sex, and Christian Society*, 214–222, 342–343, 546–549.

simple fornication between single parties at nearly double the rate. From the fifth to the tenth centuries, the surviving canon law texts in the West had no major new canons on real polygamy, and the new penitential books were silent on the topic, too.

It was the law of the state, not the law of the church that prohibited real polygamy, and it did so with growing severity. Already for more than half a millennium before the time of Jesus, Greek and Roman laws had privileged monogamy as the only form of valid marriage to produce legitimate and heritable children. By the third century CE the Roman emperors made polygamy a crime of infamy. By the sixth century, the Christian emperors and the Christian Germanic kings made polygamy a "nefarious," "infamous," and "unnatural" crime on the order of adultery and incest. By the ninth century, polygamy was a capital crime, and it remained so in many states for a millennium thereafter.

The first millennium church complemented these state laws by prohibiting constructive or quasi-polygamous conduct – having two fiancées at the same time, having a fiancée and a spouse, having a concubine and a wife, marrying two sisters in a row, or making marital and spiritual vows at the same time. All these relationships bordered on polygamy, although the church canons usually called them "adultery" not "polygamy." This had the ironic effect of subjecting quasi-polygamists to severe penance, but actual polygamists to light penance at church law. The converse was true at state law: actual polygamists faced severe criminal punishment, even the death penalty by the end of the millennium; quasi-polygamists were largely immune from state criminal sanction.

The New Testament spoke four times to the remarriage of divorcees. It said that innocent husbands who dismissed their adulterous wives could marry other single, non-divorced women, but wives had to wait until the death of their husbands, even if they were innocent. A few canons maintained these biblical rules, but most moved in opposite directions. One set of canons and penitential rules allowed divorced wives and husbands alike to remarry, after a period of penance and discernment. It was better for the divorced to marry than to burn, and this applied to husbands and wives alike. A second, ultimately dominant, set of canons prohibited both husbands and wives from remarriage unless and until their first spouse had died. Marriage was an enduring sacrament, and it died only when the first spouse died. Those who remarried beforehand were viewed as adulterers, occasionally as "bigamists" and were subject to severe penitential discipline.

The New Testament left only one passage on desertion, and that concerned spouses who had lost their faith and then physically deserted their believing spouse. A believing spouse had no duty to pursue the deserter, St. Paul made clear. But the deserted spouse also had no right to remarry until the first spouse had died, the canon law added. This was true even if a new convert to Christianity still had a defiantly pagan spouse, or if a faithful spouse had now become an "enemy of Christ" and the church, and been excommunicated or imprisoned. Reconciliation with the spiritually wayward spouse or sexual continence with oneself were the only licit options. Illicit remarriage was, again, a form of adultery. The canons recognized that sometimes an absent spouse, who had gone to war or on a dangerous trip, or who been abducted or kidnapped, could be presumed dead. In those instances, the early canons allowed the parties to remarry after a period of waiting. But if the first spouse (against all odds) returned, the parties would have to return to their first marriage: the wife faced excommunication if she refused to return to the first marriage, while the husband was given more discretion.

The New Testament left three passages permitting the remarriage of widows, and the canons maintained these rules. Following St. Paul, they discouraged remarriage, sometimes assigning penance and withholding priestly blessings from the remarried. But, the Western Church, unlike the Eastern Orthodox Church, was insistent that widows and widowers be allowed to remarry, even multiple times.

The New Testament stated three times that a bishop and deacon had to be the "husband of one wife" and a deaconess "the wife of one husband." The first millennium canon law applied these biblical rules strictly, calling a twice-married candidate for ordination or spiritual vows a "bigamist" or "digamist," occasionally a "polygamist." By the fifth century, the canon law had extended these biblical rules. The more rigorous canons permitted aspiring priests only one prior relationship with a woman – whether wife, concubine, or longstanding lover. Other canons insisted that the "one wife" in question had to be of pure virginal stock, not widowed, divorced, a prostitute, or even an actress or rape victim – a Christian echo of Mosaic laws of priestly purity. For those clergy who were still married after ordination, the more rigorous canons prohibited them either from dismissing their wives or having sex with them. And any ordained cleric, consecrated deaconess, or avowed monastic who had sex with a third party, let alone got engaged or married to another, was deposed for adultery, and under some sterner canons subject to excommunication. The "dignity" and "holiness" of the clerical office and of ecclesiastical orders required that their members abstain from sex.

At the end of the first millennium, the Western legal tradition had a patchwork of legal norms to govern real, constructive, and clerical polygamy. Of these various forms, three types of illicit double relationships attracted the most extended theoretical discussion in the first millennium and the largest number of canon laws and penitential rules – those concerning clerical polygamy, remarriage after adultery and divorce, and simultaneous spiritual and marital vows.[164] Real polygamy – and its

---

[164] See David L. D'Avray, *Medieval Marriage: Symbolism and Society* (Oxford: Oxford University Press, 2005), 131–167.

closest analogues, double engagements, and marriage plus concubinage – were the most firmly punished criminal offenses in the first millennium, but they were the least theoretically developed and defended in the surviving literature.

It was not until the High Middle Ages that the church made real polygamy a serious canon law offense, clearly separated from adultery, fornication, and other sex crimes. It was only then that the church's canon law had a system in which to situate all these illicit double associations. Once simultaneous double marriages were viewed as the core and most serious case of polygamy, it was easier to view double engagements, double vows, double sisters, double sex partners and the like as lesser forms or degrees of polygamy rather than simply another form of adultery. But it took several centuries for the medieval canonists to move toward that integrated system. And it was ultimately the theoretical musings about polygamy by a few late medieval Catholics and then the actual polygamous experiments of a few early Protestants that prompted the Catholic Church to make real polygamy a serious canon law offense that was punished by regular church courts and by the Inquisition. And the church's aggressive new laws and prosecution, in turn, triggered the secular authorities to follow suit, and put firm new criminal prohibitions against polygamy in place, several of them making it a capital offense. That is the story of the next three chapters.

4

The Medieval Case for Monogamy Over Polygamy

FIGURE 9. "The Marriage of the Virgin," from Raphael (Raffaello Sanzio of Urbino), Pinacoteca di Brera, Milan, Italy (1504).
Used by permission of Pinacoteca di Brera, Milan, Italy / Bridgeman Images.

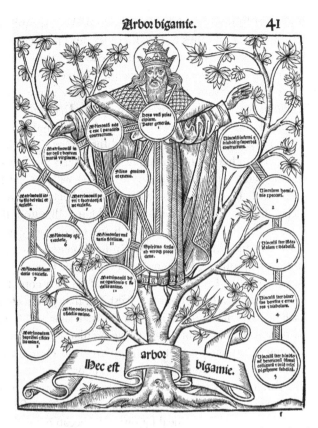

FIGURE 10. "Tree of Bigamy," Woodcut the *Summa Hostiensis* (from the facsimile edition of 1962), used by permission of Scientia Publishing.
Courtesy of the Pitts Theology Library, Candler School of Theology, Emory University.

The twelfth and thirteenth centuries were a major watershed period in the development of the Western legal tradition. This was the High Middle Ages when the clergy threw off their royal and civil rulers and established the church as an autonomous legal and political power. By 1250, the church was the one universal sovereign of the West, supreme over the sundry empires, kingdoms, territories, duchies, and cities that comprised the Western state. The church's revolutionary rise to power was part and product of an enormous transformation of Western society, politics, and culture in this period. The West was further transformed through the rediscovery and study of the ancient texts of Greek philosophy,

Patristic theology, and Roman law. The first modern Western universities were established with their core faculties of law, theology, and medicine.[1]

It was in this era that the West developed a systematic law and theology of monogamous marriage – and, in turn, a stronger and clearer case against polygamy. From the twelfth century forward, the church's canon law was systematized, first in Gratian's *Decretum* (ca. 1140)[2] and Pope Gregory IX's *Decretals* (1234),[3] then in a welter of later papal and conciliar laws that were later compiled in the *Corpus Iuris Canonici* (ca. 1586). Both the *Decretum* and the *Decretals* are important for our story because they gathered and gradually systematized the first millennium canon laws for monogamy and against polygamy, along with several Roman and Germanic laws on point. These two massive canonical collections were the starting point for most legal discussions of sex, marriage, and family life until the sixteenth century.[4] They were also the anchor texts of a living canon law system operated by the church. In the High Middle Ages, the church's canon law was not just a set of loosely enforced spiritual guidelines for the faithful. It was a sophisticated legal system whose norms and procedures were enforced by a complex hierarchy of church courts and officials throughout the West. On many subjects, the church shared power with the secular authorities. But on marriage and the family, the church claimed principal jurisdiction, leaving the secular authorities to deal with marital property and inheritance and to help enforce the church's prohibitions against sexual immorality, including various forms of polygamy.[5]

The Western church also systematized its theology of marriage in this period. That work, too, helped sharpen the Western case against polygamy. Peter Lombard's *Book of Sentences* (ca. 1153–1158)[6] is critical for our story, because it gathered many of

[1] See generally Harold J. Berman, *Law and Revolution: The Formation of the Western Legal Tradition* (Cambridge, MA: Harvard University Press, 1983).

[2] Gratian, *Decretum*, causae 27–36, reprinted in Emil Friedberg, ed., *Corpus Iuris Canonici* (Leipzig: Bernard Tauchnitz, 1879), Part I [hereafter D. – for Decretum; c – for each causa]. Anders Winroth, *The Making of Gratian's Decretum* (Cambridge: Cambridge University Press, 2000) has argued convincingly that there were, in fact, two texts of the *Decretum*, a much simpler and systematic earlier text that was then heavily amended, sometimes at the cost of coherence.

[3] See esp. *Decretales Gregorii*, bk. 4, title 1–19, in Friedberg, ed., *Corpus Iuris Canonici*, Part II [hereafter "X" – for Liber Extra].

[4] See Stephan Kuttner, *Repertorium der Kanonistik (1140–1234)* (Vatican City: Biblioteca apostolica vaticana, 1937).

[5] On the medieval canon law of marriage in action, see Charles Donahue, *Law, Marriage, and Society in the Later Middle Ages: Arguments About Marriage in Five Courts* (Cambridge: Cambridge University Press, 2007); R.H. Helmholz, *Marriage Litigation in Medieval England* (Cambridge: Cambridge University Press, 1974). On martial property, see Philip L. Reynolds and John Witte, Jr., eds. *To Have and to Hold: Marrying and its Documentation in Western Christendom, 400–1600* (Cambridge: Cambridge University Press, 2007).

[6] *Sententiae in IV libris distinctae*, bk. 4, dist. 26–42, *Patrologia Latina*, vol. 192, translated as Peter Lombard, *The Sentences*, trans. Giulio Silano, 4 vols. (Toronto: Pontifical Institute of Medieval Studies, 2010). See esp. ibid., 4:157–232.

the first millennium theological and canonical writings on point, putting them into various "distinctions," and resolving some of the tensions among them. This became the anchor text for most later medieval theological discussions of marriage and family life. Hundreds of medieval theologians wrote commentaries on Lombard's *Sentences*.[7] The most famous was Thomas Aquinas (1225–1274),[8] who left nearly 4,000 pages of commentaries on Lombard's *Sentences*, along with his equally famous *Summa Theologica* and *Summa Contra Gentiles*.[9]

In all these legal and theological writings, monogamy and polygamy came in for refined and novel discussion. Medieval writers repeated the first millennium cases against real, constructive, and clerical polygamy. But they also offered fresh new arguments based in part on their deeper understanding of monogamous marriage, based in part on their new encounters with the polygamy of medieval Muslims, then Latin American Indians, and then German Anabaptists. These developments fueled a growing legal campaign to stamp out real polygamy for good. By the sixteenth century, the Catholic Church denounced polygamy as a form of heresy, punished by the Inquisition as well as conventional church courts. The state, in turn, denounced polygamy as a capital crime against nature.

This chapter works through this medieval story. I first summarize the medieval theology of monogamous marriage and the medieval laws against real polygamy. I then work through the complex medieval arguments against Muslim forms and other forms of real polygamy, and then against various forms of successive and clerical polygamy.

MONOGAMY AS NATURAL, CONTRACTUAL, AND SPIRITUAL

The Western case against polygamy became clearer as medieval writers developed a fuller theory of monogamous marriage. Theologians, philosophers, and jurists

---

7   Frederic Stegmüller, *Repertoriorum commentarium in Sententias Petri Lombardi*, 2 vols. (Würzburg: Ferdinandum Schoningh Bibliopolam, 1947) lists 1,407 separate glosses and commentaries on Lombard's *Sentences* in the 400 years after its publication. See also G.R. Evans and Philipp W. Rosemann, eds., *Mediaeval Commentaries on the Sentences of Peter Lombard*, 2 vols. (Leiden: Brill, 2002, 2010).

8   Thomas Aquinas, *Scriptum super Libros Sententiarum Petri Lombardiensis*, in id., *Opera Omnia sancti Thomae Aquinatis Doctoris Angelici*, 13 vols. (Rome: C. de Propagandae Fidei, 1882), vol. 7, pt. 2 [hereinafter Aquinas, *Scriptum*], partly translated in Thomas Aquinas, *On Love and Charity: Readings from the Commentary on the Sentences of Peter Lombard*, trans. Peter A. Kwasniewski, Thomas Bolin, and Joseph Bolin (Washington, DC: Catholic University Press of America, 2009). Aquinas's commentary on Peter Lombard's discussion of marriage is reprinted almost verbatim in the *Supplement* to his *Summa Theologica: Complete English Edition in Five Volumes*, trans. Fathers of the English Dominican Province, 5 vols. (New York: Benziger Bros., 1947–1948), vol. 5 [hereafter ST Supp.].

9   Thomas Aquinas, *Summa Contra Gentiles*, trans. Vernon J. Bourke, 4 vols. (Notre Dame, IN: University of Notre Dame Press, 1975) [hereafter Aquinas, SCG].

of the twelfth century forward came to describe monogamous marriage as a three-dimensional institution – at once natural, contractual, and spiritual.[10]

First, medieval writers taught, marriage was a natural association, formed by the "two in one flesh" union of a man and a woman. Already in Paradise, medieval writers argued, God had commanded the first man and the first woman to "be fruitful and multiply." He had created them as social beings, naturally inclined to one another and endowed them with the physical capacity to join together and beget children. He had commanded them to help and nurture each other and to inculcate within their children the highest virtue and love of the Divine. These natural qualities and duties continued after Adam and Eve's fall into sin. But after the fall, marriage also came to serve as a remedy for the individual sinner to allay lustful passion, to heal incontinence, and to substitute a bodily union with a spouse for the lost spiritual union with God in Paradise. Rather than allow sinful people to burn with lust, God confirmed the natural institution of marriage wherein couples could direct their natural drives and desires toward the service of each other, their children, the church, and the broader society.

As a natural institution, marriage was subject to natural law. For medieval writers, natural law was not only, as the Roman law had put it, "the law that nature has taught all animals," which gave them "natural inclinations" to protect, preserve, and perpetuate themselves through procreation.[11] Natural law was also what Gratian called the "natural instincts" or "intuitions" that are unique to humans and the "common customs" and "conventions" that have emerged among humans over time.[12] These distinctly human qualities of natural law are known through reason and conscience, and often confirmed, illustrated, and sometimes corrected by the Bible.

Natural law, in this fuller human sense, helped to channel the natural drive and determination that fit persons marry when they reach the age of puberty, that they conceive children and nurture and educate them until adulthood, and that they remain bonded to their kin who are by nature inclined to serve and support each other, especially in times of need, frailty, and old age. The natural law prescribed heterosexual, life-long unions between a couple, featuring mutual

---

[10] This section distills the detailed discussion and sources in my *From Sacrament to Contract: Marriage, Religion, and Law in the Western Tradition*, 2nd ed. (Louisville, KY: Westminster John Knox Press, 2011), 77–112.

[11] *Justinian's Institutes*, 1.1.12, ed. Paul Krüger, trans. Peter Birks and Grant McLeod (Ithaca, NY: Cornell University Press, 1987) [hereafter "Inst."]; *The Digest of Justinian*, 1.1.3, ed. Theodor Mommsen and Paul Krüger, trans. Alan Watson, 4 vols. (Philadelphia: University of Pennsylvania Press, 1985) (hereafter "Dig."). See also D., Dist. 1.6–7, translated in *Gratian: The Treatise on Laws with the Ordinary Gloss*, trans. James Gordley and Augustine Thompson, O.P. (Washington, DC: Catholic University of America Press, 1993), 6–7.

[12] D. Dist. 1, c. 7 in ibid.

support and faithfulness. It proscribed incest, bestiality, buggery, sodomy, pederasty, masturbation, contraception, abortion, and other unnatural and non-procreative sexual activities and relations.[13] And it proscribed polygamy, as we shall see later in this chapter.

Second, marriage was a contract, subject to general rules of contract formation. Marriage depended in its essence on the mutual consent of the parties to be legitimate and binding, a canon law adoption of earlier Roman law. "What makes a marriage is not the consent to cohabitation nor the carnal copula," wrote Peter Lombard; "it is the consent to conjugal society that does." The form and function of this conjugal society, and the requirements for valid entrance into it, were preset by the laws of nature, as amended and emended by the laws of the church. But the choice of whether to enter this conjugal society lay exclusively with the man and the woman.[14] John Duns Scotus (ca. 1266–1308), glossed Lombard's definition with a reference to the conjugal debt: "Marriage is an indissoluble bond between a man and his wife arising from the mutual exchange of authority over one another's bodies for the procreation and proper nurture of children."[15] Hugh of St. Victor (1096–1141) stressed the requirement of exclusive conjugal fidelity: "What else is marriage but the legitimate association between a man and woman, an association in which each partner obligates (*debet*) himself to the other by virtue of mutual consent? This obligation can be considered in two ways, that one reserve oneself for the spouse, and that one not refuse oneself to the spouse."[16]

The marital contract was subject to the general principles of contract that prevailed at medieval canon and civil law. One principle was freedom of contract.[17] The validity of the marriage contract depended in its essence on the free and voluntary consent of both the man and the woman. Marriage contracts entered into by force, fear, or fraud, or through undue influence or inducement by parents, masters, or lords were thus not binding. A second principle was justice and fairness. While respecting the freedom of parties to bargain, parties could not enforce marital or marital property contracts that were unconscionable, unjust or unfair, that defied the laws of nature or the church, or that gave one party an undue advantage over the other.[18] A third contractual principle

---

[13] See sample texts in Rudolf Weigand, *Die Naturrechtslehre die Legisten und Dekretisten von Irenaeus bis Johannes Teutonicus* (Berlin: Hueber, 1967), 283–298.

[14] Lombard, *Sentences*, bk. 4, dist. 27.2, 28.4.

[15] Quoted by Theodore Mackin, *Marriage in the Catholic Church: What is Marriage?* (New York: Paulist Press, 1982), 186.

[16] Quoted by ibid., 155.

[17] Respectively, X 4.1.29; D. c. 31, q. 2, c. 1; and Hostiensis, *Summa aurea*, using translations in R.H. Helmholz, *The Spirit of the Classical Canon Law* (Athens: University of Georgia Press, 1996), 237.

[18] See Harold J. Berman, "The Religious Sources of General Contract," in *Christianity and Law: An Introduction*, ed. John Witte, Jr. and Frank S. Alexander (Cambridge: Cambridge University Press, 2008), 125–142, at 127–132; James Gordley, *The Philosophical Origins of Modern Contract Doctrine* (Oxford: Oxford University Press, 1991).

was enforceability. Absent proof of mistake or frustration, or of some condition that would render the marital contract unjust, either party could petition a court to enforce its terms and vindicate their conjugal rights under the marriage contract. Rights to spousal support, maintenance, and protection set in automatically after the couple was married, even if their marriage was not consummated. Rights to future sexual performance set in only after their first act of consensual sexual intercourse within marriage.[19]

Third, marriage between two baptized Christians was also a sacrament. Unlike other sacraments, like baptism or the eucharist, the sacrament of marriage required no formalities and no clerical or lay instruction, witnesses, or participation. The man and woman were themselves "ministers of the sacrament." The medieval church strongly encouraged the couple to seek their parents' consent, draw upon the counsel of witnesses, publicize their engagement through banns, and seek premarital counseling from a priest. The church also offered a variety of wedding liturgies to be presided over by ordained priests and to take place at home, in the church, or at the door of the church (*in facie ecclesiae*).[20] It was not until 1563, however, that the Council of Trent required a priest to witness the union, to join the spouses using whatever form of words was customary in the region, and to offer the couple a "sacerdotal benediction."[21]

Like the other sacraments, marriage was an instrument of sanctification, a channel of grace that caused God's blessings to be poured upon humanity. It transformed the relationship of a married couple, much like baptism transformed the character of the baptized. In baptism, the seemingly simple ritual act of sprinkling water on the forehead spiritually transformed the baptized party – canceling the original sin of Adam, promising the baptized party divine aid and protection in life, and welcoming the baptized believer into the sanctuary of the church, into the spiritual care of the parents and godparents, and into the communion of saints. Similarly, in marriage, the simple ritual act of a Christian man and woman coming together consensually in a sacramental marriage spiritually transformed their relationship – removing the sin of sexual intercourse, inviting them into the new creative act of

[19] James A. Brundage, "Implied Consent to Intercourse," in *Consent and Coercion to Sex and Marriage in Ancient and Medieval Societies*, ed. Angeliki E. Laiou (Washington, DC: Dumbarton Research Library and Collection, 1993), 245–256; Charles J. Reid, Jr., *Power over the Body, Equality in the Family: Rights and Domestic Relations in Medieval Canon Law* (Grand Rapids, MI: Wm. B. Eerdmans, 2004), 25–68; Rudolf Weigand, *Die bedingte Eheschliessung im kanonischen Recht* (Munich: M. Hueber, 1963); John T. Noonan, *Canons and Canonists in Context* (Goldbach: Keip, 1997), 173–198.

[20] See good samples in Mark Searle and Kenneth W. Stevenson, *Documents of the Marriage Liturgy* (Collegeville, MN: The Liturgical Press, 1992).

[21] Decree Tametsi, in H.J. Schroeder, *Councils and Decrees of the Council of Trent* (St. Louis, MO: B. Herder Book Co., 1941), 180.

procreation, promising them divine help in fulfilling their marital and parental duties, and welcoming them into the hierarchy of institutions that comprised the church.[22]

MEDIEVAL PROHIBITIONS ON REAL POLYGAMY

Canon Law

The medieval canon law texts repeated the conventional theological teaching that marriage was created as a "two in one flesh" union of a man and a woman, and that a Christian marriage symbolized the "mysterious union" of Christ and his church.[23] They repeated the Augustinian argument that marriage is a good institution (offering the goods of children, fidelity, and sacramental stability), even if celibacy and virginity are better. "Marriage populates the world, virginity populates heaven," the *Decretum* put it pithily.[24] And they repeated the traditional view that God had temporarily allowed polygamy (and incest) among the Old Testament patriarchs to enable them to "be fruitful and multiply" and to fill the empty earth.[25] Abraham and Jacob, the canonists said, committed no sin because they took their multiple wives without lust and with their first wife's permission. But Lamech sinned because his polygamy was not divinely authorized. David sinned because he behaved lustfully toward Bathsheba and murdered her husband. And Solomon sinned because he was "immoderate" in collecting a thousand wives and concubines.[26] But now everyone sins who takes a second spouse while the first is still living, for Jesus has restored the natural order of human marriages as "two in one flesh" and embodied that in his mysterious union with his bride, the one holy catholic and apostolic church.[27]

Like the Church Fathers, the medieval canonists treated this move from Old Testament polygamy to New Testament monogamy as a narrative of progress, the

---

[22] See Lombard, *Sentences*, bk. 4, dist. 26; Hugo of St. Victor, *On the Sacraments of the Christian Faith*, trans. Roy J. Deferrari (Cambridge, MA: The Medieval Academy of America, 1951), bk. 2, pt. 11.1–5, 7, 13; see further texts in Mackin, *What Is Marriage*, 20–33, 332–333.

[23] See, e.g., D. 27.1.41; 27.2.1; 29.1; 30.4.1; 32.1.12; 32.7.12; Lombard, Sent., Dist. 33.1–4. The phrase "two in one flesh" appears nine times in the *Decretum* alone. Laurent Mayali, "'Duo erunt in carne una': and the Medieval Canonists," in *Iuris Historia: Liber Amicorum Gero Delozalek* (Berkeley, CA: The Robbins Collection, 2008), 161–175, at 167.

[24] D. 32.1.12.

[25] As Alanus Anglicus put it: "sex with a second wife or concubine was allowed by a divine miracle, although it would be contrary to the natural law." Quoted in James A. Brundage, *Law, Sex, and Christian Society in the Middle Ages* (Chicago, IL: University of Chicago Press, 1987), 407.

[26] See D. 29.1; 31.1.7; 31.1.10; 32.2.2.; 32.4.1–4; 32.4.13; 32.7.12; 32.7.18–27.

[27] X 4.19.8.

discovery and development of a more refined understanding of Christian virtue.[28]
Polygamy, the argument went, was virtuous in more primitive communities, like
those of the Old Testament, where children were the principal goal of marriage,
and when many children were the most coveted sign of divine blessing. Even priests
were married in those early days to set an example for the rest.[29] But monogamy is
now the prescribed norm and form of marriage for advanced Christian civilizations.
For God now grows his church not only by the birth of new children, but especially
by the "rebirth" of new converts. And God calls his priests and nuns to be exemplars,
not of marriage, but of chastity and virginity, in imitation of Christ and the Virgin
Mary and in anticipation of heaven, where, as Jesus put it, "there will be no marriage
or giving in marriage." As the *Decretum* put it:

> For different times the Creator has different dispensations. The promise to Abraham
> was that in his seed all nations would be blessed, and that his seed would possess
> the land of his sojourning. So, leaving others in idolatry, the Lord chose Abraham
> and his sons for himself as a people peculiarly his own. Abraham rightly sought the
> multiplication of the people of God from the fecundity of many women, because
> the succession of the flesh was also the succession of the faith. Hence it said in the
> Law, "Cursed be the barren woman who does not leave offspring on the earth." For
> this reason the marriage of priests was ordered, so that through family succession
> would come succession to office.

> But, as the grace of faith was spread to all through the incarnation of Christ, it
> did not say, "Say to the house of Judah and the house of Israel," but rather "Go,
> therefore, make disciples of all nations" and "In every nation, he who fears God
> and does what is right is acceptable to him." Nor is election to the promise found
> in succession of race, but in perfect life and sincere knowledge, and as virginity is
> preferred to fecundity, chaste continence is ordered for priests.

> So Abraham and Jacob did no wrong in seeking children from slave women other
> than their wives. But now, no one may, after their example, seek fecundity in another
> woman, outside the conjugal debt [of monogamous marriage]. Their marriages are
> not to be equated with ours, or to be preferred to virginity. Nor should immoderate
> use of marriage in our time imitate the disgraceful fornication of those times.[30]

In 1201, Pope Innocent III offered a similar argument about the move from
polygamy to monogamy, and firmly prohibited real polygamy anew:

> It is read that the patriarchs and other just men, both before and after the Law, had
> many wives at once. The Gospel or Law does not seem to command the contrary....

[28] See discussion of the Church Fathers in Chapter 2, pp. 85–92.
[29] D. c. 32.7.27, quoting Augustine's *The Good of Marriage*.
[30] D. c. 32.4.2, referencing Genesis 12:3, 7; Deuteronomy 7:14; Matthew 28:19; Acts 10:35; 1 Corinthians 7:8.

But this seems contrary and hostile to the Christian faith. From the beginning one rib was turned into one woman, and divine Scripture testifies that for this case a man shall leave his father and mother, and cleave to his wife, and the two shall be one flesh. It did not say, "three or more," but "two." It did not say, "will cling to his wives," but, "to his wife...."

That truth may prevail over falsehood, we assert without any hesitation that it was never lawful for anyone to have several wives at once, unless it was allowed them by divine revelation....

This true opinion is shown by the truthful testimony given witness to it in the Gospel: "Whoever puts away his wife, except for fornication, and marries another, commits adultery." So if one cannot lawfully take another when a wife is sent away, even more obviously he cannot do so when she is kept. So it is evident that plural marriage is reprobated for either sex, since they cannot be judged differently.[31]

This 1201 papal pronouncement against polygamy was included in the *Decretals* of 1234, the most authoritative canon law text after Gratian, and it was subject to numerous conciliar echoes and juridical commentaries thereafter.[32] The Second Council of Lyon (1274), for example, stated clearly that "one man is not permitted to have several wives, nor one woman several husbands at the same time."[33] Raymond of Penyafort's *Summa on Marriage*, the standard text for law students and theology students throughout the Middle Ages, was equally clear: "Marriage is the union of a man and a woman, maintaining an undivided manner of life," Raymond wrote, echoing the Roman law. "It does not say 'of men and a woman' or 'of a man and women' because one man cannot have many wives at once or one woman many husbands." "It is clear that it was never licit to have many wives at the same time" save through the "divine dispensation" granted to the "ancient Patriarchs" who were temporarily "excused from adultery." But in our day, it is an act of "adultery" for a man or woman or woman to enter into "double contracts" for marriage, and such an act must be "sternly punished."[34]

---

[31] X. 4.19.8.

[32] See, e.g., Gottofredo da Trani, *Summa super titulis decretalium* (1519), repr. ed. (Aalen: Scientia Verlag, 1968), 40r-42r; Innocent IV, *Commentaria: apparatus in V libros Decretalium* (1570), repr. ed. (Frankfurt am Main: Minerva, 1968), title 21 ("de bigamis"); Rufinus, *Summa Decretorum*, ed. Heinrich Singer (Aalen: Scientia Verlag, 1963), 429–536; Hostiensis, *Summa Aurea* (1519), ed. Nicolai Superantii, repr. ed. (Aalen: Scientia Verlag, 1962), 40–43 ("de bigamia"); Ioannis Montaigne, Tractatus de utraque bigamia, in *Tractatus Universi Juris*, 16 vols. (Venice, 1584), vol. 9, folios 121v-132r.

[33] Heinrich Denzinger, *The Sources of Catholic Dogma*, 30th ed., trans. Roy J. Deferrari (St. Louis: B. Herder, 1957), p. 185, item 465.

[34] Raymond of Penyafort, *Summa on Marriage*, trans. Pierre J. Payer (Toronto: Pontifical Institute of Medieval Studies, 2005), 1.6, 2.1, 10.3, 10.13, 13.1–3. See also Raymond Penyafort, *Summa de iure canonico*, ed. X. Ochoa and A. Diez (Rome: Commentarium pro religiosis 1975), pt. 2, title 5 and 22S. Raimundus de Pennaforte, *Summa de Paenitentia*, ed. X. Ochoa and A. Diez (Rome: Commentarium

The church's most authoritative statement against polygamy came in the Council of Trent's decree of 1563, directed in part against a few early Protestant polygamists and a few sympathetic apologists for polygamy, both Catholic and Protestant.[35] In its Decree Tametsi, the Council declared that both the preaching and the practice of polygamy were serious crimes and heresies:

> If anyone says that it is lawful for Christians to have several wives at the same time, and that it is not forbidden by any divine law (Matt. 19:4ff.), let him be anathema.[36]

Medieval church courts prosecuted cases of real polygamy with growing alacrity after the thirteenth century, Sara McDougall and others have shown, with the volume of church court cases against polygamy reaching their apex in the fifteenth century.[37] Church courts could not shed blood, mutilate, or execute criminals as their secular counterparts could. But they could order the secular authorities to torture recalcitrant or rebellious defendants to extract confessions.[38] And they could mete out a range of "spiritual punishments" for convicted polygamists, in addition to dissolving their invalid marriages, which often had the effect of illegitimating and disinheriting any children born of the same. For less serious cases of convicted polygamy, medieval church courts ordered fines, short prison sentences, pilgrimages, and various good works of penance and purgation. For more serious cases, they ordered convicted polygamists to make public confessions, to wear humiliating signs or clothing testifying to their crime, to endure various shame rituals like processing around town with a whip at their heels or standing on a raised ladder or scaffold to be subjected to public ridicule. The most serious offenders were sentenced to the bishop's prison for several years or consigned to row in a ship's galleys, were banished after their property was confiscated, or occasionally sent to the secular authorities for execution. A number of recent case studies of medieval church courts around Europe have provided illuminating windows on a rather brisk and sometimes brutal medieval practice of punishing real polygamists.[39]

Much to the consternation of both bishops and secular authorities who competed with them, the Inquisitions in Spain, Italy, Portugal, France, the Lowlands, and

---

pro religiosis, 1976) includes provisions on rape, adultery, polygamy, concubinage, prostitution, illegitimacy, and other sexual offenses that require confession. Ibid., bk. 2, title 5; bk. 3, title 3, 19, 30. bk.

[35] See discussions later in this chapter and in Chapter 5.

[36] Denzinger, *The Sources of Catholic Dogma*, p. 296, item no. 972.

[37] See analysis and detailed primary and secondary sources in Sara McDougall, *Bigamy and Christian Identity in Late Medieval Champagne* (Philadelphia: University of Pennsylvania Press, 2012) with a summary in id., "The Punishment of Bigamy in Late Medieval Troyes," *Medium Aevum* 3 (2009): 189–204.

[38] John H. Langbein, *Torture and the Law of Proof: Europe and England in the ancien régime* (Chicago, IL: University of Chicago Press, 1974).

[39] See analysis and detailed sources in McDougall, *Bigamy*, 37–41, 97–137.

beyond also claimed jurisdiction over polygamy on grounds that polygamy was heresy, blasphemy, and perjury at once. As the Spanish Grand Inquisitor Tomás de Torquemada (1420–1498) put it, polygamy was "primarily an offense against the laws of God, and a defilement of the sacrament of marriage," and therefore needed to be expurgated root and branch.[40] In the fifteenth and sixteenth centuries, the Inquisition – eventually on both sides of the Atlantic[41] – worked hard to identify and punish polygamists. In less serious cases, they issued spiritual punishments much like the church courts. But in more serious cases of brazen or repeated polygamy by a remorseless defendant, the Inquisition could order execution by burning (live at the stake or in effigy). Their most frequent punishment was whipping and five to seven years of service in the galleys.[42] After the church's 1563 pronouncement of "anathema" on polygamy, the Inquisition stepped up its prosecution and imposed firmer sentences in places like Spain and Portugal; indeed, in some Spanish cities, up to a quarter of all Inquisition cases in the later sixteenth century concerned real polygamy.[43] But elsewhere prosecution for polygamy increasingly shifted to the secular authorities.[44]

Secular Law

Real polygamy was not only a serious spiritual offense, but also a serious secular crime in many parts of the West – save England, which left polygamy to the church courts until 1604.[45] The civil law nations on the Continent came to view polygamy,

---

[40] Quoted by Rafael Sabatini, *Torquemada and the Spanish Inquisition* (London: Stanley Paul, 1924), 168.

[41] On the operation in Spanish North America, see Chapter 10, p. 392.

[42] See detailed sources and discussion in Henry Kamen, *The Spanish Inquisition: An Historical Revision* (New Haven/London: Yale University Press, 1997), 75–80, 201, 265–267; Kim Seibenhüner, *Bigamie und Inquisition in Italien 1600–1750* (Paderborn: Ferdinand Schöningh, 2006); Allyson M. Poska, "When Bigamy is the Charge: Gallegan Women and the Holy Office," in Mary E. Giles, ed., *Women and the Inquisition: Spain and the New World* (Baltimore, MD: The Johns Hopkins University Press, 1999), 189–208. See additional sources in McDougall, "The Punishment of Bigamy."

[43] Kamen, *The Spanish Inquisition*, 265ff.; Isabel M. R. Mendes, *Bigamia em Portugal na época moderna* (Libson: Hugin, 2003); William Monter, *Frontiers of Heresy; The Spanish Inquisition from the Basque Lands to Sicily* (Cambridge, MA: Harvard University Press, 1990), 34, and Appendix 2, 328.

[44] For Italy, see Trevor Dean, "A Regional Cluster? Italian Secular Laws on Abduction, Forced, and Clandestine Marriage (Fourteenth and Fifteenth Centuries)," in Mia Korpiola, ed., *Regional Variations in Matrimonial Law and Custom in Europe, 1150–1600* (Leiden/Boston: Brill, 2011), 147–159; Cecilia Cristellon and Silvana Seidel Menchi, "Rituals Before Tribunals in Renaissance Italy: Continuity and Change, 1400–1600, in ibid., 275–287; Pierroberto Scaramella, "Controllo e repression ecclesiastica della poligamia a Napoli in età moderna: dalle cause matrimoniali al crimine di fede (1514–1799), in *Trasgessioni: Seduzione, concubinato, adulterio, bigamia (XIV-XVIII secolo)*, ed. Silvana Seidel Menchi and Deigo Quaglioni (Bologna: Il Mulino, 2004), 443–501 [hereafter "Trasgressio"].

[45] For English common law developments, see Chapter 7, pp. 290–293.

along with adultery, as grave offenses against God, nature, and the innocent spouse and children at once.[46] These nations drew on the Roman criminal laws against polygamy from the third to the sixth centuries, and sometimes drew on Germanic law as well. The classical Roman law texts, newly discovered in Europe in the late eleventh century, were the starting point for legal education in the new European universities, and the texts on polygamy came in for repeated glosses and then commentaries by the medieval civilians. By the fifteenth century, standard civil law commentaries listed polygamy either as a separate sex crime or as a special form of adultery and perjury. And their authors called for convicted polygamists to be sentenced to fines, flogging, bodily mutilation (including castration), hard labor, banishment, or execution.[47]

As European secular polities stabilized and strengthened after the twelfth century, a growing number of city and regional governments passed their own criminal prohibitions against polygamy, alongside the laws of the church, usually calling for sterner corporal punishments than the church courts allowed.[48] A few nation-states followed suit. In medieval Sweden, for example, new royal laws made intentional polygamy a capital crime to be punished by "decapitation for the male, stoning or burning for a female."[49] Doubly engaged parties, or those who sought to betroth an already engaged or married party, had to pay hefty fines to the injured party, the king, the hundred, and the bishop at once. The late medieval Swedish secular courts, Mia Korpiola has shown, heard a good number of polygamy cases, most leading to execution.[50]

---

[46] See Ludwig von Bar, *A History of Continental Criminal Law*, trans. Thomas S. Bell et al. (Boston: Little Brown, 1916), 102–103, 169–171, 286.

[47] See a good distillation of this learning in Diego Garzia de Trasmiera, *De Polygamia et Polyviria libri tres* (Palermo: Apud Decium Cyrillum, 1638), a massive three-volume setting out the law and literature on every conceivable form of plural union. For a good summary of the late medieval *ius commune* on real polygamy, see Giuliano Marchetto, " 'Primus fuit Lamech': La bigamia tra irregolarità a delitto nella dottrina di diritto commune," in *Trasgessioni*, 43–106, esp. 8off.

[48] See, e.g., the Statute of Bologna, 4.33, in Gina Fasoli and Pietro Sella, *Statuti di Bologna dell'anno 1288* (Vatican City: Biblioteca apostolica vaticana, 1937–1939), 1:197 and 1287 Statute of Ferrara, 4.55, in William Montorsi, ed., *Statuta Ferrari, Anno MCCLXXXVII*, 4.55 (Ferrara: Casa di risparmio di Ferrra, 1955), 271. See Brundage, *Law, Sex, and Christian Society*, 478, 539–540; Anna Esposito, "Adulterio, concubinato, bigamia: testimonianze della normativa statutaria della Stato pontificio (secoli XIII-XVI), in *Trasgessioni*, 21–42; Stefano Riccio, *La Bigamia* (Naples: Dott. Eugenio Jovene, 1934), 23–24.

[49] Mia Korpiola, "Rethinking Incest and Heinous Sexual Crime: Changing Boundaries of Secular and Ecclesiastical Jurisdiction in Late Medieval Sweden," in Anthony Musson, ed., *Boundaries of the Law: Geography, Gender, and Jurisdiction in Medieval and Early Modern Europe* (Aldershot: Ashgate, 2005), 102–117, at 111.

[50] Mia Korpiola, *Between Betrothal and Bedding: Marriage Formation in Sweden 1200–1600* (Leiden/ Boston: Brill, 2009), 14, 186, 213–217, 328–331; id., "Marriage Causes in Late Medieval Sweden: The Evidence of Bishop Hans Brask's Register (1522–1527)," in Korpiola, ed., *Regional Variations*, 212–247.

One of the most influential and enduring secular laws against polygamy came in the massive Spanish legal code, *Las Siete Partidas* (1250–1284) of Alfonso X of Castile. Influenced by both classical Roman law and medieval canon law learning, this code listed polygamy – whether double marriages or double engagements – as a separate sex crime:

> Men who knowingly marry a second time while their first wives are living commit manifest wickedness, and women do the same thing when aware that their first husbands are living. There are other men, who being betrothed by words relating to the present time, disregard this, and become betrothed to, and marry other women; and there are still others, being betrothed as we stated above, although they do not marry, know when women to whom they are betrothed marry others, and keep silent and permit the marriages to take place; or they themselves marry them to others who are cognizant of this. And, for the reason that from such marriages against God arise many sins and injuries, and losses and great dishonor happen to those that are deceived in this way....
>
> Therefore we order that anyone who knowingly contracts marriage in any of the ways we mentioned in this law, shall be banished to some island for the term of five years, and shall lose whatever property he possessed in the place where he contracted the marriage, and it shall belong to his son or grandson if he has any.[51]

This and related medieval Spanish prohibitions on polygamy remained in place until the nineteenth century, both in Spain and in its far flung colonial empire, especially in Central and Latin America as well as Spanish North America.[52]

By the early sixteenth century – even before the Protestant Reformation shifted many laws from the church to the state – secular criminal laws against polygamy were commonplace on the Continent, and many of the prosecutions for real polygamy were shifting from church courts to state courts. A highly influential example was the 1532 *Constitutio Criminalis Carolina*, passed for the Holy Roman Empire and drawn in large part from the earlier German code, the *Bambergensis* of 1507:

> When a married man takes another wife or a married woman another husband into holy marriage before their first marriage is over, this is a grave crime that is more serious than adultery. Although the imperial law has so far not imposed corporal sanctions on this crime, we proclaim that hereafter anyone who willingly and knowingly commits such a fraudulent crime, must be criminally punished at

---

[51] Robert I. Burns, ed., *Las Siete partidas*, 5 vols. trans. Samuel Parsons Scott (Philadelphia: University of Pennsylvania Press, 2001), vol. 5, Part 7, Title 17, Law 16, pp. 1419–1420.

[52] On the long history of anti-polygamy statutes in Spain, see http://noticias.juridicas.com/articulos/ 45-Derecho%20Civil/200504-3655132531051141.html. See also the Fuero Juzgo (ca. 1241), Part I, bk. 3, ch. 2 http://www.cervantesvirtual.com/servlet/SirveObras/80272752878794052754491/thm0000.htm.

a level no less than an adulterer is punished [adultery was a capital offense at the time].[53]

The *Carolina's* prohibition on polygamy was echoed in numerous local ordinances in the Empire, France, Italy, and the Lowlands. Catholic Poland and Protestant Hungary spared polygamists from execution, but ordered them stripped of their properties and banished for good.[54]

THE MEDIEVAL CRITIQUE OF MUSLIM POLYGAMY

It was not just the polygamy of Old Testament Jews, or modern-day philanderers, that concerned medieval writers. More disconcerting to them was the polygamy of Islam, the formidable civilization that pressed hard on the boundaries of medieval Christendom – in southern Spain, in northern Africa, and in the Middle East and Eurasia. By the mid-twelfth century, Western Christian scholars knew a good bit about this vast and sophisticated Islamic world through trade and commerce, through crusaders and explorers, through scholarly literature and exchanges.[55] They knew that Islamic law permitted pious men of sufficient means to take up to four wives in imitation of the Prophet Mohammed and unilaterally divorce and remarry up to three times.[56] From the twelfth century onward, the canon law made clear that a Muslim convert to Christianity would have to retain only his first wife, and dismiss any others.[57] Several medieval church councils also limited severely the "ruinous

53 Joseph Kohler and Willy Scheel, eds., *Die Peinliche Gerichtsordnung Kaiser Karls V: Constitutio Criminalis Carolina* (Halle: Buchhandlung des Waisenhauses, 1900), art. 121. See good discussion of the prototypes, applications, and local echoes of this important law in Johann S.F. von Boehmer, *Meditationes in Constitutionem Criminalem Carolinam* (Halle/Madeburg: Impensis Vidvae Gebaveri et Filii, 1774), 469–482. For context, see John H. Langbein, *Prosecuting Crime in the Renaissance: England, Germany, France* (Cambridge, MA: Harvard University Press, 1974).

54 See Johann Christoph Theodor Hellbach, *Selecta Criminalia eaque iam de Marito Hebraico Christiano, una uxore non contento* (Arnstadii: Schill, 1747), with samples of several cases, commentaries, and consilia in the appendix, ibid., 307–475; Transmiera, *De Polygamia et Polyviria*. See several case studies and sources in Korpiola, ed., *Regional Variations*; Jean François Poudret, *Coutumes et coutumieres: histoire comparative des droits des pays romands du XIIIe à la fin du XVIe siècle*, 5 vols. (Bern: Staempli Editions, 1998–2002), 3:24ff.

55 For medieval Christian accounts about the growth of Islam, see sources in *Corpus Scriptorum Muzarabicorum*, ed. Johannes Gil, 2 vols. (Madrid: Consejo superior de investigaciones scientificas, 1973). See discussion in Peter Biller, *The Measure of Multitude: Population in Medieval Thought* (Oxford: Oxford University Press, 2000), 76–81; Jonathan Lyon, *Islam Through Western Eyes: From the Crusades to the War on Terrorism* (New York: Columbia University Press, 2012), 43–72; N. David, "Crusades and Propaganda," in *A History of the Crusades*, 6 vols., ed. K. M. Setton (Madison: University of Wisconsin Press, 1989), 6:39–97.

56 See Islamic texts in the Introduction, pp. 18–20. For medieval discussions of this time, see, e.g., Peter Alfonsi, *Dialogue Against the Jews* [1109], trans. Irven M. Resnick (Washington, DC: Catholic University of America Press, 2006), title 5, p. 148.

57 X 4.19.8. See also Raymond of Penyafort, *Summa on Marriage*, 2.1, 10.1, 10.3, 13 pr. For later individual concessions made to polygamous converts, see Francis J. Burton, *A Commentary on Canon 1125*

commingling" of Muslims and Christians, including within the household.[58] But what was the argument against the polygamy of a people who did not accept the Christian Bible, or the canon law, or the church's authority?

Polygamy as Backward

Some medieval writers retooled the traditional narrative of progress argument to heap scorn upon Muslim polygamy. Muslim polygamists, early polemicists wrote, were "backward," "primitive," "barbaric," "lustful," "adulterous," and "incestuous."[59] They were "perennially ensnared by carnal lures" wrote French theologian, Jacques de Vitry (ca. 1160–1240), and "infected" by the same "sultry heat" of the desert that had misled Old Testament figures like Lamech and David to multiply wives out of "murderous lust." Like those ancient, primitive people of the Old Testament, Muslims today regard the procreation of many children as the highest virtue. "Among them, the more [women] a man can impregnate, the more religious he is regarded," wrote de Vitry. In fact, Muslims commit "adultery as if by divine command," and "mingle with their wives and concubines more frequently during a [religious] fast, either to satiate their lust, or so they can generate more children for the defense of their law."[60] The rapid growth of Islam that has resulted from this "excessive procreation" is "a peril to the church," warned Peter the Venerable (ca. 1092–1156). Islam already occupies "almost half the world" and its "great multitude" "threatens to crush the smallness of the Christian people."[61] Such fear-mongering was an effective tool of the crusaders and their propagandists in the eleventh through thirteenth centuries who bore down on Jerusalem and the Holy

---

Together with a History of the Legislation Contained in the Canon (Washington, DC: Catholic University of America Press, 1940), 30–62.

[58] Third Lateran Council (1179), canons 24, 25 and Fourth Lateran Council (1215), canons 68 and 70 in H.J. Schroeder, *Disciplinary Decrees of the General Councils: Text, Translation, and Commentary* (St. Louis, MO: B. Herder Book Co., 1937), 232–234, 290, 294–296. See additional examples in Andrew Holt and James Muldoon, *Fighting Words: Competing Voices from the Crusades* (Westport, CT: Greenwood World Publishing, 2008), 259–274, and discussion of the papacy's evolving attitudes toward Islam in James Muldoon, *Popes, Lawyers, and Infidels: The Church and the Non-Christian World, 1250–1550* (Philadelphia: University of Pennsylvania Press, 1979).

[59] The language is in Paul Alvarus, *Indiculus luminosus* [c. 854], reprinted in *Corpus Scriptorum Muzarabicorum*, 1:270–315; *Memoriale Sanctorum*, II.2–8, in ibid., 2:398–415. See also Alfonsi, *Dialogue*, 161, 169, and John Victor Tolan, *Petrus Alfonsi and his Medieval Readers* (Gainesville: University Press of Florida, 2003); Biller, *The Measure*, 83–85.

[60] Jacques de Vitry, *Historia orientalis*, I.vi, pp. 25–30, using the quoted excerpts in Biller, *The Measure*, 83–85, and parallel language from Peter the Venerable, quoted in J. Kritzeck, *Peter the Venerable and Islam* (Princeton, NJ: Princeton University Press, 1964), 137. See also Lyon, *The Western Idea of Islam*, 68, 71–72.

[61] Ibid.; with other quotes in Kritzeck, *Peter the Venerable*, 205, 210; Daniel, "Crusader Propaganda," 6:49; Biller, *The Multitude*, 80–81.

Land – not just to recover the birthplace of Christ but also to vanquish a formidable and growing "enemy of Christ" as they saw Islam.[62]

This would become an enduring argument against Muslim polygamy in the Western legal tradition. It flipped on its head the narrative of progress argument from the Old Testament to the New Testament. Having multiple wives and children was a virtue in primitive civilizations, the revised argument went, but it is now a vice in our more advanced day. The Old Testament patriarchs, like Abraham and Jacob, were virtuous because they operated with God's permission. Muslim polygamists do not know the true God, and are thus operating on their own lustful license. The Old Testament polygamists were trying to fill the empty world with God's chosen people who had been promised to Abraham and his legitimate seed. Muslim polygamists are trying to fill an already crowded earth with new enemies of Christ, whose law forbids them to convert to Christianity. The Old Testament patriarchs like Abraham took multiple wives not out of lust but out of respect for the wishes of his faithful wife, Sarah. Muslim polygamists operate only with zealous lust, and their first wives could never have agreed to become a subordinate or rival to a second wife, let alone a third or a fourth.

This argument about the cultural superiority of monogamy over polygamy would also become a staple in the broader Western case against polygamy. It recurred frequently as early modern colonists and missionaries faced indigenous polygamy in America, Africa, and Asia,[63] and then as nineteenth-century Americans sought to stamp out the polygamy of Mormons, Native Americans, Asian migrants, and enslaved African-Americans.[64] The origins of this argument lay in the biblical theology of the Church Fathers, who had developed it as a hermeneutical tool to explain why polygamy had been licit in the Old Testament world but was now illicit in the New. In the High Middle Ages, however, this simple exegetical move became an argument of cultural superiority designed to depict all current-day polygamists as backward, even "barbaric."

---

[62] See examples in Holt and Muldoon, *Fighting Words*; and vast sources and discussion in Christopher Tyerman, *God's War: A New History of the Crusades* (Cambridge, MA: Harvard University Press, 2006). See also texts in Jacqueline Murray, ed., *Love, Marriage, and Family in the Middle Ages: A Reader* (Toronto: Broadview Press, 2001), 502–505.

[63] See, e.g., Adhemar Esmein, *Le mariage en droit canonique*, 2 vols., repr. ed. (New York: Burt Franklin, 1968), 2:267–273; James Muldoon, ed., *The Spiritual Conversion of the Americas* (Gainesville: University Press of Florida, 2004); James Muldoon, *The Americas in the Spanish World Order: The Justification for Conquest in the Seventeenth Century* (Philadelphia: University of Pennsylvania Press, 1994); Thomas S. Kidd, *American Christians and Islam: Evangelical Culture and Muslims from the Colonial Period to the Age of Terrorism* (Princeton, NJ: Princeton University Press, 2009).

[64] See discussion in Chapter 10, pp. 429–439.

Polygamy as Harmful

William of Auvergne (ca. 1180–1249), Bishop of Paris, offered a second argument against Muslim polygamy that would also become a staple of the broader Western case against polygamy. The heart of William's argument was that the "bent love" of polygamy, as he called it, harmed men, women, children, and society alike. William started with the proposition that "nature puts males and females in the human species almost at the same level in number, without perceptible or observable excess." "Sometimes males, sometimes females die by disease or by the sword beyond the intention of nature." Sometimes there are more men than women who choose the celibate religious life. Sometimes it is the other way around. But, in the usual course, there is one man for each woman. Polygamy, by definition, "upsets this natural balance" of one-to-one sex ratios, said William. For inevitably, if one powerful or wealthy polygamist hordes more than his "natural share" of women, that will leave other men in sharper competition for the fewer women who are left. Some men will inevitably lose out altogether, and will resort to violence, fraud, and intrigue, as well as to prostitution, adultery, rape, and abduction, all to the harm of existing families and to the exploitation of girls and women. "Natural equity" thus commends monogamy over polygamy.[65]

Moreover, William continued, polygamous households can become independent powers that rival and distort the rule of legitimate political powers. Aristotle had properly seen that the "household is the foundation of the polis." And the Bible had properly defined this household to be monogamous. "What a nest is" among pair-bonding birds "is what a house is among humans," William argued. "Just as one male and one female hatch their young in one nest," eventually producing a flock of birds that mingle and migrate together, "so only one man and one woman generate in each house. Through marriage, male and female leave father and mother and cleave to each other in order to build another house for themselves." Monogamous marriages respect "the limits and the constrictions of means and affluence" of each household so that their eventual collection yields an organized and governable community.[66] By contrast, Muslim polygamous households try "to enclose cities within the narrow confines of individual houses. In their wretched blindness they conflate city and house, since they do not try to build a house before a city, but a city … within a house." This is just developmentally backwards, William

[65] William of Auvergne, "De Sacramento Matrimonii," in *Guilielmi Alverni Opera Omnia*, 2 vols. (Paris, 1674; repr. ed., Frankfurt am Main: G.m.b.H., 1963), 1:512–528, at 516–518. My discussion of William draws heavily on Biller's analysis in ibid., 19–110. I am grateful to my colleague, Philip L. Reynolds, for bringing William's and Biller's works to my attention.

[66] William of Auvergne, "De Sacramento Matrimonii," 523–524.

concluded, and inevitably results in the perpetuation of rival families and tribes not the development of a well-governed civilization.[67]

While some polygamous households become rival independent powers, William continued, just as many of them fail miserably, to the great harm of wives and children. The wives themselves must deal largely on their own with "the great pain of childbirth, the unhappiness of [other] pregnant women, the hard work and misery of feeding" and tending to their children without enough resources or help. The man, in turn, must work doubly hard to try to support all "the pregnant, child bearing, and breast-feeding women, while similarly looking after, feeding, and educating the many children." "It is obvious to those who look carefully into this, that a man of any condition, power, or wealth is overburdened" with a polygamous family. "Even a powerful and wealthy prince could hardly provide for [say] twelve children decently and competently in a way which was appropriate.... One could hardly find a man and a woman taking twelve children through to adult age while rearing them and instructing and providing for them in every way."[68] A rational and calculating man will understand this reality, of course, William's later commentators added, and this will inevitably lead him to harm his own children and commit grave moral offenses in so doing. He will either "spill his seed" upon the ground for fear of yet another pregnancy, or induce an abortion of an unwanted child. If a less than perfect child comes forth, he will smother it on birth, or sell it on the slave market with modest prospects of survival. Women and children thus suffer harm disproportionately in a polygamous household.[69]

Finally, William argued, polygamy will sometimes harm the man of the house, too. Not only will his energies and resources be dissipated upon so many competing women and children with their heavy demands. Not only will the prospect of adding new women to his harem inevitably and perennially "inflame his lust" for more – a temptation to which even the great King David succumbed in his lust for Bathsheba, bringing shame and devastation to his household and ultimately to the whole nation of Israel.[70] But ultimately, the excessive lust and sex that is endemic to a polygamist's life will actually decrease rather than increase the man's fertility. Reflecting a common biological belief of his day about the effects of too much sex, William wrote:

---

[67]   Ibid., 524. See also William of Auvergne, "De Legibus," in id., *Opera Omnia*, 1:18–102 at 53–54, and discussion and other texts quoted in Biller, *The Measure*, 72–73, 86.

[68]   William of Auverne, "De Sacramento Matrimonii, 524–526; see also Biller, *The Measure*, 72–73.

[69]   Ibid.

[70]   See more generally Albrecht Quentin, *Naturkenntnisse und Naturanschauungen bei Wilhelm bei Auvergne* (Hildesheim: Gerstenberg, 1976); Helmut Borok, *Der Tugenbegriff des Wilhelm von Auvergne (1180–1249)* (Düsseldorf: Patmos Verlag, 1979). For William's ties to Thomas Aquinas, see Amato Masnovo, *Da Gugliemo d'Auvergne a S. Tomasso d'Aquino*, 2nd ed., 3 vols. (Milan: Societa editrice Vita e Pensioro, 1945–1946).

Through its increase and vehemence the pursuit of sexual pleasure impedes the fruit of generation. For those who burn mostly with this sort of concupiscence are of little generation, or little or no fruit, and they are quickly rendered sterile and inept for generation. [This happens] either for this reason, that the seed of generation is consumed in the heat of such ardour, or because the frequency of such sexual mingling stops seed of this sort coalescing into life. This occurs in prostitute women, who rarely or never conceive.[71]

William of Auvergne's arguments against the "bent love" of polygamy presupposed biblical and canonical teachings about marriage and sexual morality. These he spelled out in detail in his massive tomes *On the Sacrament of Marriage, On Law,* and *On Virtue.*[72] But the enduring power of his argument against polygamy for the Western legal tradition lay in its appeal to the principle of harm against women, children, men, and society. William only sketched the outlines of this argument. He sometimes traded on sociological and biological assumptions that have not held up. And he ultimately could not decide whether polygamy caused too much or too little procreation, leading to some incoherence in his overall presentation. But his basic argument that polygamy causes sundry harms would become a powerful and permanent part of the Western case against polygamy. This was not just a medieval Christian theological quarrel with Muslims. This was a general legal and moral argument against a form of human reproduction that was considered to be inherently harmful, regardless of who practiced it or why they believed in it. Eventually, as we shall see in later chapters, Protestant theologians and Enlightenment liberal philosophers alike would use a similar argument from harm to denounce the experiments of later polygamists, including those of a few enterprising Christians.[73]

POLYGAMY AS UNNATURAL: THE SHIFTING NATURAL LAW ARGUMENTS

An additional reason for the enduring power of William's argument was that he appealed to the nature of human sexuality and to the natural patterns of human procreation. Natural arguments for and against polygamy had long been a divisive topic in the Western legal tradition.[74] The Church Fathers, we saw, had split on this issue. Fathers of peerless repute, like Ambrose and Basil, had condemned polygamy as "unnatural," "a beastly thing," a "violation of natural law." Other Fathers of equal orthodoxy, like Augustine and Chrysostom, had said that polygamy was "perfectly

---

[71] William of Auvergne, "De Sacramento Matrimonii," 524.

[72] William of Auvergne, "De Virtutibus," in *Opera Omnia*, 1:102–119.

[73] See discussion in Chapters 5 and 9.

[74] For patristic and scholastic sources for and against the view that polygamy is "unnatural" or "against natural law," see Montaigne, *De Bigamia*, 125r-126r.

natural" and "consistent with the natural law."[75] More was at stake in this division of opinion than idle taxonomy. "Crimes against nature" or "against natural law" were deadly serious business in the medieval and early modern world. They were mortal sins that required massive penance and severe criminal punishment as well as social evils that could trigger wars and crusades if pervasive enough.[76]

Medieval writers tried in various ways both to lower the stakes and to harmonize the contradictory teachings of the first millennium about natural law and polygamy. One technique was to distinguish between different forms of natural law. If natural law is defined as "what nature teaches all animals," then there is no question that polygamy is natural.[77] Prides of lions, herds of antelopes, even clutches of chickens all feature one dominant male and a harem of females. But if natural law is defined as the Golden Rule – "Do unto others as you would have them do to you," a teaching shared by Jews, Christians, and Muslims alike[78] – then polygamy is contrary to natural law. "A husband would by no means be willing for his wife to have another husband," Thomas Aquinas wrote. "Therefore, he would be acting against the law of nature, were he to have another wife in addition."[79] Similarly, if natural law is defined as the laws and customs common to all people, then polygamy and monogamy are both natural. "What is common to all peoples is marriage, not a single form of marriage," wrote Franciscan theologian, Alexander of Hales (d. 1245), noting the polygamy of historical Jews and current-day Muslims.[80] But if natural law is defined as the law of right reason directed to the common good, then polygamy is unnatural. More goods are enjoyed in common by men, women, and children in monogamous households than in polygamous ones.[81]

A second technique was to contrast the primary and secondary precepts of the natural law. Primary natural law precepts deal with activities that are primal, inescapable; one cannot help but obey them. For example, each person must eat, drink, and sleep to survive. Secondary natural law precepts guide activities consistent with these primary precepts, but which "vary according to the various persons, times, and circumstances." These activities are not "binding in all cases, but only in the majority."[82] So: primary precepts command that everyone must eat, drink, and sleep,

---

[75] See discussion on pp. 82–92.
[76] On the latter, see James Muldoon, *The Americas in the Spanish World Order: The Justification for Conquest in the Seventeenth Century* (Philadelphia: University of Pennsylvania Press, 1994), 78–95; Gerald Herman, "The 'Sin Against Nature' and its Echoes in Medieval French Literature," *Annuale Mediaevale* 17 (1976): 70–87.
[77] Dig., 1.1; Inst., bk. 1, ch. 2; Isidore, *Etymologies*, bk. 5, ch. 4, n. 1.
[78] See, e.g., sources and discussion in Jacob Neusner and Bruce Chilton, ed., *The Golden Rule: The Ethics of Reciprocity in World Religions* (London: Continuum, 2008).
[79] ST Supp. q. 65, art. 1.
[80] Alexander of Hales, *Glossa in quatuor libros sententiarum Petri Lombardi*, 4 vols. (Florence: Collegium S. Bonaventurae, 1951–1957), bk. 4, dist. 33.1.
[81] Ibid.; Montaigne, *De Bigamia*, 122v–123r.
[82] ST Supp q. 65, art. 2.

or they die. Secondary precepts help determine the appropriate amounts of food, drink, and sleep for each person in different circumstances.[83]

The natural law of procreation is similar, medieval writers argued, but its secondary precepts are more complex. Primary natural law precepts command that the human race must procreate. If no one has children, the human race will die out. Secondary natural law precepts, however, teach that not every person needs to procreate. Some individuals are called to a life of chastity and virginity. Others are called to marriage, and they produce children in substitution for those who do not. In addition, secondary precepts teach that some ways of procreating are more just, healthy, and beneficial than others. After all, children can be produced by rape, fornication, prostitution, concubinage, incest, polygamy, and monogamy alike. Secondary precepts, moreover, teach that procreation means not just conceiving a child, but nurturing, educating, and preparing it for independent life. Animals choose among these various methods of procreation and nurture by following their natural instincts of attraction and revulsion. Humans follow these same natural instincts, too, but they also use their reason and conscience to form norms and habits of moral behavior in response. Those who attend properly to the natural law understand that monogamy is a better form of procreation and nurture than polygamy. For polygamy is harmful to children, women, men, and society (according to the argument by William of Auvergne). Using this distinction, medieval writers concluded that polygamy is "against the natural law, not as regards its first precepts, but as regards the secondary precepts."[84] (They made similar arguments that incest, rape, fornication, prostitution, and concubinage are inferior modes of procreation.)

A third technique that medieval writers used to harmonize first millennium teachings was to distinguish among the "goods" or "goals" that are inherent to marriage – that are part of its nature.[85] Augustine had already forecast this technique by arguing that the natural good of procreation can be achieved both through monogamy and polygamy, but that the supernatural goods of fidelity and sacramental

---

[83] See Philip L. Reynolds, *Food and the Body: Some Peculiar Questions in High Medieval Theology* (Leiden/Boston: Brill Academic Press, 1999).

[84] ST Supp. 65, art. 2. See the summary of other later medieval writers by Francisco Saurez, *De Legibus, ac Deo Legislatore* (1612), bk. 2, ch. 15.25–28, in id., *Selections from Three Works*, 2 vols. (Buffalo: William S. Hein, 1995), 2:303–07, and by Thomas Sanchez, *De sancto matrimonii sacramento disputationun tomi tres* (Antwerp: Heredes Martinii Nutii et Ioannem Meurisum, 1617), bk. 7, folios 265r–269v, building on Aquinas. See also discussion in Marchetto, "Primus fuit Lamech," 6–80; Esmein, *Le Mariage*, 1:70–72. For the use of this primary and secondary precept distinction by early modern Catholic and Protestant writers, see Michael Siricius, *Uxor Una: Ex Jure Naturae et Divino, Moribus Antiquis et Constitutionibus Imperatorum et Regnum. Eruta et Contra Insultus Impugnantium Defensa* (Giessen: Typis et sumptibus Josephi Dieterici Hampelii, 1669), 47ff.

[85] See the detailed discussion in John Witte, Jr., *God's Joust, God's Justice: Law and Religion in the Western Tradition* (Grand Rapids, MI: Wm. B. Eerdmans, 2006), 322–363.

stability at work in a Christian marriage can be achieved only through monogamy.[86] Many medieval writers repeated this argument as they worked through the three Augustinian goods of fidelity, children, and sacrament that both Peter Lombard and Gratian had highlighted in their early collections. A century after Lombard, Thomas Aquinas expanded on this argument:

> Now marriage has for its principal end the begetting and rearing of children, and this end is competent to man according to his generic nature, wherefore it is common to other animals, and thus it is that the *offspring* is assigned as a marriage good. But for its secondary end, as the Philosopher [Aristotle] says, it has among men alone, the community of works that are a necessity of life, as stated above. And in reference to this, they owe one another *fidelity* which is one of the goods of marriage. Furthermore it has another end as regards marriage between believers, namely, the signification of Christ and the Church: and thus the *sacrament* is said to be a marriage good. Wherefore the first end corresponds to the marriage of man inasmuch as he is an animal: the second, inasmuch as he is a man; the third, inasmuch as he is a believer.
>
> Accordingly, plurality of wives neither destroys nor in any way hinders the first end of marriage [procreation], since one man is sufficient to get children of several wives and to rear the children born of them. But though it does not wholly destroy the second end [fidelity], it hinders it considerably, for there cannot easily be peace in a family where several wives are joined to one husband, since one husband cannot suffice to satisfy the requisitions of several wives, and again because the sharing of one occupation is a strife: thus potters quarrel with one another and in like manner the several wives of one husband. The third end [sacrament], it [polygamy] removes altogether, because as Christ is one, so also is the Church one. It is therefore evident from what has been said that plurality of wives is in a way against the law of nature, and in a way not against it.[87]

Moral philosopher, John Duns Scotus, offered a variation on this argument, and then explored the possibility of permissible polygamy. Scotus reduced the goods of marriage to two: a primary good of procreating children and a secondary good of protecting husbands and wives from the sin of sexual association with others. The primary good of procreation alone can be met by polygamy and monogamy alike, said Scotus. A man can easily impregnate one woman or several women in a night. And a woman will get pregnant once every nine months, no matter how many men share her marital bed.[88] Both spouses could thus have multiple spouses,

---

[86] See Augustine's discussion in Chapter 2, pp. 91–93.

[87] ST Supp. q. 65, art. 1.

[88] Aquinas argued that if one woman had sexual intercourse with multiple men, the good or procreation would be "considerably hindered" "because this can scarcely happen without injury to both fetus[es] if not one of them." ST 65, art. 1, reply obj. 8.

and achieve the first good of procreation. But only monogamy can serve the goods of both procreation and protection of the spouses from the sins of sexual association with others. Therefore, in entering their marriage contracts, Scotus argued, "strict justice" or "natural justice" requires "both parties" to "turn in something of their rights when they exchange promises to marry." For God "instituted as a rule that a bodily exchange [in marriage] ought to be between one person and one other person."[89]

Scotus, however, allowed that there might be extreme cases in which a man might have to practice polygamy in violation the secondary good of protection in order to achieve the primary good of procreation. The "natural justice" of polygamy in such cases turned on the extremity of the need and the quality of the permission granted to practice polygamy:

> If in some situation many men fell through war, the sword, or pestilence and there were still more women, bigamy could now be allowed, if one considers justice exclusively on the part of those who exchange and their exchanges. Then women, from their side, would have to be willing to exchange with men by giving more for less, so far as the second aim [of protection from sinful associations with others] is concerned, but equal for equal as far as the first aim [of procreation] is concerned. In terms of a correct analysis, the woman would have to will this so that the good of offspring is achieved by intercourse of her husband with another woman. There would be no deficiency here only if full justice is done, which derives from God's approval, which in this case would certainly occur and would be specifically revealed to the Church.[90]

This was more adventuresome speculation about permissible polygamy than most medieval writers offered.[91] Scotus was suggesting that it could still be naturally just for a man to take another woman into his bed in a case of extreme necessity so long as his wife consents and his action is equitably dispensed. This was the case with Abraham and Sarah who agreed that Hagar should sleep with Abraham in order to produce the children that God had promised them. Scotus did not speculate further, so far as I know, about what other needs or conditions were extreme enough to warrant consensual polygamy. Was a wife's sterility enough? Her frigidity? Her sickness or a physical condition that precluded sex? Was the husband's "burning with lust" enough to warrant polygamy, say, when his wife had deserted or separated from him? Could he have another faithful sexual relationship, short of marriage,

---

[89] John Duns Scotus, *On Bigamy, Ordinatio IV distinction* 33, *q. 1*, trans. A. Vos et al. (Washington, DC: Research Group John Duns Scotus, 2010), 3–7.

[90] Ibid., 6–7.

[91] On permissive natural law theories, see Brian Tierney, *Liberty and Law: The Idea of Permissible Natural Law, 1100–1800* (Washington, DC: Catholic University Press of America, 2014).

such as concubinage, to relieve his burning or desire for children? Scotus also left hanging the suggestion that God, now operating through the church, had to grant a dispensation from the usual rules of monogamy in order for such a second marital contract to be "fully just."[92] But who was to grant this dispensation: The pope? A bishop? A priest? A church court? And what evidence was needed and what burden of proof met to get such a dispensation? It was slippery slope questions such as these that led most medieval writers to shut the door tightly on any dispensations to practice real polygamy under any circumstances.[93]

But this was not the unanimous position. For example, theologian and philosopher, Durandus of Saint Pourçain (d. 1332), wrote that polygamy was ultimately not against natural law, even though it was against Christian law. Just as God had dispensed the polygamy of selected Old Testament patriarchs, so the pope, as God's vicar and keeper of the Christian law, had the power to grant a dispensation for polygamy by selected Christian believers.[94] Gerard Odonis (d. 1348), a French Franciscan, explained why the power of dispensation might be licit even in less extreme cases. Polygamy, after all, was not expressly prohibited by the Bible or by natural law, Odonis reasoned, but only by the church's canon law. Adultery and voluntary divorce, by contrast, were explicitly prohibited both by the Bible and by the church. So, in some cases of irresolvable marital breakdown, but chronic personal need for a sexual outlet or pressing political need for an heir,[95] polygamy might be a better solution than adultery and divorce. A pious man, seeking to obey the law of God and nature, would do well in such a case to seek a papal dispensation to practice polygamy.[96] Thomas de Vio (1469–1534), better known today as Cardinal Cajetan who first attacked Martin Luther for his heresy, wrote similarly that "having a plurality of wives is not against the law of nature" and that "a law concerning one

---

[92] Ibid., 7–9.

[93] See Montaigne, *De Bigamia*, 129r–130v. Contrast this to dispensations from clerical bigamy discussed later in this chapter, pp. 186–190.

[94] Comm. Sent. IV, q. 33, art. 1. See Joyce, *Christian Marriage*, 578–579. Durandus of Saint Pourçain (d. 1332) must not be confused with the more conservative William Durand of Mende (d. 1296). Cf. Dennis Doherty, *The Sexual Doctrine of Cardinal Cajetan* (Regensburg: F. Pustet, 1966), 203.

[95] He may have had in mind the infamous bigamy case of King Philip of France at the turn of the twelfth century who, in an evident effort to produce more male heirs, had repudiated his first wife Bertha of Holland and sought to marry one, Bertha of Montfort, who was herself already married. See discussion in Christopher L. Brooke, *The Medieval Idea of Marriage* (Oxford: Oxford University Press, 1989), 119–126; Christof Rolker, *Canon Law and the Letters of Ivo of Chartres* (Cambridge: Cambridge University Press, 2010), 230–243. This issue would come up again in the case of Henry VIII who sought to repudiate his wife Katherine and marry another woman to sire a male heir. See discussion in Chapter 5, pp. 201–209. See also the infamous ninth-century case of King Lothar II, discussed in Chapter 3, pp. 128–129.

[96] See Antonius M. Mruk, "Singularis opinion Gerardi Odonis, O.F.M., circa naturam divortii in casu adulterii," *Gregorianum* 14 (1960): 273–283, and discussion in Hillman, "Polygamy and the Council of Trent," 364–365.

wife is nowhere written in the canonical Scriptures." Polygamy is only prohibited by the positive laws of church and state, Cajetan wrote, leaving open the question whether the authors or interpreters of these positive laws could grant equitable dispensations from them.[97] A number of eminent early modern Catholics – Gerson, Tostatus, Erasmus, Bellarmine, Mersenne, Sanchez, and others – echoed these views either that polygamy was not against the natural law and/or that the pope could grant dispensations to practice polygamy in individual cases of real necessity.[98]

But that said, it must be emphasized that these were exceptions to the strong canonical position of the medieval and early modern Catholic Church that pronounced repeatedly that polygamy was against the natural law properly understood, and that no earthly authority, whether pope or emperor, had power to grant a dispensation to practice it. Indeed, the writings of both Odonis and Cajetan were censored by the Catholic church, evidently for their unduly Protestant-like speculations about polygamy.[99] (We shall return to these Protestant speculations in the next chapter.)

These natural law arguments about polygamy would become commonplaces of Catholic legal and moral thought in succeeding centuries. In fact, they echo in the writings of some Catholic natural law writings to this day.[100] But these natural law arguments, while powerful, would eventually find less appeal outside the Western Catholic world – first among sixteenth-century Protestants who chided them for their casuistry, then among eighteenth-century Enlightenment philosophers, who chided them for their religiosity, and then among modern philosophers, who chide them for their static view of law and nature.[101]

---

[97] Cajetan, *Omnia Opera Quotquot Sacrae Scripturae Expositionem Repuriuntur*, 5 vols. (Hildesheim/ New York: Olms, 2005), s.v. Genesis 16, Leviticus 18, Matthew 19:8, Mark 10:11, 1 Timothy 3:2; Titus 1:6. See Doherty, *The Sexual Doctrine of Cardinal Cajetan*, 200–205.

[98] See sources listed in Joyce, *Christian Marriage*, 578–579; Hillman, "Polygamy and the Council of Trent," 365–371; Leo Miller, *John Milton Among the Polygamophiles* (New York: Loewenthal Press, 1974), 36–38, 229–233.

[99] Ioannes Eck, *Enchiridion Locorum Adversus Lutherium, et alios hostes Ecclesiae* (Louvain: Theobaldum Paganum, 1561), 446. See also Hillman, "Polygamy and the Council of Trent," 366–367, and N. Paulus, "Cajetan und Luther über die Polygamie," *Historisches Politisches Blätter* 135 (1905), 81–100, at 95, who speculates that Cajetan's writings were indexed because they reflected the views of some Protestant reformers on permissible polygamy in cases of necessity. On this theme, see Chapter 5, pp. 205–209.

[100] See, e.g., "Marriage: Love and Life in the Divine Plan: A Pastoral Letter of the United States Conference of Catholic Bishops" (November 17, 2009), pp. 1–6, viewed at www.usccbpublishing.org. See also, from different Catholic perspectives, Robert P. George, *In Defense of Natural Law* (Oxford: Oxford University Press, 1999); Russell F. Hittinger, *The First Grace: Rediscovering the Natural Law in a Post-Christian World* (Wilmington, DE: Intercollegiate Studies Institute Publishers, 2003); Stephen J. Pope, *Human Evolution and Christian Ethics* (Cambridge: Cambridge University Press, 2007); Jean Porter, *Ministers of the Law: A Natural Law Theory of Legal Authority* (Grand Rapids, MI: Wm. B. Eerdmans, 2010).

[101] See analysis of these criticisms in Don S. Browning, "A Natural Law Theory of Marriage," *Zygon* 46 (2011): 733–760. See also Luis Cortest, *The Disfigured Face: Traditional Natural Law and its*

NATURAL PAIR-BONDING STRATEGIES OF PROCREATION

It was an additional medieval argument from nature, crystallized by Thomas Aquinas, that had a wider and more enduring appeal for the Western case against polygamy. This was an argument about the natural pair-bonding strategies of procreation that humans had learned to develop to compensate for several peculiar sexual, reproductive, and developmental tendencies. Aquinas set out this argument most fully in his *Summa Contra Gentiles*, a sophisticated work of apologetics designed in part to present the teachings of Christianity to Muslims, Jews, and other foreign "peoples" ("*Gentiles*") of the day. Here he analyzed what he considered to be the deep natural foundation of all human marriages, not just Christian marriages, as ideally monogamous, exclusive, and indissoluble unions.

Aquinas built his account in part on the extensive observations of the reproductive strategies of various animals just published by his teacher, Albert the Great (ca. 1206–1280).[102] He also built on Aristotle's teaching that humans are "marital animals" before they are "political animals" and that most men and women have a natural attraction to each other and have a natural inclination to produce "copies of themselves" as an act of self-preservation and perpetuation.[103] But Aquinas added several new insights into the unique strategies of human reproduction through enduring pair bonding, rather than through random or multiple sexual associations.

Aquinas first observed that humans are unique among other animals in producing utterly fragile and helpless infants. Unlike other young animals, human babies cannot soon run, fly, or swim away. They need nurture, protection, food, shelter, and education for a number of years – ideally from both their mother and father and their respective kin networks.

> [T]here are animals whose offspring are able to seek food immediately after birth, or are sufficiently fed by their mother; and in these there is no tie between male and female; whereas in those whose offspring needs the support of both parents, although for a short time, there is a certain tie, as may be seen in certain birds. In man, however, since the child needs the parents' care for a long time, there is a very great tie between male and female, to which ties even the generic nature inclines.[104]

Encounter with Modernity (New York: Fordham University Press, 2008); Nicholas Bamforth and David A.J. Richards, *Patriarchal Religion, Sexuality, and Gender: A Critique of New Natural Law* (Cambridge: Cambridge University Press, 2008).

[102] See Albertus Magnus, *Quaestiones super animalibus*, translated as *Questions Concerning Aristotle's On Animals*, trans. Irven M. Resnick and Kenneth F. Kitchell, Jr. (Washington, DC: Catholic University of America Press, 2008), esp. bks. 5, 9, 10, 15, 67.

[103] See Chapter 3, pp. 105–106.

[104] ST Supp., q. 41, art. 1.

"Among some animals where the female is able to take care of the upbringing of offspring, male and female do not remain together for any time after the act of generation," Aquinas continued. This is the case with cats, dogs, cattle, and other herding animals, where newborns quickly become independent after a brief nursing period. "But in the case of animals of which the female is not able to provide for upbringing of children, the male and female do stay together after the act of generation as long as is necessary for the upbringing and instruction of the offspring." In these latter cases, this inclination to stay and help with the feeding, protection, and teaching of the offspring is "naturally implanted in the male." Birds are a good example: They pair for the entire mating season and cooperate in building their nests, in brooding their eggs, and in feeding, protecting, and teaching their fledglings until they finally take flight on their own.[105]

Human beings push this pair-bonding pattern of reproduction much further, Aquinas continued, not only because their tiny children remain dependent for so much longer but also because these children place heavy and shifting demands on their parents as they slowly mature. Except in rare cases, this requires the effort of both parents and the kin structures they each represent. "The female in the human species is not at all able to take care of the upbringing of offspring by herself, since the needs of human life demand many things which cannot be provided by one person alone. Therefore it is appropriate to human nature to remain together with a woman after the generative act, and not leave her immediately to have such relations with another woman, as is the practice of fornicators." For this reason, human males and females are naturally inclined to remain together for the sake of their dependent human infant.[106]

A man will remain with the mother and care for the child, however, only if he is certain that he is the father, Aquinas continued. A woman will know that a child is hers because she carries it to term and then nurses the child thereafter. A man will know that a child is his, only if he is sure that his wife has been sexually faithful to him alone. Only with an exclusive monogamous relationship can a man be sure that he is the father if his wife becomes pregnant. And only then will a man be likely to join his wife in care for their child. "Man naturally desires to know his offspring," Aquinas wrote; "and this knowledge would be completely destroyed if there were several males for one female. Therefore that one female is for one male is a consequence of a natural instinct."[107]

[105] SCG, III-II.122.6; 124.3. See an interesting reflection on monogamy in other animals described in Jodocus Damhouder, *Praxis rerum criminalium: Gründlicher Bericht und Anweisung, Welchermassen in Rechtfärtigung peinlicher sachen nach gemeynen beschriebenen Rechten … zu behandeln* (Frankfurt am Main: Joh. Wolff, 1555), title "De Adulterio," nos. 99–108. I am grateful to Professor R.H. Helmholz for bringing this passage to my attention.

[106] SCG, III-II.122.6–7; 124.3.

[107] Ibid., 124.1; see also ST Supp., q. 41, art. 1.

Aquinas recognized that paternal certainty alone was often not enough to bind a man to his wife and child. Echoing a medieval commonplace, Aquinas believed that human males, like other male animals, craved sex with many females much more than they craved permanent attachment to women and children. But a rational man, he insisted, can be induced to care for his children and cleave to his wife because of his natural instinct for self-preservation. Once a man realizes that a given child is literally an extension of himself, a part and product of his own body and being, "flesh of my flesh, bone of my bone," he will care for the infant as he is inclined to care for his own body. And once he begins this parental process, his attachment to that child will settle and deepen, and he will remain with the child and its mother. He will come to enjoy the interaction with and growth of his child, and he will also enjoy the sexual intimacy and domestic support of his wife as the family remains together.[108]

Both faithful and indissoluble marriage, Aquinas concluded, provides the context for this parental life-long investment in children. Faithful marriage provides paternal certainty – ensuring a man that he is investing in his own children not those with whom he has no biological tie. Indissoluble marriage provides parental investment – ensuring children of the support of their parents for their many years of maturation. These children will later reciprocate when their parents grow old and fragile and enter into their own second childhood and become needy and dependent anew.[109]

To these two arguments from the nature of human reproduction and parental attachment, Aquinas added a third argument from natural justice and contractual fairness to show that monogamy was superior to polygamy in humans. Aquinas rejected polyandry (one female with multiple males) – a practice that Plato had briefly contemplated in his *Republic* and a few Christian writers had mused about, too[110] – because polyandry was naturally unjust to children. If a woman had sex with several husbands, he argued, it removed the likelihood that the children born to that woman will clearly belong to any one husband. This will undermine paternal certainty and consequent paternal investment in their children's care. The children will suffer from neglect, and the wife will be overburdened trying to care for them and trying to tend to her multiple husbands and their rampant sexual needs at once.[111]

Aquinas rejected polygyny (one male with multiple females) because it was naturally unjust to wives. Polygyny did not necessarily erode paternal certainty, Aquinas allowed. So long as his multiple wives were faithful to him alone, a man could be assured of being the father of children born in his household. But this

---

[108] Ibid.; ST II-II, q. 26, arts. 7–9.
[109] SCG, III-II.122–123.
[110] See Augustine, *De haeresibus* 5 (PL 41, 26), referenced in SCG, III-II, 124.8.
[111] ST Supp., qq. 41, 65–66; SCG, III-II, 123.3, 124.3–8.

required a man to pen up his wives like cattle, isolating them from other roving males even when his own energies to tend to them were already dissipated over the several women and children gathered in his household. While locked up at home, the wives were reduced to servants, and set in perennial competition with each other for resources and access to their shared husband. "This is not marriage, but servitude," said Aquinas. It betrayed the fundamental requirement of fidelity and mutuality between husband and wife, the undivided and undiluted love and friendship that become a proper marriage. True marital faith and "friendship consists in an equality" that should never be divided, Aquinas wrote. It requires not only forgoing sexual intercourse with another and honoring the reasonable sexual advances of one's spouse. It also requires the commitment to be indissolubly united with one's spouse in body and mind, to be willing to share fully and equally in the person, property, lineage, and reputation – indeed, in the "whole life" – of one's spouse. It is to be and bear with each other in youth and in old age, in sickness and in health, in prosperity and adversity. Polygyny undercuts all of those fundamental goods of marriage. "So, if it is not lawful for the wife to have several husbands, since this is contrary to the certainty as to offspring, it would not be lawful, on the other hand, for a man to have several wives, for the friendship of husband and wife would not be free, but somewhat servile. And this argument is corroborated by experience, for among husbands having plural wives the wives have a status like that of servants." Natural law and natural justice thus teach monogamy.[112]

Aquinas's concern for natural justice to women and children also framed his arguments against divorce and remarriage – which he regarded as a form of "successive polygamy" or "digamy," as the Church Fathers had called it. His real concern was with "voluntary divorce" – unilateral, no-fault divorce as we would call it today. This option was especially unjust to wives, Aquinas said, for they would be left vulnerable to their husband's decisions to divorce them when they became barren or lost their youthful beauty. If they had the right to divorce, Aquinas argued, many men, given their proclivity to wander sexually, would not be encouraged to develop the comfortable habits of monogamous fidelity to wife and child that the natural structure of monogamy encourages. Many women would be discarded in middle age, without support either from their husbands, who would likely go on to other women, or from their fathers, who would likely be dead at that point. (The notion that a woman could have her own career to support herself, beyond that of the cloister or church guild, was simply not within the medieval imagination.) This made divorce "naturally wrong," said Aquinas: "So if a man took a woman in the time of her youth, when beauty and fecundity were hers, and then sent her away

---

[112] Ibid.

after she had reached an advanced age, he would damage that woman, contrary to natural equity" or natural justice.[113]

Removing divorce as an option for properly married couples not only provides security for wives, but also fosters "good behavior" in the marital household, said Aquinas. The husband and wife will eventually be less prone to adultery, knowing they will have to live either alone or with their spouse, and knowing that their adulterous lover will remain forever forbidden to them, even after the death of their spouse. The marital couple will be more inclined to fix "the source of their disagreements" so as to reach "a more solid affection" for each other and their relatives, making life together more agreeable. And "they will be more solicitous in their care for domestic possessions when they keep in mind that they will remain continuously in possession of these same things."[114]

Voluntary divorce was also naturally unjust to children, Aquinas continued, for it squandered their inheritance and impeded their ability to take care of their parents when they most needed help, in their elderly return to infancy. "By the intention of nature, marriage is directed to the rearing of the offspring, not merely for a time, but throughout its whole life. Hence it is of natural law that parents should lay up for their children, and that children should be their parents' heirs. Therefore, since the offspring is the common good of husband and wife, the dictate of the natural law requires the latter to live together forever inseparably: and so the indissolubility of marriage is of natural law."[115]

This combination of natural arguments for monogamy and against polygamy in various forms would become a staple for the Western legal tradition. The core of the argument was focused on the natural needs and tendencies of men, women, and children, and the premium placed on stable monogamous marriage as the proper site for sexual exchange, mutual adult dependency, and the procreation and nurture of long dependent children. The core of the natural justice argument was focused on the injustice and harm done to women and children by the multiplication or replacement of spouses.

To these natural arguments, we shall see in a moment, Aquinas and others added theological arguments that helped to stabilize and solidify these intra-family relations and responsibilities. This strengthened his case for the exclusive and indissoluble monogamous marriages of Christians. But even stripped of its theological overlay and left to stand alone, Aquinas's arguments from nature

---

[113] ST Supp., q. 67; SCG III-II.123. Thomas added an argument against divorce that rankles modern egalitarian sensibilities: "the female needs the male, not merely for the sake of generation, as in the case of other animals, but also for the sake of government, since the male is both more perfect in reasoning and stronger in powers." Ibid., III-II.123.3.

[114] SCG III-II.123.6, 8.

[115] ST Supp., q. 67, art. 1, citing 2 Corinthians 12:14.

were powerful. They were also enduring. Many later jurists and philosophers – Catholics, Protestants, and post-Christian liberals alike – built on these early arguments to defend monogamy and denounce polygamy.[116] And today, a number of anthropologists and evolutionary scientists have shown that enduring pair-bonding is the most expedient means for humans to reproduce given the realities of long and demanding human infant dependency and the perennial sex drives of humans. Indeed, human reproduction by enduring pair-bonding is described by many modern evolutionary scientists from Claude Lèvi-Strauss to Bernard Chapais as the "deep structure" of survival that the human species has evolved.[117] In his own pre-modern way, Aquinas saw this already 750 years ago. To be sure, he called it the human nature that God has created, rather than a reproductive survival strategy that the human species has developed through millennia of evolution. But the conclusion was the same: monogamy was ultimately better than polygamy for human reproduction and flourishing.

Natural Rights within the Monogamous Family

Aquinas's insights into the natural foundations of monogamy and procreation were not only prescient of modern scientific teachings. They also helped form the foundation for an emerging medieval law of natural rights for children and their parents. The rights of the parents to marriage and procreation were based on their natural duties "to be fruitful and multiply" by licit conjunctions of "two in one flesh."[118] The rights of children were the correlatives of the duties that Christian parents owed to children. As Jesus had put it in the Sermon on the Mount:

> What man of you, if his son asks him for bread, will give him a stone? Or if he asks for a fish, will give him a serpent? If you then, who are evil, know how to give good gifts to your children, how much more will your Father in heaven give good things

---

[116] See discussion in Chapters 6, 7, and 9 in this book.

[117] Bernard Chapais, *Primeval Kinship: How Pair-Bonding Gave Birth to Human Society* (Cambridge, MA: Harvard University Press, 2008), 10. See also Peter B. Gray and Kermyt G. Anderson, *Fatherhood: Evolution and Human Paternal Behavior* (Cambridge, MA: Harvard University Press, 2010); Melvin A. Konner, *The Evolution of Childhood: Relations, Emotions, Mind* (Cambridge, MA: Harvard University Press, 2010). The topic remains controversial, however; see the essays in Laura L. Betzig et al., eds., *Human Reproductive Behavior: A Darwinian Perspective* (Cambridge: Cambridge University Press, 1988) and in Peter M. Kappeler and Joan B. Silk, *Mind the Gap: Tracing the Origins of Human Universals* (Berlin/New York: Springer, 2010).

[118] On medieval origins of modern rights talk, see Brian Tierney, *The Idea of Natural Rights: Studies on Natural Rights, Natural Law, and Church Law, 1150–1625* (Grand Rapids, MI: Wm. B. Eerdmans, 1997); R.H. Helmholz, "Human Rights in the Canon Law," in *Christianity and Human Rights: An Introduction*, ed. John Witte, Jr. and Frank S. Alexander (Cambridge: Cambridge University Press, 2010), 99–113.

to those who ask him! So whatever you wish that men would do to you, do so to them; for this is the law and the prophets.[119]

It was biblical texts such as these, together with the naturalist arguments of Aquinas and others just outlined, that inspired medieval jurists to develop the law of children's rights. By the fourteenth century, canon law and civil law texts spoke about a child's right to life and the means to sustain life, the right to care, protection, nurture, and education, the later right to emancipation from the home and the right to contract marriage, enter a profession, or join the clergy or monastery, and the right to support and eventual inheritance from their natural or adoptive parents. Furthermore, illegitimate children had special rights to oblation in a monastery or legitimation by their natural or adoptive parents. Poor children had special rights to relief and shelter. Abused children had special rights to sanctuary and foster care. Abandoned or orphaned children had special rights to foundling houses and orphanages. All these were real and actionable "subjective" rights for children that medieval church courts and state courts helped to enforce.[120] By the sixteenth century, these natural rights of domestic life were expanded and systematized by a series of Spanish and Portuguese jurists, most of them Dominicans, like Thomas, gathered at the University of Salamanca.[121]

SPIRITUAL ARGUMENTS AGAINST POLYGAMY

The foregoing medieval arguments from nature and from harm were directed primarily against real polygamy: one person with two or more spouses or fiancé(e)s at the same time. For medieval Christians, however, marriage was not just a natural institution: a union of bodies, of two in one flesh. Marriage was also a supernatural institution: a union of souls, of two in one spirit. When contracted between two baptized Christians in good standing within the church, marriage was a sacrament,

---

119 Matthew 7:9–11; ST II-II, q. 26.7–9.
120 See detailed sources and discussion in R.H. Helmholz, "Children's Rights and the Canon Law: Law and Practice in Later Medieval England," *The Jurist* 67 (2007): 39; id., "And Were There Children's Rights in Early Modern England? The Canon Law and 'Intra-family Violence' in England, 1400–1640," *International Journal of Children's Rights* 1 (1993): 23; Charles J. Reid, Jr., "The Rights of Children in Medieval Canon Law," in *The Vocation of the Child*, ed. Patrick M. Brennan (Grand Rapids, MI: Wm. B. Eerdmans, 2008), 243–265; Reid, *Power over the Body*; John Witte, Jr., *The Sins of the Fathers: The Law and Theology of Illegitimacy Reconsidered* (Cambridge: Cambridge University Press, 2009), 49–134.
121 Tierney, *The Idea of Natural Rights*, 225–315; Annabel S. Brett, *Liberty, Right, and Nature: Individual Rights in Later Scholastic Thought* (Cambridge: Cambridge University Press, 1997); Virpi Mäkinen and Petter Korman, eds., *Transformations in Medieval and Early-Modern Rights Discourse* (Dordrecht: Springer, 2006).

symbolizing and embodying the mysterious union of God and his elect, of Christ and his church.[122] This sacramental understanding of marriage not only helped to explain why real polygamy was improper for medieval Christians. It also helped to explain why other forms of plural union by aspiring priests, divorcees, and widow(er)s were considered to be improper forms of marriage as well. Let us sample these arguments a bit, understanding that the medieval discussion of these topics was far more involved than the few final pages of this chapter can capture.[123]

Polygamy and Sacramental Marriage

The heart of the sacramental argument against real polygamy was that it betrayed the model of marriage between Christ and his church as an exclusive and enduring dyadic union. Augustine had already said that the "two in one flesh" metaphor of Adam and Eve in Paradise was a prefiguration and prophesy about Christ's exclusive marriage to the church. He had also said that each Christian marriage was a miniature version of this divine marriage, a visible expression of this invisible mystery. Augustine had based this view in part on the teachings of Jesus and St. Paul, who had adduced the "two in one flesh" metaphor of Genesis to underscore the exclusive fidelity and mutual sacrifice that was expected of a Christian husband and wife.[124] He had relied even more on the description of Christian marriage in Ephesians 5:21–32:

> Be subject to one another out of reverence for Christ. Wives, be subject to your husbands as you are to the Lord. For the husband is the head of the wife just as Christ is the head of the church, the body of which he is the Saviour. Just as the church is subject to Christ, so also wives ought to be, in everything, to their husbands. Husbands, love your wives, just as Christ loved the church and gave himself up for her, in order to make her holy by cleansing her with the washing of water by the word, so as to present the church to himself in splendor, without a spot or wrinkle or anything of the kind – yes, so that she may be holy and without blemish. In the same way, husbands should love their wives as they do their own bodies. He who loves his wife loves himself. For no one ever hates his own body, but he nourishes and tenderly cares for it, just as Christ does for the church, because we are members of his body. "For this reason a man will leave his father and mother and be joined to his wife, and the two will become one flesh." This is a great

---

[122] Lombard, *Sentences*, 4.26.6; Hugh of St. Victor, *On the Sacraments*, bk. 2, pt. 11.8; Guillaume Durandus, *The Rationale Divinorum Officiorum of William Durand of Mende*, ed. Timothy M. Thibodeau (New York: Columbia University Press, 2007), 103–104.

[123] See Theodore Mackin, *Marriage in the Catholic Church: The Marital Sacrament* (New York: Paulist Press, 1989), 274–378.

[124] See Matthew 19:5; 1 Corinthians 6:16, 7:2–6.

mystery [or sacrament – translating the Greek word *mysterion*] and I am applying it to Christ and the church.

For medieval writers, Christ's mysterious union with the church was the model for each Christian marriage as an *exclusive* union. In a Christian sacramental marriage, "neither man nor woman is content to receive a divided conjugal affection," wrote Franciscan theologian, St. Bonaventura (1221–1274). After all, "God is a jealous God," and will allow no other gods before him. Yahweh is a loving husband, but he will not suffer his chosen bride Israel to "play the harlot." Christ is the faithful bridegroom who calls the church to join him in one body, indeed to be part of his body: "bone of my bone, flesh of my flesh."[125] A Christian sacramental marriage expresses and emulates this divine norm and form of exclusive marital love. A Christian who enters such a marriage in good faith may thus expect and demand exclusive faith and love from his or her spouse. That is why the New Testament takes so seriously violations of marriage – whether through a one-time act of adultery, or an occasional visit to a prostitute, or an ongoing relationship with a concubine. All these are betrayals of the unity and exclusivity that uniquely become a Christian marriage. It is an insult not only to one's spouse, but to the divine model of exclusive love that the Christian couple is called to emulate and exemplify. Polygamy is even worse, for it is a perpetual act of adultery, an ongoing defiance of God's creation ideal for marriage and its fulfillment in Christ's incarnational model of marriage.

Christ's mysterious union with the church also provided a model of marriage as an *enduring* union, one that was permanent. The Bible makes clear that Christ's love for his church is endless. God remains faithful to his beloved regardless of what they say or do. Augustine had already said that a Christian sacramental marriage was thus an inherently enduring union. It left a "permanent conjugal mark" on its participants. It created an inescapable "conjugal status" that remained with them until one spouse died.[126] Medieval writers pressed this Augustinian argument further. "The sacraments effect that of which they are made signs," Thomas Aquinas wrote. And a sacramental marriage, of necessity, takes on its divine form, much like a shadow is framed by the light that produces it.

> Since the union of husband and wife gives a sign of the union of Christ and the Church, that which makes the sign must correspond to that whose sign it is. Now, the union of Christ and the Church is a union of one to one to be held forever. For there is only one Church, as the Canticle (6.8) says: "One is My dove, My perfect one." And Christ will never be separated from His Church, for He himself says: "Behold I am with you all days, even to the consummation of the world" (Matt.

---

[125] Joyce, *Christian Marriage*, 577, quoting in part Bonaventura, *Comm. Lombard, Sent.*, 33.1; See also ST III, q. 66.3.

[126] See Augustine's discussion in Chapter 2, pp. 96–97.

28:20); and further, "we shall always be with the Lord" (1 Thess. 4:16). Necessarily, then, matrimony as a sacrament of the Church, is a union of one man to one woman to be held indivisibly, and this is included in the faithfulness by which the man and wife are bound together.[127]

Thomas bolstered this sacramental argument for exclusive and enduring sacramental marriage with the arguments from nature that we have already sampled: "According to nature's intent, marriage is oriented to the nurture of offspring. Thus it is according to the law of nature that parents save for their children and that children be heirs for their parents. Therefore, since offspring are the good of both husband and wife together, the latter's union must remain permanently, according to the dictate of the law of nature."[128] He also added a contractual argument that the couple had consensually agreed to remain together "in sickness and in health, for better and for worse," and that preserving the marital bond was more advantageous to the couple, their children, and the broader community.[129] But it was the argument from the sacramental quality of marriage that gave his argument its final cogency and canonical force in his day.

That canonical force made polygamy a form of blasphemy and heresy to medieval writers. It was a violation not only of the natural form of marriage, but even more of the supernatural norm which it embodied. For a Christian to pretend to add a second spouse while the first was still living (with him or her) and to call that new union a marriage was a deliberate insult to Christ's example and instruction. For a Christian believer or official to extend the definition of marriage to include a second or third concurrent marriage was a deliberate insult to the sacramental symbolism of Christian marriage. It was tantamount to downing a beer and a sandwich and calling that the eucharist, or diving into a pond several times and calling that baptism writ large. This simply could not be. It was not only a "legal impossibility," as Raymond of Penyafort had put it, echoing Roman law,[130] but a grave spiritual offense, too. Medieval writers labeled such misuses of the concept and institution of marriage by Christians as "heresy," "blasphemy," and "desecration" – an insult to God and his sacraments. The Council of Trent later called it "heresy" deserving of the church's "anathema."

Medieval writers offered numerous variations on this argument for monogamy and against polygamy based upon the sacramental symbolism of marriage.[131]

---

[127] SCG IV.78.

[128] Quoted by Theodore Mackin, *Marriage in the Catholic Church: Divorce and Remarriage* (New York: Paulist Press, 1984), 342.

[129] Ibid.

[130] D. c. 31.1; X.4.19.4; Raymond, *Summa on Marriage*, 3.3.

[131] See other examples in David L. D'Avray, *Medieval Marriage: Symbolism and Society* (Oxford: Oxford University Press, 2005), 131–167.

Bonaventura, for example, focused on the analogies between the exclusive love of God and his elect before the fall into sin and the enduring love of Christ and the Church after the fall:

> Now, man's original perfection consisted in the union of his soul with God through an utterly chaste, singular, and individual union of love; moreover, the remedy came from the union of the divine and human natures within the oneness of a hypostasis or Person, a oneness, that is to say, effected by divine grace as singular and individual. Therefore God decreed from the very beginning that propagation would be brought about by means of a singular and individual union of male and female. The union was to signify, before the fall, the union of God with the soul ... but after the fall, the union of God with human nature, or of Christ with the church. Hence matrimony was a sacrament both before and after the fall, but it differed as to meaning and purpose.[132]

William Durand of Mende (d. 1296), a distinguished canonist and theologian, saw first the engagement and then the marriage of a Christian couple as symbols respectively of the soul's mysterious unity with God and Christ's mysterious unity with the church:

> The first mystery is the union of the faithful soul to God through faith, love, and charity; or the union of the will to God, that is charity, which consists in one spirit between God and the just soul; thus the Apostle says: *He who clings to God is one in spirit with Him* [1 Cor. 6:17]. This mystery is signified by the union of kindred souls when the first step – the betrothal – toward carnal matrimony is taken.
>
> The second [mystery] is the union of human nature with God, which was done in the womb of the Virgin, through the Incarnation of the Word of God; or in the sharing between Christ and the Holy Church of that nature composed of flesh, to which these words apply: *The Word was made flesh, etc.* [Jn. 1:14]. This mystery is designated in the consummation of carnal marriage, through the union of bodies; not that the union itself, in which the Holy Spirit is not present, designates this mystery, but rather, that it is signified through the act of consummation....
>
> That is why one who is a bigamist or goes through with a [illicit] second marriage is at that moment cut off from the unity of the Church, because he has divided his body among many.... For the Church, which has joined herself to Christ, has never separated herself from Him, nor has He from her. A bigamist, therefore, can never signify such a unity.[133]

---

[132] Bonaventura, *Breviloquium*, trans. Erwin Esser Nemmers (St. Louis, MO: B. Herder, 1946), VI, ch. 13.2.

[133] Durandus, *The Rationale Divinorum Officiorum*, 103–104. Durandus was discussing not only "real polygamy" but also "clerical bigamy" as discussed further on pp. 72–73, 186–190.

Other medieval writers focused on the symbolic ties between "two in one flesh" and "two in one spirit." What was the "one" that was produced through sacramental marriage?[134] Some writers, like Gratian and the canonist Bernard of Parma (d. 1264), who saw consummation as critical to the sacrament, focused on the child produced by the sexual union of husband and wife. Marriage was in that sense not only a faithful act of obeying God's command to "be fruitful and multiply" and participating in a new creation with God's help. Marriage was also a symbol ultimately of the Trinitarian Godhead itself, whose Holy Spirit proceeded from "the Father and the Son," in the words of the ancient Nicene Creed.[135] Other writers, like Aquinas and Hostiensis, who saw mutual consent as the essential step of sacramental marriage, focused on the new unity of mind, status, name, friendship, household, property, and more produced through a marriage, even a marriage that was not sexually consummated or blessed with children.[136]

In his famous "Tree of Bigamy" (see Illustration 10 at the beginning of this chapter), a full folio page woodcut in his standard textbook on canon law, Hostiensis went on to depict graphically sundry divine relationships that he thought to be symbolized in and by a sacramental marriage, and sundry illicit relationships that betrayed it. On the right hand of God, who stood open-armed behind the tree, were the proper dyadic relationships symbolized by the first marriage contracted by Adam and Eve in Paradise – the union of God and the Virgin Mary; of Christ and the universal church; of the clergy and laity within the church; of the word and sacraments of the church; of baptism and marriage in a wedding liturgy; of faith and works in a Christian household. All these symbolic dyadic echoes of sacramental marriage attest to the unity of the Christian faith and the spiritual life of the Christian church. On the left hand of God and subject to divine condemnation were the false "bonds" that lead people to betray sacramental marriage – the bonds between the Devil and hell, man and sin, heresies and diabolical errors that divide the church and its people and lead them to hell. Hostiensis made clear that polygamy was on God's left hand, a diabolical doctrine, a product of the devil, and ultimately subject to condemnation and the fires of hell.[137] This was an echo of what Basil and other early

---

[134] See analysis and sources in Mayali, "Duo erunt in carna una," 168–172.

[135] See, e.g., Bernard of Parma, quoted in X. 1.21.5; Montaigne, *De Bigamia*, 124v-125r. See fuller discussion in Mayali, "Duo erunt in carna una," 168–172; Brundage, *Law, Sex, and Christian Society*, 235–243.

[136] ST Supp., q. 43, art. 3.

[137] See Illustration 5, taken from Hostiensis, *Summa*, folio 42r ("de bigamia"). This image and others like it are discussed in D'Avray, *Medieval Marriage*, 137–139; Edgar Breitenach, "The Tree of Bigamy and the Veronica Image of St. Peter's," *Art Institute of Chicago Museum Studies* 9 (1978): 30–38; H. Schadt, "Die Arbores Bigamiae als heilsgeschichtliche Schemata: Zum Verhältnis von Kanonistik und Kunstgeschichte," in *Kunst als Bedeutungsträger: Gedenkschrift für Günter Bandmann* (Berlin: Gebr. Mann, 1978), 129–147. Schadt describes seventeen different versions of these contrasting pictures of

Church Fathers had said: that polygamy was "evil," a "beastly thing," an act to be condemned like the Beast of Hell that had produced it since the days of Lamech, the first murderous polygamist.[138] Hostiensis's description was also an anticipation of what the Tridentine Fathers would say three centuries after him: that polygamy was a form of "heresy," a "mortal sin" worthy of the church's most dire pronouncement of "anathema."[139]

Polygamy and the Remarriage of Widow(er)s

This emerging sacramental argument for monogamy and against polygamy found additional elaboration in the discussion of the remarriage of widow(er)s. Formally, the medieval canon law texts made little change to the prevailing first millennium rules. Remarriage of widow(er)s was not encouraged, but it was permitted – immediately for men, after a year of waiting for women (to avoid paternity or illegitimacy issues in case of pregnancy). This was biblical teaching, Pope Innocent III wrote:

> According to the Apostle [in Romans 7:2], when her husband has died his wife is freed from him by law and has complete liberty to marry whom she wishes, but only in the Lord. So she is not to suffer legal degradation when she marries, even if it is within the time of mourning after the death of her husband, that is, within one year.[140]

Indeed, at medieval canon law a person who suffered the loss of multiple spouses could theoretically remarry multiple times.[141] Some canonists saw no reason to limit the number: "a thousand remarriages" should be allowed, wrote Hostiensis, besting Jerome's famous statement about "octogamists."[142] Others cautioned against "frequent remarriages,"[143] and this remained the dominant position in the Middle Ages. A few enterprising bishops and abbots, in fact, taxed remarrying widow(er)s and imposed higher license fees on those who remarried more than once, despite papal orders to the contrary.[144]

---

real and false marriage in late medieval and early modern book illustrations. The focus is on the bigamy of clergy discussed below, but the logic applies to what Hostiensis called both "real" and "constructive" polygamy alike. Ibid., 134–142.

[138] See discussion in Chapter 2 of this book.

[139] See discussion of this Tridentine decree on pp. 154–200.

[140] X 4.21.5.

[141] D. c. 27.1.33; 27.2.13; 31.1.11–12; 32.2.16; X.4.21.5.

[142] Lombard, *Sentences*, 4.42.7; Montaigne, *De Bigamia*, 125r.

[143] D. c. 31.1.8.

[144] See James A. Brundage, "The Merry Widow's Serious Sister," in *Matrons and Marginal Women in Medieval Society*, ed. Robert R. Edwards and Vickie Ziegler (Woodbridge, Suffolk: The Boydell Press, 1995), 33–48, esp. 37–43.

The medieval canon law became increasingly strict, however, in requiring that the widow(er) be certain of the death of the former spouse before marrying another so as to avoid even unintentional polygamy. The medieval canon law initially was not so strict. Some eleventh- and twelfth-century writers had repeated the first millennium canons that treated a good faith investigation of a spouse's death to be proof enough and left parties free from guilt or liability if a long-lost spouse returned to find the other remarried.[145] A few other canonists and civilians called for statutes of limitations or waiting periods of five, seven, or ten years before authorizing remarriage in such cases.[146] But by the thirteenth century, popes and canonists alike insisted on absolute proof of death in an effort to foreclose even unintentional cases of polygamy: "A wife should not marry without knowing for certain of her spouse's death, and indeed nor should her husband," the *Decretales* put it firmly.[147] Those who remarried without such proof risked charges of polygamy, doubly so if a long-lost spouse returned home unawares.

In a day of poor records, dangerous travel, and primitive communication, absolute proof of death was a daunting standard – especially for wives of soldiers, crusaders, traveling merchants, or seamen, or husbands of abducted, captured, or disappearing wives. One option for these abandoned spouses was to get a dispensation from a bishop or the pope to remarry even without full proof. But such dispensations were rare, expensive, by no means automatic, and thus reserved principally for the well-to-do. A second option was to remain alone. But that could be hazardous for a deserted wife with children who needed support and protection, or for those whose active libidos left them sorely tempted by "illicit loves" of various sorts.[148] So, a good number of abandoned spouses just eventually remarried secretly or moved to a new area of the country, keeping their prior marriage secret.[149] That carried two risks. If the first spouse returned, or the first marriage became known otherwise, the remarried party and the new spouse were subject to charges of bigamy as well as perjury.[150]

---

[145] D. c. 31.1.11–12; 32.2.16.

[146] See sources and literature in McDougall, *Bigamy*, 29–48.

[147] X. 4.21.2.

[148] See Ruth Mazo Karras, Joel Kaye, and E. Ann Matter, eds., *Law and the Illicit in Medieval Europe* (Philadelphia: University of Pennsylvania Press, 2008), esp. 116–129.

[149] See Michael Sheehan, "The Formation and Stability of Marriage in Fourteenth Century England: Evidence of an Ely Register," *Medieval Studies* 33 (1971): 228–263; Philippa Maddern, "Moving Households: Geographical Mobility and Serial Monogamy in England, 1350–1500," *Paregon* 24(2) (2007): 69–92; Marie-Ange Tricarico Valazza, "L'officialité de Genève et quelque cas de bigamie à la fin du moyen âge: l'empêchement de lien," *Zeitschrift für schweizerische Kirchengeschichte* 89 (1995): 99–118. See other detailed sources cited in McDougall, *Bigamy*, and id., "The Punishment of Bigamy."

[150] See examples of this in Monique Vleeschouwers-van Melkebeek, "Self-Divorce in Fifteenth-Century Flanders: The Consistory Court Accounts of the Diocese of Tournai," *Tijdschrift voor Rechtsgeschiedenis* 68 (2000): 83–98; id., "Marital Breakdown Before the Consistory Courts of Brussels, Cambrai, and Tournai: Judicial Separation *a mensa et thoro*," *Tijdschrift voor Rechtsgeschiedenis* 72 (2004): 81–89.

Their children could be branded as non-heritable bastards. And the remarried spouse would have to return to the first spouse, on pain of excommunication.[151] Second, if the doubly married party died, the surviving spouses and their legitimate children might well clash in claims to collect marital property and inheritance. An estate could easily be squandered or divided at grave cost to the intended heirs.[152]

The medieval canon law also became increasingly strict in forbidding clergy to bless these remarriages, even if one of the parties was marrying for the first time. The clergy who did so faced punishment, even suspension from office.[153] Some secular rulers followed suit in making it hard for a remarried widow to claim guardianship, dower, and legacies from her late husband and his surviving family.[154] And local communities sometimes heaped scorn on the remarried couples. Popular medieval rituals, called *charivari*, brought out rowdy crowds who would heckle newly remarried couples on their wedding night and thereafter, chanting vulgar songs and sayings to interrupt and insult their love-making and new life together. Part of this may have been a form of soft hazing that new couples often go through: showers of rice and confetti, gaudily decorated, tin-can-towing cars, and the like still face some modern couples as they leave on their honeymoons. Some of this rowdiness may well have been directed specifically at affluent widowers who scooped attractive marriage prospects from the market to the dismay of envious men in the community. But as Sara McDougall has shown, these *charivari* were also the "rowdy enforcers of public morality." They pronounced in loud lay terms the silent stigma that the church communicated in not blessing these second unions.[155] Various church councils tried to clamp down on these "blasphemous and obscene games" by fining and threatening to excommunicate participants.[156] But the medieval church had created its own "catch-22," by treating a remarriage as unworthy of its blessing and celebration, a sort of second class marriage.

Medieval canonists wrestled hard with the question whether the remarriage of a widow(er) was a still a sacrament, or only a valid – but non-sacramental – union. Some canonists thought the latter, arguing that marriage like baptism, holy orders, and extreme unction should occur just once: any further sacramental marriage was "a waste of grace."[157] Other medieval canonists thought that marriage was more akin to the sacraments of eucharist and penance, which could be repeated. They further

[151] X 4.1.19; 4.17.14.
[152] X 4.19; X. 4.21; see also Raymond of Penyafort, *Summa on Marriage*, 13.3–4.
[153] X 4.21.1–3.
[154] Ibid.
[155] McDougall, *Bigamy*, 25–26.
[156] Quoted from a synodal statute of Troy in McDougall, *Bigamy*, 26. See also Esmein, *Le marriage en droit canonique*, 2:124–125; D'Avray, *Medieval Marriage*, 142–143.
[157] See Bernard of Parma discussed in Esmein, *Le Mariage*, 2:123, and D'Avray, *Medieval Marriage*, 144.

reminded their medieval readers that it was the baptized couple's consent to the marriage, not the church's blessing, that rendered it a sacrament.[158]

Medieval theologians were divided on the question, too. Thomas Aquinas sought to split the difference, but that got him into trouble. Because "everything that is of the essence of marriage is found in a second marriage," he wrote, "a second marriage is a sacrament just like the first one." Fair enough. But, Aquinas went on, if it is a woman, a widow, who is remarrying rather than a man, "it has something of a defect in the sacrament, since it is not of one woman to one man." By contrast, if it is a man, a widower, who is remarrying a virgin, there is no such defect:

> [F]or the signification is in some way preserved even in relation to the [man's] first marriage, since Christ, even if he had a single Church as a bride, nevertheless has many persons within one Church as brides; but the soul cannot be the bride of any other but Christ, since with the demon it commits fornication, and there is no spiritual marriage there; and because of this, when a woman marries for the second time, the marriage is not blessed because of a defect of the sacrament.[159]

This explanation was not only "murky," as James Brundage aptly writes.[160] It was also dangerous. Aquinas was trying to explain both how an unblessed marriage could still be a sacrament and why the second marriages of widowers to virgins were still blessed "in some churches," while the converse was not true.[161] His resort to a sexual double standard to explain this differential treatment of widows and widowers is troublesome in our day, but it was typical in his day. More troublesome, then and now, was his statement that Christ "has many persons within one Church as brides." This brought him dangerously close to making a sacramental argument for polygamy. If Christ the bridegroom has many brides within the church, could a husband acting in imitation of Christ have many brides within his "domestic church," the Christian household? Was the real sacramental symbolism of marriage, then, Christ's relationship not with the one holy and apostolic church as a whole, but with each of its members? If that is the case, sacramental marriages could still be enduring, but need they be exclusive? Was Thomas just repeating, in lofty theological language, "the patriarchal assumption that properly speaking 'man is polygamous, woman is monogamous'?"[162] I think the answer is no. I think Thomas just made a rhetorical mistake in this passage – like Tertullian's earlier slip

[158] D'Avray, *Medieval Marriage*, 144, citing Geoffrey of Trano.
[159] Aquinas, *Commentary on the Sentences*, q. 3, art. 2, using translation in D'Avray, *Medieval Marriage*, 145–147.
[160] James A. Brundage, "The Merry Widow's Serious Sister," 42.
[161] Esmein, *Le Mariage*, 2:124–125; D'Avray, *Medieval Marriage*, 148, citing Bernard of Pavia and Hostiensis.
[162] D'Avray, *Medieval Marriage*, 148.

that a man could marry "a plurality of older widows."[163] I think he inadvertently ran together two distinct marital metaphors that were commonly used by medieval writers – one of Christ and the church, the second of God and each elect soul – and made them Christ's relations with each elect soul within the one church. This was not a mistake that Thomas or his followers repeated so far as I know. Indeed, the full weight of Thomas's arguments, as we have seen, was firmly against polygamy on natural and supernatural grounds.

Polygamy and the Clergy

Medieval writers were most concerned – or at least wrote the most – about "clerical bigamy": those who sought clerical or monastic office after being married more than once. The medieval sources occasionally called this "ecclesiastical bigamy" or "clerical polygamy," even a form of "infamy" (the ancient Roman law term for the infamous crime of polygamy). More typically, clerical bigamy was called "irregularity" or "irregular marriage," one contracted contrary to the rules (the *regula*) of the church and its clergy.[164] In one sense, the lengthy medieval discussion of this topic was an insider theological issue and not central to the emerging Western case against polygamy. But some of this discussion about clerical bigamy was animated by some of the same concerns that we have seen: to protect the nature and dignity of the sacraments and their important symbolic role in the community.

The medieval canon law repeated the first millennium canons that a prospective deacon, priest, and bishop had to be "the husband of one wife" alone. It added the rule that every cleric had to be single and celibate after ordination; even sexless marriages between clergy and their wives were forbidden after the Second Lateran decree of 1123.[165] Life-long virginity was still the ideal for every clerical candidate. But one prior marriage or a comparably longstanding sexual relationship like concubinage that had ended was tolerated in an aspiring cleric so long as the woman herself had been a virgin, not a widow, former nun, divorcee, prostitute, concubine, adulteress, fornicator, or even a victim of rape or abduction. Two or more prior marriages or sexual relationships, whether concurrent or consecutive, disqualified a candidate for ordination. Also disqualifying was a single marriage or single sexual relationship with a non-virginal woman.

---

[163] See discussion of Tertullian on p. 77.

[164] Montaigne, *De Bigamia*, 122v-123r, 125v. See Peter Landau, *Die Enstehung des kanonischen Infamiebegriffs von Gratian bis zur Glossa Ordinaria* (Cologne: Böhlau, 1966), 63–64. Brundage, *Sex, Law, and Christian Society*, 318 says that the term "irregularity" was coined by Rufinus, *Summa*, D. 25, d.p.c. 3, ed. Singer, 60.

[165] See detailed sources in Brundage, *Law, Sex, and Christian Society*, 214–223.

Clerical bigamy was a permanently disqualifying stigma to the clerical office. Sitting clergy who were discovered to have been "bigamists" or married to a non-virgin woman in an earlier life would be removed from clerical office, stripped of their benefices, banished from their clerical homes, and deprived of the privilege of forum. In more extreme cases – those in which a clerical candidate practiced real polygamy, or intentionally hid his or his wife's second relationship before seeking ordination – a cleric was subject to excommunication from the church, disqualification from state offices, and deprivation from rights to litigate in secular courts or to devise, receive, or inherit property. Dispensations from these canon law rules were possible in individual cases, although the medieval canonists disputed endlessly whether anyone lower than the pope could grant a dispensation, and whether any candidate higher than a subdeacon could receive one.[166]

These prohibitions against clerical bigamy were based on the idea that "in Christian marriage the union of one flesh represents the union of Christ with his one church.... [T]he remarried man has 'divided' his flesh, and his marital union can no longer represent the mystical Union. Because of this *defectus sacramenti*, he is not to stand in the place of Christ and to minister to his spouse," the church.[167] Christ had a single spouse, the church. The priest, as representative of Christ and holding his power, has to have a single spouse, too, the church. Already in the eleventh century, Peter Damiani (d. 1072) made clear that the logic of clerical bigamy was different from that of lay polygamy:

> [W]ith those who are joined in second marriages the focus is not on sin, but on the symbol *[sacramentum]* of the Church. For just as Christ ... is the husband of one bride, that is, of the whole holy Church, which is without doubt a virgin, since it keeps the integrity of the faith inviolably: so too each and every priest is commanded to be the husband of one wife, so that he may seem to present the image of that supreme spouse [Christ]. With [clerical] "bigamists," therefore, the issue is not the assessment of sin, but rather the form of the sacrament, and when they are excluded; it is not that a crime is being punished, but that the mystical role of the true priesthood is kept.[168]

Two centuries later, Thomas Aquinas elaborated on this argument. Second marriages by the laity were fine, he made clear, so long as the prior spouse was

[166] See D. c. 27, q. 12, 24, 40–41; c. 31.1.10; c. 33.5; X.4.17.14; Innocent IV, *Commentaria*, 112r-v; Hostiensis, *Summa*, 40–43; and summary of later medieval sources in Montaigne, *De Bigamia*, 126v-131r.

[167] Stefan Kuttner, "Pope Lucius III and the Bigamous Archbishop of Palermo," in J.A. Watt et al., eds., *Medieval Studies: Presented to Aubrey Gwynn* (Dublin: Colm o Lochlain, 1961), 409–451, at 410. See also Marchetto, "Primus fuit Lamech," 50–54, analyzing Montaigne's dependence on William Durandus.

[168] *Die Briefe des Petrus Damiani*, ed. K. Reindel (Munich: MGH, 1983), 1:464–65, using translation in D'Avray, *Medieval Marriage*, 135.

dead.[169] But second marriages by the clergy betrayed the purity of the single faithful union of Christ and his church symbolized in the sacrament of ordination or holy orders. The sacraments must "effect" and "reflect" what they symbolize, Thomas said again. "A minister is compared to his lord as an instrument to its principal.... [T]he instrument must be proportionate to the [principal]. Hence, the ministers of Christ, must be in conformity with Him."[170]

> By the sacrament of Order a man is appointed to the ministry of the sacraments; and he who is to administer the sacraments to others must suffer from no defect in the sacraments. Now there is a defect in a sacrament when the entire signification of the sacrament is not found therein. And the sacrament of marriage signifies the union of Christ with the Church, which is the union of one with one. Therefore the perfect signification of the sacrament requires the husband to have only one wife, and the wife to have but one husband; and consequently, bigamy, which does away with this causes irregularity....

> There is another consequent reason assigned, since those who receive the sacrament of Order should be signalized by the greatest spirituality, both because they administer spiritual things, namely the sacraments, and because they teach spiritual things, and should be occupied in spiritual matters. Wherefore since concupiscence is most incompatible with spirituality, inasmuch as it makes man to be wholly carnal, they should give no sign of persistent concupiscence, which does indeed show itself in bigamous persons, seeing that they were unwilling to be content with one wife.[171]

Aquinas's concern about the risk of spiritually and morally weak clerics betraying the church and its clerical offices was one that first millennium writers had already stressed.[172] It was just too risky to appoint to clerical office a person who had shown that he could not control himself sexually – who betrayed "persistent concupiscence," in Thomas's words, by entering more than one marriage. Placing such persons in clerical office would erode the moral authority and spiritual dignity of the church and the clergy. But Aquinas's other concern was that the sacrament of Holy Orders could not be opened to those who could not meet basic eligibility requirements, including the Bible's explicit command that the clergy be pure, upright, and "the husband of one wife." To allow a polygamist to become a cleric would be to insult the dignity of the sacrament of orders. It would also insult the dignity of the sacrament of marriage. Not only would it defy the New Testament

---

[169] SCG IV.63.
[170] SCG IV.74. Following the modern legal language of principal and agent, I interpolated the term "principal" in the quotation. See also ST Supp. qq. 36 and 39 on qualities required for and impediments barring receipt of this sacrament.
[171] ST Supp, q. 66, art. 1.
[172] See discussion in Chapter 2, pp. 75–76, 93–95.

ideal of Christian monogamy symbolized in both sacraments. It would also expose a lay Christian couple to the indignity of being married, pastored, and disciplined by a cleric whose own life betrayed New Testament ideals for marriage. How could the church allow a polygamous priest to bless a monogamous Christian union? This argument gained even more power after the Council of Trent in 1563 ordered every Christian marriage to be blessed by an ordained priest. For that priest to be a bigamist was a desecration of the sacraments.

These intense interior theological debates about ordination of clerical bigamists were more remote from the ongoing Western case against real polygamy. But they underscored a more general teaching that the Western legal tradition often repeated: that each individual marriage embodied, symbolized, and celebrated the community's ideal of marriage. Not just anyone could get married. Not just any union was a marriage. And, now the new point highlighted by the clerical bigamy concern, not just anyone could preside at a wedding. Weddings were special moments of enactment, actualization, and celebration of the community's monogamous ideals, and important moments for teaching and modeling these ideas. The clergy who presided over this teaching and celebration had, especially, to embody the very ideals of matrimony that the wedding was enacting. In Catholic circles, that embodiment of monogamy was symbolic: in the priest's exclusive marriage to the church in emulation of Christ's mysterious union with the church, his bride. In later Protestant circles, that embodiment was literal: the married clergy presiding at weddings were to be exemplars of faithful and exclusive monogamous marriage here and now. But the basic symbolic point was the same: that weddings were the special times to celebrate the community's monogamous ideals.

These medieval discussions of clerical bigamy added nuance to the Western understanding of degrees or grades of polygamy and the variant punishments that should attach to them. In cases of improper remarriage, the canon law, we saw, distinguished between (1) unintended or accidental remarriages (where parties remarried on the mistaken assumption that the first spouse was dead or that their first marriage had properly ended by annulment); and (2) intentional or fraudulent remarriage (where one party knowingly hid a prior marriage from an innocent spouse, knowingly engaged in "self-divorce" in defiance of the authorities, or – even worse – when the parties colluded or cooperated in the bigamy).[173]

Clerical marriage doctrine made a comparable distinction between "unintentional" and "intentional" clerical bigamists. The first group were clergy who did not think they had a disqualifying second relationship or did not know their wives were not virgins upon their marriage. For them, bigamy was, in effect, a strict liability offense. Even without intent, they were still punished as clerical bigamists, losing their

---

[173] On the practice of "self-divorce," in pp. 291–292, 404.

clerical offices, livings, and privileges, unless they could procure a dispensation. The second group were clergy who had hid or lied about their own or their wife's second sexual relationship, only to have that fraud discovered later. They suffered the same penalties as unintentional bigamists, plus they faced excommunication and severe civil punishments and were never eligible for dispensation. After the fifteenth century, these distinctions between less and more serious degrees of polygamy would become important for the laws of church and state alike. Unintentional polygamists typically were punished more lightly – with fines, imprisonment, public exposure in pillories or scaffolds, or more seriously through banishment and hard labor for a period of five years. Intentional polygamists got much harsher punishments, and the truly brazen were whipped, and sometimes executed.

Finally, these medieval discussions of clerical bigamy highlighted an additional feature about bigamy or polygamy in the Western tradition: that it was a permanent defect, an indelible offense that could result in investigation and punishment many years after the fact. A long-sitting bishop or priest could suddenly find himself defrocked for clerical bigamy or blocked from ecclesiastical promotion if there was a hint of bigamous scandal. No statute of limitations attached to the offense. This feature, too, would become important for later laws of church and state, when these rules of clerical bigamy spilled over into the realm of lay polygamy. Even unintentional/innocent polygamists, whose prior undissolved marriage was discovered long after the fact, could have their second marriage involuntarily dissolved, their children illegitimated, their property rights reassigned, and their lives disrupted by criminal sanctions and civil damages payable to first spouses and their children.

SUMMARY AND CONCLUSIONS

The Western legal tradition first systematized its sacramental theology and canon law of monogamous marriage in the twelfth and thirteenth centuries. Medieval writers treated marriage as a natural, contractual, and sacramental unit at once. Marriage is a natural association, created by God as a "two in one flesh union" designed to enable man and woman to "be fruitful and multiply" and to raise children in the service and love of God. Since the fall into sin, marriage has also become a remedy for lust, a channel to direct one's natural passion to the service of the community and the church. Marriage is a contractual unit, formed by the voluntary and mutual consent of the two parties. The marital contract prescribes for couples a life-long relation of exclusive love, service, and devotion to each other and their children – both in sickness and in health, and for better or for worse. And marriage is a sacrament for Christians, expressing and symbolizing the enduring and exclusive union between

Christ and his church. This sacramental theology placed marriage squarely within the social hierarchy of the church and within the jurisdiction of the church courts.

From the thirteenth century onward, the church courts took the lead in governing questions of marital formation, maintenance, and dissolution, as well as enforcing the norms of sexual morality. The church courts punished real polygamy (one man with two or more spouses at the same time) as a violation of the essential natural, contractual, and sacramental qualities of marriage. Polygamy was a defiance of the natural "two in one flesh" structure of marriage. It was a betrayal of man's contractual duties to his first wife and their children. And it was an insult to the sacramental ideal of marriage as an exclusive and enduring mysterious union. While medieval church courts took the lead in prosecuting polygamy, Continental secular courts and the Inquisition also competed for jurisdiction. Together these courts imposed fines and penitential works for those who mistakenly or negligently took a second wife, and more serious punishments of prison, banishment, galley service, and execution for those who knowingly cohabited with multiple wives and remained recalcitrant.

For medieval jurists and theologians, real polygamy was backward, harmful, and unnatural. It was the practice of backward communities that had not yet come to a full understanding of virtue. It put too much stock in the artificial prestige of plural wives and multiple children. It showed too little understanding of the mutual love, protection, and procreation that are the happy hallmarks of proper monogamous marriage. Such backwardness could be seen in the ancient households of Old Testament patriarchs and modern day Muslims alike.

Real polygamy was also harmful. Women are harmed because they are reduced to rival slaves within the household, exploited for sex with an increasingly sterile and distracted husband, sometimes deprived of the children they do produce, and forced to make do for themselves and their children with too few resources as other women and children are added to the household against their wishes. Children are harmed because their chances of birth and survival are diminished by their calculating fathers who might contracept, abort, smother, or sell them, and by their mothers who sometimes lack the resources, support, and protection to bring them to term, let alone to adulthood. Men are harmed because they do not have the time, energy, or resources to support their polygamous households, because their bodies cannot sustain their fertility with so many sexual demands, and because their minds and hearts cannot rest if they are always on the lookout for another shapely woman to add to their harems or for another dangerous man who will abduct his women. And societies are harmed because polygamy results in too many unattached men who become menaces to public order and morality. Moreover, polygamous households "confuse city and household," producing unfit citizens and creating ad hoc seats of power based on sheer numbers rather than on legitimate political succession.

Polygamy was unnatural as well, for it betrayed the natural pair-bonding strategies of procreation that humans needed to accommodate several peculiar natural characteristics. First, unlike most other animals, humans crave sex all the time, especially when they are young and most fertile. They do not have a short rutting or mating season, followed by a long period of sexual quietude. Second, unlike most other animals, human babies are born weak, fragile, and utterly dependent for many years. They are not ready to run, swim, or fly away upon birth or shortly thereafter. They need food, shelter, clothing, and education. Most human mothers have a hard time caring fully for their children on their own, especially if they already have several others. They need help, especially from the fathers. Third, however, most fathers will bond and help with a child only if they are certain of their paternity. Put a baby cradle on a street corner, medieval writers argued, and most women will stop out of natural empathy. Most men will walk by, unless they are unusually charitable. Once assured of their paternity, however, most men will bond deeply with their children, help with their care and support, and defend them at great sacrifice. For they will see their children as a continuation and extension of themselves, of their name, property, and teachings, of their own bodies and beings – of their genes, we now say. Fourth, unlike virtually all other animals, humans have the freedom and the capacity to engage in species-destructive behavior in pursuit of their own sexual gratification. Given the lower risks and costs to them, men are more prone to extramarital sex than women, exploiting prostitutes, concubines, and servant girls in so doing and yielding a perennial underclass of "bastards" who have rarely fared well in any culture.

Given these four factors, nature and its laws have strongly inclined rational human persons to develop enduring and exclusive marriages as the best form and forum of sexual bonding and reproductive success. Faithful and healthy monogamous marriages are designed to provide for the sexual needs and desires of a husband and wife. They ensure that both fathers and mothers are certain that a baby born to them is theirs. They ensure that husband and wife will together care for, nurture, and educate their children until they mature. And they deter both spouses from destructive sexual behavior outside the home. The natural law thus inclines men and women toward marriage, and provides them with the natural rights and duties to care for each other and for their children.

Polygamy might ensure paternal certainty, but only at too high a cost. Although a polygamous man usually has his sexual desires met, his multiple wives often do not, producing rivalry and discord in the home. Although a polygamous father may know who his children are, his children have to work hard to get his attention, affection, and resources which are dissipated over multiple wives and children. Although polygamy might seem to contain extramarital sex better than monogamy, the opposite is often true. A polygamous man, not schooled by monogamous habits, will always be tempted to add another attractive woman to his harem. A co-wife, once pushed aside by another, will be sorely tempted to test her neighbor's or servant's bed, unless threatened with grave retribution. And single men, with fewer chances to marry, will resort more readily to prostitution, seduction, and other destructive sexual behavior.

This naturalist argument was further enhanced by a moral argument designed to tilt this natural inclination more decisively in favor of monogamous and enduring marriages. It is naturally unjust to women and children, medieval writers argued, to permit fornication, adultery, polygyny, polygamy, or voluntary divorce. Each of these sexual activities erodes paternal certainty and investment in child care. It dilutes family resources, energy, and time that must now be spent on care for extra-marital children. It produces illegitimate children who are stigmatized and discriminated against throughout their lives by their extramarital birth. It brings disease, strife, and harm into the family and into the marital bed. And it detracts from the mutual support and love that husbands and wives owe to each other throughout their lives, even after their children are mature.

Among medieval Christians, marriage was not just a natural but also a sacramental union, a vital example and instantiation of the enduring and mysterious love of Christ and his Church. The sacrament of marriage elevated the natural goods of procreation and marital fidelity into a divine act, modeled on the creative act of God the Father in Paradise, and the sacrificial act of God the Son, who gave his life and body to the church. The sacrament of marriage also elevated the natural configuration of marriage. Marriage was no longer just a set of biological inclinations and moral instructions for men and women to form enduring and exclusive bonds for the sake of each other and their children. Sacramental marriage was a channel of divine grace, like baptism, penance, or the eucharist. Voluntary participation in it brought special divine blessings upon the couple, their children, and the broader communities of which they were a part. Sacramental marriage was also a channel of divine work, the means God chose not only to perpetuate the human species, but also to preserve his church.

This sacramental logic not only bolstered the medieval case against real polygamy, but also helped systematize the medieval case against clerical and successive polygamy. What all these forms of polygamy had in common was that they defied the sacramental ideal of marriage as an enduring and exclusive union modeled on Christ's mysterious union with his one holy, catholic, and apostolic church. All these unions suffered from "a sacramental defect," even if they were not all necessarily unnatural, unjust, or harmful.

On this logic, the least serious form of polygamy was "clerical bigamy" – where a candidate for clerical ordination had properly married a second time (say, after the death of his wife or the annulment of his first marriage) or married a woman who was not a virgin at the time of their marriage. Clerical bigamy of this sort, medieval writers repeatedly made clear, was not a crime. It just made the candidate ineligible to take holy orders because of the sacramental defect. It was more serious if he hid his or her wife's double relationships and assumed clerical office. But the sin and crime then was fraud, perjury, and desecration of the sacrament of holy orders, not polygamy. It was still more serious if the cleric, before or after ordination, kept multiple wives, fiancées, or concubines. But that was the sin and crime of "real polygamy," not clerical bigamy. This was a cleric who was a bigamist, not a "clerical bigamist," a critical distinction in the Middle Ages.

More serious than clerical bigamy were the too frequent remarriages of widow(er)s. Remarriage after the death of a spouse was allowed. But it was often frowned upon and discouraged, especially if repeated by someone who suffered the loss of two or more spouses. After all, St. Paul had counseled widows, especially if they were beyond child-bearing years, to forgo remarriage. Some medieval writers thought such remarriages were not sacramental, even if valid, and the canon law prohibited ordained clergy from blessing or presiding over the weddings of those who remarried. Local rowdy crowds of lay *charivari* underscored this stigma attached to remarriage by jeering at the newly married couple.

A bit more serious still were those who remarried without being absolutely sure about the death of the first spouse. These were the wives of soldiers, merchants, or crusaders, or the husbands of abducted, deserting, or runaway wives who could not be found. In the first millennium, the canon law allowed the abandoned spouse who made a good faith effort to find their lost spouse to remarry with impunity. After 1200, the canon law forbad such remarriages unless and until there was absolute certainty that the first spouse was dead. Parties who remarried without such proof risked charges of unintentional polygamy – even more so if the long gone spouse returned to the surprise of all.

The most serious case of successive polygamy was the remarriage of a divorcee before the death of the first spouse. These remarriages were not just against the counsel of Paul. They were against the express commandment of both Jesus and Paul, who called such remarriages, especially those involving divorced women, a form of adultery. Already in the later first millennium, the canon law had eventually settled on the rule that estranged parties could get divorced – in the sense of being separated from bed and board. But they could not remarry until the first spouse was dead. The medieval canon law maintained these rules, and charged prematurely remarried divorcees with polygamy. It was a less serious offense if the party thought the first spouse was dead, but was simply mistaken: that was unintentional polygamy. It was more serious if the party knew the first spouse was alive, but kept it hidden, and remarried nonetheless. This was not uncommon for those who moved to a new region and sought to start life anew. If found out, these parties were subject to charges of both adultery against the first spouse and polygamy. This was only one step short of sharing a bed with two spouses at once ("real polygamy"), and was a serious offense against the laws of church and state by the end of the Middle Ages.

5

Polygamous Experiments in Early Protestantism

FIGURE 11. "Parable of the Ten Virgins," from *Kirchen Postilla, das ist, Auslegung der Epistein vnd Evangelien.*
Courtesy of the Richard C. Kessler Reformation Collection, Pitts Theology Library.
Candler School of Theology, Emory University.

FIGURE 12. "The Harem," from John Frederick Lewis, V and A Images, London.
Used by permission of V & A Images, London / Art Resource, New York.

The Protestant Reformation that Martin Luther (1483–1546) unleashed in 1517 began
as a loud call for freedom – freedom of the church from the tyranny of the pope,
freedom of the laity from the hegemony of the clergy, freedom of the conscience
from the strictures of canon law. "Freedom of the Christian" was the rallying cry of
the early Lutheran Reformation. It drove theologians and jurists, clergy and laity,
princes and peasants alike to denounce church authorities and legal structures
with unprecedented alacrity. "One by one, the structures of the church were thrust
into the glaring light of the Word of God and forced to show their true colors,"
Jaroslav Pelikan writes.[1] Few church structures survived this scrutiny in the heady
days of the 1520s. The church's canon law books were burned. Church courts were
closed. Monastic institutions and endowed benefices were dissolved. Church lands
were seized. Clerical privileges were stripped. Mandatory celibacy was suspended.
Indulgence trafficking was condemned. Annates to Rome were outlawed. Ties to the
pope were severed. Within a generation after Luther posted his Ninety-Five Theses
on the church door of Wittenberg, the Protestant Reformation had "turned the
world upside down" and permanently destroyed the unity of Western Christendom.[2]

---

[1] Jaroslav Pelikan, *Spirit versus Structure: Luther and the Institutions of the Church* (New York: Harper
    & Row, 1968), 5.
[2] Acts 17:6. See details in John Witte, Jr., *Law and Protestantism: The Legal Teachings of the Lutheran
    Reformation* (Cambridge: Cambridge University Press, 2002).

The Protestant reformers took early aim at the medieval theology and law of marriage, including its intricate rules on polygamy. For Protestants, the Catholic Church's jurisdiction over marriage and its elaborate system of canon law was a flagrant usurpation of the magistrate's authority. The Catholic sacramental concept of marriage on which the church predicated its jurisdiction was, for most Protestants, a self-serving theological fiction. The canonical prohibition on marriage of clergy and monastics ignored the Bible's teachings on sexual sin and the Christian vocation as the reformers understood them. The church's intricate rules governing sexual desire and expression, even within marriage, were seen as a gratuitous insult to God's gift of marital love and an unnecessary intrusion on private life and Christian conscience. The canon law's long roll of impediments to engagement and marriage and its prohibitions against complete divorce and remarriage stood in considerable tension with the Protestant understanding of the natural and biblical right and duty of each fit adult to marry and remarry.

Early Protestants leaders, beginning with Luther, began to act on their new ideas about sexuality and marriage. Like Luther, many of them were ex-priests or ex-monastics who forsook their orders and vows, and married shortly thereafter – committing spiritual adultery and bigamy in so doing. New Protestant converts followed these leaders' examples by marrying, divorcing, and remarrying in open contempt of canon law rules. As Catholic Church courts and their secular counterparts began punishing these canon law offenses with growing severity, Protestant theologians and jurists rose to the defense of their coreligionists, producing a welter of new writings that denounced traditional norms and pronounced a new Protestant gospel of marriage and marital freedom.

Protestant political leaders rapidly translated this new gospel into new civil laws. Long envious of the church's jurisdiction over marriage, Protestant magistrates had new marriage laws on the books usually within a decade after accepting Protestantism. These new Protestant marriage laws together (1) shifted marital jurisdiction from the church to the state; (2) abolished monasteries and convents; (3) commended, if not commanded, the marriage of clergy; (4) rejected the sacramentality of marriage and the religious tests and spiritual impediments traditionally imposed on Christian marital unions; (5) banned secret or private marriages and required the participation of parents, peers, priests, and political officials in the process of marriage formation; (6) sharply curtailed the number of impediments to engagements and marriages that abridged the right to marry or remarry; and (7) introduced fault-based complete divorce with a subsequent right for divorcees to remarry. The Western legal tradition would not see such sweeping reforms of its marital laws again until the liberal cultural and constitutional reforms of the past half century.

These radical legal and theological changes born of the Protestant Reformation permanently changed the Western case against polygamy. The medieval church had required a celibate clergy, and deemed twice married clerical candidates to be clerical bigamists or polygamists unworthy of holy orders. The Protestant reformers called for married clerics, and cared little how often a priestly candidate or his wife had been validly married. The medieval church had allowed monastic vows to trump marital promises and had charged former monastics who married with both spiritual adultery and polygamy. The Protestant reformers abolished the monasteries and encouraged their monks and nuns to marry in exercise of their God-given freedom. The medieval church had discouraged the remarriage of widow(er)s and withheld from these unions the church's blessing, if not its sacramental seal. The reformers encouraged the widowed to remarry and welcomed them to the church's wedding altar, offering special liturgies and ministries for second marriages. The medieval canon law had treated divorce as separation from bed and board and prohibited divorcees from remarriage before the death of the first spouse. The reformers authorized absolute divorce on proof of serious fault, and encouraged divorcees to get remarried soon thereafter, doubly so if they still had strong sexual drives to control or household businesses to manage.[3]

These contrasts in approach permanently shifted the focus of Western state law to real polygamy alone. Both clerical and successive polygamy – the multiple marriages of aspiring clergy and monastics and the improper remarriages of widow(er)s and divorcees – remained important concerns for the Catholic Church and its internal canon law and, for a time, the Anglican Church and English ecclesiastical law as well.[4] But the state laws of early modern Protestant lands, and eventually the state laws of Catholic lands, too, became increasingly focused on real polygamy alone.

Real polygamy became the new focus of the Western legal tradition in no small part because it had become a temporary new reality in sixteenth-century Protestant lands. With all the radical changes that the Protestant reformers introduced to long settled marital theories and laws, some new Protestants experimented with polygamy, too, following the examples of the biblical patriarchs. A few enterprising Protestant monarchs and nobles asserted the right to take second wives as equitable dispensations from the positive law and as viable applications of the natural law. New converts to the Protestant cause abandoned their Catholic homelands and households and took new Protestant spouses, even though their first marriages to Catholic spouses were still intact. Colonial settlers, seeking freedom across the

---

3 See detailed sources and analysis of these reforms in Lutheran, Calvinist, and Anglican lands in John Witte, Jr., *From Sacrament to Contract: Marriage, Religion, and Law in the Western Tradition*, 2nd ed. (Louisville, KY: Westminster John Knox Press, 2012), 113–286.

4 These issues remain important in modern Catholic canon law. See Code of Canon Law (1983): Title VII: Marriage, Can. 1055–1165. For earlier Anglican law, see Helen L. Parish, *Clerical Marriage and the English Reformation: Precedent, Policy, Practice* (Burlington, VT: Ashgate, 2000); Richard Burn, *Ecclesiastical Law*, 8th ed. (London: A. Strahan, 1824), 1:192–193.

Atlantic, married new spouses abroad without severing their marital ties at home. Various Anabaptist groups, most notoriously those gathered in the German city of Münster in the early 1530s, took up polygamy en masse in imitation of the Old Testament patriarchs and in an effort to populate the world more quickly with true believers like themselves. A few sympathetic theologians began to write openly that polygamy was a lesser evil than adultery or divorce in individual cases, perhaps even a licit alternative to monogamy in certain communities. All the elegantly wrapped interpretations of biblical texts and teachings about polygamy inherited from the Church Fathers and medieval scholastics were ripped open and reinvestigated in the name of Christian liberty, biblical piety, and humanist inquiry. Millennium-long legal prohibitions on polygamy were openly challenged as unjust encroachments on Christian freedom.

These radical new experiments with polygamy alarmed the Catholic authorities, and eventually the Protestant authorities as well. For Catholics, such scandals were precisely the kind of social and moral fallout to be expected from Martin Luther's heretical ranting and his simple-minded calls for the priesthood of all believers to live by the Bible alone (*sola Scriptura*), unaided by a living tradition or a learned clergy.[5] The Council of Trent in 1563 included polygamy among the "new Protestant heresies" that deserved its anathema. Both the Inquisition and Catholic secular authorities went after polygamists and their apologists with a vengeance, sending hundreds of them to row in the galleys as prisoners and a few of the more brazen polygamists to swing from the gallows as a warning to the rest.[6]

By the later sixteenth century, the Protestant leadership of all denominations – Anabaptists notably included – firmly rebuked polygamy as well. Protestant theologians offered detailed new interpretations of the relevant biblical texts to show how and why traditional prohibitions on real polygamy needed to be retained, even while many other traditional teachings on sex, marriage, and family life needed to be reformed. Their arguments echoed some of the natural and contractual perspectives on monogamous marriage taught by the medieval Catholic tradition. But, in place of traditional sacramental theories, several Protestants developed new covenantal theories of marriage that defended monogamy on biblical, equitable, and utilitarian grounds, and denounced polygamy as unnatural, unjust, and dangerous. Protestant political leaders, in turn, passed firm new secular laws against polygamy, making it a capital crime if done intentionally. By the mid-sixteenth century, most Protestant lands on the Continent placed prosecution of polygamy firmly in the hands of

---

[5]   For the medieval theory of sola Scriptura, that left biblical interpretation to the papacy and church councils, see Brian Tierney, "*Sola Scriptura* and the Canonists," *Studia Gratiana* 11 (1967): 347–366.

[6]   See sources listed in Chapter 4, notes 42–44 in this volume. On the inquisition's work in the Americas, see discussion in Chapter 10, p. 392.

the state criminal courts, with church courts and consistories removing polygamy cases to them for criminal punishment. By the turn of the seventeenth century, the English common law followed suit. Parliament passed an aggressive new capital law against polygamy in 1604 and the Old Bailey and other state courts took over most real polygamy cases from the English ecclesiastical courts.

This chapter analyzes the various experiments with polygamy in the sixteenth century. It also samples some of the strongest new arguments for polygamy put forward by the apologists, most notably those of Bernard Ochino (1487–1564). The next two chapters then sample some of the emerging new Protestant theologies of monogamous marriage and their accompanying arguments against polygamy and their implementation in early modern civil law and common law lands.

HENRY VIII AND THE PROSPECTS OF POLYGAMY

Two headline cases in the early years of the Reformation put marital reform and polygamous experimentation at the center of the new rivalries between Catholics and Protestants. The first was the divorce and remarriage case pressed by King Henry VIII of England against his wife Catherine of Aragon. Real polygamy was one option considered in the heat of the battle that broke out between the king and the pope. The case eventually ended with Henry's unilateral divorce from Catherine and remarriage to Anne Boleyn – a form of successive polygamy per the medieval canon law but a solution that was eventually accepted in the English common law. The second was the notorious polygamy case pressed by Lutheran Prince Philip of Hesse who wanted to marry a second woman while retaining his first wife. Divorce and remarriage were the preferred options pressed strongly by his advisors. But Philip chose real polygamy instead, advertising to the world that Luther and his colleagues had condoned this option if his conscience absolutely demanded it. Both cases drove scholars on all sides back to the sources to weigh anew the Western case for and against polygamy.

The first case, involving King Henry VIII (1491–1547) and his bride Catherine of Aragon (1485–1536), raised intriguing technical questions of canon law.[7] The familiar facts in brief are these: Henry VIII's father, Henry VII, had come to the English throne in 1485, a victor in the bloody War of the Roses over the question of royal succession. Henry VII's first son, Prince Arthur, was his heir apparent. Arthur's

---

[7] In the vast literature, see especially Catherine Fletcher, *The Divorce of Henry VIII: The Untold Story from Inside the Vatican* (New York: Palgrave MacMillan, 2012); Henry Ansgar Kelly, *The Matrimonial Trials of Henry VIII* (Stanford, CA: Stanford University Press, 1976); Diarmand MacCulloch, *Thomas Cranmer: A Life* (New Haven, CT: Yale University Press, 1996), 41–78; G. Bedouelle and P. LeGal, *Le Divorce du Roi Henry VIII: Études et Documents* (Geneva: Travaux d'Humanisme et Renaissance, 1987).

siring of a son was critical to ensuring a male successor to the English throne for at least two more generations and averting another civil war. Prince Arthur was thus engaged as an infant to Catherine of Aragon, the daughter of Ferdinand and Isabella of Spain – an engagement that also helped seal favorable diplomatic relations between England and Spain. Arthur and Catherine were married in 1501. Prince Arthur died in 1502 – childless.

Henry VII's second son, Henry (VIII), now became heir to the throne. In a continued effort to secure peace between England and Spain, the 12-year-old Prince Henry was engaged to his brother's widow, Catherine, in 1503. This engagement of a widow to her former brother-in-law, however, raised a difficult legal question. The Mosaic law spoke three times to the issue, and not altogether clearly. Leviticus 18:16 stated: "You shall not uncover the nakedness of your brother's wife; she is your brother's nakedness." Leviticus 20:21 underscored this prohibition with a threat that the new couple "shall be childless." But Deuteronomy 25:5 provided: "[I]f brothers dwell together, and one of them dies and has no son, the wife of the dead shall not be married outside the family to a stranger; her husband's brother shall go in to her, and take her as wife, and perform the duty of a husband's brother to her." The Jewish tradition had reconciled these passages by reading the first two Leviticus passages to govern relations when both brothers are alive, and the Deuteronomy passage to govern only after one brother has died.[8] But the Christian tradition had not accepted this reading unequivocally – in part because of the fear that a brother, with more opportunity than a third party, might be tempted to seduce his sister-in-law and conspire to kill his brother (his lover's husband) in order to marry her.[9]

The prevailing Catholic canon law on the subject treated the relationship of a man and the widow of his brother as one of affinity. This relationship was an impediment to marriage and would lead to the involuntary annulment of a putative marriage contracted in violation of it. The canonists, however, had also maintained that the pope, as final interpreter of the canon law, could grant a dispensation from this and other biblical impediments in specific cases of necessity. Such dispensations were viewed as equitable exceptions to the usual rules. In this case of affinity, a dispensation could be especially compelling, given the injunction of care for a brother's widow set out in Deuteronomy 25:5. Medieval popes had exercised this power of dispensation, and waived impediments of affinity in a number of cases of budding royal and aristocratic marriages between former brothers- and sisters-in-law. Indeed, Catherine's sister Isabella was granted precisely such a dispensation from an impediment of affinity in 1500, under pressure on the papacy by her father, Ferdinand.

---

[8]   See discussion in Chapter 1, pp. 53–55.
[9]   See discussion in Chapter 3, p. 127.

On petition to Pope Julius II in 1504, therefore, Catherine was given a dispensation to marry Henry when they both came of age. They were married in 1509, just after Henry VIII had succeeded to the English throne. Catherine gave birth to six children, including two princes, but they were all stillborn or died in infancy except Mary, born in 1516. Popular sentiment of the day described this ill fate as the scourge of childlessness promised by the Mosaic law. The lack of a male successor carried more than the usual disappointment to the hopeful couple and nation. Against the backdrop of the War of the Roses, it posed a real threat of renewed civil war. In desperation – or infatuation – Henry VIII had taken a mistress named Mary and sired an illegitimate son, Henry Fitzroy. But the claim of an illegitimate child to succeed to the throne was dubious at best, and the efforts to legitimate him failed completely.[10]

Henry VIII grew disenchanted with Catherine, and by 1527, he and his advisors had come upon the legal formula to be rid of her. Henry announced that he had become convinced that his marriage to Catherine was against the law of God set forth in Leviticus 18. This law, he alleged, had been improperly waived by Pope Julius II's dispensation in 1504. It would violate his "scruple of conscience," Henry said, to continue his marriage in open violation of God's law. At the king's urging, the Archbishop of York, Cardinal Thomas Wolsey, convened a secret ex officio inquisitorial trial, which canon law empowered him to do. At trial, Henry was accused of violating the divine law of Leviticus 18 that prohibited his marriage to his brother's widow. Henry's defense was that the papal dispensation of Julius II granted him permission to marry. The promoter for the inquisitorial court then predictably attacked, at length, the procedural propriety and substantive legitimacy of the dispensation. Henry and his advisors evidently thought that this bit of legal maneuvering would end the matter. Pope Julius's 1504 dispensation from the impediment of affinity would prove to be improper and be reversed. Henry's marriage to Catherine would thus be invalid and automatically annulled. Henry would perform a requisite penance for his sin of violating Leviticus 18. He would then be free to marry again. And a new woman to marry was at hand. Everyone thought that the intended new wife was to be Mary, Henry's former mistress and mother of Henry Fitzroy. A marriage of Henry VIII and Mary could render their bastard son Henry's claim to the throne considerably stronger.[11] Henry, however, secretly desired to marry not Mary, but Mary's sister, Anne Boleyn.

---

[10] See John Witte, Jr., *The Sins of the Fathers: The Law and Theology of Illegitimacy Reconsidered* (Cambridge: Cambridge University Press, 2009), 113–114.

[11] Both civil law and canon law provided that a child could be legitimated by the subsequent marriage of its parents, but the common law of the day made no such provision. See sources and discussion in ibid., 60–62, 90, 111–115.

Confronted with these alarming new facts, Cardinal Wolsey took the case under advisement. He soon learned that the case was not nearly so easy as Henry and his counselors had hoped. First, he discovered that most canon law authorities did not think an inquisitorial court could reverse a papal dispensation, rendering any such judgment vulnerable on appeal to Rome. Second, Catherine had come to learn of the secret proceeding and stood up to fight for her marriage to Henry. She introduced a vital new fact that changed the legal question completely: her first marriage to Henry's brother, Arthur, had never been consummated through sexual intercourse. She was thus a virgin at the time of her marriage to Henry, she argued, and Henry in fact knew this. According to some canonists who still regarded consummation as critical to the formation of marriage, this meant she was technically not the wife or widow of Arthur, and no impediment of affinity precluded her marriage to Henry. According to other canonists who regarded the contract as critical to the formation of marriage, this meant that the only impediment that stood in the way of her marriage to Henry was a more minor impediment of "public honesty." This minor impediment was routinely dispensed in other cases. It could easily be covered by Julius's 1504 dispensation, or easily procured after the fact and applied retroactively. Either way, Catherine argued, the validity of Pope Julius II's dispensation was not critical, and Henry's scruple of conscience was not pressing. Then, to make the case even more difficult, Catherine demanded, as canon law allowed, that she be made a party to the case and given legal counsel, not only from England but also from abroad. What was supposed to have been a bit of secret legal maneuvering to be rid of his wife had suddenly escalated well beyond anything that Henry and his advisors could have imagined.

The case was rendered even more complicated by Henry's secret desire to marry Anne Boleyn. The same impediment of affinity under dispute in Henry's relationship with Catherine also stood in the way of Henry's intended marriage to Anne Boleyn. Having already consensually consummated his relationship with Anne's sister Mary, Henry had, by some accounts, married her, albeit bigamously. His "marriage" to Mary created a similar impediment of affinity to marrying Mary's sister, Anne Boleyn. For Leviticus 18 had likewise precluded a man from marrying his (deceased) wife's sister. Henry thus found himself in a most untenable position. In the case of his current wife, Catherine, he had just argued that the impediment of affinity could not be dispensed with, and an annulment must be granted. In the case of his intended new wife, Anne, he would have to argue that the impediment of affinity must be dispensed with, and permission to marry must be granted. The contradiction was too plain to ignore.

Henry sought to escape this dilemma by appealing to the new Pope, Clement VII, for a dispensation to marry Anne Boleyn. Clement was trapped – both by precedent and by politics. According to canon law precedents, the granting of a dispensation for Henry to marry Anne was premature, because Henry was still married to Catherine. And to dispense with the impediment of affinity in this case was tacitly to confirm the propriety of Julius II's dispensation from the impediment of affinity in 1504 and to underscore the indissolubility of Henry's first marriage to Catherine. Moreover, Clement had just surrendered to Catherine's nephew, Charles V, the Holy Roman Emperor, who had sacked Rome. Clement was in no position to alienate his captor by ill treatment of his captor's aunt, Catherine. Neither sovereign could be entirely disappointed. To assuage Henry, Clement granted him on April 13, 1528, a dispensation to marry Anne, pending resolution of his case with Catherine. To assuage Charles, Clement on the same day commissioned his own legatine inquisitorial court to rehear the case for annulment, taking the matter out of Cardinal Wolsey's discretion and placing it beyond Henry's immediate control.

On May 31, 1529, the legatine court commenced a public inquisition in England, but after six weeks of legal wrangling, the pope ordered the entire case removed to Rome. He further ordered Henry to suspend his planned marriage to Anne pending the papal court's final resolution of his case against Catherine. When Clement learned of Henry's open consorting with Anne, he issued a stern letter to Henry on January 25, 1532, threatening to excommunicate him if he did not leave Anne and return to Catherine.

Instead of leaving Anne, Henry left the pope, and took the entire English church with him. In the autumn of 1532, he impregnated Anne – with the later Queen Elizabeth. On January 25, 1533, he secretly married her, despite his existing marriage to Catherine, thus becoming a real polygamist. Two months later, he pushed through Parliament the Act in Restraint of Appeals to Rome, which placed marital jurisdiction firmly under the king and his designates. On May 28, 1533, an English inquisitorial court, convened by Thomas Cranmer, declared that the marriage of Henry and Catherine was annulled. Cranmer then ratified the secret marriage of Henry and Anne, saying nothing about the impediment of affinity between them. On April 4, 1534, Parliament confirmed Archbishop Cranmer's sentences in the Act of Succession, which guaranteed the legitimacy of their daughter Elizabeth's claim to the throne. To remove any lingering doubt about the pope's control, Henry pushed through Parliament the Supremacy Act of 1534, declaring himself and his successors to be "the only supreme head in earth of the Church of England."[12]

The Counsel of Polygamy

Few matrimonial cases, before or since, have reached this level of complexity, intrigue, and machination. As the showdown between the king and the pope

[12] 26 Henry VIII, c. 1.

escalated, various scholars and diplomats throughout Europe weighed in, trying to find a via media between them. Real polygamy was among the alternatives proposed and discussed. Rather than allow Henry to divorce innocent Catherine and marry his adulterous lover, Anne, the proposal went, perhaps it would be better for Henry to retain Catherine as his wife and simply validate his de facto marriage to Anne, too, thereby legitimating any children born to them. There was biblical precedent for this: Jacob had married his beloved Rachel, while retaining his first wife, the unwanted older sister, Leah. King David had added Bathsheba to his harem, even though he had committed adultery with her and killed her husband; their son, Solomon, succeeded David to the throne of Israel and was reputed to be a wise and noble ruler, despite his own ample polygamy. Yes, these were extreme biblical cases, but Henry's case was extreme, too. England faced a real threat of renewed civil war without a legitimate (male) successor to the throne. And there was real threat to the future of a unified Christendom if this stubborn impasse over a single royal divorce case could not be broken. The stakes were high enough to make this the kind of special case of "necessity" that allowed for an equitable dispensation from the usual rules against polygamy. A few late medieval writers had already speculated about permissible polygamy on grounds of necessity.[13] Early on, Henry's counselors had thought of this idea, too, as had Erasmus of Rotterdam whom Catherine had consulted.[14] It was time to put all this book lore into practice.

A "great divine" of the Catholic Church counseled Clement to consider offering Henry the option of polygamy instead of a fraudulent annulment.[15] Commentators then and now thought this "great divine" was Cardinal Cajetan, who had written openly that polygamy was consistent with natural law and could be used in special cases of real necessity.[16] In the fall of 1530, while the case was pending in Rome, Pope

[13] See discussion in Chapter 4, pp. 166–169; and see discussions of the polygamy option among scholars and diplomats in the 1520s and early 1530s in William W. Rockwell, *Die Doppelehe des Landgrafen Philipp von Hessen* (Marburg: N.G. Elwert'sche Verlagsbuchhandlung, 1904), 279–309; Erwin Doernberg, *Luther and Henry VIII* (Stanford, CA: Stanford University Press, 1961), 73–78.

[14] See J.S. Brewer, J. Gairdner, and R.H. Brodie, eds., *Letters and Papers, Foreign and Domestic of the Reign of Henry VIII*, 21 vols., 2nd. ed. (London: Her Majesty's Stationery Office, 1862–1920), 4:cccvii-viii and Fletcher, *The Divorce of Henry VIII*, 10–11, reporting that an English diplomat, William Knight, had in 1527 prepared a draft bull for Clement's signature permitting Henry's bigamy, though the proposal was dropped. See a comparable proposal in Erasmus of Rotterdam, *Collected Works of Erasmus: Spiritualia and Pastoralia*, eds. John W. O'Malley and Louis A. Perraud (Toronto: University of Toronto Press, 1999), Epistolae, xx, 87.

[15] The phrase is in the Letter of Dr. William Bennett to King Henry VIII (October 27, 1530), reprinted in Nicholas Pocock, ed., *Records of the Reformation: The Divorce, 1527–1533*, 2 vols. (Oxford: Clarendon Press, 1870), 1:448, 459.

[16] See Dennis Doherty, *The Sexual Doctrine of Cardinal Cajetan* (Regensburg: Verlag Friedrich Postet, 1966), 233–234; N. Paulus, "Cajetan und Luther über die Polygamie," *Historische-Politische Blätter* 135 (1907): 81–100, at 89–91; John L. Thompson, "Patriarchs, Polygamy, and Private Resistance: John

Clement VII had, reportedly, raised this counsel with envoys, who quietly asked Henry whether he would accept a dispensation to marry Anne, while still retaining Catherine as his wife. One English ambassador, Sir Gregory Casale, reported as follows to Henry VIII:

> A few days since, the Pope secretly proposed to me that your Majesty might be allowed two wives. I told him I could not undertake to make any such proposition, because I did not know whether it would satisfy your majesty's conscience. I made this answer because the Imperialists have this view, and are urging [it], but why I know not.[17]

The Bishops of Tarbes and Worcester reported similarly, in separate missives to Henry VIII, that Pope Clement had suggested to them that it might be less scandalous if Henry took Anne as his second bigamous wife rather than for him to divorce Catherine and then remarry his lover Anne, while Catherine was still living.[18] Another English ambassador in Rome, William Bennett, wrote the same thing to Henry, but then also reported that the pope's other advisors had counseled against him giving a papal dispensation for bigamy:

> Sire, shortly after my coming hither, the pope moves unto me a dispensation for two wives, which he spake at the same time so doubtfully that I suspected that he spake it for one of two purposes. The one was that I should have set it forward to your Highness, to the intent that if your Highness should have accepted it, thereby he shall have gotten a mean[s] to bring your Highness to grant that if he might dispense in this case, which is no less a case than your case is, consequently he might dispense in your Highness's case. The other was that I conjectured that it should be a thing proposed to entertain your Highness in some hope, whereby he might defer your case, to the intent that Your Grace should trust upon the same.

Calvin and Others on Breaking God's Rules," *Sixteenth Century Journal* 25 (1994): 3–27, at 8. See Chapter 4, pp. 168–169 for Cajetan's speculations on polygamy. Cajetan, however, wrote to Henry VIII directly on January 27, 1534, trying to demonstrate to him on biblical, canonical, and theological grounds that his marriage to Catherine was valid and could not be annulled. See Tommaso de Vio Cajetan, *Ad serenissimum Angliae regem fideique defensorem Henricum ius nominis octavum: de coniugio cum relicta fratis sententiae. De coniugio regis Angliae cum relicta fratis sui* (Rome: 1535), with an excerpt translated in Jared Wicks, ed., *Cajetan Responds: A Reader in Reformation Controversy* (Eugene, OR: Wipf & Stock, 2011), 38, 241ff.

[17] Letter of September 18, 1530, in Brewer et al., *Letters and Papers*, vol. 4, item 6627. Casale evidently had doubts about Henry's willingness to accept the option of bigamy because Henry had first proposed this solution to Clement, but then withdrew it in favor of seeking an annulment. Ibid., 4:cccvii-viii. See also Doernberg, *Luther and Henry VIII*, 74–76; John Cairncross, *After Polygamy Was Made a Sin: A Social History of Christian Polygamy* (London: Kegan and Paul, 1974), 57.

[18] Letter from Ghinnuci, Bishop of Worcester to Henry (received October 1, 1530), reprinted in Pocock, *Documents*, 2:5, 9; the letter of Gabriel de Grammont (Bishop of Tarbes) is described in Rockwell, *Die Doppelehe*, 302–303, and quoted in John A. Faulkner, "Luther and the Bigamous Marriage of Philip of Hesse," *The American Journal of Theology* 17 (1913): 206–231, at 222.

Then I asked His Holiness whether he was fully resolved that he might dispense in the same case, then His Holiness showed me, No; but said that a great divine showed him that he thought for avoiding a great inconvenience His Holiness might dispense in the same case; howbeit, he said he would counsel further upon it with his council. And now of late the pope showed me that his council showed him plainly that he could not do it.[19]

Lutheran theologians, when asked for their advice by English diplomats, also counseled polygamy in this case.[20] Luther agreed that Henry's marriage to Catherine was valid, and that Catherine should contest the divorce and retain her royal title. But then, echoing Erasmus's advice to Catherine, Luther wrote:

She should rather permit the King to marry a second queen according to the example set by the patriarchs, who had many wives, even prior to the law; but she herself should not agree to be excluded from the royal matrimony and from the title of the queen of England.[21]

Luther's leading Wittenberg colleague, Philip Melanchthon (1497–1560), likewise thought that Henry's first marriage to Catherine could not be broken, and he, too, counseled polygamy, even if the pope would not authorize it. Here "public utility commends a second marriage," wrote Melanchthon. "While I am loath to permit polygamy in general, in this case I would say that there is a great advantage to the kingdom and to the king's conscience for the king to take a second wife while maintaining the first. After all, polygamy is not prohibited by divine law. Nor is it that unusual" to pursue polygamy in cases of real individual necessity, as can be seen already in Pope Gregory II's letter to St. Boniface in 726 and in later cases where "popes have conceded it to others."[22] Melanchthon advised Henry to request

---

[19] Letter of Dr. William Bennett to King Henry VIII (October 27, 1530), reprinted in Pocock, ed., *Records*, 1:448, 458–459.

[20] See various examples in Preserved Smith, "German Opinion of the Divorce of Henry VIII," *English Historical Review* 27 (1912): 671–681.

[21] Letter to Robert Barnes (September 3, 1531), in *Luther's Works*, Jaroslov Pelikan and Helmut Lehman, trans. and ed. (St. Louis, MO: Concordia Publishing House, 1955–1968), 50:33, n. 40 [hereafter LW]. See two variations of the original in *D. Martin Luthers Werke: Briefwechsel*, 17 vols. (Weimar: H. Böhlau, 1930-1983), 6:178 [hereafter WA Br]; and *Dr. Martin Luthers Sämtliche Werke, Briefweschsel*, ed. Ernst L. Enders, 19 vols. (Frankfurt am Main: Heyder und Zimmer, 1884–1932), 9:88 [hereafter WA Br (Enders ed.)].

[22] The most commonly cited medieval case among early Protestants was that of crusader Graf von Gleichen, who had been captured by a Turkish sultan, but was given his freedom after he agreed to marry the sultan's daughter. He returned with his new wife to Europe only to find his first wife still alive; she welcomed him and his new wife, and they lived together, having received the church's dispensation. This story has proved to be a fiction, although the wonderful story was often repeated and even became the subject of Schubert's Opera, "Der Graf von Gleichen." There are a number of other such medieval stories of dispensation for bigamous crusaders. See, e.g., M. Michel du Perray, *Traité des*

the pope to authorize his bigamy. If the pope refused the dispensation, however, he said that Henry could "in good conscience" proceed with a second marriage to Anne, while leaving his first marriage intact, because "charity compels it."[23] A few other early Lutheran theologians opined similarly that polygamy would be better than divorce or annulment in this case, but many other early Protestants disagreed.[24] When Basil Reformer, Johannes Oeclampadius (1482–1531), for example, heard what the Wittenberg reformers had counseled, he retorted angrily: "Far be it from us to listen more to Mohammed on this matter than to Christ."[25]

PHILIP OF HESSE AND THE LUTHERAN COUNSEL OF POLYGAMY

This was not the first or last time that Luther and a few of his colleagues counseled polygamy to resolve difficult marriage cases. It must be said that Luther was utterly conventional in teaching that marriage was created by God as a "two in one flesh" union between a man and a woman with the freedom, fitness, and capacity to marry each other. Although the Old Testament patriarchs had departed from this creation norm and the Mosaic law had marginally accommodated their polygamy, he said, Jesus and Paul had called Christians back to this original "two in one flesh" form and

dispenses de mariage, de leur validité ou invalidité, et de l'état des personnes (Paris: D. Beugnié, 1719); Diego Garzia de Transmiera, *De Polygamia et Polyviria libri tres* (Palermo: Apud Decium Cyrillum, 1638), esp. bk. 1, q. 9, chaps. 1–4; bk. 2, qq. 1–12; Leo Miller, *John Milton Among the Polygamophiles* (New York: Loewenthal Press, 1974), 20–21, 204–208. Many historians, however, have disputed almost every one of the alleged papal dispensations for polygamy prior to the sixteenth century. See, e.g., Norman Hardy, "Papal Dispensations for Polygamy," *Dublin Review* 153 (1913): 266–274; and more generally George H. Joyce, *Christian Marriage* (London: Sheed & Ward, 1948), 430–452. Most of the papal "dispensations," they show, were dispensing "clerical bigamy," a much narrower issue discussed in Chapter 4, pp. 186–190.

23 Consilium of August 23, 1531, in G. Bretschneider, ed., *Corpus Reformatorum: Melanchthons Werke*, 28 vols. (New York: Johnson Reprint Corp., 1963 [1864]), 2:520–526 [hereafter CR]. Melanchthon referred to "Gregory II" as "Georgio" rather than "Gregorio." He also pointed to the story of Roman fourth-century CE Emperor Valentinian who is said to have passed a law permitting a man to marry two wives so that he could marry the beautiful Justina whom both he and his first wife Severa coveted. See *The Ecclesiastical History of Socrates, Surnamed Scholasticus or the Advocate* (London: George Bell and Sons, 1874), bk. 4, ch. 31 (pp. 252–253). Historians now think Valentinian's law is a fiction. See additional discussion later in this chapter.

24 Other early Protestants who favored bigamy (at least in Henry VIII's case) included Martin Bucer, Wolfgang Capito, Simon Grynaeus, Johannes Brenz, and Andreas Osiander. Most others opposed bigamy, and split on the question whether divorce was licit in this case, given Henry's adultery but Catherine's objection to divorce. See detailed examples in Rockwell, *Die Doppelehe*, 202–222; Hartmann Grisar, S.J., *Luther*, trans. E. Lamond, ed. Luigi Cappadelta, 6 vols. (London: Kegan Paul, 1913–1917), 4:3–79; Hastings Eells, *The Attitude of Martin Bucer Toward the Bigamy of Philip of Hesse* (New Haven, CT: Yale University Press, 1924), 30–43; Joel Harrington, *Reordering Marriage and Society in Reformation Germany* (Cambridge: Cambridge University Press, 1995), 89–91.

25 WA Br, 6:179;WA Br (Enders ed.), 9:80.

norm of marriage which remains in force today. Luther was also utterly conventional in teaching that marriage was designed for the mutual love and support of husband and wife, the mutual protection of both parties from sexual sin, and the mutual nurture and care of their children.[26]

But Luther placed greater emphasis than many on the remedial qualities of marriage to offset the pervasive sin of lust. Without marriage, Luther believed, most persons' sexuality becomes a force capable of overthrowing the most devout conscience. A person, especially a man, is enticed by his own nature to lustful leering, voyeurism, pornography, prostitution, masturbation, or fornication, and sometimes more serious sins like adultery, rape, and sodomy. "You can't be without a wife and remain without sin," Luther declared.[27] Almost everyone who chooses to "live alone undertakes an impossible task ... counter to God's word and the nature that God has given and preserves in him."[28]

This strong belief in the remedial good of marriage undergirded Luther's bitter attacks on the traditional canon law rules of celibacy. To require celibacy of clerics, monks, and nuns, he believed, was beyond the authority of the church and ultimately a source of great sin. Celibacy was for God to give, not for the church to require. It was for each individual, not for the church, to decide whether he or she had received this gift. By demanding monastic vows of chastity and clerical vows of celibacy, the church was seen to be intruding on Christian freedom and violating Scripture, nature, and common sense. By institutionalizing and encouraging celibacy, the church was seen to be preying on the immature and the uncertain. By holding out food, shelter, security, and opportunity, the monasteries enticed poor and needy parents to condemn their children to celibate monasticism regardless of whether they were naturally called to that vocation. Mandatory celibacy, wrote Luther, a former monk, is not a prerequisite to true service of God. Instead it has led to "great whoredom and all manner of fleshly impurity and ... hearts filled with thoughts of women day and night."[29]

This belief in the remedial good of marriage also informed Luther's repeated counsel that widow(er)s and divorcees remarry after a suitable period of grieving. Such parties can benefit from a new spouse, especially if they have young children to tend or busy households to manage. But more importantly, these now-single parties who have known the pleasures and warmth of sexual intimacy will be doubly

---

[26] See detailed sources and discussion in Witte, *Law and Protestantism*, 214–231, updated in Witte, *From Sacrament to Contract*, 119–135.

[27] D. Martin Luthers Werke: *Tischreden*, 6 vols. (Weimar: H. Böhlau, 1912-1921), vol. 1, no. 233 [hereafter WA TR]; LW 54:31.

[28] D. Martin Luthers Werke: *Kritische Gesamtausgabe*, repr. ed., 78 vols. (Weimar: H. Böhlaus Verlager, 1883–1987), 18:276 [hereafter WA].

[29] LW 44:243–400; LW 46:139ff.; WA 12:98.

tempted by lust in its sudden absence. St. Paul's instruction that "it is better to marry than to burn," becomes doubly imperative for them. "I'm astonished that the lawyers, and especially the canonists, are so deeply offended by digamy" or successive polygamy, Luther wrote. "Oh, how vast is the ignorance of God in man's heart that he can't distinguish between a commandment of God and a tradition of men. To have one, two, three, or four wives in succession is [in every case] a marriage and isn't contrary to God, but what's to prevent fornication and adultery, which are against God's command?"[30]

It was this same belief in the vital remedial good of marriage that led Luther to condone private polygamy as a better option than flagrant adultery or no-fault divorce – and not just in high stakes cases involving kings and dynasties.[31] Already in his 1520 manifesto on *The Babylonian Captivity of the Church*, which detailed his case for Christian freedom from the medieval canon law, Luther wrote freely – even recklessly – about this topic:

> Let us examine such a case as this. A woman is married to an impotent man, but cannot, or perhaps will not, prove in court her husband's impotence, because of the numerous items of evidence, and the notoriety, which would be occasioned by a legal process. Still she wishes to have a child, and is unable to remain continent.
>
> In addition, suppose I had advised her to seek a divorce in order to marry another, as she was content, in her conscience, to do [but] her husband would not agree to her proposal. I myself would give the further advice, that, with her husband's consent (although now really he is not her husband, but only a man who lives in the same house) she should have sexual intercourse with another man, say her husband's brother, but keeping this "marriage" secret, and ascribing the children to the putative father [her actual husband] as they call such a one....
>
> [I]f the man will not consent [to this paternal surrogacy option either], and if he does not wish to be separated, then, rather than let her burn or commit adultery, I would counsel her to contract marriage with someone else, and flee to some distant and unknown region.[32]

A bit later in this same tract, Luther added: "I prefer bigamy to divorce, yet I do not venture an opinion whether bigamy should be allowed" as a general matter.[33]

Four years later, in 1524, Luther did venture an opinion, and counseled against the general legalization of polygamy because it would cause scandal in the community

30 WA TR 3, no. 3609B, LW 54:243–244.
31 WA 29:144ff., 303ff.
32 WA 6:558–59; LW 36:103–105.
33 Ibid., 339. A couple of years later, Luther said he was really talking about surrogacy, not bigamy: If a healthy spouse desperately wants to have a child, an impotent husband or sterile wife should consent to allow their spouse to have a surrogate child by another. Martin Luther, *The Estate of Marriage* (1522), in LW 45:14–49, at 19–21, 45.

and discord in the home. "I have to confess that I cannot prohibit any man who wishes to marry several wives, nor can I say that this practice is against the Holy Bible. But I do not want that custom to be introduced among Christians, for Paul calls us to forgo some things even if they are permitted, so as to avoid scandal and to promote respectable living."[34] "All things are lawful, but not all things are helpful," Paul had written, and this adage, in Luther's view, counseled against any general practice of polygamy within the church or the state.[35] It was simply too dangerous.

In 1526, Luther repeated this counsel, but left a loophole for permissible polygamy where a person had grave needs and believed firmly in his or her conscience that God had given them a dispensation to take a second spouse:

> It is my faithful warning and counsel that Christians should not take more than one wife, not only because it is scandalous, and no Christian causes scandal but most diligently avoids it, but also because there is no word of God for it that is pleasing to him by Christians. Heathens and Turks [i.e., Muslims] may do what they please. The ancient [Old Testament] Fathers had several wives, but they were driven to this by necessity. And accordingly kings received as by inheritance the wives of their friends according to the law of Moses.

> But it is not sufficient for a Christian to be satisfied by the work of the [Old Testament] Fathers. He must have a divine word for himself, that makes it certain for him, just as they had. For where there was no necessity or cause, the ancient Fathers did not have more than one wife, as [was the case with] Isaac, Joseph, Moses, and many others. Therefore I cannot advise it (taking more than one wife), but strongly advise against it, especially to Christians, unless it may be a case of high necessity, such that the wife was leprous or similarly afflicted. Other cases however I know not how to defend.[36]

Luther repeated this teaching several more times in his private letters and in his private table talks.[37] A 1532 case in his *Table Talk*, for example, reads thus:

---

[34] Letter to Gregory Brück (January 13, 1524), in WA Br 2:458–460. In his 1523 sermons on Genesis, he commented quite conventionally – citing Augustine, Lombard, and others – that the polygamy of Lamech was sinful but that of Abraham and later patriarchs was customary in its day and not contrary to natural law. See WA 14:121, 223, 250ff., 304ff., 404ff. and other sources and discussion in Rockwell, *Die Doppelehe*, 223–252.

[35] 1 Corinthians 10:23; see also 1 Corinthians 6:12; Romans 14:19 and Luther's discussion of these texts in various letters in WA Br (Enders ed.), no. 756; WA Br. 3:140.

[36] Letter to Philip of Hesse (November 28, 1526), in WA Br 6:79. See also Heinrich Heppe, "Urkundliche Beiträge zur Geschichte des Doppelehe des Landgrafen Philipp von Hessen," *Zeitschrift für historisches Theologie* 22 (1852): 263ff. and in Rockwell, *Die Doppelehe*, 256–257. I have used the translation in Faulkner, "Luther and the Marriage of Philip of Hesse," 207–208.

[37] See, e.g., WA TR 1, no. 414, 611; WA TR 2, no. 1461; LW 50:33; LW 54:65–66. Luther's wife, Katharina von Bora, evidently had no patience with Luther's table talk speculations. A guest in his home reported this conversation, beginning with Luther talking: "'The time will come when a man will take more than one wife.' The Doctor's wife replied: 'The devil believe that.' Said the Doctor: 'The

A certain man took a wife, and after bearing several children, she contracted syphilis and was unable to fulfill her marital obligation. Thereupon her husband, troubled by the flesh, denied himself beyond his ability to sustain the burden of chastity. It is asked, ought he be allowed a second wife? I reply that one or another of two things must happen: either he commits adultery or he takes another wife. It is my advice that he take a second wife; however, he should not abandon his first wife but should provide for her sufficiently to enable her to support her life. There are many cases of this kind, from which it ought to be clearly seen and recognized that this is the law and that is the Gospel.[38]

Philip of Hesse (1504–1567), a powerful Protestant prince and vital political supporter of the Reformation, cited these Lutheran teachings in 1539, when he requested the reformers' blessing for his proposed polygamy.[39] Philip had been diplomatically married at the age of 19 to Christina, the daughter of Duke George of Albertine Saxony, an important ally for the newly Lutheranized territory of Hesse. Philip claimed that "he had never any love or desire for her on account of her form, fragrance, and manner," although this did not prevent him from having enough sex with her to produce seven children.[40] Throughout his married life, and especially as his wife grew more frigid and intemperate in later years, Philip admitted to wild sex with paramours of all sorts, male and female alike, and was rewarded with a severe rash of syphilis in 1539. He was now deeply ashamed of his conduct, confessed it fully, and sought to do better. He insisted, however, that he still needed a sexual outlet, given his strong sex drive – he reportedly had three testicles – or he would again be driven into the arms and beds of his maids and prostitutes. He had his eyes, though evidently not yet his hands, on a single, beautiful 17-year old girl, Margaret, less than half his age. He wanted to marry Margaret, while retaining his first wife, Christina. Margaret's mother, however, would not give her consent to such a bigamous marriage unless and until it was blessed by the political and religious leaders of the Reformation.

Philip thus asked Martin Bucer (1491–1551), a leading Protestant reformer from Strasbourg and a close friend of Luther and John Calvin (1509–1564), to bless this

---

reason, Ketha, is that a woman can bear only one child a year, while her husband can beget many.' Ketha responded: 'Paul says 'let each have his own wife'.'" The Doctor then replied: 'His own, but not one alone. That is not in Paul.' So he kept joking for a long time, till the Doctor's wife said: 'Before I put up with that, I would rather go back into the convent, and leave you and all your children.'" WA TR 2, no. 1461. See also Miller, *Milton*, 23.

[38] WA TR 1, no. 414; LW 54:65–66.

[39] See documents in WA 8:628–644, 9:131–35; CR 3:849–865. See discussion in Rockwell, *Die Doppelehe*; Eells, *The Attitude of Martin Bucer*; Hans J. Hillerbrand, *Landgrave Philipp of Hesse, 1504–1567: Religion and Politics in the Reformation* (St. Louis, MO: Foundation for Reformation Research, 1967); Paul Mikat, *Die Polygamiefräge in der Neuzeit* (Opladen: Westdeutscher Verlag, 1988).

[40] Quoted in Martin Luther, "Letter to Elector John of Saxony (June 10, 1540)," WA Br 9:131–135.

polygamous arrangement. Bucer instead counseled Philip to divorce his first wife and then remarry. Divorce was licit if for no other reason than Philip's own repeated and fully confessed adultery. But Philip did not want to risk public revelation of his adultery, a capital crime in his day,[41] and a source of deep public shame and scandal if revealed. He preferred to keep and support his first wife and their children, and to marry and support a second wife and family as well, which he had ample financial means to do. This, Philip argued, was in accord with the biblical examples of David, Solomon, and the other ancient kings. It also followed the biblical law of Deuteronomy 21:15 which said that "[i]f a man has two wives, the one loved, the other disliked," he has to support both wives and both sets of children. I have one wife Christina whom I "loathe," said Philip. I have another woman Margaret whom I love and desire to marry. Isn't it better for me to marry Margaret, too, rather than commit adultery with her or stage a fraudulent divorce or annulment from Christina? "I desire the means allowed by God to be used to remedy this condition," namely taking a second wife, Philip wrote to Bucer. After all:

> God allowed the Fathers in the Old Testament times – Abraham, Jacob, David, etc. – who believed in the same Christ as we, to have more than one wife. Nor was this forbidden by Christ or the apostles in the New Testament. In the Acts of the Apostles, this prohibition is not found, and Paul expressly confines only bishops and ministers to one wife.... Remember also the counsel which Luther and Melanchthon gave Henry VIII of England to the effect that he should not send away his present wife, but rather – if the necessity of the kingdom required [a] male heir – to take another. I wish to have a second wife, because God forbids adultery and permitted polygamy.[42]

And then, playing his final cards, Philip threatened that, if Bucer would not bless this arrangement, he would take his case to the Holy Roman Emperor, perhaps taking the important Lutheran territory of Hesse back to Catholicism in so doing. Or he might just change the law of Hesse to allow for polygamy, risking a dangerous confrontation with the emperor, who in 1532 had just made polygamy a capital crime in the entire Holy Roman Empire, which included Hesse.[43]

A deeply troubled Bucer took the case to Luther and Melanchthon in Wittenberg for their counsel. Within ten days, these three theologians, working with a group of fellow Lutheran theologians in Hesse, crafted a four-page response, very reluctantly agreeing to Philip's bigamy proposal. This they delivered to Philip as a formal letter

[41] See *Constitutio Criminalis Carolina*, art. 121, quoted in Chapter 4, pp. 157–158.
[42] Reprinted in CR 3:851ff., using translation in Faulker, "Luther and the Marriage," 209–210. See also Rockwell, *Die Doppelehe*, 2–6, Eells, *Martin Bucer*, 68–69.
[43] CR 3:851–853; Eells, *Martin Bucer*, 70–71.

of private counsel (called a *Ratschlag* in German) which was designed, as they said to Philip, to relieve the "longtime burden of your conscience."[44]

The reformers made clear in their letter that they did not want Philip to abandon the Lutheran church, which "is small and forsaken and truly needs pious lords and rulers" like Philip. Nor did they want Philip to go to the emperor for help. The emperor "is an untrue, false man," "holds adultery as a small sin," and "has forgotten the German way," the reformers argued. He also "lets the Turks go unattacked" and tolerates the "Saracen faith," even though both these Muslim groups practice polygamy. The message to Philip was clear: We good German Lutherans can handle this issue among ourselves.

The reformers also did not want Philip to change the local marriage law of Hesse to allow for the general practice of polygamy. This should remain a private case of equitable dispensation from the general rules of monogamy:

> Your Princely Grace knows that there is a great difference between making a common [i.e. general] law and in some one case for weighty grounds and according to divine permission using a dispensation.... [T]hink of how fearful it would be if such a law [permitting polygamy to all] were brought into the German nation, from which endless trouble would come for all the married.

The general law requiring monogamy and prohibiting polygamy must not change, the reformers continued, for

> God has instituted marriage as a society between two persons alone, and not more, so nature does not become destroyed. So we have the passage, "These two shall become one flesh," and thus it was at first. But Lamech introduced the example of having more than one wife, which is spoken of concerning him in the Scriptures as bringing in something against the first rule. Accordingly it became a custom with the unbelieving, until Abraham and his descendants took more wives; and so it came to be allowed by the law of Moses, Deut. 2[1:15], "If a man has two wives." For God allowed something to weak nature.

> But inasmuch as at the beginning and conformably to the creation, a man was not to have more than one wife, so such a law is praiseworthy and therefore to be received in the Church; and no other law is to be made against it. For Christ repeats this passage, "The two shall be one flesh" (Matt. 19), and reminds us of how it was before the time of human weakness.

---

44 The original is reprinted in CR 3:856–863, and in *Martin Luthers Briefe, Sendschreiben und Bedenken*, ed. Wilhelm Martin Leberecht de Wette, 6 vols. (Berlin. G. Reimer, 1825–1828), 6:239–244. For the quotations from this letter that follow, I have used the excellent English translation of this text in Faulker, "Luther and the Marriage," 213–216.

But that in a certain case a dispensation might be given, as for instance in the case of a captive in a strange land, who has become free and bring his [second] wife with him, or in the case of some chronic disorder such as was thought of for a time with lepers – that in such cases, with the advice of their pastor, a man may take a wife again, not to bring in a [new] law, but as counsel for his necessity, this we do not condemn. Because it is one thing to bring in a [new] law, and another to use a dispensation [from the old law].

Even a private dispensation to practice polygamy in a single case like this, however, requires great "caution," the reformers continued. Such an act must be kept quiet to avoid sullying the Prince's name or eroding his authority, or sending the wrong message to other private persons – especially the "wild nobility" who will quickly seek their own dispensations for polygamy if word gets out. And, if we are not careful, our enemies will regard us "like the Anabaptists" or the Muslim "Turks who seek to have as many wives as they wish." They will "gladly lay all blame upon [us] preachers if trouble comes" from this dispensation; "there is much to be feared."

Moreover, a dispensation to practice polygamy can be granted only in cases of dire necessity, the reformers continued in their letter, and frankly this case does not seem so dire. You, Prince Philip, already have a wife and plenty of heirs to the throne. You are sick, weak, and sleep little, and probably cannot even handle another wife. And you must lead your people by moral example, especially given that the world treats sexual sins so "lightly." You have married your first wife, Christina, for better or worse, and she is still available to you, even if currently estranged. "Many others in their married state have to exercise patience" in this situation. Your claim for dispensation is that you simply cannot control yourself sexually, and thus want a second wife to relieve your sexual urging and to quiet your conscience. That's better than your longstanding habits of "whoredom and adultery" and "other wild unchaste living" that has brought inevitable "punishment from God, sickness, and other dangers" to yourself and others. But frankly this is still a rather weak case for permissible polygamy.

But since "Your Princely Grace has finally concluded to have another wife," the reformers continued with resignation, to assuage your conscience we can give you a special dispensation in order to relieve your anguished "feelings." But this special dispensation comes with our "special admonition" that your bigamy must be kept secret, so that others may think you have merely taken Margaret as a concubine – unhappily, a "common practice" of princes in our day. We also admonish you to surround yourself with "certain trustworthy persons" so that this letter is kept quiet and that your future behavior is kept under control. "We pray Your Grace will live as a praiseworthy Christian prince, and pray God will lead and guide Your Grace to his praise and to Your Princely Grace's salvation."

The reformers wrote this private letter hastily given the political stakes involved, but also reluctantly given the moral implications of their writing. A few months thereafter, Luther reported on what drove their decision to write as they did to Philip:

> The account of his life and purpose shocked us in view of the vicious scandal that would follow, and we begged His Grace not to do it. We were then told he was unable to refrain and would carry out his intention in spite of us by appealing to the emperor or pope. To prevent this, we humbly requested him, if he insisted on doing it or (as he said) was unable to do otherwise before God and his conscience, at least to do it secretly because he was constrained by his need, for it could not be defended in public and under imperial law. We were promised that he would do so. Afterward we made an effort to help as much as we could to justify it before God with examples of Abraham, etc. All this took place and was negotiated under seal of confession, and we cannot be charged with having done this willingly, gladly, or with pleasure. It was exceedingly difficult for us to do, but because we could not prevent it, we thought that we ought at least to ease his conscience as much as possible.[45]

For all the reformers' caution and admonitions to secrecy, however, Philip shared their letter openly, and publicly celebrated his second wedding in open defiance of his own territorial laws and the new imperial laws against polygamy. This caused a great scandal in Germany. Sundry political and religious leaders in both the Catholic and Protestant worlds, including the pope and the emperor, weighed in to condemn Philip for his actions and to condemn Luther and his colleagues for condoning his bigamy.[46] The scandal only got worse when it became known that Lutheran theologian, Dionysius Melander, who had presided at Philip's second wedding with Margaret, had three wives, and that Johan Oldendorp, the leading Lutheran jurist at Philip's University of Marburg in Hesse, had two wives, too.[47] Long letters and hefty pamphlets began to pour out in caustic rebuke of the Lutheran polygamists in the early 1540s.[48] Philip and his defenders answered these charges in

---

[45] Letter to Elector John of Saxony (June 10, 1540), WA Br 9:131–135, using translation in Theodore G. Tappert, ed., *Luther: Letters of Spiritual Counsel* (Philadelphia, PA: Westminster Press, 1955), 288–291. See also WA Br 8:631ff.; WA TR 4, nos. 5038, 5046, 5096.

[46] See details in Rockwell, *Die Doppelehe*, 49–136; Eells, *Martin Bucer*, 107–153.

[47] See sources in Rockwell, *Die Doppelehe*, 86–92. On Oldendorp, see Witte, *Law and Protestantism*, 154–168.

[48] See Eells, *Martin Bucer*, 160ff. and a good summary in Michael Siricius, *Uxor Una: Ex Jure Naturae et Divino, Moribus Antiquis et Constitutionibus Imperatorum et Regnum. Eruta et Contra Insultus Impugnantium Defensa* (Giessen: Typis et sumptibus Josephi Dieterici Hampelii, 1669), 35–44 (a work dedicated to the later Landgrave of Hesse, Ludwig). See also Robert Parsons, S.J., *A Defence of the Censvre Gyven vpon Two Bookes of William Charke and Meredith Hanmer, mynysters* (Rouen: Father Parsons Press, 1582), esp. 59ff. which castigates Luther and his followers for condoning polygamy, and claims that their simple-minded calls for sola Scriptura led to the polygamous excesses of Münster discussed below.

several apologiae for polygamy.[49] Philip eventually escaped imperial prosecution for the capital crime of bigamy, but only in exchange for a one-sided treaty with the emperor that neutralized the powerful Lutheran territory of Hesse and served to break up the Schmalkald League of Lutheran polities that Philip had earlier helped to create to resist military attacks from the emperor and his Catholic allies. Those attacks came a few years later, and Philip was imprisoned by the emperor for nearly five years before returning to Hesse.

In the months and years after they had issued their letter, Luther, Melanchthon, and Bucer all tried, in vain, to contain Philip's personal and political excesses, and to explain their actions and advice in the case to their followers.[50] But the damage was done – especially when their letter to Philip was read alongside Luther's earlier remarks that polygamy was not against the natural law or the Bible, and that men and women with pressing needs to produce a child or even to relieve their lust could take a second spouse while retaining the first. This was all the ammunition their opponents needed to brand the Lutherans as vile sexual libertines, bent on destroying the divine institution and holy sacrament of monogamous marriage.

POLYGAMOUS EXPERIMENTS IN EARLY ANABAPTISM

What made the Lutheran reformers' counsel to Philip even more controversial was that Germany was already roiling with news of the polygamous teachings and practices of certain Anabaptists. Anabaptists were Protestants, but most of them wanted more radical biblical reforms than were countenanced by Lutherans, Anglicans, and Calvinists of the sixteenth century.[51] Anabaptist communities thus separated themselves from Catholics and other Protestants alike into small, self-sufficient, communities, metaphorically if not physically cordoned off from the world. These separated communities governed themselves by biblical principles of discipleship, simplicity, charity, modesty, and nonresistance. They set their own

---

[49] The fullest such text is *Dialogus Neobuli*, whose likely author was John Lening, a Lutheran pastor, whom Philip Melanchthon called "a monstrosity in body and mind," CR 4:709. The argument proceeds as a dialogue about monogamy versus polygamy in the Bible, natural law, canon law, and Roman law; see the summary of the argument in Eells, *Martin Bucer*, 185–193, and its later adaptation by Bernard Ochino discussed on pp. 223–238.

[50] Lutheran legal scholars over the next century, too, began to pile up arguments and books in defense of monogamy over polygamy and to defend Luther's actions. See discussion in Mikat, *Die Polygamiefrage*, 33–46, and texts collected in Hieronymous Bruckner, *Decisiones Iuris Matrimonialis Controversi* (Gotha: Sumptibus Jacobi Medivi, 1724), ch. 14, 476–505, which includes the Wittenberg letter to Philip in an appendix starting another round of Catholic-Lutheran invective over polygamy and Luther's role in its condonation. See discussion later in this chapter and also Miller, *Milton*, 101–110, 151–179, 333–354, on the ample seventeenth-century German literature.

[51] Walter Klaassen, *Anabaptism: Neither Catholic nor Protestant* (Waterloo, ON: Conrad Press, 1973).

internal standards of worship, liturgy, diet, discipline, dress, and domestic education. They handled their own internal affairs of property, contracts, commerce, marriage, and inheritance, so much as possible without appeal to the state or to secular law.[52] The Bible was their law.

Most early Anabaptists read the Bible's treatment of marriage, conventionally, to require strict monogamy. Peter Riedemann (1506–1556), for example, an early leader of the Hutterites, based this view on the exclusive and enduring union of Christ and the church described in Ephesians 5:

> The man should also be the husband of only one wife, even as Christ is the head of the Church. For, since marriage is a picture of the same, the likeness and indication must resemble what it indicateth. Therefore must a man have no more than one wife.[53]

Menno Simons (1496–1561), the later leader of the Mennonites, appealed to the creation order and its restoration by Jesus in defending monogamy:

> As to polygamy, we would say that scriptures show that before the Law some of the patriarchs had many wives, yet they did not have the same liberty under the Law as they had before the Law.... Each era has its own liberty and usage according to the scriptures in the matter of marriage. And under the New Testament, we are not pointed by the Lord to the usage of the patriarchs before the Law nor under the Law, but to the beginning of creation, to Adam and Eve.... Therefore we teach, practice, and consent to no other arrangement than the one which was in vogue in the beginning with Adam and Eve, namely, one husband and one wife, as the Lord's mouth has ordained.[54]

The Bible's sundry examples of polygamy in the Old Testament, however, and the absence of an explicit condemnation of polygamy in the New Testament, led a few of these widely scattered and sometimes exotic Anabaptist groups to experiment with polygamy. As the leading Anabaptist historian of his day, George H. Williams, reports, small groups of radical utopians emerged during and after the Peasants' War in Germany in 1525, and spread into middle and southern Germany. A charismatic Anabaptist leader, Louis Haetzer, was put to death in Constance in 1529, after deserting his "unregenerate" first wife and taking a second wife who was, in his view, more spiritually pure. Nicholas Frey was executed in Strassburg in 1534

---

[52] Walter Klaassen, ed., *Anabaptism in Outline* (Scottdale, PA: Herald Press, 1981), 101–114, 211–232.

[53] Peter Riedemann, *Account of our Religion, Doctrine, and Faith Given by Peter Riedemann of the Brothers Whom Men Call Hutterites*, trans. Kathleen Hasenberg, 2nd ed. (Rifton, NY: Plough Publishing House, 1970), 100. See George Huntson Williams, *The Radical Reformation*, 3rd ed. (Kirksville, MO: Sixteenth Century Journal Publishers, 1992), 777.

[54] Menno Simons, *The Complete Writings*, trans. Leonard Verduin, ed. John C. Wenger (Scottdale, PA: Herald Press, 1956), 560. See other examples of conventional monogamy among Anabaptists in Williams, *The Radical Reformation*, 776–788.

when he followed Haetzer's example and tried to get others to join him. A group of self-described Spiritualists, led by Jan van Batenburg, "preached and practiced the community of wives." They based their views in part on the Old Testament example of large polygamous households, in part on the communitarian ideals of the New Testament church. But they also drew on what some Anabaptists took to be an authoritative apostolic letter of St. Peter's successor Clement, which letter recommended that Christian "friends should have all things in common ... unquestionably including wives." This same apostolic letter, now known as a forgery, also helped to inspire "a group of Thuringian or Hessian Dreamers or Blood Friends, led by one Louis of Tüngeda" to practice "fleshly mingling as the true and sole sacrament, called *Christerie* or *Christirung*." These groups were brought up on various charges of adultery and polygamy as were groups of Anabaptists in St. Gall, Zips, and Köningsberg who followed the polygamous teachings and examples of George Volk, Andrew Fischer, Jan Willemsen, and others.[55]

The Anabaptists' most elaborate polygamous experimentation took place in the German city of Münster in the 1530s.[56] Initially this little city of some 15,000 had, like other surrounding cities, converted from Catholicism to Lutheranism. But then in 1531 with the arrival of charismatic preacher Bernhard Rothman (1495–1535), the city moved toward stricter Anabaptist views of the sacraments, especially the call for adult rather than infant baptism – a deeply controversial issue in the day.[57] The city became more radical in 1534 with the arrival of the handsome and charismatic John Beukels (ca. 1509–1536) of Leiden, who soon assumed political leadership of the city.[58] Beukels grandly declared Münster to be the "new chosen Israel," with himself as the new king, who ruled with twelve elders and with Rothman as chief preacher and propagandist. Catholics and Lutherans in the city who refused adult baptism and the new utopian dispensation and rule were banished; the few who resisted were

[55] Ibid., 781–782. See also his discussion of each of these incidents in ibid., 410–422, 1086–1087, 1113–1114. Clement's letter is quoted in ibid., 652. On the provenance of this letter, and its transmission to the Anabaptist world in Anabaptist leader Sebastian Frank's *Chronica* (1531), see ibid., 650–653. The text circulated in the early Protestant world as *Divi Clementis Recognitionum Libri X* (Basel: Bebel, 1526).
[56] See primary documents in Klemens Löffler, *Die Wiedertäufer zu Münster, 1534–35: Berichte, Aussagung, und Aktenstücke von Augenzugen und Zeitgenossen* (Jena: Dietrichs, 1923), with analysis in Williams, *The Radical Reformation*, 556–588; Cairncross, *After Polygamy*, 1–34; Norman Cohn, *The Pursuit of the Millennium* (Oxford: Oxford University Press, 1970), 261–280.
[57] See esp. Bernhardt Rothman et al., *Bekenntnise von beyden Sacramenten, Dope und Nachtmaele der Predikanten tho Munster* (Münster: Rothman, 1533).
[58] See Norbert Hürte, *Jan Bockelson, gennant Johann von Leyden, die Wiedertäufliche-König im neuen Zion* (Reutlingen: Verlag von Fleischhauer und Spohn, 1854); August Ludwig von Schlözer, *Die Wiedertäufer in Münster: Geschichte des Schneider- und Schwärmer-Königs Jan van Leyden Anno 1535* (Cologne: Kirchner, 1919); Harry C. Schnur, *Mystic Rebels: Apollonius Tyaneus – Jan van Leyden – Sabbatai Zevi-Cagliostri* (New York: Beechhurst, 1949), 87–158.

executed. This brought reprisal and attack from both Lutheran and Catholic forces marshaled from surrounding cities.

On May 25, 1534, after successfully defending the city from initial attack, Beukels decreed that the city should adopt polygamy in emulation of the Old Testament patriarchs. This, he said, would allow for a more efficient application of the biblical command to "be fruitful and multiply," and would allow the city's population to grow to the magical biblical number of 144,000 true saints needed for the Lord to return and to redeem his chosen people from their enemies. Additional orders by Beukels and sermons by Rothman enjoined all persons within the city to be married. All previous marriages were declared heathen and automatically annulled. All true believing men were commanded to marry anew – not only their first wives, if they were true believers, but others as well. Because women in Münster outnumbered men more than three to one, every woman was ordered to marry any man who would take her, and she was thereafter to submit to his biblical headship and household rule. Men in turn were expected to take and impregnate as many wives as they were able. They were not to "waste" their semen on barren, menstruating, pregnant, or nursing wives. Each man has the "seed and gift of God," Rothman declared, and he has the capacity to "fructify" several women at a time. "He is therefore left free, especially because of [our community's] need, to take more than one fruitful woman in marriage."[59] To set an example for the rest, John Beukels took at least fifteen wives and bragged loudly: "the man with the most wives was the best Christian."[60] Rothman, too, married nine wives and preached repeatedly about the biblical merits of this new polygamous regime within the "newly restored Zion" of Münster.[61]

While many devout men and women in the city initially accepted this new polygamous regime, complaints soon began to pour in to the authorities. One group of women, including eighteen young girls, complained that they had been coerced into marriage and been forced to have sexual relations with much older husbands; three pre-pubescent girls, in fact, had died from the grossly premature sexual activity. In response, the authorities allowed women who could prove they had married under duress to bring a public action to divorce their husbands; some

---

[59] Bernard Rothman, "Restitution Rechter und Gesunder Christlicher Lehre [1534]," in Robert Stupperich, ed., *Die Schriften Bernhard Rothmanns* (Münster: Aschendorff, 1970), 208–283 at 264. See discussion in C. Arnold Snyder, *Anabaptist History and Theology* (Kitchener, ON: Pandora Press, 1995), 282.

[60] Löffler, *Die Wiedertäufer zu Münster*, 159; Cairncross, *After Polygamy*, 14, quotes a local chronicler, Heinrich Gresbeck, who reported that the men "stormed through the whole town and invaded every house where there was a woman, girl or maid, four or even six men in succession, each trying to outbid the other in his number of wives." Ibid., 14.

[61] Rothman, "Restitution Rechte."

200 of the 2,000 women who entered polygamous marriages that year successfully divorced soon thereafter, although many other wives stayed put, fearing reprisals from their husbands or the authorities.[62]

A second group of married women complained about the growing rancor within their expanding polygamous households. A local chronicler, Heinrich Gresbeck, no friend of polygamy, reported as follows:

> There was fierce resentment in the town among the women where two or three lived together and shared a husband. There was no end to abuse and bickering among them. For the first wife always wished to be closest to her husband, and so did the new wives.... Thus they could not get along together, and there never was any peace. Complaints streamed in every day to the prophets, the preachers, and the Twelve Elders. At first the authorities put the refractory wives in prison. But in vain. Then Rot[h]man brandished the much graver threat of the sword which cowed them for a time.[63]

Six executions of women followed. Four of them were wives who protested the addition of other wives to their household. One was a woman who refused to have sex with her husband, and told him to take his pick from the other wives he had brought into the home against her wishes. Another was a woman who took on a second husband in evident retaliation for her husband taking on a second wife. They were all slain by the sword.[64]

Alarmed by this escalating brutality, several local preachers and town leaders organized to capture and imprison Beukels, and to try to dissuade him from his growing radicalism. He escaped prison, and butchered forty-eight of these insurrectionaries in a mass public execution; a few later critics suffered the same fate. In the months ahead, Beukels and his fellow leaders grew increasingly ruthless, fanatical, and erratic as they sought to build up their biblical utopia. Beukels now pronounced himself to be the new "king of the world" and held an exotic feast in the city square, even as the population was starving from an increasingly effective military siege of the city. When one of Beukels's wives dared to criticize him, he dragged her and his entire harem into the marketplace, and beheaded her and trampled her corpse for all to see.[65]

As word of this savagery spread, an alliance of military forces put the city under even stricter siege in the winter and spring of 1534 and 1535, and eventually captured

[62] Williams, *The Radical Reformation*, 568–570; Cairncross, *After Polygamy*, 15–19.
[63] Löffler, *Die Wiedertäufer zu Münster*, 115–116, using translation in Cairncross, *After Polygamy*, 17–18. Gresbeck's full account is published as Heinrich Gresbeck and Carl Adolf Cornelius, *Berichte der Augenzeugen über das münsterische Wiedertäuferreich*, repr. ed. (Münster: Aschendorff, 1983 [1853]).
[64] Ibid., 15–19.
[65] Williams, *The Radical Reformation*, 570–574.

it on June 25, 1535. The armies killed virtually all the remaining inhabitants either in battle, or in executions thereafter. Beukels and other leaders were systematically tortured in public. Before his execution, Beukels was closely questioned about his views of polygamy. He admitted that it was an "innovation" in his day. But it was hardly new, he said. The Old Testament patriarchs practiced it: "why therefore should it not be allowed to us?" "Better several wives than several whores," he added with a smirk. His captors found little convincing or amusing in his argument, and executed him by slow torture with red-hot tongs. His mangled body, and the bodies of two other leaders, were hung in cages from the local church, and the city returned to Catholicism.[66]

PRESSING THE CASE FOR POLYGAMY: BERNARD OCHINO

Münster's experiment with polygamy and its brutal ending were seared onto the memory of the Western tradition. It would remain the most famous mass polygamous experiment on Western Christian soil until the Mormon experiments in nineteenth-century North America.[67]

Sundry critics of the day and since saw the Münster story as a textbook example of the grave harms that are too often associated with polygamy. Here, they charged, a group of young men, giddy with lust and theocratic pretensions, combined charisma, brutality, and biblical platitudes to force a gullible Christian community to adopt their utopian vision of polygamy. Old couples were forced to end their marriages and start again. Young girls and women were coerced into premature and unwanted marriages; even little pre-pubescent girls were fair game, and three of them were literally raped to death. Husbands collected wives like spiritual trophies, measuring their faith by the size of their harems and nurseries. Wives were used and then spurned when they were pregnant or nursing or when the next wife was added to the harem. Polygamous households were filled with bickering wives and children, who were then cowed into silence with threats of the sword. Wives who still objected, or who rejected their husband's sexual advances to protest the unwanted polygamy, were summarily executed. Community dissenters and critics of these utopian excesses were summarily banished or executed.

Already in the twelfth and thirteenth centuries, critics like William of Auvergne had warned of the inevitable harms that polygamy inflicted on children, women, men, and society as a whole.[68] Biblical scholars had pointed out that even the most pious biblical polygamists and their families fared miserably. Münster was grim proof

---

[66]   Ibid.; Cairncross, *After Polygamy*, 23–27.
[67]   See discussion in Chapter 10, pp. 429–439.
[68]   See discussion in Chapter 4, pp. 161–163.

of the enduring wisdom of these traditional warnings about the inherent dangers of polygamy, critics warned. But this was not the polygamy of some ancient biblical patriarch or distant Muslim sultan. This was polygamy right in the heartland of Western Christendom. "Never again" was the lesson drawn by the Catholic and Protestant leadership of the day – including eventually all Anabaptist groups, too. Whatever ambivalence early Protestants may have still felt toward polygamy before then, Münster cured them. By the mid-sixteenth century, the Western legal and theological tradition in both Catholic and Protestant lands turned resolutely against real polygamy.[69]

But this was not the unanimous sentiment of the West. Famous apologists for liberty – from Sebastian Castellio and Bernard Ochino in the sixteenth century to Heinrich Heine and Karl Marx in the nineteenth century – lamented the brutality inflicted on this little Anabaptist town.[70] Left on its own, and with liberty to experiment, these critics argued, this early biblical utopia would likely have died a natural death, particularly if the traditional assumptions about the inherent harms of polygamy proved true. But this polygamous community might just have given the West the quiet little laboratory it needed to test out alternative forms and forums of effective procreation in place of monogamy. After all, monogamy has always been accompanied by adultery, concubinage, prostitution, rape, and other exploitations of women and the production of bastard children who never fare well in any society. Just maybe, these critics concluded, the Münster polygamists could have proved polygamy to be a better procreative strategy for all parties concerned – men, women, children, and society as a whole.[71]

Moreover, these critics continued, the brutality of the Christian establishment in this case far outweighed the actual harms of polygamy. It was Beukels's growing madness in the face of oppression, not his polygamy per se, that led him to his brutal excesses in those final months. And even those excesses have likely been exaggerated by the propagandists marshaled after the fact to condemn the Münsterites who were now dead and incapable of correcting the record. Just pile up the bodies on both sides, and you can see that the Catholic and Lutheran oppressors of Münster were much harsher than the Münsterites themselves.[72]

A few other advocates of the day defended this early Anabaptist experiment with polygamy using variations both on traditional arguments and on the new teachings of the Protestant Reformation. First, they argued, following the Church Fathers,

---

[69] This is the thesis of the next two chapters.

[70] See Richard Landes, *The Varieties of the Millennial Experience* (New York/Oxford: Oxford University Press, 2011), 303–304.

[71] Cohn, *The Pursuit of the Millennium*, 261–280.

[72] Cairncross, *After Polygamy*, 26–33.

polygamy was not only consistent with natural law, but was in fact a natural and spiritual necessity, given that the Anabaptists were the only true Christians left who needed to fill the earth with like-minded children before Christ could return. Second, polygamy had been practiced by the ancient patriarchs, and there was nothing wrong if the new leaders of the Anabaptist community emulated them. If Abraham is the father of faith and Solomon the exemplar of wisdom, why should we not follow their examples of how to live life well? By what criteria and on whose authority do we make decisions about what aspects of the patriarchs' lives are virtuous, what odious? Either they are spiritual role models, or they are not. Third, the Protestant Reformation was all about discarding obsolete and odious institutions that impeded the true worship of God and the full exercise of Christian liberty. If other Protestant reformers could upend church, state, and family alike in the process of radical reform, why could the Anabaptist reformers not now upend marriage, too, in order to bring greater and purer reform as they saw it? Who are these other Protestants, of all people, to say that some biblically based reforms of marriage are fine but others are not? Is protest against unbiblical practices not the very essence of being a Protestant? Finally, Anabaptist apologists argued, marriage was God's recipe for human procreation and God's remedy for sexual sinfulness. Everyone should be allowed to be married, and every woman should be given the maximum opportunity to have children properly through a marriage. Rather than letting individuals burn with passion, or depriving them of the maximum chance to have children, or forcing unwanted bastards to bear the inevitable sins of extramarital sex that monogamy occasions, why not just allow for polygamy? Polygamy ultimately serves the needs of men, women, and children alike. All these became familiar arguments among the pro-polygamy advocates in the sixteenth and seventeenth centuries, and would be repeated when controversies over polygamy occasionally broke thereafter.

One of the most elaborated such defenses of polygamy came from the learned and lively pen of distinguished Italian scholar, Bernard Ochino.[73] Ochino was a former heralded leader of the Franciscan order, a few of whose medieval proponents had already countenanced polygamy.[74] He had converted to the Protestant cause in the early 1540s and was initially drawn to Genevan reformer, John Calvin, who befriended him. He became a pastor of Italian Protestant churches in Augsburg and then Strasburg, and wrote several sharp attacks on Catholic theology and papal government. Forsaking his monastic vows, he also married (one wife) and had four

---

[73] For biographical studies, see Karl Benrath, *Bernardino Ochino von Siena: Ein Beitrag zur Geschichte der Reformation*, 3rd ed. (Neiuwkoop: B. de Graaf, 168); Roland Bainton, *Bernardino Ochino* (unpublished manuscript, 1965; available in the Library of Congress).

[74] See discussion in Chapter 4, pp. 167–169; for the examples of Gerard Odonis and Durandus of Saint Pourçain, both Franciscans.

children. Ochino's clever writings attracted the attention of Archbishop Thomas Cranmer in England, who invited him to England where he became a canon in Canterbury in 1547 and pastor of an Italian congregation in London. There he continued to preach and write sharp anti-Catholic invectives. But when Queen Mary came to the throne and sought forcibly to return England to Catholicism, Ochino fled for his life in 1553. He went back to Geneva, but arrived just as the smoke was clearing from the stake of Michael Servetus, whom the Genevan authorities had just executed for heresy. Ochino was horrified by this execution, and he sharply criticized Calvin and his colleagues for betraying their own earlier teachings on religious liberty.[75] He moved to Zurich, where he continued to preach and to write, but now with much stronger Anabaptist sympathies.

In one of these writings – his *Thirty Dialogues*, published in 1563, the same year that the Council of Trent declared its anathema on polygamy – Ochino offered a series of Socratic musings about the cogency of various standard theological doctrines. Included was a lengthy dialogue about "whether in some instances an individual man should make his own decision under the inspiration of Almighty God to marry a second wife."[76] Ochino's interlocutors went over many of the same biblical passages that apologists for Henry VIII and for Philip of Hesse had used in defense of polygamy.[77]

Ochino's dialogue features a man named "Telipolygamous." Let us call him "Teli" for short. Teli was seeking advice from a friend about whether he could take a second wife while still married to a first. His friend defended monogamy on grounds of Scripture, tradition, and natural law. Teli cleverly refuted him each time by bringing up contrary arguments from the same sources. After sixty-five pages of jousting, the two left hanging the suggestion that, because there is no clear biblical or moral commandment against polygamy, the decision about the propriety of polygamy was best left to the judgment of each individual Christian conscience. Ochino's dialogue anticipated many of the arguments for and against polygamy that

[75] See Williams, *The Radical Reformation*, 964–965; John Witte, Jr., *The Reformation of Rights: Law, Religion, and Human Rights in Early Modern Calvinism* (Cambridge: Cambridge University Press, 2007), 67–70, 94–103.
[76] See *Bernardini Ochini Senensis Dialogi XXX* (Basel, 1563), Dialog XXI, pp. 186ff. An English translation of this dialogue was published, during the permissive Commonwealth era in England, as *A Dialogue on Polygamy, Written Originally in Italian* (London: John Garfield, 1657), and also included, with revisions, in *The Cases of Polygamy, Concubinage, Adultery, and Divorce* (London: E. Curli, T. Payne, J. Chrichley, and J. Jackson, 1732), 1–66. It was recently published again as *A Dialogue on Polygamy*, Don Milton, ed. (n.p.: Born Again Publishers, 2009). I am using the 1657 edition hereafter and have modernized the spelling and punctuation. I have not been able to find a copy of the original Latin text to check this translation.
[77] In fact, Ochino's dialogue seems to have been modeled in part on the 1542 *Dialogus Neobuli*, written by one of Philip of Hesse's apologists in the heat of the battle over Philip's polygamy. Eells, *Martin Bucer*, 154–222, provides a detailed account of the provenance and argument of this tract.

the West would see over the next four centuries – especially the biblical arguments. So, let us linger over this text for a few pages to see the arguments unfold.

The dialogue began with Teli reporting that his wife was both barren and frigid. He was burning with lust and needed a sexual outlet, and he also wanted to have a legitimate child to raise in the faith. His conscience prevented him from taking a concubine, or from staging a divorce or annulment, let alone outright killing his wife. He had prayed and meditated on the Bible, but found no express command against polygamy. He thus came to the conclusion that it would be best to take a second wife, while continuing to support the first. Teli asked his friend whether this was permissible.[78]

His friend said no, reminding him of the creation story of Adam and Eve, and the fact that God had created but one wife for the man. "Had it been his divine pleasure, that a man should have a plurality of women, doubtless he would have created more than one [wife], especially in the world's infancy, when propagation was so much more necessary than ever after." The point of the story is that God created humans to be monogamous.[79]

But this was a "mere act of God" to relieve Adam's loneliness, Teli retorted. It was not an eternal command about marriage that required "strict imitation" by every other man thereafter. It is just a story about the first man and the first woman. There is no command in this story, save God's command to "be fruitful and multiply," which is much easier with multiple wives than with just one. If God had meant this mere act of creating but one woman for Adam to be the norm for all men in all ages, he would have said so. Moreover, if God's mere act of giving one woman to Adam is taken as a command for all humanity, why is God's act of clothing the first humans in skins not a command for all future forms of clothing, rendering the sundry cloth and wool fashions in vogue today a violation of God's norm for human attire? And, in turn, if monogamous marriage truly is a command of God for all men, why is the voluntary single life by those capable of marriage not also a violation of God's norm?[80]

The Bible offers two options for adults, his friend replied, either marriage or singleness if one has the gift of continence. But if marriage is chosen, it must be with one wife alone. "Having more wives than one is utterly repugnant to the very essence of real matrimony."[81]

How is polygamy "repugnant," Teli countered? I want a real wife for sex, companionship, and children, and I don't have one. My wife is barren and frigid, and

[78] Ochino, *A Dialogue on Polygamy*, 1–3.
[79] Ibid., 3.
[80] Ibid., 3–4.
[81] Ibid., 5.

I am now lonely, burning with lust, and without a child, heir, and future congregant and citizen whom I am willing and able to nurture and educate. The Bible states that God's real purpose in giving Eve to Adam was to relieve his loneliness and to allow him to be fruitful and multiply. Those are the real purposes of marriage, and those purposes are frustrated in my marriage. So, why can't I marry a second wife, as "both the Word of God and the examples of the saints" and the patriarchs allow? "You have not cleared it up to me, that the having of one more wife is repugnant to marriage, otherwise than by saying that God gave to Adam one, but no more." But that still begs the question of why the mere act of God giving Eve to Adam has become the universal norm for marriage.[82]

His friend tried again. Monogamy is the norm for marriage because Genesis 2:24 goes on to say after describing the creation of Eve for Adam: "Therefore a man shall leave his father and mother, and cleave unto his wife, and the two shall become one flesh." Therein lies the command for monogamous marriage: it says that a man must "cleave unto his wife," not his "wives."[83]

But why is that to be taken as an exclusive relationship, Teli shot back. After all, the Old Testament also commands a man to "love his neighbor" – stated in the singular. Does that mean he can only love one neighbor, not more? Of course not, said his friend. He can and must love all his neighbors. But it says, "love your neighbor" (stated in the singular), Teli responded. What the command really means, came his friend's reply, is "thou shalt love every one of thy neighbors."[84]

Aha, said Teli, spotting his opening: If you can read "love your neighbor" (stated in the singular) that way, why can't you read "he shall cleave unto his wife" (also stated in the singular) the very same way? Why can't the text mean: "he should cleave unto every woman who is his wife" just as he should love every person who is his neighbor. Because, his friend replied, it says that "the two shall become one flesh" – not the three or four shall become one flesh. Not so, Teli replied: the original Hebrew text in Genesis, repeated by Jesus, says only "*they* shall become one flesh." And "they" can refer to any number of wives. We have been misled by our translators, who have betrayed their preferences for monogamy by rendering "they" as "the two" shall become one flesh.[85]

But it is not possible for more than two to become one flesh, his friend answered. That cannot be right, Teli replied, leaving his friend to use his sexual imagination about a ménage de trois or an orgy. In fact, St. Paul says the opposite. In 1 Corinthians 6:16, he warned each Christian man, including each husband, not to visit a prostitute

[82] Ibid., 5–6.
[83] Ibid., 6–7.
[84] Ibid., 7.
[85] Ibid., 7–9.

because he would then become "two in one flesh with her," too, even though he was already "two in one flesh with his wife." "If a man, while he cleaves to a harlot, becomes, as St. Paul says, one body with her, notwithstanding he has a wife, should he not much more become one flesh with her if he makes her his [second] wife?"[86]

To this argument, Teli's friend had no real answer, so he just repeated his charge that polygamy is morally repugnant: "Say what you will: to have more than one wife is a thing filthy, dishonest, and quite contrary, no destructive to the holy state of matrimony."[87]

Undeterred by this general charge of repugnancy, Teli pressed his biblical arguments further. Abraham, Jacob, David, Solomon, and other ancient men of God practiced polygamy without destroying marriage, he argued. Why can I not follow their examples? Because those ancient patriarchs were "frail sinners," his friend replied. But where is their sin and punishment, Teli rejoined? God never punished these ancient polygamists, nor even criticized them. Yes, King David was punished. But that was not for taking Bathsheba as a plural wife, but for committing adultery with her and murdering her husband as well in order to marry her. His polygamy was not the problem; the sins of adultery and murder were what led to his punishment. In fact, God rewarded his polygamy by giving David and Bathsheba a son Solomon, who became David's great successor. No other Old Testament polygamist was punished at all. "Peruse the Scriptures throughout," Teli challenged his friend, "and you will not find a single syllable of God's having prohibited a plurality of wives." In fact, the Mosaic law in Deuteronomy 21:15–17, which is God's own law given to his elect people and designed to make them a holy nation, expressly permits polygamy in providing: "If a man has two wives, the one loved and the other disliked, and they have borne him children," the man must make testamentary provision for both sets of children. This passage makes clear that the children of both wives are legitimate and heritable, and that "not only the first, but all the succeeding marriages are lawful, seeing God himself did approve and bless them."[88]

God did not approve the ancient Israelites' sins of polygamy, his friend replied. He only tolerated them, like he tolerated their sins of voluntary divorce (what we today call unilateral, no-fault divorce). God indulged his ancient people because of "the hardness of their hearts." But just because they were not punished does not mean that they did not sin or did not deserve punishment. But, again, how do you know they were sinful, Teli pressed further? After all, in the Old Testament world, "those things are permitted which are neither hindered, forbid[den], nor punished."

---

[86] Ibid., 9.
[87] Ibid., 9.
[88] Ibid., 9–12.

But neither the natural law nor the Mosaic law gives a hint of hindering, forbidding, or punishing polygamy. The only legal word we find is the provision in the Mosaic law that facilitated the inheritance of the children of polygamy.

His friend tried an argument from self-evidence: "Plurality of wives was then, as it is now, so apparently vicious, filthy, and indecent, that it was needless for Moses to forbid it." You cannot be serious, Teli said, pouncing on this weak miss. After all, adultery, murder, theft, and the like are even more vicious, filthy, and indecent than polygamy. They are prohibited by the natural law and by the laws of other ancient nations as well. Yet Moses prohibited these acts in the Decalogue, which is "an express epitome of the laws of nature." But he says nothing against polygamy. The reality is that the Mosaic law is silent about polygamy not because it is so obviously wrong that it requires no special prohibition, but because it is so obviously right for everyone, except for priests who are commanded to have only one wife.[89]

His friend tried again: God as creator of the law has power to dispense even the laws of nature, and he evidently did so in the case of Abraham, Jacob, David, and other ancient patriarchs and kings. But these divine dispensations did not undermine or cancel the natural laws against polygamy for all men. Only those with special divine dispensation were free from condemnation for their polygamy. And that is clear from the story of Lamech, the first polygamist in the Bible. He did not receive God's dispensation, and he thus committed grave sin in taking two wives. And his sin of polygamy led him to the even graver sin of murder.[90]

But how do you know Lamech was the first polygamist, Teli inquired? And why should his polygamy be a sin or related to his murder which clearly was a sin under both natural law and later Mosaic laws? "We may reasonably conjecture this," his friend answered, "that his having two wives was displeasing to God; since the said murder is mentioned presently after." There is nothing in the biblical text that supports this reading, Teli shot back – either that his polygamy or murder are related, or that God was displeased with him for having two wives. It was his murder that was wrong (just as David's murder of Uriah was wrong). God's displeasure with Lamech had nothing to do with his polygamy.[91]

Exasperated with Teli's relentless rejoinders to his Old Testament interpretations, his friend turned to the New Testament for fresh arguments. He started with St. Paul's statement in 1 Corinthians 7 that celibacy is better than marriage, even though marriage is better than burning with lust. Marriage, he argued, is inferior to celibacy because "married people, being entangled with worldly affairs, are not so free to pray and preach up and down and do good to others, as those who are single.

[89] Ibid., 13–15, 20–22. See also ibid., 28–32, regarding priestly monogamy.
[90] Ibid., 16–17.
[91] Ibid., 15–19.

Now, if the having one wife brings along with it so many impediments [to spiritual life], one may readily conjecture what a plurality of wives will do. Therefore, to have more than one [wife] is absolutely unlawful."[92]

Maybe that is true for a bishop or a deacon in the church, Teli replied. As St. Paul says in 1 Timothy 3, a cleric must be "the husband of one wife" alone so he does not become so distracted with domestic affairs that he cannot attend properly to his spiritual office. But that is not true of everyone else who is not saddled with such heavy spiritual duties. Because Paul specifically commanded clergy to have only one wife, it is "easy to comprehend that he allowed other men to have more."[93] New Testament Christians, just like Old Testament Jews, must have practiced polygamy. And both Testaments thus included a specific prohibition against priestly polygamy in order to enable these religious leaders to discharge their spiritual functions fully. But both Testaments thereby left everyone else free to practice polygamy. Moreover, the New Testament expressly prohibited prostitution, fornication, concubinage, and sundry other sexual sins among new Christians, even though some of these sexual acts had been permitted under the Mosaic law and the ancient Middle East more generally. But the New Testament said nothing about polygamy, evidently leaving that traditional practice in place for new Christians, too.[94]

That under-reads the New Testament, said Teli's friend. St. Paul says clearly in 1 Corinthians 7 that "every man should have his own wife" – not "wives." And, in turn, "every woman shall have her own husband" – not "husbands." Therefore, just "as a wife ought to be proper and peculiar to her husband, and not to appertain to other husbands, so the husband ought to be appropriated to his first wife, and not common to others." Moreover, a "plurality of wives is repugnant to the matrimonial contract in which both man and woman reciprocally yield up to each other, during life, the honest use of their respective bodies.... And a man having once granted the honest use of his body to his wife, he may not afterwards give the same to any other." The marriage contract is an exclusive bilateral contract, and gives each spouse a monopoly over the other's body.[95]

But that Pauline passage only proves that the first wife might have to consent to the addition of a second wife, Teli came back. Sarah consented to Abraham taking Hagar, and many wives would give their consent, too, if they were "given to

---

[92] Ibid., 21.

[93] The argument then veered into a discussion of clerical polygamy and successive polygamy by widows and divorcees, with Teli pressing the argument that God created marriage as a good institution to be repeatedly enjoyed, and his friend standing firm on the traditional Catholic argument that only the laity may marry more than once, and then only after the death of the first spouse. Ibid., 20–28.

[94] Ibid., 28–32.

[95] Ibid., 32–33.

understand, that it is not sinful for their husbands, with their permission, to take to them other wives."[96]

But Sarah is the only biblical wife to give her consent to her husband's polygamy, his friend replied. And even then, it did not go well for Hagar, the second woman. Sarah grew jealous of Hagar and her son Ishmael, and eventually compelled Abraham to drive them out, with only God's intervention sparing them from death in the wilderness. There is no evidence that David or Solomon or any of the other Old Testament patriarchs sought their first wife's permission, and their households were even more rancorous than Abraham's.[97]

Teli, stumbling after this firm rejoinder, tried to poke apart his friend's contractual argument for monogamy. There is no requirement that the first wife expressly consent to a second wife, he argued, so long as she "tacitly acquiesced" in it. Moreover, there is nothing in the marriage contract to give the wife a monopoly over her husband's body: when "a man granted to his wife the use of his body, he gave it not up to her so entirely as utterly to bereave himself of all power to participate in the same to other wives" – either at the same time, or after the death of the first wife.[98]

"No man can marry a second wife without wronging his first," Teli's friend replied, with indignation. "Nor is it credible that wives did ever cordially consent to their husbands doing them such manifest injury as to marry others." The marital contract is an exclusive one, and gives the wife exclusive rights to her husband's body. Anything less than an exclusive relationship would do harm to the woman, and – by implication – her children.[99]

It is not self-evident to me that every woman would or even should withhold her consent to a second wife, Teli tried again. If the first wife is barren, frigid, sick, intemperate, or even pregnant or nursing, it would be "unjust" for her to object to her husband taking a second wife, regardless of what the marital contract says. Justice and fairness must always trump the particulars of any contract, including a marriage contract. But even if a wife is healthy and fertile, "she ought to be satisfied with having, at certain meet times, the enjoyment of her husband's society, and to leave him at liberty" to consort "as he sees proper among his other wives." As long as the man treats his first wife well and honors her "reasonable" conjugal rights to sex, what is the harm to her if he takes another wife?[100]

Part of the problem is the slippery slope, his friend replied. If a man can take a second wife, it would be equally just for a wife to have a second husband, too. For sometimes men cannot or will not have sex, or cannot have children, or are unable

[96] Ibid., 33.
[97] Ibid., 34.
[98] Ibid., 34–35.
[99] Ibid., 34–35.
[100] Ibid., 34–35, 40.

to meet their wife's other reasonable needs. If we accept the argument that justice can trump the terms of the marital contact, "it is seemingly more just, or at least less unjust," that both spouses be allowed to have multiple others.[101]

No, only the man can have multiple wives, Teli replied, citing the arguments against polyandry already raised by Augustine and Aquinas.[102] First, men can produce multiple children with multiple wives, while a woman can produce only one child at a time, however many husbands she has. Second, without being certain of their paternity, none of the husbands will nurture, educate, or protect any child born to the wife. This will lead to "disorder, dissension and confusion" within the home, to the detriment of the children. Third, the Bible says that the husband is the "head" of the wife, not the other way around. A body can have many members, but only one head; it would be "most monstrous" to have multiple heads but one only member in a marital household. Inevitably, with each husband vying to assume his natural place at the head of his wife, there will be endless discord, inconvenience, and fighting within the household.[103]

But discord is just as common among multiple wives, Teli's friend came back. Look at the biblical examples of Sara and Hagar, Leah and Rachel, Hannah and Peninnah. Their "perpetual dissensions" are evidence of God's "displeasure at men having a plurality of wives." More than two in one flesh brings trouble.[104]

But family discord cannot be the test of the validity of polygamy, Teli replied, now stepping back from his argument about the discord occasioned by multiple husbands. After all, biblical siblings like Cain and Abel, or Jacob and Esau fought all the time; that does not mean God disfavors more than one child in a home. Daughters and mothers-in-law fight all the time, too, in the Bible and today; that does not mean God does not want marriages or ongoing relationships between parents and their adult children. Likewise here, Teli concluded, rivalry among plural wives does not mean God does not want polygamy. You cannot draw divine prescriptions against polygamy from biblical descriptions of the patriarchs' troubles with polygamy.[105]

Teli's friend, having stood on firm ground for a few rounds of the argument, now retreated to a weak syllogism. Christians need pleasure more than discord in their marital lives. There is more discord with many wives than with one wife, even for great men of faith like the Old Testament patriarchs. Therefore, Christians should have one wife. That weak rejoinder allowed Teli to take control of the argument again. Even if you are right, he said, the relative pleasure or discord of any actual marriage does not bear on its lawfulness. Monogamous and polygamous households

[101] Ibid., 35.
[102] See discussions on pp. 89 and 172.
[103] Ochino, *A Dialogue on Polygamy*, 35–37.
[104] Ibid., 37–38.
[105] Ibid., 38.

alike have times of pleasure, and other times of discord. That is just life, and you cannot judge the norms or forms of marriage based on that. The Old Testament makes clear that polygamy is "consistent with the elevated degree of faith and perfection. Nor can I apprehend from whence you can be assured that some [Jews and] Christians have not a call from the Almighty to cohabit with sundry wives."[106]

Teli's friend repeated his generic repugnancy argument that polygamy is "dishonest, indecent, and filthy." That is just "hypocritical sanctity," Teli now shot back indignantly. You are elevating the monogamous customs of Christians to a universal norm and imputing that norm to the Bible, even though the Bible provides examples of polygamy among its leading patriarchs and makes provision for them in the later Mosaic law.[107]

His friend tried the familiar argument from necessity to explain the patriarchs' polygamy. The only time polygamy was allowed in the Bible was "when the world was thinly populated" and it is only then that this practice "was, perhaps, expedient." But now with the world filled, there is no need for polygamy.[108]

What is your worry, Teli replied, that the world will have too many people and not enough resources to sustain them? Surely God would not allow that.[109] My concern is not so much scarcity of resources, his friend replied – thereby giving away a familiar medieval argument that polygamy can produce too many children for a family or community to handle.[110] No, said his friend, it is rather "the scandal and offense" of allowing a "detestably filthy ... even diabolical" thing in the Christian community."[111]

Teli tried a different argument from necessity: What if a man felt truly called by God to take a second wife because of his extreme necessity? His friend rejected the hypothetical: "[H]e who already has one wife has no need to take another; neither will he be thereunto called by impulse divine." That is just not true, Teli persisted, as my own case illustrates. What if that first wife is the very cause of his need; she neither prevents him from burning with lust nor produces children for him. Is that not precisely the kind of case of necessity where polygamy should be allowed?[112]

His friend replied with the medieval canon law argument that the practice of polygamy in this case was adultery not necessity.[113] After all, Jesus had said in Matthew 19 that "if any man puts away his wife, except for adultery, and shall marry another,

---

[106] Ibid., 39.
[107] Ibid., 39.
[108] Ibid., 40.
[109] Ibid., 40.
[110] See discussion on pp. 75, 159–161.
[111] Ochino, *A Dialogue on Polygamy*, 41.
[112] Ibid., 41–42.
[113] See discussion in Chapter 4, pp. 152–158.

he commits adultery." If taking a second wife after dismissing the first is adultery, his friend reasoned, then surely having two wives at the same time is an even worse form of adultery. Moreover, if the woman is unjustly divorced, her husband makes her an adulteress if she marries another, and he himself becomes an adulterer because his first marriage is still intact despite his purported divorce. Either way, the second marriage is adultery, which is clearly prohibited by both biblical testaments.[114]

Jesus's statements are about divorce and remarriage, not polygamy, Teli replied. They prohibit a man from divorcing his wife if she does not commit adultery. And, they prohibit a man from marrying an adulterous divorcee. But if neither the husband nor his wife have committed adultery, there is nothing in this passage to prevent the husband from taking a second wife so long as she herself is not an adulterous divorcee. "You so force and strain this interpretation of yours that it is in the greatest danger of breaking."[115]

Well, if Scripture does not convince you, what about nature, Teli's friend tried again. "Irrational creatures" like birds procreate by pair-bonding. "Rational" humans should therefore do so, too. Why are birds, of all creatures, exemplary for humans, Teli replied. Many other male animals have harems, and even some birds like chickens do, too. Because, "by divine ordinance, and for man's benefit, one cock has many hens, much more is it the Almighty's pleasure that a man may have several women, for the propagation of men, whom he so tenderly loves, and so highly prizes."[116]

Ah, but Noah only put one male and female of each animal species in the ark, said his friend. So what! Teli shot back: now there are many more females around than males. And that is true of the human species, too. If there were exact 1:1 sex ratios in all creatures, monogamy might make sense. But even among humans "God creates a greater number of females," making polygamy possible and even necessary for propagation.[117] His friend was not convinced by this empirical claim. It is not all clear that God and nature produce more females than males, he replied. Yes, men might die more often in battle and shipwreck or for crime. But women have a "tenderer constitution," and often die early or in childbirth. Nature generally leaves males and females in roughly equal numbers, making monogamy the most natural form of marriage.[118]

Not only nature, but also utility commends monogamy, Teli's friend continued. "[I]t is a very difficult task for a man to distribute his affection and benevolence

---

[114] Ibid., 42–44.
[115] Ibid., 43–44.
[116] Ibid., 44–45.
[117] Ibid., 45–46.
[118] Ibid., 45–47.

equally and impartially among several wives, which, yet, must be done where polygamy is admitted," as in the case of the Muslims. A man will also have a favorite wife; even Mohammed favored Aisha. "When a man has but one wife, a reciprocal love is better preserved than if he had a plurality; and in case of any quarrel between a man and his single wife, they are more easily reconciled. Amidst a plurality of wives, contrary opinions abound, and there never wants a comfortless scene of discord and distraction."[119]

But polygamy itself is "no enemy to concord and charity," Teli pushed back; "the fault lies not in polygamy, but in the fractious dispositions of those discording females."[120] Not so, said his friend: "polygamy is repugnant" not only to charity and concord, but to "natural reason" and to "natural law," too. And that is why it causes discord in the home. How so, Teli asked. Many nations and peoples, who live by the natural law, do practice polygamy. Socrates, the wisest of the ancient Greeks, who knew the natural law as well as anyone, practiced polygamy.[121] "Polygamy was, and still is, practiced as a beneficial custom, most profitable to mankind by advancing propagation." And, Mosaic law, which God himself authored as he authored the natural law, allowed for polygamy. "If plurality of wives had been repugnant to reason, certainly, neither would Moses have connived at it, those holy good patriarchs have practiced it, nor the Almighty have suffered it."[122]

It is only we European Christians, Teli pressed on, who insist on monogamy as an expedient "piece of prudence" designed to "prevent noise and confusion" within the household. Frankly, it does not work. For in Christian Europe, too, sexual and domestic "vice has abounded, and still does, if not more, yet not one jot less, than in any other part of the universe."[123]

But it was the pagan Roman emperors who first prohibited polygamy, his friend countered, and our own Holy Roman Emperor today still condemns it. And the Christian emperors banned concubinage, too, because of their insistence on a single woman for each man. That certainly did not keep these pious Christian emperors, or the Germanic rulers after them, from practicing polygamy, Teli replied, citing sundry examples. Moreover, my interest is what the natural law requires or permits, not "what men in power will, or will not" prescribe or practice. "Nature's laws are immutable. And, if in Abraham's time it was consonant to reason to have a diversity of wives, and deemed a matter neither dishonest nor unjust ... we must confess

[119] Ibid., 47.
[120] Ibid., 48.
[121] Teli seems to be confusing Socrates, the fifth century BCE Greek philosopher with Socrates Scholasticus, the fifth century CE author of *The Ecclesiastical History of Socrates*. See n. 23 to this chapter.
[122] Ibid., 49–50.
[123] Ibid., 50.

it to be now, in our days, likewise just, honest and expedient.... [T]o condemn polygamy, is for man to prefer himself to God, who never did condemn it, and to assume a greater degree of perfection than He."[124]

But, surely, the church's law is superior to natural law among Christians, said Teli's friend. And that ecclesiastical law condemns polygamy. Not so, said Teli, working through the same canons that we surveyed in Chapter 3. All those canons do is prohibit clerical polygamy, and that is just what the Bible does as well with its "husband of one wife" rule in 1 Timothy 3. "Had the authors of those canons looked upon polygamy itself to have been repugnant to Scripture, Christian charity, and the common good of mankind, they, assuredly, would have excommunicated all those who had more than one wife" and inflicted "grievous corporal punishments" as well. But nothing of the kind can be found in the early councils or canon law rules. Yes, medieval canon law became clearer in condemning polygamy, but those medieval canonists were just importing into the church the man-made laws of the Roman state. But even so, popes and bishops, beginning with Gregory II in his 726 letter to St. Boniface, offered dispensations to practice polygamy in individual cases.[125]

Teli's friend had no counterargument, but just dug in his heels: "All you can utter, should you plead till doomsday, will never convince me that it is either decent, reasonable, or lawful for a man to have more than a single wife." "The whole [Christian] world has believed polygamy to be unlawful; nor can any man have more than one wife, without giving all imaginable offense, which by all ought carefully to be avoided. Besides, God wills us to be obedient to our magistrates. And they are so far from allowing polygamy, that they will put to death the man who is proved to have two wives."[126]

Maybe so, said Teli, but this imperial law also allows a monogamously married man to surround himself with concubines and prostitutes with virtual impunity. And the canon law allows a priest who is married to the church to keep concubines and prostitutes and to commit all kinds of other vile sexual acts with impunity. Maybe you should think again about privileging these man-made laws of church and state above the laws of nature.[127]

The laws of nature call men to be fruitful and multiply through marriage. The more marriages, and the more opportunities for marriage, the better for men, women, children, and society alike, Teli concluded with a flourish:

A man cannot transmit to posterity a more honorable memorial of his name than by leaving behind him children virtuously educated. And what greater folly can

---

[124] Ibid., 51–54.
[125] Ibid., 54–61. Ibid., 61, mistakenly says "Gregorius III," not II.
[126] Ibid., 62.
[127] Ibid. 63–64.

be imagined than, under a show of holiness, to shun holy matrimony, as a thing profane, which nevertheless has been ordained by God, is dictated by nature, is persuaded by reason, was confirmed by Christ, has been and is praised by writers sacred and profane, authorized by all laws, unanimously approved by all nations, and whereunto we are invited by the example of the best men? On the other hand, what more inhumanly barbarous than to hate matrimony, the desire whereof we have implanted by nature? What more ungrateful to nature, the world, and our own species, than not to beget children, as our ancestors and parents have begot us? For my part, I make account, that such men are murderers of as many of they might have begotten, had they embraced matrimony; except, peradventure, they are carried by a divine impulse to lead a single life. Questionless, it is a sort of manslaughter, not only to cause abortion or sterility by drugs, or the like, but also to shun matrimony, without very just cause.[128]

I am not against marriage, but against polygamy, his friend replied simply. But what am I supposed to do now, with a frigid and sterile wife? Teli returned to his starting point. Pray for continence, was his friend's reply. I have tried; it does not work, Teli admitted. Pray more, and have more faith, said his friend, leaving Teli alone.[129]

Ochino captured in this little dialogue virtually all the disputed biblical texts and many of the historical and pragmatic arguments that would come into the discussion of polygamy in succeeding centuries. A century after him, we shall soon see, the English poet and philosopher, John Milton would lift up all these texts and arguments again and press hard for the permissibility of polygamy. And, after Milton, each time the censors fell asleep or were put out of work, new apologists pressed these arguments further. Each time these arguments came up, they were condemned with an array of arguments, some variations on old arguments, some inventions of new ones. But it was Ochino who had laid his fingers on many arguments that traditional critics of polygamy needed, and still need, to answer.

SUMMARY AND CONCLUSIONS

Great revolutions, Harold J. Berman tells us, always pass through radical phases before they reach an accommodation with the tradition they had set out to destroy. During that radical phase, each revolution explodes with iconoclastic new ideas and experiments that rethink and reorder much that was considered sound, settled, and sacred in the tradition.[130] Sex, marriage, and family life are often among the

[128] Ibid., 64–65.
[129] Ibid., 65.
[130] Harold J. Berman, *Law and Revolution: The Formation of the Western Legal Tradition* (Cambridge, MA: Harvard University Press, 1983); id., *Law and Revolution II: The Impact of the Protestant Reformations on the Western Legal Tradition* (Cambridge, MA: Harvard University Press, 2003).

first ideas and institutions to be so radicalized as individuals brimming with their new-found freedoms follow their passions, and as authorities covetous of new power vie for control of the household.[131]

This pattern of revolution was certainly at work during the sixteenth-century Protestant Reformation. From the start, Lutheran, Anglican, Calvinist, and Anabaptist reformers radically rejected traditional Catholic teachings on clerical celibacy, the sacramentality of marriage, the many impediments to engagement and marriage, the many restrictions on sex within marriage, and the prohibitions on divorce and remarriage. Protestant magistrates challenged the church's canon law of marriage, and issued sundry new secular statutes on sex, marriage, and family life to be newly enforced by the secular courts. And Protestant clergy and laity experimented with all manner of marital forms and norms, sexual acts and associations that would never have been countenanced before Martin Luther posted his Ninety-Five Theses in 1517.

In this first generation of heady Protestant reform, the traditional theology and law of polygamy came under new attack and experimentation as well. Political leaders like Henry VIII and Philip of Hesse and their apologists considered polygamy as a viable option for them to satisfy their lusts and to guarantee heirs to succeed them to the throne. Theological leaders like Luther, Erasmus, and Melanchthon ultimately considered polygamy a better choice than brazen adultery or no-fault divorce to resolve hard marital cases. The most adventuresome were selected Anabaptists, most notably in Münster, who thought polygamy was a spiritual duty for all members of the community to channel their natural passions toward the production of more saints in emulation of the Old Testament patriarchs and in anticipation of the return of the Lord. This Münster experiment proved to be a textbook example of the many harms that polygamy had already occasioned in biblical times: rape, coerced marriage, household rivalry, abused wives and children, lustful patriarchal excess, battery and murder, social destruction, and warfare.

These early experiments with polygamy, however, soon drew to themselves ever more sophisticated defenses. Apologists for royal polygamy issued thick propaganda pamphlets in defense of their patrons, and in defiance of their ample critics in church and state. Apologists for Anabaptist polygamy raked through the Bible and the tradition in search of spiritual prototypes and theological warrants for their newly chosen lifestyle. Smart free-thinkers like Bernard Ochino cracked open long sealed arguments from Scripture, tradition, and nature to cast reasonable doubt on monogamy as the only, or even the best, form and forum of love, support, nurture, and education. Was polygamy not, in fact, countenanced by nature and the Bible,

[131] See examples of revolutionary experiments and reforms of sex, marriage, and family life during the fifth, twelfth, sixteenth, and eighteenth centuries, in my *From Sacrament to Contract.*

and exemplified by some of the great heroes of the West – Abraham, David, and Solomon? Should polygamy not at least be an option for loveless and childless spouses eager for sex, companionship, and children? Would faithful polygamy not be a better deterrent to the sins of fornication, prostitution, concubinage, adultery, and bastardy that faithless monogamy always produces? Would more marriages made available through polygamy not be better for men, women, children, and society, or at least better for spinsters, widows, bastards, and orphans otherwise left to fare perilously on their own? Do Scripture, nature, justice, fairness, and common sense, in short, not condone polygamy more than condemn it? These were the new challenges that the Western tradition had to answer.

And answer it would. In the next two chapters, we examine the emerging Western case against polygamy – first in Calvinist civil law circles in Geneva, then in Anglican common law circles in England. Ochino's arguments for polygamy in particular, we shall see, came in for long and caustic rebuke, and Ochino himself would be convicted for heresy and blasphemy and banished with his family from Protestant Zurich.[132] Each of his arguments from Scripture, nature, utility, and tradition were flipped on its head in favor of monogamy over polygamy.

---

[132] See discussion in Chapter 6, pp. 255–256, and Chapter 8, pp. 330–331.

6

The Calvinist Case Against Polygamy and
Its Civil Law Influence

FIGURE 13. "Adam and Eve," from Lucas Cranach, Samuel Courtauld Trust, The Courtauld Gallery, London.
Used by permission of Samuel Courtauld Trust, The Courtauld Gallery, London, UK / Bridgeman Images.

FIGURE 14. "The Meeting of Jacob and Rachel," from Franz August Schubert, Private Collection.
Used by permission of Peter Nahum at The Leicester Galleries, London, UK / Bridgeman Images.

Alarmed by the polygamist experiments and speculations unleashed by the Reformation, both Catholic and Protestant authorities in the sixteenth century came down hard on polygamy. The Catholic Council of Trent pronounced "anathema" on the practice in 1563. The Inquisition, together with the church courts and secular courts of Catholic lands in Europe and their colonies, doubled their resolve to stamp out polygamy for good. The index of prohibited books eventually included a long roll of pro-polygamy tracts, not least those that we have seen by Cajetan, Luther, Ochino, and the Münsterites.[1] The Holy Roman Empire in 1532 ordered that polygamy should be punished as sternly as adultery, making it a capital crime in serious cases.[2] Catholic Spain and France repeated these provisions, and Catholic Poland ordered convicted polygamists to be banished for good.[3] Early modern Protestant magistrates in Germany, Scandinavia, the Netherlands, Scotland, and

---

[1]　See *Index Auctorum et Librorum* (Rome: Ex officina Saluini, 1559) (http://www.aloha.net/~mikesch/ILP-1559.htm#B).

[2]　Josef Kohler and Willy Scheel, eds., *Peinliche Gerichtsordnung Kaiser Karls V: Constitutio Criminalis Carolina* [1532], repr. ed. (Aalen: Scientia Verlag, 1968), art. 121.

[3]　See discussion in Chapter 4, pp. 155–158.

England ordered various levels of punishment for convicted polygamists – fines, public confessions, shame punishments, flogging, hard labor, banishment, and occasionally execution.

The growing range of punishments of polygamy set out in these statutes reflected a growing refinement in the degrees of polygamy that were criminalized. In early modern Protestant lands, the crime of polygamy came to encompass four types of illicit plural relationships. In order of growing severity, they were cases when one party: (1) engaged a second party, while already engaged to a first; (2) engaged a second party, while already married to a first; (3) married a second party, while already engaged to a first; and (4) married a second party, while already married to a first. Adding even more fiancé(e)s or spouses compounded the defendant's problems; each new relationship was a new case of polygamy that could be separately prosecuted. Each case of polygamy became more serious if the defendant's conduct proved knowing or intentional, rather than accidental or unintentional. Each case also became more serious if other parties knowingly participated in or winked at the second contract. In those cases, accomplice liability charges could lie against the other fiancé(e) or spouse or their respective children or families who were in on the fraud, the parents who knowingly consented to the second union, and the minister or magistrate who just married the second couple without properly ascertaining their eligibility for marriage.[4]

Sundry such polygamy cases crowded onto the dockets of Protestant state courts in the sixteenth century and thereafter, producing a steady stream of judgments over the next three centuries. Most Protestant laws rejected self-divorce or self-annulment as an excuse for polygamy, and even engagement contracts had to be carefully broken before a party was free to engage or marry another. But most Protestant laws also rejected private engagement or marriage contracts that did not involve parents, peers, pastors, and political officials, making it harder for a party to become doubly contracted. When someone did engage a second party while already being engaged to a first, the authorities generally upheld the first engagement and administered spiritual and sometimes criminal sanctions for entering the second. When someone was engaged to one and married to another, the authorities generally upheld the marriage contract and administered both severe spiritual discipline and firm

---

[4] On Genevan developments, see discussion later in this chapter. On this differentiations of types or degrees of polygamy in other legal systems in late medieval and early modern polities, see Diego Garzia de Trasmiera, *De Polygamia et Polyviria libri tres* (Palermo: Apud Decium Cyrillum, 1638); Giuliano Marchetto, "'Primus fuit Lamech': La bigamia tra irregolarità e delitto nella dottrina di diritto commune," in *Trasgessioni: Seduzione, concubinato, adulterio, bigamia (XIV–XVIII secolo)*, eds. Silvana Seidel Menchi and Deigo Quaglioni (Bologna: Il Mulino, 2004), 43–106; Anna Esposito, "Adulterio, concubinato, bigamia: testimonianze della normativa statuturia della Stato pontificio (secoli XIII-XVI), in ibid., 21–42; Johann Christoph Theodor Hellbach, *Selecta Criminalia eaque iam de Marito Hebraico Christiano, una uxore non contento* (Arnstadii: Schill, 1747).

criminal sanctions. When someone was found in a double marriage, not only was the second marriage annulled, but the second couple could face severe criminal punishment – execution if this was a brazen or repeated offense, or if the polygamy was compounded by other felonies like adultery, child marriage, rape, or serious marital property fraud.[5] All this became standard practice both at civil law and at common law in early modern Protestant lands. These state laws and cases followed a good bit of the practice of some medieval courts,[6] but now with a much stronger emphasis on imposing firm criminal sanctions for polygamy alongside providing civil remedies for breaching the impediment of precontract.

This chapter samples one such Protestant legal system in action, that of sixteenth-century Geneva after its conversion to Protestantism in 1536. Before sampling a few cases, I first analyze the underlying theology of monogamous marriage developed by two of its founding leaders, John Calvin (1509–1564) and his successor Theodore Beza (1519–1605). Both of these Protestant titans were French-trained classicists, theologians, and jurists who left a massive body of writings that influenced broader Protestant scholarship for centuries thereafter.[7] Both of them were politically and legally active in Geneva and surrounding polities, crafting dozens of new statutes and legal opinions, and sitting on hundreds of marriage and family cases that appeared before the Genevan Consistory each year.[8] Together, they and their coworkers engineered a sweeping reform of sex, marriage, family life, lore, and law based on the biblical idea of marriage as a covenant rather than a sacrament. Both of them condemned polygamy at length in their writings and sermons, and both were active in the prosecution and punishment of polygamists in Geneva. Beza, furthermore, answered in detail the polygamous speculations of Bernard Ochino that we sampled in the last chapter. And he participated as an expert in Ochino's trial for heresy, which led to Ochino's eventual banishment from the Protestant community.

[5]   See, e.g., William G. Naphy, *Sex Crimes From Renaissance to Enlightenment* (Stroud, Gloucestershire/ Charleston, SC: Tempus Publishing, 2002), 33–54.

[6]   See discussion of medieval church courts in Chapters 4 and 7 of this book.

[7]   See *Ioannis Calvini opera quae supersunt omnia*, eds. G. Baum et al., 59 vols. (Brunswick: 1863–1900) [hereafter CO]; Theodore Beza, *Tractationum Theologicarum*, 2nd ed., 3 vols. (Geneva: Excvdebat Evstathivs Vignon, 1582) [hereafter TT]; and samples of their main writings in critical English edition in John Witte, Jr. and Robert M. Kingdon, eds., *Sex, Marriage and Family in John Calvin's Geneva*, 2 vols. (Grand Rapids, MI: Wm. B. Eerdmans, 2005, 2015) [hereafter SMF 1 and 2].

[8]   The statutes are collected in Emile Rivoire and Victor van Berchem, eds., *Les sources du droit du canton de Genève*, 4 vols. (Aarau: H.R. Sauerländer 1927–1935). The consistory court records are collected in Robert M. Kingdon et al., eds., *Registres du Consistoire de Genève au Temps de Calvin*, 21 vols. (Geneva: Droz, 1996) [hereafter RC]. Samples of both sources in critical English edition appear in SMF 1 and 2.

JOHN CALVIN ON THE COVENANT OF MARRIAGE
AND THE EVILS OF POLYGAMY

John Calvin's case for monogamy and against polygamy was built on a covenantal model of marriage that he developed in place of the medieval Catholic sacramental model.[9] The Bible, Calvin pointed out, describes marriage only once as a *mysterion* (Eph. 5:32), a term that, in his view, was mistranslated in the Latin Bible as *sacramentum*.[10] But the Bible describes marriage forty-six times as a covenant (*b'rith*; *foedus*). The Old Testament analogizes Yahweh's covenantal relationship with Israel to the special relationship between husband and wife. Israel's disobedience to Yahweh, in turn, becomes a form of "playing the harlot." Idolatry, like adultery, can lead to divorce, and Yahweh the metaphorical husband threatens this many times, even while calling his metaphorical wife Israel to reconciliation. These covenantal images of marriage, divorce, and reconciliation recur repeatedly in the Old Testament books of Hosea, Isaiah, Jeremiah, Ezekiel, and Malachi, on all of which Calvin commented at length.[11]

The Bible also speaks about marriage as a covenant in its own right, Calvin continued. The Prophet Malachi's formulation is the fullest:

> You cover the Lord's altar with tears, with weeping and groaning because he no longer regards the offering and accepts it with favor at your hand. You ask, "Why does he not?" Because the Lord was witness to the covenant between you and the wife of your youth, to whom you have been faithless, though she is your companion and your wife by covenant. Has not the one God made and sustained for us the spirit of life? And what does he desire? Godly offspring. So take heed to yourselves, and let none be faithless to the wife of his youth. "For I hate divorce, says the Lord the God of Israel, and covering one's garments with violence, says the Lord, the God of hosts. So take heed to yourselves and do not be faithless."[12]

Just as God draws the elect believer into a covenant relationship with Him, Calvin argued, so God draws husband and wife into a covenant relationship with each other. Just as God expects constant faith and good works in our relationship with him, so God expects connubial faithfulness and sacrificial works in our relationship with our spouses. "God is the founder of marriage," Calvin wrote:

---

9. See detailed sources and discussion of Calvin's views in SMF 1 and 2 and in John Witte, Jr., *From Sacrament to Contract: Marriage, Religion, and Law in the Western Tradition*, 2nd ed. (Louisville, KY: Westminster John Knox Press, 2012), 159–216.

10. See John Calvin, *The Institutes of the Christian Religion* [1559], trans. John T. McNeill, ed., Ford Lewis Battles (Philadelphia, PA: Westminster Press, 1960), 4.19.34.

11. In the order of their appearance, see Comm. Isaiah 1:21–22; 54:5–8; 57:3–10; 61:10–11; 62:4–5 (1551); Serm. Deut. 5:18, 22:22 (1555); Comm. Harm. Gospel Luke 1:34–38 (1555); Comm. Ps. 16:4, 45:8–12, 82:1 (1557); Lect. Hosea 1:1–4, 2:19–20, 3:1–2, 4:13–14, 7:3, 9–10 (1557); Lect. Zec. 2:11, 8:1–3 (ca. 1560); Lect. Mal. 2:13–16 (ca. 1560); Lect. Jeremiah 2:2–3, 25; 3:1–5, 6–25; 13:27; 23:10; 31:32, 51:4 (1563); Comm. Harm. Law Deut. 11:26–32 (1563); and Lect. Ezek. 6:9, 16:1–63 (1564).

12. Malachi 2:13–16.

When a marriage takes place between a man and a woman, God presides and requires a mutual pledge from both. Hence Solomon in Proverbs 2:17 calls marriage the covenant of God, for it is superior to all human contracts. So also Malachi [2:14–16] declares that God is as it were the stipulator [of marriage] who by his authority joins the man to the woman, and sanctions the alliance.... Marriage is not a thing ordained by men. We know that God is the author of it, and that it is solemnized in his name. The Scripture says that it is a holy covenant, and therefore calls it divine.[13]

God participates in the formation of the covenant of marriage through his chosen agents on earth, Calvin believed. The couple's parents, as God's "lieutenants" for children, instruct the young couple in the mores and morals of Christian marriage and give their consent to the union.[14] Two witnesses, as "God's priests to their peers," testify to the sincerity and solemnity of the couple's promises and attest to the marriage event.[15] The minister, holding "God's spiritual power of the Word," blesses the union and admonishes the couple and the community of their respective biblical duties and rights.[16] The magistrate, holding "God's temporal power of the sword," registers the parties, ensures the legality of their union, and protects them in their conjoined persons and properties. This involvement of parents, peers, ministers, and magistrates in the formation of the marriage covenant was not an idle or dispensable ceremony. These four parties represented different dimensions of God's involvement in the marriage covenant. They were essential to the legitimacy of the marriage itself. To omit any such party in the public formation of the marriage was, in effect, to omit God from the marriage covenant.

God also participates in the ongoing marriage covenant through the daily instruction of the natural law and the Bible, which these same four parties must help communicate to the new couple and to their eventual children, too.[17] The covenant of marriage is grounded "in the creation and commandments of God," and "in the order and law of nature," Calvin believed.[18] At creation, God ordained the structure of marriage to be a lifelong union between a fit man and a fit woman of the age of consent. God assigned to this marriage three interlocking purposes: (1) the mutual love and support of husband and wife; (2) the mutual procreation and nurture of children; and (3) the mutual protection of both parties from sexual sin.[19] In nature, man and woman enjoy a "common dignity before God" and a common function of "completing" the life and

[13] Serm. Eph. 5:22–26, 31–33; see also Serm. Deut. 5:18.
[14] Comm. Harm. Law Lev. 19:29; Serm. Deut. 5:16; Comm. and Serm. 1 Cor. 7:36–38; Serm. and Comm. Eph. 6:1–3.
[15] Comm. I Thess. 4:3; Comm. I Peter 2:9; Institutes (1559), 4.18.16–17.
[16] Serm. Eph. 5:31–33.
[17] The congregational baptismal vows underscore this communal responsibility for children. See texts collected in SMF 2, chap. 5.
[18] Comm. Gen. 2:18; Comm. Deut. 24:1–4; Comm. Mal. 2:15; Comm. Matt. 19:3–9 and Mark 10:2–12; Consilium in CO, 10/1:239–241.
[19] Comm. Gen. 1:27; 1:28, 2:18; 2:21; 2:22; Comm. 1 Cor. 9:11; Comm. Eph. 5:30–32; Serm. Eph. 5:28–30.

love of the other.[20] In marriage, husband and wife are "joined together in one body and one soul," but then assigned "distinct duties" within the household.[21] God has appointed the husband as the head of the wife. God has appointed the wife, "who is derived from and comes after the man," as his associate and companion –literally his "help meet."[22] "The divine mandate [in Paradise] was that the husband would look up in reverence to God, the woman would be a faithful assistant to him, and both with one consent would cultivate a holy, friendly, and peaceful intercourse."[23]

The covenant of marriage is a "sacred contract," Calvin wrote, that depends in its essence on the mutual consent of both the man and the woman. "While all contracts ought to be voluntary, freedom ought to prevail especially in marriage, so that no one may pledge his faith against his will."[24] "God considers that compulsory and forced marriages never come to a good end.... [I]f the husband and the wife are not in mutual agreement and do not love each other, this is a profanation of marriage, and not a marriage at all, properly speaking. For the will is the principal bond."[25] When a woman wishes to marry, she must thus not "be thrust into it reluctantly or compelled to marry against her will, but left to her own free choice."[26] "When a man is going to marry and he takes a wife, let him take her of his own free will, knowing that where there is not a true and pure love, there is nothing but disorder, and one can expect no grace from God."[27] Any marital contract that is formed in violation of these essential requirements of consent must be annulled.

The covenant of marriage, even if properly formed, remains a conditional performance agreement, Calvin went on. Unlike the sacraments of baptism and the Eucharist, which are permanent marks of grace, marital covenants have built into them conditions of mutual performance. Marital covenants, like all covenants, recognize the possibility of breach and consequent dissolution. Fundamental breaches of a marriage covenant by adultery or desertion can result in divorce. Yes, God "hates divorce," as Malachi said, but God allows for divorce, as Moses, Jesus, and Paul all provided. Calvin and the laws of Geneva that he drafted recognized the right of each spouse to divorce on grounds of adultery and desertion, and to remarry, with the guilty party responsible to pay postmarital support and maintenance to the innocent first spouse and children. This, too, was part of the freedom inherent in the covenant of marriage – the freedom to end a covenant that had been fundamentally betrayed by the other party.[28]

[20] Comm. Gen. 1:27.
[21] Comm. Gen. 2:18, 22.
[22] Comm. Gen. 2:18. See also Comm. 1 Cor. 9:8, 11:4–10.
[23] Comm. Gen. 2:18.
[24] Comm. Josh. 15:14.
[25] Serm. Deut. 25:5–12.
[26] Comm. Gen. 24:57.
[27] Serm. Deut. 25:5–12. See other examples in SMF 1:20–30.
[28] See detailed sources in SMF 2, ch. 9; Robert M. Kingdon, *Adultery and Divorce in Calvin's Geneva* (Cambridge, MA: Harvard University Press, 1995).

Although both marital parties have freedom of contract, Calvin emphasized, they were not free to marry just anyone. Many of the terms of the marital covenant were preset by the laws of nature and the Bible. Parties could not marry or have sex with blood relatives, children, eunuchs, or animals. Nor could they form temporary marriages, tolerate concubinage, prostitution, or adultery, or get divorced and remarried without just cause. Instead, God and nature had designed marriage to be a monogamous union between a fit man and a fit woman presumptively for life, Calvin said, echoing medieval teachings. This arrangement promoted essential trust and reliance between husband and wife. It also fostered paternal certainty and joint parental investment in fragile and dependent children, who, as Aquinas had already emphasized, need both parents to help them through their long infancy and childhood.[29] Stable marriages also provided ongoing care for spouses and children as they moved through their lifecycles and depended intermittently on their natural kin network for support. And this arrangement ensured that the marital household remained a stable institutional cornerstone for church, state, and society alike.[30] Calvin worked out an elaborate covenant theology and law of sex, marriage, and family life from these starting premises.

Calvin used this same covenantal logic to put what would remain the principal Calvinist case against polygamy. Polygamy was a pressing concern for Calvin – in part because some Protestants had experimented with polygamy (as we saw in the last chapter), and in greater part because the Old Testament included several examples of polygamists, including such leading patriarchs as Abraham, Jacob, David, and Solomon. How could Calvin, with his strong *sola Scriptura* ethic, insist that Bible-believing Christians follow these great Old Testament patriarchs in so much else, yet denounce their polygamy so vehemently and denounce anyone who sought to emulate the patriarchs in their polygamous practice?

Calvin denounced polygamy because he believed that God had prescribed monogamy as an "order of creation." God created one man and one woman in Paradise, and brought them together in holy matrimony. This first marriage of Adam and Eve, he believed, set the norm and form for all future marriages, and it distinguished proper sexual relationships among humans from the random and multiple sexual associations of other animals who also operated in accordance with a general natural law. After recording the story of the creation and coupling of Adam and Eve, Moses wrote: "Therefore shall a man leave his father and his mother, and shall cleave onto his wife: and the two shall become one flesh."[31]

---

[29] See discussion in Chapter 4, pp. 170–175.

[30] See detailed sources in SMF 1, chs. 4–10; Cornelia Seeger, *Nullité de mariage divorce et séparation de corps a Genève, au temps de Calvin: Fondements doctrinaux, loi et jurisprudence* (Lausanne: Société d'histoire de la Suisse romande, 1989).

[31] CO 10/2:255, 258, quoting Genesis 2:24, Matthew 19:5, I Corinthians 6:20, and Ephesians 5:32.

Calvin read the phrase the "two *shall* become one flesh" as a divine command. By this phrase, God commanded monogamous marriage as the "most sacred" and "primal" institution. And God also condemned polygamy as "contrary to the order and law of nature" for humans, a teaching which he believed Moses, Jesus, and Paul all confirmed in their repeated references to this creation story and its commandment of "two in one flesh." At creation, God could have created two or more wives for Adam, as he did for other animals. But he chose to create one. God could have created three or four types of humans to be the image of God. But he created two types: "male and female he created them." In the Mosaic law, God could have commanded his chosen people to worship two or more gods as was common in the day, but he commanded them to worship one God and remain in exclusive covenant with him. In the Gospel, Jesus could have founded two or more churches to represent him on earth, but he founded one holy catholic and apostolic church, for which he made infinite loving sacrifices. Marriage as an "order of creation" and as a covenantal "symbol of God's relationship with his elect" involves two parties and two parties only. "[W]hoever surpasses this rule perverts everything, and it is as though he wished to nullify the very institution of God," Calvin concluded.[32]

Whereas monogamy was commanded at creation, polygamy became commonplace already soon after Adam and Eve's fall into sin. The first polygamist in the Bible was Lamech, a descendent of the first murderer, Cain. Calvin denounced Lamech, for he knowingly "perverted" the "sacred law of marriage" that "two shall become one flesh." Whether driven by lust or by a lust for power, Lamech upset the "order of nature" itself in marrying a second wife. Lamech's sin of polygamy begat more sin. Many of Israel's greatest patriarchs and kings – Abraham, Jacob, Gideon, David, Solomon, Rehoboam, and others – succumbed to the temptation of polygamy.[33]

Although polygamy may have been customary in that early day, Calvin continued, the Bible's account of the chronic discord of these polygamous households should be proof enough that polygamy brought trouble. Each polygamist described in the Bible became distracted by multiple demands on his time and energy and multiple divisions of his affections. His wives competed for his attention and approval, and "ensnared" and "stifled" his mind of all "manly good sense," making him "effeminate" and prone to bad judgments. His parents became torn in their devotion to their daughters-in-law. His children vied for his property and power. In

---

[32] CO 23:50–51; John Calvin, *Sermons sur la Genèse*, ed. Max Engammarre, 2 vols. (Neukirchen-Vluyn: Neukirchener Verlag, 2000), 1:139–149; Comm. Gen. 1:27; CO 7:214; Serm. Deut. 21:10–14, Comm. Harm. Law Ex. 20:3–6; Comm. Eph. 5:31; Serm. Eph. 5:31; Lect. Ezek. 16; Serm. Deut. 21:15–17.

[33] Comm Gen. 4:19.

King David's polygamous household, the sibling rivalry escalated to such an extent that the step- and half-children of his multiple wives raped and murdered each other. And that was after King David had already killed the husband of Bathsheba whom he lustfully coveted and wanted to add to his harem. Take one step down the slippery slope of sinful polygamy, Calvin concluded, and even the greatest kings slide all the way down into a vast pool of sin.[34]

It was for that reason, said Calvin, that the Mosaic law repeated the natural law of monogamy, ordering that even a king must not "multiply wives for himself, lest his heart turn away" (Deut. 17:17).[35] The point of this Mosaic rule – and its New Testament echoes that each bishop and priest must be "the husband of one wife" (1 Tim. 3:2, Titus 1:6) – was not that polygamy was permitted to everyone except for kings, bishops, and priests. The real point was that these political and religious leaders, who had the power and resources to take multiple wives, were to set moral examples for their people by following the monogamous ideal set out in the creation order and natural law.[36]

But it was not just biblical kings with their hundreds of wives who suffered from the compounding sins of polygamy, Calvin went on. Jacob's long travail with his two wives, Rachel and Leah, was a simple but sobering illustration of these evils of polygamy under any circumstance (Gen. 29–31). The biblical story is detailed, and Calvin returned to it often. Jacob's uncle Laban had tricked him into marrying his elder daughter, Leah, instead of Rachel whom Jacob loved. Jacob, after working for seven years to get this privilege, had reluctantly married Leah. A week later, he got permission to marry her sister Rachel as well but only in exchange for seven more years of labor. Both Laban and Jacob thereby "pervert[ed] all the laws of nature by casting two sisters into one marriage bed," and forced them to spend their "whole lives in mutual hostility." But it was not so much the incest as the polygamy that caused all the problems. After his second marriage, Jacob did not accord Leah "adequate respect and kindness"; indeed, he "hated" her, even though he slept with her regularly and God "opened her womb" so that she produced many sons for him. Jacob loved Rachel, but she produced no children, placing her in hostile competition with her sister Leah. Escalating the hostility, Rachel gave Jacob her servant Bilhah who produced two sons for Jacob. Leah countered by giving Jacob

[34] Comm. Gen. 4:19,16:1–6, 22:19, 26:34–35, 28:6–9, 29:27–30:34, 31:33–42; Comm. Harm. Law Deut. 17:17; Lect. Mal. 2:15–16; Serm. 1 Sam. 1:6; Serm. 2 Sam. 13.
[35] Comm. 1 Tim. 3:2; Comm. Titus 1:6.
[36] Ibid.; Comm. Harm. Law Deut. 17:17. Although he refers here to the problems of Solomon's polygamy, Calvin left no commentary on 1 Kings 11:3–8, where Solomon's wives are reported to have led him to worship other gods. Calvin also left no commentary on Judges 8:30 and 2 Chronicles 11:18ff reporting on the polygamy of Gideon and Rehoboam.

her servant Zilpah who produced yet another son. All the while, Jacob continued to sleep with Rachel, who finally conceived and had a son Joseph. This only escalated the feud between Rachel and Leah and the sins of their children and the children of their concubines.[37]

For Calvin, this entire scandalous affair proved that "there is no end of sinning, once the divine institution" of monogamous marriage is breached. Jacob's fateful first step of committing polygamy led him to commit all manner of subsequent sins – incest, concubinage, adultery, lust, and then even more polygamy. Jacob's initial sin was perhaps excusable; he was after all tricked into marrying Leah and had to work seven more years for the right to marry his beloved Rachel. His subsequent sins, however, were an utter desecration of God's law. Calvin blamed Rachel as well, rebuking her for her "petulance," her blasphemy and lack of faith, her abuse of her servant Bilhah, and her complicity in Jacob's concubinage, adultery, and polygamy.[38]

Jacob could well have minimized some of this rampant sin by divorcing Leah, before marrying Rachel, Calvin argued. For Calvin, divorce was "a lighter crime" than polygamy – a position directly opposite to that argued by Luther, Melanchthon, Erasmus, and others.[39] After all, said Calvin, the Mosaic law did allow a Jewish man to divorce his wife for her "uncleanness" or "indecency," and to remarry any eligible woman thereafter, save his ex-wife if she had since remarried.[40] Jesus and Paul allowed for divorce and remarriage, too, albeit on narrower grounds of adultery and desertion.[41] The Bible's express provision for divorce created a hierarchy of proper marital conduct for believers. Marriage for life was best. Divorce and remarriage were acceptable. But polygamy was never allowed, for it was a desecration of the primal form and norm of marriage.[42]

Calvin drove home this argument by appealing to the covenantal description of marriage in Malachi 2. The King James Version captures nuances in the passage (reflected in Calvin's French Bible, too) that he stressed:

> Because the Lord hath been a witness between thee and the wife of thy youth, against whom thou has dealt treacherously; yet she is thy companion, the wife of thy covenant. *And did not he make one? Yet he had the residue of the Spirit. And wherefore one? That he might seek a godly seed.*[43]

---

[37] Comm. Gen. 29:27–30:3.
[38] Comm. Gen. 29:27–31, 30:1–3.
[39] See discussion in Chapter 5, pp. 205–218.
[40] Deuteronomy 24:1–4.
[41] Matthew 19:6–9; 1 Corinthians 7:15.
[42] Lect. Mal. 2:14–16; Comm. Harm. Gospel Matt. 19:5–6.
[43] Malachi 2:15–16 (KJV, emphasis added).

Calvin read this passage as a confirmation of monogamy and as a condemnation of polygamy. The point of this passage, he said, is that at creation God "breathed his spirit" of life into "one" woman, Eve. God had plenty of spirit left to breathe life into more women besides Eve. But God chose to give life to Eve only, who alone served to "complete" Adam, to be "his other half." And it was this monogamous union only that could produce "godly seed" – that is, legitimate children.[44]

Malachi furthermore had made each individual marital covenant between husband and wife part and product of the covenant between God and his elect. Both the husband and the wife must be faithful to this covenant, Malachi made clear, just as God remained faithful to his elect bride of Israel. For a husband to wander after another woman – whether a lover, prostitute, concubine, or a second wife – was now not just an act of adultery, but an act of blasphemy, an insult to the divine example of covenant marriage that God, the metaphorical husband, had offered to each human husband living under God's covenant. Husbands must follow God's example of offering "covenant love" to their wives, remaining faithful to them even in the face of "violence," trouble, or betrayal. Husbands must also follow God's example in living both by the letter and the spirit of the traditional law of divorce. There is still a place for divorce in cases of deep rupture of the relationship. "God hates divorce," Malachi says, but God does not prohibit it. Instead, God calls husbands not to divorce lightly on grounds of mere "uncleanness" (as Deuteronomy 24 put it), nor to divorce harshly "covering their garments with violence" (as Malachi 2 put it). To breach one's marital covenant lightly or violently, Malachi teaches, is tantamount to breaching one's covenant with God. For those who do so, God "no longer regards or accepts" their offerings or worship – a sure sign of divine condemnation.

While both divorce and polygamy are deviations from the ideal of life-long monogamy, Calvin argued, "polygamy is the worse and more detestable crime." Divorce for cause was allowed by God. Polygamy enjoyed no such license, and was expressly forbidden even to kings and bishops. The children of divorced parents remained legitimate heirs. But the bastard children of a second wife or concubine inherit nothing. Both the Roman law and the Mosaic law confirmed this, Calvin argued. Roman law prohibited all bastards from inheriting property, and treated the children of polygamy as bastards.[45] Mosaic law provided the same, albeit less directly. Deuteronomy 21:15–17 reads:

> If a man has two wives, the one loved and the other disliked, and they have both borne children, both the loved and the disliked, and if the first-born son is hers that is disliked, then on the day when he assigns his possessions as an inheritance to his

---

44 Ibid.; Comm. 1 Tim. 3:2; Comm. Titus 1:6; Comm. Harm. Gosp. Matt. 19:3–9.
45 See texts in my *The Sins of the Fathers: The Law and Theology of Illegitimacy Reconsidered* (Cambridge: Cambridge University Press, 2009), 49–72.

sons, he may not treat the son of the loved as the first-born in preference to the son of the disliked, who is the first-born, but he shall acknowledge the first-born, the son of the disliked, by giving him a double portion of all that he has, for he is the first issue of his strength; the right of the first-born is his.

Calvin offered a novel interpretation of this passage that others in his day, like Ochino, had taken to be a clear biblical endorsement of polygamy. This law cannot be about a man having "two wives" at the same time, Calvin argued, but having two wives in succession after the man had divorced the first wife whom he "dislikes." The Mosaic law protects the inheritance of the first set of legitimate children against unscrupulous divorced fathers who might be tempted to favor the legitimate children of their second wife. By contrast, children of polygamy, beginning with Ishmael, the first-born son of Abraham and Hagar, are illegitimate bastards who deserve and receive no inheritance.[46] Indeed, two chapters after this Deuteronomy 21 passage, the Mosaic law bars bastards even "from the assembly of the Lord … until the tenth generation."[47] Later Old Testament passages – including those from the same Prophets who had introduced the marital covenant metaphor – ordered that bastards be "cut off" and "cast out" of their homes, if not out of the community altogether. Because bastards cannot inherit, and because the children of second wives beginning with Ishmael are bastards, Calvin concluded, Deuteronomy's discussion of the heritability of the children of "two wives" must be about two "successive wives," not two wives at the same time.[48]

Having made so much of this distinction between permissible divorce and prohibited polygamy, Calvin dismissed out of hand traditional Catholic arguments that the remarriage of divorcees or widow(er)s was a form of successive polygamy, or "digamy." "I do not consider polygamy to be what the foolish papists have made it," Calvin declared derisively. Polygamy is about marriage to two or more wives at once, as is practiced today among Muslims. It has nothing to do with remarriage to a second wife after the first marriage is dissolved by divorce or death.[49] For Calvin, that was the end of the matter, and he left it to his handpicked successor Theodore Beza to elaborate this argument.

[46] Genesis 25:5–9.

[47] Deuteronomy 23:2.

[48] For relevant passages, see Judges 11:1–3; Ezra 9:10–11:44; Hosea 2:4–5; Jeremiah 31:29, Ezekiel 18:2–3; Lamentations 5:7; Sirach. 3:11 23:24–26; Wisdom 3:16–17, 4:6. But cf. Genesis 48:22, where Joseph (son of Jacob's second wife Rachel) did receive an inheritance. For Calvin's discussions of inheritance issues, see Comm. Harm. Law Deut. 21:15–17; Comm. Harm. Law Deut. 23:2; Serm. Deut. 23:1–3; Comm. Gen. 21:8–18. 25:1–6; Comm. Gal. 4:21–31 with excerpts in SMF 2, ch. 13. For direct rejoinders to this interpretation, see the discussion of John Milton and Martin Madan later in this chapter and in Chapter 8, pp. 332–334, 341. See also the more conventional interpretation of this passage by Theodore Beza later in this chapter.

[49] Lect. Mal. 2:15–16.

THEODORE BEZA VERSUS BERNARD OCHINO:
POLYGAMY AS UNBIBLICAL AND UNNATURAL

Beza was the first rector of the famous Genevan Academy when it opened in 1559, and he served as the Academy's leading professor of theology until his retirement four decades later. After Calvin's death in 1564, he also stood at Calvin's pulpit, sat in his consistory seat, and assumed his role as legal advisor and diplomat for Geneva.[50] Beza was the leading light of the French Calvinist movement until the seventeenth century, and his work remained in print in multiple translations for another century thereafter.[51]

Among his numerous writings, Beza produced two critical tracts that helped refine the Calvinist case for monogamy and against polygamy. One tract, *On Annulment and Divorce* (1569),[52] was a systematic exposition on the covenantal model of monogamous marriage, and its detailed implications for the laws of marital formation, maintenance, and dissolution. Included in that tract was a firm defense of remarriage after death or divorce, and a sharp attack on the "superstitious sanctimony" of Tertullian and many later theologians and canonists who opposed second marriages after death or divorce. "We know polygamy is opposed by the divine law," Beza wrote, but second marriage is permitted in the Bible. To call a second marriage polygamy, bigamy, or digamy is just "foolish."[53]

Beza expounded on these themes at far greater length in his tract *On Polygamy, and Divorce* (1568/1573), a 334-page "refutation" of these same "Montanist" attacks on marriage and remarriage,[54] as well as a "refutation" of traditional prohibitions against "clerical bigamy."[55] Like Calvin and other Protestants, Beza believed that divorce was permissible, sometimes essential, if one spouse committed adultery, desertion, or a capital crime.[56] Beza also believed that, after divorce or death of the

[50] See Paul Geisendorf, *Théodore de Bèze* (Geneva: Droz, 1967); Eugène Choisy, *L'État chrétien calviniste a Genève au temps de Théodore de Bèze* (Geneva: C. Eggimann & cie, 1902).

[51] See Beza, TT. Missing from this collection is his important but controversial political work which was published anonymously in 1574 and in modern critical edition as *Du Droit des Magistrats*, ed. Robert M. Kingdon (Geneva: Droz, 1970), and in translation as *Concerning the Rights of Rulers Over Their Subjects and the Duties of Subjects Toward Their Rulers*, trans. Henri-Louis Gonin (Cape Town/ Pretoria: H.A.U.M., 1956) [hereafter Beza, *Rights*].

[52] Theodore Beza, *De repudiis et divortiis* (Geneva: Vignon, 1569, 1573), reprinted in Beza, TT, 2:50ff. I am using the 1573 edition.

[53] Ibid., 175–177.

[54] See Theodore Beza, *Tractatio de polygamia, in qua et Ochini apostatae pro polygamia, et Montanistarum ac aliorum adversus repetitas nuptias argumenta refutantur: addito veterum canonum et quarundam civilium legum ad normam verbi divini examine* (Geneva: Apud Eustathium Vignon, 1573 [1568]), 40–199.

[55] Ibid., 200–335.

[56] See Beza, *De Repudiis et Divortiis*, 163–214 (for remarriage after adultery), 214–244 (after desertion), and 244–255 (after capital crime), and Beza, *De Polygamia*, 40–69 (after spouse's death). Beza added capital crime as a ground for divorce on the argument that even if the spouse was not executed, his

other spouse, remarriage was commendable, even essential for those with minor children to raise, household businesses to manage, or sexual drives to control. He recommended a time of healing and recovery after the end of a prior marriage. In cases of desertion, he further urged the deserted party to act "in good conscience and fairness" to find the deserter first before filing for divorce or a declaration of death. But thereafter, he said, remarriage was a commendable practice, one or more times if needed, as the laws of Geneva properly made possible.[57]

The most salient part of Beza's *On Polygamy* for our purposes was his forty-page attack on the arguments for real polygamy offered by Bernard Ochino.[58] Ochino's tongue-in-cheek "dialogue," we saw in the last chapter, adroitly pressed the case for polygamy on biblical, natural, and utilitarian grounds. The volume was a brisk seller in its day, although it was soon censored by Catholic and Protestant authorities. When Ochino's volume reached Geneva in 1563, Beza immediately condemned it as an "apostasy" and "heresy" – terms that Beza had already put to grim effect in his defense of Geneva's execution of Michael Servetus for heresy.[59] It did not help Ochino's cause that it was Sebastian Castellio, the robust defender of Servetus and sharp critic of Calvin, who had translated Ochino's tract into Latin and commended it in a robust preface to the new publication. Beza's attack on Ochino's views on polygamy, which he distilled into an opinion letter, was a key piece of evidence used by the Zurich authorities to prosecute Ochino later that year. The Zurich authorities found him guilty of heresy and banished the frail 76-year-old and his four children in mid-winter of 1564. Ochino wandered through Germany and Poland in search of refuge, and died the following year in Moravia where he was buried.[60]

Four years later, in his tract *On Polygamy*, Beza sought to bury Ochino's arguments for polygamy as well, expanding his earlier opinion letter into a forty-page

---

actions made him worthy of death, and thus dead to his spouse who was now a widow(er) with the right to remarry.

[57] Beza, *De Repudiis et Divortiis*, 222, 235–237.

[58] Beza, *De Polygamia*, 3–40. For other early Protestant refutations of these pro-polygamy arguments, see, e.g., Johannes Gerhard, *Loci Theologici … Tomus Septimus, De Conjugio* (Jena: Typis & Sumptibus Tobiae Steinmanni, 1657), secs. 202–226 (pp. 104–119); Henning Arnisaeus, *De Jure Connubiorum Commentarius* (Frankfurt am Main: Impensis Iohannis Thimij, typis Andreae Eichorn., 1613), ch. 4, pp. 184–211; Friedrich Spanheim, *Dubia Evangelica in tres partes distributa* (Geneva: Sumptibus Petri Chouët, 1639), sect. 122; Jacob Cats et al., *Patriarcha bigamos* (Rudolphopoli: [s.n.], 1821); *Faces Augustae: sive poemeta* (Dordrecht: Sumptibus Matthiae Havii & typis Henrici Essaie, 1643); Michael Siricius, *Uxor Una: Ex Jure Naturae et Divino, Moribus Antiquis et Constitutionibus Imperatorum et Regnum. Eruta et Contra Insultus Impugnantium Defensa* (Giessen: Typis et sumptibus Josephi Dieterici Hampelii, 1669), 35–44, 101–163. See discussion in Miller, *Milton Among the Polygamophiles*, 55–57.

[59] See Theodore Beza, *De haereticis a civili Magistratu puniendis* (Geneva: Vignon, 1554).

[60] See Henry Martin Baird, *Theodore Beza: The Counsellor of the French Reformation, 1519–1605* (New York: G.P. Putnam's Sons, 1899), 275ff.; Tadataka Maruyama, *The Ecclesiology of Theodore Beza: The Reform of the True Church* (Geneva: Droz, 1978), 70ff.

attack on his views. Ochino had argued that polygamy was biblical and natural. The Old Testament patriarchs and kings, he argued, practiced polygamy with impunity, producing many godly children. The Mosaic laws of inheritance established rules for a man with "two wives" and children from each. The Bible nowhere prohibits polygamy, although it prohibits many other sexual crimes. The biblical metaphor of "two in one flesh" is not a command about the number of wives, because the Bible says that a married man can become "two in one flesh" with a prostitute, too. The Bible's talk of a husband "cleaving to his wife" is no more exclusive a relationship than a man "loving his neighbor"; just as a man must love every person who is his neighbor, so he must cleave to every woman who is his wife. And the Pauline "conjugal debt" gives a wife no monopoly over her husband's body. Instead, it obliges the husband to satisfy fully his wife's sexual needs, but obliges the wife to consent to his taking another wife if she cannot satisfy his sexual needs or his need for an heir, as Sarah did in consenting to Abraham's taking of Hagar to produce Ishmael.[61]

Beza rejected Ochino's arguments, echoing and elaborating some of Calvin's arguments in so doing. Yes, Beza said, a few of the biblical patriarchs and kings did practice polygamy– perhaps out of necessity to fill the empty earth. But only a few of these ancient men did so, beginning with Lamech. Most men did not practice polygamy, and Ochino exaggerates the number who did.[62] The necessity to produce many children that drove a few of these early men to polygamy no longer obtains with the earth now full and with many children no longer an essential sign of divine favor and social standing. That some of these ancient men produced godly sons and heirs through polygamy as well as through incest, adultery, prostitution, or rape does not condone any of their actions, even if God did not punish them. It testifies instead to God's "unique goodness" in harvesting good from evil, and dealing so patiently with human sin. After all, these ancient patriarchs were just sinful men (just like we all are), albeit men of great faith and favor in God's sight (as are a few people today). Modern-day believers can take no more instruction from their polygamy than they can take from the biblical stories of Lot's incest with his daughters, Gilead's sex with a prostitute, or David's adultery with Bathsheba – all of which produced children who proved important in the history of salvation.[63] God's silence in the face of such sins does not constitute his blessing of their activities, any more than God's silence in the face of our own sins today makes them right in his eyes. God "is merciful and gracious, slow to anger and abounding in steadfast love."[64]

---

[61] See discussion in Chapter 1, pp. 41–42 in this volume, and in Witte, *Sins*, 11–26.

[62] Beza, *De Polygamia*, 5–6.

[63] Ibid., 5–6, 27–28 (referencing Genesis 19:30–37; Judges 11:1–3; 2 Samuel 11).

[64] Psalm 103:8.

But that does not change the fact that polygamy is "repugnant to honest nature" and natural law.[65]

The laws of God and nature do condemn polygamy, Beza went on in answering Ochino's argument.[66] Indeed, polygamy violates four of the Ten Commandments of the Decalogue, the single most important statement and summary of both biblical law and natural law. First, polygamy violates the Commandment against adultery – sexual misconduct which other biblical laws and many other legal systems clearly and repeatedly condemn.[67] Marriage, Beza wrote, "comprises an agreement concerning the indivisible joining of life" with one's spouse, and a pledge to "make exclusive use" of one's own spouse alone in all conjugal matters. Adultery is a betrayal of the exclusive relationship of trust and fidelity that marriage demands, and a violation of the rights and privileges that each spouse has in the life, body, and property of the other. A husband's one-time sexual tryst with a third party is already adultery; indeed even looking lustfully at another woman constitutes adultery, Jesus says in Matthew 5:28. Far worse is a husband's ongoing sexual relationship with a prostitute or concubine; each sexual act with her is adultery. But the worst form of adultery is polygamy, where a man seeks to legitimize his adultery under "the cover of legal marriage." This whole unfaithful relationship of polygamy is perpetual adultery, or adultery writ large.[68]

The New Testament said as much, Beza continued, in treating adultery as a violation of the primal "two in one flesh" form and norm of marriage set at creation. Paul said that a husband who has sex with a prostitute becomes "two in one flesh" with her.[69] Ochino had argued that this passage shows that a man can join in "one flesh" with two women or two wives at the same time. Nonsense, said Beza. To join "two in one flesh" with a prostitute is to break the "two in one flesh" union with one's wife. A man cannot be two in "one flesh with a prostitute and with his wife at

---

[65] Ibid., 4–10. See also Theodore Beza, *The Psalmes of Dauid: Truely Opened and Explaned by Paraphrasis, According to the Right Sense of Euery Psalme*, trans. Anthony Giblie (London: Iohn Harison and Henrie Middleton, 1580), s.v. Psalm 103.

[66] On Beza's natural law theory – that combines biblical laws (moral, juridical, and even ceremonial), moral laws, natural law, and the common law of nations – see Beza, TT 1:53–54; Beza, *Rights of Rulers*, 24–26, 64–66; Theodore Beza, *Lex Dei moralis, ceremonialis et politica* (Geneva: Apud Petrum Santandreanum, 1577); id., *Propositions and Principles of Divinity, Propounded and Disputed in the University of Geneva* (Edinburgh: Robert Waldegrave, 1591), cap. 34ff. and running comments throughout id., *Psalmorum Davidis et aliorum Prophetarum* (London: Excudebat Thomas Vautrollerius, 1580). See analysis in John Witte, Jr., *The Reformation of Rights: Law, Religion, and Human Rights in Early Modern Calvinism* (Cambridge: Cambridge University Press, 2007), 93–94, 127–133, 138–140.

[67] Beza, *De Polygamia*, 13, and his detailed discussion of adultery in Beza, *De Repudiis et Divortiis*, 179–214, esp. 180–182, 190–195, 285–290.

[68] Beza, *De Polygamia*, 12–14, 28–29.

[69] 1 Corinthians 6:16.

the same time." The wife is now free to divorce her husband for his adultery. Only if she forgives him, and takes him back, is their marital "two in one flesh" union restored. But if the man returns to the prostitute, after his wife has forgiven him, the marriage is again broken. And if he tries to maintain both his marriage and his resort to prostitution, he is a polygamist and adulterer at once.[70]

Jesus said the same, Beza continued, in arguing that an illegal divorce and remarriage creates adultery, too: neither a man nor a woman can be two in one flesh with more than one spouse. In Matthew 19, Jesus said that a husband may divorce his wife for her adultery and remarry thereafter with impunity. But if he divorces his wife without just cause, and marries another he has committed adultery against his first wife. And if his unjustly divorced wife gets remarried, she commits adultery, too, with her first (former) husband and second (current) husband both accomplices to her adultery. Beza read this passage to apply equally if the wife files for divorce with or without cause and each of the ex-spouses gets remarried. Jesus's main point in this passage, Beza concluded contrary to Ochino, is not to create loopholes for a second marriage even without adultery. It is, instead, to underscore that adultery is a breach of the covenant of marriage, and that a second marriage without a lawful divorce based on proven adultery or desertion violates the "two in one flesh" norm, making it not only adultery, but also polygamy. For Ochino to argue that Jesus's teaching on adultery and divorce allows a man to form several "two-in-one-flesh" unions with impunity so long as his first wife or wives consent thereto, Beza concluded, is plain "blasphemy."[71]

Second, polygamy is not only a form of adultery, but also a form of theft, Beza continued. And theft, too, is clearly prohibited by the laws of God and nature, specifically by the Commandment "thou shalt not steal." In polygamy, both the husband and the second wife steal the first wife's contractual rights, her marital property, and the spousal support to which she is entitled. Polygamy is not just a breach of the husband's marital contract with his first wife and a betrayal of the exclusive conjugal debt that he owes to his first wife. It is also blatant theft of the first wife's exclusive rights to her husband's body, protection, support, and estate. And the more wives that a man has "the less that is left" for the first wife, the ultimate theft victim. Polygamy is theft from a man's children, too, who are deprived of the full material and moral support of their father, which is "wicked and nefarious." Deuteronomy 21:15–17 makes modest provision for children of polygamy, by insisting that the children of the first spouse get their share of the inheritance, Beza argued, reading this text more conventionally than Calvin had done. "But what is this to the forum of conscience?" It is certainly not a commendation of polygamy

[70] Ibid., 36–38.
[71] Ibid., 35–39. See also Beza, *De Repudiis et Divortiis*, 198–210.

but a humane concession to the needs of innocent children who will otherwise be "robbed" by the "lust" of their polygamous fathers.[72]

Third, building on this last point about a man's "lust," Beza argued that polygamy also violates the Commandment: "Thou shalt not covet … thy neighbor's wife [or] maidservant." Following Protestant convention, Beza read this no coveting Commandment as a prohibition against both temptations toward and attempted crimes against a neighbor's household and its members.[73] Coveting a neighbor's wife or maidservant, Beza argued, thus constitutes attempted theft from the neighbor, attempted adultery against one's own wife, attempted complicity in the adultery of the neighbor's wife, and ultimately attempted polygamy, too. The most notorious such case was that of David and Bathsheba, the wife of Uriah described in the Bible. David's coveting of Bathsheba started the downward spiral into double adultery, murder, and polygamy. Given these risks, Beza argued, the very availability of polygamy as a valid marital option triggers perennial violations of this Commandment not to covet. As the story of David and Bathsheba tragically reveals, having a valid polygamy option available inflames a man's lust, "making even a modest man whorish" because he will always be on the lookout for another wife. This betrays an essential good and goal of marriage, namely, curbing lust and removing sexual temptation. And it betrays the most sublime biblical commandment of all – to "love thy neighbor as thyself." So, Beza concluded, polygamy violates the no coveting Commandment, too.[74]

Fourth, Beza hinted, and later commentators made clear, polygamy also violated the Commandment: "Thou shalt not bear false witness." The letter and spirit of this Commandment, Beza wrote, is that a person must not only speak truthfully but must also keep his or her word and promise. There are few promises more precious to keep than the promise of marriage, where both parties vow solemnly to have and hold their spouse faithfully and exclusively, "forsaking all others," and remaining

---

[72] Ibid., 12–16, 19, 24–25. Beza followed Calvin's argument that the Mosaic law of "levirate marriage" – the obligation of a brother ("levir" in Hebrew) to take in and have children with his deceased's brother's widow set out in Deuteronomy 25:5–10 – was not an "exception" to the prohibition against polygamy or incest. Levirate marriage, in Calvin and Beza's view, was permissible, not required, and then allowed only if the surviving brother was single at the time and only if the widow consented to the new marriage. See ibid., 16–17; Calvin, Serm. Deut. 25:5–12 and further texts and discussion in SMF 1:120–121, 314–318.

[73] Ibid. On this reading of the Decalogue by Calvinists, see also Christoph Strohm, *Calvinismus und Recht* (Tübingen: Mohr Siebeck, 2008), esp. 133–136, 314–317; John Witte, Jr., *Law and Protestantism: The Legal Teachings of the Lutheran Reformation* (Cambridge: Cambridge University Press, 2002), 113–114, 125–127, 158–161; and the later tradition expounded in David Van Drunen, *Natural Law and the Two Kingdoms: A Study in the Development of Reformed Social Thought* (Grand Rapids, MI: Wm. B. Eerdmans, 2010) and Stephen Grabill, *Rediscovering the Natural Law in Reformed Theological Ethics* (Grand Rapids, MI: Wm. B. Eerdmans, 2006).

[74] Beza, *De Polygamia*, 24–25.

together for better or worse, in sickness and in health, until they are parted by death.[75] There are few breaches of promise more grave than violating this exclusive marital vow by making the same exclusive vow to a second spouse or fiancé(e). Beza did not say this explicitly in his brief against Ochino. But he did say, elsewhere, that the breach of any contractual promise, including an engagement or marital promise, was a violation of the Commandment not to bear false witness. And he also made clear that it is both adultery and polygamy for a person to enter into a double engagement, a double marriage, or back-to-back engagements and marriages with two or more parties.[76]

These four Commandments of the Decalogue – prohibiting adultery, theft, coveting, and promise-breaking – separately and together, condemn polygamy, Beza concluded. The Bible is thus not at all silent about polygamy, as Ochino had argued. Anyone attentive to the letter and spirit of the Bible can see that God speaks loudly against it. Malachi and the other Prophets underscored this teaching by commending anew the "two-in-one-flesh" monogamous norm of marriage announced already at creation and exemplified in the faithful union of Yahweh and his chosen bride Israel. Jesus and St. Paul did the same by invoking the metaphorical monogamous marriage of Christ and the Church.[77] And if that is not biblical proof enough, Beza continued echoing Calvin, the Old Testament is filled with horror stories that warn us about the ample discord that beset even the holiest and noblest of polygamous households. Yes, Beza acknowledged, Ochino has a point that domestic discord is not unique to polygamy. But the "mutual hatred" and "evil competition" of rival wives "alights especially upon polygamy," for it is fundamentally an unnatural and unjust relationship. The addition of a new wife to the household inevitably triggers the retaliation of the first wife who is acting in legitimate defense of herself, her property, her household, her bed, her marriage, her husband. A wife's self-defense against so fundamental a betrayal of the covenant of marriage, Beza said, is both natural and just.[78]

Because polygamy is so "unnatural" and so "unjust," Beza continued, other advanced civilizations attentive to the natural law have also condemned the

---

75   For the Marriage Liturgy used in Geneva, see SMF 1:445–480, esp. 464–467.
76   Beza, *De Polygamia*, 39–40; TT 2:76–77, 98–99. See elaboration of this point by later Protestants below in this chapter and in Chapter 7 in this book. See further the Genevan cases punishing the adultery and infidelity of fiancé(e)s in SMF 1, chap 12.
77   Beza expounded on this dyadic imagery of marriage at length in his late-life sermons on the Song of Songs: *Sermons sur les trois premiers chaptres du cantique des Cantiques, de Salomon* (Geneva, 1586), translated as *Master Bezaes sermons upon the three first chapters of the Canticle of Canticles* (Oxford: Joseph Barnes, 1587), ch. 1, sermons 1–6. Beza's panegyric here about monogamy says little about polygamy, but condemns adultery and all other illicit sexual unions.
78   Beza, *De Polygamia*, 12–13. For Beza's interweaving of the rights of resistance and self-defense in the home and in the state, see Witte, *The Reformation of Rights*, 129–133.

practice, even without direct access to the Bible. The best examples are ancient Greece and Rome. Long before the advent of Christianity and with only the natural law to guide them, these ancient cultures prohibited polygamy and prescribed monogamy. This is evidence of "the natural law in action," Beza argued. Good classicist that he was, Beza could list sundry early Greek and Roman laws against polygamy, and show their ongoing use in the medieval and early modern *ius commune*. Yes, he noted, there were occasional concessions to polygamy by and for individual rulers ancient and modern. But these exceptions did not undermine the dominant reality that Western law before and after its Christianization viewed polygamy as unnatural and unjust. All these laws, Beza wrote, "make it clear that polygamy is none other than the covering of that wandering lust of honest nature, and that men, with only the single light of nature guiding them, recognized that such infamy must be condemned."[79]

Ochino had made much of the relative silence of the early church and its canons in condemning polygamy, and had suggested that the medieval church's later adoption of these laws was merely political. Beza read this history through the lens of church-state relations. For the first 1,200 years, he said, the state principally punished polygamy, while the church disciplined sexual acts and alliances at the edges of polygamy. That is exactly how church and state should divide their responsibilities. Polygamy is first and foremost a crime, and the state, not the church, should punish crime. The church called the faithful to a higher form of moral discipline than the state could. It was only when the late medieval church usurped the state's jurisdiction, Beza argued, that the canon law made polygamy a sexual crime prosecuted by the church courts. It may well be that the medieval church's motivation to take over this prosecution was political, Beza allowed. But that does not mean the criminalization of polygamy itself was improperly motivated or something new. Polygamy was always a crime in the West, even if it has been intermittently punished by different authorities.[80]

Ochino had also made much of Paul's instruction that a bishop or priest must be the "husband of one wife." Because only a cleric is told to have one wife, Ochino had argued, a lay person must be allowed to have more than one. Not so, said Beza. Paul is talking here prudentially about a minister's fitness for church office. A minister who has been widowed or divorced often may simply not be stable or strong enough for church ministry. A minister who has had multiple households

[79] Beza, *De Polygamia*, 24–26, 38–39.
[80] Ibid., 26–28. Beza dealt with church-state relations and ecclesiastical government in his tracts *A Briefe and Pithie Summe of the Christian Faith Made in the Form of a Confession*, trans. R.F. (London: Roger Ward, 1589), bk. 5 and *The Judgment of a Most Reverend and Learned Man from Beyond the Seas, Concerning the Threefolde Order of Bishops: With a Declaration of Certaine Other Waightie Pointes, Concerning the Discipline and Government of the Church* (London: Robert Walgrave, 1585).

and now has many children to tend to, might be too distracted to be able to engage fully in "the administration of the Word." And a congregation that is served by an oft-married minister might not have the resources to support his extra-large family. That is why the "husband of one wife" rule is in place. Nothing in this speaks to the propriety of polygamy.[81]

Beza made equally fast work of Ochino's linguistic games with other biblical phrases, treating them as parlor tricks that missed the larger point and context of all these passages. Ochino, for example, had said that the mere act of God in giving one woman to Adam was no more normative for marriage than the mere act of God clothing the first couple in skins was normative for clothing. But, Beza replied, the Genesis passage that reports the creation of Eve goes on to say that a "man *shall* cleave unto his wife and the two *shall* become one flesh." Moses, Malachi, Jesus, and Paul all repeated this, saying nothing about skins or clothing fashions. The nature of marriage is about the essentials, the forms of fashion are not.[82] Ochino had also said that for a man "to cleave unto his wife" is no more exclusive a relationship than for him to "love his neighbor." He may love many wives just as he must love many neighbors. But, said Beza, it is obvious from the full context of the Bible that a man has many neighbors, all of whom he must love, while a man has only one wife, whom he must love exclusively as if she were his own body.[83]

Ochino had pressed various utilitarian arguments for polygamy as well. If there were more polygamy, he argued, there would be fewer divorces. The opposite is true, said Beza. There would be more divorces because the first wife would want out of her marriage – as was the case in Münster, he might have added, where 200 wives divorced their polygamous husbands in the first year.[84] Moreover, as Calvin had already pointed out, divorce is allowed by the Bible and natural law, while polygamy is not.[85] If having one wife is good for a man's health, Ochino had further argued, having multiple wives must be even better. Nonsense, Beza argued. That is like saying because a man needs food and drink, he should consume unlimited quantities. "Moderation" is the norm in all things, and in marriage God sets that norm of moderation by providing "one wife" to satisfy a man's needs, because "it is not good that the man should be alone."[86]

[81]   On marriage of bishops and other church offices, see Beza, *De Polygamia*, 17–18, 201–206, 242–244.
[82]   Ibid., 30–32.
[83]   Ibid., 32–34.
[84]   See related discussion in Chapter 5, pp. 221–222.
[85]   Ibid., 18–19.
[86]   Ibid., 20–22, citing Genesis 2:18.

GENEVAN CASES ON POLYGAMY AND PRECONTRACT

Polygamy was a serious crime in Protestant Geneva, as it was in other early modern Protestant lands. In Geneva, cases of open and intentional polygamy went directly to the Genevan City Council for prosecution and punishment. If convicted, polygamists were banished, sometimes after being whipped, imprisoned, and subjected to various shame penalties. Repeat polygamists, or those who compounded their polygamy with other felonies, were executed.[87]

But it was not just brazen double marriages that attracted the attention of the Genevan authorities. They also investigated other double relationships or contracts that could constitute polygamy of a lesser degree.[88] The first tribunal to hear these lesser forms of suspected polygamy was an important new institution that Calvin had created for the city, called the Consistory. The Consistory, which combined city officials and church ministries on two benches, acted at once as a preliminary hearings court and as a mediation and reconciliation tribunal. It had power to administer spiritual sanctions: admonition and confession, bans from the Eucharist, and excommunication in serious cases. But if the case required criminal punishment or civil sanctions, the Consistory would remove the case to the Council to handle.

In each new case of suspected polygamy, the Genevan authorities were required to check whether either the man or the woman had a first contract of engagement or marriage that required annulment. This issue came up quite regularly. For Geneva was a haven for refugees and émigrés, and the prior marital histories of these new residents often required investigation before a new marriage could be authorized. The 1546 Marriage Ordinance that Calvin had drafted for Geneva provided for this specifically:

> To avoid all the frauds that are committed in these matters, let no foreigner coming from a distant country be admitted to marriage unless he has good and certain testimony, either by letters or by respectable people, worthy of faith, that he has not been married elsewhere, and also of his good and respectable behavior; and let the same be observed with respect to girls and women.[89]

The 1552 case of Blaise de la Croys and his fiancée Yrlande was typical of the kind of inquiry that often came up.[90] Blaise and Yrlande had just moved to Geneva from

---

[87] See Kingdon, *Adultery and Divorce*, 62, 129ff.; William G. Naphy, *Calvin and the Consolidation of the Genevan Reformation* (Louisville, KY: Westminster John Knox Press, 1994), 31. See also E. William Monter, "Crime and Punishment in Calvin's Geneva, 1562," in Richard C. Gamble, ed., *Calvin's Work in Geneva* (New York: Garland Publishing, 1992), 271–277.

[88] On the division of authority between the consistory, that exercised spiritual discipline over sin, and the council that meted out criminal punishment and civil remedies, see sources and analysis in SMF 1, ch. 2.

[89] Translated in SMF 1: 51–61.

[90] RC VII, 70, 71v.

a Catholic town in Provence. Before moving, they had already become engaged. They now wanted to get married in Geneva. The Consistory questioned them and their witnesses whether any precontract or other impediment stood in the way of marriage. Yrlande, it turned out, was a former nun who had relinquished her vows. She had later met Blaise whom she found to be a good man. Both sets of parents had consented to their marriage. But, as a former nun, Yrlande would not have been able to marry in a Catholic territory. That may well have prompted the couple's move to Geneva. Previous monasticism was no impediment to marriage in Geneva. Finding no other precontract or impediment, the Consistory approved the match.

Not all cases proved so easy. During their investigations, the Consistory came upon a good number of cases where one or both parties had entered into more than one engagement or marital contract at a time. What follows are samples of these cases from the Genevan records, arranged in escalating order of gravity.

Engagement-Engagement

In simple cases of back-to-back engagements, the Consistory would generally uphold the first engagement contract. If the first engagement contract was somehow imperfectly formed or subject to a legitimate condition that had been breached, however, the Consistory would annul that first engagement contract and uphold the second.[91]

A good example is the 1557 case of Philiberte Chapuis and her two fiancés, Anthoine and Pierre.[92] Philiberte was first engaged to Anthoine. Four months later, she became engaged to Pierre. A distraught Anthoine appeared before the Consistory seeking to annul Philberte's second engagement, and to have her compelled to marry him. Philiberte's defense was that she and Anthoine had made their contract in secret and that Anthoine had failed to give her an engagement gift. Moreover, she argued that her aunt, who was also her guardian, had not consented to this match, and indeed feared that Philiberte and Anthoine were second cousins who could not marry in any event because of incest laws. Accordingly, her aunt had found Pierre as a substitute whom Philiberte was happy to marry.

There was enough contradiction in the testimonies of Philiberte and her aunt to give the Consistory some pause. They sent the two women and Philiberte's two purported fiancés to the Council to sort out the testimony. The Council eventually imprisoned Philiberte briefly, apparently for perjuring herself concerning the whereabouts of her parents. But the Council also dissolved her first engagement with Anthoine because it was contracted secretly – without witnesses or parental

[91] See examples in Seeger, *Nullité de mariage divorce et séparation*, 348–352.
[92] RC XII, 48v, 52–52v, 60, 62.

consent, a ground for annulment in Calvin's Geneva. They ordered Philiberte to marry Pierre instead. It was the secrecy of her first engagement to Anthoine that was fatal in the Council's judgment. The other two allegations in Philiberte's defense against Anthoine would not have been sufficient. Failure of dowry was not a ground for annulment of engagements in Geneva.[93] And, as second cousins, the parties were too distantly related to make out an incest impediment.[94]

A 1552 case of Pierre Saultié involved allegations of three sequential engagements. Pierre first became engaged to a woman in Chézery, and gave her an engagement gift. She conditioned her consent on her parents' consent, however, and her parents would not approve the match. The woman returned Pierre's gift, and Pierre assumed the engagement was over. He then moved to Présilly and became engaged to a second woman, and gave her an engagement gift. This engagement was apparently made with the condition that Pierre remain in Présilly under the rule of the local lord. Pierre did not want to remain in the town under that lord's authority, so he broke this engagement, too, although without retrieving his engagement gift. He then became engaged to yet a third woman, also in Présilly, and then moved to Geneva. The Consistory regarded Pierre's conduct as altogether improper and sent him and his witnesses to the Council to "get to the bottom of the matter."

The Council's record for the case does not survive. It is likely that Pierre's second engagement promise would have been enforced, after he had been punished for his polygamous engagement with the third fiancée. Engagement contracts conditioned on parental consent could be annulled in the absence of such parental consent.[95] Thus the first engagement to the woman from Chézery would have been broken. But engagement contracts conditioned on less material considerations – such as relocation to a new city or procurement of a job – could not be so easily broken. Unless the lord of Présilly who insisted that Pierre live in the town under his rule happened also to be the parent or guardian of Pierre's second fiancée, this condition would not have been considered material enough to justify an annulment. Pierre would thus have been bound to this second engagement contract. That made his third engagement contract a prima facie act of polygamy.

The Consistory came down even harder on parties who compounded their multiple engagements with other crimes. In a 1561 case, for example, Claude Plantain had become engaged to a woman named Jeanne who was a ward of Maurice and Françoise Gaillard.[96] The Gaillards, as guardians, had consented to this union. Claude, however, grew disenchanted with Jeanne. Without seeking annulment of

---

93 See Marriage Ordinance (1546), item 14, in SMF 1:51–61.
94 Given what her aunt testified, Philiberte and Anthoine were at best second cousins. This did not trigger an impediment of affinity at Genevan law, although it would have at medieval canon law.
95 See SMF 1, ch. 4–5.
96 RC XVII, 94; XVIII, 70, 73v.

his first engagement to Jeanne, Claude became engaged to Jeanne's older sister, also named Claude. This sister Claude was also a ward of the Gaillards, and they encouraged this engagement when Claude rejected their younger ward Jeanne. This seemed to be incest piled upon polygamy, and the Consistory sent Claude to the Council for close investigation. Claude did not help his cause by disappearing for a year. When the authorities came upon Claude a year later, they came down hard. The Consistory summoned a battery of witnesses against him. Despite their conflicting testimony, the Consistory thought this case was sufficiently serious to send Claude, his two purported fiancées, and their guardians to the Council. All five parties involved, including Claude who was a Genevan citizen, were banished from the city and ordered not to return on pain of whipping or worse.[97]

Marriage-Engagement

To engage a second party after being engaged to a first was bad enough. To engage a second party, while being *married* to a first was worse. The gravity of this offense could be seen in a 1542 case.[98] Four or five years before, Pierre Rapin had become properly engaged to Pernette Maystre. He had given her a piece of property as his engagement gift. The couple had been properly married, and now had a child. In the months before the case, the couple had become estranged. They no longer slept together, and Pierre was given to lengthening absences from the marital home. This raised suspicions. Two months before the case was filed, Pierre became engaged to another woman named Franceyse. They had sexual intercourse. Franceyse testified, however, that "she did not consent to his company," which suggests that Pierre may have raped her. Moreover, she said, Pierre left her shortly thereafter "because she did not give him any money."

Calvin, on behalf of the Consistory, urged the Council to punish Pierre Rapin's offense. The Council's sentence was severe. Rapin was condemned to a public whipping and to "carrying a miter on his head," a form of shame punishment. He was then banished from the city and forced to abandon his property "under penalty of the gibbet." This was rather severe punishment, but Pierre was guilty not only of polygamy but also of adultery with Franceyse. Moreover, the authorities might well have suspected him of rape and fraud as well, although these charges were evidently not pursued. He was lucky to have escaped with his life.

During Calvin's tenure, the Genevan authorities continued to punish firmly parties found guilty of contracting new engagements while they were already married. A good example is the 1559 case of Charles Fournat which involved self-divorce.[99]

---

[97] Reported by Naphy, *Sex Crimes*, 48.
[98] RC I, 6–7.
[99] Reported in Naphy, *Sex Crimes*, 50–51.

Charles was a fervent new convert to the Reformed cause, who had recently moved to Geneva from the Catholic city of Rouen. Shortly after his arrival, he became engaged to Thomasse de Reancourt. The parties thereafter were summoned before the Consistory on charges of premarital fornication. During the investigation, the Consistory learned from several witnesses that Charles was already married and that his wife was alive and well in Rouen. When confronted with this evidence of his polygamy, Charles defended himself by saying that his wife had committed adultery four years before and had thereby not only "ruptured the oath of marriage" but also "given him a serious illness," probably syphilis. His first marriage was over, Charles insisted, leaving him free to marry another.

Charles's marriage may have been over in fact, but not in law, the Consistory determined. Charles had not sought an annulment or divorce of his first wife, and he was thus still married. It made no difference that the Catholic authorities in Rouen would not hear a case of divorce. Charles should have brought an ex parte divorce action against his first adulterous wife after he moved to Geneva and before he became engaged to Thomasse. A private person had no power to dissolve a marriage; only a properly authorized tribunal could make this judgment. Charles was found guilty both of deserting his wife in Rouen and committing polygamy with Thomasse in Geneva. Notwithstanding his new fervency for the Reformed cause, which the authorities acknowledged, the Council sentenced him to the public humiliation of carrying a torch through the streets, and then banished him from the city and ordered him not to return on pain of whipping.

Engagement-Marriage

For the Genevan authorities, an engagement was a serious contract much like a marriage contract. To have sex with a third party in breach of one's engagement contract was considered to be an act of adultery.[100] To marry a third party after engagement to another was an act of polygamy.

The seriousness with which the authorities took such cases of back-to-back engagement and marriage can be seen in a tangled and tawdry case that went on for more than a year in 1555 and 1556.[101] The case began before the Council. Denis Potier testified that he had earlier proposed the marriage of his daughter Marthe to Ameyd Varo who was courting her. Ameyd had refused the marriage. Shortly thereafter Denis had approved Marthe's marriage to Andre Dumonet. After her wedding night, Marthe was found to be already pregnant; she gave birth to a healthy son within six months of the wedding. Her former lover Ameyd, not her husband Andre, turned out to be the father. Ameyd had revealed as much in several secret

---

[100] See examples in SMF 1, ch. 12.
[101] RC X, 59v, 61–62, 80, 81, 85v, 88v; RC XI, 3–3v, 29, 50v, 91.

love letters he had sent to Marthe, which her husband Andre had discovered. When confronted with these letters, Ameyd pled guilty to charges of fornication, and the Council imprisoned and fined him.

These same love letters suggested to the Council that Ameyd and Marthe might well have been engaged to be married as well. Ameyd denied any such engagement, and testified that he had already been engaged to another woman in Antwerp, and was in fact trying to annul that engagement. This testimony only compounded Ameyd's problem, for now the Council suspected both parties of polygamy – Marthe for marrying Andre after her engagement to Ameyd, Ameyd for engaging Marthe after his engagement to the woman in Antwerp. The Council sent the whole case to the Consistory for close investigation.

Before the Consistory, Marthe testified that Ameyd had indeed promised to marry her. That was why she had yielded to his sexual advances and had kept his secret love letters, despite the risk of being found out. She further testified that when Ameyd spurned her she "wanted to die." When she found out she was pregnant, she sought medical advice on how to abort the child. When her efforts at abortion failed, she quickly married André apparently under some pressure from her father.

Ameyd again insisted that he had made no such engagement promise to Marthe, for he was already engaged to a woman in Antwerp. He was trying to have that engagement annulled for lack of parental consent, but had to date not been successful. He loved Marthe more than the Antwerp woman but could not and would not promise to marry her until he had broken off this prior engagement. He further testified that he had tried to explain all this to Marthe's father Denis, but Denis would not see him.

Denis at first denied Ameyd's whole story as a self-serving cover-up and angrily denounced Ameyd before the Consistory. The Consistory had little reason to trust Denis's credibility, however. They had just heard Marthe's testimony that Denis had pressured her into marrying Andre quickly, and likely suspected that he was trying to cover up her fornication and find support for her illegitimate son. Moreover, the Consistory discovered that Denis had also just carried his new baby grandson to baptism, and had him registered as the son of Andre, Marthe's husband, in a further attempt to cover up the illegitimacy. Andre, it turned out, had not consented to any of this, and indeed now wanted out of his marriage to Marthe altogether.

The case bounced back and forth between the Consistory and the Council for the next half year. The Council investigated Ameyd and Marthe under oath several times and imprisoned Ameyd for a time evidently because of his recalcitrance and perjury. It became quite clear to the authorities that Marthe had married Andre while believing that she was already engaged to Ameyd. The Consistory sent Calvin himself to the Council to impress on them the gravity of her offense. The Council ultimately fined her heavily, dissolved her marriage with Andre, and barred her from marriage to anyone else, consigning her to effective "widowhood." The Consistory banned her from the Eucharist, admitting her only a half year later when she did another full confession. Calvin later sought the Council's permission to allow her to remarry after a further time of repentance.

It also became quite clear to the authorities that Ameyd did not believe himself engaged to Marthe, because of his engagement to the Antwerp woman. This was apparently ample mitigation in their mind. The Council fined him, too, but barred him from marriage for only a year to "consider his conscience." They also determined that his engagement to the woman in Antwerp was no longer binding. The Consistory banned him from Communion as well, and readmitted him several months later when he did full confession for his sins.

Most cases of engagement to one party followed by marriage to another were not nearly so complicated.[102] What this case illustrates is how seriously Calvin and the Genevan authorities took this offense. Especially notable was their emphasis on the *intent* to commit polygamy, rather than the proof of polygamy. It was because Marthe *believed* she was already engaged to Ameyd when she married Andre that she was punished so severely for her polygamy. But the legality of both her contracts was suspect. Her engagement contract to Ameyd was never proved to exist, even if she intended or believed its existence. Her marriage contract to Andre was vulnerable to attack on two fronts: Marthe was not fully compos mentis when she entered that marriage contract, and her father had evidently coerced her into this marriage as part of the cover up. Such a marriage might well have been annulled if attacked directly on grounds of lack of consent by Marthe.

Moreover, Marthe's punishment of forced permanent widowhood was a rather harsh sentence. She was now forced to be a single mother of an illegitimate child. The child's father, Ameyd, was ready and willing to marry her and support the child, and after a year of forced bachelorhood would be able to do so. Perhaps it was this reality that prompted Calvin to go back to the Council to have Marthe's sentence of forced widowhood reduced.

Marriage-Marriage

One marriage contract followed by another was the purest case of polygamy, and the Consistory sent these cases swiftly to the Council with recommendations of stern punishment. Claude du Noyer found this out in 1558.[103] The Consistory summoned him to answer charges that he was married to two wives. He admitted the offense, saying he had earlier married a woman and had produced children who were now

[102] See other examples in Seeger, *Nullité de mariage divorce et séparation*, 348–352.
[103] RC XII, 149.

fully grown. Ten years ago, apparently without dissolving the first marriage, he had married a second woman and had moved with her to Geneva. Although Claude had remained faithful to his second wife, he was routinely drunk and had not registered himself as a *habitant*. The Consistory had little sympathy for him. They banned him from Communion, and urged the Council to "purge" him from the city. The Council imprisoned Claude, and then banished him on pain of whipping if he returned. They must have also annulled his second marriage, although there is no such order in the record.

Not only the doubly married spouse, but also the second spouse could be punished for being an accomplice to polygamy. This happened to Robert Cuysin in a 1552 case.[104] Six years before, Robert had married a woman (whose name is not revealed in the records). At the time, the woman had claimed she was a widow. Friends of her former husband had told Robert that the man had died. He had thus married the woman. After the marriage, however, Robert found out that his wife's former husband was still alive, but had remarried and was living in the town of Lyon.

The Consistory was suspicious of Robert's story. They summoned Mrs. Cuysin to testify. She admitted that she had married another man ten years before but had left him. After she had remarried Robert, however, her first husband had sought to have her marriage to Robert annulled by a court in Lyon. She had refused the Lyon court's subpoena: apparently, her first husband had then received a proper ex parte dissolution of his first marriage to her, and later had married another woman. When pressed, Mrs. Cuysin admitted that she would be happy to return to her first husband if he wanted her back – hardly a vote of confidence about her marriage to Robert Cuysin.

This was all too much for the Consistory. They sent Mr. and Mrs. Cuysin to the Council, recommending that they be separated while the case was pending. On investigation, the Council annulled the Cuysin's six-year marriage because the woman had "remarried before her first husband had done so." Both Cuysins were then banished from Geneva – the woman for her polygamy, her second husband for being an accessory to the same offense. In the Council's judgment, Robert Cuysin should have inquired about the legality of his marriage once his wife's first husband was found to be alive. The Council must have determined that his failure to inquire was willful blindness to the offense, if not a deliberate cover up.

Polygamists in Geneva could face the death penalty if they compounded their offense with other crimes. This can be seen in the 1564 case of Marie Binot.[105] Marie had first been married to a Pierre Sachet in Thonon, a nearby town on Lake Geneva. She says she was divorced in 1563 on account of her adultery, and

[104] RC VII, 16, 18.
[105] Reported in Kingdon, *Adultery and Divorce*, 129–135; the case records are in SMF 2, ch. 8.

ordered to remain single for at least a year – a typical precaution in case of pregnancy and the need to establish paternity. Well before that year had expired, however, she had moved to Lausanne, and become engaged to a second man, Antoine Rebout. She says that she discovered that Rebout was already engaged to another woman, so she walked out on him and moved to Geneva. Almost immediately, at the urging of a hostess at a local inn, Marie became engaged to a third man, Claude Michod, and promptly bedded him in the same inn – all still within the year of her first alleged divorce.

When the Genevan authorities got word of her philandering, they mounted a full-scale inquiry, suspecting her of polygamy or prostitution. The Consistory first checked closely with their Thonon counterparts to see if Marie's first marriage had in fact ended, and her rights to remarriage conditioned. It appears that no divorce had been finalized, and she had been ordered to wait until it was. The Consistory checked with their Lausanne colleagues whether Marie's second engagement contract was validly entered and ended. It became clear that Lausanne law regarded her as still engaged, pending a formal declaration of annulment. They grilled the hostess whether she knew of Marie's prior relationships, making her a knowing accomplice to the bigamous engagement to Claude. They grilled Claude on suspicion either that he was making a frivolous engagement promise in order to seduce Marie, or in fact knew about her engagement but wanted to beat his rivals to the marriage altar. An engagement promise followed by premarital sex was serious business in Geneva. It was more serious if Claude knew Marie was already engaged or married to someone else: that would make him an adulterer and bigamist, too. And they grilled Marie repeatedly in hopes of extracting a confession.

Marie professed innocence, despite the introduction into evidence of an incriminating letter that suggested that she was having sex with yet another man. The Consistory sent the entire case and all the parties to the city Council for closer investigation. The third man, Claude, and the hostess who had encouraged him to propose to Marie, were both charged with accomplice liability to bigamy and fornication and forced to endure shame punishments and short prison sentences. Marie was tortured repeatedly, and ultimately confessed not only to multiple marriage promises but also to several affairs with other men, both single and married. She was duly convicted for bigamy, prostitution, fornication, adultery, and contempt of court, and was executed by drowning.

SUMMARY AND CONCLUSIONS

The foregoing cases illustrate the seriousness with which this one set of influential Protestants on the Continent took up the crime of polygamy and reshaped the civil law in response. There are dozens more such polygamy cases in the sixteenth-century

Geneva archives,[106] and many hundreds more such cases in the consistory and city court records of other early modern Calvinist communities in France, Germany, the Netherlands, Scotland, and England.[107] Calvin and Beza helped to lay the theological foundations for this fresh new criminal punishment of polygamy in Calvinist and other Protestant lands. For them, polygamy violated the order of creation, the ideals of covenantal union, and the commandments of the Law and the Gospel on which the covenant of marriage was based. At creation, God could have created two or more wives for Adam. But he chose to create one. God could have created three or four types of humans to be the image of God. But God created two types: "male and female he created them." In the Law, God could have commanded his people to worship two or more gods, but he commanded them to worship one God. In the Gospel, Christ could have founded two or more churches to represent him on earth, but he founded one holy catholic and apostolic church as his chosen bride. Marriage, as an order of creation and as a symbol of God's covenant relationship with his elect, Calvin and Beza argued, involves two parties and two parties only. To say or do otherwise was "blasphemy" and "heresy."

Following tradition, Calvin, Beza, and their followers argued that polygamy was too often the cause or consequence of other harms – to men, women, children, and society alike. William of Auvergne and other medieval writers had already pressed this argument from harm. Calvinists repeated it and used it to condemn not only modern-day polygamists but also biblical polygamists, who in their view sinned gravely by taking more than one wife at a time. Just look at the chaos of the polygamous households of Abraham, Jacob, and David. Just look at the diffusion of their energies and resources and the perennial strife of their wives and children. If even the great patriarchs of salvation history could not make polygamy work, who are we to try? The point of the many biblical stories of polygamy, Calvin and Beza insisted, was not to illustrate an alternative form of marriage but to show how dangerous it was to violate God's natural law of monogamy.

Also following tradition, Calvinists argued that polygamy may have been customary in more primitive cultures that needed many children for labor, prestige, power, and social standing, if not divine confirmation. Even the greatest men of faith in the Bible privileged this custom of polygamy over the natural law of monogamy. But in more advanced civilizations resort to polygamy is no longer licit or necessary. This was another iteration of the "narrative of progress" argument that the early Church Fathers had introduced as a biblical hermeneutic to explain Old Testament

---

[106] See Seeger, *Nullité de mariage divorce et separation*, 115, 341–352.

[107] On diaspora Calvinist communities, see, e.g., Philip Benedict, *Christ's Churches Purely Reformed: A Social History of Calvinism* (New Haven, CT: Yale University Press, 2002), and Richard C. Gamble, ed., *Articles on Calvin and Calvinism*, 14 vols. (New York/London: Garland Publishing, 1992), vols. 13–14.

polygamy, and that medieval and early modern Catholic writers had used in their rebuke of Jewish, Muslim, and indigenous polygamy.[108]

More original to the Western case against polygamy was Beza's argument that polygamy violated the laws of God and nature, particularly as distilled in the Ten Commandments. Polygamy, he said, was at once an act of perpetual adultery, brazen theft, blatant promise-breaking, and covetous endangerment of the neighbor. Polygamy thereby broke the Commandments against adultery, theft, promise-breaking, and coveting, and the analogs of these Commandments in other natural law systems recognized by pre-Christian Greeks and Romans. At the same time, Beza continued, polygamy violated the natural rights that were corollaries to these natural law duties. It breached the first wife's natural rights to marital fidelity and trust, to marital property and security, and to contractual expectations and reliance on her husband's fidelity to the marriage contract. It breached the children's natural rights to inheritance and support, and to the undiluted care, nurture, and education of their father. And it breached the neighbor's natural rights to the security and privacy of his household and the safety of his wife, daughters, and maidservants from the covetous exploits of neighboring men.

This appeal to both natural law and natural rights to condemn polygamy was a new argument in the Western case against polygamy for the early Protestant world. It had parallels in the natural law and natural rights arguments of sixteenth-century neo-scholastics in Salamanca who echoed and elaborated the rights arguments of Thomas Aquinas and the medieval canonists.[109] Beza retooled the traditional argument that polygamy was naturally harmful to wives, children, and society into a new argument that polygamy violated the natural rights of wives, children, and neighbors as well. This was a shift in emphasis from the objective wrongs of polygamy to the subjective rights that it violated. Both Calvin and Beza had come to embrace the general idea of subjective natural rights that could be claimed against public authorities and private parties alike. The strongest foundation for natural rights, they had argued, was the natural law. And the best formulation of the natural law was the Decalogue. For them the Decalogue's natural duties not to kill, steal, commit adultery, speak falsely, or covet gave rise to the corollary natural rights to life, property, fidelity, contract, and privacy.[110]

---

[108] For the Church Fathers' and medieval scholastics' narrative of progress arguments, see Chapters 2 and 4 in this book, pp. 85–92, 159–161.

[109] For earlier natural rights discussions in the medieval and early modern Catholic tradition, see discussion in Chapter 4, pp. 175–176; and elaboration in Brian Tierney, *The Idea of Natural Rights: Studies on Natural Rights, Natural Law and Church Law, 1150–1625* (Grand Rapids, MI: Wm. B. Eerdmans, 1997); Charles J. Reid, Jr., *Power over the Body, Equality in the Family: Rights and Domestic Relations in Medieval Canon Law* (Grand Rapids, MI: Wm. B. Eerdmans, 2004).

[110] See sources in Witte, *The Reformation of Rights*, 57–58, 114–118, 139–140.

With four of the Ten Commandments of the Decalogue breached by polygamy (no adultery, theft, false testimony, or coveting), it became easy for Calvinists to condemn polygamy as doubly unnatural – a violation of natural law and natural rights alike. Calvin helped lay all the premises for this argument, but he did not press it to this logical conclusion. Beza and later Calvinists made this move. They argued that polygamy was not only objectively wrong but also subjectively harmful. It was not only a violation of the natural law of God but also a violation of the natural rights of God's children. Many other later Protestants – Lutherans and Anglicans especially – pressed these same arguments, as did several Enlightenment philosophers and Scottish, English, and American common lawyers who built on their views. We shall watch these rights-based arguments against polygamy unfold in succeeding chapters.[111]

If a man could not contain himself, Calvin and Beza insisted contrary to earlier Protestants, it was better for him to divorce his wife rather than to marry a second wife while his first marriage remained intact. Divorce was allowed by Moses, and even recognized by Jesus and Paul; polygamy was not. Children of divorce remained legitimate heirs; children of polygamy were bastards to be cast out like Abraham had cast out Ishmael and cut him off from any inheritance. Marriage to one spouse was best. Divorce from the first spouse and marriage to a second was tolerable. Polygamy was anathema.

[111] See discussions in Chapter 9, pp. 363–372, and Chapter 10, pp. 425–429.

7

The English Case Against Polygamy

Theology, Politics, and the Early Modern Common Law

MATRIMONY.

FIGURE 15. "Matrimony," from *The Book of Common Prayer and Administration of the Sacraments*, Church of England.
Courtesy of the Pitts Theology Library, Candler School of Theology, Emory University.

FIGURE 16. "The Babylonian Marriage Market," from Edwin Longsden Long, Royal
Holloway and Bedford New College, Surrey, United Kingdom.
Used by permission of Royal Holloway and Bedford New College, Surrey,
UK / Bridgeman Images.

The new criminalization of polygamy that took place on the Continent after
the Reformation took longer to develop in England. It was only in 1604 that
Parliament for the first time declared polygamy to be a capital crime prosecuted
in the secular courts. Before then, polygamy questions remained within the
jurisdiction of the English church courts, which operated with medieval canon
law rules and procedures. This did not mean that England was soft on polygamy.
Notorious polygamists could still be punished, but under a different regime. The
English church courts annulled second marriages and engagements when there
was still a valid first marriage, and ordered spiritual sanctions on intentional
polygamists and their accomplices – public penance, various shame punishments,
and excommunication in serious cases. They looked to the secular courts to make
appropriate dower and other marital property settlements for innocent duped
fiancées, spouses, and children. In serious cases of brazen polygamy, secular
courts could also impose corporal punishments – flogging, prison, mutilation,
banishment, even execution. But the crime for which these parties were punished
was usually not polygamy, but perjury or adultery. Unlike their Continental
counterparts, medieval England did not have separate secular statutes prohibiting
polygamy.

   This began to change in the sixteenth century. Alarmed by the polygamous
experiments and speculations unleashed by the Reformation, notably during

Henry VIII's battles with the papacy, Anglican theologians adopted and adapted a new Protestant theology of monogamous marriage that left no room for polygamy, even for kings or nobles. These theologians repeated some of the sacramental and covenantal logic of monogamy set out in Catholic and Calvinist sources. But they also emphasized the critical public goods of a stable domestic commonwealth and its salutary influence on the broader commonwealths of church and state. This "commonwealth model of marriage" had no place for polygamy or other domestic unions that would jeopardize the health of the household and its members, and by extension the stability of the broader commonwealth and its citizens. Polygamy was trouble, English writers insisted, and too often the cause or consequence of sundry other harms and crimes. It needed to be firmly prohibited by both church and state authorities alike. The spiritual penalties traditionally imposed by the church courts alone were considered too light a regimen; such moral maladies and dangerous practices required the stronger medicine of the criminal law, too. By the end of the reign of Queen Elizabeth (the daughter of Henry VIII's polygamous union with Anne of Boleyn), English theology and culture had settled firmly in favor of criminalizing polygamy for the sake of protecting both monogamy and the orderly English commonwealth built on its foundation.

Elizabeth's successor, King James I and his Parliament passed the 1604 Polygamy Act that made intentional bigamy or polygamy a capital crime. Other laws passed in the early years of James's reign sought to rein in easy annulments, easy desertion, and self-divorce, especially among the lower classes. Still other laws sought to nullify private or secretly contracted marriages and second marriages that lacked parental consent, two witnesses, civil registration, and the church's blessing. Together, these new laws raised the threshold for valid marriage formation but closed the door firmly on divorce, save by a rare private bill passed by Parliament. Once validly married, spouses were bound for life. Those who took a second fiancée or wife, in defiance of these new laws, now did so at their peril.

This chapter tells this story of the gradual English theological and legal settlement against polygamy. It then reviews a few of the hundreds of polygamy cases that emerged in the more than two centuries that the 1604 Polygamy Act was the law of the land.[1] The next chapter samples a few of the radical English experiments with polygamy, especially during the brief Interregnum period of 1642–1660, and then the growing body of liberal, sometimes radical, English literature that pressed the case for polygamy.

---

[1] Throughout this chapter, I have modernized the spelling and punctuation of the historical sources quoted, but retained the original spelling and punctuation in the books and articles cited.

THE THEOLOGICAL AND CULTURAL CASE AGAINST POLYGAMY

Theological Teachings

Although a few English divines flirted perilously with polygamy in the heady days of King Henry VIII's great marital dispute with Catherine, they settled quickly against polygamy. A good example is Thomas Cranmer (1489–1556), the Archbishop of Canterbury. After his appointment in 1533, Cranmer had helped to end Henry VIII's marriage with Catherine of Aragon and legitimate his remarriage to Anne of Boleyn.[2] For the next twenty years as clerical head of the Anglican Church, he pushed for many Protestant reforms of sex, marriage, and family life in England. But Cranmer was resolutely opposed to polygamy, and he condemned both Lutherans and Anabaptists in his day for their openness to polygamy. He wrote firmly to Lutheran reformer, Andreas Osiander, who had endorsed Philip of Hesse's polygamy: there is no "excuse when you allow a man after a divorce while the man and woman are both living to contract a fresh marriage, and, what is still worse, even without a divorce allow one man to have several wives."

> These two things are expressly and undeniably contrary both to the nature of marriage, which does not make two but one flesh, as well as also to the scriptures, as will be seen from Matthew 19, Mark 10, Luke 16, Romans 7, 1 Corinthians 7: from which passages it is clear that, according to the institution of the apostles, and therefore of Christ himself, one person ought to be joined in matrimony with one person, and that persons so joined together cannot again contract marriage until the death of one of the parties shall have happened.... [Polygamists are] the supporters of the law of Mahomet rather than Christianity. If they do the latter, let them beware how they allow what Christ, the apostles, evangelists, and moreover, the consent of the whole church, from its commencement up to this day, hath strictly forbidden.[3]

It is also no excuse for modern-day Christians, like Anabaptists, to justify their polygamy by adverting to the examples of Old Testament patriarchs, Cranmer continued. The polygamy of these ancient men – like their incest, adultery, fornication, concubinage, and prostitution – may have been "customary" sexual practices in their day. But their polygamy and other sexual acts were nonetheless "sinful" and contrary to the "law and morality" set down at creation, and revealed anew in Christ. "May Christ the great God deign to avert from his holy church such foul, incestuous, and portentous marriages, both now and in unto the day of the Lord!"[4]

[2] On this case see Chapter 5, pp. 201–208 in this book.
[3] Letter of Andreas Osiander (December 27, 1540), in Thomas Cranmer, *Miscellaneous Writings and Letters of Thomas Cranmer*, ed. John E. Cox (London: The Parker Society, 1843), 404–408.
[4] Ibid.

Cranmer did his part to try to stamp out the "foul" and "portentous" polygamy that had crept into shadows of the new Protestant churches and commonwealth of England. In 1540, he directed church vicars and other clerical supervisors to "detect and present to their ordinary all adulterers and fornicators, and such men as have two wives living, and such women who have two husbands living, within their parishes."[5] In 1548, he joined the Lord Chancellor of England in calling on the church courts of England to "proceed against such as had or should hereafter have two wives ... and to punish such offenders according to the ecclesiastical laws, that others might be afraid to fall into such insolent and unlawful acts."[6] In the proposed "Reformation of Ecclesiastical Law" of 1552, Cranmer and the committee called on the state, too, to take strong measures against polygamy:

> [W]e want polygamy to be done away with by our laws, and we think it right that in a marriage there should be only one sole spouse, for in this way was marriage established by God in the first place. And so if anyone has taken more than one wife, he must send away all the latest ones, and keep only the one whom he first took in hand, (if she wishes to acknowledge him as her husband); but to the others who will be turned out, he shall grant a dowry to each one, and he will make amends to the church in addition, subject to whatever punishment the judge will reckon suitable for such an enormity. Then too, the worthlessness of women will be penalized by punishment if knowingly they delivered themselves to the same man and if any faults of theirs can be apprehended in this misdeed.[7]

This all became standard lore among later Anglican theologians who condemned polygamy as unbiblical, unnatural, unjust, unwise, and unsafe. Bishop John Hooper (1500–1555), for example, declared polygamy to be a "form of adultery," which violated at once the natural law of creation, the Mosaic law against adultery, the Gospel's call that only "two join in one marital flesh," and the long tradition of civil, canon, and common laws prohibiting polygamy. "For as the beginning of matrimony was but one man and one woman created and married together; no more should there be now in one matrimony."[8] Cranmer's confessor, Thomas Becon (1511–1567), declared

5   Ibid., 157.
6   See also the royal proclamation of April 24, 1540, calling on the ecclesiastical courts to "proceed against such as had or should hereafter have two wives ... and to punish such offenders according to the ecclesiastical laws, that other might be afraid to fall into such insolent and unlawful acts." John Strype, *Memorials of Archbishop Cranmer*, 3 vols. (Oxford: T. Combe, 1848), 2:1.141–143; see also Letter of Richard Hilles to Heinrich Bullinger (June 18, 1548), in *Original Letters Relative to the English Reformation* (Cambridge: The University Press, 1846), 261–264, at 263.
7   James C. Spalding, ed., *The Reformation of the Ecclesiastical Laws of England, 1552* (Kirksville, MO: Sixteenth Century Journal Publishers, 1992), 95.
8   John Hooper, *The Ten Commandments* (Cambridge: Cambridge University Press, 1843), 386–387.

polygamy to be a grave insult to the enduring and exclusive union of Christ and the church that is the model of every Christian marriage. Each man, said Becon, is to love, cherish, and sacrifice for his wife, for she is now "bone of his bone, flesh of his flesh." Following Christ's example, a man must "so dearly love his wife, that he not only not touch any other woman, but also that he refrain both his eyes and the thoughts of his heart from coveting any strange flesh." For, as Christ taught, even to look longingly at another woman was not only to covet her but also to commit adultery with her.[9]

Fifty years later, Cambridge theologian, William Perkins (1558–1602), who straddled the Anglican and Puritan Calvinist worlds of England, denounced polygamy as a betrayal of the exclusive "covenant of marriage" between a man and a woman. By that covenant, "the man is to love, cherish, and comfort his wife, whereas if he should take unto him another besides her, he should greatly vex his first wife." A polygamist "plays a very dishonest part with her, to whom he was before lawfully married." Following Calvinist convention, Perkins had less trouble than Cranmer and some other early Anglican divines in countenancing remarriage after fault-based divorce; but remarriage before divorce or annulment was, for him, anathema.[10] Also following Calvinist convention, influential theologian William Ames (1576–1633) added Malachi 2 to the biblical texts that Cranmer had used, making this addition to underscore the unique "covenant" form and fidelity of marriage set out in the Bible.

> Marriage is the individual joining of one woman and woman by lawful consent for a mutual communication of their bodies and community of life together. It is of one man and one woman. Gen. 2:22; Mal. 2:15; Matt. 19:4, 5; 1 Cor. 7:2; Lev. 18:19. The perfection of friendship and the mutual duties of marriage cannot be reached except between one and one. Therefore, polygamy, even that which prevailed with the ancient fathers, was always a violation of the laws of marriage.[11]

Anglican and Anglo-Calvinist writers roundly condemned Old Testament patriarchs and present-day polygamists alike for violating the laws of God and nature that favored faithful monogamy and thereby bringing inevitable trouble to their families and communities.[12] Citing the same biblical texts as William Ames, Robert

9   Thomas Becon, *The Catechism of Thomas Becon, S.T.P.*, ed. John Ayre (London: The Parker Society, 1844), 334–337.
10   William Perkins, *The Works of that Famous and Worthy Minister of Christ in the University of Cambridge, M.W. Perkins: The Third and the Last Volume* (London: John Legatt, 1613), 677.
11   William Ames, *The Marrow of Theology*, trans. John D. Eusden (Durham, NC: The Labyrinth Press, 1968), 318 (internal numbered paragraph breaks omitted). See comparable views in Henry Hammond, *A Letter of Resolution to Six Quares of Present Use in the Church of England* (London: J. Flesher, 1653), 83–91.
12   A few earlier theologians were more benign in their treatment of the patriarchs. Hugh Latimer, in a 1549 sermon preached before King Edward VI, declared: "although the Kings among the Jews had liberty to take more wives than one, we may not therefore attempt to walk inordinately.... Christ limiteth unto us one wife only, and it is a great thing for a man to rule one wife rightly and ordinately." Hugh Latimer, *Sermons*, ed. George E. Corrie (Cambridge: Parker Society, 1844), 94.

Sharrock (1630–1684) depicted polygamy as "a sin against nature," "a virulent species of adultery" that brings "constant trouble and unrest to the household," "chronic hatred, discord, and fighting among rival wives and children," and inevitable suffering in the community.[13] Edward Leigh (1602–1671) argued that polygamy "is a swerving from God's first institution" and that the Old Testament "patriarchs lived and died in the sin of polygamy."[14] James Gordon (1541–1620) stated boldly that polygamy always runs "contrary to the law of nature," and that even the great men of faith in the Old Testament had acted against nature.[15] William Slatyer (1587–1647) regarded the Old Testament patriarchs' polygamy, along with their adultery, bestiality, incest, and sodomy, as "unclean" acts driven by the "hardness of their hearts" and the inferiority of their morals.[16] William Charke (d. ca. 1617) believed that Abraham's polygamy "had brought upon him and his kingdom a great sin," that Jacob's incestuous polygamy, although the product of Laban's trickery, was still without excuse, and that King David should have repented for his polygamy as much as for his adultery and murder.[17] William Gouge (1575–1653) and his son Thomas (1609–1681) likewise thought that the many troubles of David's household were proof positive that his polygamy "was ever a sin." Particularly the rivalry, rape, and murder of "the children of those various wives proved crosses unto him."[18] Andrew Willet (1562–1621) thought that biblical and modern polygamists alike were "not guided by reason" or conscience but "void of all judgment in their actions, being carried away with their preposterous and precipitate affections." Every polygamist, said Willet, is a "vile person" "void of all judgment both in divine and human things" and bent on lustfully sowing the seeds of "their own destruction."[19]

[13] Robert Sharrock, *Judicia seu legume censurae de variis incontentiae, speciesbus adulterio, polygamia & concubinatu, fornication, stupor, raptu, peccatis contra naturam, incest & gradibus prohibitis* (Oxford: H. Hall, 1662), 25–29.

[14] Edward Leigh, *A Systeme or Body of Divinity, Consisting of Ten Books* (London: A.M. for William Lee, 1654), 369; see also Lisa Shirley Loughead, "The Perception of Polygamy in Early Modern England" (Ph.D. Diss., Dalhousie, 2008), 102. This work has since been published as Lisa Shirley Loughead, *The Perception of Polygamy in Early Modern England* (Halifax, NS: Dalhousie University Press, 2008), but I have had access only to the dissertation.

[15] James Gordon, *A Treatise on the Unwritten Word of God, Commonly Called Traditions*, trans. William Wright (London?: English College Press, 1614), 28.

[16] William Slatyer, *The Compleat Christian, and the Compleat Armour and Armoury of a Christian* (London: n.p., 1643), 394ff. See Loughead, "The Perception of Polygamy in Early Modern England," 113.

[17] William Charke, *A Treatise Against the Defense of the Censure* (Cambridge: Thomas Thomas, 1586), 279–280.

[18] William Gouge and Thomas Gouge, *A Learned and Very Useful Commentary on the Whole Epistles to the Hebrews* (London: Joshua Kirten, 1655), 184–185.

[19] Andrew Willet, *Hexapla* (London: 1611), 83–85, 155. See also Loughead, "The Perception of Polygamy in Early Modern England," 66–67.

Travel Diaries

These attacks on polygamists as irrational, lustful, barbaric, and morally inferior became rhetorically sharper at the turn of the seventeenth century, when missionaries, merchants, travelers, and colonists confronted polygamy in the brave new worlds of Africa, Asia, the Americas, and the Ottoman Empire.[20] The polygamous practices of the ancient Jewish patriarchs became less of a focus, especially after the great English jurist John Selden (1584–1654) documented carefully how medieval Judaism had rejected the Mosaic toleration of polygamy because of its inherent injustice to women and children and the hard strife that it occasioned in polygamous households, beginning already with Abraham.[21] More interesting – and more intimidating for some – were the polygamous practices of Muslims and various Indigenous Peoples whom the English occasionally encountered in the new world. In the early seventeenth century, polygamy became – in Lisa Loughead's apt phrase – a "boundary marker" between the cultivated, disciplined Christian people of England who maintained faithful monogamy, and the barbaric, unruly, pagan peoples of the uncivilized world who practiced faithless polygamy.[22]

The African travel diary of John Leo (Africanus) (ca. 1490 – ca. 1550), published for the first time in English in 1600, helped set this "boundary maker" in the English mind. Although some northern Africans were sophisticated, subtle, and civil, Leo wrote, several tribal indigenous peoples whom he encountered were "barbarians." Leo called them a "vile and base people," woefully "ignorant of natural, domestic, and commonwealth matters," and "principally addicted unto treason, treachery, murder, theft, and robbery." "They have neither judges nor lawyers, by whose wisdom and counsel they ought to be directed. They are utterly unskillful in trades and merchandize [and] live a miserable, toilsome, wretched, and beggarly life: they are a rude people," "born and bred to theft, deceit, and brutish manners." "Hardly shall you find so much as a spark of piety in any of them." "They lead a savage and beastly life."[23]

---

[20] On the rise of traveler writings, see Peter Hulme and Tim Youngs, eds., *The Cambridge Companion to Travel Writing* (Cambridge: Cambridge University Press, 2002), 17–52; Barbara Korte, *English Travel Writing*, trans. Catherine Matthias (New York: Palgrave, 2000).

[21] John Selden, *Uxor Ebraica: seu, De nuptiis et divortiis ex jure civili, id est divino et Talumudico veterum ebraeorum libri tres* (Frankfurt an der Oder: Sumptibus Jeremiae Schreii, 1673), bk. 1, ch. 8–9.

[22] Loughead, "The Perception of Polygamy in Early Modern England," 108.

[23] John Leo, *The History and Description of Africa*, trans. John Pory (1600), reprinted in *Amazons, Savages, and Machiavels: Travel and Colonial Writing in English, 1550–1630*, ed. Andrew Hatfield (New York: Oxford University Press, 2001), 139–151. The full text is published in modern edition as John Leo, *The History and Description, and of the Notable Things therein Contained*, ed. Robert Brown, 3 vols. (Burlington, VT: Ashgate, 2010).

Leo ascribed this "barbarism" in part to the rampant polygamy of these African communities. In their polygamous households, he observed, "lust reigns" supreme, and no matter how many wives and concubines they already have, polygamous men always "seek out other paramours for their liking," dragging home their sexual favorites to add to their harems. This inevitably sets out bitter jealousy among the wives who treat each other in "a savage and brutal manner," setting the household in perennial uproar. It also teaches boys and girls alike "no compassion at all," let alone morality or sexual virtue. Many of these children, boys and girls alike, become promiscuous, and the whole lustful cycle repeats itself in the next generation.[24]

Fynes Moryson's (1566–1630) *Observations of the Ottoman Empire* (1617) issued comparable invectives against Muslim polygamy. Moryson was impressed with the sophisticated culture, wealth, architecture, and literary achievements of the Ottoman Empire; indeed, he saw Muslim civilization as a formidable threat to Christian Europe. But Moryson described the "Turks" as a hard, corrupt, tyrannical, and lustful people – prone and primed by their faith to the "sin of polygamy." Some Muslim men, said Moryson, keep different wives in different cities "to avoid the strife of women." Other men gathered their multiple wives under one roof, adding others as their lusts demanded and their means allowed. "They buy free women to be their wives," or they buy "conquered women" at a lesser price to be their concubines, Moryson wrote.[25]

A few years later, John Trapp (1601–1669) looked up from his biblical exegesis long enough to say triumphantly that Muslims, in contrast to pious Christians, were a "vile race" given to sexual excess, evidenced not only by their polygamy, but also by their "adultery," sodomy, and "coupling with beasts."[26] Pierre Charron (1541–1603), a French favorite of the Anglican clergy, insisted that all these sexual sins were connected among "the Jews, Mahometans, and other barbarous nations" that are given to such "infinite excesses, debaucheries, and adulteries" for the sake of venting their lust and promoting "the vast increase" of their populations to the peril of Christian Europe. It is polygamy, not monogamy that inflames sexual sin and destroys marital fidelity:

[C]ommon experience demonstrates that in much the greatest part of married persons, what they complain of as confinement and constraint, does by no means cool and destroy, but promote and heighten the affection, and render it more dear and strong, by keeping it more entire and unbroken. Especially in men of honest

24 Ibid.
25 Fynes Moryson's *Observations of the Ottoman Empire* (1617), in Hatfield, ed., *Amazons, Savages, and Machiavels*, 166–178.
26 John Trapp, *A Commentary or Exposition upon the Four Evangelists* (London, 1647), 42; see similar views in George Abbot, *Vindicae Sabbathi* (London, 1641), quoted by Loughead, "The Perception of Polygamy in Early Modern England," 114–116.

principles, and good dispositions, which easily accommodate their humors, and make it their care and study to comply with the tempers of the person to whom they are thus inseparably united. And as for the debaucheries and flyings out alleged against us, the only cause of them is the dissoluteness of men's manners, which a greater liberty, though so great, will never be able to correct or put a stop to. And accordingly we find that adulteries were every whit as rife in the midst of polygamy and divorce; witness the example of David in particular who became guilty of this crime, notwithstanding the multitude he had of wives and concubines of his own. On the contrary, these vices were not known for a long while together in other countries, where neither polygamy nor divorce were ever permitted; as in Sparta, for instance, and at Rome, for a considerable time after the founding of that city.[27]

Samuel Purchas's (ca. 1575–1626) massive collection of travel and pilgrimage reports from around the world, first published in England in 1613, added further fuel to the ugly picture of Muslim polygamy, and its corrosive effects on women and society:

Mahomet allows four wives, besides they take liberty to keep as many women as they are able, only the priests content themselves with one. Notwithstanding this polygamy, the hot jealousies of the lustful Mahometans are such, that they will scarce endure the brothers or fathers of their beloved wives or women, to have speech with them, except in their presence; and time, by this restraint, hath made it odious for such women to have the reputation of honesty, to be seen at any time by strangers. But if they dishonor their husbands' beds, or being unmarried are found incontinent professing chastity rather than they shall want punishment, their own brothers will be their executioners, who for such unnatural acts [of killing their sisters] shall be commended rather than questioned.[28]

Purchas's collection also included descriptions of Asian polygamy, which involved the husband's exploitation of first wives when he pursued a younger second wife. One diary entry made clear that if "the man beginneth to thrive, and hath means to buy another wife, he may not buy her without the consent of the first wife" or without payment to her. But, inevitably thereafter:

[H]is first wife waxing old, and her mind not so much addicted unto lust, if he perceiveth it, then he cleaveth unto his younger wife, to have his pleasure with her, and ever after esteeming most of her, maketh his old wife do the housework, giving her meat and drink as long as she liveth, and putting her not away, but she is forced to serve the young wife, and shall never trouble herself with anything but only to

---

[27] Pierre Charron, *Of Wisdom*, trans. George Stanhope (London: J. Tonson et al., 1729 [1608]), vol. 2, bk. 1, ch. 46, pp. 468–489 ("On Marriage"), at 485–486.

[28] Samuel Purchas, *Pvrchas his Pilgrimes*, 4 vols. (London: William Stransby, 1625), vol. 3, bk. 9, ch. 6, sec. 9 (p. 1478).

eat and drink well, to have a care to please her husband, and to do whatsoever he commandeth.[29]

These early modern traveler reports on the new world can be duplicated at great length. It must be said that polygamy was only a very minor feature in the dozens of seventeenth-century traveler reports that I have read, some of which went on for many hundreds of pages describing endless details of the lives of these foreign peoples. But when these early modern travelers did encounter and report on polygamy, they treated it with moral scorn and outrage. This was of a piece with the reports of medieval chroniclers and crusaders who had used polygamy, among other features, to contrast what they thought was the virtuous civilization of Christianity with the backward civilizations of Islam.[30] These traveler reports served a comparable role in early modern England: to confirm the "boundary marker" between the civilized monogamy of Christian England and the barbaric polygamy of the pagan new world.

THE COMMONWEALTH MODEL OF MONOGAMOUS MARRIAGE

It is telling that these traveler reports depicted the new world polygamists as "ignorant of natural, domestic, and commonwealth matters" and that they blamed polygamy for some of the "excesses, debaucheries," and other social pathos of these "barbarian" peoples. For "domestic" and "commonwealth matters" were closely tied in the early modern English development of what can be called a "commonwealth model" of monogamous marriage.[31] This new commonwealth model taught that a stable monogamous marital household was essential to the stability of the broader commonwealth of England and to the discipline of its citizens. By contrast, a polygamous household, with the inevitable harms it visited on men, women, and children alike, would inevitably erode the stability of the state and the capacity of its citizens.

Already in 1560, Anglican divine Thomas Becon had insisted that "marriage is a little commonwealth" created "for the common good" of the broader commonwealth of church, state, and society.[32] Later Anglican and Anglo-Puritan writers built on this view. In 1590, William Perkins put it thus: "[M]arriage was made and appointed

[29] Ibid., vol. 2, bk. 7, ch. 2, sec. 4 (p. 930).
[30] See discussion in Chapter 4, pp. 159–161.
[31] On this model, see detailed discussions in John Witte, Jr., *From Sacrament to Contract: Marriage, Religion, and Law in the Western Tradition*, 2nd ed. (Louisville, KY: Westminster John Knox Press, 2011), 217–286.
[32] *The Booke of Matrimonie both Profitable and Comfortable for all Them that Entende Quietly and Godly to lyue in the Holy State of Honorable Wedlocke* (c. 1560), in ibid., 1, bk. 12 (STC 1710), folio DCxlix.

by God himself to be the foundation and seminary of all sorts and kinds of life in the commonwealth and the church.... [T]hose families wherein the service of God is performed are, as it were, little churches; yea, even a kind of paradise on earth."[33] Robert Cleaver (ca. 1561 – ca. 1625) opened his famous 1598 tract *A Godly Form of Householde Gouernment* with an oft-repeated maxim: "A household is as it were a little commonwealth, by the good government whereof, Gods glory may be advanced, the commonwealths which standeth of several families, benefited, and all that live in those families may receive much comfort and commodity."[34] William Gouge premised his massive 1622 tome *Of Domestical Duties* on the same belief that "the family is a seminary of the church and the commonwealth," and indeed in its own right, "a little church, and a little commonwealth, whereby a trial may be made of such as are fit for any place of authority, or subjection in Church or commonwealth."[35] Daniel Rogers (1573–1652) agreed: "Marriage is the preservative of chastity, the seminary of the commonwealth, seed-plot of the church, pillar (under God) of the world."[36] Such sentiments "represent the consensus" of those writing on marriage in the late sixteenth and early seventeenth centuries.[37]

The dozens of household manuals and catechisms of the day described in detail the reciprocal duties of loving care that husband and wife, parent and child owed to each other at different stages of the life cycle. Faithful maintenance of this hierarchy of domestic duties, Robert Cleaver believed, was the best guarantee of order, stability, and discipline within the domestic commonwealth.

> For as in a city, there is nothing more unequal, than that every man should be like equal: so it is not convenient, that in one house every man should be like and equal another. There is no equality in that city, where the private man is equal with the magistrate, the people with the senate, or the servants with the master, but rather a confusion of all offices and authority. The husbands and wives are lords of the house.... The husband without any exception is master over all the house, and hath as touching his family more authority than a King in his own kingdom. The wife is ruler of all other things, but yet under her husband.[38]

---

[33] Perkins, *Works*, 3:418–419. See paraphrase in Robert Pricke, *The Doctrine of Superioritie, and of Subjection, Contained in the Fifth Commandment of the Holy Law of Almightie God* (London: Ephraim Dawson & T. Downe, 1609), A8–9.

[34] Robert Cleaver, *A [G]odly Form of Householde Gouernment* (London: Thomas Creede, 1598), 1.

[35] William Gouge, *Of Domesticall Duties: Eight Treatises* (London: John Haviland, 1622), 17, 27, Epistle, sig. 2v.

[36] Daniel Rogers, *Matrimoniall Honour* (London: Philip Nevil, 1642), 17.

[37] Susan Dwyer Amussen, *An Ordered Society: Gender and Class in Early Modern England* (Oxford: Basil Blackwell, 1988), 38.

[38] Cleaver, *Householde Gouernment*, 174–175.

Faithful maintenance of these domestic duties and offices was also the best guarantee of order within the broader commonwealths of church and state, Cleaver insisted. Indeed, properly functioning marriages and households were indispensable to civic flourishing. "[I]f masters of families do not practice at home catechizing, and discipline in their houses and join their helping hands to magistrates and ministers," social order and stability will soon give way to chaos and anarchy.[39] "[I]t is impossible for a man to understand to govern the commonwealth, that doth not know to rule his own house, or order his own person, so that he that knoweth not to govern, deserveth not to reign."[40]

This last emphasis of the public and political goods of a stable domestic commonwealth was common lore among Cleaver's fellow divines. "A conscionable performance of household duties ... may be accounted a public work," William Gouge wrote. For "good members of a family are likely to make good members of church and commonwealth."[41] "[M]ost of the mischiefs that now infest or seize upon mankind throughout the earth, consist in, or are caused by the disorders and ill government of families."[42] "There was never any disorder and outrage, in any family, church, or commonwealth" when domestic offices were respected and domestic duties discharged, Robert Pricke insisted. For domestic duty and discipline allow persons "to rise up to the knowledge of the sovereign Lord, and to give unto him the reverence and honor due to his divine majesty." It also teaches them not only the personal virtues but also the civic habits that "upholdeth, and continueth all these estates, degrees, and orders" of the broader commonwealth.[43] Daniel Rogers wrote more generally that a stable marriage and household served as "the right hand of providence, supporter of laws, states, orders, offices, gifts, and services, the glory of peace, ... the foundation of countries, cities, universities ... crowns, and kingdoms."[44]

This English commonwealth model of marriage deliberately transformed the idea of patriarchy at work among the Old Testament polygamists. In ancient days, it was normal for the patriarch, wielding unlimited power within his own household, to gather as many wives, concubines, and maidservants as his means and energy allowed. Women and children were badges of honor and prestige, and the more a man had the higher his social station. By contrast, a patriarch in this new Christian commonwealth model of marriage had no license for polygamy. His

[39] Ibid., Preface, A4.
[40] Ibid., 4–5.
[41] Gouge, Of Domesticall Duties, 17, 27.
[42] Richard Baxter, A Christian Directory (1673), quoted by Mary Shanley, "Marriage Contract and Social Contract in Seventeenth Century English Political Thought," Western Political Quarterly 32 (1979): 79.
[43] Pricke, The Doctrine of Superioritie, B2.
[44] Daniel Rogers, Matrimoniall Honour (London: Philip Nevil, 1642), 17.

loving rule over his wife and children was rooted in the natural order of creation with its "two in one flesh" ethic, and it was modeled on the mysterious relationship between Christ and his one holy catholic and apostolic church. The Christian patriarch's duty as a husband was to give faithful, loving, and sacrificial care and protection to his wife above all others, even above himself. To defy this mysterious monogamous model of marriage by adding a second wife betrayed essential Christian teachings about the nature and purpose of marriage which lay at the heart of this commonwealth model.

Polygamy betrayed not only essential Christian teachings, but also vital political goods. As both biblical stories and traveler diaries about polygamy underscored, a polygamous household had none of the loving order, discipline, and peace that the household needed to be a stable pillar for an orderly society and a steady source of disciplined and productive citizens. Too often in polygamous households, wives were commodified, exploited, and abused; children were neglected, undereducated, and made rivals; men were too tempted by their lawful lustful pursuits of other wives to attend to their domestic duties or provide their children with healthy models of the good moral life. Inevitably, this spelled rancor and violence among the competing wives and children in the home, and unruly habits, ignorance, and immorality in the next generation. Polygamy, as the Western tradition had long taught, was simply too often the cause, corollary, or consequence of serious harms and crimes to be countenanced in this commonwealth model of marriage.

To the early seventeenth-century English mind, the state was not only well served by a properly functioning monogamous household. The state was, in fact, modeled on that household. King James said as much in 1603, the year before his Parliament passed the Polygamy Act of 1604. Just like the paterfamilias ruled over his wife, children, and servants within the orderly and united domestic commonwealth that bore his family name, so the paterpoliticus, the king, ruled over England, Scotland, and Wales, united in the political commonwealth of Great Britain.

> What God hath conjoined then, let no man separate. I am the head and all the whole isle is my lawful wife; I am the head, and it is my body.... I hope therefore no man will be so unreasonable as to think that I ... a Christian King under the Gospel, should be a polygamist and husband to two wives; that I being the head, should have a divided and monstrous body.[45]

---

[45] James I., "A Speech as it was Delivered in the Upper House of the Parliament to the Lords Spirituall and Temporall, and to the Knights, Citizens, and Burgesses there assembled, on Monday the XIX Day of March 1603," in *King James VI and I: Political Writings*, ed. J.P. Sommerville (Cambridge: Cambridge University Press, 1994), 136. See the excellent contextualization of this text in Anne McLaren, "Monogamy, Polygamy, and the True State: James I's Rhetoric of Empire," *History of Political Thought* 25 (2004): 446–480, esp. 469–475.

Three years later, King James returned to this metaphor: It is "no more possible ... for one king to govern two countries contiguous ... than for one head to govern two bodies, or one man to be husband of two wives."[46] James I would spend a good deal of time thereafter defending this "divine right of kingship," with this metaphor of patriarchal monogamous marriage front and center. James was hardly alone. A long series of royal apologists defended this view, using the same image of an interwoven domestic and political commonwealth predicated on monogamy. One of the most famous of these apologists was Robert Filmer (ca. 1588–1653), John Locke's later antagonist, whom we shall see again in a couple of chapters. In his *Patriarcha* of ca. 1638, Filmer sought to prove that the domestic and political commonwealths are essentially the same, both rooted in the creation story of the monogamous marriage of Adam and Eve, and both subject to the absolute authority of the male head ruling over a unified body.[47]

This commonwealth model of monogamous marriage would be duplicated, with endless variations, in the Anglo-American Protestant world thereafter. In this very traditional, conservative form, it seemed a rather counterintuitive argument for monogamy. The stronger the patriarchy, the stronger the monogamy was the gist of it. One could follow the steps of the argument without necessarily accepting the monogamous conclusion. After all, a monarch could, and indeed sometimes did, rule two different peoples: think of the Spanish Holy Roman Emperor in the day, or the later House of Orange that ruled both the Netherlands and England. A husband could, and sometimes did, rule two wives and their children whether in one home or two: think of the traveling Turkish merchant with separate households in two cities, as just reported by Moryson, let alone the sundry biblical polygamists with their ample harems. What constrained an English patriarchal husband from following this possible polygamous path was his Christian duty to love and care for his one wife alone and their children and his civic duty to maintain an orderly and disciplined household which was easier do with one wife than with several. To the early modern Englishman who took the Bible and the monarchy as absolutes, this traditional formulation of the commonwealth model of monogamy was convincing. For the ongoing Western case against polygamy, this traditional formulation would

[46] James I., "A Speech Delivered the Last Day of March, 1607," in *Political Writings*, 162.
[47] Robert Filmer, *Patriarcha and other Political Works*, ed. Peter Laslett (Oxford: Oxford University Press, 1949). See similar formulations in John Wing, *The Crown Conjugall; or, The Spouse Royall* (London: John Beale for R. Mylbourne, 1632) (STC 25845); Dudley Digges, *The Unlawfulnesse of Subjects Taking up Armes Against their Soveraigne* (s.l., s.n., 1644); William Lawrence, *Marriage by the Morall Law of God Vindicated [and] The Right of Primogeniture in Succession to the Kingdoms of England and Scotland* (London, 1681). See James Daly, *Sir Robert Filmer and English Political Thought* (Toronto: University of Toronto Press, 1979); G.J. Schochet, *Patriarchalism in Political Thought: The Authoritarian Family and Political Speculation and Attitudes Especially in Seventeenth Century England* (New York: Basic Books, 1975).

prove less enduring. It was not until this commonwealth model was revolutionized – first during the Puritan Revolution of the mid-seventeenth century, and then by the liberal Enlightenment thinking beginning with John Locke – that it was transformed into a more enduring argument for monogamy over polygamy. We shall watch these developments in the next chapters.

THE ENGLISH LAW AGAINST POLYGAMY

The Inheritance

Although polygamy was not listed as a separate common law crime in England until the Polygamy Act of 1604, it was long regarded as a serious moral offense in England. Anglo-Saxon kings put polygamy alongside adultery and incest as grave violations of divine law. The laws of King Ethelred (ca. 994) and of King Canute (1027), for example, both provided that a man shall "have no more wives than one, and that shall be his wedded wife, and he who seeks to observe God's law aright and to save his soul from hell-fire shall remain with the one [wife] as long as she lives."[48] Two centuries later, the famous text of *Bracton On the Laws and Customs of England* provided: "One may not have two lawful wives at the same time, since marriage is the joining together of a man and a woman, holding to a single tenor of life; it does not say of men and a woman, nor of a man and women, because one man cannot have several wives nor one woman several husbands *de jure*, though he may have several *de facto*."[49] When a case of suspected de jure polygamous marriage or de facto concubinage or adultery does come up, the text continued, "an inquiry of this kind belongs to the ecclesiastical forum."[50]

[48] See these and other sources cited in Chapter 4, p. 114. Early Britons and Saxons, however, according to ancient lore going back to Julius Caesar, had been rampant polygamists. See, e.g., John Milton's list of bigamous kings in his *History of Great Britain*, in *The Works of John Milton*, 18 vols. ed. Frank Allen Patterson (New York: Columbia University Press, 1931–1938), 10:16, 51, 117, 131–132, 230, 241, 246–247; see also Leo Miller, *John Milton Among the Polygamophiles* (New York: Loewenthal Press, 1974), 117–120, 325–327.

[49] *Bracton on the Law and Customs of England*, trans. and ed. Samuel E. Thorne, 4 vols. (Cambridge, MA: Belknap Press, 1968–1977), 3:363, citing the *summae* on marriage by medieval canonists Raymond of Penyafort and Tancred. For Bracton's incorporation of canon law and civil law authorities into his discussion of the English common law, see Frederic W. Maitland, ed., *Select Passages From the Works of Bracton and Azo* (London: Barnard Quaritch, 1895), esp. xxiv–xxv.

[50] *Bracton on the Laws and Customs of England*, 3:384. See also ibid., 2:271, 3:362, 373. Matthew Bacon, *The Abridgement of the Law*, ed. John Bouvier (Philadelphia, PA: T. & J.W. Johnson, 1852), 2:107–111, reports that among "the very early inhabitants of the island" of England a second marriage incurred a forfeiture of dower.

Since the mid-twelfth century, the medieval church courts in England had almost exclusive jurisdiction over cases of fornication, adultery, and "such like" sexual offenses, including polygamy.[51] Church or state officials brought a few of these polygamy cases on their own. But the vast majority were raised when interested private parties sued, defended, intervened, or were subpoenaed in a marriage or inheritance case.[52] The point of entry or dispute usually concerned the technical impediment of precontract.[53] A typical case of precontract involved an already married person who sought to engage or marry someone else. That person's previous marital contract (the "pre-contract") would render the second contract null and void. If the first contract proved valid, the second contract would be dissolved, regardless of the parties' wishes and even if it had been fully executed, consummated, and had yielded children. Even a longstanding putative marriage of a happy couple with children and grandchildren could be undone by a precontract impediment. Only if the parties could secure a rare papal dispensation could the second marriage contract stand, and the first marriage be dissolved. The stakes were high in these cases: annulment could illegitimate children,[54] deprive wives of their dower rights and heirs of their legacies, and expose parties to spiritual and sometimes civil sanctions.[55]

Precontract cases were fairly common in medieval England. Secretly contracted marriages were valid. Local marriage registration rolls were uneven, sometimes nonexistent. Many parties were ignorant of the technical rules of marital dissolution and remarriage. Deserted spouses sometimes gave up after a few years of searching for their mates and remarried, as did the lonely and vulnerable wives of long missing soldiers, sailors, prisoners, or traveling merchants. Some disgruntled spouses just moved out of their homes and home towns and started their marital lives afresh in a new place. Until the fifteenth century, the English still exercised a considerable degree of "lay control over marriage and divorce," the leading canon law historian, R.H. Helmholz, has shown, and both "secret marriage" and "self-divorce" were viewed as viable forms

---

[51] 13 Edw. 1. Medieval secular authorities occasionally sought to take over polygamy cases, but to no avail. See, e.g., the collection of sources in Nathaniel Bacon and John Selden, *A Historical and Political Discourse of the Lawes of England From the First Times to the End of Queen Elizabeth*, 2 vols. (London: John Starkey, 1689), 1:145–147.

[52] On English medieval church court procedure, see R.H. Helmholz, *Marriage Litigation in Medieval England* (Cambridge: Cambridge University Press, 1974); Charles Donahue, Jr., *Law, Marriage, and Society in the Later Middle Ages* (Cambridge: Cambridge University Press, 2007), 33–41.

[53] See detailed sources and discussions in James A. Brundage, *Law, Sex, and Christian Society in the Middle Ages* (Chicago: University of Chicago Press, 1987), 207, 252–253, 318–319, 343, 405–408, 477–479. For basic canon law texts, see Gratian, *Decretum*, c. 28.2–3, 31.1, 32.1, 6–7, 33.2, 34.1–2, 35.9, 36.2; Gregory IX, *Decretales*, 4.2, 7, 21.

[54] See statutes and early cases in John Brydall, *Lex Spuriorum or the Law Related to Bastardy Collected from the Common, Civil, and Ecclesiastical Laws* (London: Assigns of Richard and Edward Atkins, 1703), 69–71.

[55] See discussion in Chapter 4, pp. 151–158, 182–186.

of marital formation and dissolution, especially in rural communities.[56] This was not so much impiety, anti-clericalism, or antinomianism at work. It was just as much the continuation of longstanding customs of marital self-governance that went back to early Anglo-Saxon days.[57]

It is often when those privately married or self-divorced parties got engaged or remarried to another that their troubles began. A first spouse, long thought dead or gone for good, might surprisingly reappear to object to their spouse's second engagement or marriage to another. A second spouse might learn of his or her spouse's secret past marriage and now want out or want the first marriage dissolved before staying in. A "shotgun wedding" ordered for a newly pregnant couple might reveal that one of them was married already. A publication of engagement banns, or the final call in the marital liturgy to "speak now or forever hold your peace" might reveal an existing marriage. A widow or heir to a first marriage might challenge the claims of the widow or heir to an improper second marriage, or vice versa. A stray word or loud boast at a drunken party or in an unguarded moment about one's other marriage might set off the local rumor mill and prompt the local authorities to investigate.[58] In all such cases the parties would march to the church court for resolution of their dispute.

In an exhaustive study of late medieval church court records, my great legal history professor, Charles Donahue, has turned up a good number of such cases of precontract in the diocesan courts of York and Ely (as well as on the Continent). For example, in 215 marriage cases in York between 1300 and 1499, Donahue shows that 46 percent of the cases involved precontract – cases challenging prior engagement or marriage contracts. They were brought by either the first or second spouse, and roughly divided between male and female litigants. "All other issues pale in comparison with the defense or claim of precontract," writes Donahue.[59] He finds comparable ratios of precontract cases in the diocese of Ely, although the case records there are thinner.[60] Helmholz and others have found similar patterns

---

[56] Helmholz, *Marriage Litigation*, 59.

[57] See George Elliott Howard, *A History of Matrimonial Institutions*, 3 vols. (Chicago: University of Chicago Press, 1904), 1:276–286.

[58] Helmholz, *Marriage Litigation*, 57–66. See also R.H. Helmholz, "Marriage Contracts in Medieval England," in *To Have and To Hold: Marrying and its Documentation in Western Christendom: 400–1600*, eds. Philip L. Reynolds and John Witte, Jr. (Cambridge: Cambridge University Press, 2007), 260–286; Frederik Pedersen, "Marriage Contracts and the Church Courts of Fourteenth-Century England," in ibid., 287–331.

[59] See Donahue, *Law, Marriage, and Society*, 70–72.

[60] Ibid., 229–230. See also the Cambridge University Press online supplement to this volume, p. 402, questioning the lower numbers of ca. 40 percent of precontract cases for Ely raised by Michael Sheehan, "The Formation and Stability of Marriage in Fourteenth Century England: Evidence of an Ely Register," *Medieval Studies* 33 (1971): 228–263, and reprinted in id., *Marriage Family and Law in Medieval Europe: Collected Studies*, ed. J.K. Frage (Toronto: University of Toronto Press, 1996), 38–76.

in other medieval English church courts in Canterbury, Rochester, Lichfield, and London.[61] The proportion of English church court cases involving precontract impediments – and indeed marital issues altogether – did fall off sharply by the end of the fifteenth century as the canon law rules and church court procedures became more routinized, and as other legal topics came to dominate the church court dockets. But these precontract cases remained a staple of medieval marriage litigation.[62]

The sixteenth-century English Reformation initially made little change to this. Yes, when the dust of Henry VIII's great marriage dispute with the papacy finally settled in the mid-1530s, it was now Parliament, not the papacy, that laid down the statutory laws of sex, marriage, and family life, supplemented by Convocation's canons. And, yes, it was now the English Court of Delegates, not the papacy, that heard final appeals from local church court decisions. But marriage law and litigation in sixteenth-century Reformation England "continued to look much as it had during the Middle Ages"[63] – the treatment of polygamy notably included. Indeed, sixteenth-century English ecclesiastical law was more traditional than sixteenth-century Catholic canon law on the Continent. For England did not recognize the reforms of the Catholic Council of Trent in 1563, including its new pronouncement of anathema on polygamy as a separate canon law crime. While Continental church officials, including the Inquisition, were prosecuting polygamists with a fresh vengeance, this took longer to develop in England. The sixteenth-century English church courts continued to hear a few cases involving annulment (or disinheritance) on grounds of precontract as well as a few cases of slander or defamation where a plaintiff claimed injury for being falsely accused of

---

[61] Helmholz, *Marriage Litigation*, 57–66; Shannon McSheffrey, *Marriage, Sex, and Civic Culture in Late Medieval London* (Philadelphia: University of Pennsylvania Press, 2006), 23–25, 38–39, 117–118.

[62] Helmholz, *Marriage Litigation*, 58–59; R.H. Helmholz, *The Oxford History of the Laws of England: Volume 1, The Canon Law and Ecclesiastical Jurisdiction from 597 to the 1640s* (Oxford: Oxford University Press, 2004), 206–234. See, e.g., Martin Ingram, *Church Courts, Sex, and Marriage in England, 1570–1640* (New York/Cambridge: Cambridge University Press, 1987), 68, who documents that of 686 presentments arising from an episcopal visitation in Wiltshire in 1566, only 7 cases involved bigamy or precontract issues. See also William Hale, *A Series of Precedents and Proceedings in Criminal Causes: Extending from the Year 1475 to 1640, Extracted from Act-Books of Ecclesiastical Courts in the Diocese of London* (London: F. & J. Rivington, 1847), cases 36, 45, 220, 295, 306, 323, 327 (7 cases of precontract or bigamy out of 829 included from this period).

[63] Helmholz, *Marriage Litigation*, 69–70. For studies, see ibid., 70–79; Ronald A. Marchant, *The Church Under the Law: Justice, Administration, and Discipline in the Diocese of York 1560–1640* (Cambridge: Cambridge University Press, 1969); Eric Josef Carlson, *Marriage and the English Reformation* (Oxford: Blackwell, 1994), esp. 105–180. See compilation of statutes and cases in Richard Burn, *Ecclesiastical Law*, 8th ed., 4 vols.(London: A. Strahan, 1824), 2:433–512; John Godolphin, *Repertorium Canonicum*, 3rd ed. (London: Assigns of R. & E. Atkins, 1687), 492–513.

bigamy or polygamy. But there were fewer such cases on the sixteenth-century books than in the prior two centuries.[64]

The English church courts did begin to ramp up the number of official prosecutions of suspected polygamists, particularly if no children were involved.[65] "The late Elizabethan ecclesiastical authorities," Oxford historian, Martin Ingram, concludes after a lengthy study, were increasingly "vigilant in the pursuit of witting or unwitting bigamists.... At least in some cases the efforts of the courts were supported by strong local opinion; it was said of a couple living bigamously at Castle Combe in 1594 that 'all the country thereabouts for the most part crieth out threat, for that they are suffered to live so offensively.' Moreover, detected offenders were dealt with rigorously; bigamous couples were ordered to separate and the guilty enjoined severe penances. Overall, the evidence of prosecutions suggests that, certainly by the end of the sixteenth century," polygamy was not as easy to commit with impunity as some writers have alleged.[66]

Polygamy and the Reforms of Marriage Law

The church courts in Reformation England were likely feeling pressure not only from the theologians but also from the secular authorities to step up their prosecution of polygamy. Already in 1548, a royal proclamation condemned "unlearned and evil-disposed persons" for spreading "evil and perilous opinions against God's law and the good order of the realm, some teaching that a man may forsake his wife and marry another, his first wife yet living, and likewise the wife may do to the husband; other[s teaching], that a man may have two wives or more at once ... so that by such evil and fanatical opinions some hath not been afraid indeed to marry and keep two wives."[67]

That same year of 1548, the Privy Council, in an unusual move, censured William Parr, Lord Marques of Northampton, for his "strange" decision to have two wives at once, which caused "great and manifold disorders and inconveniences within the

---

[64] See Ingram, *Church Courts*, 68–70, 149–151,175–190. For other examples, see Ralph Houlbrooke, *Church and the People During the English Reformation 1520–1570* (Oxford: Oxford University Press, 1979), 70–71 (citing cases from Winchester and Norwich); Carlson, *Marriage and the English Reformation*, 83, 89, 95; Bernard Capp, "Bigamous Marriage in Early Modern England," *The History Journal* 52 (2009): 537–556.

[65] 32 Henry VIII c. 38, repealed by 2 & 3 Edward VI, c. 3, and 1 & 2 Mary c. 8 (both of which allowed for full enforcement of precontract impediments), partly revived by 1 Eliz. c. 1 s. 12.

[66] Ingram, *Church Courts*, 176, 179 (internal case citations omitted). See examples of interesting later sixteenth-century cases in Capp, "Bigamous Marriage," 542ff.; Martin Ingram, "Spousals Litigation in the English Ecclesiastical Courts, c. 1350–1640," in *Marriage and Society: Studies in the Social History of Marriage*, ed. R.B. Outhwaite (New York: St. Martin's Press, 1981), 35–57.

[67] Paul L. Hughes and James F. Larkin, eds., *Tudor Royal Proclamations*, 3 vols. (New Haven, CT: Yale University Press, 1964–1969), 422–423 (item no. 303). See additional discussion in Carlson, *Marriage*, 83.

realm." Parr protested that his first wife was an adulteress, and he had left her for a second wife. Fair enough, said the Council, but that purported adultery would have to be proved in a church court, which could at best grant him a right to separate from his first wife, not to marry a second. The Council ordered him to dismiss his second wife as was "consonant with the Word of God."[68] In 1552, Parr was able to secure a rare special act of Parliament permitting his divorce and remarriage.[69] But several other English men in the sixteenth century who resorted to such self-help were prosecuted by church and state authorities alike and forced to end their second marriages.[70]

These prosecutions evidently did little to stem the growing tide of polygamous unions in England. In a later session, Parliament heard all manner of stories of divorce, polygamy, incest, murder, and related problems. Archbishop Whitgift's (ca. 1530–1604) notes on the session about cases of polygamy were no doubt sobering to him:

> In Suffolk near Sir Edward Waldegraves, one married a woman lawfully one day: And she carried away from him, and the next day [he] married another by license. With whom she liveth at this day, her husband being alive....
>
> One badger of Tyerhil in Worcestershire, married two wives, and the second by a license. And finding two wives, chargeable, cut the second wife's throat, and was hanged....
>
> One Sermishair had two wives, and said to be divorced from them both. And afterwards married the Bishop's daughter of Litchfield and Coventry, that now is. Who was formerly married to one Pleested; but from him, divorced. Sermishair's elder brother married one of his divorced wives, and it is said Pleested the other....
>
> One known to the sheriff of Sussex was contented for a sum of money to acknowledge himself an adulterer, which he was not; and in open court his wife was divorced from him, and married with his consent to another man, by a license....
>
> One married two sisters in Oundel, in the country of Northampton.
>
> One married two sisters of Duddington, in the same county.
>
> One married his brother's wife, of Easton, by Stanford.[71]

[68] J.R. Dasent, ed., *Acts of the Privy Council*, 32 vols. (London: Eyre and Spottiswoode, 1890–1907), 2:164–165.
[69] Houlbrooke, *Church Courts*, 70–71.
[70] See cases cited in ibid., 71, and Capp, "Bigamous Marriage," 540–541. See also contemporaneous discussion in Edmund Bunny, *Of Divorce for Adulterie* (Oxford: n.p., 1612), 2r–3v.
[71] John Strype, *The Life and Acts of John Whitgift* (London: T. Horne et al., 1718), Appendix 36, 222–223; see also ibid., 508–510, and Simonds D'Ewes and Paul Bowles, *The Journals of all the Parliaments*

And on and on these tales of sexual woe and wonder went. Queen Elizabeth I was evidently so scandalized by such reports that she told the Commons she "would take remedial action."[72]

It was actually Elizabeth and her retinue, however, who had blocked earlier efforts to quash these kinds of offenses, in part as an effort to protect the church courts from secular interference. For example, the "Reformation of Ecclesiastical Law," first proposed in 1552 and reintroduced in Elizabeth's Parliament in 1571, had included a provision calling for stern punishment for polygamists: "[W]e want polygamy to be done away with by our laws, and we think it right that in a marriage there should be only one sole spouse, for in this way was marriage established by God in the first place."[73] The legal "Reformation" as a whole was blocked. But a 1581 Parliamentary bill sought again to make polygamy a felony punishable by the secular courts.[74] When that bill died, too, Parliament and Convocation shifted their efforts to shoring up the rules of marital formation and dissolution so as to make clearer when a marriage was validly made, when a putative marriage was validly broken, and when a party was free to marry another.[75]

Before 1604, the formation of a valid marriage in England required only a mutual promise of marriage stated in the present tense ("I take you for my husband/wife") between a man and woman with freedom, fitness, and capacity to marry each other. Even a future promise ("I promise to take you as my wife/husband") followed by consensual sexual intercourse constituted a valid marriage. No parental consent, testimony of witnesses, publication of banns, or religious ceremonies were necessary, although some couples did marry with all these formalities.[76] In 1604, a comprehensive new set of Canons and Constitutions Ecclesiastical required parental consent for parties under 21 years of age, and public banns and church consecration for all couples intending marriage.[77] But these same Canons also

---

of the Reign of Queen Elizabeth, rev. ed. (London: John Starkey, 1682), 555–562; Capp, "Bigamous Marriage," 541.

[72] Ibid., 541.

[73] James C. Spalding, ed., *The Reformation of the Ecclesiastical Laws of England, 1552* (Kirksville, MO: Sixteenth Century Journal Publishers, 1992), 95.

[74] T.E. Hartley, ed., *Proceedings in the Parliaments of Elizabeth I*, 3 vols. (Wilmington, DE: M. Glazier, 1981–1995), 1:529–530.

[75] See sources and discussion in Carlson, *Marriage*, 85–87; Witte, *From Sacrament to Contract*, 248–254.

[76] For the law at the end of the Tudor Reformation, see Henry Swinburne, *A Treatise of Spousals or Matrimonial Contracts* (written circa 1591) (London: S. Roycroft, 1686), 45–108; *The Lawes Resolutions of Womens Rights, or, The Lawes Provision for Women* (London: Assigns of John More, Esq., 1632), 51–115; *Baron and Feme. A Treatise of the Common Law Concerning Husbands and Wives* (London: Assigns of Richard and Edward Atkyns, Esq., 1700), 28–50.

[77] Edward Cardwell, ed., *Synodalia: A Collection of Articles of Religion, Canons, and Proceedings of Convocations in the Province of Canterbury*, 2 vols. (Oxford: Oxford University Press, 1842), 1:305,

confirmed the traditional "licensing exception," which eventually undercut these publicity rules.[78] "Licensed marriages" were initially reserved for rare cases where necessity, such as imminent travel or military service, demanded an abbreviated engagement without banns or ceremony. At first, only the Archbishop of Canterbury and a few of his delegates were formally authorized to issue marital licenses, and they were expected to demand the presence of two good and honorable witnesses, strict proof of no prior impediment or pending marital litigation affecting the couple, and formal proof of parental consent from both sets of parents.[79] But this licensing exception came to be treated as an attractive alternative method of marrying without the involvement of church, family, or community. Licensing officials proliferated, licensing requirements eroded, and false licenses abounded. Couples who sought to marry secretly or quickly could easily steal away to a remote parish to be married, or make their way to one of the many licensing booths that sprang up around the Fleet Prison and near the ports. This "underground marital industry," as Lord Hardwicke would later call it, thrived despite the increasingly stern prohibitions of Parliament and Convocation against it.[80] Only in 1753 did Parliament try to put a stop to this "clandestine marriage" industry for good by passing Lord Hardwicke's Act that made banns, witnesses, parental consent for minors, and consecration prerequisites for every valid marriage, and voided marriages that defied these formation steps.[81]

Marriages, once validly contracted could be dissolved either by annulment (which allowed remarriage) or divorce (which did not). An order of *annulment* required proof of one of the impediments to marriage that survived Tudor statutory reform – a blood or family relationship between the parties prohibited by Leviticus, a precontract to an earlier marriage by one of the parties, coercion, fraud or mistake in the formation of the marriage, or proven impuberty, frigidity, or impotence discovered shortly after the wedding.[82] Once a marriage was annulled, the parties were generally free to remarry, at least the innocent and healthy party. Annulments had hidden costs, however, beyond the costs of litigation. The annulment dissolved

---

Canons 100, 101. The age of consent for marriage was 12 for girls, 14 for boys. Swinburne, *A Treatise of Spousals*, 45–54.

[78] See Acts and Proceedings of Convocation (1604), item VI, in Cardwell, ed., *Synodalia*, 2:580, 583 (only chancellors granted licenses for marriage).

[79] Cardwell, ed., *Synodalia*, Canons 101, 103. Per Canon 104, no parental consent was required for the marriage of an emancipated widow or widower.

[80] See sample documents listing complaints in ibid., 1:380, 412; 2:707, 711–712, 724, 731, 770, 794.

[81] Formally called "Act for the Better Preventing of Clandestine Marriage," 26 Geo. II, c. 33. See R.B. Outhwaite, *Clandestine Marriage in England, 1500–1850* (London: Hambledon Press, 1995); Lawrence Stone, *Road to Divorce; A History of the Making and Breaking of Marriage in England* (New York and Oxford: Oxford University Press, 1995), 96–137; Stephen Parker, *Informal Marriage, Cohabitation, and the Law 1750–1989* (New York: St. Martin's Press, 1990).

[82] See 1597 Constitutions and Canons Ecclesiastical in Cardwell, ed., *Synodalia*, 1:152–155, 161–163.

a woman's right to collect dower interests in her former husband's estate,[83] and it illegitimated any children born of the first union.[84]

A decree of *divorce* required proof of adultery, desertion (for more than seven years), or protracted ill treatment.[85] Until the mid-nineteenth century, a decree of divorce in England was an order for separation from bed and board alone, with no right of remarriage for either party while the other spouse was still alive. The 1604 Canons underscored this traditional rule by ordering church court judges to enjoin divorced parties to "live chastely and continently; neither shall they during each other's life, contract matrimony for any other person. And, for the better observation of this last clause, the said sentence of divorce shall not be pronounced, until the party or parties requiring the same have given good and sufficient caution and security into the court, and they will not in any way break or transgress the said restraint or prohibition."[86] Judges faced a one-year suspension from office for failure to extract this pledge.[87] Divorced parties who did remarry prior to the death of their ex-spouse (or presumed death in cases of desertion) faced prosecution for polygamy.

The 1604 Polygamy Act

In 1604, the English Parliament for the first time in its history made polygamy a secular crime in England – and a capital crime at that. The new polygamy law was entitled: "An act to restrain all persons from marriage until their former wives and former husbands be dead." It was part and product of the secular authority's efforts to bring marriage formation and dissolution under stricter legal control, and to end the exploitation of women and children occasioned by self-divorce and private remarriage. The full Act reads:

> For as much as diverse evil disposed persons being married, run out of one country into another, or into places where they are not known, and there become to be married, having another husband or wife living, to the great dishonour of God, and utter undoing of diverse honest men's children, and others;

---

[83] Sir Edward Coke, *The First Part of the Institutes of the Lawes of England* (London: Societie of Stationers, 1628), folios 32, 33v, 235; id., *The Third Part of the Institutes of the Lawes of England* (London: M. Flesher, 1644), 93. This was remedied in part by the later introduction of alimony to mitigate the loss to an innocent wife. See Helmholz, *Roman Canon Law*, 77–79; Godolphin, *Repertorium*, 508–513.

[84] Burn, *Ecclesiastical Law*, 1:118–135.

[85] See a contemporary critique in W[illiam] H[eale], *An Apologie for Women, or Opposition to Mr. Dr. G. his Assertion … That it was Lawful for Husbands to Beate Their Wives* (Oxford: Joseph Barnes, 1609), and discussion in J.M. Biggs, *The Concept Of Matrimonial Cruelty* (London: University of London Press, 1962).

[86] Cardwell, ed., *Synodalia*, Canon 107.

[87] Ibid., Canon 108.

[I.] Be it therefore enacted ... that any person or persons within His Majesty's dominions of England and Wales, being married, or which hereafter shall marry, do at any time at the end of the said session of this present Parliament, marry any person or persons, the former husband or wife being alive; that then every such offence shall be [a] felony, and the person and persons so offending shall suffer death as in cases of felony, and the party and parties so offending shall receive such and the like proceeding, trial, and execution in such county where such person or persons shall be apprehended, as if the offence had been committed in such county where such person or persons shall be taken or apprehended.

II. Provided always, that this Act, nor anything therein contained, shall extend to any person or persons whose husband or wife shall be continually remaining beyond the seas by the space of seven years together, or whose husband or wife shall absent him or herself the one from the other by the space of seven years together, in any parts of within His Majesty's dominions, the one of them not knowing the other to be living within that time.

III. Provided also, and be it enacted by the authority aforesaid, that this Act, nor anything herein contained, shall extend to any person or persons that are or shall be at the time of such marriage divorced by any sentence had or hereafter to be had in the ecclesiastical court; or to any person or persons where the former marriage hath been or hereafter shall be by sentence in the ecclesiastical court declared to be void and of no effect; nor to any person or persons for or by reason of any former marriage had or made, or hereafter to be had or made, within [the] age of consent.

IV. Provided also, that no attainder for this offence, made [a] felony this act, shall make or work any corruption of blood, loss of dower, or disinhersion of heir or heirs.[88]

This 1604 Polygamy Act remained on the books until it was replaced by new acts of 1828 and 1861 which made polygamy a non-capital crime, punishable by up to seven years of "transportation" or two years of prison.[89]

The 1604 Polygamy Act created a new relationship between church courts and state courts in the prosecution of polygamy. English state courts, for the first time since Anglo-Saxon days, now had jurisdiction over polygamy, with power to punish convicted polygamists with a range of criminal sanctions, including execution in grave cases. But church courts still retained jurisdiction over marital formation and dissolution, with power to judge the validity of a marriage, to issue orders of annulment or divorce, and to impose a range of spiritual sanctions on delinquent parties, including excommunication in cases of serious sin. This continued into the nineteenth century.

[88] 1 Jac. 1, c. 11 (spelling and capitalization modernized). See Coke, *The Third Part of the Institutes,* cap. 27, page 88.

[89] 9 Geo. 4, c. 31; see parallel Irish Statute 10 Geo. 4, c. 34, s. 20.

This created three possible scenarios in a typical polygamy case. First, if it was clear from the evidence, or if the church court on request found that a defendant had two or more valid intact marriages, that defendant was a polygamist and subject to prosecution and criminal punishment by the secular court. Second, if the church court had properly *annulled* or "voided" one of the defendant's two marriages, the defendant's second marriage was not an act of polygamy. The defendant would be acquitted of any crime of polygamy and free from both church court discipline and secular court punishment. Third, if the church court had properly granted the defendant a *divorce* (meaning a separation) but the first spouse was still alive, the defendant's second marriage was still an act of polygamy, albeit a less serious crime. Absent aggravating factors, such defendants were usually not criminally punished very much, but would be sent to a church court for spiritual discipline and for the annulment of their second marriage.[90] The secular courts, in turn, would make the necessary adjustments to dower and other marital property. Those three scenarios seem to have been the intent of the Polygamy Act, and that was how the English courts came to interpret and apply it.[91]

The 1604 Polygamy Act was designed to provide relief to long deserted spouses who wanted the freedom to remarry. The medieval canon law, as we saw,[92] had required such parties to furnish absolute proof of the death of their long-gone spouse before they could remarry – an impossible burden of proof in many cases. This posed a "heartbreaking dilemma" for many lonely spouses, and especially for mothers with young children.[93] If they remained single, these mothers and their children were often condemned to poverty and exploitation. If they remarried without proof of their first husband's death, they were vulnerable to charges of bigamy and the spiritual sanctions that followed, including a state court order that illegitimated and thus disinherited any children born from the second marriage.

---

[90] Coke, *Third Part of the Institutes*, cap. 29, page 89; Matthew Hale, *Pleas of the Crown* (London: Richard Atkyns et al. 1678), 1:693ff.; William Blackstone, *Commentaries on the Law of England*, 4 vols. (Oxford: Clarendon Press, 1765–1769), 4:164.

[91] See, e.g., *R. v. Middleton*, Kelyng 27 (1638); *R. v. Williams*, March. 101 (1641). But see *R. v. Porter*, Cro. Car. 461 (1637) and the pre-1604 Act case of *Rye v. Fulmainde*, Moo. K.B. 683 (1602) where a mere divorce decree (as separation of bed and board) did not spare the defendant charges of bigamy when he married again. See discussion in G.W. Bartholomew, "Origin and Development of the Law of Bigamy," *The Law Quarterly Review* 74 (1958): 259–271, at 261–265; Lewis Dibdin, *English Church Law and Divorce* (London: J. Murray, 1912), 52–55, 82–85.

[92] See discussion in Chapter 4, pp. 182–186.

[93] Helmholz, *Roman Canon Law*, 166. See James A. Brundage, "Widows and Remarriage: Moral Conflicts and Their Resolution in Classical Canon Law," in *Wife and Widow in Medieval England*, ed. Sue Sheridan Walker (Ann Arbor, MI: University of Michigan Press, 1993), 17–32. Occasionally women deserted their husbands, too. See Sara Butler, "Runaway Wives: Husband Desertion in Medieval England," *Journal of Social History* 40 (2006): 337–359.

Henry VIII's Parliament had passed a law urging courts to limit the prosecution of bigamy charges in cases when minor children were involved, but this law was repealed by Edward VI's Parliament and only partly reinstated by Elizabeth's. The 1604 Act sought to resolve this dilemma for good by building in a clear statute of limitations on desertion. If deserters who remained hidden somewhere within Great Britain for seven years, or if even good faith travelers "beyond the seas" remained away for more than seven years, the abandoned spouse at home could remarry with impunity. Those who remarried within the seven-year window on the good faith assumption that their first spouse had died sometimes could still face charges of polygamy if the spouse unexpectedly turned up.[94] It was prudent to wait seven years before remarriage, but at least there was now relief available to the patient.

The 1604 Polygamy Act was also designed to shield minors from youthful marital mistakes or arranged marriages that might later put them in the frame for polygamy. If a person of the age of consent (12 for girls, 14 for boys) but under 21 years old got consensually married and had procured their parents' consent to the marriage as well, that marriage was valid, and would count against them if they were charged with polygamy. But if the minor had been forced into an arranged marriage by their parents, or had contracted their marriage without parental consent, that first marriage was presumptively invalid. If later charged with polygamy, those parties could defend themselves by challenging the validity of this first premature marriage. That defense became stronger still after Lord Hardwicke's Act of 1753 made parental consent for a minor's marriage a clear requirement for the validity of the marriage.

In application, the 1604 Polygamy Act did allow a polygamist to escape capital punishment on the technical grounds of "benefit of clergy."[95] This was a new variation on an ancient privilege long enjoyed by the English clergy. "Benefit of clergy" had a confusing relationship to polygamy, and it is worth taking a moment to lay it out.[96] The privilege of "benefit of clergy" – sometimes called the "privilege of forum" – started in the early twelfth century in England. It was then that English church officials began to insist that clergy charged with serious crimes be free from the jurisdiction of secular courts and instead be tried by their clerical peers in church courts. Criminal cases that started in secular courts had to be removed (or at least could be appealed once sentence was already passed) to the church courts if the clerical defendant claimed benefit of clergy. Pleading this privilege could save the defendant's life. Secular courts

---

94 *R. v. Gibbons,* 12 Cox 237 (holding that there was bigamy); cf. *R. v. Moore,* 13 Cox 544 (holding there was no bigamy). See James Fitzjames Stephen, *A History of the Criminal Law of England,* 3 vols. (London: MacMillan, 1883), 2:117–118.

95 See Coke, *Institutes,* 1:194ff.

96 See Matthew Hale, *Pleas of the Crown,* 323–390; Blackstone, *Commentaries,* 4:358; Joseph Chitty, *A Practical Treatise of the Criminal Law,* 5 vols., repr. edn. (New York: Garland Press, 1978 [1816]), 1:666–690; Stephen, *History,* 1:459–475.

had power to order convicted felons whipped, mutilated, or executed, while church courts could issue only non-corporal penance and purgation.[97] In 1350, the "benefit of clergy" privilege was extended not only to regular clergy (bishops, priests, deacons, and monks) but also to "secular clergy" (subdeacons, doorkeepers, readers, and others).[98] Over the next century, it was extended still further to any man who could read or write, regardless of his clerical status. But it was notoriously withheld from women, even learned abbesses and nuns.[99] This created a two-tier system of criminal law. The illiterate masses and all women, regardless of their education, were subject to execution for felonies by the secular courts. The clergy and the educated male laity were not. A 1487 statute imposed a modest limit; those who did successfully plead "benefit of clergy" in one case were branded on the hand or thumb with the first letter of their crime ("M" for murderer; "R" for rapist, "K" for kidnapper, and the like), so that they could not claim this benefit again if indicted for committing this same offense a second time.[100]

Now here is the confusing connection with polygamy. A new Parliamentary law of 1276, the Statute on Bigamy ("Statutum de Bigamus") prohibited "clerical bigamists" in England from claiming this privilege of benefit of clergy in criminal cases.[101] "Clerical bigamists," were not "real polygamists," however – one man with two or more wives. They were instead clergy who, before their ordination, had been lawfully married to two or more wives in a row, or who had been married once but to a widow, divorcee, prostitute, or other woman who was not a pure virgin on their wedding day.[102] Medieval canon law, as we saw, said that no man with that marital or sexual history could properly be ordained.[103] But, inevitably, some of these candidates for ordination did take holy orders. Some had kept their prior marital lives secret. Others had mistakenly thought their brides were virgins, but they were not.

---

[97] Bracton, quoted in Stephen, *History*, 1:456–460.

[98] 25 Edw. 3, st. 3.

[99] See, e.g., Year Book for 34 Henry VI, p. 49 a b. Luke Owen Pike, *A History of Crime in England*, 2 vols., repr. ed. (Montclair, NJ: Patterson Smith, 1968), 1:483.

[100] 4 Henry VII, c. 13. See also 1 Edw. VI, c. 12, s. 14 repealing 28 Henry VIII c. 1, s. 7. See Stephen, *History*, 1:462.

[101] 4 Edw. 1, c. 5 (1276) and 18 Edw. 3, c. 2 (1344). The 1276 statute reads: "Concerning men twice married, called Bigami, whom [the pope] by a Council of Lyons [in 1274] hath excluded from all Clerks Privilege.... It is agreed and declared before the King and his Council, that the same Constitution shall be understood in this wise, that whether they were Bigami before the same Constitution or after, they shall not henceforth to be delivered to the Prelates, but Justice shall be executed upon them, as upon other Lay people."

[102] See discussion of clerical bigamy in Chapter 4, pp. 186–190. See also Richard Burn, *Ecclesiastical Law*, 8th ed. (London: A. Strahan, 1824), 1:192–193; for elaboration see V. Bullard and H. Chalmer Bell, eds., *Lyndwood's Provinciale: The Text of the Canons Therein Contained, Reprinted from the Translation Made in 1534* (London: The Faith Press, 1929), bk. 3, tit. 3.1–2.

[103] See discussion in Chapter 4, pp. 186–190.

Still others had thought one of their preordination sexual relationships had not been a marriage, but it was. When these now sitting clergy were found out, the church courts or their religious superiors charged them with "clerical bigamy." Whether witting or unwitting, these clerical bigamists if convicted were put out of clerical office.[104] Unless they could get a rare papal dispensation, they were defrocked, stripped of their benefices and privileges, and, in cases of serious fraud, they were excommunicated. The Council of Lyon had formalized this canon law rule for the universal church in 1274 at the instigation of Pope Gregory X. The Parliamentary law of 1276 echoed this canon law provision and made this exclusion part of English secular law as well. It said that a proven clerical bigamist could claim no benefit of clergy. So, if that defrocked former cleric was indicted for a serious felony, like murder, rape, kidnapping, treason, grand larceny, or the like, he could be tried in a secular court and could make no claim of benefit of clergy. If convicted, he was subject to harsh corporal punishment, including execution.[105]

Some writers have read this 1276 law to say that the common law thereby made bigamy or polygamy a capital crime – indeed, one so serious that even a cleric could not claim benefit of clergy if duly convicted.[106] This misreads the statute. The "bigamy" at issue in the statute is not "real polygamy" but "clerical bigamy." The statute does not directly or indirectly make polygamy a secular capital crime. It says only that clerical bigamists, in the technical canon law sense of the term, cannot plead "benefit of clergy" to escape secular jurisdiction if charged with a capital crime like murder. As the 1276 law put it: "Justice shall be executed upon them, as upon other lay people." And that lay justice could include execution.

The 1604 Polygamy Act opened a new chapter on the relationship between polygamy and the privilege of benefit of clergy. English law, by this point, allowed clergy to be married, and all the fastidious medieval concerns about "clerical bigamy" had largely fallen aside.[107] The 1604 act criminalized only "real polygamy" – having

---

[104] The judgment of whether there was a clerical bigamy in the first place remained within the jurisdiction of the church courts. See Nathaniel Bacon and John Selden, *An Historical and Discourse of the Law and Government of England*, 3 vols., 4th ed. (London: Daniel Browne and Andrew Millar, 1739), 1:29.

[105] See Sir Edward Coke, *The Second Part of the Institutes of the Laws of England* (London: W. Clarke and Sons, 1809), 271–274. See also Coke, *The First Part of the Institutes*, 80a-80b, n. 1.

[106] See, e.g., William O. Russell, *A Treatise on Crimes and Misdemeanors*, 2 vols. (Boston: Wells and Lilly, 1824), 1:282; Ellis Lewis, *An Abridgement of the Criminal Law of the United States* (Philadelphia: Thomas, Cowperthwait, 1847), 116; John Comyns, *A Digest of the Laws of England*, 5 vols. (London: H. Woodfall, 1762–1767), 4:765; J.L.J. Edwards, "Mens rea and Bigamy," *Current Legal Problems* 2 (1949): 47–67, at 48.

[107] See details in Helen L. Parish, *Clerical Marriage and the English Reformation: Precedent Policy Practice* (Burlington, VT: Ashgate, 2000); Carlson, *Marriage and the English Reformation*, 37–66. A 1547 statute, 1 Edw. VI, c. 12 had in fact repealed the 1276 law and allowed both clerical bigamists and real polygamists to plead benefit of clergy. This law, in turn, was repealed during Mary's reign.

two or more spouses at once. Both clergy and laity, and both men and women, could now be charged with real polygamy. And both clergy and laity, and both men and women (after 1691), too, could claim "benefit of clergy."[108] The power to exercise this privilege no longer turned on one's clerical or even one's educated status. It turned on a single test: whether the defendant could read the opening verse of Psalm 51: "Have mercy on me, O God, according to thy steadfast love." Clergy and laity who successfully pled "benefit of clergy" using these new rules were still treated a bit differently – with vestiges of the medieval rules still in operation. Ordained Anglican clergy (and peers) who successfully pled this privilege were excused from all punishment, were not branded on the thumb, and were free to claim the privilege again if indicted for polygamy. But all laity (and all non-Anglican clergy) could still be imprisoned for up to a year, and were usually branded on the thumb with a "B" or "P" (for bigamist or polygamist) so they could not plead this privilege again. Any person, clerical or lay, who failed to plead the privilege, or who failed to recite Psalm 51 passage accurately, could be punished for their polygamy, including by execution.[109]

A series of statutes in the eighteenth and nineteenth centuries gradually removed the lingering inequities of this system. A 1705 statute removed the literacy requirement altogether, and let anyone plead "benefit of clergy," leaving vulnerable only the most ignorant or poorly represented defendants.[110] A 1717 statute allowed courts to condemn convicted polygamists, even if they had successfully pled benefit of clergy, to transport for up to seven years.[111] Finally, an 1827 statute abolished the "benefit of clergy" for all persons in all crimes, including polygamy.[112]

A new 1828 polygamy statute declared polygamy to be a non-capital felony punishable by up to seven years of transport or two years of prison, and with no distinction left between clergy and laity, men and women, literate or illiterate.[113] This was confirmed in the 1861 Offenses Against the Persons Act, a comprehensive

---

See discussion in John G. Bellamy, *Criminal Law and Society in Late Medieval and Tudor England* (New York: St. Martin's Press, 1984), 115–179, esp. 148–149.

[108] 21 Jas. 1, c. 6 for larceny, and extended to all felonies by 3 & 4 W. & M., c. 9 and 4 & 5 W. & M., c. 24.

[109] This happened in 1677 to Richard Hazlegrove, who was convicted for having two wives, but executed because he failed to recite the Psalm properly. The Court said the result was "a little severe" and urged parents to educate their children to read. Case of Richard Hazlegrove (July 11, 1677), transcribed on http://www.oldbaileyonline.org/ (consulted August 12, 2013), case no. t16770711a-6. [Future cases cited as "OB no."]

[110] 5 Anne, c. 6 (1705). I am passing over the short-lived attempt by the Commonwealth authorities in the later 1640s and 1650s to retain polygamy as a capital offense, but to abolish benefit of clergy, and instead give court the power to reprieve, and Parliament the power to pardon. See Stephen, *History*, 1:209–210.

[111] 5 Geo. 1, c. 11 (1717).

[112] 1827, 7 & 8 Geo. 4, c. 28, s. 6.

[113] 9 Geo. 4, c. 31, ss.; see parallel Irish Statute 10 Geo. 4, c. 34, s. 20.

criminal law that remains on the books in England, and is echoed in many countries in the British Commonwealth.[114] With ample amendment and a gradual softening of punishments, these polygamy provisions remain in place in England, although the crime is now rarely prosecuted as a separate criminal offense, and it remains a civil offense yielding damages to the innocent spousal victim(s) and leading to annulment of the putative marriage(s).[115]

THE PROSECUTION OF POLYGAMY IN EARLY MODERN ENGLAND

In the 224 years that the 1604 Polygamy Act was the law of England, the Old Bailey in London and various assize and appellate courts around England heard hundreds if not thousands of criminal cases of polygamy – although exactly how many is unclear. The *All English Law Reports* lists 368 cases touching "bigamy" and 51 more cases touching "polygamy" from 1604 until the new statute of 1828 was enacted. These *Reports* are far from complete. A great number of court records from these earlier centuries did not survive, and many cases went unreported officially by the courts, even if sometimes reported by local chroniclers, newspapers, or private diarists.[116] University of Warwick historian Bernard Capp, for example, in a penetrating study, finds some 350 cases of polygamy all told in later sixteenth and seventeenth-century England, as reported in these various sources.[117] Capp's family law colleague, Rebecca Probert, in a thorough study of English marriage law in "the long eighteenth century," references 168 bigamy trials from 1715 to 1755.[118]

---

[114] U.K. Stat. 1861, c. 100, s. 57. See Russell, *A Treatise on Crime and Misdemeanors*, 944–977 for English developments, and discussion of other common law countries in the Introduction of this book.

[115] Stephen Cretney, *Family Law in the Twentieth Century: A History* (Oxford: Oxford University Press, 2005), 72–74; Rebecca Probert, *Family Law in England and Wales* (Alphen aan den Rijn: Kluwer Law International, 2012), sec. 488.

[116] See Andrew Knapp and William Baldwin, *The New Newgate Calendar; Being Interesting Memories of Notorious Characters, Who Have been Convicted of Outrages on the Laws of England, During the Eighteenth Century*, 6 vols. (London: Albion Press, 1810) includes a number of interesting cases and related materials on prosecutions for bigamy and polygamy.

[117] Capp, "Bigamous Marriage" and broader contextual discussion in Bernard Capp, *When Gossips Meet: Women, Family, and Neighborhood in Early Modern England* (Oxford: Oxford University Press, 2003); id., *England's Culture Wars: Puritan Reformation and its Enemies in the Interregnum, 1649–1660* (Oxford: Oxford University Press, 2012), esp. 144–145 (showing continued vigorous prosecution of bigamy during the Interregnum). See also see also J.A. Sharpe, *Crime in Seventeenth-Century England: A County Study* (Cambridge: Cambridge University Press, 1983), 67–68 (listing twenty-one indictments for bigamy in Essex assize courts – seventeen men and four women; one man was hanged, four men were condemned to die but pled clergy; three women were ordered executed, but even without clergy all three were reprieved; the remaining thirteen were acquitted or at least there is no record of punishment).

[118] Rebecca Probert, *Marriage Law and Practice in the Long Eighteenth Century: A Reassessment* (Cambridge: Cambridge University Press, 2009), esp. 39ff. and 191ff. See other examples in Joanne Bailey, *Unquiet Lives: Marriages and Marriage Breakdown in England, 1660–1800*

Standard criminal law handbooks in the nineteenth century turn up several new polygamy cases a year, as the prosecution for this offense escalated both before and after the 1828 and 1861 statutory reforms.[119] A number of collections of cases from the seventeenth through nineteenth century include entries on bigamy or polygamy. Every decade or two throughout this early modern period a sensational polygamy case captured the headlines, and was published as a free standing pamphlet.[120] A few of these cases have given rise to wonderful narrative histories by modern historians to enlighten our understanding.[121]

A superb online collection of cases from 1674 to 1913 in the Old Bailey, London's central criminal court, holds a total of 2,384 criminal cases of bigamy or polygamy (out of a grand total of 197,000 plus criminal cases).[122] Of all these bigamy cases, 507 were brought under the 1604 Act before the 1828 statutory reform.[123] Of these 507 cases, 6 of them ended with execution – two women, four men. In 110 cases, the defendants successfully pled benefit of clergy and were branded – 14 women, 96 men. In fifty-nine cases, the defendants were sentenced to transport for seven

---

(Cambridge: Cambridge University Press, 2001), 184–187. For earlier and overlapping lists of cases, see Chilton L. Powell, *English Domestic Relations, 1487–1653* (New York: Russell & Russell, 1972 [1917]); Bacon, *The Abridgement of the Law*, 2:107–111; Blackstone, *Commentaries*, 4.13; Leonard Shelford, *A Practical Treatise on the Law of Marriage and Divorce* (London: S. Sweet, 1841), secs. 223–231.

[119] See, e.g., Henry Roscoe, *A Digest of the Law of Evidence in Criminal Cases*, 3rd. Am. ed., ed. T.C. Granger (Philadelphia, PA: T. & J.W. Johnson, 1846), 308–326. See also three unreported cases on bigamy in D.R. Bentley, ed., *Select Cases from the Twelve Judges' Notebooks* (London: John Rees, 1997), 48–49, 152–153, 170–171, 176–182.

[120] For both these individual cases and collections of criminal cases including on polygamy and bigamy, see the entries in the electronic source *The Making of Modern Law, Trials 1600–1926* (Gale).

[121] See, e.g., cases described in Lawrence Stone, *Uncertain Unions* (Oxford: Oxford University Press, 1992), 232–274 and more cases later in this chapter. See, in addition, John Butler, *The True State of the Case of John Butler* (London: s.n., 1697), an interesting case of an Anglican priest, whose wife refused to have sexual relations let alone children with him, which he remedied by taking a second wife as a purported concubine, following Old Testament precedent; he was convicted for bigamy and wrote a long defense of his actions in ibid. For a couple of later interesting cases, see, e.g., Arvel B. Erickson and Fr. John R. McCarthy, "The Yelverton Case: Civil Legislation and Marriage," *Victorian Studies* 14 (1971): 275–291; Gail Savage, ""More than One Mrs. Mir Anwaruddin: Islamic Divorce and Christian Marriage in Early Twentieth-Century London," *Journal of British Studies* 47 (2008): 348–374.

[122] See http://www.oldbaileyonline.org/ (consulted August 12, 2013). This valuable resource provides transcripts, and many facsimiles of all the criminal cases reported in the *Old Bailey Proceedings* from 1674 to 1913, and of the *Ordinary of Newgate's Accounts* between 1676 and 1772, the two most reliable and expansive sources that have survived.

[123] I have omitted from these numbers the 1828 cases, because they do not make clear whether they are applying the 1604 act or the 1828 act. There are twenty-three defendants charged for bigamy in 1828 – eighteen men, five women. Of the eighteen male defendants – four were transported, eight were imprisoned (from two to twenty-four months), the rest were acquitted or there is no punishment recorded. Of the five female defendants – one was transported, one imprisoned for three months, one found guilty but released on her own recognizance, and the cases against the remaining two ended inconclusively.

years – one woman, fifty-eight men. In thirty-two cases, they were sent to prison from two weeks to two years – two women, thirty men. In five cases, they were simply fined – all men. In 211 cases, the defendants were found not guilty – 67 women, 144 men. Eight cases, all involving men, ended inconclusively.

It is worth noting several clear patterns in this 500-plus case sample from England's most important criminal court – although it must be stressed that this was just one of many courts that heard polygamy cases. First, polygamy remained very much "a male crime," in Sara McDougall's apt phrase, as it had been in the Middle Ages.[124] Both men and women were equally subject to the 1604 Act. But only 19 percent of the Old Bailey cases (95 of 507) were brought against women. Fully 70 percent of these women defendants (67 of 95) were acquitted; an additional 15 percent of them (14 of 95) successfully pled benefit of clergy, escaping with a branded thumb. Fewer than 5 percent of these women defendants faced harsh punishment: two went to prison, one was transported, and two were executed (both in the seventeenth century). Men were prosecuted much more frequently, and punished much more severely for practising bigamy or polygamy. More than 81 percent of the polygamy cases were brought against men. Men were severely punished through imprisonment, transportation, or execution in 22 percent of these cases, compared to 5 five of the women. And men were acquitted in only 35 percent of these cases, women in more than 70 percent.

Second, although the 1604 Polygamy Act declared bigamy or polygamy to be a capital felony, executions for polygamy were rare. Only 6 out of the 507 defendants in the Old Bailey were executed, and all these took place before 1693. There were no doubt more executions ordered for convicted bigamists by the Old Bailey before 1674, the first year from which we have records. There were certainly more executions ordered by criminal courts outside of London. But the number of executions for polygamy is very small – perhaps surprisingly so, given the moral outrage heaped upon this crime by jurists and theologians alike. The privilege of "benefit of clergy" was the real safety net: 22 percent (110 of 507) of Old Bailey defendants successfully pled benefit of clergy and escaped execution.

Third, transportation for seven years was the preferred harsh punishment for particularly brazen polygamists, and after 1717 it could be imposed even on those who successfully pled benefit of clergy. Some 11 percent (58 of 507) of the defendants, all but one of them men, were so sentenced. Transportation was usually a form of banishment to a penal colony – often North America, after 1787 Australia as well, and occasional other outposts in the vast British Empire. Convicts were often put to hard work on the "hulks" – think of Charles Dickens's *Great Expectations* – that

---

[124] Sara McDougall, "Bigamy: A Male Crime in Medieval Europe," *Gender and History* 22 (2010): 430–446.

provided passage over, and they could be sold as indentured servants, a few times as slaves, to the ship captains or on arrival to their grim new home.[125]

Fourth, imprisonment was a relatively rare form of punishment in these cases, imposed on only 6 percent (32 of 507) of the defendants, with sentences rarely over a year. Imprisonment for any crime was not a common form of long-term punishment in England before the nineteenth century, and a good number of such convicts were held in private prisons or had their sentences commuted into indentured servitude.[126]

Fifth, the vast majority of cases involved a party with two spouses only, rather than multiple spouses. A few traveling cads did keep multiple wives in different cities, or just rotated through a series of wives without bothering to end their prior marriages. They were the ones who were usually sentenced to death, although most pled benefit of clergy and escaped with branding. A good example is the 1676 case against an unnamed handsome charlatan who ultimately seduced seventeen wives around England. The trial record is worth quoting:

> [F]or about five years last past or more he has made it his business to ramble up and down most parts of England pretending himself a person of quality, and assuming the names of good families, and that he had a considerable Estate per Annum, though in Truth he was old sutor ultra Crepidam, a Knight of the Order of the famous Crispin, being originally by profession a Shoemaker, and not many years since a Journeyman; but on the pretensions aforesaid, where ever he came if he heard of any rich Maid, or wealthy widow at their own disposal, he would very formally make Love to them, wherein being of handsome taking presence, and Master of a voluble insinuating tongue, he commonly succeeded to engage their easy affections. And having inveigled them to marry him, and for some small time enjoyed their persons, and got possession of their more beloved Estates, he would march off in Triumph with what ready money and other portable things of value he could get, to another strange place, and there lay a new plot for a second Adventure, but was at last discovered in the West, and apprehended, and at the great charge of the Prosecutor brought up by Habeas Corpus hither, but however subtly he behaved himself heretofore, I conceive he failed in his politics, when being brought to the Bar and demanded what he could say for himself why judgment should not pass upon him, whereas 'tis believed he might have had the benefit of the Clergy, he obstinately waived that, and insisted for Transportation, which being not thought convenient to be granted, because he stood charged in the Sheriff's custody with an Action of a thousand pounds, he thereupon received sentence with the rest to be hanged.[127]

---

[125] J.M. Beattie, *Crime and the Courts in England, 1660–1800* (Princeton, NJ: Princeton University Press, 1986), 450–618.

[126] Ibid., 573–610.

[127] Case of May 10, 1676, OB no. t16760510-1.

Mary Stokes presented a comparable case, albeit a rarer one for women in the day. She married four men in the space of five years, slept with them a few nights – the second husband got just one night – and then made off with their property. She then moved down the road and took up with the next handsome wealthy man she could find. A scandalized judge accused her of being "an idle kind of a Slut," and ordered her executed.[128]

Although these sensational cases made for good gossip, news, and occasional plays and novels, most polygamy cases involved rather ordinary people who had gotten remarried and were now charged with bigamy or polygamy. The cases were often brought at the instigation of their first or second spouse, or of an interested family member or third party. Occasionally an aggressive church or state official instigated prosecution. Many of the cases turned on the simple factual question whether the defendant had two valid marriages intact at once. Defendants' honest and reasonable mistakes of fact or law did not exonerate them, but these mistakes often lessened their punishment. Defendants who were impoverished, abused, manipulated, or otherwise victimized by their first spouses and were trying to make thin ends meet by forming a second marriage, tended to get more sympathy. The more knowing and deliberate the defendant was in entering a second illegal marriage the more likely it was that severe punishment would follow. Defendants who compounded their crime by stealing marital property, abandoning their minor children or pregnant wife, or leaving massive debts for the abandoned spouse and family to cover generally faced harsher punishments. Those who bragged about their multiple marriages or defamed their abandoned spouses and families also got harsher punishment. So did those who changed their names, posted false banns, or manipulated the legal process to gain the hand of their second spouse.

Female Defendants

A typical case against a woman brought under the 1604 Polygamy Act was the Crown's prosecution of Mary Picart.[129] Mary had been properly married more than twenty years before to Jean Gandon – in a church wedding with witnesses. Jean's brother testified that the couple had two or three children, but Jean had since become old and decrepit. Mary was still more lively and adventuresome. One day, she went into London, and got drunk with one Philip Bouchain. They went to a Fleet Street marriage licensor, and Philip paid a license fee for them to marry on

---

[128] Case of Mary Stokes (December 6, 1693), OB no. t16961206-14. See a few other notorious cases in Capp, "Bigamous Marriage," 546–547.
[129] Case of Mary Picart, alias Gandon (1725), in James Montagu, ed., *The Old Bailey Chronicle*, 4 vols. (London: S. Smith, 1788), 1:377–378.

the spot, which they did in a brief ceremony. The drunken couple then collapsed into bed together, only to be interrupted loudly a few hours later by Mary's relatives who ordered her home and him out. Philip had evidently passed out, because he remembered nothing of getting married. Mary, too, denied any second marriage though she remembered vaguely the brief ceremony. Both insisted that they had not had sex with each other. Because the second marriage was not consummated, the jury acquitted her. They could well have convicted her, because consummation was not a condition for a valid marriage. But execution for an interrupted one night drunken tryst was evidently too much for the jury.

A 1726 case against Mary Jane Bennett also ended in acquittal, this time because the first marriage was declared void.[130] When she was 14, Mary had gone to live with an Italian man, named Dr. Letart, to serve as his interpreter. He "debauched" her, getting her pregnant. He then threatened to kill her or to "send her to Brideswell" if she would not marry his friend Peter Dorfille. If she would marry Peter, Letart promised to maintain and compensate her handsomely. She married Peter, but Letart then abandoned her and "never took the least notice of her." Peter proved to be a "poor weakly Thing," a "Tool of a Husband," who did nothing and took whatever she earned. Despondent, Mary eventually took up with Thomas Smith, was impregnated by him, and now wanted to marry him. She told Thomas she was a widow, and they were promptly married by a Fleet licensor. Mary was then indicted for bigamy under the 1604 Act. The jury acquitted her, finding no evidence of a lawful first marriage to Peter given Letart's coercion and extortion, and probably taking pity on her for being so exploited.

Pity was also evident in a later case against a destitute woman, Mary Burns.[131] Seven years earlier, Mary had wed Richard Winter. They lived as husband and wife for a few months. He then enlisted in the military and went away on foreign service, never to return. Just over a year after Richard's departure, a desperately poor Mary wed one Francis Burns, and the new couple produced two children. After the seven year statute of limitations for desertion built into the 1604 Act had expired, Mary must have thought she was free. But an ambitious local official had her prosecuted for bigamy, since she had married within a year of her first husband's departure, not after seven years of waiting. The trial court evidently convicted her, but the case was appealed to the King's Bench, whose judges were divided. The dissent thought the 1604 Polygamy Act created a presumption that the absent party was alive for the first seven years, and could only be presumed dead thereafter. Any other rule, the dissent said, would allow a woman to "marry a week after her husband's departure" but

---

[130] *Select Trials at the Session-House in the Old-Bailey for Murder, Robberies, Rapes, Sodomy, Coining, Frauds, Bigamy, and other Offences*, 4 vols. (London: J. Applebee, 1742), 3:32–33.
[131] The Case of Tywning, Gloucestershire, 106 Eng. Rep. 407 (1819).

leave her free from prosecution unless and until her first husband returned within seven years of the first wedding. The majority ruled in Francis's favor, holding that the first husband Richard could be presumed dead, which the ensuing seven years of his absence confirmed. That was a more defendant-friendly reading of the statute than many courts offered.[132]

It was not so much the court's pity as the defendant's own resilience and eloquence that saved Mary Moders, a well-educated and well-heeled German woman, who was being "framed" for bigamy.[133] Mary had moved from Germany to England on her own, leaving her vulnerable, both because she was a foreigner and because a woman without a male protector could be easily exploited in that day. Sure enough, Thomas Stedman and his father had heard of her considerable wealth, and they sought repeatedly to bully her into marrying young Thomas. At one point, they dragged her in front of a justice of the peace to be married, but the judge refused them. At another point, they had her imprisoned on trumped up charges to pressure her. They stole her valuable jewelry and clothing. But, at least according to Mary, she refused the marriage. When Mary later married another man, John Carleton, the bitter elder Stedman had her indicted for bigamy. He first had her charged in a Dover court for marrying a man called "Day" before her marriage to Carelton. Mary was acquitted on that bigamy charge. He then had her indicted again, now on grounds that she had already married his son, Thomas, too. The prosecutor sought to prove Mary's first marriage to Thomas but ultimately had only one witness to the wedding, and that witness seemed to have been paid rather handsomely for his testimony. There was no marriage registration, no priest or clerk, no other witnesses to the wedding or indeed to the couple's life thereafter, save again this not so credible single witness.

The judge grew suspicious. When he inquired into how Thomas and his father had come upon Mary's goods, they claimed that they were now marital property, and Thomas was properly keeping them as the husband and controller of the marital property. The judge cross-examined other prosecuting witnesses who later came forward, and their stories against Mary also fell apart. The elder Stedman was said to have been offering ample bribes to have still other witnesses appear against Mary, but no credible witness came forward. Mary gave a lengthy and eloquent speech, calmly reciting the facts of the Stedman family vendetta against her, although their motives were not clear from the trial record. The judge could, and probably should, have thrown out the case at this stage, but he put it to the jury. His jury instructions,

---

[132] See comparable result in Case of Rebecca How (July 5, 1749), OB no. t17490705-85.

[133] The case record is in T.B. Howell, ed., *A Complete Collection of State Trials and Proceedings for High Treason and Other Crimes and Misdemeanors from the Earliest Period to the Year 1783*, 42 vols. (London: T.C. Hansard et al., 1816), col. 273–284.

however, reminded them of the high stakes: "You have heard what defence she hath made for herself.... If you believe ... the single witness [for the prosecution] speaks the truth so far forth to satisfy your conscience that that was a marriage, she is guilty. You see what the circumstances are, it is penal; if guilty, she must die; a woman has no [benefit of] clergy, she is to die by the law." The jury declared her not guilty, to the great applause of a spell-bound courtroom.

Not all women defendants escaped liability. Mary Stoakes compounded her crime with fraud and was more severely punished.[134] In 1688, she married Thomas Adams before several witnesses. In 1692, she left Thomas and married William Carter, again before several witnesses. But she soon left William, too, changing her name to Mary Elliott, and holding herself out to yet another man as a single maid with an estate. She was tried and convicted for polygamy. She escaped execution by claiming benefit of clergy, newly available to women, and was branded on the thumb.

Elizabeth Wood Lloyd proved even more brazen.[135] In 1812, she had married Thomas Lloyd, a baker. Around 1816, she began consorting with a sailor, suspiciously named Captain Bligh, and the couple would take a room together when he was between voyages. Thomas found her out, and told her in front of Bligh and other witnesses: "If you like the sailor better than me, you had better go with him." Bligh gave Thomas five shillings and made off with Elizabeth. Whether Bligh and Elizabeth ever formally married is unclear, but in 1822 she was formally married to William Henry Truss, signing the marriage registration as "Betty Wood Louther Bligh, the widow of Captain Bligh." Truss later found out about her prior marriage to Thomas, and he promptly left her, albeit after giving her a rather handsome severance. But seeking to end the marriage, and recoup his settlement, Truss had Elizabeth prosecuted for polygamy. She was convicted and sentenced to seven years transport.

One of the most famous bigamy cases in this period involved Elizabeth Chudleigh, the eventual Duchess of Kingston. In 1754, she married the Honorable Augustus John Hervey in a proper church wedding. In 1768, however, she sued Hervey in a church court for "jactitation," a technical private claim alleging that Hervey had boasted that he was married to another woman besides the Duchess.[136] She won her jactitation case against Hervey, and the church court declared her "free from all matrimonial contracts and espousals with him." Less than a month after winning her case, Elizabeth married her lover, a nobleman, Evelyn (a man) Pierpoint, Duke of Kingston, by special license from the Archbishop of

---

[134] *The Trials of all the Felon Prisoners, Tried, Cast, and Condemned, This Session at the Old Bailey* (London: n.p., 1798), 6.

[135] Case of Elizabeth Wood Lloyd (April 6, 1826), OB no. t18260406-790.

[136] See Franciscus Clarke, *Praxis Francisci Clarke omnibus qui in foro ecclesia* (Dublin: Nathanielem Thompson, 1666), 145–147.

Canterbury. The timing and the seeming connivance of the Archbishop made the Crown authorities suspicious. In 1775, they indicted the new Duchess for her bigamy in being married to both Hervey and Pierpoint at the same time. With ample contestation about jurisdiction by distinguished lawyers arrayed on both sides, the case was first removed to the King's Bench, and then eventually to the House of Lords, where the Duchess was tried de novo for her bigamy. Counsel for the Duchess sought to have the case dismissed on grounds that her first marriage to Hervey had been dissolved by the church court. The prosecutor charged that her claim "was wickedly accomplished by practising a concerted fraud upon a court of justice," designed to get a "fabricated" and "collusive sentence" upon her innocent first husband Hervey. She was a bigamist, the prosecutor concluded, and the Duchess must thus bear "the inconvenient consequences of guilt … which God and the order of nature" and with it the common law have set against bigamy. The House of Lords ultimately found that they were not bound by the church court's judgment in the first "jactitation" case that her marriage to Hervey was over. They convicted the Duchess for bigamy. She successfully pled benefit of clergy. As a peer she escaped even branding, although not ample embarrassment given the media sensation surrounding the case.[137]

A few uninformed pamphleteers and scandalmongers suggested that the second marriage of Elizabeth Chudleigh and Evelyn Pierpoint was, in fact, an early lesbian marriage. This was not true in the Kingston case. But it had been a closer question in the 1719 case of Catherine Jones. In 1713, Catherine had married John Rowland, who then went abroad. Six years later, she married one Constantine Boone, only to have John return and have her indicted for polygamy. Catherine defended herself by saying that she discovered after her second wedding that Constantine was a hermaphrodite and that "the female sex prevailed over that of the male." Constantine wore female clothing and was given to knitting and other "female activities," Catherine said. The jury on hearing this acquitted Catherine of the bigamy charge, and the court opined: "We can only express our astonishment that a hermaphrodite should think of such a glaring absurdity as the taking [of] a wife."[138]

---

[137] The Duchess of Kingston Case (April 1776), 168 Eng. Rep. 175–177, and more fully reported and quoted in Matthew Hale and Charles Runnington, *History of the Law*, 5th ed. (1794), 39–50, and in *The Laws Respecting Women as they Regard their Natural Rights* (London: J. Johnson, 1777), 327–337. See the full case record in *The Trial of Elizabeth Duchess Dowager of Kingston for Bigamy* (London: Charles Bathurst, 1776). The Duchess's colorful sexual history has attracted ample commentary. See detailed sources and discussion in Matthew J. Kinservik, *Sex, Scandal, and Celebrity in Late-Eighteenth-Century England* (New York: Palgrave, 2007).

[138] "Singular Case of Catherine Jones" (September 5, 1719 in the Old Bailey), in *The Making of Modern Law, Trials 1600–1926* (Gale).

Male Defendants

Although most courts gave women charged with bigamy the benefit of the doubt, particularly before they could plead the benefit of clergy, they tended to treat male defendants more firmly, even when the facts seemed to call for leniency. Take the case of William Morgan Manners.[139] He had married Eliza Redkison in a proper church wedding. Shortly after their honeymoon, Eliza took up with an old boyfriend. William moved their marital home to another town in an effort to end the affair. But one day, when William was traveling, Eliza disappeared taking much of their marital property with her. William made sixteen attempts to persuade her to come back home, but Eliza's boyfriend threatened to shoot him if he returned. William waited three years, and then got remarried to Susan Anderson. He was convicted for bigamy. An unsympathetic court sentenced him to seven years transport.[140]

John Fisher lost any hope of getting the court's sympathy because of his perjury and premarital sex.[141] In June, 1812, he had married Mary Arlett in a church wedding. She was apparently already pregnant because in November that year, John testified that she promptly "left her home with all the child's clothes, and everything she could lay h[o]ld of, and left me only just enough to put on in the morning." He spent time settling their ample debts and then sought to start over by changing his name to John Ingram. Holding himself out as a bachelor, he married Ruth Elcock four years after his first marriage to Mary. His bigamy and perjury were discovered, and he was convicted for seven years of transport.[142]

Not all cases ended so badly for male defendants.[143] For example, George Brickle testified that he had his heart broken by his first wife, Sara Harding, whom he married in 1810 and professed to love dearly. But, he said, "she turned out everything that was base, and has had children by other men." She then left George for good, although exactly how many years ago was not clear enough to fit easily within the statute of limitations for desertion. A crushed George eventually married Christiana Massey in 1821. He was still convicted for bigamy, but the jury "strongly recommended to mercy." He was fined one shilling and discharged.

Brazen polygamists, particularly those who compounded their offense with serious crimes, found no sympathy from the Old Bailey and other criminal courts.[144]

---

[139] Case of William Morgan Manners (September 12, 1821), OB no. t18210912-95.

[140] See same results on similar facts in Case of Henry Sanders (April 17, 1822), OB no. t18220417; Case of Thomas Sale Denby (May 22, 1822), OB no. t18220522-165. But see Case of John W.K. Kitchingmam (July 3, 1822), OB no. t18220703-23 who received only one year of prison on similar facts.

[141] Case of John Fisher (July 10, 1816), OB no. t18160710-77.

[142] Same result in another perjury Case of John Harwood (December 6, 1820), OB no. t18201206-156.

[143] Case of George Brickle (July 15, 1824), OB no. t18240715-46.

[144] Case of Thomas Brown (Sept. 9, 1747), OB no. t17470909-22.

The case of Thomas Brown provides a good example. Brown, a tobacconist in London, had properly married a maidservant named Ann Mussels in February 1747. Six months later, he picked up a second woman, Susannah Watts, in a local pub, courted her briefly, and then promptly married her in a proper ceremony. They went on a honeymoon, and he then took her home. His first wife Ann raised the roof when Thomas arrived with his new wife, and a mortified Susannah had him prosecuted for bigamy. Given his long criminal record already, which included earlier charges of robbery and rape, the court said "they hoped they should live to see this crime punished with death." But Thomas successfully pled benefit of clergy.

Samuel Taylor aggravated his bigamy with fraud, theft, and desertion of his pregnant wife.[145] Seventeen years earlier, he had properly married Mary Hayter, but the couple had separated by mutual consent, and Mary had then taken in another woman and did not want him back. Sixteen years after that first marriage, Taylor held himself out as a widower and married Harriet le Sturgeon. She got pregnant, and he left her in her seventh month, taking some of her goods, too. He was convicted for bigamy and got seven years of transport. John Maude left his wife Harriet of thirteen years and their six children. He pretended to be a bachelor and married Esther Barrett, and sired another child by her. He was convicted for bigamy and perjury and sentenced to seven years transport.[146] John Crooks left his pregnant wife once, returned to impregnate her again, and then left her and their two young boys for good, rendering them impoverished wards of the local parish.[147] Crooks then bragged to someone that "he had a great many wives." Local authorities began to look into his case and found an earlier marriage still intact. They prosecuted John for bigamy, and he was sentenced to seven years transport.[148] All three men were lucky to have escaped with their lives.

Lewis Houssart, a French emigrant barber living in England, was not so lucky.[149] In 1723, Lewis had married Elizabeth Heren in a church wedding before several witnesses. A parish clerk testified to the new marriage with Elizabeth, but he also mentioned that Lewis was rather nervous after the wedding for no seeming reason. That raised the court's suspicions. They subpoenaed another pastor serving in the French émigré community who testified that he had, in fact, several years earlier married Lewis to another woman named Ann Rondeau. That name was familiar to the court because Ann had just been murdered. Lewis was called back for investigation, now on suspicion both of bigamy and murder. He eventually admitted

---

[145] Case of Samuel Taylor (October 28, 1818), OB no. t18181028-148.
[146] Case of John Maude (December 1, 1789), OB no. t18191201-109. See similar result in Case of John Mackiah Collins (April 17, 1782), OB no. t18220417-121.
[147] Case of John Crooks (January 9, 1822), OB no. t18220109-134.
[148] See similar result in Case of William Guy (April 9, 1923), OB no. t18230409-175.
[149] *Select Trials at the Session-House in the Old-Bailey*, 2:72–87.

knowing Ann, but denied that they were ever married. He also cast ample aspersions on Ann's character and chastity to the great chagrin of her family. Ann's brother testified that Ann and Lewis had been married, and claimed that Lewis in fact had murdered her. Lewis was then tried for murder, too. The evidence was largely circumstantial, but the court had lost all sympathy for him. He was convicted and hung. It was not clear whether he tried to plead benefit of clergy, but his broken English testimony recorded in the case suggests that he could not have recited Psalm 51 accurately enough to escape.

Robert Fielding, Esq. was also convicted of bigamy, but he escaped execution by successfully pleading benefit of clergy.[150] The facts sound like a Jane Austen novel. Fielding, a handsome bachelor but also a high society rake, was in hot pursuit of a new widow, Barbara, the Duchess of Cleavland and former mistress of King Charles II. Using his legal connections, he had checked on her will, and found her legacy of some 80,000 pounds inducement enough. He began pursuing her through intermediaries and letters in August 1704. The Duchess's servants evidently did not like Robert, because they secretly protected her against his pursuits, burning one of his letters of inquiry and blocking his agent's efforts to see her. Robert was not so easily put off. When he took up his pursuit in person, one of the servants, the comely Mary Wadsworth, dressed up like the Duchess, and allowed Robert to see her through a window on one of Robert's frequent visits to the home. This made Robert doubly eager to meet the Duchess, and he kept trying to find a way. The servants then had Mary go to meet Robert at his home, holding herself out as the Duchess. Robert was infatuated, and after a lengthy interview, proposed marriage to her. A demur Mary eventually accepted. Robert collected a Roman Catholic priest who married them on the spot. They consummated their marriage that night, and slept together several more times in coming weeks as she prepared her move into his home. Robert gave Mary gifts, money, furniture, and clothing. He also gave her an expensive wedding ring. He wrote her several letters thereafter always addressed to "his wife," "the countess of Fielding," and the like. Mary became pregnant. The pretense continued for the next six months. Robert then discovered who Mary was, a penniless maidservant, and he promptly threw her out. He then resumed his pursuit of the Duchess, whom he married in November 1705. But when he began to abuse his new wife, the Duchess, and was then found sleeping with her granddaughter

---

[150] *The Arraignment, Trial, and Conviction of Robert Fielding, Esq. for Felony in Marrying Her Grace, the Duchess of Cleavland; His First Wife, Mrs. Mary Wadsworth Being Then Alive at the Session of the Old-Bailey* (London: John Morphew, 1708). A 1736 edition of this same record is entitled *The Trial of Robert Fielding, Esq. on Wednesday, December 4, 1706, in the Fifth Year of the Reign of Queen Anne* (London: R. Snagg, Fleet Street, 1736).

as well, whom he impregnated, the Duchess sued him and brought him up on criminal charges.[151]

Robert was then charged with bigamy. Part way through the case, the judge seemed to be leaning in favor of Robert's argument that his first marriage to Mary was void because of his mistake of marrying "this false woman." There was also a serious question of whether the Catholic priest could officiate at a proper English wedding, and whether he had even administered the proper marital vows.[152] But then Robert overplayed his hand. He argued that Mary could not validly marry him anyway, because she had already been married for two years to another man, Lilly Brady. Robert triumphantly produced a copy of her marriage registration from the Fleet and urged the court to charge her with bigamy, not him. Counsel for Mary cleverly turned that argument against Robert. For Robert to charge Mary with bigamy was to admit that he had married her, too, as his marriage to her was the indictable second marriage. Robert sought to escape his dilemma by petitioning a church court to annul his marriage with Mary on grounds of precontract, fraud, or mistake. The church court eventually did so, but not before the criminal court convicted him under the 1604 Polygamy Act. He pled benefit of clergy, was branded on the thumb, and sent away on payment of bail in lieu of prison.

It ultimately went better for James Cooke who was accused of bigamy in the Old Bailey in 1812, but only after the remarkable persistence of his second wife led to his pardon.[153] Nine years before, in 1799, Cooke had married one Jane Browning in a private church wedding. He said he was under 21 at the time, but had not secured his parent's consent, which Lord Hardwicke's Act of 1753 now required for every valid marriage of a minor. Some two years after her marriage to Cooke, Jane had an affair. Cooke promptly left her and never saw her again until the trial nine years later. After leaving Jane, Cooke had sought advice from legal counsel who told him in an opinion letter, later submitted into evidence, that his first marriage was void because of the lack of parental consent, and would certainly be void if the parties remained absent from each other for seven years. Cooke waited the requisite seven years, and shortly thereafter was properly married to Sophia Sanders, and the new couple then had a child. Cooke was indicted for bigamy, which the prosecutor grandly declared to be "one of the most heinous in the catalogue of human offences." Cooke appeared pro se before a jury and a notoriously obstreperous judge. The judge credited the prosecution's rather thin and controverted evidence of Cooke's "intentional and malicious" bigamy, and blocked and discredited much of Cooke's evidence. The

[151] See Amanda Foreman, "Valentine's Revenge," *Smithsonian* (February 2014): 29–31, 102.
[152] See Probert, *Marriage Law and Practice*, 136–137.
[153] *The Remarkable Trial of The Honourable James Stamp Sutton Cooke, Accused of Bigamy at the Old Bailey, on the 14th of April, 1812* (London: F. Marshall, 1823).

judge also said that, notwithstanding Lord Hardwicke's Act, Cooke's first marriage with Jane was valid unless and until a church court declared it void. He led the jury with biased instruction; they convicted him immediately, and the judge sentenced Cooke to seven years transport. His "second" wife Sophia organized an appeal, summoned a battery of witnesses and officials, including Cooke's original lawyer, to document the trial judge's obvious bias and misinterpretation of the law. For good measure, she also brought an action in the church court, which annulled the first marriage between Cooke and Jane. When the trial judge still refused to budge, Sophia sought a royal pardon which was granted and Cooke freed.

Although Cooke could not convince the trial judge of this fact, Lord Hardwicke's Act of 1753 generally made it easier for defendants charged in polygamy cases. Each marriage in question had to be formed by parental consent if the parties were under 21, and had to feature two or more witnesses, civil registration, publication of banns, and a wedding ceremony. Failure of any of these requirements would automatically void a marriage, without necessary resort to a church court proceeding. The secular court could simply weigh the evidence of failure of formation, and – if proved – the defendant could be acquitted for polygamy. The Cooke court was evidently suspicious that he had invented the absence of parental consent: Cooke was very close to 21 at the time of his first marriage, and there was some evidence that his parents may have, in fact, been dead. The Cooke court was also likely irked that it was Cooke, the deserter, not his deserted first wife Jane, who was claiming the seven year window on desertion. But many other courts, hearing bigamy cases, held that lack of parental consent of either marriage was a sufficient defense to polygamy.[154]

Sometimes an irregularity in the formation of one of the marriages allowed the court at least to mitigate the punishment of a defendant rather than exonerate him. This can be seen in a 1794 case of John Taylor in the Old Bailey.[155] In 1771, John had married Sara Marshall in a proper church wedding. The marriage was evidently never consummated, and Sara, who was incapable of sexual intercourse, eventually persuaded the long suffering John to marry another younger woman. In 1792, John married Margery Sophia Richardson, with his first wife's approval. All was going well until "some great reformer of morals," as the defense called him, had John prosecuted for the "abominable and atrocious felony" of bigamy. There was enough dispute about the character and motivations of the prosecutor and the quality of the evidence against the defendant to give the court pause. But they hung their light sentence on the stated suspicion that the second marriage had not been properly formed. John was given a two-week prison sentence and small fine.

---

[154] See, e.g., *Rex v. Williams*, 168 Eng. Rep. 660 (1802).
[155] R. *v. John Taylor* (November 11, 1794), OB no. t17941111-44.

Thomas Wardropper, a butcher, was also very lightly punished on suspicion that his first marriage was invalid.[156] He had married Ann Archer in 1787, but there was some evidence he was coerced to marry her and that he was drunk on the wedding day, further impeding his consent. This was evidently a shotgun wedding, because the couple had a child shortly before or after the wedding. They were soon estranged, and Anne seems to have gone to France, leaving Thomas to care for the child. In 1791, Thomas was persuaded to marry the "beautiful" Alice Doyle, who was the ward of one of his friends and eager to have Alice married off. Thomas and Alice were properly married, and lived together with the child for more than a year. But then Alice discovered Thomas's prior marriage to Ann and moved out on her own. Alice then began taking up with a Mr. Douglas, who provided her with ample furnishings, and evidently came over regularly to test the bed. Douglas wrote Thomas one or more letters trying to force him to end his marriage with Alice so he could marry her. With that failing, he instigated the prosecution of Thomas for bigamy. After hearing all this tawdry and self-serving testimony, the court concluded that this "is not one of those cases in which severe punishment ought to be inflicted." Thomas was fined one shilling and discharged.

A shotgun wedding was also one of the marriages at issue in the 1803 case of Charles Butler.[157] In 1791 at the age of 20, local parish officers had charged him with impregnating a servant girl, Lydia Blackwell. They threatened to prosecute him for his fornication, unless he would marry her immediately. They dragged him to church to be married to her, giving him, still a minor, no time to consult with his parents. Right after the wedding, Lydia left Charles for good, and their child died shortly after birth. She was later married in 1798 and had several more children by her new husband. In 1800, well after the seven-year statute of limitations on desertion, Charles married Elizabeth Field, and they had a child, and established a good business. Elizabeth's mother evidently learned of Charles's prior marriage to Lydia. She had him arrested for bigamy, and she and Elizabeth sold all of his property and business while he was in prison. The court concluded that both marriages were probably valid, but sentenced him to only six months in prison, probably thinking that he had suffered enough.

The treatment of foreign marriages and divorces was a major issue for English courts given the vastness of the British Empire into Asia, Africa, and the Americas. A person's monogamous marriage contracted abroad was generally recognized in England, making any second marriage contracted in England a prima facie crime of polygamy.[158] If the person's foreign marriage was ended by annulment or absolute

---

[156] Case of Thomas Wardropper (December 6, 1797), OB no. t17971206-2.
[157] Case of Charles Butler (July 6, 1803), OB t18030706-44.
[158] *R. v. Jacobs*, 168 Eng. Rep. 1217 (1826). The converse was not true; forming a second marriage abroad was not an act of bigamy in England. *R. v. Forsyth*, 168 Eng. Rep. 512 (1798).

divorce by the judgment of a foreign court, however, a second marriage in England was legal. In turn, if a person lawfully married in England contracted a second marriage abroad, they could not be charged for polygamy in an English court. But if a person lawfully married in England, got a divorce or annulment of that marriage in a foreign court, their subsequent remarriage in England could lead to a charge of polygamy, for the English courts would not recognize this foreign dissolution of a valid English marriage.[159]

SUMMARY AND CONCLUSIONS

Already in Anglo-Saxon times, England condemned polygamy as a serious moral offense deserving of "hell-fire." But until 1604, it was left to church courts to punish polygamists using spiritual punishments. Like their Continental counterparts, English church courts dissolved invalid second engagements and marriages of convicted polygamists, often leading secular courts to illegitimate their children in so doing. The church courts also issued a range of spiritual punishments (except fines) to convicted polygamists – penitential works, public confessions, shame rituals, and property confiscation.

Although a few English divines condoned and a few English nobles and commoners practiced polygamy in the heady days of Henry VIII's Reformation, English theologians quickly condemned polygamy as unbiblical, unnatural, unjust, unwise, and unsafe. They further condemned present-day polygamists in Africa, Asia, the Americas, and the Ottoman Empire as irrational, lustful, barbaric, and morally inferior. Travel diaries describing the polygamy of various exotic peoples around the world quickly became popular. Their unforgiving descriptions of polygamists served to strengthen England's self-image as a holy, faithful, sophisticated, God-fearing nation, and to provide a "boundary marker" between them and the barbaric polygamists of the pagan world.

English writers treated the monogamous family as a little commonwealth whose proper ordering and functioning was essential to the stability and flourishing of the political commonwealth of England. The domestic commonwealth, they believed, was ordained by God and nature as a hierarchical structure under the enduring and exclusive authority of the husband and father. Women served as a helpmate and co-ruler of this little commonwealth, while children were expected to love and obey their parents who had been given authority over them. Polygamy was viewed as a betrayal of the exclusive covenant of marriage between a man and a woman, and it

---

[159] See Burn, *Ecclesiastical Law*, 3:110–112; for later developments, see G.W. Bartholomew, "Polygamous Marriages and English Criminal Law," *Modern Law Review* 17 (1954): 344–359; J.H.C. Morris, "The Recognition of Polygamous Marriages in English Law," *Harvard Law Review* 66 (1953): 961–1012.

caused crippling harm not only to wives and children, but also to church, state, and society whose new members would be deprived of the essential virtues, habits, and exemplars needed to thrive outside the home.

Parliament enforced these monogamous ideals by taking firm control over English marriage and family law in the course of the later sixteenth and seventeenth centuries. It worked hard to stamp out the medieval practice of self-marriage and self-divorce. It instituted firm new marital formation rules of parental consent, two witnesses, civil registration, and church consecration for valid marriage. It restricted divorce to very rare cases that could occasion a special bill in Parliament, and it truncated impediments to rein in a runaway annulment practice. When private licensing arrangements to make marriage, and simple desertion and remarriage practices continued, Parliament enacted the 1604 Polygamy Act that made polygamy a serious crime, punishable by the secular courts. But the Act also provided relief for long-deserted parties, by allowing them to remarry if abandoned for more than seven years.

Using this 1604 law, both individual victims of desertion or double marriage as well as church or state officials could initiate indictment of parties for polygamy. Other interested parties also had standing to press polygamy claims, effectively as private attorneys general. Thousands of polygamy cases came before the criminal tribunals of England, not least the famous Old Bailey, the central criminal court in London, which heard more than 500 such cases under the 1604 Act. Convicted parties faced punishments ranging from fines and short imprisonment, to transportation to a penal colony or execution orders, although almost all those convicted for a capital felony successfully pled benefit of clergy. The vast majority of polygamy cases were brought against men, and convicted men were punished far more severely than women. The 1604 Polygamy Act, while eventually replaced by Acts of Parliament in 1828 and 1861 that made polygamy a non-capital crime, was a model for the common law world and broader British Commonwealth. Particularly North American colonies and states, as we shall see two chapters hence, used the basic structure of the 1604 Polygamy Act until the twentieth century.

8

The Early Modern Liberal Case for Polygamy

FIGURE 17. "In the Harem," from Juan Gimenez y Martin, Dahesh Museum of Art, New York.
Used by permission of Dahesh Museum of Art, New York, USA / Bridgeman Images.

By 1650, England and other early modern Western lands had rested their case against polygamy, confident that God and nature, morality and justice were on their side. The radical experiments with polygamy born of the Protestant Reformation were now finally refuted as unbiblical, unnatural, and unjust. The experiences of polygamy discovered through travel, trade, and colonization in the new world were now firmly rebuked as pagan, barbarian, and uncivilized. Polygamy, it was thought, had betrayed its inherent dangers and harms clearly enough that it could be comfortably criminalized. It was thought that only a few self-serving cads,

FIGURE 18. "Fantasia in a Harem," from Gianni Dagli Orti.
Used by permission of Gianni Dagli Orti / the Art Archive at Art Resource, New York.

aristocrats,[1] and cultural iconoclasts engaged in this practice, and they were to be prosecuted – and banished to penal colonies or sent to the gallows if they persisted. For the next two centuries, mainstream Western churches, states, and societies settled down to rest comfortably again on the foundation of monogamy, with censors, clerics, and criminal courts keeping polygamous ideas and practices in proper check. This early modern settlement against polygamy would remain the norm in the West until a fresh batch of polygamous experiments in nineteenth-century America eventually forced the issue of polygamy back onto everyone's agenda.

But this did not mean that Western speculations about or arguments for polygamy just ended. After all, those stories of biblical polygamists remained there to be read, and not everyone bothered with or believed the official interpretations that

---

[1] The most notorious of these was William Cowper (1664–1723), Lord Chancellor of England, who was said to had two wives at the same time – Elizabeth Culling and Judith Booth – and then after Judith died, he married yet another, Mary Clavering. He was exposed by Mary de la Rivère Manley's *Secret Memoirs and Manners of Several Persons of Quality* (1709). See Leo Miller, *John Milton Among the Polygamophiles* (New York; Loewenthal Press, 1974), 139–141, with other English examples in ibid., 136–145.

explained away these biblical texts. After all, some of the great fathers of the church –
Augustine, Chrysostom, Erasmus, Luther, and others – had said polygamy was
natural, and not everyone read these titans through the glosses of their critics and
detractors. After all, those traveler and missionary diaries about polygamy in Africa,
Asia, and the Americas continued to multiply, and not everyone was convinced that
all these reports could be so easily dismissed as pagan barbarism, especially when it
became clear that some of these new world Christian converts gave up their many
gods more easily than they gave up their many wives. And, after all, the obvious raw
advantage of polygamy for repopulating early modern lands devastated by war and
disease or for providing more homes for fatherless children and single women kept alive
the "necessity" and "utility" arguments for polygamy.

Already during the interregnum in England, from 1640–1660, when censorship was
temporarily lifted, the press churned out a whole series of interesting new pamphlets,
briefs, poems, and novels about polygamy. In the next two centuries, when freedoms of
speech, press, and religion became ever greater cultural and constitutional realities, a
steady flurry of pro-polygamy tracts cluttered the comfortable consensus about monogamy.
Each time a major new pro-polygamy tract came out, a series of counter-tracts followed,
aiming to push aside these arguments. Church and state alike responded mostly with
their traditional arguments against polygamy, and doubled the efforts of the secular courts
to stamp out polygamy. The more novel and interesting arguments against polygamy
eventually came from the pens of Enlightenment liberals. These new architects of
modern liberalism and liberty, despite their rejection of Christian establishments if not
Christianity altogether, nonetheless denounced polygamy as contrary to nature, utility,
fairness, and common sense as well as to the rights of women, children, and men alike.
The more radical the arguments for polygamy became, the more sharply honed this
liberal Enlightenment case against polygamy became.

This chapter samples a few of the new arguments for polygamy that emerged in
the liberal literature of the seventeenth and eighteenth centuries; I have drawn in
part on the pioneering work of Leo Miller and John Cairncross.[2] The next chapter
works through the liberal case against polygamy put forward by the Enlightenment
philosophers and jurists.

POLITICAL BROADSIDES FOR POLYGAMY IN ENGLAND

After finally settling down under the long reigns of Queen Elizabeth and King
James, the English world was again "turned upside down" by the English

---

[2]   Ibid.; John Cairncross, *After Polygamy Was Made a Sin: The Social History of Christian Polygamy*
(London: Routledge and Kegan Paul, 1974). See also Paul Mikat, *Die Polygamiefrage in der frühen
Neuzeit* (Opladen: Westdeutscher Verlag, 1988).

Revolutions of 1640 and 1689.[3] The 1640 Revolution was, in part, a rebellion against the excesses of the political commonwealth, headed by James's son, King Charles I (1600–1649). The landed aristocracy and merchants chafed under oppressive royal taxation raised to support unpopular wars. Clergy and laity suffered under harsh new establishment laws that drove religious nonconformists first out of their families and churches, then out of England altogether. Much of the country resented the increasingly belligerent enforcement of royal measures by the prerogative courts – Star Chamber, Admiralty, High Commission, and Requests. When Parliament was finally called into session in 1640, after an eleven-year hiatus, its leaders seized power by force of arms. Civil war erupted between the supporters of Parliament and the supporters of the monarch. The Parliamentary party prevailed and passed an Act "declaring and constituting the People of England to be a commonwealth and free state." Parliament abolished the kingship, and the deposed King Charles was tried, convicted for treason, and beheaded. Parliament also abolished the aristocratic House of Lords and declared that "supreme authority" resided in the people and their representatives. Anglicanism was formally disestablished, and episcopal ecclesiastical structures were replaced with congregational and Presbyterian forms. "Equal and proportional representation" was guaranteed in the election of local representatives. England came under "the democratic rule" of Parliament and the Protectorate of Oliver Cromwell (1599–1658).[4]

After Cromwell died in 1658, the Commonwealth government eventually collapsed. King Charles II (1630–1685), son of the executed Charles I, returned to England, reclaimed the throne in 1660, and restored traditional monarchical government and pre-revolutionary law. This Restoration era was short-lived. Charles II proved to be an immoral "merry Monarch." His brother King James II (1633–1701), a Catholic no less, began to betray tyrannical tendencies as his father had done. Within three years, Parliament forced James II to abdicate the throne in favor of the new dynasty of William and Mary. This was the Glorious Revolution. It established government by the King *in Parliament* and introduced a host of new guarantees to English subjects in the 1689 Toleration Act and Bill of Rights, including freedom of speech.[5]

Like the Protestant Reformation a century before, the English Revolutions unleashed a new round of intense new speculation about the fundamentals of

---

3 Christopher Hill, *The World Turned Upside Down: Radical Ideas during the English Revolution* (New York: Viking Press, 1972).

4 See detailed sources and discussion in John Witte, Jr., *The Reformation of Rights: Law, Religion, and Human Rights in Early Modern Calvinism* (Cambridge: Cambridge University Press, 2007), 209–276; Harold J. Berman, *Law and Revolution II: The Impact of the Protestant Reformations on the Western Legal Tradition* (Cambridge, MA: Harvard University Press, 2006), 190–230.

5 1 William & Mary, st. 2, c. 2, c. 18.

sex, marriage and family life. Freed temporarily from the censors in the 1640s and 1650s, and then given fuller freedoms of speech after 1689, a few English writers proposed all manner of alternatives to traditional norms and forms of monogamous marriage – from the salutary to the prurient. For example, in 1643 Gerrard Winstanley (1609–1676), the leader of the Diggers, suggested, against prevailing patterns of parentally controlled and male-initiated marriages, that "every man and every woman shall have the free liberty to marry whom they love, if they can obtain the love and liking of that party whom they should marry, and neither birth nor portion shall hinder the match, for we are all of one family mankind." Winstanley, like many others, urged England to develop the right of both husbands and wives to divorce for cause and to remarry thereafter. And, in a further effort to protect women and children, he urged that a man who impregnated a single woman be forced to marry her and that convicted adulterers and rapists be executed, and their estates used to support any children whom they left, whether legitimate or illegitimate.[6]

Several pamphleteers in the 1640s and 1650s urged polygamy as an expedient marital solution to the surplus of single women and widows left to compete for the few men who were left, many of them "frosty-bearded usurers" who had skipped or survived the wars of the day. Would it not be better, read *The Widowes Lamentation* of 1642, for these women to join together with one "young, lusty husband" instead of remaining single and miserable, or worse producing bastards that imposed further care and cost on the commonwealth if the bastard survived at all?[7]

Another pamphleteer in 1658 proposed that polygamy was the best solution to the scourge of fornication, bastardy, and infanticide then besetting England. Too often fornicating couples cannot get married, and desperate new mothers abort their children or quietly smother them upon birth, despite clear new criminal laws against this.[8] "Does not the blood of many thousand infants cry against the rigor of those laws not permitting their fathers to espouse their mothers, and legitimate them

---

[6] Gerrard Winstanley, *The Law of Freedom in a Platform, or True Magistracy Restored*, ed. R.W. Kenny (New York: Schocken Books, 1941), 146–147 ; and see discussion of his views by Martin Madan later in this chapter.

[7] See Anonymous, *The Virgins Complaint for the Losse of their Sweet-harts by these Present Wars* (London: Henry Wilson, 1642), 3; *The Widowes Lamentation for the Absence of their Deare Children and Suitors* (London: s.n. 1642), 6, with other texts in Lisa Shirley Loughead, "The Perception of Polygamy in Early Modern England" (Ph.D. Diss., Dalhousie, 2008), 95–97. See also Cairncross, *After Polygamy*, 81, reporting that the regional council of Catholic Franconia in Germany, with the local bishops' approval, temporarily authorized men to take two wives in an effort to encourage local repopulation after the devastating loss of life in the Thirty Years War.

[8] "An Act to Prevent the Destroying and Murthering of Bastard Children," 21 Jac. c. 27. See also Mark Jackson, *New-Born Child Murder: Women, Illegitimacy and the Courts in Eighteenth-Century England* (Manchester: Manchester University Press, 1996); J.M. Beattie, *Crime and the Courts in England, 1660–1800* (Oxford: Clarendon Press, 1986), 113–124.

to the world?" The polygamous Muslim Turks do not abort or kill their children; they just add the new mothers to their harems. As a result, Muslims are now a formidable population threatening the very existence of Christendom, whose pious Christian subjects are forced to throw their infant children on scrap heaps. This is so because the "popish" laws of monogamy have misinterpreted the laws of nature and the teachings of Scripture; these laws deprive a man of his natural right and his natural duty to marry every single woman whom he impregnates.[9]

Commonwealth lawyer Francis Osborne (1593–1659) also looked wistfully upon Turkish polygamy as a more expedient means to repopulate England. It was also, to him, a more efficient way to run a government, given the many more kin-based political alliances that could be forged across polygamous families.[10] Additionally, Osborne thought that polygamy was a far better form and norm of domestic life than "the perpetual slavery" of monogamy. In an oft-reprinted misogynist rant, *Advice to a Son*, Osborne lamented that "English laws are composed so far in favor of wives, as if our ancestors had sent women to their Parliaments" – heaven forbid! Monogamous marriage is "like a trap set for flies," with just enough ointment of "voluptuousness" to turn a man's head, and just enough promise of "a lick at [the] honeypot" that a man will walk into the snare. But once married, a man is stuck for life, no matter how barren, frigid, diseased, profligate, abusive, weak, ugly, or nasty his wife inevitably becomes. Monogamy is "a padlock on the liberty of men," restricting them to their single marital beds for fear of adultery charges, but forcing them to accept and support every child their wives drag back into the marital homes, no matter who has fathered them.[11] How can this monogamous madness be the law, Osborne cried out, when women are by nature "the weaker vessels" deserving of subordination and when the holy patriarchs, who walked and talked with God, multiplied wives and concubines without reproach. The fault lies with the church whose "wily priests" made "single wedlock" a matter of "divine right" and imposed the "heavy punishment" of death on polygamy. Mandatory monogamy for the laity is as unnatural and unnecessary as mandatory celibacy is for the clergy, Osborne concluded. Polygamy is the more natural and expedient course.[12]

---

9 Anonymous, *Remedy for Uncleanness or Certain Queries Propounded to his Highness the Lord Protector* (London: s.n., 1658), 1–6.

10 Francis Osborne, "Political Reflections on the Government of the Turks," [c. 1656], in id., *The Works of Francis Osborne*, 10th ed. (London: A. and J. Churchill, 1701), 249–262.

11 This refers to the common law rule that any child born to a married woman was strongly presumed to be the legitimate child of her husband. See John Godolphin, *Repertorium Canonicum*, 3rd ed. (London: Assigns of R. & E. Atkins, 1687), 482; R.H. Helmholz, "Bastardy Litigation in Medieval England," *American Journal of Legal History* 13 (1969): 361–383, at 370–371.

12 Francis Osborne, "Advice to a Son in Two Parts," in Osborne, *Works*, 28–39. See a comparable misogynist rant by Osborne's contemporary Thomas Browne in *Religio Medici & Other Writings of Sir Thomas Browne* (London: J.M. Dent & Co., 1906).

Pushing the procreative efficiencies and sexual pleasures of polygamy, novelist Henry Neville (1620–1694) described a polygamous utopia on an isolated *Isle of Pines* in the south Pacific which featured "open sex as lust gave us liberty" between a man and four women marooned there; they and their children proved free and fecund enough to yield an imaginary island population of some 10,000 to 12,000 when discovered a few decades later.[13] A radical group of self-styled "Ranters" sought to make this sexual utopia a reality in mid-seventeenth-century England. They called for the abolition of monogamous marriage, considering it "the fruit of the curse" for "one man to be tied to one woman, or one woman tied to one man."[14] "A man should not have sex with but one woman apart from another, but all in one, and one in all.... [T]he bed is large enough to hold them all."[15] "Give up thy stinking family duties, and the Gospel ordinances as thou callest them," wrote leading Ranter, Abiezer Coppe (1619–1672); "for under them all there lies snapping, snarling, biting."[16]

These libertine views of sexuality, procreation, and marriage were further encouraged during the Restoration by the ribald life of King Charles II, the Stuart king purportedly tasked after 1660 with restoring traditional English law, religion, and morality.[17] Charles evidently took the "restoration" to mean that he should go all the way back to King Henry VIII and emulate his abusive and promiscuous sexual habits, too. Saddled with another queen named Catherine who produced him no heir, Charles and his retinue began to cast about for alternative procreative means. Without a legitimate heir, Charles's younger brother, James, stood to succeed him. But James was a Catholic, whom few in Protestant England were eager to have on the throne; England was still smarting, even a century later, from their last Catholic monarch, "bloody Queen Mary." Some advisors pressed Charles to get a divorce or annulment. Others suggested they spirit Queen Catherine away to a colony or nunnery, so that Charles could declare himself deserted and thus entitled to remarry under the 1604 Polygamy Act. None of this came to pass. Charles did keep himself dutifully busy with sundry mistresses who rotated at a rather brisk

---

[13] Henry Neville, *The Isle of Pines* (London: T. Cadell, 1668), 12. See discussion of this and other utopian literature favoring polygamy in Owen Aldridge, "Polygamy in Early Fiction: Henry Neville and Denis Veiras," *Modern Language Association* 65 (1950): 464–472; see also Cairncross, *After Polygamy*, 103–138 on French utopian literature on polygamy, often intermixed with the diaries of travelers to the Ottoman Empire, Africa, and south Asia.

[14] John Holland, *The Smoke of the Bottomless Pit: A More True and Fuller Doctrine of those Men which call Themselves Ranters; or the Mad Crew* (London: John Wright, 1651), 4.

[15] *A Justification of the Mad Crew in their Waies and Principles* (London: s.n., 1650), 147.

[16] Abiezer Coppe, *A Second Fiery Flying Roule: To all the Inhabitants of the Earth, Specially the Rich Ones* (London: s.n., 1649), 12, reprinted with additional tracts in Andrew Hopton, ed., *Abiezer Coppe: Selected Writings* (London: Aporia Press, 1987). See additional quotes and discussion in Loughead, "The Perception of Polygamy in Early Modern England," 80–82.

[17] See Miller, *Milton*, 111–115, 320–324; Cairncross, *After Polygamy*, 150–152.

pace through his royal bedchamber. But these women produced only bastards who could not properly succeed him. Perhaps polygamy was the better way forward. In 1671, Charles and one of his mistresses, Louise de Kéroualle, had a "mock wedding" "performed with all the traditional solemnities."[18] From their union came a son, Charles Lennox, whom his father thought worthy of the throne. But given that he was born of either bigamy or adultery, this son, too, was a nonheritable bastard. James eventually took the throne in 1685, only to be ousted three years later in the Glorious Revolution.

Charles's colorful sex life caused a little flurry of polygamous speculation among the literati of the day, even though by then the censors were back on the job.[19] For example, in his famous poem, "Absalom and Achitopel," John Dryden (1631–1700) captured the promiscuous but fruitless life of this "merry monarch." He dubbed Charles the new "David" and Queen Catherine "Michal."

> In pious times e'r Priest-craft did begin
> Before Polygamy was made a sin;
> When man, on many, multiply'd his kind,
> E'r one to one was, cursedly, confind;
> When nature prompted, and no law deny'd
> Promiscuous use of Concubine and Bride;
> Then Israel's Monarch, after Heaven's own heart,
> His vigorous warmth did, variously, impart
> To Wives and Slaves; and wide as his Command,
> Scatter'd his Maker's image through the Land.
> Michal, of Royal Blood, the Crown did wear;
> A Soyl ungratefull to the Tiller's care:
> Not so the rest; for several Mothers bore
> To Godlike David several Sons before.
> But since like slaves his bed they did ascend
> No True Succession could their Seed attend.[20]

While Dryden and his generation might have been quietly snickering at the hapless polygamist king, a generation later, female novelist and playwright, Delarivier Manley (1663–1724), herself the victim of a fraudulent and bigamous husband, would issue a much more sardonic critique of Charles's polygamy and that of his libertine court. This would open a new line of early feminist critique of

---

[18] Miller, *Milton*, 114.

[19] On the shifting forms and effects of English censorship laws, see Donald Thomas, *A Long Time Burning: A History of Literary Censorship in England* (New York: Praeger, 1969); Frank Fowell and Frank Palmer, *Censorship in England* (New York: Barnes and Noble Digital Library, 2011).

[20] John Dryden, *Absalom and Achitopel*, lines 1–16, quoted in Miller, *Milton*, 115.

polygamy that would strengthen in the next two centuries (as we shall see in the next chapter).[21]

Such were some of the poems, punditries, and political broadsides that pressed the case for polygamy in early modern England. Some of these writings were "porno-utopian."[22] Others were born of cultural envy or worry, especially concerning Muslim polygamy. Others were born of vulgar misogyny, the raw desire of men to have more women and more sex with impunity. Others were born of pragmatism, pressing polygamy as a solution to the problems of too many single women, too many abortions and infanticides, too many fatherless children, too many unruly youth. Others were born of anti-clericalism, if not antinomianism, a rebellion against those old ("popish") laws that encroached on the people's new-found rights and liberties. These early modern arguments would recur with endless variations in succeeding centuries; some of them are still at the heart of the modern liberal and libertarian case for polygamy today. Whatever the motivation of their early modern authors, none of these tracts came to much in their day, and certainly none of them succeeded in changing the official teachings of the English church and state in favor of monogamy alone.

THE LIBERAL BIBLICAL CASE FOR POLYGAMY

A more sober and serious wave of opinion in favor of polygamy came from the pens of theologians and philosophers who could not be so easily dismissed in that early modern religious era, especially when they pressed their case for polygamy on the strength of the Bible. Erasmus, Luther, Melanchthon, and a few other early Protestant reformers, we saw, could not say that the Bible condemned polygamy outright, and their views were known in early modern England. English jurist, John Selden, had likewise made clear that the Old Testament condoned polygamy and that a millennium of rabbinic jurisprudence had supported polygamy, too, albeit with ever greater reluctance. This finding, too, was well known in elite academic and literary circles. Even more provocative was Bernard Ochino's 1563 tongue-in-cheek defense of polygamy, which first appeared in English translation in 1657.

John Milton

The fullest biblical argument for polygamy in early modern England came from the prodigious pen of English poet and philosopher John Milton (1608–1674). Milton was an avid and admiring reader of Ochino's work on polygamy; he may have been its translator, too.[23] Milton had already shocked the English world with

---

[21] See discussion in Chapter 9, pp. 369–372 and in Bernadette Andrea, *Women and Islam in Early Modern English Literature* (Cambridge: Cambridge University Press, 2000), 85–117.

[22] Ibid., 109 (quoting Adam Beach).

[23] See Miller, *Milton*, 24–33, 214–219; Cairncross, *After Polygamy*, 139–150.

four lengthy tracts, published from 1643 to 1646, that defended the "Christian right" to divorce as part of a broader set of civil rights and liberties. In 500-plus pages of erudite, furious, sarcastic, and bare-fisted prose, Milton pressed his case for divorce. He made sweeping appeals to Scripture, nature, utility, justice, history, fairness, common sense, and more, and produced all manner of counter-textual and counterintuitive arguments to press his case for the natural and biblical right to divorce and remarriage. He was roundly denounced in his day, but he ultimately proved prophetic in anticipating arguments three centuries later for the right to unilateral divorce and remarriage at common law.[24]

By contrast to his furious argument for divorce, Milton's argument for polygamy was a much calmer, patient scholarly sifting of biblical evidence for and against polygamy. This he tucked into his equally calm and erudite two-volume *Investigations into Christian Doctrine*, a major defense of a literal "sola Scriptura" theology.[25] But this tract was lost on the world until it was rediscovered in 1823. Pieces of Milton's argument for polygamy set out in the tract were known and echoed in his day.[26] His notebooks, too, with their sundry scribbles and squibs on past polygamy were known. But his biblical discussion of polygamy in full never appeared until 1823. Even then, the tract was still considered deeply controversial, and it became more so as arguments for and against polygamy escalated in nineteenth-century America and England.[27]

Milton began his discussion quite conventionally. Marriage "if it was not commanded, was at any rate instituted, and consisted in the mutual delight, help and society of husband and wife, though with the husband having greater authority." It is "a very intimate relationship instituted by God for the procreation of children or of the help and solace of life."[28]

But there is nothing said here of "one man with one woman," Milton continued, now treading on more tender ground. Indeed, to read a commandment of monogamy into these biblical passages is to charge Abraham and many other men of faith with "constant fornication and adultery" and to consign all the children of Abraham and of the covenant to perpetual bastardy. Thus either polygamy is a true form of marriage, or else all children born in it are bastards and forever "barred from the

---

[24] See Witte, *The Reformation of Rights*, 248–259.
[25] The tracts is reprinted as *Two Books of Investigations into Christian Doctrine Drawn from the Sacred Scriptures Alone* (ca. 1658–ca. 1660), reprinted in Don M. Wolfe, gen. ed., *Complete Prose Works of John Milton*, 7 vols. (New Haven, CT: Yale University Press, 1953–1980), 6:117–807 [hereafter CPW].
[26] See Miller, *Milton*, 121–135, 327–330. For example, almost all the biblical arguments in the 1658 pamphlet Anonymous, *Remedy for Uncleanness* match Milton's almost exactly.
[27] See discussion in Chapter 10, pp. 416–438. For one attack on Milton's newly published tract, see S.E. Dwight, *The Hebrew Wife: or the Law of Marriage Examined in Relation to the Lawfulness of Polygamy and ... Incest* (New York: Leavitt, Lord & Co., 1836).
[28] CPW 6:355.

assembly of the Lord," as Deuteronomy 23:2 commands. This latter proposition is "absolutely absurd and even downright blasphemous." So, the question, said Milton, is whether the Bible regards marriage to be monogamy alone, or includes polygamy too. After sifting through the texts, Milton concluded that both monogamy and polygamy were permissible by the Bible, even if monogamy was favored.[29]

Milton lined up the biblical passages commonly adduced to support monogamy alone, and he knocked them down one-by-one. Echoing Ochino's arguments, he made short work of the "two in one flesh"/ "cleave unto his wife" passages in Genesis 2:24 and Matthew 19:5. These passages are descriptions not prescriptions. The original texts say *"they* shall be one flesh," not *"the two* shall become one flesh." And a man can certainly become "one flesh" with more than one woman at a time – as Paul says in 1 Corinthians 6:16 in his warning about becoming "one flesh" with a prostitute.[30]

The language "cleave unto his wife" – not "wives" – is no implied command for monogamy, Milton continued. A man can (and should) love more than one neighbor at a time even though the command says: "love thy neighbor" in the singular. A man can (and should not) covet all of his neighbor's maidservants, even though the Commandment speaks only of one "maidservant." In using the singular, the Bible is not implying that a man can have only one neighbor, or his neighbor only one maidservant. Likewise, the "cleave unto his wife" passage is not saying that a man can have only one wife. The Bible uses "the singular not in a numerical sense, but as designating the species of the thing intended." Thus the Bible means that a man must cleave unto every woman who is his wife. That reading becomes even more obvious when you consider a father's relationship with each of his sons, Milton said: "his paternal relationship towards them all will be various, but towards each one it will be single and complete in itself." So here, "if anyone has several wives, his relationship toward each one will be no less complete, and the husbands will be *one flesh* with each one of them, than if he had only one wife." "It follows, then, that polygamy is neither forbidden nor opposed by this so-called commandment."[31]

Malachi 2, a favorite of Calvinist and Anglo-Puritan monogamists, does not help much either, Milton continued. Yes, Malachi 2:14–15 calls a man to remain faithful to "the wife of thy covenant." And then, obliquely, the passage goes on: "And did not he make one? Yet he had the residue of the Spirit. And wherefore one? That he might seek a godly seed." This is hardly a clear and convincing endorsement of monogamy alone, Milton argued. "It would certainly be far too rash and dangerous," on the authority of such an "obscure passage," to command monogamy to be an

[29] Ibid., 6:355–356.
[30] Ibid., 6:356–358.
[31] Ibid., 6:357–358.

absolute "article of faith." Moreover, this is just one of many passages in a long "allegorical fiction" that several of the Old Testament prophets used to describe God's relationship with his fictitious bride, Israel. But, even this running allegory includes polygamy, Milton pointed out. For Ezekiel 23 says that "God has taken two wives, Aholah and Aholibah. He would certainly not have spoken about himself like this at such great length, not even in a parable, nor adopted this character or likeness at all, if the thing itself had been intrinsically dishonorable or base." Given that textual reality, why is Malachi 2's oblique reference to monogamy taken as normative for our day, while Ezekiel 23's open talk of divine polygamy is ignored?[32]

Matthew 5:32 is not dispositive of the question of polygamy either, Milton continued. There Jesus says: "That whosoever shall put away his wife, saving for the cause of fornication, causeth her to commit adultery: and whosoever shall marry her that is divorced committeth adultery." Catholic and Protestant writers alike read this passage to say that because it is adultery to reject a first wife and marry a second it is even more obviously adultery to marry a second wife while retaining the first. But this does not necessarily follow, Milton argued. The man "who rejects his first wife and marries another, is not said to commit adultery because he marries another, but because when he married the second wife he did not keep the first though he ought to have behaved like a dutiful husband to her as well." A man who takes a second wife has to perform his duties to both of them. The Bible says as much in Exodus 21:10: "If he take him another wife; her [the first wife's] food, her raiment, and her duty of marriage, shall he not diminish."[33]

There is no dispositive word for monogamy in 1 Corinthians 7 either, Milton continued. Here Paul provides that "every man [shall] have his own wife" and that "the husband hath not power of his own body, but the wife." But there is no monopoly implied in this: a man can have multiple wives, and they can share power over his body. This is especially so because there are times of menstruation, pregnancy, and childbirth when some wives cannot exercise their power over his body, and the man in turn has no power over their bodies at these times. The only New Testament men who must each be "the husband of one wife" are bishops and deacons, Milton observed, so "they could carry out the ecclesiastical duties which they had undertaken more diligently."[34]

The upshot of all these texts, Milton concluded, is that while the Bible favors monogamy, it also "clearly admit[s] polygamy." This can be seen not only in the passages already adduced, but in many others as well, Milton argued. Take Leviticus 18:18, which provides: "Neither shalt thou take a wife to her sister, to vex her, to

---

[32] Ibid., 6:360–361, 365.
[33] Ibid., 6:361–362.
[34] Ibid., 6:362.

uncover her nakedness, beside the other in her life time." The implication of this passage, said Milton, is that while a man may not marry his wife's sister during his wife's lifetime, he may take an unrelated woman as a second wife, while his first wife is still alive. Sisters will fight for the same husband, as was the case with Jacob, Rachel, and Leah; hence the precaution to wait to marry the second sister until the first sister is dead. But there is no such restraint in marrying an unrelated second wife.[35]

Or take Deuteronomy 17:17, which orders that "a king shall not multiply wives for himself, lest his heart turn away; nor shall he greatly multiply for himself silver and gold." The passage does not prohibit polygamy outright, but only excessive wife-taking that turns a man's heart away – presumably away from God and his existing wives. Similarly, the passage does not prohibit saving money, but only excessive wealth accumulation that again turns a man's heart away. Remember, too, said Milton, these limits are imposed only on kings with massive responsibilities of office. Nothing is said about wife or wealth accumulation by all other men.[36] (Milton could have added here another favorite text, Deuteronomy 21:15–17, which makes provision for the inheritance of this accumulated wealth: "if a man has two wives, the one liked, the other disliked," he must support the children of both wives. This is an echo and continuation of Exodus 21:10, which says the man must support both wives, too.)

These are not dead legal letters in the Bible, Milton continued. The Old Testament reports story after story of polygamy among the ancient Israelites, who lived under this Mosaic law. The biblical chroniclers reported that good and righteous biblical leaders like Solomon, Joash, Jehoida, Asa, Gideon, Elkanah, Rehoboam, Caleb, Manasseh, the sons of Issachar, and others took multiple wives. The biblical prophets celebrated that the royal house of Israel housed "threescore queens and fourscore concubines, and virgins without number" (Song of Songs 6:8). These "abundant examples of men whose holiness renders them fit patterns for imitation" all underscore that "polygamy is allowed by the law of God," Milton wrote. "Who could believe that so many of the best men sinned throughout so many ages, either through ignorance or because their hearts were hardened? Who could believe that God would have tolerated such a thing in his people? Let that rule so common among theologians hold good here if anywhere: The practice of the saints interprets the commandments."[37]

The one biblical polygamist who was singled out for his sin was King David, Milton acknowledged. Scholars like Theodore Beza have read this story as a general

---

warning about the sins and dangers of polygamy. But, Milton pointed out, these pro-monogamists conveniently ignore what God in fact said to David through his prophet Nathan in 2 Samuel 12:8: "And *I gave thee* thy master's house, and *thy master's wives* into thy bosom, and gave thee the house of Israel and of Judah; and if that had been too little, I would moreover have given unto thee" more. Here, God himself says he gave David his multiple wives, and God would have given more if he had properly asked. David's polygamy was not the problem, Milton argued. The problem was that he took another wife, Bathsheba, on his own, and by means of adultery and murder no less. He broke Deuteronomy 17:17's command that a king must not multiple so many wives that his heart turns away from God.[38]

Gilbert Burnet

Building on Ochino but going beyond him, Milton put into English play most of the important and contested biblical texts about polygamy. These texts would come in for endless discussion thereafter. A few other biblical passages came into the discussion, too. For example, in 1670, future Anglican Bishop, Gilbert Burnet (1643–1715) in his youthful support of King Charles II's bigamy, argued as follows: "Marriage is a contract founded by the laws of nature, its end being the propagation of mankind." God may have formed marriage in Paradise as "the perfectest coalition of friendship and interest" of one man and one woman. But we are now living after the fall into sin, which has brought "frigidity, barrenness, unchastity, crossness of humors," and much more within the marital home and bed. One solution to this often grim domestic reality is divorce, which Moses, Jesus, Paul, and other ancient peoples allowed. Another solution, and one perhaps fairer to women and children, is polygamy which is "the natural right of mankind" and was exercised happily and innocently by a number of biblical patriarchs for the sake of producing children. Sometimes, the Bible even made polygamy a religious duty, as in the Mosaic law of "levirate marriage." In Deuteronomy 25, Moses orders a brother (a *levir*) to marry his dead brother's wife in order that she may have the children needed to continue the family line. The Bible imposes this duty on the brother, Burnet argued following the Talmud, without regard for whether he is already married, and gives the widow the right to accuse and rebuke him publicly if he fails in his duty. The New Testament says nothing against any of these Old Testament practices and precepts of polygamy. "What God made necessary in some cases, to any degree, can in no case be sinful in itself, since God is holy in all his ways: And thus far it appears that polygamy is not contrary to the law and nature of marriage."[39]

---

[38] Ibid., 6:363–364.
[39] Gilbert Burnet, *Two Dissertations Written by the Late Bishop Burnet, viz., I. A Defence of Polygamy. Proving That It Is Not Contrary to the Law and Nature of Marriage; and That an Express Prohibition*

Although Scripture and nature allow and sometimes even require one man to have multiple wives, Burnet went on, they do not allow one woman to have multiple husbands. Such polyandry may have been common among the "Amazons who made use of men only as stallions," or the ancient Britons who allegedly "had no less than 10 or 12 husbands apiece." But this domestic arrangement, Burnet argued (echoing Ochino and Aquinas before him), was "against the law of nature, according to which the male as the most perfect is the head and master of the woman." Moreover, polyandry is a far less efficient form of reproduction than polygamy, because one husband can impregnate many wives at once, but one wife can have only one pregnancy at a time, no matter how many husbands she has. Moreover, the wife's natural passion and her many husbands' repeated demands for sex will endanger her pregnancy. Some wives might even be barren, making all the marital sex entirely fruitless. Polyandry would further lead to bitter rivalry among the husbands within the household. It would lead to the "confusion of several seeds" within the woman, jeopardizing her health and that of her children – a common biological assumption in that day. And with so many husbands having sex with the same wife, "it would be impossible for a father to know his own child." Without paternal certainty, none of the husbands or fathers "would take care of the children" properly within the home, rendering them public wards without proper nurture, education, and role models. From that the whole commonwealth would suffer.[40]

Every generation or two thereafter, an adventuresome preacher or pamphleteer would voice similar biblical arguments for polygamy – and very occasionally against polyandry.[41] The volume of this literature should not be exaggerated. Polygamy was hardly "a doctrine daily defended in common conversation and often in print," as one exuberant writer put it in 1724, in an evident effort to draw attention to his

---

of It Is No Where to Be Found in Scripture, 3rd ed. (London: E. Curll, 1731 [1670], 7–8. This argument for both polygamy and concubinage was elaborated by another Anglican divine, John Butler, *The True State of the Case of John Butler ... of a Lawful Concubinage in a Case of Necessity* (London: s.n., 1697). See also Thomas Graham, *A Marriage Sermon Called a Wife Mistaken* (London: s.n., 1710) (listing Old Testament provisions and precedents for polygamy).

[40] See Burnet, *Two Dissertations*, 9–16. See comparable arguments in Thomas Salmon, *A Critical Essay Concerning Marriage* (London: Charles Rivington, 1724), 81–84.

[41] For a later English example, see James Edward Hamilton, *A Short Treatise on Polygamy, or, The Marrying and Cohabiting with More Than One Woman at the Same Time, Proved from Scripture, to be Agreeable to the Will of God* (Dublin: n.p., 1786). For a German example, see Miller, *Milton*, 162–179, on the colloquy occasioned by Samuel Friedrich Willenberg's disputation that polygamy was not against biblical law, divine law, the natural law, or the law of nations and thus should be allowed in individual cases of conversion from Islam or native religion that practiced polygamy, when a wife is frigid, diseased, or incapacitated, or a wife is barren and the husband or the dynasty he represents is in pressing need for an heir.

long but plain book on the topic.[42] Indeed, each brave soul who did make a serious argument for polygamy in this period was soon drenched by a storm of criticism.

THEOLOGICAL UTILITARIAN ARGUMENTS FOR POLYGAMY

These storms of criticism became more violent when a few writers combined their liberal biblical exegesis with liberal public policy arguments that favored polygamy. This "theological utilitarianism," we will see in the next chapter, was generally directed to more conservative ends, with the "secular utilitarianism" of a Jeremy Bentham or John Stuart Mill often serving as the liberal answer. But in the seventeenth and eighteenth centuries, a few liberal theologians pressed the argument that the Bible allowed for polygamy for a number of sound policy reasons that were so good that they should convince the modern state to allow polygamy, too.

Johann Leyser

An early exponent of this method was the German writer Johann Leyser (1631- ca. 1685). Once a promising academic, Leyser lost credibility when he began to write idiosyncratically in defense of polygamy. His theological utilitarian arguments were not so much the problem. Instead, his writings were pulsing with such venomous hatred for women and with so many wild-eyed arguments and assertions drawn from every conceivable scrap of writing no matter how bizarre in assertion and doubtful in provenance that he quickly became a scholarly and social pariah. His earlier writings were more conventional, especially his "100 arguments" in favor of polygamy, framed as a *Political Discourse Between Polygamy and Monogamy About Polygamy or Plural Wives* (1676).[43] Some of these arguments at least were akin to the political broadside arguments we just read, and to the biblical arguments for polygamy in Milton, Ochino, and others. But Leyser soon outdid himself with his hefty magnum opus, *Polygamy Triumphant* (1682), nearly 600 pages of prolix prose and strangulating footnotes.[44] Historian Leo Miller has taken on the immense task of analyzing this densely written Latin tract and its many sources and reported generously on what his research has found.[45]

The most relevant part of this work for our purposes here is Leyser's relentless claim that biblical-style polygamy was good for men, women, and children, and for

---

[42] Patrick Delaney, pseud. Phileleutherus Dubliniensis, *Reflections Upon Polygamy and the Encouragement Given to that Practice in the Old Testament* (London: J. Roberts, 1734), 1.

[43] J[ohann] L[eyser], *Politischer Discursus zwischen Polygamo und Monogamo von der Polygamia oder Vielweiberey* (Freiburg: Apud Henricum Cunrath, 1676).

[44] Johann Leyser, pseud. Theophilo Aletheo, *Polygamia Triumphatrix* (Lund: n.p., 1682).

[45] Miller, *Milton*, 60–95, 250–308. See also Cairncross, *After Polygamy*, 81–98.

church, state, and society alike. He called "on all earthly powers and magistrates highest and lowest to become the patrons of polygamy," writes Miller, marshaling "his case methodologically and in encyclopedic style. With an earnestness positively pathetic he calculates the benefits that would accrue from plural marriage." Let us just take one passage from Leyser to illustrate all the private and public goods that would purportedly come from polygamy in our day:

> It will help expand the family fortune. The wives will vie with each other in bringing up the husband's children and thereby avoid the temptation to be unfaithful. It helps young men, for they can tranquilly marry girls whom they have seduced while drunk. Wives will have their arrogance and ill-temper put down, as well as their other vices, and their virtues, in mind and in body will increase. Girls will have everything to gain, because it will be easier to marry, and their health and reputation will no longer run any risk from their enforced singleness. It will help the traders who fare to distant lands and are obliged to keep their liaisons secret to the great detriment of the state and their conscience. Poor sailors will be able to marry another wife, possibly a rich one. The old will renew their youth, like the eagle, at the contact of a youthful Abigail [King David's beautiful polygamous wife]. Children, whose mother is absent or ill, will be reared by the other women of the household, a far better arrangement than the use of servants. And parents will have an easier time bringing up their children and finding husbands for their daughters. Farmers will have many more trusty hands to help them till their fields, and kings and nobles will, like Solomon, extend their power and wealth by fruitful alliances. Pastors will benefit, since there will be more baptisms and marriages. The Church will gain with the decline in infanticide, whoremongering and uxoricide. And the Gentiles and Turks will flock to the true faith once polygamy is no longer forbidden.[46]

Gottfried Leibniz (1646–1716), a leading German scientist and philosopher of the day, picked up on Leyser's very last point about the utility of polygamy for missionaries. "[I]t is a great mistake to imagine that polygamy is absolutely against the divine law or natural law; and if not for this dream the Christians would have had much greater progress in the Indies where they will never succeed except by force or by permitting polygamy, which has been established there for several thousand years; I remain in agreement that monogamy is definitively better and more conformable to good order, but what is the best is not always absolutely necessary." And again with respect to the church's refusal to allow Chinese converts to Christianity to continue polygamy, Leibniz wrote: "I do not see why so much of a racket is made over it, and I am convinced that the Pope and the Church generally can grant plural

---

[46] Quoted by Cairncross, *After Polygamy*, 89. See also Miller, *Milton*, 73–74. I have not been able to find this passage in Leyser's writings to check the translation.

marriages and genuine divorces 'because of the hardness of their heart' as in the Old Testament."[47]

Leyser was "polygamy's prophet," Miller says, and, Leibniz notwithstanding, he was a prophet without much honor anywhere.[48] He traveled throughout much of Western Europe hawking his pamphlets and books and preaching on street corners to any who would listen about the glories of polygamy. Few were convinced, and every publisher rejected his *Polygamy Triumphant*, leaving him to publish a few copies on his own. His writings did temporarily startle the establishment, and at least eight scholars in his day took the time to debunk his arguments about the biblical validity and modern utility of polygamy, publishing such tracts as *Monogamy Victorious*[49] and *Monogamy Triumphant*.[50] But Leyser was soon dismissed and forgotten as a heretical eccentric.

Martin Madan

A more sophisticated exemplar of theological utilitarianism was Martin Madan (1726–1790), a one-time Oxford playboy who later trained in law and theology. He became an Anglican cleric with Methodist sympathies and for a time a hospital chaplain, too. In 1780, Madan pressed his case for polygamy in a substantial two-volume tract entitled *Thelyphthora, Or a Treatise on Female Ruin*.[51] The "female ruin" that concerned him was the rampant sexual exploitation of women in his day through seduction, fornication, adultery, prostitution, concubinage, rape, and various other deviant means by which "the hungry males of our species" use women to their peril and often to the peril of their unwanted children, too, who are aborted, smothered, or abandoned. Madan had seen the fallout of all this first hand as a hospital chaplain in London. There he came upon too many ravaged maidens now saddled with unwanted children, botched self-abortions, or infanticide charges. Far too many of these maidens, said Madan, were abandoned by their families, parishes,

---

47 Gottfried Wilhelm Leibnitz, Letters of September 2/12, 1691 and November 13/23, 1691 to Ernst, Landgrave of Hesse-Rheinfels and Letter of quoted in Miller, *Milton*, 108–109.

48 Miller, *Milton*, 60. One ally was Lorenz Beger, *Kurze doch unpartheyisch und gewissenhaffte Betrachtung dess in dem Natur- und Göttlichen Recht gegründeten heiligen Eh[e]standes* (Heidelberg, n.p. 1679). I have not been able to lay hold of this tract, and depend on the brief description of Beger's comparable argument for polygamy for reasons of utility and necessity in Cairncross, *After Polygamy*, 95–96.

49 Johannes Brussman, *Monogamia Victrix: a Criminationibus vindicata quibusvis* (Frankfurt am Main: n.p., 1679).

50 Elias Schneegaas, pseud. Antonius de Mara, *Monogamia Triumphans* (Brunswick: n.p., 1696). For other tracts, see Miller, *Milton*, 151–178 with detailed citations in ibid., 250–308.

51 Martin Madan, *Thelyphthora; or, a Treatise on Female Ruin, in its Causes, Effects, Consequences, Prevent, and Remedy Considered on the Basis of the Divine Law*, 2 vols. (London; L. Dodsley, 1781), esp. 1:74–319 ("on polygamy").

and society alike, and forced to make do on their own. For Madan, the cure-all for all this sexual pathos and "female ruin" was a well-regulated and transparent institution of monogamy and polygamy, modeled in part on ancient biblical laws. He pressed this case in a massive work of 800 pages, with follow up letters and pamphlets.

Madan rested much of his case on the Bible. He largely repeated the arguments from Ochino, Milton, Burnet, and others whom have we sampled, although now with a much closer sifting of the original Hebrew and Greek texts, and with a steady series of jabs and jousts with theologians past and present who had read the Bible to condemn polygamy. Madan also repeated John Selden's analysis of early rabbinic opinion in favor of polygamy. He included some long, quite amateurish tours of legal and religious history, and made a few weak stabs at comparative ethnography. And he distracted himself with long digressions on transubstantiation doctrine, the trinity, ecclesiology, and the like that bore rather little on his case, save as further instances of what he considered to be bad biblical exegesis. Madan was in dire need of a good editor.

One interesting new argument that did come tumbling out of all these pages was that polygamy had become even more necessary after Jesus restricted the right to divorce. In Old Testament times, divorce and polygamy existed side by side as alternatives to monogamy. In Matthew 19, Jesus rebuked the rabbis for extending the husband's unilateral right to divorce to the point of making "marriage little better than a pretense for gratifying their lusts, divorcing one in order to take another, and thus profaning the holy ordinance of the Lord." An indulgent God had permitted the Jews this "monstrous practice" because of the "hardness of their hearts" and for fear that those ancient men would otherwise harm or kill their unwanted wives and children. Jesus was now calling the faithful back to a more limited practice of divorce and remarriage. But all along, Madan noted, in both the Old Testament world and the New, the faithful men of God practiced polygamy, too, "with no trace of sorrow, remorse, or repentance," and with no hint of divine censure. When he tightened the laws of divorce, Jesus also increased the need for polygamy as a remedy for those men whose wives would not or could not have sex, bear children, or carry their share of household duties. The less divorce there could be, the more polygamy there had to be, said Madan. Else men would be even more inclined to harm or kill their unwanted wives or stage adulteries to drive them away. Surely that was not Jesus's intent.[52]

Madan also added a couple of new observations about Old Testament polygamy. He zeroed in on the story of good King Joash, who had restored the law of the Lord in ancient Israel. The Bible reports: "Joash did what was right in the eyes of the Lord all the days of Jehoida the priest. Jehoida got for him two wives, and he had sons

---

[52] Ibid., 1:75–88, 185–188; 2:4–34.

and daughters."[53] Milton had already shown how King David got his multiple wives directly from God.[54] Madan added that Joash got his two wives from God, too, now through his high priest, and he was rewarded with children. Some scholars, said Madan, pretend that this was really about Joash getting two wives in succession, after the death or divorce of the first wife. But a plain reading of the Hebrew text is that God gave him two fertile wives at once, either as a reward for or as an example of doing what was "right in the eyes of the Lord."[55]

A plain reading of Deuteronomy 21:15–17 yields the same endorsement of polygamy, said Madan. "If a man has two wives," the text reads, he has testamentary obligations to the children of both wives. John Calvin and others had insisted that this text had to be about two wives in a row, because bastards cannot inherit or even enter into the temple, and biblical children of polygamy starting with Ishmael are bastards. Not so, said Madan. The Hebrew text again is clearly talking about a man having two wives at the same time, and requiring a man to provide not only for both his wives (per Exodus 21:10) but also for the children of both wives upon his death. Moreover, said Madan, plenty of biblical children of polygamy did inherit, and that is because they were not viewed as bastards. Think of the inheritance of all the sons of Jacob, Rachel, and Leah (reported in Genesis 49). Or think of Samuel, the son of Elkanah the polygamist. Samuel not only inherited from his father but in fact became a priest serving in the very temple from which bastards are explicitly banned by the Mosaic law.[56] Bastards do not inherit; legitimate children do. Children of polygamy are legitimate and thus can inherit. Ishmael was disinherited not because he was a child of polygamy, but because he was a bastard, the child of Abraham's maidservant, Hagar, and "a wild ass of a man" at that, the Bible says.[57]

Madan also supplemented Milton's critique of the traditional argument that a Christian marriage was monogamous because it was modeled on both the exclusive covenant of Yahweh and his elect and the mysterious union of Christ and the church. Much like Milton, he argued that the Old Testament covenant metaphor was hardly a template for monogamy, because God himself is said to have married two wives in Ezekiel 23. Moreover, God's covenant love for his chosen people as a whole is matched by God's covenant love for each individual Israelite who remained faithful to the covenant and the law of God.[58] The same is true with the New Testament analogy of Christ's relationship with his church, Madan added. Yes, Christ is mysteriously united with the one holy, catholic, and apostolic church. But

---

[53] 2 Chronicles 24:2–3.
[54] 2 Samuel 12:8.
[55] Madan, *Thelyphthora*, 1:91–96, 115–116.
[56] 1 Samuel 1–2; Deuteronomy 23:2.
[57] Madan, *Thelyphthora*, 1:105–115, 262–264.
[58] Ibid.

already in New Testament days there were many different kinds of churches, and many more individual believers within them, each with a mysterious relationship with Christ. There are many more such churches today, with varieties of Protestants, Catholics, and Orthodox, each of them representing in part the one holy catholic and apostolic church. Each believer, each congregation, and each denomination has a distinct loving relationship with Christ, reflecting the mysterious union. There is no monogamy in this metaphor.[59]

Madan buried his constructive project of public policy reform near the end of his lengthy biblical arguments and exegetical jousting about polygamy. His principal concern was saving wives and children of his day from "the ruin" brought on by rampant extramarital sex – whether consensual, collusive, or coerced.[60] His other concern was the danger of chronic depopulation brought on by contraception, abortion, infanticide, sterility, venereal disease, and more that often accompany extramarital sex.[61] Madan's remedy was much more marriage – whether monogamous or polygamous. He rooted his concern and his remedy in the Mosaic law requirement that "*every man* marry the virgin he lies with."[62] This Mosaic law, he said, was designed "for the preservation of the female from ruin and prostitution." A deflowered single woman in that ancient day, even a rape victim, was often prostituted, stoned, or sold into slavery. To put a stop to this abuse, the Mosaic law required every man to marry each single woman he ravaged, and to see to the support and inheritance of his new wife and of any children born of their sexual intercourse. The despoiled woman's father might and may object, the Bible makes clear, but then the man would still have to pay a dowry as a price for his violation of her and as support for her and her children thereafter. This, too, might be expedient in our day, said Madan.[63]

It did not matter whether this man was already married, Madan went on, for the Mosaic law made ample provision for polygamy. The Bible says clearly that "virgins could not be seduced and taken as appetite might prompt, and then abandoned and forsaken as licentiousness might incline." Instead, the Bible says "that monogamous and polygamous contracts were equally valid and binding, equally lawful as to the inheritableness of the issue." "Whoredom and fornication," Madan wrote, are "inimical to those bonds of human society" and "introductory of all manner of confusion and wickedness, inconsistent with the law of marriage, and the probable causes of ruin and destruction to the female sex. Therefore, as seduction and

---

[59] Ibid., 1:240–242.
[60] Ibid., 1:68–96.
[61] Ibid., 1:100–106, 2:249–266.
[62] Exodus 22:16; Deuteronomy 22:28–29.
[63] Madan, *Thelyphthora*, 1:254–266.

dereliction must, in the very nature of things, lead to these, the positive law of God forbids any man to take a virgin, and then abandon her."[64]

This right and duty of a man to marry and support every woman he ravages is "a perpetual obligation of the moral law," Madan continued.[65] And polygamy makes it all possible, even if monogamy remains the more common and even the preferred practice. Once polygamy is "divested of all the nonsense of human reasoning, [and] is set in its true scriptural light, as not sinful in itself, but, in some cases, highly expedient," then it should be clear that it is "highly criminal" for a man "to seduce and abandon to prostitution and ruin, those who have a most indefensible claim upon him for safety and support." This rule requiring a man to marry the single woman he ravages would be a most effective "check upon the licentiousness of mankind" and a deterrent to the "lust, treachery, and cruelty of mankind" who "act without control."[66]

Biblical Israel, Madan argued, provides a good model of how to regulate such destructive sex by balancing options of monogamy, polygamy, and divorce and holding men fully accountable for their extramarital sex and procreation. The polygamy of ancient Israel was "not that wild, licentious practice of it, which is now maintained at the [public] expense." Nor was it a form of polygamy that lacks "all decency" and even "humanity" toward women, as is sometimes practiced today "among the Mahometans." Ancient Israel, said Madan, made "a holy and sober use of marriage, circumscribed by holy laws and institutions," with polygamy "in all cases permitted, in some commanded. And what was the consequence to the state? A numerous issue, which contributed to its riches and strength – the demand for women in marriage increased, and few were left either to a burden or disgrace to it." "While this system was reverenced and observed, we read of no adultery, whoredom, and common prostitution of women among the daughters of Israel; no brothels, street-walking, venereal disease; no child-murder" – "either by procuring abortion, or by destroying in or after birth."[67]

"Our making polygamy [a] felony has destroyed it," Madan went on, citing modern statutes. "But in what respect are we gainers by this? Why, we have gained what Israel never saw, till they regarded the divine law as little as we do – thousands of women" reduced to "prostitution and destruction" with neither the state nor the church powerful enough to force "their seducers to do that justice, which reason, nature, and the divine law entitle them to demand," namely to marry and support their wives and children.[68]

---

[64] Ibid., 1:281–282, 288–289.
[65] Ibid., 1:282.
[66] Ibid., 1:289–291; see also ibid., 1:99–105.
[67] Ibid., 1:288–289; 2:263–264.
[68] Ibid., 2:264–265. For Madan's argument, see Oscar Sherwin, "Madan's Cure-all," *The American Journal of Economics and Sociology* 22 (2006): 427–433, 543–549.

The only real and substantial difference between the ancient Jews and the [modern day] Christians is this. The former took a plurality of women whom they maintained, protected and provided for agreeably to God's word. The latter take a plurality of women and turn them out to ruin and destruction not only against God's word but against every principle of justice and humanity. Or in other words, if the Jew took as many as he could maintain, the Christian ruins as many as he can debauch.[69]

One can easily imagine the scorn that Madan's blistering indictment of prevailing theology and public policy occasioned in his day. In nineteen books, and sundry letters and shorter pieces published over the next decade, Madan was pilloried for his bad biblical exegesis, selective proof-texting, Hebraic romanticism, sloppy social engineering, naïve economics, moral licentiousness, misguided alarmism, salacious preoccupations, and more.[70] Some critics thought Madan's massive book was just an elaborate self-indictment for his own earlier playboy life. Others thought it a self-serving brief in support of men keeping mistresses or pimping prostitutes in a veritable "Mahometan paradise." Only a man of "libertine principles and licentious inclinations could so speculate," wrote one critic. Maybe the best response to Madan would be "to oblige him to put his own doctrine into practice and marry a patriarchal number of wives. A round dozen of spouses altogether, would, I doubt not, soon make him ... wish he had thrown his manuscript into the fire."[71] All this opprobrium was predictable, although the unflappable Madan – a faithful and

---

[69] Quoted by Cairncross, *After Polygamy*, 175, citing generically Madan's *Thelyphthora*, although I could not find this nice pithy quote. It might be in some of Madan's correspondence that I do not have access to.

[70] For a full listing of Madan's critics, see Miller, *Milton*, 146–148 and a summary of their criticisms in ibid. 148–150; Cairncross, *After Polygamy*, 178–181. Of these, I have been able to review carefully Sir Richard Hill, *The Blessings of Polygamy Displayed, in an Affectionate Address to the Rev. Martin Madan; Occasioned by his late work, entitled Thelyphthora; or, A Treatise on Female Ruin* (London, J. Matthews etc. 1781); Henry Moore, *A Word to Mr. Madan or Free Thoughts on his late Celebrated Defence of Polygamy* (Bristol: W. Pine, 1781); Thomas Wills, *Remarks on Polygamy &c. in Answer to the Rev. Mr. M-d-n's Thelypthora* (London: T. Hughes and F. Walsh; R. Baldwin; and W. Otridge, 1781); Anonymous, *Martin's Hobby Houghed and Pounded: or, Letters on Thelyphthora, to a Friend, on the Subjects of Marriage and Polygamy* (London: J. Buckland 1781); John Towers, *Polygamy Unscriptural or Two Dialogues between Philalethes and Monogamus, in which the Principal Errors of the First and Second Editions of the Revd. Mr. M-d-n's Thelyphthora are Detected*, 2nd ed. (London: Alex. Hogg et al., 1781); John Smith, *Polygamy Indefensible: Two sermons ... Occasioned by a Late Publication, entitled "Thelyphthora"* (London: Alexander Hogg, 1780); Anonymous, *An Heroic Epistle to the Rev. Martin M-d-n author of a Late Treatise on Polygamy* (London: R. Faulder, 1780); Anonymous, *A Letter to the Rev. Mr. Madan, Concerning the Chapter of Polygamy, in his Late Publication, entitled Thelypthora* (London: Fielding and Walker, 1780). See also the collection of twenty-seven letters by Madan answering the criticisms of various pastors, a lawyer, and a lady in *Letters on Thelyphthora: With Occasional Prologue and Epilogue by the Author* (London: J. Dodsley, 1782). I review the liberal arguments by James Cookson and Mary Wollstonecraft against Madan in the next chapter.

[71] These last quotes are collected in Moore, *A Word to Mr. Madan*, 18–29.

pious Christian husband by all accounts and loving father of five children – stood firm in rejoining his critics.

More surprising, and more important for the ongoing Western case against polygamy, were the responses from critics who were attracted to Madan's solicitude for the rights of women and children, even if they rejected his "cure-all" of polygamy. Madan's concern for the exploitation and ruin of girls and women was admirable, these critics allowed. But Madan's remedy of mandatory marriage and polygamy suffered from the same fundamental flaw as the malady of female sexual exploitation. It instrumentalized women, making them mere pawns in vital activities like sex and marriage they did not and could not then control. The better way to protect the rights of women, the argument went, would be to give all women the rights and privileges that all men have to work and participate in society, to vote and contribute to the laws and policies that govern them, and to make their own free and unbiased determinations of what domestic arrangements worked best for them and their children. As Madan critic Henry Moore (1732–1802) put it, "When nations grow more polished and refined by the cultivation of the nobler sciences and arts; when an enlarged and liberal manner of thinking and good taste prevail, the [female] sex rise higher in estimation, proper justice is done to their real accomplishments, and they are allowed" to make their own judgments about sex, marriage, and family life.[72]

Many women in such a liberated society would likely still choose monogamous marriages, Moore and other critics said. Other women might choose the single life, with or without children, especially if they had independent wealth. But what is critical is that this choice should be the woman's, not anyone else's. Forcing a woman to accept polygamous marriage to a man who had exploited her – and who had likely exploited his other wives, too – was hardly a proper "vindication of the rights of the woman" in a civilized society.[73] Mary Wollstonecraft (1759–1797), we shall see in the next chapter, would give this emerging women's rights argument against polygamy its classic formulation, building in part on different natural rights and domestic rights arguments that the Western legal tradition already had in place.[74]

It would take longer, we shall see two chapters hence, for children's rights advocates to rise to Madan's concerns for the rights of children. After all, there was something basically sound and sensible to the modern mind in forcing a man to take care of the children whom he fathered. The issue was whether polygamy was the best setting to give that paternal support. A stable polygamous home, providing children with a

[72] Ibid., 41–42.
[73] See Mary Wollstonecraft, A *Vindication of the Rights of Woman* [1791], repr. ed. (Oxford: Oxford University Press, 2008), discussed in detail in Chapter 9.
[74] See Eileen Hunt Botting, *Wollstonecraft, Mill and Women's Human Rights* (New Haven, CT: Yale University Press, 2016).

daily relationship with both their mother and father, looked better than some of the alternatives in that early modern day, at least in theory. Until the later nineteenth century, the common law did not recognize the law of adoption or many forms of legitimation of bastard children. It did not have universal free schooling or regular and stable government programs of social welfare for children, although the church wardens provided some support. The choices facing an unwanted bastard child and the child's mother were thus often times rather grim. Many were put out to nurse or lease, dumped into orphanages or apprentice programs, or consigned to menial labor or even indentured servitude. Civil law lands did offer adoption and legitimation, and Catholic lands did open their cloisters to abandoned children, but these still remained hard options to pursue en masse.[75] It was only when modern writers began to compare the experiences and performances of children in monogamous versus polygamous households, that children's rights advocates, at least in the West, moved decidedly in favor of monogamy.

SUMMARY AND CONCLUSIONS

Like the Protestant Reformation of the sixteenth century, the revolutions and wars of the seventeenth and eighteenth centuries periodically put polygamy back onto the table for discussion. Unlike the Reformation era, there were now no Münster-like polygamous communes or theological heavyweights pushing the case for polygamy. A few royals and aristocrats in England and on the Continent still experimented a bit with polygamy. A number of lesser writers issued political broadsides in favor of polygamy or even utopian communes of open sex and no marriage. But their efforts moved neither church nor state in their day, and they gave the Restoration censors after 1660 plenty of copy to slash and burn, and gave the prosecutors a few sensational cases to press in court.

A bit more serious for the tradition were the writings of John Milton, Gilbert Burnet, Johann Leyser, Martin Madan, and others who argued that the Bible quite clearly allowed for polygamy alongside monogamy. Their views not only reopened debate about the biblical and theological case for monogamy, challenging anew Catholic and Protestant conventions; they also presented strong new utilitarian arguments for polygamy as a cure-all for the sexual exploitation of women who were impregnated by "the hungry males of our species" and then left to fend for themselves and their children. A mandatory system of polygamy in such cases of exploitation, the argument went, would both deter sexual intercourse outside of marriage and hold men accountable for the extramarital children they did conceive. Polygamy

---

[75] See John Witte, Jr., *The Sins of the Fathers: The Law and Theology of Illegitimacy Reconsidered* (Cambridge: Cambridge University Press, 2009), 107–130.

was, after all, the system that God had ordained in the Mosaic law to ensure that women and children were cared for, and this should still be a useful option for a modern Christian society that purported to rest its ultimate beliefs and policies on the Bible. It was certainly a better system than the current practice of abortion, infanticide, and bastardy. These writings on the biblical and utilitarian values of polygamy, though provocative, were not taken seriously by the establishment, and they yielded little legal or social change in their day. Yet they helped set the stage for the Enlightenment refutations of polygamy, which we examine in the next chapter.

9

The Liberal Enlightenment Case Against Polygamy

FIGURE 19. "Brothel," from Jose Gutierrez Solana.
Album of the Art Resource, New York.

FIGURE 20. "Prisoners for the Harem," from Dionisio Baixeras-Verdaguer.
Used by permission of the Private Collection Look and Learn / Bridgeman Images.

From the eighteenth century forward, Western Protestants and Catholics on both sides of the Atlantic continued to debate the biblical cases for and against polygamy, using the increasingly refined tools of biblical form criticism, biblical archeology, and more. Western Christian missionaries to Africa, Asia, the Middle East, and beyond continued to press their church leaders at home to allow polygamy among new Christian converts, and were usually met with the traditional "Heavens, no!" Christian travelers, ethnographers, and anthropologists continued to uncover and analyze exotic new varieties of polygamy in dark rainforests, distant islands, and windy tundras, and some used these observations to bolster the traditional argument that monogamy was the mark of advanced Christian civilizations, polygamy the badge of primitive barbarism. These internal theological reflections about polygamy have continued to be important for Western Christian self-identity, marital theology, and church discipline to this day. And an important new chapter in these discussions has now opened with the rapid globalization of Christianity, especially in the Global South where polygamy is more common.

But after the eighteenth century, the intense internal theological discussions about polygamy became less and less important for the ongoing Western *legal* case against polygamy. Part of the reason is that straight biblical arguments for and against polygamy did not produce a clear winner. Both sides had their proof texts. It took a larger and longer narrative to make the theological case against polygamy, and few jurists and judges would now sit still long enough to hear it, at least when they were on their legal jobs. For Christianity was being systematically disestablished in most modern Western legal and political systems. "Disestablishment of religion" meant that Christianity was no longer the compulsory or even the privileged religion of the nation, and Christianity could no longer count on the state to give it preferential support or to do its legal bidding.[1] Comparable forms of religious "disestablishment" were occurring in philosophy, science, and epistemology, whose exponents now sought truth and guidance in other sources besides the Bible and in other methods besides theology.[2] Even a decisive biblical or theological case against polygamy by itself was no longer reason enough for the state to prohibit it. The case against polygamy now needed to be pressed on philosophical, scientific, and other nonreligious grounds as well in order to pass legal and cultural muster.

In an important sense, making the nonreligious case against polygamy was nothing new for the Western tradition. Already the ancient Greeks and Romans, long before the birth of Christianity, had prohibited polygamy for reasons of nature, friendship, domestic efficiency, political expediency, and more.[3] These nonreligious arguments had always remained at the foundation of the ongoing Western case against polygamy. Medieval Catholic and early modern Protestant writers, we saw, built elaborate natural law, natural rights, and natural justice arguments against polygamy on this nonreligious foundation, and then built more elaborate sacramental and covenantal frameworks for monogamy on top of that.[4] And all along – from the earliest church fathers' observations about Old Testament polygamy to the latest traveler diaries about new world polygamy – Western writers had observed that polygamy often did not work well; it was too often the cause or consequence of other harms and crimes, particularly to women and to children, but also to moral, social, and political order and organization.

---

[1] On the meaning and evolution of the concept of "disestablishment of religion," see T. Jeremy Gunn and John Witte, Jr., eds., *No Establishment of Religion: America's Original Contribution to Religious Liberty* (Oxford: Oxford University Press, 2012).

[2] See Ernst Cassirer, *The Philosophy of the Enlightenment*, trans. Fritz C.A. Koelln and James P. Pettegrove, repr. ed. (Princeton, NJ: Princeton University Press, 2009).

[3] See discussion in Chapter 3, pp. 104–113.

[4] See discussions in Chapters 4, 6, and 8.

The new question forced by the gradual disestablishment of religion was whether the Western legal case for monogamy over polygamy was strong enough even without its theological overlay. If stripped of the heavy biblical, sacramental, and covenantal logics of monogamy, would the remaining non-theological arguments against polygamy still be cogent? Were those non-theological arguments now so closely intertwined with theological arguments that they could no longer be teased out separately or imagined on their own? Were those theological arguments so relentlessly religious that they could no longer be reconstructed into more generic and philosophical forms? That was the new challenge as the Western tradition gradually moved into a post-establishment, and eventually a post-Christian phase.

This challenge was taken up by Western Enlightenment liberals both before and after the formal disestablishment of religion. The Enlightenment was no single, unified movement, but a series of diverse ideological movements, in various academic disciplines and social circles throughout Europe and North America from the seventeenth to the nineteenth centuries. It featured a new emphasis on rationalism, empiricism, individualism, contractarianism, liberalism, and more, and a growing distaste for, sometimes a violent rebuke of, traditional Christian forms and norms. While a few early Enlightenment figures – such as Hugo Grotius and Baron Montesquieu – regarded polygamy as natural even if repulsive, most Enlightenment writers did not. Indeed, for all their iconoclasm against Christianity on so many other fronts, most liberal Enlightenment writers before the twentieth century accepted many traditional norms and teachings on sex, marriage, and family life, including its teachings on monogamy and against polygamy. But, rather than adducing the Bible and Christian theology as their highest authorities, these Enlightenment writers sought to build a philosophical account of why monogamy was best – using natural, rational, utilitarian, pragmatic, and empirical arguments designed to be cogent even to those with different religious convictions.

Some of these Enlightenment writers drew increasingly sophisticated inferences from pair-bonding patterns and reproductive strategies among some animals, building on medieval insights as well as the budding sciences of biology and anthropology. Some uncovered the common forms and norms of marriage that were shared by advanced peoples around the world, building on the budding sciences of ethnography and anthropology. Some developed a practical, prudential, and commonsense logic of what worked best for husbands and wives, parents and children to exercise and enjoy their natural rights and duties in the household. Some developed women's rights and children's rights arguments that pressed the state to remove those domestic legal norms and structures like polygamy that jeopardized these fundamental rights.

Part of this Enlightenment argument about monogamy and polygamy was its own natural theological exercise – to show the existence of a common natural theology or set of teachings about the nature of marriage that Christianity shared with the many other religions and cultures. Part of it was a philosophical exercise – to prove the existence, if not the truth, of traditional marital forms and norms, much like others sought to prove on rational grounds the existence of God against the growing ranks of skeptics and atheists. Part of it was a historical exercise – to retrieve and reconstruct some of the philosophical and rational core of marriage and family life developed by classical writers before Christianity, neo-classical movements being highly fashionable in many modern Western universities and intellectual circles. And part of this was a jurisprudential exercise – to create a common law of marriage and family life that would form part of a more universal law of nations that could transcend, if not pacify, the many European nations that had been so perilously fraught with bloody religious warfare.

HUGO GROTIUS AND THE NATURAL LAW OF
SEX, MARRIAGE, AND FAMILY LIFE

In light of this last point, it is not so surprising that it was Hugo Grotius (1583–1645), the so-called father of international law, who was among the first liberals to press for a strong natural law of marriage as part of his broader theory of international law. Among legal historians, Grotius is famous for his path-breaking writings on the laws of war and peace and on the laws of prize and the sea which became so critical to the development of modern international law.[5] Among church historians, Grotius is (in)famous for defending his fellow Dutchman, Jacob Arminius, against charges of "Pelagianism," an act which won Grotius a prison sentence for heresy. What is forgotten by some legal historians is that Grotius was also an avid student of the neo-Thomist writings of the Spanish school of Salamanca and that he drew (with ample attribution) a number of his cardinal legal ideas directly from such Catholic luminaries as Francisco Vitoria (ca. 1483 – ca. 1546), who wrote in the century before him. Indeed, some historians now call Vitoria, rather than Grotius, the father of international law.[6] What is forgotten by some church historians is that Grotius was a rather distinguished theologian in his own right and not just an

---

5 Hugo Grotius, *De Jure Belli ac Pacis*, trans. Francis W. Kelsey (Oxford: Clarendon Press, 1925), with alternative translation in id., *The Rights of War and Peace*, trans. Jean Barbeyrac, ed. Richard Tuck (Indianapolis, IN: Liberty Fund, 2005). See also id., *Commentary on the Law of Prize and Booty*, trans. and ed. Martine Julia van Ittersum (Indianapolis, IN: Liberty Fund, 2006); id., *The Free Sea*, trans. Richard Hakluyt, ed. David Armitage (Indianapolis, IN: Liberty Fund, 2004).

6 James Brown Scott, *The Spanish Origins of International Law: Volume 1, Francisco de Vitoria and his Law of Nations* (Oxford: Oxford University Press, 1934). For a good sampling, see Antonio Truyol Serra, ed., *The Principles of Political and International Law in the Work of Francisco de Vitoria* (Madrid: Ediciones Cultura Hispanica, 1946).

amateur layman seduced by free-will liberals. Grotius wrote several commentaries on the New Testament, a learned tract on church-state relations and ecclesiastical law, several pamphlets of Christian devotion, and a richly textured work of Christian apologetics.[7] Drawing on diverse Catholic, Protestant, and classical sources, and using the tools of theology, jurisprudence, and natural philosophy alike, Grotius set upon a life-long quest for religious and political peace.[8]

Crafting a common legal understanding of exclusive and enduring marriage was an important part of this effort. "The union of the sexes, whereby the human species is continued, is a subject well worthy of the highest legal consideration," Grotius wrote. For, as Aristotle taught us, marriage is the "seedbed of the republic," the first natural association, and "the first school" of morality, virtue, and good citizenship. To get this institution right was essential to creating coherent national communities, which needed internal stability before they could work toward any kind of international legal harmony. Grotius also regarded marriage as a "natural right" of all men and women, echoing both Catholic and Protestant teachings. Even slaves and captives should be granted this right to marry, Grotius insisted contrary to civil law precedents, given that marriage is "the most natural association" known to humankind. He regarded celibacy as an option for those few with unique abilities or disabilities, but thought that celibacy was "repugnant to the nature of most men" and women and that its mandatory imposition on the clergy was a source of "grave sin."[9]

Both in his legal and in his theological writings, Grotius showed full command of and respect for biblical norms and conventional Christian teachings on monogamous marriage. He adverted repeatedly to the axial biblical texts of Genesis 1 and 2, Matthew 19, Corinthians 7, and Ephesians 5, some of which he further glossed in his New Testament commentaries. He pored over the Mosaic laws of marriage and the Pauline household codes. He cited frequently the marital writings of Augustine, Aquinas, Vitoria, and hundreds of other classical and Christian authorities. "Christianity is by far the most excellent of all possible religious systems," he wrote proudly, in no small part because "Christians are commanded to preserve

---

7   See Hugo Grotius, *Opera omnia theologica*, 3 vols. (London: Mosem Pitt, 1679); id., *Explicatio trium utilissimorum locurum N. Testamenti* (Amsterdam: Joh. and Cornelium Blaev, 1640); id., *De imperio summarum potestatum circa sacra*, 4th ed. (The Hague: Adriani Vlacq., 1661); id., *De veritate religionis Christianae* (Oxford: William Hall, 1662), translated as *Hugo Grotius on the Truth of Christianity*, trans. Spencer Madan (London: J. Dodsley, 1782).

8   Among many studies, see recently, with ample bibliographies, Florian Mühlegger, *Hugo Grotius, ein christlicher Humanist in politischer Verantwortung* (Berlin: de Gruyter, 2007); J.P. Heering, *Hugo Grotius as Apologist for the Christian Religion* (Leiden: Brill, 2004). On his theory of marriage, which is understudied, see Hubert Rinkens, "Die Ehe und die Auffassung von der Natur des Menschen im Naturrecht bei Hugo Grotius (1583–1648), Samuel Pufendorf (1632–1694), und Christian Thomasius (1655–1728)" (Ph.D. Diss., Frankfurt am Main, 1971).

9   Grotius, *Truth*, 108–109; Grotius, *War and Peace*, 2.4.21, 2.5.8.

indissoluble the sacred obligations of the marriage vow, by mutual concessions and mutual forbearance" of husband and wife, each "bearing an equal part in all the duties of the marital estate."[10]

But to build his natural law framework, Grotius was more interested in what the law of nature itself could teach us about sex, marriage, and family life independent of the Bible and theology. That was in part the challenge he set for himself by uttering his "impious hypothesis": natural law would exist even if "we should concede that which cannot be conceded without the utmost wickedness, that there is no God, or that the affairs of men are of no concern to him."[11] It was the further challenge he set by his definition of natural law whose contents and commandments were to be rationally self-evident:

> The law of nature is a dictate of right reason, which points out that an act, according as it is or is not in conformity with rational nature, has in it a quality of moral baseness or moral necessity; and that, in consequence, such an act is either forbidden or enjoined by the author of nature, God.
>
> The acts in regard to which such a dictate exists are, in themselves, either obligatory or not permissible, and so it is understood that necessarily they are enjoined or forbidden by God. In this characteristic the law of nature differs not only from human law, but also from volitional divine law.[12]

When deliberated purely rationally, without the aid of the Bible or "volitional divine law," Grotius concluded, natural law confirms a number of traditional Christian teachings of sex, marriage, and family. But not all traditional Christian teachings, including those against polygamy, could be so easily supported on natural law grounds alone, Grotius insisted. The Bible, he said, does not prescribe or proscribe anything "which is not agreeable to natural decorum." But the "laws of Christ do oblige us" to conduct that goes well beyond "what the law of nature already requires of us." Those who believe that Scripture and nature command exactly the same conduct are fooling themselves, Grotius observed. They will be "strangely embarrassed" when they try "to prove that certain things which are forbidden by the Gospel, such as concubinage, divorce, and polygamy, are likewise condemned by the natural law." While "reason itself informs us that it is decent to refrain" from such deviations from enduring and exclusive monogamous marriages, natural law does

---

10 Grotius, *Truth*, 327–329; Grotius, *Explicatio trium utilissimorum locurum N. Testamenti*, s.v. Matt. 19:1–9, Ephesians 5:32, and distillation of his fuller theological views in the lengthy notes by Jean Barbeyrac in Grotius, *War and Peace*, 2.5.9, n. 7, and repeated citations to Scripture and Christian authorities in ibid., 2.5.1–23. A full list of his sources is in Grotius, *De Jure Belli ac Pacis*, 889–930.

[11] Grotius, *De Iure Belli ac Pacis*, Prolegomena, 11.

[12] Ibid., 1.1.10.

not necessarily prohibit them outright; religious sanction and biblical commands must be added.[13]

With these distinctions in mind, Grotius began to sort through what features of marriage "are necessary to marriage according to the law of nature" alone, and what are required "only according to the Gospel."[14] He sometimes was content simply to show the overlaps between Christian and "heathen" marital practices, evidently thinking this was proof enough of the natural qualities of these practices. "The instances are numerous," he wrote, "wherein heathens are observed to have inculcated, severally, the very same principles and duties which are collectively enjoined by our [Christian] religion: they teach us, for example, that ... the intentional adulterer is guilty of the actual sin of adultery; ... that a man should be the husband of one wife; that the marriage covenant should be inviolable."[15]

Grotius sometimes combined the common patterns of animals with the common customs of advanced civilizations to demonstrate what he thought was natural. For example, he condemned "the promiscuous enjoyment of all women in common," which some ancients and "savage" peoples practiced and which even Plato had commended in his *Republic*. Such practices would reduce the state to "a common brothel," Grotius concluded, violating the natural rights especially of women and children.[16] "Even some of the brute animals" observe natural law far better, for "they are seen to observe a sort of conjugal obligation" at least in their production of offspring. "Far more just and reasonable it is, therefore, that man, the most excellent and most distinguished of all animals, should not be suffered to derive his origin from casual and uncertain parents, to the total extinction of those mutual ties, the filial and the parental affections." Observing the natural law, humans have thus learned "to ensure the certainty of the bond between parents and children" by tying procreation to enduring marriages so "that confusion of offspring may not arise." And because of the long period of human infantile dependency, humans have further learned to treat monogamous marriage as a "real friendship," "a perpetual and indissoluble union," "a full participation and mutual connection both of body and soul."

> The superior advantage of this institution, in respect to the proper education of children, is a truth as obvious as undeniable. Monogamy was even the established custom of some particular pagan nations; among the Germans, for example, and the Romans: and herein the Christians also follow their example, on a principle of justice, in repaying, on the part of the husband, the entire and undivided affection

---

[13] Grotius, *War and Peace*, 1.2.2–3, 1.2.6.
[14] Ibid., 2.5.9.
[15] Grotius, *Truth*, 221–222.
[16] See discussion in Chapter 2, p. 83.

of the wife; while, at the same time, the regulations of domestic economy may be better preserved under one head and mistress of the family; and all those dissensions avoided which a diversity of mothers must create among the children.

Genesis 1 and 2 further confirms this natural preference for monogamous marriage, said Grotius. Because "God gave to one man one woman only, it sufficiently appears what is best" for the marriages of the human race.[17]

Grotius's argument for monogamy, albeit cryptic, was a textbook restatement of the natural configuration of marriage expounded earlier by Thomas Aquinas and by the Spanish neo-Thomists whom he had read closely.[18] The gist of the argument was that enduring and exclusive monogamous marriages were essential to ensuring parental certainty for their children. And parental certainty, particularly for the father, was essential so that both parents would bond with their children who are born helpless and remain utterly dependent upon their parents for survival for many years.

While monogamy is the naturally preferred form of marriage and forum for sex, Grotius continued, he could not say that polygamy was automatically rendered "void by the law of nature only." After all, a number of animals – from chickens and cattle to lions and wolves – are polygamous and fare quite well. A number of biblical patriarchs and kings were polygamous, and they thrived with God's blessing. A number of advanced civilizations like Muslims are polygamous, and they are strong. So long as a man's multiple wives remain faithful to him, and he himself has sufficient resources to support his large family, the natural conditions of paternal certainty and joint parental investment in his children can still be achieved. Grotius thought that polygamy was a "reprehensible" exploitation of women and an indulgence of a barbaric man's "brutal appetite." And he praised the institution of monogamous marriage taught by Christianity. But he concluded that it takes "the law of Christ" to "condemn polygamy outright"[19] – turning the tables on fellow Protestants, especially the rival Dutch Calvinists of his day, who had said that the law of nature and its distillation in the Ten Commandments clearly rejected polygamy.[20]

Grotius had less trouble condemning polyandry – one woman with multiple husbands – as contrary to natural law. But he did so with a heavy-handed patriarchal argument that contradicted his own starting and startling egalitarian assumption that in a marriage, the man and woman share "an equal part in all the duties of the marital estate."[21] A marriage "contracted with a woman, who already has a husband,

---

[17] Ibid., 109–111; Grotius, *War and Peace*, 2.5.8–10.
[18] See discussion earlier in this chapter.
[19] Grotius, *Truth*, 109–110, 328; Grotius, *War and Peace*, 2.5.9–10.
[20] See discussion in Chapter 6, pp. 257–260.
[21] Grotius, *Truth*, 327–329.

is void by the law of nature, unless her first husband has divorced her; for till then his property in her continues." "In its natural state," Grotius explained, a marriage "puts the woman, as it were, under the immediate inspection and guard of the man: for we see, even among some beasts, such a sort of society exists between the male and female." In human marriages, too, "the authority is not equal; the husband is the head of the wife in all conjugal and family affairs; for the wife becomes part of the husband's family, and it is but reasonable that the husband should have the rule and disposal of his own home."[22]

The gist of Grotius's argument was that polyandry was unnatural because the natural law gives a man exclusive dominion over his wife's person, property, and contracts – what common lawyers call the doctrine of "coverture," but now cast in natural law terms. This argument not only contradicted Grotius's starting premise that men and women have an equal and natural right to marry, but it also made little sense. Men by nature share property and power all the time – else no civilization could ever emerge from the state of nature. Moreover, bees, ants, and other animals sometimes operate successfully with matriarchies: why should they count any less than a herd of cattle in describing the contents of natural law, especially as the orderliness of beehives served Grotius's later arguments about the natural legal order. Many later Enlightenment philosophers rejected Grotius's arguments against polyandry, instead condemning this practice with more egalitarian natural law and natural rights rationales that they thought sufficient to condemn polygamy, too. They also rejected Grotius's further argument that the natural law permits fathers to sell, enslave, or lease their children.[23] For most later natural law theorists, these arguments were just a thin natural law apologia for the traditional unlimited power of the paterfamilias in Roman law.

DOES NATURAL LAW ALONE PROHIBIT POLYGAMY?

Given his stature as one of the great natural law thinkers of early modern times, and one of the early architects of a new common law of nations, Grotius set the terms for much of the early Enlightenment debate about the natural law of sex, marriage, and family life. Like Grotius, many later Enlightenment writers used this same natural configuration of marriage to argue in support of many traditional norms and forms of sex, marriage, and family life. And a few of these Enlightenment writers, like Grotius (and like a few of the church fathers and medieval scholastics before him), doubted whether natural law by itself condemned polygamy.[24]

---

[22] Ibid., 2.5.8, 2.5.11.

[23] Ibid., 2.5.5.

[24] For a good summary of arguments pro and con, see Johann Wolfgang Textor, *Synopsis of the Law of Nations*, trans. John P. Bate (Washington, DC: Carnegie Institution, 1916), ch. 3, secs. 28–38.

Samuel von Pufendorf

For example, the prolific Lutheran jurist and historian of Sweden Samuel von Pufendorf (1632–1694) fully endorsed Grotius's account of the natural configuration of marriage. The reality of lengthy infant dependence, Pufendorf wrote, gave humans a "strong natural inclination" toward exclusive and enduring marriages and a "strong natural abhorrence" toward sex outside of marriage – even though "man is an animal always ready for the deed of love." If natural law had not channeled this strong male sex drive toward marriage and men were permitted to have random sex "like cattle in heat," they would do nothing to help the mothers and children who need them. "What man would offer his support unless he were sure he was the father" of her child? "What man would undertake the care of any but his own offspring, whom it is not easy to pick out when such free license prevails?" Sexual intercourse confined to marriage was a "natural necessity" for mankind and a "natural duty" for each man, Pufendorf concluded.[25]

But Pufendorf – echoing Grotius as well as the early Lutherans whom he also deeply respected – thought that both monogamy and polygamy could achieve these natural goods and goals of marriage. Polygamy may be condemned for many reasons in an advanced civilization, he wrote, but it could not be condemned altogether on natural law reasoning alone, although polyandry could. In his lengthy tract expounding a "universal jurisprudence" for the world, Pufendorf wrote:

> But, as touching polygamy, it is certain, indeed, that the form in which several men have one wife together is utterly abhorrent from nature and the end of matrimony; but that one man should be united at the same time with several women, although it is now believed among Christians to have been forbidden by a divine law, is, nevertheless, in itself by no means repugnant to the law of nature. For it is not necessary that, just as a wife ought to grant the use of her body to no man but her one husband, so ought a husband to do the same to no other woman but his only wife. For the former regulation is necessary so as to secure certainty about offspring.

[25] Samuel von Pufendorf, *De Jure Naturae et Gentium libri octo*, trans. C.H. and W.A. Oldfather (Oxford: Clarendon Press, 1934), 6.1.2, 6.1.4. See also ibid., 6.1.1–36; id., *Elementorum Jurisprudentiae Universalis libri duo*, trans. W.A. Oldfather, repr. ed. (New York: Oceana Publications, 1964), 37–39, 275–294; id., *The Whole Duty of Man According to the Law of Nature*, trans. Andrew Tooke, eds. Ian Hunter and David Saunders (Indianapolis, IN: Liberty Fund, 2003), 174–184; Samuel von Pufendorf, *The Divine Feudal Law: Or, Covenants with Mankind Represented*, trans. Theophilus Dorrington, ed. Simone Zurbuchen (Indianapolis, IN: Liberty Fund, 2002), 47–51. See analysis in Erik Wolf, *Grosse Rechtsdenker der deutschen Geistesgeshichte*, 4th ed. (Tubingen: J.C.B. Mohr, 1963), 311–370; Leonard Krieger, *The Politics of Discretion: Pufendorf and the Acceptance of Natural Law* (Chicago: University of Chicago Press, 1965). See the popularization of Pufendorf's views, as well as those of Grotius, in Jean Jacques Burlamaqui, *The Principles of Natural and Politic Law*, trans. Thomas Nugent (Indianapolis, IN: Liberty Fund, 2006 [1747]), 1.4.7. This work was often cited by the American founders and early nineteenth-century judges and jurists.

But, in truth, that a man should spend upon appeasing the lust of one woman all the vigor which was sufficient to raise up offspring among a number of women, does by no means seem to be ordered by nature.

But those reasons which have to do with jealousy between the wives, domestic discord, hatred on the part of stepmothers to be continued also among the offspring themselves are valid only among those nations in whom the dispositions of women are too elevated. Such are most women today among Europeans, where he who is himself not beholden to his wife performs with vigor the office of a man. But, in truth, among the Asiatics and others, where women are left merely the glory of obedience, several wives no more disturb domestic peace than elsewhere the preposterous lust for commanding [*imperandi libido*] on the part of a single virago.

And yet it must altogether be the finding that *polygamy*, formerly allowed for very weighty reasons, has later been prohibited by positive laws. But this feature also has been added to matrimony from the positive law of God.[26]

Christian Thomasius

Pufendorf's friend Christian Thomasius (1655–1728), also a distinguished Lutheran legal and political thinker in Germany, went further and thought that the natural law standing alone permitted polygamy, polyandry, and even concubinage in dire circumstances. Thomasius agreed with Grotius and Pufendorf – and Martin Luther and Philip Melanchthon before them – that "the positive law of Christ," set out in the New Testament, condemned polygamy, and that the church could properly ban polygamists from its midst. He also praised the Western legal tradition from antiquity to the present day for making polygamy a crime, and for wisely recognizing a hierarchy of degrees of polygamy based on the defendant's state of mind and the number of extra spouses he took.[27]

But the natural law itself, Thomasius said, without "divine positive law" superadded, does not condemn polygamy or plural unions outright. If natural law is defined as "what nature has taught all animals," polygamy is obviously acceptable, given how many animals practice polygamy and how some practice polyandry, too. If it is defined as what is common among the nations or "what was rooted in the Noahide law," polygamy is still acceptable because it is marriage that is natural and common to all humans, not one particular form of marriage; many nations ancient and modern practice polygamy. If natural law is defined as "what is good for

---

[26] Pufendorf, *Elementorum Jurisprudentiae*, Observation 5.7.
[27] Christian Thomasius and Georg Beyer, *De Crimine Bigamiae: Vom Laster der zwiefachen Ehe* (Leipzig?: Johannis Georgi, 1715), secs. 5–8, 44–74; id., *De Bigamie Praescriptione* (Leipzig: Johannis Georgi, 1685), passim.

the preservation and perpetuation of the human race," polygamy is still permissible given its procreative efficiency, especially if there is a scarcity of men. If natural law is defined as what natural reason teaches to be good for humanity, polygamy is still not entirely forbidden, because a rational person may be put in circumstances in which polygamy can still be reasonably treated as a better option than open fornication, communal sex, or "lust unbounded." Nor does such rational calculus rule out concubinage (either the single concubinage of Rome or even the multiple concubinage of the Hebrew Bible) if the alternatives are "lust unbounded," women unprotected, "children untutored," or dynasties in peril. "Some dire social condition" might make each of these plural unions necessary to preserve and perpetuate the human race, wrote Thomasius.[28]

There are certainly many "secondary reasons" that might make polygamy and polyandry less attractive than faithful monogamy, Thomasius allowed. Polygamy is often plagued by "jealousy, domestic discord, the unkindness of stepmothers, which is continued in the offspring, and other domestic inconveniences." If polyandry and "the community of wives were allowed, then many quarrels would break out between men over attractive women. A pregnant woman would lack assistance, because none of the men would help her unless he knew she was pregnant with his child. That is impossible [to know] in this kind of community. Then the education of the child, which none of the men would want to undertake for the same reason, would be laborious and involve a lot of effort for the woman on her own, who would barely be able to manage. Finally relatives would not be sufficiently distinct, and there could also be no patrimonies. And once these have been removed, a great part of the advantages that sustain and adorn human life would go under." Polyandry is thus "barely permissible and closer to being prohibited than being commanded" by the natural law. In the end, natural law makes monogamy better than polygamy, and polygyny better than polyandry, but none of these domestic arrangements can "be attacked on the basis of natural law" alone.[29]

---

[28] Thomasius and Beyer, *De Crimine Bigamiae*, secs. 9–20; Christian Thomasius, *Institutiones jurisprudentiae divinae, in positiones succincte contractae in quibus hypotheses illustris Puffendorfi circa doctrina juris naturalis apodicti demonstrantur & corroborantur* (Frankfurt and Leipzig: Sumptibus Mauritii Georgii Weidmanni, 1688), 88–89, 96, 137–143, 182–194, translated as id., *Institutes of Divine Jurisprudence With Selections from Foundations of the Law of Nature and Nations*, trans. and ed. Thomas Ahert (Indianapolis, IN: Liberty Fund, 2011), bk. 3, chap. 2.200–219; bk. 3, chap. 3.77–90; id., *Shediasma inaugurali juridicum de Concubinatu* (Halle?: n.p., 1713), bk. 3, ch. 2.27–36, 3.23–31. On Thomasius's broader liberal project, see Ian Hunter, *The Secularization of the Confessional State: The Political Thought of Christian Thomasius* (Cambridge: Cambridge University Press, 2007).

[29] Thomasius, *Institutes*, bk. 3, ch. 2.203, 204, 207, 211. See comparable arguments in Thomas Salmon, *A Critical Essay Concerning Marriage* (London: Bible and Crown in St. Paul's Church Yard, 1724), 86–102; Patrick Delaney, pseud. Phileleutherus Dubliniensis, *Reflections upon Polygamy and the Encouragement Given to that Practice in the Old Testament* (London: J. Roberts, 1734), 108–136.

Baron Montesquieu

The distinguished French political philosopher and man of letters Baron Charles-Louis de Montesquieu (1689–1755) agreed that "it is a thing extremely delicate to fix exactly the point at which the laws of nature stop, and where the civil laws begin." And it is an equally delicate task to know "in what cases, with regard to marriage, we ought to follow the laws of religion, and in what cases we should follow the civil laws." For the reality is that "it has happened in all ages and countries, that religion has been blended with marriages. When certain things have been considered as impure or unlawful, and [have] nevertheless become necessary, they were obliged to call in religion, to legitimate in the one case, and to reprove in others."[30] But in this day of contested religious claims, Montesquieu continued, the critical question is whether there are alternative norms and "auxiliary expedients" besides religion that can channel nature or school natural inclinations in the direction of exclusive and enduring monogamous marriages.

In the case of polygamy, Montesquieu thought that climate and geography had a lot to do with what nature taught about marriage and what a religious or civil law system could effectively offer. In the hotter climates of Africa, Asia, and the Middle East, Montesquieu wrote, polygamy was more natural. In those hot climates, there were many more females than males. Moreover, girls reached puberty much earlier and were thus married at "eight, nine, or ten, years of age" long before they had developed their own reason, capacity, and self-sufficiency. Young women in these hot climates were thus often reduced to the production of children and were rendered utterly dependent on their husband and his extended family to provide for them and their children. When their reason finally did set in, these now older wives took on new roles of caring for their growing children and working for the extended household as their husband took in younger and more fertile wives to add still more infant children. "It is therefore extremely natural, that, in these places" an organized legal system of polygamy, like that of Islam, should thrive, Montesquieu wrote. For Islamic law catered to the natural inclination in those "hot climates" toward polygamy and then put legal limits on any man's temptation to exploit women and children still further: limiting polygamy only to men who have the means to support his wives and children, and limiting the number of wives and divorces that even a wealthy man could have.[31]

By contrast, said Montesquieu, the colder climates of Europe and North America are more naturally conducive to monogamy. There the ratio of males and females

---

[30] Montesquieu, *The Spirit of Laws*, 16.13–14, in *The Complete Works of Montesquieu*, 4 vols. (London: T. Evans, 1777), 2:218.

[31] Ibid., bk. 16.2–3, 6; bk. 26.10. See also Montesquieu, *Complete Works*, vol. 3, letter cxiv.

is much closer, and often there are more males than females in a local population. Moreover, these cold weather women reach puberty much later, and they are fully mature both in body and in reason by the time they are ready for marriage. This "naturally introduce[s] a kind of equality between the two sexes, and, in consequence of this, the law of having only one wife." Northern women have more choice in marriage, because there are more men around. And these more mature women are too strong and self-sufficient to be reduced to mere breeders and servants within a man's household. "Thus the law, which permits only one wife, is physically conformable to the climate of Europe, and not to that of Asia. This is the reason why Mahometanism was so easily established in Asia, and with such difficulty extended in Europe; why Christianity is maintained in Europe and has been destroyed in Asia; and, in fine, why the Mahometans have made such progress in China and the Christians so little."[32]

But climate and geography, and the local laws and customs that have accommodated them, Montesquieu continued, cannot be the only forum in which the wisdom, justice, or propriety of polygamy are tested. For humans are not just passive pawns of their natural environment, nor slaves to the laws and customs they have inherited. Polygamy has to be judged by what is good, just, and expedient for all men, women, children, and society alike. And measured on those scales, Montesquieu concluded, polygamy falls far short:

> With regard to polygamy in general, independently of the circumstances which may render it tolerable, it is not of the least service to mankind, nor to either of the two sexes, whether it be that which abuses, or that which is abused. Neither is it of service to the children; for one of its greatest inconveniences is that the father and mother cannot have the same affection for their offspring; a father cannot love twenty children with the same tenderness as a mother can love two. It is much worse when a wife has many husbands; for then paternal love is only held by this opinion, that a father may believe, if he will, or that others may believe, that certain children belong to him....
>
> Besides, the possession of so many wives does not always prevent their [the husband's] entertaining desires for those of others; it is with lust as with avarice, where thirst increases by the acquisition of treasure.... [A] plurality of wives leads to that passion which nature disallows, for one depravation always draws on another.[33]

Many of Montesquieu's observations about the effects of climate and geography on female sexual and rational development, male-female ratios, and propensities toward polygamy or monogamy did not hold under later scientific scrutiny. But what

---

[32] Montesquieu, *The Spirit of Laws*, 16.2, 4. See also Montesquieu, *The Complete Works*, vol. 3, ch. 20: "The Conquests of Justinian. Some Account of his Government."

[33] Montesquieu, *The Spirit of Laws*, bk. 16.6.

did hold up was his insistence that the case for monogamy over polygamy had to be judged on other grounds besides nature and natural law, custom and common practice. What also held up was his general judgment that polygamy causes too much harm to women, children, and men alike to be countenanced by a society even if this practice were considered "permissible" by nature.

One line of argument against polygamy that emerged among other Enlightenment liberals appealed to the natural rights of women and children that were too often violated by polygamy and to the correlative political duties of the state to eradicate this harmful condition by prohibiting polygamy. This was a signature contribution of John Locke at the end of the seventeenth century, and it grew in prominence both among common lawyers like William Blackstone and women's rights advocates like Mary Wollstonecraft in the next century. A second line of argument appealed to common sense, prudence, and natural justice to argue against polygamy. This was the main contribution of the Scottish Enlightenment figures like Henry Home and David Hume. A third line of argument, exemplified by William Paley, made direct appeals to private and public utility, and even early pragmatic calculus. These lines of argument from natural rights, common sense, and social utility often appeared woven together. But each line of argument added something distinctive to the Western case for monogamy over polygamy. For analytical purposes it is worth tracing each of them in turn, even though some repetition will result.

NATURAL RIGHTS ARGUMENTS AGAINST POLYGAMY

A number of Enlightenment philosophers and jurists argued that polygamy violated the natural rights of women and children, and that the state must respect and protect these natural rights by prohibiting and punishing polygamy. Natural rights arguments for monogamy and against polygamy were not new. Medieval Catholic writers had advocated the natural rights and domestic rights of women and children based on the biblical duties of husbands to their wives and parents to their children.[34] Early modern Protestants had treated polygamy as a violation of the woman's natural rights to fidelity, property, promise, and privacy, and the children's natural rights to household property – rooting each of these rights claim in the duties of the Decalogue.[35] Enlightenment liberals pressed for the rights of women and children, too, but now on increasingly secular grounds. They also emphasized the equality of husbands and wives within a monogamous marriage, and the correlative rights and duties of parents and children at different

---

[34] See discussion in Chapter 4, pp. 175–176.
[35] See discussion in Chapter 6, pp. 257–260.

stages of the life cycle. Polygamy for them compromised all of these domestic ideals, and must thus be criminalized.

John Locke

English philosopher John Locke (1632–1704) offered an influential early account of these natural rights within the household, drawing his arguments both from human nature and from the creation story. Locke designed his theory of marriage to refute the patriarchal theories that fellow Englishman Robert Filmer (1588–1653) had used to support the traditional "commonwealth model of marriage" that we analyzed earlier.[36] In his *Patriarcha* of ca. 1638, Filmer argued that God had created the patriarchal domestic commonwealth, headed by the paterfamilias, as the source of the hierarchical political commonwealth headed by the king. God had created Adam and Eve as founders not only of the first marriage and family, but also of the first state and society. Adam was the first husband but also the first ruler. Eve was the first wife, but also the first subject. Together with their children, they comprised at once a domestic and a political commonwealth. All persons thereafter were, by birth, subject to the highest male head, descended from Adam.[37]

Locke responded to Filmer first by flatly denying any natural or necessary connection between the political and domestic commonwealths, between the authority of the paterfamilias and that of the magistrate. "[T]he power of a magistrate over a subject," he wrote, "may be distinguished from that of a father over his children, a master over his servant, a husband over his wife, and a lord over his slave." The "little commonwealth" of the family is "very far from" the great commonwealth in England "in its constitution, power and end." "[T]he master of the family has a very distinct and differently limited power, both as to time and extent, over those several persons that are in it; … he has no legislative power of life and death over any of them, and none too but what a mistress of a family may have as well as he."[38]

Locke responded next by denying Filmer's patriarchal interpretation of the creation story in Genesis. God did not create Adam and Eve as ruler and subject, but as husband and wife, said Locke. Adam and Eve were created equal before God: "male and female he created them." Each had natural rights to use the bounties of Paradise. Each had natural duties to each other and to God. After the fall into sin, God expelled Adam and Eve from Paradise. He increased man's labor in his

---

[36] See discussion in Chapter 7, pp. 285–290.
[37] Robert Filmer, *Patriarcha and other Political Works*, ed. Peter Laslett (Oxford: Oxford University Press, 1949).
[38] John Locke, *Two Treatises on Government*, ed. Peter Laslett (Cambridge: Cambridge University Press, 1960), II.2, II.86.

use of creation. He increased woman's labor in the bearing of children. He said to Eve in Genesis 3:16: "thy desire shall be to thy husband, and he shall rule over thee." These words, said Locke, which Filmer called "the original grant of government, were not spoken to Adam, neither indeed was there any grant in them made to Adam; they were a punishment laid upon Eve." These words do not abrogate the natural equality, rights, and duties with which God created Adam and Eve, and all persons after them. They do not render all wives eternally subject to their husbands. And they certainly do not, as Filmer insisted, give "a father or a prince an absolute, arbitrary, unlimited and unlimitable power over the lives, liberties, and estates of his children and subjects."[39]

Men and women were born free and equal in the state of nature, Locke argued, now moving to a more general logic of natural law and natural rights. But "God having made man such a creature, that, in his own judgment, it was not good for him to be alone, put him under strong obligation of necessity, convenience, and inclination to drive him into society." "The first society" to be formed after the state of nature "was between man and wife, which gave beginning to that of parents and children." This "conjugal society," like every other society, "is made by a voluntary compact between man and woman: and tho' it consists chiefly in such a communion and right in one another's bodies, as is necessary to its chief end, procreation; yet it draws with it mutual support and assistance and communion of interest too, as necessary not only to unite their care, and affection, but also necessary to their common offspring, who have a right to be nourished and maintained by them, till they are able to provide for themselves."[40]

Locke thus grounded the nature of marriage and the family in a set of natural rights and duties. It was a natural right for a man and woman to enter into a mutually consensual marital contract. It was a natural duty for them to render procreation an essential condition of whatever marital contract they entered. It was a natural condition of children to be born helpless and thus a natural right for them to be nurtured, educated, and raised to maturity by the parents who conceived them. This triggered the natural duty of their parents to remain together in marriage in order to raise their children. Locke based this network of natural domestic rights and duties on the natural configuration of marriage and family life that was now a commonplace understanding of the Enlightenment:

> For the end of conjunction between male and female, being not barely procreation, but the continuation of the species, this conjunction betwixt male and female ought to last, even after procreation, so long as is necessary to the nourishment and support of the young ones, who are to be sustained by those that got them, till they

[39] Ibid., I.9, II.47, 86, 98.
[40] Ibid., II.77, 78, 83.

are able to shift and provide for themselves... whereby the father, who is bound to take care for those he hath begot, is under an obligation to continue in conjugal society with the same woman longer than other creatures, whose young being able to subsist of themselves, before the time of procreation returns again, the conjugal bond dissolves of itself, and they are at liberty.[41]

The logical end of Locke's argument was that childless couples, or couples whose children were of age and on their own, should be free to divorce, unless they had found some other "communion of interest" to sustain their marriage. Locke dithered on the question of divorce and remarriage. It was not essential to his argument to speak definitively on the subject, and he knew the dangers of loose literary speculation on it given the heated English politics of his day and the firm common law prohibitions against it. In his private diary, he wrote quite brashly in a way that seemed to countenance not only remarriage but perhaps even a form of concurrent concubinage: "He that already is married may marry another woman with his left hand.... The ties, duration, and conditions of the left hand marriage shall be no other than what is expressed in the contract of marriage between the parties."[42] In his *Two Treatises* and other publications, however, he only flirted with the doctrine of divorce and remarriage, suggesting delicately that the matter be left to private contractual calculation.

The other logical end of Locke's argument was that polygamy was a violation of the natural rights of wives and children, and the natural equality of husband and wife within the marital estate. Locke did not say this clearly. He said obliquely that polygamy was not a proper "moral relation" because it compromised a man's "readiness to acknowledge and return kindness received," including presumably from his wife and children.[43] He suggested that polygamy, like other forms of promiscuity, was a "sin."[44] He said more explicitly that a guarantee of liberty of conscience and religious toleration did not prevent the state from punishing "the dishonesty and debauchery of men's lives" – which, for Locke, included "arbitrary

---

[41] Ibid., II.79–80.

[42] Diary Entry, quoted in editor's note to ibid., II.81–82. The term "left-hand marriage" was a term of art in Locke's day to describe the so-called morganatic relationship between a nobleman and a common woman, whose disparate social status precluded marriage. This was viewed as an exclusive and permanent union, sometimes blessed by the medieval and early modern church. The women were supported during the relationship and gained truncated inheritance rights. Children born of these unions were considered legitimate, and received support during their father's lifetimes, but could not inherit from him. It is not clear whether Locke is referring to this kind of arrangement alongside a monogamous marriage – making it a form of concubinage – or subsequent remarriage after ending the first marital contract.

[43] John Locke, An Essay Concerning Human Understanding, ch. 27, in *The Works of John Locke*, 10 vols. (London: Thomas Tegg, 1823), 1:28ff.

[44] John Locke, *Essays on the Law of Nature*, ed. W. von Leyden (Oxford: Clarendon Press, 1954), 171.

divorce, polygamy, concubinage, simple fornication," adultery, and incest. These sexual "immoralities," said Locke, cannot "be exempt from the magistrate's power of punishing them" just because their proponents happen to call them "articles of faith, or ways of worship." Polygamy, incest, adultery, and the like are "simply wrong," said Locke, and must be prohibited without exception, religious liberty notwithstanding.[45] This echoed Locke's earlier statement that polygamy and divorce are not so much matters of religion or conscience but "things either of indifference or doubt" – the "adiaphora" or unessentials of the faith. A magistrate may limit or prohibit these activities to protect "the welfare and safety of his people" and to avoid the "greater inconveniences than advantages to the community" that these activities occasion. "[A] toleration of men in all that which they pretend out of conscience they cannot submit to, will wholly take away all the civil laws and all the magistrate's power, and so there will be no law, nor government, if you deny the magistrate's authority in indifferent things, over which it is acknowledged on all hands that he has jurisdiction."[46]

This was an early statement of an important argument about the proper and necessary limits of religious freedom and human rights claims to practice polygamy. This argument for such limitations would grow in the Western legal tradition, especially in America, to reject the claims of religious polygamists who claimed religious freedom exemptions from general criminal laws prohibiting polygamy.[47] Locke saw this religious freedom argument for polygamy exemptions looming already in the later seventeenth century, and he cut it off cleanly.

William Blackstone

While Locke provided much of the new philosophical foundation for natural rights within the family, William Blackstone (1723–1780) helped situate these natural rights ideas within the Anglo-American common law of the family as well. The "rights and liberties of women" in various stations in life were amply discussed at common law before Blackstone.[48] But, in his influential *Commentaries on the Law of England* (1765),

---

45 John Locke, "A Third Letter Concerning Toleration" [1692], ch. 3, in *The Works of John Locke*, 5:2ff.
46 John Locke, "An Essay Concerning Toleration" [1667], sec. 2, in John Locke, *A Letter Concerning Toleration and Other Writings*, ed. Mark Goldie (Indianapolis, IN: Liberty Fund, 2010), 110–111.
47 See discussion in Chapter 10, pp. 429–439. For a sixth-century Roman law exemption for Jewish polygamists, see discussion in Chapter 1, p. 55.
48 See, e.g., John Doddridge and Thomas Edgar, *The Lawes Resolutions of Womens Rights: or, The Lawes Prouision for Women* (London: John More Esq., 1632); Elizabeth Chudleigh Bristol, *The Laws Respecting Women: As They Regard their Natural Rights* (London: J. Johnson, 1776). For seventeenth- and eighteenth-century rights talk in England, see my *The Reformation of Rights: Law, Religion, and Human Rights in Early Modern Calvinism* (Cambridge: Cambridge University Press, 2007), esp. 213–220, 260–271.

the leading textbook on the common law for the next century, Blackstone sought to give an account of the natural foundations of these rights, especially for women and children within the marital household. He cited Grotius, Locke, Pufendorf, Montesquieu, and other Enlightenment philosophers to argue that exclusive and enduring monogamous marriage was the best way to ensure paternal certainty and joint parental investment in children who are born vulnerable and utterly dependent on their parents' mutual care.

> Montesquieu has a very just observation upon this head: that the establishment of marriage in all civilized states is built on this natural obligation of the father to provide for his children: for that ascertains and makes known the person who is bound to fulfill this obligation: whereas, in promiscuous and illicit conjunctions, the father is unknown; and the mother finds a thousand obstacles in her way – shame, remorse, the constraint of her sex, and the rigor of laws – that stifle her inclinations to perform this duty.[49]

"The duty of parents to provide for the maintenance of their children is a principle of natural law," Blackstone continued. It is "an obligation, says Pufendorf, laid on them not only by nature herself, but by their own proper act, in bringing them into the world." "The main end and design of marriage [is] to ascertain and fix upon some certain person, to whom the care, the protection, the maintenance, and the education of the children should belong."[50]

Echoing Locke, Blackstone set out the reciprocal rights and duties that the natural law imposes upon parents and children. God and nature have "implant[ed] in the breast of every parent" an "insuperable degree of affection" for their child once they are certain the child is theirs, Blackstone wrote. The common law confirms and channels this natural affection by requiring parents to maintain, protect, and educate their children, and by protecting their rights to discharge these parental duties against undue interference by others. These "natural duties" of parents are the correlatives of the "natural rights" of their children, Blackstone further argued. Once they become adults, children acquire reciprocal natural duties toward their parents:

> The duties of children to their parents arise from a principle of natural justice and retribution. For to those who gave us existence, we naturally owe subjection and obedience during our minority, and honour and reverence ever after; they, who protected the weakness of our infancy, are entitled to our protection in the infirmity of their age; they who by sustenance and education have enabled their offspring to prosper, ought in return to be supported by that offspring, in case they stand in

---

[49] William Blackstone, *Commentaries on the Laws of England*, 4 vols. (Oxford: Oxford University Press, 1765), 1.16.1.

[50] Ibid., I.15.1, 1.16.1, 1.16.3.

need of assistance. Upon this principle proceed all the duties of children to their parents, which are enjoined by positive laws.[51]

Blackstone was more liberal and tolerant than most common lawyers of his day in treating traditional sexual crimes, especially when children were not involved. But he was unequivocal in condemning polygamy, placing it among "offenses against the public health, and the public polic[y] or economy."

> [P]olygamy can never be endured under any rational civil nations, the fallaciousness of which has been fully urged by many sensible writers; but in northern countries the very nature of the climate seems to reclaim against it; it never having obtained in this part of the world even at the time of our German [Saxon] ancestors, who, as Tacitus informs us, "thought it to be singularly barbaric, and were content with a single wife instead." It is punished therefore by the laws of ancient and modern Sweden with death. And with us in England ... it is a [capital] felony.[52]

Women's Rights Advocates

A number of Blackstone's English contemporaries thought the criminal punishment of polygamy was essential to protecting the natural rights and liberties of women and the natural equality of husbands and wives, fathers and mothers within the martial home. Polygamy violates "all the privileges and immunities" and "rights and prerogatives transmitted down" to the "she-patriots" of our nation, wrote Unitarian minister and political commentator Henry Moore (1732–1802). Indeed, polygamy is "no less than high treason against the female state." It condemns women to become "absolute slaves to every whimsy, and caprice of an imperious, an unreasonable, or a drunken husband, in terror of being deprived at once of every domestic privilege, for every slight or even imaginary offence." She is "starved too after his death," given the wide distribution of her polygamous husband's estate which has already been thinned by so many demands on it by his many wives and children during his lifetime. This is no way to treat any woman or to honor her "natural rights," said Moore. Only a culture that views women as "stupid asses," to be worked hard or even as "monsters" to be controlled could contemplate the idea of polygamy. Polygamy might work "only for those eastern regions where men buy their wives, as farmers do their cattle, at so much per head—where the females are trained up to be slaves, and kept as slaves during life – where they are regarded either as mere instruments of pleasure, or as mere household drudges and beasts of burden." But

[51] Ibid., 1.16.
[52] Ibid., 4.13.

this simply cannot be in modern-day England. For here women "are free-born, and their bosoms are yet warm with the flame of British liberty."[53]

English philosopher and minister James Cookson (1752–1835) also condemned polygamy as a violation of "the just rights of Eve's fair daughters." Polygamy violates "the reciprocal rights of husband and wife" that are the foundation of every just marital contract, he wrote. "[I]n polygamous contracts the obligations are not mutual; therefore, both are not equally bound, and this defect cannot but be highly injurious to civil society." A polygamist will inevitably show "partiality" to one wife and her children over others. Some wives will be amply supported, but not all. Some children will be educated, but others, "like their mothers," will be "rejected or despised," and "condemned to the most servile offices, and doomed to ignorance and wretchedness, without any prospect of attaining that rank in life which otherwise they might." This will ultimately destroy the essential kinship bonds among the children, who, "being begotten upon different mothers who mortally hated each other, and instilled the same sentiments into their children, did not think themselves relations in blood, so much as rivals in interest."

> It is confirmed by all experience that polygamous contracts are totally destructive of domestic happiness; and jealousies, animosities, and the implacable hatred thereby excited between mothers, and eventually between their children, which, if they do not break out into crimes quite intolerable to society, have such malignant influence, that the duties of relationship are disregarded, and in this state of things, order and filial subordination cannot exist; the first principles of civil society, which appear to me to be, in some measure, founded on parental authority originally, are stabbed in their vitals.[54]

"The scheme of a plurality of wives at once," Cookson continued, "is nothing but a scheme of debauchery" leading to unchecked tyranny of men over women. "It would put an end to matrimonial endearments, and wives would be nothing but the slaves of prostitution" – coveted for their beauty, used for sexual pleasure and procreation, and then cast out of her marital bed to make room for the next wife. In polygamy as it now exists in the East, "the women are treated as the most abject slaves, shut up in a seraglio, and guarded like prisoners" by mean-spirited eunuchs, themselves literally cut off from marriage because a few rich men have hoarded all the women. The wives they guard are "abject servants of their surly lords, their mere drudges, compelled to perform every laborious part of the domestic business, without any will of their own, and considered as beings only calculated for the

---

[53] Henry Moore, *A Word to Mr. Madan or Free Thoughts on His Late Celebrated Defence of Polygamy* (Bristol: W. Pine, 1781), 9–14, 41–51.

[54] James Cookson, *Thoughts on Polygamy Suggested by the Dictates of Scripture, Nature, Reason, and Common-Sense* (Winchester: J. Wilkes, 1782), 406–409, 420–421, 442.

gratification of brutal appetite." This is no way to live in "nations where the women are esteemed as they ought to be, and enjoy an equality of rights with men."[55]

In her famous *Vindication of the Rights of Woman*, feminist critic and educator Mary Wollstonecraft (1759–1797) built on Locke, Cookson, and Moore to condemn polygamy as a "depravation" of the "natural rights of woman" and an insult to the "inherent dignity" of each woman. Polygamy, Wollstonecraft wrote after reading several travel narratives about the practice, routinely involves the "degradation," "domestication," and instrumentalization of women. Polygamy is not a function of climate or geography as Montesquieu or his followers would have us believe, but the product of a calculated prejudice against women. It aims to deprive a wife of fair and equal treatment within the home, and "that share of physical love which, in a monogamous condition, would all be" hers. But even more, it perpetuates the idea that "woman must be inferior to man, and made for him." It treats a woman as a mere pretty, demur, and passive "toy of man," to be shaken and rattled "whenever, dismissing reason, he chooses to be amused," although inevitably he will grow tired of this one toy, especially when it becomes worn or damaged, and he will acquire another and then another. Polygamy measures a woman's value and virtue in society merely by her physical beauty, by her fecundity, by her capacity to bear and raise children. It says to a woman that her main vocation in life is to "procreate and rot."[56]

Wollstonecraft's argument against polygamy was also an argument against traditional patriarchal forms of monogamy where husbands ruled their wives without check or restriction, and confined them to procreation and menial household duties. "The divine right of husbands, like the divine right of kings, may, it is to be hoped in this Enlightened age, be contested without danger," she wrote. We cannot be seduced by "the same arguments that tyrannic[al] kings and venial ministers have used, and fallaciously assert that woman ought to be subjected because she has always been so." Custom is not nature, and the long habit of penning and domesticating women in a "gilted cage," does not make it right. Men have their "natural freedom," rights, and dignity. Women do, too. "It is time to effect a revolution in female manners – time to restore to them their lost dignity – and make them a part of the human species, labour by reforming themselves to reform the world."[57]

The reform of the world that Wollstonecraft had in mind was for men and women to be treated equally in private and public life, and given the education and opportunity to develop their minds and capacities to fit their native talents. Men might be stronger in body on average, and women might have more capacity and thus responsibility

---

[55] Ibid., 412–417.
[56] Mary Wollstonecraft, *A Vindication of the Rights of Woman and A Vindication of the Rights of Men*, ed. Janet Todd, pbk. ed. (Oxford: Oxford University Press, 2008), 100, 103, 133, 141–142.
[57] Ibid., 108, 112–113.

in the production and nursing of infant children, Wollstonecraft allowed. And that might suggest different roles within the public and private spheres for a time, and different training to prepare for the unique vocation of motherhood. "But I still insist," Wollstonecraft argued, "that not only the virtue, but the knowledge of the two sexes should be the same in nature, if not in degree, and that women, considered not only as moral, but rational creatures, ought to endeavor to acquire human virtues (or perfections) by the same means as men, instead of being educated like a fanciful kind of half being." "Liberty is the mother of virtue, and if women be, by their very constitution, slaves, and not allowed to breathe the sharp invigorating air of freedom, they must ever languish like exotics, and be reckoned beautiful flaws in nature."[58]

If a woman is given the freedom and education to develop her full capacity of reason, virtue, and character, Wollstonecraft insisted, the monogamous marriage that she chooses to enter will be so much better. The marriage will be a union of "equal moral beings," a "dyadic perfectionist friendship,"[59] between partners who can sustain and support each other throughout a lifetime. A properly educated woman will make a true friend and partner to her husband, and not just a sexual plaything while they are newlyweds, a useful mother as children grow up, but then a dispensable burden to her husband when beauty, sex, and children are no longer the priority. She will also make a much better mother, teacher, and role model for their children, preparing them properly to rise to their full potential and contribution:

> Contending for the rights of woman, my main argument is built on this simple principle, that if she be not prepared by education to become the companion of man, she will stop the progress of knowledge and virtue; for truth must be common to all, or it will be inefficacious with respect to its influence on general practice. And how can *woman* be expected to cooperate unless she know why she ought to be virtuous? unless freedom strengthen her reason till she comprehend her duty, and see in what manner it is connected with her real good? If children are to be educated to understand the true principle of patriotism, their mother must be a patriot; and the love of mankind, from which an orderly train of virtues spring, can only be produced by considering the moral and civil interest of mankind; but the education and situation of *woman*, at present, shuts her out from such investigations.[60]

SCOTTISH COMMONSENSE ARGUMENTS AGAINST POLYGAMY

These English natural rights arguments against polygamy had parallels in other legal systems and cultures, including the United States, as we shall see in the next chapter.

---

[58] Ibid., 103, 106–107.
[59] This phrase is from Eileen Hunt Botting, *Wollstonecraft, Mill and Women's Human Rights* (New Haven, CT: Yale University Press, 2016), ch. 2, n. 56.
[60] Wollstonecraft, *A Vindication of the Rights of Woman*, 143–149.

In making their arguments these natural rights advocates pointed out various harms that polygamy visited on women and children – a feature of polygamy that some earlier natural law theorists had also raised. Various Scottish Enlightenment figures also pointed to these harms, and wove them into a commonsense, prudential, and even pragmatic argument against polygamy. "Rights talk" was part of this Scottish discourse, but "wrongs talk" was the real focus of their argument. For them, polygamy simply did not make any sense given the natural configuration of human sexuality and enduring pair bonding strategies needed for effective procreation. And other forms of plural sexual union – notably, adultery, concubinage, and no-fault divorce and remarriage – did not make much sense either. Indeed, as David Hume put it, they would prove to be "the doom of all mortals."

Henry Home

The writings of Henry Home (1696–1782), known as Lord Kames of Scotland, were a particularly good example of this style of commonsense argument. A leading man of letters and a leading justice of the Scottish high court, Home wrote extensively on law and politics, religion and morality, history and economy, art and industry. He was best known for his brilliant defense of natural law, principally on empirical and rational grounds. Home sought to prove the realities of virtue, duty, justice, liberty, freedom, and other natural moral principles, and the necessity for rational humans to create various offices, laws, and institutions to support and protect them. Although his rationalist methodology and naturalist theology rankled the orthodox Christian theologians of his day, Home wanted to give his natural law and commonsense argument a more universal and enduring cogency. A devout and life-long Protestant, he believed in the truth of Scripture and the will of God. But he wanted to win over even skeptics and atheists to his legal and moral arguments and to give enduring "authority to the promises and covenants" that helped create society and its institutions.[61]

Among many other institutions and "covenants," Home defended monogamous marriage as a "necessity of nature," and he denounced polygamy as "a vice against human nature." Home recognized, of course, that polygamy was commonplace among some animals.[62] He also recognized that polygamy had been practiced in

---

[61] See Henry Home, *Essays on the Principles of Morality and Natural Religion* [1779], 3rd ed., ed. Mary Catherine Moran (Indianapolis, IN: Liberty Fund, 2005), esp. Part I, Essay 2, chaps. 6 and 9, and the study of Ian Simpson Ross, *Lord Kames and the Scotland of his Day* (Oxford: Oxford University Press, 1972); William C. Lehmann, *Henry Home, Lord Kames, and the Scottish Enlightenment: A Study in National Character and in the History of Ideas* (The Hague: Martinus Nijhoff, 1971).

[62] See Henry Home, *Sketches of the History of Man, Considerably Enlarged by the Latest Additions and Corrections of the Author*, ed. James A. Harris (Indianapolis, IN: Liberty Fund, 2007), 3 vols., Book I, Sketch VI, Appendix: "Concerning Propagation of Animals and Care of Progeny."

early Western history and was still known in some Islamic and Asiatic cultures in his day. But, Home insisted, polygamy exists only "where women are treated as inferior beings," and where "men of wealth transgress every rule of temperance" by buying their wives like slaves and by adopting the "savage manners" of animals. Among horses, cattle, and other grazing animals, he argued, polygamy is natural. One superior male breeds with all females, and the mothers take care of their own young who grow quickly independent. For these animals, monogamous "pairing would be of no use: the female feeds herself and her young at the same instant; and nothing is left for the male to do." But other animals, such as nesting birds, "whose young require the nursing care of both parents, are directed by nature to pair" and to remain paired till their young "are sufficiently vigorous to provide for themselves."[63]

Humans are the latter sort of creature, said Home, for whom pairing and dual parenting are indispensable. Humans are thus inclined by nature toward enduring monogamous pairing of parents – indeed, more so than any other creature given the long fragility and helplessness of their offspring. Home expanded on the natural configuration of marriage and the importance of human childhood dependency for the construction of marriage. He added new insights as well from the budding science of cultural development (anthropology as we now call it):

> Man is an animal of long life, and is proportionally slow in growing to maturity: he is a helpless being before the age of fifteen or sixteen; and there may be in a family ten or twelve children of different births, before the eldest can shift for itself. Now in the original state of hunting and fishing, which are laborious occupations, and not always successful, a woman, suckling her infant, is not able to provide food even for herself, far less for ten or twelve voracious children.... [P]airing is so necessary to the human race, that it must be natural and instinctive.... Brute animals, which do not pair, have grass and other food in plenty, enabling the female to feed her young without needing any assistance from the male. But where the young require the nursing care of both parents, pairing is a law of nature.[64]

Not only is the pairing of male and female a law of nature, Home continued. "Matrimony is instituted by nature" to overcome humans' greatest natural handicap to effective procreation and preservation as a species – their perpetual desire for sex, especially among the young who are the most fertile. Unlike most animals, whose sexual appetites are confined to short rutting seasons, Home wrote, humans have a constant sexual appetite which, by nature, "demands gratification, after short intervals." If men and women just had random sex with anyone – "like the hart in rutting time" – the human race would devolve into a "savage state of nature"

---

[63] Ibid., Sketch V, 204, Sketch VI, 261, 263, 271, 278.
[64] Ibid., Sketch VI, 263–264.

and soon die out. Men would make perennial and "promiscuous use of women" and not commit themselves to the care of these women or their children. "Women would in effect be common prostitutes." Few women would have the ability on their own "to provide food for a family of children," and most would avoid having children or would abandon them if they did. Marriage is nature's safeguard against such proclivities, said Home, and "frequent enjoyment" of marital sex and intimacy "endears a pair to each other," making them want only each other all the more. "Sweet is the society of a pair fitted for each other, in whom are collected the affections of husband, wife, lover, friend, the tenderest affections of human nature."

> The God of nature has [thus] enforced conjugal society, not only by making it agreeable, but by the principle of chastity inherent in our nature. To animals that have no instinct for pairing, chastity is utterly unknown; and to them it would be useless. The mare, the cow, the ewe, the she-goat, receive the male without ceremony, and admit the first that comes in the way without distinction. Neither have tame fowl any notion of chastity: they pair not; and the female gets no food from the male, even during incubation. But chastity and mutual fidelity [are] essential to the human race; enforced by the principle of chastity, a branch of the moral sense. Chastity is essential even to the continuation of the human race. As the carnal appetite is always alive, the sexes would wallow in pleasure, and be soon rendered unfit for procreation, were it not for the restraint of chastity.[65]

Polygamy violates this natural design and strategy for successful procreation through enduring marital cohabitation, Home argued. First, monogamy is better suited to the roughly equal numbers of men and women in the world. "All men are by nature equal in rank; no man is privileged above another to have a wife; and therefore polygamy is contradictory" to the natural order and to the natural right of each fit adult to marry. Monogamous pairing is most "clearly the voice of nature." It is echoed in "sacred Scripture" in its injunction that "two" – not three or four – shall become "one flesh" in marriage. If God and nature had intended to condone polygamy, there would be many more females than males.[66]

Second, monogamy "is much better calculated for continuing the race, than the union of one man with many women." One man cannot possibly provide food, care, and nurture to the many children born of his many wives. Their wives are not able to provide easily for their young when they are weakened from child labor and birth, needed for nursing, or distracted by the many needs of multiple children. Some of

---

[65] Ibid., Sketch VI, 264, 267, 269–270. Later, Home condemned mandatory celibacy and abstinence within marriage as "ridiculous self-denial," an "impudent disregard of moral principles," and the "grossest of all deviations, not only from sound morality, but from pure religion" and natural law. Ibid., Book III, Sketch III, 888–890.

[66] Ibid., Sketch VI, 265–266.

their children will be neglected; some will grow up impoverished, malnourished, or undereducated; some will inevitably die. "How much better chance for life have infants who are distributed more equally in different families."[67]

Third, monogamy is better suited for women. Men and women are by nature equal, Homes argued at length. Monogamous marriage is naturally designed to respect this natural gender equality, even while recognizing the different roles that a husband and wife play in the procreation and nurture of their children. Thus marriage works best when a husband and wife have "reciprocal and equal affection" as true "companions" in life, who enjoy each other and their children with "endearment" and "constancy." Polygamy, by contrast, is simply a patriarchal fraud. Each wife is reduced to a servant, "a mere instrument of pleasure and propagation" for her husband. Each wife is reduced to competing for the attention and affection of her husband, particularly if she has small children and needs help in their care. One wife and her children will inevitably be singled out for special favor, denigrating the others further and exacerbating the tensions within the household which cause the children to suffer, too. Packs of wolves might thrive this way, but rational humans cannot. Combining natural instinct with rational reflection, humans have discovered that monogamy is the "foundation for a true matrimonial covenant" between two equal adults.[68]

Fourth, monogamy is better designed to promote the fidelity and chastity humans need to procreate, nurture, and educate their children through adulthood, and to provide them with models of effective marriage and parenting that they will emulate. Monogamy induces husbands and wives to remain faithful to each other and to their children, come what may. Polygamy, by contrast, is simply a forum and a catalyst for adultery and lust. If a husband is allowed to satisfy his lust for a second woman whom he can add as a wife, his "one act of incontinence will lead to others without end." Soon enough, he will lust after yet another wife and still another – even the wife of another man, as the biblical story of King David's lust for Bathsheba tragically illustrates. The husband's bed-hopping, in turn, will "alienate the affections" of his first wife, who will embark on her own bed-hopping. Such "unlawful love" will only trigger more and more rivalries among husbands, wives, and lovers in which all will suffer. Moreover, by sharing another man's bed, the wife might well require her husband "to maintain and educate children who are not his own." This most men will not do unless they are uncommonly smitten or charitable. Polygamy simply "does not work," Home wrote. "Matrimony between a single pair, for mutual comfort, and for procreating children implies the strictest mutual

[67] Ibid., Sketch VI, 266; Sketch VIII, 484.
[68] Ibid., Sketch VI, 261, 267–268, 287–311.

fidelity." Polygamy leads men, women, and children to "domestic wreckage," whose damaging effects will only compound in the next generations.[69]

Even children understand that monogamous marriage is "an appointment of nature," Home concluded. As infants they bond with both their mothers and fathers and when they grow older they work to keep the couple together. "If undisguised nature shows itself anywhere, it is in children," Home wrote. "They often hear, it is true, people talking of matrimony; but they also hear of logical, metaphysical, and commercial matters, without understanding a syllable. Whence then their notion of marriage but from nature? Marriage is a compound idea, which no instruction could bring within the comprehension of a child, did not nature cooperate." From the "mouths of babes" come profound truths about our most basic institution.[70]

Frances Hutcheson

Home's extended argument for monogamy and against polygamy was typical of the arguments used in Scottish Enlightenment circles. Some of these writers supplemented these with arguments from Scripture and Christian tradition, but most, like Home, sought to prove their case on rational and empirical grounds so much as possible. For example, the great Scottish philosopher of common sense Frances Hutcheson (1694–1746) grounded his argument for the natural law of monogamy, fidelity, and exclusivity again on the natural needs of mothers and children:

> Now as the mothers are quite insufficient alone for this necessary and laborious task, which nature also has plainly enjoined on both the parents by implanting in both that strong parental affection; both parents are bound to concur in it, with joint labor, and united cares for a great share of their lives: and this can never be tolerable to them unless they are previously united in love and stable friendship: as new children also must be coming into life, prolonging this joint charge. To engage mankind more cheerfully in this laborious service nature has implanted vehement affections between the sexes; excited not so much by views of brutal pleasure as by some appearances of virtues, displayed in their behavior, and even by their very form and countenances. These strong impulses plainly show it to be the intention of nature that human offspring should be propagated only by parents first united in stable friendship, and in a firm covenant about perpetual cohabitation and joint care of their common children. For all true friendship aims at perpetuity: there's no friendship in a bond only for a fixed term of years, or in one depending upon certain events which the utmost fidelity of the parties cannot ensure.[71]

---

[69] Ibid., Sketch V, 204; Sketch VI, 270, 287–289.

[70] Ibid., Sketch VI, 265.

[71] Frances Hutcheson, *Philosophiae Moralis Institutio Compendiaria, With a Short Introduction to Moral Philosophy*, ed. Luigi Turco (Indianapolis, IN: Liberty Fund, 2007), 218.

"Nature has thus strongly recommended" that for humans all sex and procreation occur within a "proper covenant about a friendly society for life," Hutcheson continued. "The chief articles in this covenant" are mutual fidelity of husband and wife to each other. A wandering wife causes the "greatest injury" to her husband by bringing adulterine children into the home who dilute his property and distract him from "that tender affection which is naturally due to his own [children]." A wandering husband causes great injury to his wife and children by allowing his affections and fortunes to be squandered on prostitutes, mistresses, and lovers. (Hutcheson's commentators added the dangers of tracking in syphilis and other sexual diseases, too, through his illicit sex.) Other articles of the "natural marital covenant," Hutcheson wrote, include "a perpetual union of interests and pursuits" between husband and wife, a mutual commitment to "the right education of their common children," and a mutual agreement to forgo separation and divorce. It is against reason and human nature, Hutcheson wrote, "to divorce or separate from a faithful and affectionate consort for any causes which include no moral turpitude; such as barrenness, or infirmity of body; or any mournful accident which no mortal could prevent." Such "libertinism" is "not only unjust, but also unnatural." Divorce should be allowed only in cases of adultery, "obstinate desertion, capital enmity, or hatred and such gross outrages as take away all hopes of any friendly society for the future or a safe and agreeable life together."[72]

David Hume

Similarly, the famous Scottish philosopher David Hume (1711–1776) for all his skepticism about traditional morality, thought traditional legal and moral norms of sex, marriage, and family life to be both natural and sensible. Hume summarized the natural configuration of marriage crisply: "The long and helpless infancy requires the combination of parents for the subsistence of their young; and that combination requires the virtue of chastity and fidelity to the marriage bed."[73]

Hume used many of the same arguments that Home had mustered against polygamy. This "odious institution," he called it, replaced the natural equality of the sexes with a form of slavery and tyranny. Polygamy led to "jealousy and competition among wives." Moreover, said Hume, polygamy forced a man, distracted by his

[72] Ibid., 220–222. See also Frances Hutcheson, *Logic, Metaphysics, and the Natural Sociability of Mankind*, eds. James Moore and Michael Silverthorne (Indianapolis, IN: Liberty Fund, 2006), 206–207.
[73] David Hume, *Enquiries Concerning the Human Understanding and Concerning the Principles of Morals* [1777], 2nd ed., ed. L.A. Selby-Bigge (Oxford: Clarendon Press, 1902; 2nd impr., 1963), 206–207.

other wives and children, to confine his other wives to the home – by physically threatening, binding, or even laming them, by isolating them from society, or by keeping them so sick, poor, and weak they could not leave, or be attractive enough for another man to steal. All this is a form of "barbarism," with "frightful effects" that defy all nature and reason.[74] No rational woman with any common sense would willingly accept such "tyranny" and "slavery," said Hume. Nor would rational men and societies with any commonsense accept such a role for their wives.

> We are, by nature, their lovers, their friends, their patrons: Would we willingly exchange such endearing appellations, for the barbarous title of master and tyrant? In what capacity shall we gain by this inhuman proceeding? As lovers, or as husbands? The lover, is totally annihilated; and courtship, the most agreeable scene in life, can no longer have place, where women have not the free disposal of themselves, but are bought and sold like the meanest animal. The husband is as little a gainer, having found the admirable secret of extinguishing part of love, except its jealousy. No rose without its thorn; but he must be a foolish wretch indeed, that throws away the rose and preserves only the thorn....
>
> The bad education of children, especially children of condition, is another unavoidable consequence of [polygamy]. Those who pass the early part of life among slaves [their mothers], are only qualified to be, themselves, slaves and tyrants; and in every future intercourse, either with their inferiors or superiors, are apt to forget the natural equality of mankind.... Barbarism appears, from reason as well as experience, to be the inseparable attendant of polygamy.[75]

Hume offered similar natural and utilitarian arguments against "voluntary divorce" and remarriage – what the tradition regarded as successive polygamy. Many in Hume's day argued for divorce as a natural expression of the freedom of contract and a natural compensation for having no recourse to polygamy despite a man's natural drive to multiple partners. "The heart of man delights in liberty," their argument went; "the very image of constraint is grievous to it." Hume

---

[74] David Hume, *Essays Moral, Political, and Literary*, rev. ed., ed. Eugene F. Miller (Indianapolis, IN: Liberty Fund, 1987), Essay XIX "On Polygamy and Divorces," pp. 182–187.

[75] Ibid., XIX.9–13. Drawing on Hume, Adam Smith wrote similarly that "polygamy was on many accounts much inferior to monogamy of every sort. With regard to the wives it produces the greatest misery, as jealousy of every sort, discord, and enmity must inevitably attend it. The children also must be greatly neglected in every shape and lead but a very wretched life. The servants must all be slaves and entirely under the power of their master. With regard to the [polygamous] man himself, to whose happiness or rather pleasure the good of all the rest seems to be sacrificed, he also has no great enjoyment. He is racked by the most tormenting jealousy and has little enjoyment from the affections of his family or the intercourse of other men. It is also detrimental to population, and besides it is very hurtful to the liberty of the people." Adam Smith, *Lectures on Jurisprudence*, eds. R.L. Meek, D.D. Raphael, and P.G. Stein (Indianapolis, IN: Liberty Fund, 1978), 159. See more generally ibid., 150–173, 442–449.

would have none of this. To be sure, he recognized that divorce was sometimes the better of two evils – especially where one party was guilty of adultery, severe cruelty, or malicious desertion, and especially when no children were involved. But, outside of such circumstances, he said, "nature has made divorce" without real cause the "doom of all mortals." First, with voluntary divorce, the children suffer and become "miserable." Shuffled from home to home, consigned to the care of strangers and step-parents "instead of the fond attention and concern of a parent," the inconveniences and encumbrances of their lives just multiply as the divorces of their parents and stepparents multiply. Second, when voluntary divorce is foreclosed, couples by nature become disinclined to wander, and instead form "a calm and sedate affection, conducted by reason and cemented by habit; springing from long acquaintance and mutual obligations, without jealousies or fears." "We need not, therefore, be afraid of drawing the marriage-knot, which chiefly subsists by friendship, the closest possible." Third, "nothing is more dangerous than to unite two persons so closely in all their interests and concerns, as man and wife, without rendering the union entire and total. The least possibility of a separate interest must be the source of endless quarrels and suspicions." Nature, justice, and prudence alike require their "continued consortium."[76]

THE UTILITARIAN CASE AGAINST POLYGAMY

The natural law, natural rights, and commonsense arguments of the Enlightenment that we have seen all sought to make the case against polygamy on non-theological grounds. The Bible and traditional theologians, if referenced at all, were used only as examples or illustrations of broader principles that were equally evident in secular texts and equally cogent on secular grounds. One final line of argument against polygamy to emerge from Enlightenment writers was based on the principles of public and private utility. "Theological utilitarianism," we saw in the last chapter, was one of the methods used by Johann Leyser and Martin Madan, among others, to defend polygamy. Their technique was to show that the Bible had good policy reasons to blend the options of monogamy, polygamy, and divorce in biblical times, and those policy reasons were still useful in the present day. A number of Enlightenment writers pushed firmly against this appeal to utility.

William Paley

The writings of William Paley (1743–1805), a Cambridge philosopher and, later, an Anglican cleric, provide a good illustration. Paley was known in his day as a

---

[76] Hume, *Essays Moral, Political, and Literary*, 187–190.

"theological utilitarian." He sought to define those natural principles and practices of social life that most conduce to human happiness – in this life and in the next. Those principles and practices, he said, could be variously sought in Scripture and tradition, divine law and natural law, morality and casuistry – all of which, for Paley, contributed and came to "the same thing; namely, that science which teaches men their duty and the reasons of it."[77]

Marriage is among the natural duties and rights of men and women, Paley wrote, for it provides a variety of private and public goods. His list of marital goods was a nice distillation of traditional arguments:

1. The private comfort of individuals, especially of the female sex....
2. The production of the greatest number of healthy children, their better education, and the making of due provision for their settlement in life.
3. The peace of human society, in cutting off a principal source of contention, by assigning one or more women to one man, and protecting his exclusive right by sanctions of morality and law.
4. The better government of society, by distributing the community into separate families, and appointing over each the authority of a master of a family, which has more actual influence than all civil authority put together.
5. The same end, in the additional security which the state receives for the good behaviour of its citizens, from the solicitude they feel for the welfare of their children, and from their being confined to permanent habitations.
6. The encouragement of industry ... and morality.[78]

Paley worked systematically through the respective "natural rights and duties" of husband and wife, parent and child. In marriage, a husband promises "to love, comfort, honor, and keep his wife" and a wife promises "to obey, serve, love, honor, and keep her husband" "in every variety of health, fortune, and condition." Both parties further stipulate "to forsake all others, and to keep only unto one another, so long as they both shall live." In a word, said Paley, each spouse promises to do all that is necessary to "consult and promote the other's happiness." These are not only Scriptural and traditional duties of marriage. They are natural duties, as can be seen in the marital contracts of all manner of cultures, which Paley adduced in ample number. These natural duties, in turn, give the other spouse "a natural right" to enforce them in cases of adultery, "desertion, neglect, prodigality, drunkenness, peevishness, penuriousness, jealousy, or any levity of conduct which administers

77 William Paley, *Principles of Moral and Political Philosophy* [1785], ed. D.L. LeMahieu (Indianapolis, IN: Liberty Fund, 2002), 1–25. See also D.L. LeMahieu, *William Paley: A Philosopher and His Age* (Lincoln, NE: University of Nebraska Press, 1976).
78 Paley, *Principles*, 167–168.

occasion of jealousy." What St. Paul called the "mutual conjugal rights" of husband and wife are simply one way of formulating the natural rights that husband and wives enjoy the world over.[79]

If the couple is blessed with children, the parents have a "natural right and duty" to provide for the child's "maintenance, education, and a reasonable provision for the child's happiness in respect of outward condition." A parent's rights to care for their children "result from their duties" to their children, said Paley.

> If it be the duty of a parent to educate his children, to form them for a life of usefulness and virtue, to provide for them situations needful for their subsistence and suited to their circumstances, and to prepare them for those situations; he has a right to such authority, and in support of that authority to exercise such discipline as may be necessary for these purposes. The law of nature acknowledges no other foundation of a parent's right over his children, besides his duty towards them. (I speak now of such rights as may be enforced by coercion.) This relation confers no property in their persons, or natural dominion over them, as is commonly supposed.[80]

But a parent "has, in no case, a right to destroy his child's happiness," Paley went on, and those that do will suffer punishment, if not lose custody of their child. Moreover, while parents have a right to encourage and train their children to a given vocation and to give their consent to their children's marriages, "parents have no right to urge their children upon marriages to which they are averse." Children, in turn, have "a natural right to receive the support, education, and care" of their parents. They also have a "natural duty" to "love, honor, and obey" their parents even when they become adults, and to care for their parents when they become old, frail, and dependent.[81]

Paley worked systematically through the various sexual sins that deviated from the private and public goods of marriage, and the natural rights and duties of the household – now marshaling natural, rational, and utilitarian arguments against them. He included briefs against fornication, prostitution, adultery, concubinage, polygamy, incest, rape, no-fault divorce, and polygamy. Although he marshaled strong arguments against each of these, he considered fornication, adultery, and polygamy to be the most serious because they caused the most injury to the most parties, and thus had the least utility for the couple, their children, and society at large.

Paley opposed fornication – "sex or cohabitation without marriage" – mostly because it "discourages marriage" and "diminishes the private and public goods"

[79] Ibid., 194–196.
[80] Ibid., 196–198.
[81] Ibid., 210.

it offers "by abating the chief temptation to it. The male part of the species will not undertake the encumbrance, expense, and restraint of married life, if they can gratify their passions at a cheaper price; and they will undertake anything rather than not gratify them." Paley recognized that he was appealing to general utility, but he thought an absolute ban on fornication was the only way to avoid the slippery slope to utter sexual libertinism. "The libertine may not be conscious that these irregularities hinder his own marriage ... much less does he perceive how *his* indulgences can hinder other men from marrying; but what will he say would be the consequence, if the same licentiousness were universal? or what should hinder its becoming universal, if it be innocent or allowable in him?"[82]

Fornication furthermore leads to prostitution, Paley went on, with its accompanying degradation of women, erosion of morals, transmission of disease, production of unwanted and uncared for children, and further irregularities and pathos. Fornication also leads naturally to a tradition of concubinage – "the kept mistress," who can be dismissed at the man's pleasure, or retained "in a state of humiliation and dependence inconsistent with the rights which marriage would confer upon her" and her children. No small wonder that the Bible condemned fornication, prostitution, concubinage, and other such "cohabitation without marriage" in no uncertain terms, said Paley, with ample demonstration. But, again, in these injunctions the Bible is simply reflecting the natural order and moral sense of mankind:

> Laying aside the injunctions of Scripture, the plain account of the question seems to be this: It is immoral, because it is pernicious, that men and women should cohabit, without undertaking certain irrevocable obligations, and mutually conferring certain civil rights; if, therefore, the law has annexed these rights and obligations to certain forms, so that they cannot be secured or undertaken by any other means, which is the case here (for, whatever the parties may promise to each other, nothing but the marriage-ceremony can make their promise irrevocable), it becomes in the same degree immoral, that men and women should cohabit without the interposition of these forms.[83]

Adultery harms the innocent spouse as well as the couple's children, said Paley. For the betrayed spouse, adultery is "a wound in his [or her] sensibility and affections, the most painful and incurable that human nature knows." For the children it brings shame and unhappiness as the vice is inevitably detected and discussed. For the adulterer or adulteress, it is a form of "perjury" that violates their marital vow and covenant. For all parties in the household, adultery will often provoke retaliation and imitation – another slippery slope to erosion of marriage and the unleashing of

[82] Ibid., 168–169.
[83] Ibid., 169–173.

sexual libertinism and seduction. Both nature and Scripture thus rain down their anathemas against it.[84]

Polygamy is adultery writ larger, Paley continued. It not only violates "the constitution of nature and the apparent design of the Deity" in creating men and women as equals and creating equal numbers of men and women. Its unnatural qualities are made even clearer in the many "bad effects" it occasions. Polygamy causes

> contests and jealousies amongst the wives of the same husband; distracted affections, or the loss of all affection, in the husband himself; a voluptuousness in the rich, which dissolves the vigor of their intellectual as well as active faculties, producing that indolence and imbecility both of mind and body, which have long characterized the nations of the East; the abasement of one half of the human species, who, in countries where polygamy obtains, are degraded into mere instruments of physical pleasure to the other half; neglect of children; and the manifold, and sometimes unnatural mischiefs, which arise from a scarcity of women. To compensate for these evils, polygamy does not offer a single advantage. In the article of population, which it has been thought to promote, the community gains nothing: for the question is not, whether one man will have more children by five or more wives than by one; but whether these five wives would not bear the same or a greater number of children to five separate husbands. And as to the care of the children, when produced, and the sending of them into the world in situations in which they may be likely to form and bring up families of their own, upon which the increase and succession of the human species in a great degree depend; this is less provided for, and less practicable, where twenty or thirty children are to be supported by the attention and fortunes of one father, than if they were divided into five or six families, to each of which were assigned the industry and inheritance of two parents.[85]

Paley opposed "frivolous" or "voluntary" divorce and remarriage as well, using arguments from natural law and general utility against this species of "successive polygamy." Like many other Protestants and Enlightenment philosophers, he thought that divorce and remarriage of the innocent spouse was both natural and necessary in cases of adultery, malicious desertion, habitual intemperance, cruelty, and crime. But Paley was against voluntary divorces or separations for "lighter causes" or by "mutual consent," on grounds of nature and utility. Such "lighter" divorces were "obviously" against natural law if the couple had dependent children, Paley thought. "It is manifestly inconsistent with the [natural] duty which the parents owe to their children; which duty can never be so well fulfilled as by their cohabitation

---

[84]   Ibid., 176–180.
[85]   Ibid., 182–183.

and united care. It is also incompatible with the right which the mother possesses, as well as the father, to the gratitude of her children and the comfort of their society; of both which she is almost necessarily deprived, by her dismission from her husband's family."[86]

"Causeless," "voluntary," and "lighter divorces," unilaterally sought, are not so obviously against natural law for childless couples, Paley argued, but they are still "inexpedient" enough to prohibit. If such divorces are available, especially on a unilateral basis, each spouse will be unnaturally tempted to begin pursuing their own separate interests rather than a common marital interest. They will begin hoarding their own money, developing their own friendships, living more and more independently. "This would beget peculation on one side, mistrust on the other, evils which at present very little disturb the confidence of married life." The availability of such divorces will further discourage spouses to reconcile their conflicts or "take pains to give up what offends, and practice what may gratify the other." They will have less incentive to work hard "to make the best of their bargain" or "promote the pleasure of the other." "These compliances, though at first extorted by necessity, become in time easy and mutual; and, though less endearing than assiduities which take their rise from affection, generally procure to the married couple a repose and satisfaction sufficient for their happiness." And the availability of such divorces will heighten the natural temptation of each spouse, especially the husband, to succumb to "new objects of desire." However much in love they were on their wedding day, and however hard they try, men are "naturally inclined" to wander after "the invitations of novelty" unless they are "permanently constrained" to remain faithful to their wives even as they lose their "youthful vigor and figure." Thus, "constituted as mankind are, and injured as the repudiated wife generally must be, it is necessary to add a stability to the condition of married women, more secure than the continuance of their husbands' affection; and to supply to both sides, by a sense of duty and of obligation, what satiety has impaired of passion and of personal attachment. Upon the whole, the power of divorce is evidently and greatly to the disadvantage of the woman: and the only question appears to be, whether the real and permanent happiness of one half of the species should be surrendered to the caprice and voluptuousness of the other."[87]

Paley's natural law and theological utilitarian arguments for monogamy and against polygamy and related sexual offenses would find enduring provenance among many utilitarians into the nineteenth century. The most famous of these utilitarians, Jeremy Bentham (1748–1832), endorsed most of these same propositions that Paley had set forth, even though Bentham famously eschewed the natural law

---

[86] Ibid., 186, 190.
[87] Ibid., 187–189.

and natural rights language that had so inspired Paley's theory of marriage. Bentham thought that traditional commendations of monogamy and condemnations of polygamy and other sexual offenses could be rationalized on utilitarian principles alone. He quoted with favor Montesquieu's rejection of polygamy as "useless."[88]

SUMMARY AND CONCLUSIONS

Scores of Enlightenment philosophers and jurists from the seventeenth century on defended traditional Western norms of monogamous marriage using this surfeit of arguments from nature, reason, custom, fairness, prudence, utility, pragmatism, and common sense. Some of these writers were inspired, no doubt, by their personal Christian faith, others by a conservative desire to maintain the status quo. But most of these writers pressed their principal arguments for monogamy and against polygamy on non-biblical grounds. And they were sometimes sharply critical of the Bible – denouncing St. Paul's preferences for celibacy, the Mosaic provisions on unilateral male divorce, and the tales of polygamy, concubinage, and prostitution among the ancient biblical patriarchs and kings. Moreover, most of these writers jettisoned many other features of the Western tradition that, in their judgment, defied reason, fairness, and utility – including, notably, the establishment of Christianity by law and the political privileging of the church over other associations. Their philosophical call for enduring and exclusive monogamous marriage was not just a rationalist apologia for traditional Christian family values or a naturalist smokescreen for personal religious beliefs. They defended traditional family norms not out of confessional faith, but out of rational proof; not just because they uncritically believed in them, but because they worked.

Their starting naturalist argument was one that Thomas Aquinas and other medieval writers had already introduced into the tradition and that various Spanish neo-scholastics had elaborated in the sixteenth century with a natural law and natural rights framework. The heart of the argument was that exclusive and enduring monogamous marriages are the best way to ensure paternal certainty and joint parental investment in children who are born vulnerable and utterly dependent on their parents' mutual care and remain so for many years. Exclusive and enduring monogamous marriages, furthermore – and this was a new emphasis in the Enlightenment – are the best way to ensure that men and women are treated with equal dignity and respect, and that husbands and wives, parents and children

[88] *The Works of Jeremy Bentham*, ed. John Bowring, 11 vols. (Edinburgh; William Tait, 1843), 1:119–121, 348–357, 55, 2:499, 531–532; 3:73, 202–203; 6:63, 522; 7:579–581. See Mary Sokol, "Jeremy Bentham on Love and Marriage," *American Journal of Legal History* 30 2009): 1.

provide each other with mutual support, protection, and edification throughout their lifetimes, adjusted to each person's needs at different stages in the life cycle.

This Enlightenment naturalist argument for stable monogamous marriages drew on complex ideas concerning human infant dependency, parental bonding, paternal certainty and investment, and the natural rights and duties of husband and wives, parents and children vis-à-vis each other and other members of society. But it also emphasized more heavily than the tradition a feature of human nature that every legal system must deal with, namely that most human adults crave sex a good deal of the time, especially when they are young and most fertile. The Enlightenment philosophers thus presupposed that husbands and wives must work hard to remain in open and active communication with each other, and maintain active and healthy sex lives even when – indeed, especially when – procreation was not or no longer possible. Robust sexual communication within marriage was essential for couples to deepen their marital love constantly and to keep them in their own beds, rather than their neighbor's. And marital sex sometimes was even more important when the home was (newly) empty, and husbands and wives depended so centrally on each other (not on their children) for their daily emotional fulfillment.

The Enlightenment arguments, furthermore, outlawed many other types of sexual activities and interactions, even those practiced in less developed human societies. Polygyny was out because it fractured marital trust and troth, harmed wives and children, privileged patriarchy and sexual slavery, and fomented male lust and adultery. Polyandry was out because it created paternal uncertainty and catalyzed male rivalry to the ultimate detriment of the children. Prostitution and fornication were out because they exploited women, fostered libertinism, deterred marriage, and produced bastards. Adultery was out for some of the same reasons, but even more because it shattered marital fidelity and trust, diffused family resources and parental energy, and risked sexual disease and physical retaliation of the betrayed spouse. No-fault divorce was out because it eroded marital fidelity and investment, jeopardized long-term spousal support and care, and squandered family property on which children eventually depended. By the twentieth century, similar natural law and natural rights arguments were used to stamp out the discrimination that the common law still retained against spinsters, wives, and illegitimate children.

The Enlightenment philosophers furthermore highlighted the many public and private goods that monogamous marriage brought to husband and wife, parent and child, state and society, and the many harms that were associated with the practice of polygamy. This utilitarian argument, too, was continuous with the tradition, but the philosophers now abstracted it from biblical teachings. Pre-modern writers, we saw, praised monogamous marriage for the many benefits it brought. And, they read the biblical accounts of polygamy as fair warning that this institution was not only inexpedient, immoral, unnatural, and unjust, but that it also inevitably fostered criminal wrongdoing. Polygamy often caused or came with fraud, trickery, intrigue, lust, seduction, coercion, rape, incest, adultery, murder, exploitation and coercion of young women, jealousy and rivalry among wives and their children, dissipation of family wealth and inequality of treatment and support of household members, banishment and disinheritance of disfavored children, and more. Not in every case, to be sure, but in so many cases that these had to be seen as the inherent and inevitable risks of polygamy. Even the most pious and upright biblical patriarchs incurred these costs when they experimented with this unnatural institution.

Enlightenment writers repeated this long list of harms and crimes associated with the practice of polygamy. But they now used comparative cultural examples rather than biblical examples to drive home their point. The Enlightenment philosophers presented these harms and crimes as prima facie evidence that polygamy was ultimately unnatural for humans. But they now made general appeals to human anthropology and evolutionary science to drive home their argument rather than adducing the creation story of "two in one flesh" or covenant or sacramental metaphors based on God and his people.

Even the most robust natural law theorists of early modern and modern times, however, understood that the natural law of sex, marriage, and family could not do it all, because it was not self-executing. The natural law might strongly incline humans to behave in certain ways in their sex, marriage, and family lives, and many humans in fact follow these inclinations without prompting. But the reality is that humans (unlike most animals) have free will, and a good number of folks choose to stray on occasion from the naturally licit path; some miscreants stray all the time. Natural law needs the positive laws of the state and the sturdy examples and constraints of the culture to teach these basic norms of sex, marriage, and family life to the community, to encourage and facilitate citizens to live in accordance with them, to deter and punish citizens when they deviate to the harm of others, and to rehabilitate and redirect them to healthier relationships consistent with the norms of natural and civil liberty.

10

The American Case Against Polygamy

FIGURE 21. "Detail of a Fan: The Marriage Contract," from Alfredo Dagli Orti. Used by permission of the Alfredo Dagli Orti / Art Resource, New York.

FIGURE 22. "Brigham Young hiding in a wardrobe while his many wives attack two new brides," from American School.
Used by permission of the Private Collection. Peter Newark Pictures / Bridgeman Images.

The Enlightenment arguments in favor of monogamy and against polygamy, and other sexual crimes were staples for the Anglo-American common lawyers of the eighteenth to twentieth centuries. It was precisely the rational, utilitarian, and even pragmatic formulation of these arguments that made them so appealing to jurists as they sought to create a common law of marriage that no longer depended on ecclesiastical law, church courts, or theological arguments. Particularly in America, the disestablishment of religion mandated by the federal and state constitutions made direct appeals to the Bible and to Christian theology an insufficient ground by itself for cogent legal arguments concerning marriage. Even in England, which retained its Anglican establishment, many common lawyers were equally eager to cast their argument in the natural and utilitarian terms of the Enlightenment, rather than the biblical and theological terms of the tradition. It was one thing to say that "Christianity is part of the common law," as Anglo-American lawyers had long said.[1] It was quite another thing to say that the common law is part of Christianity. That

---

[1] See, e.g., Thomas M. Cooley, *A Treatise on the Constitutional Limitations Which Rest upon the Legislative Power of the States of the American Union*, 3rd ed. (Boston: Little Brown, 1874), 471–473. Cooley wrote: "It is frequently said that Christianity is part of the law of the land. In a certain sense, and for certain purposes, this is true. The best features of the common law, and especially those

would simply not do. The Enlightenment philosophical distillation of the strongest traditional arguments for monogamy and against polygamy was thus attractive to the common lawyers.

This chapter traces the American case against polygamy from early colonial days to the twentieth century. Because the nineteenth-century federal government case against Mormon polygamy is very well known in the literature, I summarize that part of the story more briefly, pointing you to the best literature on point. Less well known are the many colonial and early state laws against polygamy, and the theories of monogamy versus polygamy that emerged among nineteenth-century jurists and social scientists; those are the main focus of the pages that follow and provide the background to the U.S. Supreme Court's cases upholding the criminal prohibitions on polygamy against Mormons.

THE EMERGING AMERICAN LAW OF
MONOGAMY AND POLYGAMY

The Colonial Inheritance

The American colonies inherited the teachings and laws of marriage and family life from their European mother countries. Catholic models of sacramental monogamous marriage came to direct application in Spanish North American colonies, beginning already in the sixteenth century. Before the United States acquired the territories of Louisiana (1803), the Floridas (1819), Texas (1836), New Mexico (1848), and California (1848), these colonies were under the formal authority of Spain, which had millennium-long prohibitions against polygamy.[2] These colonies were also under the formal jurisdiction of the ecclesiastical provinces of Santo Domingo, Havana, and Mexico. The Catholic clergy and missionaries to these American frontier regions taught the sacramental theology of marriage. The ecclesiastical hierarchy, aided by the secular courts, enforced the canon laws of

which relate to the family and social relations; which compel the parent to support the child, and the husband the wife; which make the marriage tie permanent and which forbid polygamy, have either been derived from, or have been improved and strengthened by, the prevailing religion and teachings of its sacred book. But the law does not attempt to enforce the precepts of Christianity, on the ground of their sacred character or divine origin. Some of these precepts are universally recognized as being incapable of enforcement by human laws, notwithstanding they are of continual and universal obligation. Christianity therefore is not part of the law of the land, in the sense that would entitle the courts to take notice of and base their judgments upon it, except so far as they should find that its precepts have been incorporated in, and thus become a component part of, the law." Ibid., 472. See also Stuart Banner, "When Christianity was Part of the Common Law," *Law and History Review* 16 (1988): 27–62.

[2] See sources and discussion in the Introduction, p. 14 and in Chapter 4, p. 157.

marriage. This included the Decree *Tametsi* issued by the Council of Trent in 1563, with its anathemas on polygamy as well as on divorce and remarriage.[3]

The Spanish Inquisition operated in the Spanish colonies of North and Central America. Local records show that the inquisitors worked hard to break up the plural marriages of the colonists and to punish knowing polygamists rather severely. In an impressive archival study, social historian Brian Boyer has found 2,305 cases of bigamy or polygamy brought before the Inquisition in colonial Mexico between 1535 and 1789.[4] Suspected polygamists were accused or denounced before the Inquisition, and their cases preliminarily investigated. Many cases stopped there, with the parties admonished or instructed to do better. But if there was evidence of knowing or intentional polygamy, the inquisitors subjected the defendant and his or her accomplices to a formal trial, which could include the use of torture to extract a confession. Parties found guilty of polygamy, or complicity in the polygamy of others, faced a range of punishments and purgations tailored to the gravity of their offense. Intentional polygamists, especially recidivists, faced serious punishment, Boyer documents: "one or two hundred lashes, as one was paraded through the main streets of Mexico, with a crier shouting one's crime. Afterward came a long and brutalizing confinement of galley servitude for a term of five to seven years – if one survived."[5] In addition to the work of the Spanish Inquisition among the colonists, local secular authorities, armed with new royal decrees from Spain in 1530 and 1551, worked hard to stamp out the polygamy of indigenous peoples in new Spain, a campaign that went on, with episodes of real brutality, for more than two centuries.[6]

Protestant models of marriage were more influential in colonial America, particularly in the thirteen original colonies that became the first American states. Before the American Revolution of 1776, the Atlantic seaboard was a veritable

---

[3] See Hans W. Baade, "The Form of Marriage in Spanish North America," *Cornell Law Review* 61 (1975): 1–89; David J. Weber, *The Spanish Frontier in North America* (New Haven, CT: Yale University Press, 1992).

[4] Richard Boyer, *Lives of the Bigamists: Marriage, Family, and Community in Colonial Mexico* (Albuquerque: University of New Mexico Press, 1995), 7–9.

[5] Ibid., 232; see examples of individual male and female defendants, in ibid., 196, 207; John F. Chuchiak IV, ed., *The Inquisition in New Spain, 1536–1820: A Documentary History* (Baltimore, MD: John Hopkins University Press, 2012), esp. 5–11, 132–135, 154–155, 218–223, 371, 374, 380, 385. See additional case studies in Alexandra Parma Cook and Noble David Cook, *Good Faith and Truthful Ignorance; A Case of Transatlantic Bigamy* (Durham, NC: Duke University Press, 1991); Ramón Gutiérrez, *When Jesus Came, The Corn Mothers Went Away: Marriage, Sexuality and Power in New Mexico, 1500–1846* (Stanford, CA: Stanford University Press, 1991), 246–247.

[6] See detailed sources and discussion in Sarah Pearsall, "'Having Many Wives' in Two American Rebellions: The Politics of Households and the Radically Conservative," *American Historical Review* (October 2013): 1000–1028, evidently a preview to her forthcoming title *Beyond One Man and One Woman: A History of Early American Polygamy*.

checkerboard of Protestant pluralism (with Catholic strongholds in Maryland). Lutheran settlements were scattered throughout colonial Delaware, Maryland, Pennsylvania, and New York. Calvinist communities (Congregational, Puritan, Presbyterian, Reformed, and Huguenot) were strong in New England, and in parts of New York, New Jersey, Pennsylvania, and the coastal Carolinas and Georgia. Evangelical and Free Church communities (Baptists, Methodists, and Quakers especially) found strongholds in Rhode Island and Pennsylvania and were scattered throughout the new states and far onto the frontier, especially after the Great Awakening of 1720–1780. The largest groups of colonists were Anglicans (called Protestant Episcopalians after 1789) who were strongest in Virginia, Maryland, Georgia, and the Carolinas, but had ample representation throughout the original thirteen states and beyond. Indeed, on the eve of the American Revolution, all thirteen American colonies were formally part of the Bishopric of London and formally subject to English ecclesiastical law.

These plural Protestant polities, although hardly uniform in their marital norms and habits, were largely united in their adherence to the basic marital teachings of the Protestant Reformation. They rejected Catholic views of marriage as an unbreakable sacramental union under the church's jurisdiction, and instead favored the view of marriage as a conditional and breakable covenant or contract under the state's jurisdiction. They generally allowed for divorce on proof of adultery and desertion, and encouraged remarriage of the divorced and widowed after a waiting period. They encouraged ministers to be married and rejected the complex medieval laws of clerical bigamy. New England Calvinist colonies allowed eligible couples to choose to marry before a justice of the peace or a religious official.[7] Southern Anglican colonies, following the *Book of Common Prayer*, insisted that such marriages be contracted "in the face of the church" and be consecrated by a properly licensed religious official. Calvinist communities in the north granted local civil courts jurisdiction over issues of divorce, annulment, child custody, and division of the postmarital estate. Anglican communities in the south insisted that only the legislature should hear and decide such cases and issues.[8] These jurisdictional differences between north and south softened after the American Revolution, when judicial control of marital dissolution gradually became the norm, although the respective roles of church and state, and of courts and legislatures, in

---

[7] See Judith Areen, "Uncovering the Reformation Roots of American Marriage and Divorce Law," Uncovering the Reformation Roots of American Marriage and Divorce Law," *Yale Journal of Law and Feminism* 26 (2014): 29–85.

[8] See detailed study in George Elliott Howard, *A History of Matrimonial Institutions*, 3 vols. (Chicago, IL: University of Chicago Press, 1904).

marital formation and dissolution remained contested in some states well into the nineteenth century.[9]

All thirteen American colonies on the Atlantic seaboard privileged monogamy and criminalized polygamy. This was, in part, a simple application of English law. The founding colonial charters issued by England granted the colonists an ample measure of self-governance, but they also ordered the local authorities to abide by the law of England.[10] The Polygamy Act issued by the English Parliament in 1604 was thus the presumptive law of the colonies, too, even though the Act on its face applied only to "persons within His Majesty's dominions of England and Wales."[11] Colonial Virginia accepted this straightforwardly: "The laws of England against bigamy, or having more than one wife or husband shall be put in execution in this country."[12] Colonial South Carolina and Maryland just repeated the substance of this 1604 law in their own local penal codes and enforced them following their own procedures.[13]

Anne Thompson of colonial Maryland, for example, was convicted for "having two husbands," but she escaped execution by pleading benefit of clergy and was branded on the hand. She appealed her conviction to the General Council, and she was pardoned after promising the authorities she would "cleave" to her first husband and live with him thereafter "soberly and honestly."[14] Robert Holt of Maryland was indicted for polygamy, too. So was the minister who helped him end his first

---

[9] See, e.g., Norma Basch, *Forming American Divorce From the Revolutionary Generation to the Victorians* (Berkeley/Los Angeles: University of California Press, 1999); Thomas E. Buckley, *The Great Catastrophe of My Life: Divorce in the Old Dominion* (Chapel Hill: University of North Carolina Press, 2002); Richard H. Chused, *Private Acts in Public Places: A Social History of Divorce in the Formative Era of American Family Law* (Philadelphia: University of Pennsylvania Press, 1994).

[10] See, e.g., Charter of Massachusetts Bay (1629), ¶8, in The Avalon Project: Documents in Law, History, Diplomacy (http://avalon.law.yale.edu/17th_century/mass03.asp). On colonial charters, see Anthony Pagden, "Law, Colonization, Legitimation, and the European Background," in Michael Grossberg and Christopher Tomlin, eds., *The Cambridge History of Law in America*, 3 vols. (Cambridge: Cambridge University Press, 2008), 1:1–31.

[11] See discussion in Chapter 7, pp. 298–305.

[12] Acts of Assembly (1657–1658) in W.W. Hening, ed., *The Statutes At Large; Being A Collection Of All The Laws Of Virginia, From The First Session Of The Legislature, In The Year 1619*, 13 vols. (New York: R. &. W. & G. Bartow, 1823), 1:434. See Hugh F. Rankin, *Criminal Trial Proceedings in the General Court of Colonial Virginia* (Charlottesville: University Press of Virginia, 1965), 146–147, on two bigamy cases.

[13] *An Alphabetical Digest of the Public Statute Law of South-Carolina*, 3 vols. (Charleston, SC: John Hoff, 1814), title 132, vol. 2:119–120; John F. Grimké, *The South-Carolina Justice of Peace*, 3rd ed. (New York: T. & J. Swords, 1810), 353; John B. Colvin, *Magistrate's Guide and Citizen's Counsellor; Being a Digest of those Laws of Maryland Most Necessary to Be Known* (Fredericktown, MD: n.p., 1805), 146–147 (referencing law of 1706, c. 9).

[14] The case is reported in Raphael Semmes, *Crime and Punishment in Early Maryland* (Baltimore, MD: Johns Hopkins University Press, 1938), 205.

marriage and enter the second; he was indicted for complicity in Holt's bigamy. Holt said he had left his first wife because of her repeated adultery that had already brought two adulterine children into his home, and he wanted no more of her. He and the minister were eventually granted amnesty, but evidently on the condition that Holt return to his first wife. When Holt took up with his second wife anew, he was indicted for bigamy a second time, but he died before trial.[15]

Other colonies simply enforced the substance of the 1604 Polygamy Act of England without at first having their own local statute on point. In 1639, for example, colonial Massachusetts authorities prosecuted James Luxford for "having two wives." His second marriage was annulled and his first wife eventually divorced him. James was "obliged to give all he had to his wife last married, for her and her children, was fined £100, put in the stocks and banished" from the colony.[16] Likewise, in 1644, "the marriage of John Richardson to Elizabeth Frye was annulled on proof that he had a former wife living in England."[17]

In 1647, the Massachusetts authorities issued their own polygamy law to deal with parties who had spouses in England, and were now committing adultery or entering polygamous unions in the new world:

> [D]ivers persons, both men and women, living within this jurisdiction, whose wives and husbands are in England, or elsewhere by means whereof, they live under great temptations here and some of them committing lewdness and filthiness here amongst us, others make love to women and attempt marriage, and some have attained it, and some of them live under suspicion of uncleanness, and all to the great dishonour of God, reproach of religion, commonwealth, and churches.[18]

The 1647 law ordered these philandering parties to "repair to their said relations by the first opportunity of shipping" or to have their spouses join them in the new world – no small demand given the expense and danger of trans-Atlantic passage in that day.[19] In 1672, Henry Jackson was indicted under this new law "for lying, in saying he was single and attempting marriage with several" women, although he already had a wife "across the seas" whom he had evidently abandoned. For his

---

[15] Ibid., 205–206. See also Lawrence Friedman, *Crime and Punishment in American History* (New York: Basic Books, 1993), 197–201.

[16] Case of December 3, 1639, in *Massachusetts Colonial Records*, 1:283 and in William H. Whitmore, ed., *Colonial Laws of Massachusetts: Reprinted from the Edition of 1672* (Boston: Rockwell and Churchill, 1890), 99 n.

[17] *Massachusetts Colonial Records*, 2:86; Howard, *History of Matrimonial Institutions*, 2:159. See also John Demos, *A Little Commonwealth: Family Life in Plymouth County* (New York: Oxford University Press, 1970), 92–93, reporting the early case of a Plymouth colonist charged with having wives in Boston, Barbados, and England.

[18] *Colonial Laws of Massachusetts*, 101–102.

[19] Ibid.

repeated offenses he was whipped with twenty lashes, ordered to the pay the court its costs for prosecution, and was bound for the next ship out of town.[20] A number of other men and women in the colony were fined and sent back home to rejoin their spouses across the Atlantic or to bring them back, lest they again be tempted to adultery or polygamy.[21]

A 1694 Massachusetts law made intentional polygamy a capital crime, modeled in large part on the 1604 Polygamy Act of England.[22] Sarah Forland was convicted under the statute for having two husbands, but she successfully pled benefit of clergy and was branded on the hand.[23] The new Massachusetts law, however, also provided that if a colonist were deserted by his or her spouse for three years without hearing a word, the deserting spouse could be presumed dead, leaving the party at home free to remarry with impunity.[24] And, if a married party discovered that his or her spouse was married to another, they could sue privately for annulment and the right to remarry, and often with a draw on the marital property of their bigamous spouse. Harvard family historian, Nancy Cott, has found fifteen such private bigamy cases in Massachusetts from 1692 to 1786, eleven of them leading to annulment.[25]

A series of seventeenth- and eighteenth-century colonial Connecticut laws also ordered the annulment of any second marriage with a right of the innocent spouse

---

[20] Reported in Howard, *History of Matrimonial Institutions*, 2:159, 332.

[21] See cases in ibid., 2:159–160, and table of cases in ibid., 2:333, 341–344, listing a bigamy case of Elizabeth and Ezekiel Eldrige (December 26, 1752) and a bigamy case of Rachel and John Wormley (August 14, 1765), both leading to annulment. See also Edmund S. Morgan, *The Puritan Family: Religion and Domestic Relations in Seventeenth Century New England*, rev. enl. ed. (New York: Harper & Row, 1966), 31ff.

[22] Nathan Dane, *General Abridgement and Digest of American Law*, 8 vols. (Boston: Cummins, Hilliard, & Co., 1824), vol. 6, chap. 198, art. 10. Members of the established Congregational churches could also be subject to ecclesiastical discipline, doubly so if they successfully escaped execution by pleading benefit of clergy. See examples in Emil Oberholzer, *Delinquent Saints: Disciplinary Action in the Early Congregational Churches of Massachusetts* (New York: Columbia University Press, 1956), 117–126.

[23] N.E.H. Hull, *Female Felons: Women and Serious Crimes in Colonial Massachusetts* (Champaign-Urbana: University of Illinois Press, 1987), 114.

[24] Act of December 2, 1698 in *The Charter and General Laws of the Colony and Province of Massachusetts Bay* (Boston: T.B. Wait, 1814), chap. 56, pp. 321–322; see also Howard, *History of Matrimonial Institutions*, 2:340.

[25] *The Charter and General Laws of the Colony and Province of Massachusetts Bay*, 284–285. For annulment and divorce practice in this colony, see Nancy F. Cott, "Divorce and the Changing Status of Women in Eighteenth-Century Massachusetts," *William and Mary Quarterly*, 3rd ser. 33 (1976): 586–614, esp. 597–599. Cott has found fifteen Massachusetts annulment cases on grounds of bigamy brought between 1692 and 1786: in nine of twelve cases brought by wives, and two of three brought by husbands, the marriages were annulled. See also later developments analyzed in Nancy F. Cott, "Eighteenth Century Family and Social Life Revealed in Massachusetts Divorce Records," *Journal of Social History* 10 (1976): 20–43 and more generally id., *The Bonds of Womanhood: "Woman's Sphere" in New England, 1780–1835* (New Haven, CT: Yale University Press, 1977).

to remarry. If the bigamist continued to live with his or her second spouse, the law ordered both parties to the second marriage to be prosecuted for adultery. They were to be whipped on their backs, branded on their foreheads with an "A" for adultery, and made to wear visible halters around their necks while in public; if caught without their halters, they were to be brought before the justices again, and whipped with twenty more lashes.[26]

The Duke of York's Book of Laws (1665–1675) for colonial New York made polygamy a capital felony tantamount to adultery. The laws recognized that the hard scrabble life of the colony made it impossible to follow the letter of the *Book of Common Prayer* in forming a marriage. But, at least to prevent polygamy, the Duke's law required each newly marrying couple to swear before a justice of the peace or a religious minister that "they are not under bonds of matrimony with any other person living." If it was later proved that they had lied and "thereby attained a double marriage for the said perjury the party or parties offending [were to] be bored through the tongue with red hot iron and moreover proceeded against as in a case of adultery," at the time a capital offense.[27] The innocent victim of a bigamous marriage was free to marry thereafter, but any of the spouses who had colluded in the bigamy could be charged as accomplices and severely punished. The Duke's laws also dealt with the common problem of deserted spouses, and allowed for remarriage after five years of hearing nothing from the other spouse, who could now be presumed dead.[28]

The Great Law of Pennsylvania (1682–1700), crafted by the Quaker leader William Penn, was considerably more liberal than many other colonial laws on crime and punishment. But it still prescribed life imprisonment for knowing polygamists.

> Whosoever shall be convicted of having two wives or two husbands at one and the same time shall be imprisoned all their lifetime in the house of correction, at hard labor, to the behoof of the former wife and children; And if a man or woman being unmarried, do knowingly marry the husband or wife of another person, he or she shall be punished after the manner aforesaid."[29]

A 1705 amendment provided further that the bigamist "be whipped on his or her bare back thirty-nine lashes" before being put to a life sentence of hard labor.[30]

---

[26] *Acts and Laws of His Majesty's English Colony of Connecticut in New-England in America* (New-London: Timothy Green, 1750), 7, 146.

[27] The Duke of York's Laws 1665–1675, in *The Colonial Laws Of New York From The Year 1664 To The Revolution*, 5 vols. (Albany, NY: James B. Lyon, 1896), 1:21, 46.

[28] Ibid., 46–47. See also Howard, *History of Matrimonial Institutions*, 2:376 reporting a 1664 case of Anneke Adriaens who was released from her bigamous husband and free to marry.

[29] *Charter To William Penn, And Laws Of The Province Of Pennsylvania, Passed Between The Years 1682 and 1700* (Harrisburg, PA: Lane S. Hart, 1879), p. 194, item 8.

[30] William Graydon, *The Justices and Constables Assistant. Being a General Collection of Forms of Practice* (Harrisburg, PA: John Wyeth, 1805), 52; Richard Bache, *The Manual of a Pennsylvania Justice of the Peace*, 2 vols. (Philadelphia: W.P. Farrand, 1810–1814), 2:160–161.

Liberal Rhode Island, too, treated polygamy as a serious form of adultery. A 1749 statute provided that both a convicted adulterer and polygamist "shall be punished, by being publicly set on the gallows in the daytime, with a rope about his or her neck, for the space of one hour; and in his or her return from the Gallows to the Gaol, shall be publicly whipped on his or her naked back, not exceeding thirty stripes; and shall stand committed to the gaol of the county wherein convicted, until he or she shall pay all costs of prosecution."[31]

State Statutes

Although the American Revolution transformed the constitutional law of the former colonies now states, it left intact much of their private and penal law, including the colonial and English laws against polygamy. These laws were only gradually changed by piecemeal state legislation issued over the course of the nineteenth and early twentieth centuries. Many of the new state criminal statutes against polygamy were modeled on the English 1604 Polygamy Act and its 1828 and 1861 reforms, albeit with widely variant punishments and several adjustments to local circumstances.[32]

The 1816 law of the District of Columbia, modeled on English and typical American state laws of the day and enacted by the United States Congress, provided as follows:

If any person within the District of Columbia, being married, or shall hereafter marry, do or shall marry any person, the former husband or wife being alive, every such offence shall be a felony, and the person so offending, shall be punished by fine not exceeding five thousand dollars, and confinement at hard labour, or in solitude, not exceeding ten years, or either of them at the discretion of the court.

Provided, that nothing herein contained shall extend to any person whose husband or wife shall be continually remaining out of the jurisdiction of the United States, or whose husband or wife shall absent him or herself, the one from the other by the space of seven years together, the one of them not knowing the other to be living within that time.

And provided also, that nothing herein contained shall extend to any person that shall be, at the time of such marriage, divorced by lawful authority, or to any person whose former marriage shall have been by lawful authority declared void, nor to

---

[31] *Acts and Laws of the English Colony of Rhode-Island and Providence-Plantations, In New England, in America* (Newport, RI: Samuel Hall, 1767), 6.

[32] On the general reception of British common law in the new American states, see Elizabeth Gaspar Brown and William W. Blume, *British Statutes in American Law, 1776–1836*, repr. ed. (New York: DeCapo Press, 1974); on the reception of British marriage and family laws, see Göran Lind, *Common Law Marriage: A Legal Institution for Cohabitation* (Oxford: Oxford University Press, 2008), 139–150.

any person by reason of any former marriage which shall have been had or made within [i.e., before] the age of consent.[33]

A few years later, the State of New York issued a similar law for "the offense of *bigamy*, or as it might more properly be termed, *polygamy*," now lightening considerably the harsh capital laws inherited from colonial days:

> Every person having a husband or wife living, who shall marry any other person, whether married or single, shall, except in the following cases, be adjudged guilty of bigamy, and liable to be punished by imprisonment in a state prison for a term not exceeding five years.

These provisions do not extend to the following cases:

1st. To any person by reason of any former marriage, whose husband or wife, by such marriage, shall have been absent for five successive years, without being known to such person, within that time, to be living; nor

2nd. To any person by reason of any former marriage, whose husband or wife by such marriage shall have absented himself or herself from his wife or husband, and shall have been continually remaining without the United States, for the space of five years together; nor

3rd. To any person by reason of any former marriage which shall have dissolved by the decree of a competent court for some cause other than adultery of such person; nor

4th. To any person by reason of any former marriage which shall have been pronounced void by the sentence or decree of a competent court, on the ground of the nullity of the marriage contract; nor

5th. To any person by reason of any former marriage contracted by such person within the age of legal consent and which shall have been annulled by the decree of a competent court; nor

6th. To any person by reason of any former marriage who shall have been sentenced to imprisonment for life.[34]

The New York statute imposed the same five-year imprisonment plus a $500 fine on any person who "shall, knowingly, marry the husband or wife of another." If a person had three spouses or more at the same time, the statute called for separate charges and punishments for each additional spouse.[35]

---

[33] *Code of Laws for the District of Columbia, Prepared Under the Authority of the Congress of the 29th of April, 1816* (Washington, DC: Davis & Force, 1819), 181.

[34] 2 Revised Statutes 687, in Oliver L. Barbour, *A Treatise on the Criminal Law of the State of New York*, 2nd ed. (Albany, NY: Gould, Banks, 1852), 211–212.

[35] Ibid.

Most American state statutes in the nineteenth and early twentieth centuries had comparable language.[36] Some states imposed firmer punishments. Both Tennessee and North Carolina left polygamy as a capital offense "against health, morality, and decency," and both states still executed intentional polygamists in the 1820s and 1830s,[37] denying convicted defendants benefit of clergy.[38] Pennsylvania, by contrast, had the most lenient treatment of polygamy: while its prerevolutionary law had imposed on convicted polygamists whipping and life imprisonment with hard labor, a 1790 Pennsylvania law reduced their punishment to two years of hard labor. An 1807 law gave state judges discretion to parole such convicts after three months. Another law of 1785 allowed parties to remarry after being deserted for more than two years, and spared them from polygamy charges if the first spouse returned thereafter.[39]

Most state statutes fell between these extremes, and ordered that convicted polygamists be sentenced to various combinations of prison, hard labor, and fines. The statutory trend was to lighten the punishment in each successive reform of the penal law, although polygamy remained on the books as a serious felony. Virginia was typical. In its new 1788 criminal law, endorsed by Thomas Jefferson (1743–1826), Virginia still treated polygamy as a capital crime.[40] An 1819 law, however, reduced the punishment to up to ten years in the state penitentiary.[41] New law reforms in 1839 and 1848 reduced the punishment still further to one to five years in the penitentiary.[42] Similarly, an 1809 law in Maryland ordered convicted polygamists to serve one to nine years in the penitentiary, and ordered courts to give the first wife one-third of the convict's real and personal property – effectively as a prepayment of her dower

---

[36] See a good collection in Francis Wharton, *Treatise on the Criminal Law of the United States*, 4th ed. (Philadelphia: Kay and Bro., 1857), bk. 6, ch. 9.

[37] See, e.g., *State v. Norman*, 13 N.C. 222 (June, 1829); *Ewell v. State*, 14 Tenn. 363 (1834).

[38] *Laws of the State of Tennessee, Including those from North Carolina Now in force in this State*, 2 vols. (Knoxville, TN: Heiskell & Brown, 1821), 2:629–630. An 1874 Tennessee state prison survey found only three bigamists among the 897 convicts. See John Berrien Lindsley, *On Prison Discipline and Penal Legislation: With Special Reference to the State of Tennessee* (Nashville, TN: Robertson Association, 1874), 38.

[39] *Laws of the Commonwealth of Pennsylvania*, 5 vols. (Philadelphia: John Bioren, 1810), 1:29–30, 2: ch. 122; 4:393.

[40] *Statutes at Large ... of Virginia*, 12:695. But see Thomas Jefferson, "Outline of Bill for Proportioning Crimes and Punishments," where Jefferson said that convicted rapists, polygamists, and sodomists should be castrated. *The Papers of Thomas Jefferson*, ed. Julian P. Boyd, 40 vols. (Princeton, NJ: Princeton University Press, 1950–1968), 2:663–664.

[41] 1 Rev. Code of 1819, c. 106, s. 19 in W.W. Henning, *The New Virginia Justice*, 3rd ed. (Richmond, VA: J. & G. Cochran, 1820), 450.

[42] James M. Matthews, *Digest of the Laws of Virginia of a Criminal Nature* (Richmond, VA: West & Johnson, 1861), 68.

interests in her husband's estate.[43] An 1817 Georgia law fined convicted polygamists up to $5,000 and ordered them to serve up to three years of hard labor in the state penitentiary.[44] An 1821 Maine law ordered solitary confinement up to three months, followed by hard labor up to five years.[45] An 1829 Rhode Island law retained the colonial custom of setting convicted polygamists on the gallows with a rope about his or her neck, for the space of one hour, and then to pay a $1,000 fine and serve up to two years in prison.[46] An 1833 Louisiana law assigned convicted polygamists one to five years of hard labor.[47] An 1867 New Jersey law assigned convicted polygamists up to ten years in state prison and a $1,000 fine. An 1869 Michigan law assigned up to five years in state prison plus a fine of up to $500.

Like the 1604 Polygamy Act in England, the new American state statutes on polygamy required proof that the defendant had two or more valid marriages intact at the same time. The required proof of marriage varied greatly from state to state, but marriage licenses, testimony by self or others, cohabitation of the parties in a common household, having children, servants, property, or businesses together, and the like was usually evidence enough of a marriage. The American law on the subject was made more complicated by the recognition of "common law" marriage – a long-standing cohabitation between a man and a woman that was never licensed, formalized, or celebrated, but nonetheless treated as a valid marriage. Even double common law marriages could lead to bigamy charges.[48] Voidable second marriages (on grounds, say, of coercion, prematurity, or lack of parental consent) were also still considered valid marriages for purposes of bringing bigamy charges. The tendency of many nineteenth-century courts in polygamy cases was to insist on strong proof of the validity of the first marriage, with an authenticated marriage license the ideal evidence, while being rather relaxed about evidence of the second marriage. "The presumption favoring the validity of a later marriage," writes Göran Lind after a massive study of nineteenth-century state cases, traditionally was "one of the strongest presumptions in the law" of domestic relations.[49]

If, before the second marriage, the defendant's first marriage had ended by an order of annulment, absolute divorce, or the (presumed) death of a long absent first spouse, the defendant could not be charged with bigamy or polygamy. Like the

[43] *The Laws of Maryland*, 3 vols. (Baltimore, MD: Philip H. Nicklin & Co., 1811), 3:464–465; Ellis Lewis, *An Abridgement of the Criminal Law of the United States* (Philadelphia: Thomas, Cowperthwait, 1847), 116.
[44] *Digest of the Laws of the State of Georgia* (Milledgeville, GA: Grantland & Orme, 1822), 365.
[45] *Laws of the State of Maine*, 2 vols. (Brunswick, ME: J. Griffin, 1821), 1:77–78.
[46] *Reports of the Prison Discipline Society*, 3 vols. (Boston: T.R. Marvin, 1855), 1:253.
[47] Edward Livingston, *A System of Penal Law for the State of Louisiana* (Philadelphia: James Kay, 1833), 455.
[48] Lind, *Common Law Marriage*, 227–228.
[49] Ibid., 207–249.

English church courts, American secular courts annulled marriages on proof of an impediment such as incest, infancy, lunacy, impotence or sterility, lack of consent, and more. They also could use the added impediment of miscegenation (prohibited marriages between whites and nonwhites) as well as slavery (slaves could not marry anyone, including a fellow slave) that would result in annulment. Unlike England, however, American state courts offered absolute divorce (not just separation from bed and board) on proven grounds of adultery and desertion. Parties who had a divorce decree were generally free to remarry, sometimes after a mandatory period of waiting.

In cases of desertion, states varied on how long the first spouse had to be deserted before they could get a divorce or at least could be presumed to be widowed and thus free to remarry with impunity from polygamy charges. Two years was the shortest waiting period; in most states, five to seven years of uninterrupted and unexplained absence of the first spouse, especially overseas or on the distant Western frontier, was enough to create the presumption of death and trigger the right to remarriage. Deserted parties were wise to wait out the statutory period before remarrying. But if they did wait and then remarried, the unexpected reappearance of their first spouse would not lead to polygamy charges, though either spouse could sue for annulment or divorce.

In practice, these basic criminal laws of bigamy yielded complex rulings and precedents concerning evidence, procedure, and sentencing, as well as conflict of laws issues both between the states and between the United States and foreign countries.[50] Moreover, proving the fact of bigamy or polygamy in a court was also an important factor in non-criminal cases of divorce, alimony, marital property settlements, child support and custody, inheritance, insurance claims, pension claims, and more.[51]

State Prosecution and Punishment of Polygamy

It is impossible to know the actual number of criminal cases of polygamy in nineteenth-century America, let alone the actual number of practicing polygamists.

---

[50] For good overviews, see Francis Wharton, *A Treatise on the Criminal Law of the United States*, 7th rev. ed., 3 vols. (Philadelphia: Kay and Bros., 1874), 2:804–820; Joel Bishop, *Commentaries on the Law of Statutory Crimes*, 2nd ed. (Boston: Little Brown, 1883), 368–390; Robert Desty, *A Compendium of American Criminal Law* (San Francisco: S. Whitney, 1882), 224–234.

[51] See the standard treatise of Joel Bishop, *Commentaries on the Law of Marriage and Divorce*, 4th ed., 2 vols. (Boston: Little Brown, 1864). For the effect of desertion and bigamy on new federal pension claims during and after the Civil War, see Beverly Schwartzberg, "'Lots of Them Did That': Desertion, Bigamy, and Marital Fluidity in Late-Nineteenth-Century America," *Journal of Social History* 37 (2004): 573–600, on pensions.

Concurrent polygamy in the form of one man living with two or more wives in the same home, or keeping multiple wives in different locales, was relatively rare – and a number of the sensational cases involving Mormons and others were prosecuted, as we shall see later in this chapter. Much more common but harder for authorities to detect and prove was serial polygamy, in the form of a husband or wife who remarried "after losing or leaving their first mates," but not bothering to get a divorce or annulment of the first marriage.[52] Less common, though more sensational, Stanford legal historian Lawrence Friedman reports, was the "swindler, whose modus operandi consisted of duping women into marriage, extracting their money, or some of it, and moving on."[53]

In a day of poor records, an open frontier, easy mobility across state lines, no national marriage registry, and high burdens of proof, most of these "bigamous unions did not result in criminal prosecutions."[54] Those cases that were prosecuted typically yielded simple jury verdicts of guilty or not guilty, and the cases ended there – without opinions and many times without any formal case record either. There is nothing comparable in nineteenth-century America to the Old Bailey records of the original trials that we sampled in the earlier chapter on the English common law of polygamy.[55] We do have stray reports of individual cases in America,[56] and a few sensational cases have been analyzed closely.[57] Some state court libraries and reporters did keep a register of verdicts or results, sometimes a full record of the evidence of these cases. Even so, too many of these local case registers and records did not survive the wars, fires, floods, damp, and mold that destroyed so many early American archives. And those archival records that have survived have not been

---

[52] Michael Grossberg, *Governing the Hearth: Law and the Family in Nineteenth-Century America* (Chapel Hill: University of North Carolina Press, 1985), 120.

[53] Lawrence M. Friedman, "Crimes of Mobility," *Stanford Law Review* 43 (1991): 637–658, at 641–642.

[54] Hendrik Hartog, *Man and Wife in America: A History* (Cambridge, MA: Harvard University Press, 2000), 87.

[55] See discussion in Chapter 7, pp. 305–319.

[56] See, e.g., *The Extraordinary and Singular Law-Case of Joseph Parker who Indicted as Thomas Hoag alias dictus Joseph Parker for bigamy at the Court of Oyer and Terminer, held in the City of New York* (Baltimore, MD: G. Keatinge's Bookstore, 1808). See other cases reported in Hartog, *Man and Wife*, 88–90; Beverly J. Schwartzberg, "Grass Widows, Barbarians, and Bigamists: Fluid Marriage in Late Nineteenth-Century America" (Ph.D. Diss. University of California, Santa Barbara, 2001), which also includes a good bibliography.

[57] One of the most interesting was the fifty-seven-year battle – including seventeen cases before the U.S. Supreme Court – of Myra Clark Gaines to secure her massive inheritance from her wealthy father. The main initial point of contest was whether she was the illegitimate child of her father's bigamous marriage and thus could not inherit. She was ultimately declared legitimate and heritable. See Elizabeth Urban Alexander, *Notorious Woman: The Celebrated Case of Myra Clark Gaines* (Baton Rouge: Louisiana State University Press, 2001); Nolan B. Harmon, *The Famous Case of Myra Clark Gaines* (Baton Rouge: Louisiana State University Press, 1946).

comprehensively or systematically indexed or digested, nor have most of their cases on the criminal law of polygamy been carefully studied.

We do have some evidence of American polygamy law in action in a few interesting case studies. Timothy Gilfoyle, for example, has analyzed the bigamy prosecution of 260 separate individuals in the Court of General Sessions in New York City between 1800 and 1879. Some 85 percent (222 of 260) of these cases were against male defendants, the vast majority of them white working class men, 38 percent of them first generation immigrants. Thirteen of these men cohabited with two or more wives simultaneously; they all got stiff prison sentences. Most of the men just left their wives out of anger, dissatisfaction, lustful pursuit of another, in search of work, or in retaliation for their wife's adultery, frigidity, abuse, or neglect of household duties. After a time, these men remarried, sometimes two or three more times, and were then found out. Most of the thirty-eight female defendants had been abandoned by their husbands; several of them were still saddled with young children and with ample debts, and remarried out of a desperate need for help and support. A few wives left on their own because of chronic abuse or neglect by a wastrel or drunken husband. "In essence, these 19th-century couples treated bigamy as an informal means of common-law divorce," Gilfoyle writes.[58] In a day when formalized legal divorce was expensive, time-consuming, and available only on proof of hard fault, self-divorce was often attractive, especially for couples who had only a little property at stake or who could not afford to miss work or travel to the court to litigate their cases.[59]

Before 1860, Gilfoye shows, the New York courts were more tolerant of this practice of self-divorce, given the widespread ignorance of the shifting state laws on divorce, remarriage, and bigamy. Just over half of the defendants before 1860 were convicted, but only 11 percent (7 of 62) of these convicts went to prison – and then only for a few months, the longest for two years. During and after the Civil War, however, conviction and prison rates for polygamy spiked. From 1860 to 1879, 73 percent (53 of 73) of convicted polygamists in New York were sent to prison, several of them for the state maximum sentence of five years, including with hard labor. According to Gilfoyle, this new firmness in the prosecution of polygamy reflected the new emphasis after the Civil War on the sanctity of monogamous marriage, the new Victorian norms of sexual morality that were being enforced with alacrity in the state, and the new progressive era emphasis on a man's responsibilities to care for his wife and children.[60] Other studies have shown a growing stigmatization and punishment of men who deserted their wives and children who thereafter often

---

[58] Timothy J. Gilfoye, "The Hearts of Nineteenth-Century Men: Bigamy and Working-Class Marriage in New York City, 1800–1890," *Prospects* 19 (1994): 135–160, at 141.

[59] Hartog, *Man and Wife*, 87–92.

[60] Gilfoye, "The Hearts of Nineteenth-Century Men," 136–141, 150–152.

became public wards – a problem greatly exacerbated by the American Civil War of 1861–1865 that left so many widows and orphans who also needed care. It was bad enough that these men had deserted their first families without cause; it was worse if they married anew, making it even harder for them to offer the first families any support.[61]

In another study of the western district of territorial Arkansas, Roger Tuller found 17 cases of bigamy in a total of 12,042 cases docketed for the years 1875–1896. Of these cases, twelve were against men, five against women. By contrast to their counterparts in New York, these defendants got off rather lightly, even when the notorious "hanging judge" Isaac G. Parker presided. George Chappel had married six wives in a row and was damned with so much hostile testimony from his wives that he had to plead guilty and throw himself on the mercy of the court; he got three years in the penitentiary and a $200 fine. James Holley, who had abandoned two wives and two sets of minor children and then married yet a third wife, got three years and a $500 fine. Matthew Flannigan, who was married a second time before he had completed his divorce suit against his first wife got six months and a $100 fine. One female defendant with two husbands, Sarah Green, pled guilty and got three months in prison and a $100 fine.[62]

Beverly Schwartzberg has explored sixty-two overlapping polygamy cases in this same Arkansas territorial court and found comparable patterns. Of the sixty-two cases, forty-five were filed against men, seventeen against women. The punishments were again quite lenient: an average sentence of 19.5 months for male defendants, usually less than 3 months of prison, if any, for female defendants. The most severely punished were intentional bigamists, who secretly kept wives in different locales, and then made things worse by perjuring themselves or committing other forms of fraud. The most severely punished was Willis Lytle who got five years and a $500 fine for his polygamy and perjury.[63]

Schwartzberg shows further that "marital fluidity" was commonplace in many other places on the open western frontier, especially during and after the Civil War, where the already poor state and territorial marriage registration records were rent asunder even more. Parties moved in and out of marriages a great deal more easily in this era and area than would be the case in the twentieth century. Some parties also exploited the toleration of polygamy and fluid marital bonds among some Native

---

[61] See, e.g., sources and discussion in Martha May, "The 'Problem of Duty': Family Desertion in the Progressive Era," *Social Service Review* 62 (1988): 40–60; Lillian Brandt, *Five Hundred and Seventy-Four Deserters and their Families* (New York: The Charity Organization Society, 1905); Schwartzberg, "Grass Widows, Barbarians, and Bigamists," 55–57, 79–88.

[62] See, e.g., Roger Tuller, "Bigamy in the Indian Territory, 1878–1890," *West Texas Historical Association Year Book* 68 (1992): 100–112.

[63] Schwartzberg, "Grass Widows, Barbarians, and Bigamists," 160–206.

American Indian tribes, intermarrying Native American women while already married elsewhere.[64] It was often only when the widows sought pension benefits from the government or dower and inheritance rights from their late husbands' estates that the man's multiple marriages came to light.[65] As French observer of American family life, Duvergier De Hauranne, wrote in 1866: it was the "legal chaos" of postbellum America that facilitated such easy polygamy, with "the great number of double, triple, and quadruple marriages discovered each year by female jealousy" and lawsuits over the dead polygamists' estates.[66]

Lawrence Friedman has shown that even in the more settled and populated regions of the East Coast and Midwest, polygamy remained a crime "characteristic of this mobile society." Nineteenth-century America was "a society of immigrants and migrants – of restless, transient people who shuttled across the vast face of the landscape" and moved easily across social, economic, legal, cultural, and religious barriers. With few means to track them, and no universal marriage registry to identify them, it was relatively easy for nineteenth-century Americans to practice polygamy if they wished, and relatively hard for the individual state authorities to catch them.[67] The principle of federalism that gave each state its own family law system without an overarching national family law made it very difficult for authorities to track plural marriages across state lines. And even when they did catch a polygamist, the authorities generally did not throw the whole statutory book at them, unless the defendants proved to be truly brazen, abusive, and remorseless.

A few surviving surveys of nineteenth-century prison populations provide some further evidence of this relative leniency in the prosecution and punishment of polygamists. The State of New York, for example, whose statute required that convicted polygamists serve up to five years in state prison, had rather few imprisoned polygamists.[68] Between 1817 and 1836 there were 34 convicted bigamists out of some 3,000 state prisoners in Auburn, NY;[69] 12 out of 668 felons in New York City; 3 out of 26 felons in Oneida; 4 out of 190 felons in Albany, 1 out of 115 felons in Syracuse.[70] A comparable survey of Connecticut inmates in the 1830s listed 14 bigamists out

[64] On native American marriages and polygamy, see, among other studies, John Phillip Reid, *The Law of Blood: The Primitive Law of the Cherokee Nation* (New York: New York University Press, 1970), 113–122; and a study of early Indian family practices in Ann Marie Plane, *Colonial Intimacies: Indian Marriage in Early New England* (Ithaca, NY: Cornell University Press, 2001).

[65] Schwartzberg, "Grass Widows, Barbarians, and Bigamists," 207–333, 376–392; see also Hendrik Hartog, "Marital Exits and Marital Expectations in Nineteenth-Century American," *Georgetown Law Journal* 80 (1991): 95–129.

[66] Quoted in Schwartzberg, "Grass Widows, Barbarians, and Bigamists," 249.

[67] Friedman, "Crimes of Mobility," 638–641.

[68] Wharton, *Treatise on the Criminal Law* (4th ed.), 552.

[69] *Reports of the Prison Discipline Society*, 3 vols. (Boston: T.R. Marvin, 1855), 3:8.

[70] Ibid., 3:13–17, 68.

of a total of 1,293 prisoners.[71] Likewise, a south Boston prison in 1838 had only one prisoner for bigamy out of a total of fifty-seven prisoners,[72] even though Massachusetts statutes also called for up to five years of state prison for bigamy.[73] National prisoner surveys in 1880 showed only 257 polygamists (242 of them males) out of 57,958 prisoners total in the entire nation. In 1890, there were 342 polygamists (322 males) out of 82,329 prisoners, with 2.57 years the average length of their sentence.[74]

State Appellate Cases

And even these prison sentences were sometimes shortened or ended after the parties appealed to the state appellate or state supreme courts. The number of reported state appellate cases involving bigamy or polygamy is not large. A comprehensive survey of these appellate cases in all state courts between 1860 and 1900 that I commissioned from my students Brian Kaufman and Christopher Huslak turned up 193 cases – 179 with male defendants, 14 with female defendants. These 193 cases come from forty states and the District of Columbia. In twenty-four states, there were only three or fewer cases. The majority of the cases were from the South – Texas leading the way with twenty-five, followed by Alabama with fifteen, Georgia with ten, Kentucky, North Carolina, and Missouri each with nine, and Arkansas with six. Of the original Atlantic seaboard states, only Massachusetts with thirteen cases and New York with eight had more than a couple such cases each.[75]

Many of these appellate cases turned on technical challenges to the indictment, evidence, or jury instruction in the case below, and 39 percent (75 of 193) of the bigamy convictions were vacated or reversed, although a good number of cases were remanded for further proceedings. Almost all of these cases involved a deserting spouse who just remarried another spouse or two without (properly) ending the prior marriage(s). Only a couple of these state appellate cases, in states on the western frontier, involved Mormon or Native American polygamy.[76]

[71] Ibid., 3:46.
[72] Ibid., 2:76, 82.
[73] Wharton, *A Treatise on the Criminal Law* (4th ed.), 552.
[74] Schwartzberg, "Grass Widows, Barbarians, and Bigamists," 49, n. 68, citing Frederick H. Wines, *Report of the Defective, Dependent, and Delinquent Classes of the Population of the United States as Returned at the Tenth Census, June 1, 1880*, repr. ed. (New York: Norman Ross Publishing, 1991), 504–510; id., *Report on Crime, Pauperism and Benevolence in the United States at the Eleventh Census*, repr. ed. (New York: Norman Ross Publishing, 1995), Pt. I, 18–19, Pt. II, 343, 372–382, 499.
[75] See Brian W. Kaufman and Christopher Huslak, "Polygamy State Law Case Analysis in the United States from 1860 to 1900" (unpublished report on file with the author).
[76] See, e.g., *United States v. Kuntze*, 2 Idaho 446 (1889) (technical attack on cohabitation issue); *Innis v. Bolton*, 2 Idaho 407 (1888) (failed First Amendment attack on required oath disavowing polygamy as a condition to vote); *Wooley v. Watkins*, 2 Idaho 555 (1889) (same).

Many of the appellate cases in nineteenth-century American state courts turned on whether the prosecutor had adequately proved that the defendant had two valid marriages intact at the same time. A good number were simple, routine cases. In an 1840 Illinois case, for example, Daniel Jackson was indicted for marrying Sara Hartwell in 1836, and then marrying Nancy Solomon in an adjacent county. He pled not guilty. The prosecutor produced a certified copy of the marriage certificate of the first marriage. The jury found him guilty and sentenced him to eighteen months in prison. The Illinois Supreme Court affirmed the judgment.[77] By contrast, in an 1875 Alabama case, an African-American woman named Brown was convicted and imprisoned for bigamy on the testimony of a single witness who said that Brown had been married to Noah Wilson and lived with him a few years before separating, and thereafter married Joe Tunstall and lived with him. There were no marital licenses, children, or marital property in evidence, nor any proof that the person who presided over the purported second marriage had license to marry her. The jury still convicted her. The Alabama Supreme court reversed the lower court's decision. Mere cohabitation, the court said, is no proof of marriage: "If it was, every case of living in fornication or adultery would establish a marriage or case of bigamy."[78] Appellate courts would routinely affirm and overturn convictions on simple facts like this.

Although a marriage license was the best evidence of a valid first marriage, it could also be proved by longstanding cohabitation, children, joint property interests, public reputation, and the statements of the parties themselves.[79] An 1890 North Carolina case involved a woman named Parker who had married her husband at the age of 13, had lived with him for twenty years, and borne him ten children. She then left him and married another man, and was indicted for bigamy. She argued that her first marriage was invalid because she was under-aged at the time of their wedding and the marriage was unlicensed and uncelebrated. That just made her first marriage voidable, said the court. Her twenty years of cohabitation and ten children thereafter were ample enough proof that a common law marriage was ratified by practice. She was found guilty and imprisoned for bigamy.[80] Similarly in an 1899 Texas case, the defendant appealed his five-year prison sentence for bigamy on the argument that the state had not produced the actual license of his first marriage. But there was ample testimony that the defendant had lived with his

---

[77] *Jackson v. The People* (1840), in *Reports of Cases at Law and in Chancery Argued and Determined in the Supreme Court of Illinois* (Cambridge, MA: Harvard Press, 1841), 3:231.

[78] *Brown v. State*, 52 Ala. 338, 340 (1875).

[79] See, e.g., *Schwartz v. Ohio*, 7 Ohio C.D. 43, 855 (1896). This evidence was given special weight if the defendant lived with two or more wives. See *United States v. Tenney*, 2 Ariz. 127 (1886) (prosecution under the federal Edmund Act of 1882).

[80] *State v. Parker*, 106 N.C. 711 (1890).

first wife for several years and produced several children with her, and that they had long held themselves out as husband and wife. There was also disputed testimony from the justice of the peace who had presided at his first wedding. This was enough for the Texas court to uphold the conviction on appeal. "A rule of construction as contended for by the appellant would bastardize children whose parents believed they were legally married, and who were not conscious of violating any law, human or Divine."[81]

Appellate courts would reverse convictions, however, if prosecutors could not prove a valid first marriage. In an 1858 Michigan case, Robert Lambert was convicted for marrying Mary Jane Brown in Michigan in 1857, while being already married to Nancy Mulholland in New Jersey since 1855. The evidence for his first marriage consisted of hazy hearsay testimony from a police officer who overhead defendant's conversations about being married to his first wife, as well as an undated and non-authenticated copy of a marriage certificate. The appellate court found the evidence insufficient to prove a valid first marriage, and they reversed Lambert's conviction.[82]

Similarly, in an 1891 Missouri case, defendant Cooper made clear to Lavina Atkins and to her father and friends that he wanted to marry her. In fact, Cooper and Lavina lived together in Missouri for two and a half years, holding themselves out as husband and wife, and transacting business and acquiring property in both their names. But their marriage was never licensed or celebrated in Missouri. There was disputed evidence that Cooper may have acquired a marriage license in Kansas, but he was under-aged at the time, and neither set of parents would consent to the marriage. Nor was a marriage certificate in evidence. Cooper then abruptly left Lavina and married a second woman, Eva Alexander, a few days later. He was indicted for polygamy. The trial judge instructed the jury that if they thought Cooper's relation with Lavina constituted a marriage, they could convict him. He was found guilty of bigamy, and sentenced to four and a half years in prison. The Supreme Court of Missouri reversed the decision, arguing that the prosecutor had to prove that Cooper had a valid first marriage, not leave it to the jury to decide based on these disputed facts and leading judicial instructions. With no marriage license in evidence, and with insufficient time to make out a common law marriage between Cooper and Lavina, Cooper could not be a bigamist.[83]

The appellate courts were considerably more lax about proof of a second marriage used to support a bigamy charge. Even voidable second marriages were enough. In

---

[81] *Waldrop v. State*, 41 Tex. Crim. 194, 198 (1899).
[82] *People v. Lambert*, 5 Mich. 349 (1858).
[83] *State v. Cooper*, 103 Mo. 266 (1891).

an 1876 Michigan bigamy case, the defendant argued that his second marriage was void, because he was an African-American and his second wife was white, and their marriage violated the state's miscegenation rules. The Supreme Court of Michigan upheld the bigamy charge: "It is the appearing to contract a second marriage, and the going through the ceremony, which constitutes the crime of bigamy, otherwise it could never exist in ordinary cases, as a previous marriage always renders null and void a marriage that is celebrated afterwards." The "two elements of illegality in the case" – the bigamy and the miscegenation – do not cancel each other out.[84] In an 1893 Texas case, the defendant was married to his first wife, but she had left him. Three years later, he seduced a second woman and was arrested. His father and the state district attorney told him that if he married the second seduced woman they would drop charges of seduction. They further told him that his first marriage was void because his first wife had left him, leaving him free to remarry. He did so and was indicted and convicted for bigamy and sentenced to two years in prison. His appeal failed. Mistake of law was not a defense, the appellate court held, even if that mistake originated with the district attorney.[85]

Similarly, in an 1862 New York case, John Hayes, who was already married to Sarah Blair, was charged with bigamy for marrying Jane White as well. John's pursuit of Jane looks like a persistent seduction gone too far. He met Jane at a hotel in Brooklyn, and courted her briefly. She told John she was not worthy of him, being poor, illiterate, and already had a bastard child. John persisted, and they were engaged. They tried to move into a flat together, but were refused because they were not married. John then brought in a man purporting to be a minister who married them privately, and left him a dubious marriage certificate that Jane never saw nor could she have read it. The couple cohabitated and slept together thereafter, although John told Jane to keep the marriage quiet, because it might ill effect an inheritance he purportedly had coming. He was indicted and convicted for bigamy. He appealed, arguing that there was no real proof of his second marriage to Jane. The appellate court upheld the conviction, arguing that his seductive intrigue was "so wicked as to exclude favorable presumptions in his behalf." There was sufficient evidence of mutual consent, consecration, and certification – however fraudulently arranged by the defendant – for a jury to conclude that there was a second marriage, and thus a sufficient ground for conviction for bigamy.[86]

In a number of these appellate cases, the defendant's lawyers unsuccessfully pushed the courts to make the prosecution's burden of proof even harder. In an 1859

[84] *People v. Brown*, 34 Mich. 339, 341 (1876), quoting in part *Regina v. Brawn*, 1 C. & K. 144 (Lord Denman).
[85] *Medrano v. State*, 32 Tex. Crim. 214 (1893).
[86] *Hayes v. People*, 5 Parker Crim. Rep. 325 (N.Y., 1862); aff'd 25 N.Y. 390 (1862).

Texas case, for example, Daniel Gorman first married Louisa Shack in Mississippi; five months later, he married Elizabeth Jane Cleaveland in Texas. He confessed he had two wives, and he was indicted and convicted for bigamy. On appeal, Gorman argued that the prosecutor had failed to prove that "his first wife was still living," as the statute required. "The presumption of [my] innocence outweighs the presumption" of her being alive was the argument. The Supreme Court of Texas would have none of it, given the proximity of the two marriages in time and location, and given the defendant's confession of a double marriage. It did not help Gorman's cause that, on appeal, his first wife Louisa proved to be very much alive, even if the prosecutor had not proved that fact during the trial.[87]

The question of presumptions came up in a bit more complex case of *Gibson v. Mississippi* (1860). Gibson had married Maria Williams in 1855. He abandoned her and then married Ann Cochran in 1857. He was indicted for bigamy. At trial, Gibson argued that his first marriage to Maria was invalid because she had already been married to a man called Williams since 1849. Maria and other witnesses testified for the prosecution that her first husband Williams had reportedly been drowned, leaving Maria a widow free to remarry Gibson; they also said that Gibson knew all this before his marriage to Maria. Gibson insisted that the state must prove absolutely that Williams was dead before his first marriage with Maria could be deemed valid and the basis for a bigamy charge. The trial court refused to give that instruction to the jury, and Gibson was found guilty of bigamy. The appellate court upheld the conviction. Not only had Maria been deserted long enough to presume the death of her first husband and her right to marry Gibson, the appellate court concluded. But even if that were not the case, Gibson would then be guilty of adultery against Maria, and deserving of punishment anyway, notwithstanding these "clever lawyer's tricks."[88]

"Clever lawyer's tricks" were also on display in an 1895 Mississippi case. In 1880, Crawford had married Susan Driggers in Georgia. In 1888, she divorced him in Alabama, evidently for his adultery. As punishment, the Alabama divorce decree prohibited Crawford from remarrying any other woman during Susan's lifetime. In 1893, with Susan still alive, Crawford married Florence King in Alabama. In 1894, with Susan now dead but Florence still alive, he married Roxie Gregory in Mississippi. He was indicted for bigamy. Crawford defended himself by saying that his marriage to Florence was invalid, because it violated the Alabama divorce decree. He thus had only one wife. The Mississippi Supreme Court rejected this argument as "wretched formality." Crawford was certainly guilty of contempt of the Alabama

[87] *Gorman v. State*, 23 Tex. 646 (1859).
[88] *Gibson v. State of Mississippi*, 9 George 313 (Miss., 1860).

court order prohibiting his remarriage before Susan's death, the court allowed. "He may be criminally punished, but with him the punishment must stop. To extend the penalty to the second wife ignorant of her husband's violation ... [and] further to the helpless and unsinning offspring of a second wife, would, it seems to us, be not only cruel and unjust, but would be, moreover, a departure from the humane spirit of the law, which views every marriage with favour."[89]

Some skillfully represented defendants did escape bigamy charges if they could prove one of the marriages void. In a 1900 New York case, for example, Corbett was charged with bigamy for marrying Sarah Hayden in Ohio in 1889 and Ida Cook in New York in 1897. His defense was that his marriage to Sara Hayden was void because he had already been married to Sara Blois in Massachusetts since 1881. Sara Blois was apparently now dead, but his marriage to Sara Hayden, he said, had been void from the start. Hence his third marriage to Ida Cook was valid and not a form of bigamy. The trial court refused to allow the jury to consider this fact, and Corbett was sentenced to three and half years in prison. The New York appellate court reversed the conviction.[90]

Clever legal arguments like this found rather little favor in the Supreme Court of North Carolina, which routinely came down hard on suspected polygamists. Thomas Norman found this out in an 1829 case. Thomas had married Mary Baker in 1819. He then left her, and nine years later married Peggy Sillaner. He was indicted for bigamy, then still a capital crime in the state. Thomas first argued that he had divorced Mary, but he could not produce an authentic divorce certificate. He then argued that the bigamy statute allowed him to remarry with impunity after seven years of absence from his first wife. The court rejected this argument. Although desertion for seven years might exonerate the deserted party (Mary) from a later charge of bigamy under the statute, said the Court, it does not exonerate the deserter (Thomas). Moreover, the statute requires that Thomas prove "not knowing his or her said husband or wife to be living within that time." Thomas evidently knew that his first wife was still alive, even though he had not contacted her. He was thus convicted and sentenced to death.[91]

It went only a bit better for Thomas Patterson in an 1842 North Carolina case, and only because the legislature had in the interim made polygamy a non-capital crime. Patterson had married Deadama Kidwell in Tennessee in 1823. He then married Leah Carter in North Carolina in 1828. He denied the first marriage. But several witnesses testified to their marriage before a Baptist minister, and to their

[89] Crawford v. State, 18 So. 848, 849 (Miss., 1895). But see People v. Constantine Faber, 1 N.Y. Crim. R. 115 (1883) (when a statute forbids an adulterer to remarry until the death of the first spouse, a subsequent marriage is void, and cannot support a case for bigamy).

[90] People v. Corbett, 14 N.Y. Crim. R. 532 (1900).

[91] State v. Norman, 2 Dev. 222 (N.C. 1829).

life together as husband and wife which had yielded five children. Other witnesses testified that the Pattersons had separated after a fight, and that a few years later Thomas Patterson and the children left the area. Patterson also denied the validity of his second marriage to Leah Carter. But he was contradicted by Leah's angry father who was scandalized by Patterson's fraud and betrayal of his daughter. The jury found Patterson guilty of bigamy, which the court described not only as an injury to the first and second wives but equally a serious form "of violating an institution, necessary to the very existence of civil life." The trial judge ordered him fined $10, forced to pay the court costs, imprisoned for three months, branded on the cheek with a "B" (for bigamist), and whipped with thirty-nine lashes on his bare back. His appeal failed.[92]

The North Carolina court's hostility to polygamy was sometimes combined with seeming racism as well, as could be seen in an 1882 case. Whitford was an African-American slave who in 1857 had purported to marry another slave Dinah Hancock before an unlicensed preacher who was also a slave. North Carolina slave codes in the day forbade slaves from all marriages. The couple lived continuously together until 1880, long after the abolition of slavery in 1865. Whitford then left Dinah, and married another woman, Sylvia Bryant, and was indicted for bigamy. He argued that because he could not have validly married Dinah he did not need to divorce her either. He was convicted for bigamy anyway on grounds that his ongoing cohabitation with Dinah after their emancipation from slavery made her his common law wife. The North Carolina Supreme Court affirmed the conviction.[93]

The Whitford case was one of dozens of polygamy cases in southern courts that involved former slaves, who could not marry while slaves, but whose marital status was unclear after slavery was abolished. Their remarriages thus raised questions about polygamy.[94] Several former slave states dealt with this by statute. Georgia's law of 1866 concerning "the marriage of persons of color" was typical: "if such persons continue to live together as man and wife, it will be bigamy for one of them to marry a third person." Stephen King, a former slave, was convicted under this statute. He had been living as if married with another slave Nancy Moreland until 1865, but after a fight he had promptly left her. Well after the 1866 statute came into effect, he returned to Nancy, and the couple lived and slept together off and on again, but they did not marry. Eventually they fought again, and King moved away for good. He later married Henrietta Grubbs in 1869. He was indicted for bigamy, and the jury found him guilty. On appeal, the Supreme Court of Georgia reversed the decision,

92 *State v. Patterson*, 2 Ired. 346 (N.C. 1842).
93 *State v. Whitford*, 86 N. C. 636 (1882).
94 For additional context, see Patrick Q. Mason, "Opposition to Polygamy in the Postbellum South," *Journal of Southern History* 76 (2010): 541–578.

saying that this violated both the letter and spirit of the 1866 law, which was designed to "cure the evil of ... a large number of cases among slaves where the marriage tie was very loose." Under these "peculiar circumstances," "a moralist will not judge them harshly, and it is perhaps a wise public policy not to inflict upon them severe penalties for failing ... to comprehend the sacredness of the marriage tie."[95]

As some of the forgoing cases illustrate, a first marriage in another American state or another country could be used to support a bigamy indictment. So long as the foreign marriage was considered valid in the place where it was made, a second marriage in one's home state could lead to charges of bigamy. A number of these appellate cases involved first marriages contracted in Europe, Canada, or another American state or territory. When parties appealed their convictions on grounds that their first marriage was invalid because the foreign jurisdiction had different marriage formation rules than their home state, their arguments were routinely rebuffed.[96] Comity and recognition of foreign marriages was the norm. As a South Carolina appellate court put it: "Our population consists ... of emigrants from all the States, and from every quarter of the globe – consisting of persons apparently standing in the relation of husband and wife, and to establish a rule that their declarations and cohabitation should not be evidence of that relationship, would be to unloose the bands, and bastardize the issue of a considerable portion of the citizens of this State."[97] There were limits on this principle of comity to guard against polygamy. As the Supreme Court of Louisiana put it: "If an inhabitant of Turkey should emigrate with several wives to this State, his women would not have the status of wives here, although legally married at home, because our law condemns polygamy." Polygamy cannot be "forced upon this state by such devices."[98]

This same principle of comity informed judgments about the effect of a foreign divorce on a bigamy case. This is nicely illustrated in an 1856 Alabama case. Allen Thompson married his first wife in Alabama in 1838. Ten years later, he left her and their two children, and moved to Arkansas. He lived there for two years, and then successfully filed an ex parte divorce action against his first wife, who knew nothing about this. Thompson then moved back to Alabama and married a second woman in 1853. He was indicted and convicted for bigamy in Alabama and sentenced to two years in prison. The Supreme Court of Alabama reversed, holding that the Arkansas divorce decree ended the first marriage, leaving Thompson free to

---

[95] *King v. Georgia*, 40 Ga. 244, 247–248 (1869). But cf. *Kirk v. State*, 65 Ga. 159 (1880) (where defendant living with a woman in 1866 and thereafter married another was convicted).

[96] See, e.g., *Commonwealth v. Kenney*, 120 Mass. 387 (1876) (re: Irish marriage ceremony and Canadian cohabitation as husband and wife were both sufficient to prove a first marriage).

[97] *State v. Hilton*, 3 Rich. 434, 437 (S.C. 1827). See also *Warner v. Commonwealth*, 2 Va. Cas. 95 (1817) (showing how this rule departed from English precedent).

[98] *Succession of Cabellero v. Executor*, 24 La. Ann. 573, 582 (1872).

remarry in Alabama. "The State has a deep concern in marriage, both for its fruits, and its influence upon society," the Court wrote. Although fraudulently procured foreign divorces will not be recognized, "we are of the opinion that just principles of comity, the preservation of good morals, the peace of society, and the happiness of families, demand the recognition of the authority of the tribunals of any country in pursuance to its laws, to grant a divorce in favor of a party in good faith domiciled in that country."[99] This was standard lore in other state cases.

It was incumbent upon the defendant to prove the divorce, however. Susan Boyer of Massachusetts found this out the hard way. She had married James Boyer in 1850. She married Henry Follett in 1863 and was indicted and convicted for polygamy. She alleged that she was divorced from James, but had no proof. On appeal, she said the burden was on the state to prove she was not divorced, not the other way around. The Supreme Juridical Court of Massachusetts rejected her argument. "In the present case, the defendant could, with perfect ease, show the affirmative, to wit, that she was legally divorced from her former husband, if such were the fact, and the government could not, without great difficulty, show the negative. Proving that she was not divorced in this state would not prove that she was not legally divorced in some other and distant state."[100]

Courts were sometimes more lenient when the defendant made an honest and reasonable mistake of fact about the divorce. An Ohio case against John Stank is a good example. Stank was a new German immigrant, illiterate in both German and English. He was married in 1879, but his wife left him after three weeks, and he knew nothing of her whereabouts. Four years later, he wanted to get a divorce so he could get remarried. He consulted a lawyer – aptly named "Mr. Ambush" – who procured for him what turned out to be a fictitious divorce decree and a fake "license to remarry." Thinking he was now free, Stank married a second woman, only to have his first wife reappear to have him charged with bigamy. The trial court convicted him, and he was sent to prison. Stank appealed, arguing that he lacked all intent to commit this felony. The Ohio appellate court agreed and reversed his conviction.[101]

Only a few of these state appellate cases offered any theoretical reflection on monogamy versus polygamy, or any lengthy rationale for the criminalization of polygamy by the state legislatures. But on occasion, the judges would look up from the technicalities of the cases before them, and say a few words about the virtues and values of monogamy over polygamy. Monogamous marriages, several courts emphasized, "is the most important of human transactions; it is the very basis of

---

[99] *Thompson v. State*, 28 Ala. 12, 18–19 (1856).
[100] *Commonwealth v. Boyer*, 7 Allen 306, 308–309 (Mass. 1863).
[101] *Ohio v. Stank*, 9 Ohio Dec. Repr. 8 (1883).

the whole fabric of civilized society."[102] By contrast, they described polygamy as "barbarous," "inconsistent with true civilization,"[103] and "contrary to the law of nature."[104] Polygamy is "not only a violation of the positive law, but also involv[es] such a serious disturbance to the whole social fabric, the peace and good order of society, the legitimacy of children, and the succession of estates."[105] "No greater offense against the marriage obligation could be committed, no grosser infidelity perpetrated, and no baser indignity put upon the faithful wife or husband than by the crime of bigamy."[106] Polygamy exists only in countries that have "a low estimate of the marriage contract" and a "deplorable laxity, if not licentiousness of morals." "[T]he reasons against polygamy ... are traced to the creation of man. The creation was dual and sexual; two and only two, one male and one female, wedded in the bowers of Paradise, God himself declaring the union."[107]

On very rare occasion, these state appellate courts also addressed claims of polygamists for the civil or religious right to practice polygamy contrary to prevailing criminal law. The Supreme Court of Ohio addressed this squarely. The Ohio state constitution gives full protection of religious liberty and liberty of conscience, the court wrote. But:

> Religious liberty does not consist in the right of any sect to oppose its views to the policy of a government. Such a claim would end in simple intolerance of all not in accordance with the sentiments of the particular sect.... There are sects who believe in polygamy, and adopt it as a part of their religion. But, however conscientious they may be in entertaining such notions, if one of them should come into Ohio, and bring with him his wives, his religious scruples would not protect him on an indictment for polygamy.... No plea of religion should shield a murderer, ravisher, or bigamist; for community would be at the mercy of superstition, if such crimes as these could be committed with impunity because sanctioned by some religious delusion.[108]

THE AMERICAN CASE FOR MONOGAMY OVER POLYGAMY

These nineteenth-century state statutes and cases against polygamy reflected prevailing Anglo-American ideas about the essential place of monogamous marriage

---

[102] *McReynolds v. Tennessee*, 45 Tenn. 18, 21 (1867).
[103] *Compo. v. Jackson Iron Co.*, 50 Mich. 578, 585 (1883).
[104] *Pennegar v. State*, 10 S.W. 305, 306 (Tenn. 1889); *Commonwealth v. Lane*, 113 Mass. 458 (1873).
[105] *Ohio v. Stank*, at 12.
[106] *Ralston v. Ralston*, 13 Pa. C.C. 597 (1896) (this is a private divorce case, not a polygamy prosecution). See comparable views in *Dickson v. Dickson's Heirs*, 9 Tenn. 100, 112–113 (1826).
[107] *Head v. Head*, 2 Ga. (Kelly) 191, 207–208 (1847).
[108] *State v. Powell*, 54 Ohio St. 324, 341–342 (1898).

in the organization of a civilized nation. Polygamy was a threat not only to the private goods and rights of women and children, but also to the public goods and needs of a well-organized society. Religious or cultural arguments for and practices of polygamy could thus not be countenanced.

An influential early statement of this idea in America came from Harvard jurist and later Supreme Court Justice Joseph Story (1779–1845). Like his English counterparts, Story was an avid reader of Enlightenment philosophers, and he drew heavily on the Scottish, English, and Continental writings that we sampled in the previous chapter. Story was also an avid student of comparative legal history and conflict of laws, and he studded his writings with all manner of ancient, medieval, and early modern sources on the origin, nature, and purpose of monogamous marriage.

> Marriage is treated by all civilized nations as a peculiar and favored contract. It is in its origin a contract of natural law.... It is the parent and not the child of society, the source of the city, a sort of seminary of the republic. In civil society it becomes a civil contract, regulated and prescribed by law, and endowed with civil consequences. It most civilized countries, acting under the sense of the force of sacred obligations, it has had the sanctions of religion superadded. It then becomes a religious, as well as a natural and civil contract; for it is a great mistake to suppose, that because it is the one, therefore it may not likewise be the other.[109]

For Story, marriage is a civil contract dependent in its essence on the mutual consent of a man and a woman with the freedom and capacity to marry each other. But marriage is also "more than a mere contract," Story insisted, for it also has natural, religious, and social dimensions, all of which the positive law of the state must take into account. The state's positive law of marriage must especially reflect the natural teaching that marriage is a monogamous union presumptively for life; that marriage channels the strong human sex drive toward marital sex which serves to deepen the mutual love between husband and wife; that marriage provides a stable and lifelong system of support, protection, and edification for husbands and wives, parents and children.[110]

The positive law of the state must also outlaw dangerous sex crimes that are deleterious to the nature and purpose of marriage, Story continued. These crimes include polygamy, incest, fornication, adultery, and "light divorce" as well as desertion, abuse, neglect, and disinheritance. All these offenses violate the other spouse's and children's natural rights, Story wrote, citing Paley, Blackstone, and Locke whom we encountered in the last chapter. "A heathen nation might justify

---

[109] Joseph Story, *Commentaries on the Conflict of the Laws, Foreign and Domestic, In Regards to Contracts, Rights, and Remedies, and Especially in Regard to Marriages* (Boston: Hilliard Gray, 1834), sec. 108.

[110] Ibid., secs. 108–199, with quotes on ibid., pp. 26, 87, 104.

polygamy, or incest, or contracts of moral turpitude, or exercises of despotic cruelty over persons, which would be repugnant to the first principles of Christian duty." But not so here, Story insisted. Normally, America will honor a contract made in a foreign country on the traditional conflict of laws principle that "if it is valid there, it is a valid everywhere." But "the most prominent, if not the only known exceptions to this rule, are those respecting polygamy and incest," since they are "repugnant to the public policy of a civilized nation."[111]

Chancellor James Kent of New York (1763–1847), another early systematizer of American law, also lifted up the civil, natural, and religious dimensions of monogamous marriage in his 1826 *Commentaries on American Law*, modeled on Blackstone's *Commentaries on English Law*:

> The primary and most important of the domestic relations is that of husband and wife. It has its foundation in nature, and is the only lawful relation by which Providence has permitted the continuance of the human race. In every age it has had a propitious influence on the moral improvement and happiness of mankind. It is one of the chief foundations of social order. We may justly place to the credit of the institution of marriage a great share of the blessings which flow from the refinement of manners, the education of children, the sense of justice, and cultivation of the liberal arts.[112]

Like Blackstone and Story, Kent cited various English common lawyers and Enlightenment philosophers in support of his argument for exclusive and enduring monogamous marriages and against polygamy. Polygamy, said Kent, is an "odious institution" that Blackstone had properly placed among offenses against "public health, policy, and economy." All polygamous marriages are "null and void," and the Anglo-American common law has properly punished them as serious crimes.[113]

> The direct and serious prohibition of polygamy contained in our law, is founded on the precepts of Christianity, and the laws of our social nature, and it is supported by the sense and practice of the civilized nations of Europe. Though the Athenians at one time permitted polygamy, yet, generally, it was not tolerated in ancient Greece, but was regarded as the practice of barbarians. It was also forbidden by the Romans, throughout the whole period of their history, and the prohibition is inserted in the Institutes of Justinian. Polygamy may be regarded as exclusively the feature of Asiatic manners, and of half-civilized life, and to be incompatible with civilization, refinement, and domestic felicity.[114]

---

[111] Ibid., p. 104. In ibid. sec. 114, Story writes further: "Christianity is understood to prohibit polygamy and incest; and therefore no Christian country would recognize polygamy, or incestuous marriages."

[112] James Kent, *Commentaries on American Law*, 4 vols. (New York: O. Halsted, 1826–1830), 2:72.

[113] Ibid., 2:72–185. *Dane's Abridgement*, vol. 6, ch. 198, art. 10 includes polygamy as "a crime against religion and morality."

[114] Kent, *Commentaries* (1854 ed.), 2:45.

In support of this last quote, Kent cited the work of Francis Lieber (1800–1872), a German-American jurist, philosopher, and social scientist whose writings were standard college texts in their day and would help shape later Supreme Court cases denouncing Mormon polygamy. Lieber emphasized the natural justice and utility of monogamy not only for the couple and their children, but also for the democratic state and its citizens. "The family cannot exist without marriage, nor can it develop its highest importance, it would seem, without monogamy. Civilization, in its highest state, requires it, as well as the natural organization and wants of man." The "Western world," said Lieber, from the classical Greeks and Romans to the modern advanced nations of Europe and North America, "acknowledge with one voice, not only marriage, but monogamy, to be of the last importance for the cause of human advancement."[115]

Lieber distilled the traditional Western argument, going back to Thomas Aquinas, that a stable monogamous family was essential to meeting fully the many needs of fragile children who remain long dependent on both their mother and father.[116] But he went beyond Aquinas to show how a stable monogamous family distinctly cultivates in its members healthy norms and habits of love and respect, rights and duties, loyalty and dependence, caring and sharing, authority and liberty, participation and public spiritedness that are essential to a thriving citizenry in a democratic state:

> Of all animals, man is born not only in the most helpless state, but the infant requires the nurture of its mother long after it has ceased to derive its nourishment from her, which cause not only a physical but an intellectual education. Hence the fact that the attachment between human parents and their offspring is far more enduring than between other animals. The education lasts so long, the child requires the care, protection, and guidance of its parents for so extensive a period, that they may have other children before the first is able to take care of itself. From this circumstance, and the continuity of conjugal attachment which is not, as with other animals, limited to certain seasons, originates the perpetuity of the conjugal union, as well as a mutual attachment among the children, while with other animals no connection, or a very limited one indeed, exists between the offspring of the various seasons.

[115] Francis Lieber, *Manual of Political Ethics, Designed Chiefly for the Use of Colleges and Students at Law*, 2nd rev. ed., ed. Theodore D. Woolsey (Philadelphia: J.B. Lippincott, 1890), 103–104, 141–142. See also the interesting discussion of Lieber, and the Supreme Court's use of his writings in upholding the conviction of Mormon polygamists, in Maura Strassberg, "Distinctions of Form or Substance: Monogamy, Polygamy, and Same-Sex Marriage," *North Carolina Law Review* 75 (1996–1997): 1501, 1518–1523.

[116] See discussion in Chapter 4, pp. 170–174.

The protracted state of the child's dependency upon the parents produces habits
of obedience, respect, and love, and, at a more advanced period, a consciousness
of mutual dependence. The family, with its many mutual and lasting relations,
increasing in intensity, is formed. The members of the family soon discover
how much benefit they derive from reciprocal assistance, and from a division of
occupation among them, since man is placed in the world without strong and
irresistible instincts which are given to other animals for protection or support,
and which seems to increase in specific intensity the lower the animal stands in
the scale of animate creation, thus approach more and more the plant, which lives
without any self-action – an absolute slave to season, clime, and soil. So little is
man instinctive, that even his sociality, so indispensable to his whole existence, has
first to be developed. He is led to it, indeed, by the natural relations between the
progenitors and their offspring.... It is in the family, between parents and children,
and sisters and brothers, that those strong sympathies and deep-rooted affections
grow up which become the vital spark of so many good actions....

With them is mingled and a thousandfold entwined all that attachment which
expands into patriotism – that warm devotion to our country which loves to dwell
in every noble heart, and without which no free state can long exist. The love of
our parents, of our children, of our brothers and sisters, makes patriotism, a thrilling
reality.... The family is the focus of patriotism. Public spirit, patriotism, devotion
to our country, are nurtured by family ties, by the attachment to our community.[117]

Polygamy, by contrast, Lieber continued, obstructs human advancement by
enslaving women, exploiting child labor, eroding education, foreclosing choice,
and privileging rich men who may be inferior in habit, mind, and virtue. Polygamy
furthermore obstructs democracy by privileging patriarchy and hierarchy, denying
liberty and equality, and creating powerful "despotic" households and communities
that rival rather than serve the broader democratic polity. With no small amount
of cultural smugness, Lieber spent pages contrasting the "patriarchal," "barbarian,"
and "backward" "Asiastic," African, and "Moslem" peoples that countenanced
polygamy with the advanced, liberated, and egalitarian Western cultures that
prescribed monogamy.[118]

Lieber emphasized that monogamy was not just biblical or Christian doctrine writ
large; indeed he lamented the polygamy of the biblical patriarchs. Monogamy, he
said, was a feature of all "enlightened" and "civilized" peoples, from pre-Christian
Greeks and Romans to modern-day liberals and anyone else who understood the
social conditions for the development of an advanced civilization.

[117] Lieber, *Manual of Political Ethics*, 103–104, 141–142 (paragraph breaks added).
[118] Ibid., 139; Francis Lieber, *Essays on Property and Labor, as Connected with Natural Law and the
Constitution of Society* (New York: Harper & Brothers, 1841), 18–19, 103–142, 387ff. See a comparable
argument, focusing on pre-Christian Greek and Roman law precedents in Leonard Shelford, *A
Practical Treatise on the Law of Marriage and Divorce* (London: S. Sweet, 1841), 1–5, 223–231.

Monogamy is sanctioned by our religion, indeed, as everything pure and holy is, but monogamy goes beyond our religion. It is "a law written in the heart" of our race.... Monogamy does not only go with the Western Caucasian race, the Europeans and their descendants, beyond Christianity, it goes beyond Common Law. It is one of the primordial elements out of which all laws proceed, or which the law steps in to recognize and to protect.... [M]onogamic marriage, is one of the "categories" of our social thoughts and conceptions, therefore, of social existence.[119]

Lieber's argument – although culturally smug, even xenophobic in some of his later-life statements – was a new variation on an old Western argument about the superiority of monogamy over polygamy. Already in the fourth and fifth centuries, we saw, the Church Fathers had posited a narrative of progress from the permissible polygamy of Old Testament Israel to the more virtuous monogamy of the New Testament world.[120] In the ninth to eleventh centuries, the Jewish Rabbis had explained that monogamy was fairer for men, women, children, and society than the polygamy that the ancient Mosaic law had permitted; polygamy, the Rabbis concluded, was just too much "trouble" to be countenanced.[121] In the twelfth and thirteenth centuries, Christian theologians and jurists had made the same argument to contrast the monogamous habits of Western Christendom with the polygamous habits of Muslims in their day.[122] In the seventeenth and eighteenth centuries, European observers of the non-Western world had made marriage a "boundary marker" between what they considered to be the cultivated, disciplined Christian people of the West who maintained faithful monogamy, and the barbaric, unruly peoples of the pagan world who practiced faithless polygamy.[123] There was nothing new in Lieber's comparisons between the cultural inferiority of polygamy and the cultural superiority of monogamy. This was a standard Western argument.

There was also nothing new in Lieber's argument about the harms of polygamy that were visited disproportionately on women and children. Eight hundred years before, medieval Rabbis and Christian scholars alike had pointed out the sundry harms, crimes, and abuses that too often attended polygamous households, both in earlier biblical times and in their own day.[124] Christian writers argued further that real polygamy as well as successive polygamy after no-fault divorce violated the natural rights of wives, children, and other dependents in the household. This theme was echoed and elaborated by early modern Protestants who argued at length

---

[119] Francis Lieber, "The Mormons: Shall Utah be Admitted into the Union?" *Putnam's Monthly* 5 (March, 1855): 225–236, at 234.
[120] See discussion in Chapter 2, pp. 85–93.
[121] See discussion in Chapter 1, pp. 59–63.
[122] See discussion in Chapter 4, pp. 159–161.
[123] See discussion in Chapter 7, pp. 282–285.
[124] See discussions in Chapter 1, pp. 52–55, pp. 59–63, and Chapter 3, pp. 73–75.

about the harms polygamy caused to the wife's rights of contract, property, fidelity, and equality and the children's rights to be raised in a wholesome and nurturing family environment with their father and mother together. Enlightenment writers repeated all of these arguments, stressing further that the harms of polygamy to women and children were often visited on society both by creating new dependents on social welfare but also a new generation of children not schooled in the norms and habits needed to thrive and contribute as responsible adult citizens.[125] Lieber was just repeating a well-worn Western argument that real polygamy and successive polygamy caused too much harm, and did too much wrong to rights.

And there was nothing new in Lieber's observation that the health and stability of the marital household and political commonwealth were essentially linked. Aristotle had already called the household a vital source of the polis, and this view echoed endlessly in the Western tradition.[126] The seventeenth-century English "commonwealth model" had repeated these ancient insights, calling the marital household a "little commonwealth" and "little school" where husbands and wives, parents and children, learned the norms and habits of authority and liberty, learning and responsibility, caring and sharing that were essential for them to participate fully and properly as patriotic citizens in an organized republic. The monogamous household, the English commonwealth model taught, cultivated better civil habits and moral virtues in the citizenry than a polygamous household.[127]

What was new was Lieber's evolutionary argument that monogamy was conducive to democracy while polygamy trapped cultures in despotism. In the development of civilization, he argued, modern liberal democracy and orderly constitutional government were the apex if not telos of social progress. And only monogamy could produce the virtues and habits necessary for its gradual development and continued maintenance thereafter. Polygamy, by contrast, retarded the development and progress of society toward civilization. It "fetter[ed] the people in stationary despotism," said Lieber, and left them under the "tyrannical rule" of the "patriarchal principle" – as can be seen today in the "backward cultures" and brutal political regimes that dominate Asia, Africa, and the Middle East.[128] Lieber cited German

---

[125] See discussion in Chapter 8, pp. 373–385.

[126] Lieber, *Manual of Political Ethics*, 1:110–113, 125.

[127] See discussion in Chapter 7, pp. 285–290, on the English commonwealth model. See also Sarah Barringer Gordon, "'The Twin Relic of Barbarism'; A Legal History of Anti-Polygamy in Nineteenth-Century America" (Ph.D. Diss., Princeton, 1995), 35: "The argument for the relationship between democracy and monogamy reflects the tradition[al] argument the state reflects and is dependent upon the individual families that make up its constituents. In this view a tyrannical husband (like a slaveholder, a man who has too much power over those dependent on him) would be unfit to participate in the reasoned debate of democratic politics, but would instead constantly seek to replicate the tyrannical policies of his home in the political arena."

[128] Lieber, *Manual of Political Ethics*, 1:125.

social scientist, Arnold Heeren (1760–1842), who had written that "polygamy at once produces domestic tyranny, by making woman a slave and man a tyrant; and society at large thus becomes a combination, not of fathers of families but of household tyrants." Because of this, Heeren continued, "no nation practising polygamy has ever attained to a true republican constitution, nor even that of a free monarchy."[129]

Heeren and Lieber were writing in the 1820s to 1840s, well before America's encounter with Mormon polygamy. They were early exponents of a powerful new school of social scientists, on both sides of the Atlantic, who were tracing the development of law, politics, and society, and the respective roles of polygamy and monogamy within this development.[130] Many of these social scientists were taken with the new evolutionary theories of natural and human development that were cresting in the nineteenth century, now amply aided by growing collections of field research and ethnographic data.[131] Many of them were also taken with the new ideas of social progress, born of Enlightenment optimism.[132] Many of these social scientists thought that polygamy was an early and inferior form of family life that degraded women and children. "The effect of polygamy in increasing the number of married women is beyond dispute," wrote Thomas Malthus (1776–1834) in his famous work on world populations. But in many parts of the world where it is practiced, polygamy has "also led to squalid and hopeless poverty" for all but favored wives and children and inevitable "enslavement" and "misery" for most of the rest of the family.[133] "Polygyny is an offense against the feelings of women, not only among highly civilized peoples, but even among the rudest savages," wrote Edward Westermarck (1862–1939) at the conclusion of his leading study of the history of marriage. Even "among monogamous savage or barbarous races, the position of women is comparatively good."[134]

[129] A.H.L. Heeren, *Historical Researches in the Politics, Intercourse, and Trade of the Principal Nations of Antiquity*, 4 vols. (London: H.G. Bohn, 1846–1850), 1:16–17; see discussion in John David Pulsipher, "The Americanization of Monogamy: Mormons, Native Americans and the Nineteenth-Century Perception that Polygamy was a Threat to Democracy" (Ph.D. Diss., Minnesota, 1988), 109–112.

[130] See a good summary of this literature in Howard, *Matrimonial Institutions*, 1:3–151, esp. 132–151 on theories of development from polygamy to monogamy.

[131] See generally Laura L. Betzig, *Despotism, Social Evolution, and Differential Reproduction* (Somerset, NJ: Aldine Transaction, 2008).

[132] See, e.g., the old classics of John B. Bury, *The Idea of Progress* (London: MacMillan and Company, 1921); Carl L. Becker, *The Heavenly City of the Enlightenment Philosophers* (New Haven, CT: Yale University Press, 1932). On nineteenth-century formulations, see Ernst Cassirer, *The Problem of Knowledge: Philosophy, Science, and History Since Hegel*, trans. William H. Woglom and Charles W. Hendel (New Haven, CT: Yale University Press, 1950).

[133] Thomas Robert Malthus, *An Essay on the Principles of Population* (London: John Murray, 1826), I.VII.18, I.VIII.6, 12.

[134] Edward Westermarck, *The History of Human Marriage* (London/New York: MacMillan, 1891), 496–504; see detailed sources in Howard, *History*, 1:142–151 distilling this social science literature at the turn of the twentieth century.

Talk of "savages" and "barbarians" grates harshly against the modern ear. But in the nineteenth century, this was standard social scientific terminology to describe earlier stages of human and social development. One of the most influential such accounts in America came from Henry Lewis Morgan (1818–1881), a lawyer, businessman, and anthropologist, who was well read in ancient civilizations, and wrote extensively on African and Native American Indian social structures.[135] In his famous 1877 title, *Ancient Society*, Morgan posited three stages of human social development over hundreds of thousands of years – from the stage of "savagery" to the stage of "barbarism" to the stage of "civilization" with "lower, middle, and upper forms" of each stage. The gradual evolution from one stage to the next turned on the development of a number of interdependent factors, said Morgan: subsistence, government, language, religion, property, family, household life, and architecture. The more differentiated and sophisticated each of these factors became, the greater the advance toward civilization.[136]

At stage one, in Morgan's account, savages had little subsistence beyond what they hunted and gathered, little language beyond gestures, signs, and pictures, little government beyond a strongman or a small tribe, little concept or division of property, and only fluid forms of sexual partnering and reproduction. At stage two, barbarians developed farming tools, agriculture, and domesticated animals, spoken languages and dialects, larger tribes, clans, and confederacies of government, communal divisions of property, and more stable households usually gathered around a patriarch and his wives and children, very occasionally a matriarch with her husbands and children. At stage three, civilized peoples have sophisticated food production, diet, and sundries trade, complex written and spoken alphabets and languages, sophisticated political and legal systems separated from families, clans, and personalities and bound by rules of law and constitutional order, a refined concept of private property and economics – all grounded ultimately on a properly functioning monogamous family and independent household structure.[137]

[135] See Henry Lewis Morgan, *Systems of Consanguinity and Affinity of the Human Family* (Washington, DC: Smithsonian Institution, 1868); id., *The Indian Journals, 1859–62*, ed. Leslie A. White (Ann Arbor: University of Michigan Press, 1959); id., *League of the Iroquois* (New York: Corinth Books, 1851); id., *Houses and House-Life of the American Aborigines* (Chicago: University of Chicago Press, 1965 [1881]).
[136] Henry Lewis Morgan, *Ancient Society, Or Research in the Lines of Human Progress from Savagery Through Barbarism to Civilization* (New York: Henry Holt and Company, 1877), esp. 3–18, 383–522.
[137] Ibid. Building on Karl Marx, Friedrich Engels drew Morgan's insights to a different conclusion, viz., that monogamy was a later stage of class struggle between men and women, which eventually would move toward true communism that abolished the marital family altogether. See esp. Frederick Engels, *The Origin of the Family, Private Property, and the State* [1884], trans. Ernest Untermann (Chicago: Charles H. Kerr and Co., 1902), 35–40, 74–101. See other sources discussed in Richard Weikart, "Marx, Engels, and the Abolition of the Family," *History of European Ideas* 18 (1994): 657–672. For later implementation of these ideas in the Soviet Union against both Christian

"The evolution of the monogamian family," Morgan wrote, comes at the boundary line between "the upper stages of barbarism and [the first] stage of civilization." Indeed, the legal establishment and social protection of monogamy was a precondition for the final move from barbarism to civilization. And the maintenance of the monogamous family thereafter was inextricably tied to the protection of life, liberty, and property in an orderly democratic society under constitutional government governed by the rule of law. To remove or dilute any of these fundamentals of civilization, especially the monogamous family, said Morgan, would be to return to barbarism.[138]

THE AMERICAN CAMPAIGN AGAINST "BARBARIAN POLYGAMY"

It was sentiments such as these that helped to drive the American campaign to eradicate polygamy in the nineteenth and twentieth centuries. This campaign was further supported by a fresh Christian reawakening and Victorian moral reformation in the later nineteenth century that sometimes saw monogamous marriage as a unique and superior feature of the Christian West. But it was fueled even more by longstanding Western arguments against polygamy that had been newly repackaged by these social science arguments that made monogamy a cornerstone of Western civilization.

One concern driving this campaign was what we already saw in the state cases analyzed earlier in this chapter: the escalation of marital fluidity and desertion, self-divorce and remarriage, especially on the frontier, and even more during and after the Civil War that proved so devastating to families. It did not help that a few free-love and sexual radicals from the 1830s to 1860s were praising this liberalization of traditional family norms and advocating all manner of new utopian forms of domestic relations, including polygamy and sexual communes.[139] Strict new state legislation about the rules and procedures of monogamous marriage, divorce, and remarriage followed in the second half of the nineteenth century, together with aggressive prosecution of deserters and successive polygamists as we saw. Deserting polygamists, particularly those who left a dependent spouse and minor children

---

monogamy and Muslim polygamy, see Harold J. Berman, "Soviet Family Law in the Light of Russian History and Marxist Theory," *Yale Law Journal* 56 (1946): 26–57; F.J.M. Feldbrugge, "Criminal Law and Traditional Society: The Role of Soviet Law in the Integration of Non-Slavic Peoples," *Review of Socialist Law* 3 (1977): 3–51.

[138] Morgan, *Ancient Society*, 462.

[139] See, e.g., Raymond Lee Muncy, *Sex and Marriage in Utopian Communities: 19ᵗʰ-Century America* (Bloomington: Indiana University Press, 1973), esp. 12–14, 169–171; Hal D. Sears, *The Sex Radicals: Free Love in High Victorian America* (Lawrence: The Regents Press of Kansas, 1977); John Spurlock, *Free Love: Marriage and Middle-Class Radicalism in America, 1825–1860* (New York: New York University Press, 1988); Louis J. Kern, *An Ordered Love: Sex Roles and Sexuality in Victorian Utopias – The Shakers, the Mormons, and the Oneida Community* (Chapel Hill: University of North Carolina Press, 1995); see further analysis and sources in Cott, *Public Vows*, 68–71, 107–112.

without support, were now actively pursued by the authorities, with stronger interstate cooperation after the Civil War in chasing down deserters. Many of these deserting polygamists were ordered to pay restitution and support for their first wives and dependents. Before the New Deal laws of the 1930s, American families, churches, and voluntary organizations provided the vast bulk of charity and social welfare, making essential a stable family structure, and ongoing spousal and parental support in cases of breakdown.

A second concern driving the American campaign against polygamy was the plight of the nearly four million newly emancipated African-Americans, whom the state slave codes had forbidden to marry. Some state statutes and cases after 1865, as we saw, sought to regularize their informal unions and enforce the norms of faithful monogamy among these newly recognized families.[140] More important for a time was the new federal Bureau of Refugees, Freedman, and Abandoned Lands created by the Reconstruction Congress in the aftermath of the Civil War. This Freedman Bureau, as it was called, implemented new marriage rules and procedures to allow African Americans to marry monogamously as well to reunite broken families and to make provision for the hundreds of thousands who were injured, impoverished, widowed, and orphaned during the Civil War.[141] The Bureau worked hard to undo at least some of the devastation visited on the lives of former slaves, and to force recalcitrant states to cooperate in vindicating their rights to marry. "I praise God for this day!" wrote one African American to the Freedman Bureau in gratitude. "I have long been praying for it. The Marriage Covenant is the foundation of all our rights. In slavery, we could not have *legalized* marriage; *now* we have it."[142] These state and federal reforms had more sinister motives, too: to stamp out the marital fluidity and suspected polygamy among some of these once-enslaved African Americans who were thought to have carried this "African" practice with them.

These more sinister concerns about polygamy were more overt in the American campaign to "civilize" Native American Indians. The tragic treatment of Native Americans by American federal and state authorities – and already by colonial authorities before them – is well known. The policies of enforced "civilization" escalated in the later nineteenth century. Echoing earlier laws, an 1867 federal statute ordered Natives to be forcibly removed from their ancestral home lands, and placed

---

[140] See cases discussed earlier in this chapter and Grossberg, *Governing the Hearth*, 129–140.

[141] See Cott, *Public Vows*, 83–94.

[142] Quoted by ibid., 89–90. See also the excellent work of Frances Smith Foster who shows the deep culture of monogamous marriage in African-American communities, both before and after Emancipation. Frances Smith Foster, *"Til Death or Distance Do Us Part": Love and Marriage in African America* (New York/Oxford: Oxford University Press, 2010); id., *Love & Marriage in Early African America* (Hanover, NH: University Press of New England, 2008). See further Peggy Cooper Davis, *Neglected Stories: The Constitution and Family Values* (New York: Hill and Wang, 1998).

on reservations in Oklahoma, the Dakotas, and beyond. Other federal laws ordered Native children taken from their homes and tribes and put in boarding schools to learn Western Christian values, beliefs, and lifestyles. Other federal and state laws ordered each Native American man to reject his "plural wives" and take up his role as head of the monogamous household, providing for his wife and children in their private home and participating in public as a responsible democratic citizen. An 1887 federal law instituted a policy of breaking up Native American ancestral lands and community properties and establishing nuclear monogamous families in private property allotments. A new federal Bureau of Indian Affairs, with agents fanned out across the Western frontier and on the reservations, implemented these new federal laws. Federal Courts of Indian Offenses were set up to enforce them against the recalcitrant. Those Native American tribes that resisted these "civilizing" efforts were eventually crushed by the military in a series of epic battles on the frontier, including the infamous Wounded Knee Massacre of 1890.[143]

All these federal policies were designed, in part, to implement nineteenth-century American ideals of moving Native Americans from "barbarism" to "civilization." The firm imposition of monogamy was considered to be an essential first step in that effort. Native Americans, it was believed, were "addicted to polygamy," and breaking them from that habit, even by brute force, was a federal priority.[144] The Commissioner of the Bureau of Indian Affairs reported thus to Congress in 1878:

> In the process of Indian civilization, it is necessary to build from the foundation, and therefore it is proper to begin with family relations. There are at the present time no valid marriages among the Indians.... The whole proceeding [of marriage] is a mere matter of bargain and sale, in which women are disposed of without their consent, and very much like cattle in the market. There is nowhere any limit to the number of wives (as they are called) which an Indian may have, and by their custom he can change the occupants of his lodge as often as he chooses. As our civilization is opposed to polygamy, some decisive action should be taken regulating and establishing [monogamous] marriage in all Indian communities.[145]

Reports from agents of the Bureau of Indian Affairs repeatedly addressed the local efforts to stamp out Native American polygamy in implementation of new federal laws of monogamy. One agent complained about the Native custom of arranged polygamous marriages and their deleterious effects on young women: "The practice of marrying off girls at the early and tender age so frequently done is most injurious and reprehensible. It cannot fail to produce rapid diminution of any race that

[143] Cott, *Public Vows*, 120–123; Pulsipher, "The Americanization of Monogamy," 81–96, 133–141, 145–149, 166–170.
[144] Annual Report of the Red Lake Agency (1877), quoted in ibid., 134.
[145] Annual Report of the Commissioner of Indian Affairs (1878), 456–460, quoted by ibid., 138–139.

habitually practices it.... The husbands are selected by the parents, and thus the child is remanded back to barbarism after it had just fairly commenced its course of preparation for civilized life" through the new schooling programs.[146] By contrast, another enthusiastic agent reported as follows in 1883: "I am happy to report that polygamy, one of the greatest obstacles to civilization, is fast disappearing among the Indians of this reservation. The teacher and myself lecture upon this subject every Sabbath after Sunday school is over, and our lectures to them seem to meet the hearty approval of the chiefs and headmen, some of whom have recently discarded their extra wife. None of the young men who have espoused wives during the past year have taken more than one."[147]

Native Americans were not the only group that the federal government targeted as "barbarians" that practiced polygamy. Asian immigrants, mostly Chinese who came in the mid-nineteenth century to work on the transcontinental railroad and other public works, faced repeated harassment from nativists and officials because of their suspected polygamy as well as their rampant use of prostitutes. Asian women thought to be polygamous wives or prostitutes were routinely excluded or deported by federal immigration officials and with them their children. These exclusionary efforts were reinforced by a firm new federal immigration law of 1875 that barred entry to anyone under contract for "lewd and immoral purposes" and that further penalized Americans who sought to bring these parties into the United States. That immigration law was extended in 1907 to exclude "persons who admit their belief in the practice of polygamy," leading to routine exclusion not only of Asian immigrants, but also Muslims from various parts of the world.[148] Polygamists were put on the same immigration exclusion list "as paupers, the insane, felons, and those with a loathsome or dangerous disease," writes Nancy Cott. "After anarchists were also excluded (as a result of the assassination of President McKinley by a reputed anarchist), polygamists and anarchists always appeared in sequence as excludable, deportable, and ineligible for citizenship, as if disloyalty to monogamy were equivalent to overthrowing the government."[149] In the intellectual milieu of the day that saw faithful monogamy, orderly government, private property, and peaceful civilization as interdependent variables, this association was easy to press; the Congressional record is filled with such rhetoric.

---

[146] Annual Report of the Pawnee Agency (1880), quoted by ibid., 135.

[147] Annual Report of the Western Shoshoni Agency (1883), quoted by ibid., 136–137.

[148] For detailed treatment, see Kerry Abrams, "Polygamy, Prostitution, and the Federalization of Immigration Law," *Columbia Law Review* 105 (2005): 641–716; and Claire A. Smearman, "Second Wives' Club: Mapping the Impact of Polygamy in U.S. Immigration Law," *Berkeley Journal of International Law* 27 (2009): 382–447

[149] Cott, *Public Vows*, 139.

The Mormon Question

The American campaign against polygamy reached its apex in the massive half-century effort to stamp out Mormon polygamy. As we saw in the Introduction to this book, the Mormon Church, or Church of Jesus Christ of Latter-Day Saints, was one of scores of new churches to emerge in America during the Second Great Awakening in the nineteenth century.[150] Its founding prophet Joseph Smith (1805–1844) had developed a new scripture to supplement the Christian Bible – the *Book of Mormon*, which he published in 1830. He had further developed a separate Book of Doctrines and Covenants in 1843 which became the doctrinal and disciplinary backbone of the Mormon Church thereafter. The Mormon faithful were called to form new communities centered on a temple, devoted to a common "Law of Consecration and Stewardship," and especially committed to missionary work. This new faith featured a number of new teachings, such as the efficacy of proxy baptism for the dead, the preexistence of man, and a metaphysical materialism that stood in tension with the traditional biblical story of the creation ex nihilo. Such novel teachings and practices, and the ardent advocacy of them by Mormon missionaries, soon led to severe repression of the Mormon Church. The church was driven from New York to Ohio, and then to Missouri and Illinois. After severe rioting and the murder of Joseph Smith and his brother in 1844, the Mormon believers escaped and migrated to the American frontier under the new leadership of Brigham Young (1801–1877). They settled in the Salt Lake area which became the United States Territory of Utah in 1850. That made the Mormon settlers subject to Congress and the federal courts until Utah was declared an independent state in 1896.

Most new religious communities born of the Second Great Awakening, especially those on the distant frontier, were left to themselves and most died out after a generation or two. But the Mormon Church continued to attract national attention, in part because of its novel teachings, in part because it was growing so rapidly both in the United States and abroad. This attention soon escalated to alarm when an 1852 manifesto from the church's leadership announced that Mormons believed in and practiced real polygamy. For one man to have several wives, the manifesto stated, was an appropriate and biblical form of communal living. It was illustrated by the ancient Hebrew patriarchs and facilitated by the Mosaic law. It was an effective and efficient way to meet the biblical command to "be fruitful and multiply." And it increased the opportunities for all women, even when men were scarce, to enjoy the spiritually salutary steps of marriage and motherhood which Mormons believed

---

[150] Nathan O. Hatch, *The Democratization of American Christianity* (New Haven, CT: Yale University Press, 1989); see details in Edwin S. Gaustad, Philip L. Barlow, and Richard W. Dishno, *New Historical Atlas of Religion in America* (Oxford: Oxford University Press, 2001).

would continue eternally in the celestial life hereafter. No one in the Mormon Church was commanded to practice polygamy. But those who could practice polygamy were encouraged to do so, especially if there were single marriageable women in the community who did not have marital prospects.

Joseph Smith had evidently been privately teaching and practicing polygamy already in the later 1830s, certainly by 1841. He set forth his formal views on celestial marriage and polygamy in the 1843 Doctrine and Covenants, making them part of official Mormon teaching and practice:

> [I]f any man espouse a virgin, and desire to espouse another, and the first give her consent, and if he espouse the second, and they are virgins, and have vowed to no other man, then is he justified; he cannot commit adultery for they are given unto him; for he cannot commit adultery with that that belongeth unto him and to no one else.

> And if he have ten virgins given unto him by this law, he cannot commit adultery, for they belong to him, and they are given unto him; therefore is he justified.

> But if one or either of the ten virgins, after she is espoused, shall be with another man, she has committed adultery, and shall be destroyed; for they are given unto him to multiply and replenish the earth according to my commandment.[151]

To set an example for the reticent, Brigham Young and other church leaders took several wives. They provided further guidelines and household manuals for men, women, and children to live properly and piously within a polygamous family.[152]

When word of Mormon polygamy got out in the early 1850s, it prompted a nationwide crusade against the Mormon Church. Not only was Mormon polygamy considered to be a flagrant affront to long cherished monogamous norms of American and Western civilization. But this news hit just as the nation was waging bitter battles to abolish chattel slavery and to secure further rights for women and children. It was very easy to castigate polygamy as yet another species of slavery and patriarchy. Indeed, polygamy and slavery were considered to be among the "twin relics of barbarism," as the Republican Party put it already in its 1856 platform.[153]

---

[151] *The Doctrine and Covenants of the Church of Jesus Christ of Latter-Day Saints*, Section 132, 61–63. See discussion of the emerging theology of plural celestial marriage in Brian C. Hales, *Joseph Smith's Polygamy*, 3 vols. (Salt Lake City, UT: Greg Kofford Books, 2013), Volume 3: "Theology," esp. pp. 149–161.

[152] See, e.g., "Orson Pratt's 27 Rules of Celestial Marriage" (1853), reprinted in Janet Bennion, *Polygamy in Primetime: Media, Gender, and Politics in Mormon Fundamentalism* (Waltham, MA: Brandeis University Press, 2012), Appendix, 293–304, and discussion in ibid., 23–55. See generally Richard S. Van Wagoner, *Mormon Polygamy: A History* (Salt Lake City, UT: Signature Books, 1986).

[153] The phrase was coined by abolitionist Ebenezer Rockwood Hoar. See Eric Foner, *Free Soil, Free Labor, Free Men: The Ideology of the Republican Party Before the Civil War* (Oxford: Oxford University Press, 1995), 130.

After the Civil War and the Reconstruction Amendments finally and forcibly abolished slavery and servitude, it became doubly imperative in the minds of many to abolish its "barbaric twin," polygamy, as well. Representative Hamilton Ward of New York put it thus: "[A]fter redeeming [the nation] from the stain of human slavery," war-weary but resolute Americans must summon "the manhood [and] nobility" to fight again to rescue polygamous Mormon wives and children who are "slaves to a system worse than death."[154]

Both before and after the Civil War, the nation was inundated with novels, plays, cartoons, sermons, pamphlets, broadsides, autobiographies by former polygamous wives, and learned tracts directed against polygamy – although Mormon and other sympathetic voices were raised in strong support of polygamy, too.[155] In her definitive study, University of Pennsylvania legal historian Sarah Barringer Gordon has shown brilliantly the pervasiveness and power of all these media in feeding the American frenzy over "the Mormon question."[156]

Much of the sweeping anti-Mormon discourse in the later nineteenth century traded on familiar Western arguments against real polygamy. Polygamy, the anti-Mormon argument frequently went, harmed young girls who were tricked, coerced, or religiously commanded to enter marriages with older men, and had too little education and too few means of escape when inevitably neglected or replaced by another favorite wife. Their plight, other critics pointed out, was exacerbated by the liberal Mormon practice of unilateral male divorce that allowed men to banish women who failed to fall in line, thereby reducing these wives to servile accomplices to their crime. Women and children within the home were placed into competition with each other for ever scarcer resources, and reduced to "white slaves," anti-polygamist Alfreda Eva Bell put it. They were bought and sold like the black chattel slaves of the South by wealthy and powerful men, and hunted down and restored to their husband-masters in the event of their desertion of the polygamous home. They were "required to do all the most servile drudgery." They were "painfully impressed with their utter inferiority" to their male rulers and regularly "subjected to personal violence and ... corporal punishment."[157] Congressman Justin Morrill of Vermont, author of a new federal law criminalizing polygamy, echoed these

[154]   Cong. Globe, 41st Congress, 2nd Sess., 2144 (1870). See further such rhetoric in Stephen Eliot Smith, "Barbarians within the Gates: Congressional Debates on Mormon Polygamy: 1850–1879," *Journal of Church and State* 51 (2009): 587–616.
[155]   See detailed sources and analysis in Sarah Barringer Gordon, *The Mormon Question: Polygamy and Constitutional Conflict in Nineteenth Century America* (Chapel Hill and London: University of North Carolina Press, 2002), 85–118.
[156]   Ibid.
[157]   Alfreda Evan Bell, *Boadicea: The Mormon Wife* (Baltimore, MD: A.R. Orton, 1855), 34–54, quoted and analyzed in Gordon, *The Mormon Question*, 47.

sentiments, arguing that polygamy was a form of both "slavery and tyranny." It tore "the enduring passion of love from the heart and install[ed] in its place the rage of jealousy" between the plural wives and their many children. It degraded women and their offspring to "the level of mere animal."[158]

The first wives of polygamy in particular, the argument continued, were betrayed in their essential roles as chief rulers, educators, and exemplars of morality and virtue within the monogamous home. "Homes are the rock on which this Republic is built," declared women rights advocate, Angie Newman, in her testimony to Congress. "Homes where one woman reigns as queen sitting upon a throne whose honor knows neither compromise nor division."[159] This "republican motherhood" theme became an important part of the argument for women's rights within the household on which both conservatives and liberals of the day could agree.

Polygamy, furthermore, licenses and encourages male lust for sex, power, and patriarchal excess, the critics argued. It induces inevitable restlessness on the part of some males to add more women to their harems. It invites inevitable repression and ostracism of rival males eager to find a wife or lover among the scant supply of women who are left to them. It restricts marriage to the richest and most powerful, not necessarily the fittest and most virtuous males of the community. Such conduct might be acceptable in a Muslim seraglio or an Asian or African tribal village, the argument went on. But it simply could not be countenanced in a civilized Christian land. "The Christian and moral male was one who controlled sexual appetite through the institution of monogamy and demonstrated virility through the law of manliness, especially manifested by his chivalry for the mother of the home."[160]

Finally, polygamy creates religious power structures that rival the legitimate power of the state. Particularly in the United States Territory of Utah, the argument went, the leadership of the Mormon church has already gained disproportionate influence in the governance of the community. Both the individual polygamous leaders of the church and the Mormon Church as a whole have amassed huge portions of property and now control a good deal of the local economy and work force. They compel their congregants, workers, and family members to support their warped polygamous policies and to vote for new officials who will do the same. They collude to evade federal laws and policies, and to suborn the perjury and contempt of their individual members. And when government officials seek to restore legal and moral order in the territory, the Mormons confront them with boycotts, guns,

---

[158] Speech of Hon. Justin S. Morrill of Vermont: on Utah territory and its laws–polygamy and its license, delivered in the House of Representatives, February 23, 1857 (Washington, DC: Office of the Congressional Globe, 1857), 10. See Gordon, *The Mormon Question*, 62–69.

[159] Quoted in Joan Smyth Iversen, *The Antipolygamy Controversy in U.S. Women's Movements, 1880–1925: A Debate on the American Home* (New York/London: Garland Publishing, 1997), 140.

[160] Ibid., 145–146.

riots, and violence. This simply cannot be. In short order, one Congressional report put it, "all the evils which must follow unlimited power of the church to take and hold lands and other property ... are beginning to show themselves in our own country." "Ecclesiastics clothed with property" now seek "to control the state and master its fate."[161]

America is a land constitutionally committed to no establishment of religion, and to the separation of church and state, the argument continued. No religion or region that defies this most basic element of American constitutional order can be allowed to stand. Theocracies are a thing of the past, and are no longer countenanced anywhere in America. Evangelical preacher Lyman Beecher had earlier captured the dangers of such a religio-political compound in a single word – "treason" – and such views were oft-repeated.

> It is a union of church and state, which we fear, and to prevent which we lift up our voice; a union which never existed without corrupting the church and enslaving the people, by making the ministry independent of them and dependent on the state, and to a great extent a sinecure aristocracy of indolence and secular ambition, auxiliary to the throne and inimical to liberty. No treason against our free institutions would be more fatal than a union of church and state.[162]

Because Utah and some of the other western areas where the Mormons settled were U.S. territories, Congress had general authority to pass laws regulating sex, marriage, and family life. Congress exercised this authority with increasing sternness in an effort to stamp out Mormon polygamy. An 1862 law made polygamy a federal crime in all United States territories, including Utah, echoing an earlier Congressional polygamy law of 1816 that governed the District of Columbia. An 1882 law disqualified real polygamists, as well as men cohabiting with more than one woman, from holding political office, voting in elections, and sitting on juries. Other federal statutes used ever more sweeping definitions of plural unions to try to capture the skillfully evasive polygamists in Utah and surrounding territories – only seventy-eight of whom ultimately could be found and indicted. Additionally, these laws required parties to swear oaths denying the practice or advocacy of polygamy, and subjected them to close scrutiny for even suspected beliefs in polygamy. An 1887

---

[161] House Report on the Edmunds-Tucker Bill, quoted by Gordon, *The Mormon Question*, 187.

[162] Lyman Beecher, *A Plea for the West*, 2nd ed. (Cincinnati, OH: Truman and Smith, 1835), 78–79, evidently repeated by Henry Ward Beecher, "Plea for Religious Liberty; A Thanksgiving Sermon Preached in Plymouth Church, Brooklyn, in 1883." See Gordon, *The Mormon Question*, 197. On the multiple meanings of disestablishment of religion and separation of church and state in the nineteenth century, see sources and discussion in T. Jeremy Gunn and John Witte, Jr., eds., *No Establishment of Religion: The America's Original Contribution to Religious Liberty* (New York/Oxford: Oxford University Press, 2012).

law called for the forfeiture of the Mormon Church's property if it persisted in its preaching and practice of polygamy.[163] The Congressional debates over these laws are teeming with invective against polygamy and the Mormons who practiced it.[164]

The Mormons repeatedly challenged technical aspects of these laws, appealing more than a dozen times to the Supreme Court, but to little avail. Four of these Supreme Court cases addressed challenges that these congressional laws violated the Mormons' free exercise of religion as protected by the First Amendment to the United States Constitution. *Reynolds v. United States* (1879) appealed a conviction under the criminal law against polygamy. *Murphy v. Ramsey* (1885) challenged the constitutionality of a federal law disenfranchising known or suspected polygamists.[165] *Davis v. Beason* (1890) appealed a conviction for false swearing of a mandatory oath renouncing polygamy.[166] *Church of Jesus Christ of Latter Day Saints v. United States* (1890) challenged the government's dissolution of the Mormon Church's corporate charter and confiscation of its property.[167] In each case, the Mormon parties claimed that they had a free exercise right to participate in voluntary polygamy as their faith encouraged, and they thus sought religious liberty exemptions from compliance with Congressional laws.

The Supreme Court would have none of it, and upheld the federal laws and policies each time. Many of the philosophical and social science arguments against polygamy that had been absorbed into Anglo-American common law over the prior three centuries came through loudly in the Court's opinions. In *Reynolds*, for example, Chief Justice Waite wrote for the Court:

> Polygamy has always been odious among the northern and western nations of Europe, and, until the establishment of the Mormon Church, was almost exclusively a feature of the life of Asiatic and of African people. At common law, the second marriage was always void (2 Kent, Com. 79), and from the earliest history of England polygamy has been treated as an offence against society. After the establishment of the ecclesiastical courts, and until the time of James I., it was punished through the instrumentality of those tribunals.... By the statute of 1 James I. (c. 11), the offence, if committed in England or Wales, was made punishable in the civil courts, and the

---

[163] 12 Stat. 501–502 (1862); 22 Stat. 30–32 (1882); 18 *Congressional Record* 585–593 (January 1887). Other laws are quoted and analyzed in *Murphy v. Ramsey*, 114 U.S. 15 (1885) and *Cannon v. United States*, 116 U.S. 55 (1885). See analysis of these and other statutes and cases in Gordon, *The Mormon Question*, 119–146; Edwin Brown Firmage and R. Collin Mangrum, *Zion in the Courts: A Legal History of the Church of Jesus Christ of Latter-Day Saints*, pbk. ed. (Champaign–Urbana: University of Illinois Press, 2001), 160–262; Van Wagoner, *Mormon Polygamy*, 89–132.

[164] Kelly Elizabeth Phipps, "Marriage and Redemption: Mormon Polygamy in the Congressional Imagination, 1662–1887," *Virginia Law Review* 95 (2009): 435.

[165] 114 U.S. 15 (1885).

[166] 133 U.S. 333, 341–342 (1890).

[167] 136 U.S. 1 (1890) and the companion case *Romney v. United States*, 136 U.S. 1 (1890).

penalty was death. As this statute was limited in its operation to England and Wales, it was at a very early period re-enacted, generally with some modifications, in all the colonies. In connection with the case we are now considering, it is a significant fact that on the 8th of December, 1788, after the passage of the act establishing religious freedom, and after the convention of Virginia had recommended as an amendment to the Constitution of the United States the declaration in a bill of rights that "all men have an equal, natural, and unalienable right to the free exercise of religion, according to the dictates of conscience," the legislature of that State substantially enacted the statute of James I., death penalty included, because, as recited in the preamble, "it hath been doubted whether bigamy or polygamy be punishable by the laws of this Commonwealth." 12 Hening's Stat. 691. From that day to this we think it may safely be said there never has been a time in any State of the Union when polygamy has not been an offence against society, cognizable by the civil courts and punishable with more or less severity.

In the face of all this evidence, it is impossible to believe that the constitutional guaranty of religious freedom was intended to prohibit legislation in respect to this most important feature of social life. Marriage, while from its very nature a sacred obligation, is nevertheless, in most civilized nations, a civil contract, and usually regulated by law. Upon it society may be said to be built, and out of its fruits spring social relations and social obligations and duties, with which government is necessarily required to deal. In fact, according as monogamous or polygamous marriages are allowed, do we find the principles on which the government of the people, to a greater or less extent, rests. Professor Lieber says, polygamy leads to the patriarchal principle, and which, when applied to large communities, fetters the people in stationary despotism, while that principle cannot long exist in connection with monogamy. Chancellor Kent observes that this remark is equally striking and profound. 2 Kent, Com. 81, note (e).

An exceptional colony of polygamists under an exceptional leadership may sometimes exist for a time without appearing to disturb the social condition of the people who surround it; but there cannot be a doubt that, unless restricted by some form of constitution, it is within the legitimate scope of the power of every civil government to determine whether polygamy or monogamy shall be the law of social life under its dominion.[168]

Justice Matthew continued this thought five years later in *Murphy v. Ramsey*, underscoring the importance of the monogamous marriage for the establishment of a free society and an orderly democratic government:

For certainly no legislation can be supposed more wholesome and necessary in the founding of a free, self-governing commonwealth ... than that which seeks to establish it on the basis of the idea of the family, as consisting in and springing from

[168] 98 U.S. at 164–166.

the union for life of one man and woman in the holy estate of matrimony; the sure foundation of all that is stable and noble in our civilization; the best guaranty of that reverent morality which is the source of all beneficent progress in social and political improvement.[169]

The congressional power to pass pro-monogamy and anti-polygamy laws in promotion of the health, safety, welfare, and morality of the community, the Supreme Court continued in *Davis* (1890), could not be compromised by judicial creations of free exercise exemptions from these laws. To exempt Mormons polygamists, or their accessories, from compliance with general criminal laws against polygamy, Justice Field thundered for the Court, would "shock the moral judgment of the community … [and] offend the common sense of mankind."

> Bigamy and polygamy are crimes by the laws of all civilized and Christian countries. They are crimes by the laws of the United States, and they are crimes by the laws of Idaho. They tend to destroy the purity of the marriage relation, to disturb the peace of families, to degrade woman and to debase man. Few crimes are more pernicious to the best interests of society and receive more general or more deserved punishment.[170]

Justice Bradley drove home these sentiments in the Court's opinion in the 1890 *Latter Day Corporation* case, drawing on the sentiments of Henry Lewis Morgan and other social scientists to write: "The organization of a community for the spread and practice of polygamy is, in a measure, a return to barbarism. It is contrary to the spirit of Christianity and of the civilization which Christianity has produced in the Western world." It is a "sophistical plea" to claim free exercise protection for this "nefarious doctrine." For the Court to grant free exercise protection in this case would invite all manner of specious evasions of the criminal law – even religious excuses for human sacrifice and suicide, the Court reasoned. "The state has a perfect right to prohibit polygamy, and all other open offenses against the enlightened sentiment of mankind, notwithstanding the pretense of religious conviction by which they may be advocated and practiced."[171]

Confronted with these sweeping congressional laws and Supreme Court cases, Wilford Woodruff, the presiding officer of the Mormon Church, issued a new manifesto in 1890 on behalf of the church's leadership disavowing any further participation in polygamy and urging church members to follow. On October 6, 1890, a Mormon Church conference accepted this new manifesto. Although polygamous ideas and practices lingered for a generation, giving rise to internal

---

[169] 114 U.S. at 45.
[170] 133 U.S. at 336–337, 341–342.
[171] 136 U.S. at 48–50.

ecclesiastical disputes and cases,[172] by 1906, the Mormon Church had made the preaching and practice of polygamy a ground for excommunication.[173]

In response to the 1890 manifesto, Congress returned the Mormon Church's property in 1894. Utah became a new state in 1896. Its new state constitution, at the insistence of Congress, expressly prohibited polygamy and mandated the separation of church and state.[174] Similar anti-polygamy measures were included, on Congress's insistence, in the new constitutions of other western states that had experienced Mormon or Native American polygamy – Arizona, Idaho, New Mexico, and Oklahoma.[175]

As we saw in the Introduction to this book, a small group of self-defined "Fundamentalist Latter Day Saints" broke off from the mainline Mormon Church in the 1890s and have quietly maintained their polygamous practices to this day in small, isolated communities scattered throughout the sparsely populated western states of America as well as Canada and Mexico.[176] Three times the authorities have moved on these polygamous communities en masse. In 1944, state and federal authorities arrested forty-six suspected polygamists in a community in Short Creek, Arizona. In 1953, state authorities mounted a second, badly bungled, raid against the same Short Creek community, charging residents not only with polygamy, but "insurrection," according to the Arizona governor. Men and women of the community alike were indicted for perpetrating or aiding the commission of "statutory rape, adultery, bigamy, open and notorious cohabitation, contributing to the delinquency of minors, marrying the spouse of another, and an all-embracing conspiracy to commit all these crimes, along with various instances of income tax evasion, failure to comply with Arizona's corporation laws, misappropriation of school funds, improper use of school facilities, and falsification of public records."[177] All 263 children in the community were plucked from their parents and put in

---

[172] See, e.g., Firmage and Mangrum, *Zion in the Courts*, 322ff.

[173] See Elizabeth Harmer-Dionne, "Once a Peculiar People: Cognitive Dissonance and the Suppression of Mormon Polygamy as a Case Study Negating the Belief-Action Distinction," *Stanford Law Review* 50 (1998): 1295–1347, esp. 1331–1340.

[174] Constitution of Utah (1896), Art. I, sec. 4; Art. III, sec. 1.

[175] Ariz. Const. Art. XX, par. 2; Idaho Const. Art. I, sec. 44; N.M. Const. Art XXI, sec. 1; Okla. Const. Art I., sec. 2.

[176] See sources cited in previous note and in the Introduction, pp. 3–8; Ken Driggs, "After the Manifesto: Modern Polygamy and Fundamentalist Mormons," *Journal of Church and State* 32 (1990): 367–389; Cardell K. Jacobson and Laura Burton, eds., *Modern Polygamy in the United States: Historical, Cultural, and Legal Issues* (Oxford: Oxford University Press, 2011).

[177] "Statement of Arizona Governor Howard Pyle," in Martha Sonntag Bradley, *Kidnapped From That Land: The Government Raids on the Short Creek Polygamists* (Salt Lake City: University of Utah Press, 1993), 141. See summary in Martha Bailey and Amy J. Kaufman, *Polygamy in the Monogamous World: Multicultural Challenges for Western Law and Policy* (Santa Barbara, CA: Praeger, 2010), 102–104, and detailed analysis in Jacobson and Burton, eds., *Modern Polygamy in the United States*.

state protective custody, while their parents were prosecuted. All but one of the children were eventually returned to their families. The prosecutions eventually fizzled out, too: twenty-six Fundamentalist Mormon men were given suspended plea-bargained sentences while all the women in the community were exonerated. This clumsy raid sought to trade on the same national "hysteria" about polygamy that the nineteenth century cases had occasioned, but it was a legal, political, and public relations disaster.

Although the Fundamentalist Mormons faced another and more effective raid on their Yearning for Zion Ranch in 2008, as we saw in the Introduction, most cases thereafter featured prosecution of individual Fundamentalist Mormons who lived in open defiance of state polygamy laws, and then aggravated their offenses with other crimes. A good recent example is *Utah v. Green* (2004). Tom Green was a Fundamentalist Mormon charged with four counts of bigamy for maintaining multiple and overlapping relations with nine wives, with whom he produced twenty-five children who were now destitute and living largely on social welfare. He was also charged with first-degree felony rape for marrying and impregnating one of his wives when she was 13 years old and he 37. He was convicted on the four counts of bigamy and one count of statutory rape. He appealed, arguing, inter alia, that the state's bigamy statute violated his rights to the free exercise rights of religion.

The Utah Supreme Court made short work of his free exercise argument. The state bigamy statute was neutral and generally applicable, the court concluded, and was properly applied in this case. "Any individual, who violates the statute, whether for religious or secular reasons, is subject to prosecution." The bigamy statute properly regulates and restricts the institution of marriage, and is designed to prevent "marital fraud" and the misuse of governmental benefits associated with marital status. "Most importantly," the Court continued, "Utah's bigamy statute serves the State's interest in protecting vulnerable individuals from exploitation and abuse. The practice of polygamy, in particular, often coincides with crimes targeting women and children. Crimes not unusually attendant to the practice of polygamy include incest, sexual assault, statutory battery, and failure to pay child support."[178] Several other recent cases against brazen Fundamentalist Mormon polygamists reached the same result with similar reasoning.[179]

The *Green* Court's final statement is a textbook example of a Western argument about polygamy that goes back for nearly 2,000 years: polygamy is too often the cause, corollary, or consequence of many other crimes and harms, especially to women and children. Polygamy too often caused or came with fraud, trickery, intrigue,

[178] 99 P. 3d 820, 828–830 (2004).
[179] See, e.g., *Utah v. Holm*, 2006 UT 31, 137 P. 3d. 726 (UT Sup. Ct.); *Arizona v. Fletcher*, 199 P. 3d 663 (Az. Ct. App. 2008). See also sources cited in the Introduction, pp. 3–8.

lust, seduction, coercion, rape, incest, adultery, murder, exploitation and coercion of young women, jealousy and rivalry among wives and their children, dissipation of family wealth and inequality of treatment and support of household members, banishment and disinheritance of disfavored children and more. Moreover, the *Green* case illustrates other harms of polygamy that are more specific to the modern democratic welfare state: social and educational deprivation of women and children in polygamous households, abuse and ostracism of young boys and poorer men who compete for brides, rampant social welfare abuses, and isolation of polygamous households and communities. To be sure, these harms are not featured in every case, but in enough cases that the American courts have found that the firm maintenance and application of criminal laws against polygamy remain warranted.[180]

SUMMARY AND CONCLUSIONS

The United States provided a large new laboratory to test the Western case for monogamy over polygamy. Although the American colonies and young states broke with many other inherited traditions from Europe, they repeated and strengthened traditional polygamy laws, making it a capital crime until the mid-nineteenth century. Although the American states and nation outlawed Christian establishments and granted religious freedom for all, they gave no corner to the polygamy of ancient Native Americans or of upstart new faiths like Mormonism. Although many social practices and policies of American life became more open, liberal, and inclusive in the course of the nineteenth and early twentieth centuries, anti-polygamy measures became sterner, both for polygamists who kept more than one spouse in the same home, and for deserters who abandoned their first wives and children and got married again.

The American case for monogamy over polygamy was, in part, yet another variation on millennium-long Western arguments against the practice: that polygamy was harmful to women, children, men, and society alike; that polygamy violated the natural rights and duties of the marital household; that polygamy betrayed the fundamental equality of husbands and wives and the equal treatment owing to their children; that polygamy was too often the cause, corollary, or consequence of sundry other harms and crimes; and that polygamous communities became laws unto themselves and eventually threatened the power and integrity of political government. Classical, Christian, and Enlightenment formulations of these old arguments all appealed to American writers, and they repeated them endlessly in both scholarly and diverse popular media.

---

[180] See Maura Strassberg, "The Crime of Polygamy," *Temple Political and Civil Rights Law Review* 12 (2003): 353–431.

Nineteenth-century American writers added an important evolutionary argument against polygamy, namely that in the development of human civilization, monogamy was conducive to democracy while polygamy trapped cultures in despotism. This repackaged a traditional argument about the social and political utility of monogamy. It was a commonplace of classical and common law learning to link the health of the household to the stability of the state. English and American writers alike had called the marital household a "little commonwealth" where husbands and wives, parents and children, learned the norms and habits of authority and liberty, learning and responsibility, caring and sharing that were essential for them to participate fully and properly as patriotic citizens in an organized and peaceful republic. The monogamous household, this commonwealth model taught, cultivated better civil habits and moral virtues in the citizenry than a polygamous household. American social scientists like Francis Lieber and Henry Lewis Morgan added an evolutionary dimension to this discussion. In the development of human societies, they argued, modern liberal democracies, bound by the rule of law and based on a concept of private property and market economy, were the apex if not telos of social progress. Only monogamy, the argument went, could produce the virtues and habits necessary for its gradual development and continued maintenance thereafter. Polygamy, by contrast, retarded the development and progress of society toward civilization. It trapped people in a stage and state of "barbarism," that too often featured political tyranny, patriarchal rule, the deprecation of women and children, and little protection for life, liberty, or property. Monogamy was the cornerstone of Western civilization, and any departure from it would be a return to barbarism.

This was not idle academic talk. This social scientific logic of monogamy helped to drive the American campaign in the nineteenth and twentieth centuries to stamp out the (suspected) polygamous practices of African-American slaves, Native American Indians, Chinese-American immigrants, and the burgeoning Mormon Church and its later splinter group, the Fundamentalist Latter Day Saints. Both Congress and various federal courts and agencies led this national campaign against polygamy, and they were supported fully by the United States Supreme Court that applauded their efforts to prevent America from a "return to barbarism." Victorian morality, Christian theology, Enlightenment philosophy, and plain old tradition also helped support America's resolute opposition to polygamy. Even more significant was America's epic battle against slavery that underscored the nation's growing concern for chronic domestic abuses and systematic deprivations. Polygamy and slavery were paired as "twin relics of barbarism" that needed to be expurgated root and branch, even at the cost of grave violence and massive bloodshed.

The statutes and cases against polygamy that emerged in this long American campaign against polygamy remain the law of the land today. Every American state still criminalizes polygamy, and federal immigration laws still bar polygamists from entry. *Reynolds* and its progeny are still good law. Not only have the results of these Supreme Court's polygamy cases been repeatedly affirmed by the United States Supreme Court and lower federal courts,[181] but the reasoning of these cases has also been repeated by a number of courts in the twentieth century.[182] Whether modern privacy and religious liberty law will eventually bring change to these old laws was the topic we mooted in the Introduction to this book, and we shall return to it next in the Concluding Reflections.

[181] See, e.g., *Employment Division v. Smith*, 494 U.S. 872, 879, 882, 890 (1990).
[182] See, e.g., recently *Bronson, Cook, and Cook v. Swenson*, 394 F. Supp. 2nd 1329 (UT Dist. Ct., 2005); *Bronson v. Swenson*, 500 F. 3rd 1099 (Ct. App. 10th Circuit, 2007); *Potter v. Murray City*, 760 F. 2nd. 1065 (Ct. App. 10th Cir., 1985); *Cleveland v. United States*, 329 U.S. 14 (1946).

Concluding Reflections

FIGURE 23. "Muslim Polygamy."
Used by permission of the Thomson Reuters Library.

FIGURE 24. "Wedding Cake Visual Metaphor with Figurine Cake Toppers." Used by permission of SuperStock.

"If a thing has been practiced for two hundred years by common consent, it will need a strong case under the [Constitution] to affect it," United States Supreme Court Justice Oliver Wendell Holmes, Jr. once wrote.[1] If a thing has been practiced for 2,000 years and more, the case to affect it must be very strong, indeed. The purpose of this volume has been to uncover and set out the Western historical case for monogamy over polygamy over the past two plus millennia, and to analyze the criminal prohibitions against polygamy that have resulted. The challenge of the next few decades will be to determine whether this case against polygamy is still cogent in a rapidly globalizing Western culture dedicated to the constitutional protection

---

[1]   *Jackman v. Rosenbaum*, 260 U.S. 22. 31 (1922).

of human rights, domestic liberty, sexual autonomy, religious freedom, and cultural self-determination for all consenting adults.

With the cultural and constitutional battles over same-sex marriage now deeply joined in many parts of the West, the next battles about domestic life will certainly include polygamous marriage. The first cases challenging the constitutionality of traditional Western criminal prohibitions against polygamy have been filed – with an American federal district court striking first in declaring unconstitutional Utah's state laws against polygamy.[2] The first sustained scholarly arguments for legal toleration if not state recognition of polygamy have been pressed – with various liberals and libertarians, Muslims and Christians, philosophers and social scientists, multiculturalists and counter-culturalists finding themselves on the same side.[3] The first wave of popular media portrayals of good polygamous families in America has now broken with shows like "Big Love" and "Sister Wives" stoking the cultural imagination and sympathy much like "Ozzie and Harriet" and "The Bill Cosby Show" had done for prior generations.[4] Just as same-sex advocates moved first against

---

[2] *Brown v. Buhman* (D.C Utah, December 13, 2013). For a contrary recent case, with detail distillation of literature about the inherent harms of polygamy, see Reference re: Section 293 of the *Criminal Code of Canada*, 2011 BCSC 1588. Kenya, a former English colony that maintains portions of the common law, also recently passed a law authorizing a man to have an unlimited number of wives, while still prosecuting a woman for having two husbands. See http://www.cnn.com/2014/05/01/world/africa/kenya-polygamy-law/index.html?iref=allsearch.

[3] For good recent discussions and bibliographies, see Lori G. Beams and Gillian Calder, *Polygamy's Rights and Wrongs: Perspectives on Harm, Family, and Law* (Toronto/Vancouver: University of British Columbia Press, 2014); Mark A. Goldfeder, *Revisiting Polygamy* (Waltham, MA: University Press of New England, 2015); Stefan Kiesbye, ed., *At Issue: Polygamy* (Detroit, MI: Greenhaven Press, 2013). Beyond these, I found especially helpful and challenging the various perspectives on polygamy in these recent sources: Martha Bailey and Amy J. Kaufman, *Polygamy in the Monogamous World: Multicultural Challenges for Western Law and Policy* (Santa Barbara, CA: Praeger, 2010), 133–188; Gary S. Becker, *A Treatise on the Family*, rev. pbk. ed. (Cambridge, MA: Harvard University Press, 2003), 80–107; Thom Brooks, "The Problem with Polygamy," *Philosophical Topics* 37 (2009): 109–122; Cheshire Calhoun, "Who's Afraid of Polygamous Marriage? *San Diego Law Review* 42 (2005): 1023–1044; Andrew F. March, "Is there a Right to Polygamy? Marriage, Equality, and Subsidizing Families in Liberal Public Justification," *Journal of Moral Philosophy* 8 (2011): 244–270; Philip L. Kilbride and Douglas R. Page, *Plural Marriage for Our Times: A Reinvented Option?* 2nd ed. (Santa Barbara, CA: Praeger, 2012); Dan Markel, Jennifer M. Collins, and Ethan J. Leib, *Privilege or Punish: Criminal Justice and the Challenge of Family Ties* (Oxford: Oxford University Press, 2009), 127–140; Ronald Den Otter, "Is There Really Any Good Argument Against Plural Marriage?" (http://works.bepress.com/cgi/viewcontent.cgi?article=1000&context=ronald_den_otter); Richard A. Posner, *Sex and Reason* (Cambridge, MA: Harvard University Press, 1992), 243–259; Shanya M. Sigman, "Everything Lawyers Know about Polygamy is Wrong," *Cornell Journal of Law and Public Policy* 16 (2006): 101–185; Maura I. Strassberg, "The Challenge of Polyamory," *Capital University Law Review* 31 (2003): 439–563; id., The Crime of Polygamy," *Temple Political and Civil Rights Law Review* 12 (2003): 353–431; Gregg Strauss, "Is Polygamy Inherently Unequal?" *Ethics* 122 (2013): 516–544.

[4] See, e.g., Janet Bennion, *Polygamy in Prime Time: Media, Gender and Politics in Mormon Fundamentalism* (Waltham, MA: Brandeis University Press, 2012).

the criminalization of sodomy and then for the recognition of same-sex unions and marriage, so pro-polygamy advocates aim first to repeal traditional criminal laws against polygamy, and then to include polygamy as an alternative form of valid marriage recognized by the state.[5]

Many modern liberals argue that the state must facilitate and support the consensual intimate relationships of all its citizens – straight or gay, temporary or permanent, sexual or non-sexual, monogamous or polygamous. Many modern libertarians argue that the state has no business interfering in the private domestic lives of its citizens unless and until there is tangible harm to a victim. Both schools of modern political thought – and the numerous variations on them – support the repeal of traditional criminal laws against polygamy. Many liberals go further to call for state recognition of polygamy, too. Feminist theorists, queer theorists, critical race theorists, and multicultural theorists offer all manner of variations on these basic arguments, although notable scholars in each of these schools of thought oppose state recognition of polygamy while supporting same-sex marriage.[6]

Many modern Muslims, Fundamentalist Mormons, and other faith communities add arguments from religious freedom and self-determination, religious equality and nondiscrimination to press their case for polygamy. Every Western nation (save Australia), they point out, has robust constitutional guarantees of religious freedom

---

[5] Already in 1972, the National Coalition of Gay Organizations advocated the repeal of "all legislative provisions that restrict the sex or number of persons entering into a marriage unit and exten[sion of] legal benefits of marriage to all persons who cohabit regardless of sex or numbers." See William N. Eskridge, Jr., "Challenging the Apartheid of the Closet: Establishing Conditions for Lesbian and Gay Intimacy, Nomos, and Citizenship, 1961–1981," *Hofstra Law Review* 25 (1996–1997): 817–970, at 841. My thanks to Professor Risa L. Goluboff for this bringing this text to my attention.

[6] Within this vast literature, see, e.g., Michel Alexandre, "Big Love: Is Feminist Polygamy an Oxymoron or a True Possibility?" *Hastings Women's Law Journal* 18 (2007): 3–30; Vaughn Bryan Baltzly, "Same-Sex Marriage, Polygamy, and Disestablishment," *Social Theory and Practice* 38 (2012): 333–362; David L. Chambers, "Polygamy and Same-Sex Marriage," *Hofstra Law Review* 26 (1997): 53–83; Adrienne D. Davis, "Regulating Polygamy: Intimacy, Default Rules, and Bargaining for Equality," *Columbia Law Review* 110 (2010): 1955–2046; Emily J. Duncan, "The Positive Effects of Legalizing Polygamy; 'Love is a Many Splendored Thing'," *Duke Journal of Gender Law and Policy* 15 (2008): 315–337; Elizabeth F. Emens, "Monogamy's Law: Compulsory Monogamy and Polyamorous Existence," *New York University Review of Law and Social Change* 29 (2004): 277–376; Jaime M. Gher, "Polygamy and Same-Sex Marriage: Allies or Adversaries Within the Same-Sex Marriage Movement," *William and Mary Journal of Women and the Law* 14 (2008): 559–603; Sara Song, *Justice, Gender, and the Politics of Multiculturalism* (Cambridge: Cambridge University Press, 2007), 142–168; Maura I. Strassberg, "Distinctions of Form or Substance: Monogamy, Polygamy, and Same-Sex Marriage," *North Carolina Law Review* 75 (1997): 1501–1624; Adrien Katherine Wing, "Polygamy in Black America," in Adrien Katherine Wing, ed., *Critical Race Feminism: A Reader*, 2nd ed. (New York: New York University Press, 2003), 186–194.

on the books for individuals and groups. Every Western nation furthermore is a signatory to the binding 1966 International Covenant on Civil and Political Rights, with its robust protections of freedom of thought, conscience, and belief for all peaceable believers – human rights norms that are echoed and elaborated in many other international human rights instruments, not least those guaranteeing religious and cultural self-determination, freedom of association and various rights to marriage and family life. Even if nonbelievers do not have the right to practice polygamy, the argument goes, surely the voluntary faithful of these religious communities must be given the right to follow the examples and instructions of their founding Prophets in taking multiple wives. Surely, the leaders of these religious communities should be respected if a polygamous family chooses to be governed by religious law rather than by state law.[7]

Some modern Christian missionaries have argued further that Western churches should accept new converts to the Christian faith who wish to maintain their polygamous households. After all, many of these men would rather give up their multiple gods than give up their multiple wives who offer them sex, love, labor, prestige, and heirs. After all, marriage is only an earthly thing: in heaven "they neither marry nor are given in marriage," Jesus had said.[8] After all, the global church has found so many other ways to accommodate and enculturate the local customs of its new converts, at least as a stepping stone toward adoption of more common Christian practices in the next generation or two. After all, Catholic and Protestant churches, especially since the 1960s, have been champions of religious freedom and human rights for all. How can the church deny religious freedom to its own new members?[9]

It is not within my brief as a legal historian to analyze all these current arguments or to advocate for or against polygamy. I personally support monogamy and oppose polygamy. But it would take a new book, longer than this one, to engage all the modern literature and arguments responsibly. My aim is more modest: to set this modern debate in full historical context, to retrieve and reconstruct the main historical arguments about polygamy, and try to checkmate some of the partial and distorted "law office" histories that have already gathered around this issue.

[7] See discussions in the Introduction and in Chapter 10 of this book. See, e.g., the collection of articles and literature cited in Joel A. Nichols, ed., *Marriage and Divorce in a Multicultural Context: Multi-Tiered Marriage and the Boundaries of Civil Law and Religion* (Cambridge: Cambridge University Press, 2013).

[8] Mark 12:25.

[9] See, e.g., the classic of Eugene Hillman, *Polygamy Reconsidered: African Plural Marriages and the Christian Churches* (Maryknoll, NY: Orbis Books, 1975) and recent literature cited in E.M. Baloyi, "Critical Reflections on Polygamy in the African Context," *Missionalia* (2014): 164–181; Timothy W. Jones, "The Missionaries' Position: Polygamy and Divorce in the Anglican Communion, 1888–1988," *Journal of Religious History* 35 (2011): 393–408.

BIBLICAL ARGUMENTS

What should be clear from the previous ten chapters is that the Western case against polygamy is markedly different from the case against same-sex relations. The Western case against same-sex relations was (and for some still is) based first and foremost on the Bible. The Mosaic law commanded firmly: "You shall not lie with a male as with a woman; it is an abomination."[10] "If a man lies with a male, as with a woman, both of them have committed an abomination; they shall both be put to death."[11] The Apostle Paul declared ominously that "the wrath of God is revealed from heaven against all ungodliness and wickedness" including specifically the acts of "sodomites," "sexual perverts," and others who succumbed to "dishonorable passions": "women [who] exchanged natural relations for unnatural, and men [who] likewise gave up natural relations with women and were consumed with passion for one another, men committing shameless acts with men and receiving in their own persons the due penalty for their error."[12] While some modern scholars see ambiguity in these passages,[13] the Christian tradition until recently treated these texts as a clear condemnation of same-sex intimacy.[14]

It was thus the church not the state that led the first campaigns against same-sex activities and unions in the Western tradition. The early canons of the church prohibited sodomy, buggery, transvestism, and other stated forms of "fornication" and "perversion," spiritually sanctioning such sins, and excommunicating recalcitrant sexual sinners. These prohibitions became more detailed and severe in the Germanic penitential literature that followed, and even more so in high medieval canon laws and scholastic texts. Sex between men was singled out as a particularly vile form of "unnatural" sin, even more so if it involved a cleric.[15] Although a few churchmen may have winked at occasional same-sex unions and

---

[10] Leviticus 18:22.
[11] Leviticus 20:13.
[12] Romans 1:18–19, 24–27; 1 Corinthians 6:9–10; 1 Timothy 1:10.
[13] See, e.g., Derrick S. Bailey, *Homosexuality and the Western Christian Tradition*, repr. ed. (Hamden, CT: Archon Books, 1975); John Boswell, *Christianity, Social Tolerance, and Homosexuality: Gay People in Western Europe from the Beginning of the Christian Era to the Fourteenth Century* (Chicago, IL: University of Chicago Press, 1980), esp. 106–112; id., *Same Sex Unions in Premodern Europe* (New York: Villard Books, 1994); Mark D. Jordan, ed., *Authorizing Marriage: Canon, Tradition, and Critique in the Blessing of Same-Sex Unions* (Princeton, NJ: Princeton University Press, 2006); William Stacy Johnson, *A Time To Embrace: Same Gender Relationships in Religion, Law, and Politics* (Grand Rapids, MI: Wm. B. Eerdmans, 2007).
[14] See detailed references in James A. Brundage, *Law, Sex, and Christian Society in Medieval Europe* (Chicago, IL: University of Chicago Press, 1987), 57, 73–74, 147–149.
[15] See references in ibid., 212–214, 313–314, 398–400, 534–535.

even quietly blessed a few of them in special liturgies,[16] one cannot rewrite this history by anecdote. The overwhelming teaching and practice of historical Catholic, Orthodox, and Protestant churches was to condemn same-sex relations.

Roman law, for its first 1,000 years, allowed same-sex acts and relationships – although only heterosexual couples of the proper class could contract valid marriages and produce heritable children and widow(er)s.[17] It was only after the fourth-century Christian conversion of Emperor Constantine that these biblically based laws against same-sex activities slowly soaked into Roman law. By the sixth century, the Christian Roman Emperor Justinian called sex between men an "abominable," "abhorrent," and "reprehensible vice" that is so "contrary to nature" that "even the beasts" forgo such practices. Since the biblical days of Sodom, Justinian declared, such "unnatural acts" have "brought the wrath of God" unto any community that countenanced them. "Severe measures" were thus needed to stamp out these acts for good.[18] This classic Christian condemnation of sodomy and same-sex activities was echoed and elaborated in the civil law, canon law, and common law traditions thereafter.[19] By the twelfth and thirteenth centuries, church and state courts worked together to mete out severe punishment against convicted "sodomists," including death by burning, beheading, or hanging (by their testicles and penises, no less!) for egregious offenders.

By marked contrast to same-sex relations, not a single command against real polygamy appears in the Bible. The Mosaic law, in fact, contemplated polygamy in cases of seduction, enslavement, poverty, famine, or premature death of one's married brother, and it made special provision for the maintenance and inheritance of multiple wives and children in those cases. More than two dozen polygamists appear in the Hebrew Bible. Almost all of them were good and faithful kings, judges, or aristocrats, and not one of them was punished for practicing polygamy per se.[20] While the New Testament condemned a wide range of sexual practices of the Jewish, Greek, and Roman cultures of the day, it, too, was silent on polygamy, save for its special rules that a bishop or deacon had to be "the husband of one wife"

---

[16] See esp. Boswell, *Christianity, Social Tolerance, and Homosexuality*; Mark D. Jordan, *Blessing Same-Sex Unions: The Perils of Queer Romance and the Confusions of Christian Marriage* (Chicago: University of Chicago Press, 2005).

[17] See discussion in Chapter 3, pp. 104–107. See also Brundage, *Law, Sex, and Christian Society*, 48.

[18] *Justinian's Institutes*, ed. Paul Krüger, trans. Peter Birks and Grant McLeod (Ithaca, NY: Cornell University Press, 1987), 4.18.4; Justinian, *Novellae* 77, pr. 1; 141 pr. 1, in T. Lambert Mears, ed., *The Institutes of Gaius and Justinian: the Twelve Tables, and the CXVIIIth and CXXVIIth Novels* (Clark, NJ: Lawbook Exchange, 2004 [1882]).

[19] See esp. Mark D. Jordan, *The Invention of Sodomy in Christian Theology* (Chicago: University of Chicago Press, 1997).

[20] King David was condemned for his adultery with Bathsheba and murder of her husband, not his polygamy. He still added Bathsheba to his harem, and she produced King Solomon, his successor. See discussion in Samuel, 11–12.

and a deaconess "the wife of one husband." The laity were commanded to "flee fornication," but in all the long New Testament lists of sexual sins illustrating what "fornication" means, not a word appears about real polygamy.[21]

Accordingly, the Christian Church, for its first 1,000 years, said and did rather little about real polygamy, although the practice persisted among first-millennium Jews, seventh- through tenth-century Muslims, and various Indigenous groups in the Middle East, Africa, and Asia. A few early Church Fathers called polygamy a dangerous betrayal of the natural ideals of marriage as a creation of "two in one flesh." Others criticized the spousal rivalries and family unrest of biblical and contemporary polygamists.[22] But in the fifth century, the preeminent Western Church Father, St. Augustine, called real polygamy a "perfectly natural" form of sexual interaction and an efficient means of procreation, too. The Old Testament polygamists, said Augustine, committed no offense "either against nature, or against common custom, or against positive law." "When polygamy was a common custom, it was not a crime; it now ranks as a crime because it is no longer a custom," having been mostly stamped out by Roman criminal law.[23] By the same token, the early canon law of the church said virtually nothing against real polygamy. Only a few cryptic canons on point have survived from the first millennium, and they called for real polygamists in the church to be punished at about the same level as petty thieves.[24]

It was the state – not the church – that led the campaign against real polygamy in the West. Already half a millennium before the advent of Christianity, both Greek and Roman laws treated polygamy as a form of "barbarism" and domestic "tyranny" that violated the natural human need for pair-bonding.[25] "Love is born into every human being," Plato wrote famously in the fourth century BCE; "it calls back the halves of our original nature together; it tries to make one out of two and heal the wound of human nature.... 'Love' is the name for our pursuit of wholeness, for our desire to be complete."[26] In extension of these ideas, early Roman laws also banned a man from having a wife and a concubine at the same time, even if they lived in separate households or cities. By the third century CE, the pre-Christian Roman emperors declared real polygamy to be a crime of infamy, whose punishment their imperial successors gradually escalated. Polygamy was declared a capital crime in the ninth century, and so it remained in much of the West until the nineteenth

---

[21] See discussion in Chapter 2, pp. 68–73.
[22] See discussions in Chapter 2, pp. 79–84, 119–120, 123–126.
[23] See discussion in Chapter 2, pp. 88–90.
[24] See discussion in Chapter 3, pp. 119–120, 123–126.
[25] See discussion in Chapter 3, pp. 104–107.
[26] See discussion in Chapter 3, pp. 104–105.

century.[27] With the exception of medieval England, it was the state courts of the West that, for nearly two millennia, took the lead on punishing real polygamy.

It was only in the twelfth and thirteenth centuries, after the medieval church developed a robust sacramental theology and canon law of monogamous marriage, that it came to condemn polygamy clearly as a heretical violation of the exclusive and enduring marital sacrament. It was only then that the scholastic thinkers of the day marshaled a refined arsenal of natural law and natural justice arguments against real polygamy. It was only then that the church courts – and for a time the Inquisition, too – joined the state courts in punishing real polygamists. And it was only then that polygamy was made a formidable boundary marker between "true Christians" and various Jews and Muslims, Asians and Africans, heretics and free thinkers who preached or practiced polygamy.

But even then the Christian tradition wavered in its opposition to polygamy. Late medieval Catholic luminaries like Cardinal Cajetan went back to Augustine, and said that polygamy was a "perfectly natural" option in cases of personal or political necessity.[28] Sixteenth-century Protestants like Martin Luther went back to the Bible, and ultimately considered consensual polygamy a better biblical option than brazen adultery or no-fault divorce to resolve hard marital cases.[29] This led a few early modern Christian communities like the Anabaptists in Münster to experiment with biblical polygamy anew.[30] It also led a few free thinkers like Bernard Ochino and John Milton to suggest that allowing polygamy might be a better way to end prostitution, rape, fornication, concubinage, adultery, and bastardy than insisting on monogamy alone.[31] It was only when the Council of Trent in 1563 issued its final confirmation of the sacramentality of monogamous marriage and its forceful anathema on the heresy of polygamy that this internal speculation about polygamy finally ended in Catholic circles.[32] In turn, it was only when Protestants came to treat marriage systematically as a divine covenant modeled on God's exclusive relationship with his elect or as a "little commonwealth" at the foundation of the commonwealths of church and state that Protestants had the theological machinery needed to declare anew that monogamy is the only valid form of marriage.[33] Marriage, early modern Catholics and Protestants together now clearly said, was created as an enduring and exclusive "two in one flesh" union, rooted in the natural order of creation, and modeled on the mysterious relationship of God and his elect, Christ and his church. Western

[27] See discussion in Chapter 3, pp. 107–114.
[28] See discussion in Chapter 5, pp. 168–169.
[29] See discussion in Chapter 5, pp. 205–217.
[30] See discussion in Chapter 5, pp. 218–223.
[31] See discussions in Chapters 5, pp. 223–238, and Chapter 8, pp. 330–335.
[32] See discussion in Chapter 4, pp. 154–155.
[33] See discussions in Chapter 6, pp. 245–254, and Chapter 7, pp. 285–290.

states responded by reconfirming their traditional capital laws against polygamy, and resuming principal responsibility for the punishment of real polygamy.

"So what?!" a modern skeptic might say to all this history. So what if, more than two millennia ago, sodomy happened to be born a biblical sin and polygamy a Roman crime. So what if the first millennium church took the lead in punishing sodomy and the first millennium state took the lead in punishing polygamy. So what if it took until the High Middle Ages or even the early modern Reformation era for church and state to combine their forces coherently in condemning and punishing both sodomy and polygamy. The reality is that for at least half a millennium the Christian Church and the Christian state together branded sodomy and polygamy as unnatural sins and crimes, and together condemned and punished as sexually deviant anyone who felt naturally drawn to same-sex or plural unions. Under the hot bright lights of modern constitutional liberty, these centuries-old sex "crimes" look equally prejudiced and problematic. Because consensual sodomy and same-sex unions (if not marriages) are now constitutionally protected, consensual polygamy and other forms of polyamorous union should be protected, too. Clever reconstruction of the variant ancient pedigrees of these purported crimes avails us little today. Dusty historical arguments about what is natural and unnatural are just not good enough anymore.

NATURAL ARGUMENTS

But there are striking differences between the traditional natural arguments against same-sex unions and those against polygamous unions. The heart of the traditional natural argument against same-sex relations was that they are by nature "non-generative." However consensual and loving, same-sex intimacy simply cannot produce a child, which the Western tradition teaches is the ultimate end and good of sexual intercourse. And having a child is essential for the preservation of the human race and for the perpetuation of one's own family name, business, identity, memory, and more. Like every other animal, Aristotle already put it in the fourth century BCE, "a male and female must unite for the reproduction of the species," and humans are thus born with "the natural impulse ... to leave behind them something of the same nature as themselves."[34] Same-sex partners simply cannot procreate together, rendering their sexual intimacy "unnatural."

Moreover, the traditional natural argument went, "even the beasts" do not engage in same-sex activities, despite their lack of reason and conscience. Many animals do kill and eat each other, take each other's homes, food, mates, and offspring, and ignore other creatures in peril, even those of their own species. All of this violates

---

[34] See discussion in Chapter 3, pp. 100–106.

basic natural laws of homicide, theft, adultery, family, and charity that humans have discovered and learned to implement through the use of their reason and conscience. But "even the beasts," following natural instincts alone, know that same-sex activities are "unnatural," even repulsive. If even the beasts instinctually know better, the traditional argument went, even the most irrational and irresponsible humans should also know that same-sex desires, relations, and activities are "unnatural."

Finally, the human sexual body itself reflects what is natural, the tradition taught. A penis can slide into a vagina easily and comfortably, while anal penetration requires artificial lubrication and often causes pain. Vaginal intercourse can bring intense orgasmic pleasure to both parties in a way that oral sex cannot, absent simultaneous masturbation and "spilling of seed" by the party performing fellatio or cunnilingus. Face-to-face missionary vaginal sex brings the couple's whole bodies more closely together in intimacy than any other sexual positions. We might blanch or roll our eyes at these distinctions today, using our imaginations or Internets to find exceptions and counterexamples. But, historically, those differences between male-female and same-sex intimacy were taken as important evidence that the natural end or telos of the human sexual body was for straight sex, not gay or lesbian sex.

All of these traditional natural arguments against same-sex relations are seriously disputed today, and their erosion has helped topple traditional Western laws against sodomy, same-sex unions, and in some places same-sex marriage.[35] But none of these traditional natural arguments applies to polygamy. Procreation is not only possible; it is enhanced by having multiple wives rather than one. Polygamy is not only known in nature but is the predominant form of reproduction in most animals, including more than 95 percent of all higher primates; pairing birds, voles, and a few other animals are the monogamous exception.[36] The human body is not only capable of having multiple sex partners, but allows a man to impregnate several women in a night, although a woman can have only one pregnancy at a time no matter how many men she takes into her bed. That is why Augustine and many later Western sages like Hugo Grotius thought that only polygyny not polyandry was a "perfectly natural" form of procreation. And that is why the current erosion of the traditional

[35] See, e.g., Michael J. Perry, *Human Rights in the Constitutional Law of the United States* (Cambridge: Cambridge University Press, 2013), 112–157; id., *Constitutional Rights, Moral Controversy and the Supreme Court* (Cambridge: Cambridge University Press, 2009), 93–130. For a recent defense of these traditional natural arguments against same-sex and alternative forms of marriage, see Sherif Girgis, Ryan T. Anderson, and Robert P. George, *What is Marriage? Man and Woman: A Defense* (New York: Encounter Books, 2012).

[36] See Melvin Konner, *The Evolution of Childhood: Relations, Emotion, Mind* (Cambridge, MA: Belknap Press, 2010), 452–462; id., *The Tangled Wing: Biological Constraints on the Human Spirit*, rev. pbk. ed. (New York: Henry Holt, 2002), 268–270, 323–337.

natural argument against same-sex relations has little bearing on the Western case against polygamy.

The traditional natural argument against polygamy was of a different order. Nearly eight centuries ago, the great Dominican scholar, Thomas Aquinas, put the argument clearly, and it became a commonplace of Western thought and law thereafter, especially among Enlightenment liberals and common law jurists who took it as axiomatic.[37] Human beings, Thomas argued, are distinct among the animals in having perennial sex drives rather than annual mating seasons. They produce vulnerable babies who need the support of both their mother and father for a long time in order to survive and thrive. Women bond naturally with children; men do so only if they are certain of their paternity. Exclusive and enduring monogamous unions are the only way that humans can at once have regular sex, paternal certainty, and joint caretaking for their young children. Humans have thus learned by natural inclination and hard experience to the contrary to develop enduring pair-bonding strategies as the most effective means of reproduction.

Polyandry (one wife with multiple husbands) is naturally unjust to children, Aquinas continued. If a woman has sex with several husbands, it removes the likelihood that any child born to that woman will clearly belong to any one husband. That will undermine paternal certainty and consequent paternal investment in their children's care. The children will suffer from chronic neglect and deprivation, and the wife will be overburdened trying to care for them and trying to tend to her multiple husbands and their rampant sexual needs at once.

Polygyny (one man with multiple wives) is naturally unjust to wives and children. It does not necessarily erode paternal certainty. So long as his multiple wives are faithful to him alone, a man can be assured of being the father of any children born in his household. But this requires a man to pen up his wives like cattle, isolating them from other roving males even when his own energies to tend to them are already dissipated over the several women gathered in his household. It places half-siblings in competition for every scrap of food, shelter, and paternal attention, and sets their mothers against each other and especially against rival stepchildren in the household. "This is not marriage, but slavery," said Aquinas. It betrays the fundamental requirements of fidelity and mutuality of husband and wife, of the undivided and undiluted love and friendship that become a proper marriage. It also betrays the fundamental bond between parents and children reflected in the Mosaic Commandment to "honor your father and mother so that your days may be long." And it betrays the fundamental command of love of Jesus to "let the children come"[38] to receive love, support, protection, nurture, and education from their

---

[37] See discussion in Chapter 4, pp. 170–175, and Chapter 9, pp. 352–357, 372–380.

[38] Mark 10:14.

parents, families, and broader communities. Polygamy is thus unnatural, unjust, and unfair, Thomas concluded. It violates the natural law of God.

Later Catholic and Protestant writers argued that polygamy violates not only the natural law of God but also the natural rights of wives and children. Calvinist jurist Theodore Beza put this argument clearly nearly five centuries ago.[39] Beza took the Ten Commandments of the Bible to be the best summary of the natural law, but he saw parallel commands in many other formulations of the natural law. He argued that polygamy violates the commandments against adultery, theft, false testimony, and coveting at once. Polygamy is a form of adultery that breaches a man's duty to be faithful to his first wife alone. It is a form of theft that breaches his duty to provide sufficient material support for his wife and their children even after his death. It is a form of false witness that breaches his duty to honor his promise of marital fidelity. And polygamy is a form of coveting that breaches a man's duty not to lust after his female neighbor, as the lustful King David did in drawing the already married Bathsheba into his already full harem.

Each of these natural duties about fidelity, property, honesty, and respect rooted in the Decalogue has correlative natural rights that polygamy also breaches, Beza continued. Polygamy breaches the first wife's natural rights to marital fidelity and trust, to ongoing marital property and material security, and to contractual expectations and reliance on her husband's fidelity to the marriage contract. It breaches the children's natural rights to proper support and inheritance, and to the undiluted and unharried care, nurture, and education of their father and mother together. And polygamy breaches a neighbor's rights to have an equal opportunity to marry without having most of the eligible women hoarded in one harem or having his own wife or daughters subject to the covetous privations of a powerful polygamous neighbor. Polygamy was thus doubly unnatural, Beza concluded, a violation of natural law and natural rights alike.

This was a critical shift in emphasis from the natural wrongs of polygamy to the natural rights that it violated. Polygamy was now viewed not only as objectively wrong but also subjectively harmful. It violated not only the natural law of God but also the natural rights of God's children. Early modern Catholics and Protestants drew on these formulations in their new critique of the polygamy of Old Testament patriarchs, Ottoman Turks, and traditional Africans and Asians alike. Particularly during the age of discovery in the sixteenth to eighteenth centuries, both travelers' diaries and colonial chronicles were filled with invective against the "unnatural" practice of polygamy in the New World, and the natural rights violations of women and children that this practice occasioned.[40]

---

[39] See discussion in Chapter 6, pp. 254–262.
[40] See discussion in Chapter 7, pp. 285–290.

Liberal philosophers and common law jurists from the seventeenth century onward drew directly on these traditional natural law and natural rights arguments against polygamy, even while they supported the legal disestablishment of Christianity. Most liberals posited natural rights as "inherent" in human nature or the state of nature rather than commanded in the Bible or the order of creation. But they came to the same conclusion as earlier Christians that polygamy violated the natural rights and liberties especially of women and children. Seventeenth-century English philosopher John Locke, for example, regarded polygamy as a violation of the natural-born equality of men and women, and the natural rights of children to be properly nurtured and fully supported by both their mother and father until they were fully emancipated. For Locke, the natural laws favoring monogamy trumped religious arguments for polygamy, and he would allow no religious liberty exemptions from criminal prohibitions on polygamy.[41] A century later, leading common law jurist William Blackstone condemned polygamy as a "singularly barbaric" violation of the reciprocal natural rights and duties of husbands and wives, parents and children, which no modern civilization could countenance. Polygamy for him was a grave offense against public health and public order.[42] Eighteenth-century women's rights advocate Mary Wollstonecraft castigated polygamy for privileging men and degrading women, forcing them to compete with other women in their own household, especially the more nubile and fertile young women whom their husbands would inevitably drag home to replace them when they grew barren or lost their good looks. A woman is not just a temporary object of beauty or dispensable channel of procreation, Wollstonecraft insisted. A woman is a full citizen who must be given the right, education, and opportunity to choose her own public and private vocations, and to enjoy her natural-born liberty and equality within her own home if she chooses to marry.[43] Scottish philosophers Henry Home and David Hume argued that polygamy would breed tyrannical patriarchy or servile submissiveness in children, depending on their and their mother's place in the polygamous home. Children of polygamy simply cannot learn the healthy balances of authority and liberty, equality and respect, property and responsibility that they need to survive, let alone thrive. For Home and Hume, and nineteenth-century American writers who echoed them, this was no way to treat the natural rights of the child.[44]

"So what?!" a modern skeptic again might say to all this talk about natural law, natural justice, or natural rights. Traditional "natural" arguments against polygamy are no more convincing than traditional "biblical" or "theological" arguments. After

[41] See discussions in Chapter 9, pp. 364–367.
[42] See discussion in Chapter 9, pp. 367–369.
[43] See discussion in Chapter 9, pp. 370–372.
[44] See discussions in Chapters 9 and 10, pp. 373–380, 419–421.

all, modern philosophers and linguists have made clear that "nature" talk is just a thin and movable cover for the imposition of underlying religious and cultural preferences and prejudices. They have proved that "irrefutable" principles of reason or "objective" facts of nature are always conditioned by a community's levels of socialization and scientific knowledge. They have shown that "self-evident" truths are only temporary normative stopping points in endlessly evolving cultures.[45] Take the "naturalist" argument for exclusive and enduring heterosexual marriages that Thomas Aquinas introduced and nearly eight centuries of Western jurists and philosophers thereafter repeated. Today, genetic testing has made paternity much easier to establish. Contraceptives have made extramarital sex much safer to pursue. Artificial reproductive technology, adoption, and surrogacy (maybe cloning soon, too) have made reproduction readily available to men and women, straights and gays, single and married, couples or communes. And the welfare state is there to help all these parents if they or their children have need. What Aquinas took as objective "natural" conditions about human sexuality and heterosexual pair-bonding strategies of reproduction were, in fact, conditioned by the level of science, economy, and politics of his day.[46] As conditions changed, domestic arrangements have changed, too. LGBTQ advocates have used this evolutionary insight to open the door to same-sex equality and marriage. Polygamy advocates can and must do the same, the argument goes.

Shifting the discourse from "natural law" to "natural rights" arguments against polygamy only compounds the problem, the skeptical argument continues. After all, natural rights – or "universal human rights" as we now call them – are also cultural constructs. They are rooted in and reflective of the values and beliefs of the Western cultures that first named and used them. Theodore Beza and other early modern Christians were at least honest in rooting these natural rights firmly in the Bible and the order of creation. But post-Christian liberals have rooted these rights in the shifting sands of human nature and the state of nature. Jeremy Bentham was perhaps a bit too harsh in calling all this "nonsense upon stilts."[47] Oliver Wendell Holmes, Jr. was perhaps a bit too cynical in calling a human right "only the hypostasis of a prophecy," a mere prediction of what might happen to "those who do things said to contravene it."[48] But the reality is that human rights are just normative

---

[45] See recitation and critique of these arguments in Don S. Browning, "A Natural Law Theory of Marriage," *Zygon* 46 (2011): 733–760.

[46] Don Browning and I respond to this argument in our forthcoming volume, *From Contract to Covenant: What Christianity Offers Modern Marriage Law*.

[47] See texts collected and analyzed in Jeremy Waldron, *"Nonsense Upon Stilts": Bentham, Burke, and Marx on the Rights of Man* (London/New York: Methuen, 1987).

[48] Oliver Wendell Holmes, Jr., "Natural Law," *Harvard Law Review* 32 (1918): 40–44, at 42.

totems of a community's ideals, procedural means to enforce a favored set of social and institutional relationships. Calling these rights "natural" or "human" does not change the reality that most purportedly "universal" human rights in vogue today are principally Western (Christian) constructions of value and belief. They have little salience or cogency in polygamous communities around the world that have chosen to reject rights talk, or at least Western formulations of them. How do you answer a sincere good faith Muslim who claims his or her right to practice polygamy under the Universal Islamic Declaration of Human Rights? Or an Indigenous African who anchors his or her claim to polygamy in the South African Bill of Rights? Can you really tell them that their rights claims and documents are wrong? On what grounds? Maybe Bentham was on to something after all.[49]

HARM ARGUMENTS

But even if we reject the validity of human rights, we cannot deny the reality of human wrongs. Even if we reject the capacity of the state to prohibit fault, we cannot deny the state the power to punish harm. And even if a global human rights campaign against polygamy might be out, a Western insistence on maintaining monogamy alone might still be in. For the most enduring argument in the Western tradition is that polygamy is too often the cause, consequence, or corollary of harm, especially to the most vulnerable populations.[50] And that argument about the harms of polygamy still has resonance today.

Some 1,800 years ago, ancient Jewish Rabbis and early Church Fathers alike warned that polygamy was "trouble" even when practiced by the most noble and God-fearing men and women. Think of Abraham with Sarah and Hagar, Jacob with Rachel and Leah, Elkanah with Hannah and Peninnah: All of these households suffered bitter rivalry between their wives, bitter disputes among their children over inheritance and political succession, deadly competition among the half-siblings that ultimately escalated to incest, adultery, kidnapping, enslavement, and banishment. Think of the great King David who murdered Bathsheba's husband to add her to his already ample harem. Or King Solomon with his "thousand wives" who led

---

[49] I answer some of these arguments against (natural) rights talk in my contributions to John Witte, Jr. and Frank S. Alexander, eds., *Christianity and Human Rights: An Introduction* (Cambridge: Cambridge University Press, 2010); John Witte, Jr. and M. Christian Green, eds., *Religion and Human Rights: An Introduction* (Oxford: Oxford University Press, 2012) and in John Witte, Jr., *The Reformation of Rights: Law, Religion, and Human Rights in Early Modern Calvinism* (Cambridge: Cambridge University Press, 2007).

[50] On vulnerability theory, see Martha A. Fineman, "The Vulnerable Subject and the Responsive State," *Emory Law Journal* 60 (2010): 251–275; id., "Beyond Identities: The Limits of an Antidiscrimination Approach to Equality," *Boston University Law Review* 92 (2012): 1713–1770.

him into idolatry, and whose children ended up raping, abducting, and killing each other, precipitating civil war in ancient Israel.[51]

Some 800 years ago, William of Auvergne and other observers of Middle Eastern polygamy argued that the "bent love" of polygamy was inevitably, if not inherently, harmful. Women are harmed because they are reduced to rival slaves within the household, exploited for sex with an increasingly sterile and distracted husband, sometimes deprived of the children they do produce, and forced to make do for themselves and their children with too few resources as other women and children are added to the household against their wishes. Children are harmed because their chances of birth and survival are diminished by their calculating fathers who might contracept, abort, smother, or sell them, and by their mothers who sometimes lack the resources, support, and protection to bring them to term, let alone to adulthood. Men are harmed because they do not have the time, energy, or resources to support their polygamous households, and because their minds and hearts cannot rest if they are always on the lookout for another woman to add to their harems or for another dangerous man who will abduct his women. And societies are harmed because polygamy results in too many unattached men who become menaces to public order and morality, and creates too many ad hoc seats of domestic power which are based on sheer numbers rather than on legitimate political succession or election.[52]

Some 500 years ago, European critics of Münster documented the harms done when religious leaders gained power over an isolated polygamous community. There a group of young men, giddy with lust and theocratic pretensions, combined charisma, brutality, and biblical platitudes to force a gullible Christian community to adopt their utopian vision of polygamy. Old couples were forced to end their marriages and start again. Young girls and women were coerced into premature and unwanted marriages; even little prepubescent girls were fair game, and were literally raped to death. Husbands collected wives like spiritual trophies, measuring their faith by the size of their harems and nurseries. Wives were used and then spurned when they were pregnant or nursing or when the next wife was added to the harem. Polygamous households were filled with bickering wives and children, who were then cowed into silence with threats of the sword. Wives who still objected, or who rejected their husband's sexual advances to protest the unwanted polygamy, were summarily executed. Community dissenters and critics of these utopian excesses were summarily banished or executed.[53]

Some 150 years ago, American critics of Mormon polygamy found much the same thing on the Western frontier. First, they charged, polygamy harmed young girls who

[51] See discussion in Chapter 1.
[52] See discussion in Chapter 4, pp. 161–163.
[53] See discussion in Chapter 5, pp. 221–223.

were too often tricked, coerced, or commanded to enter spiritual marriages with older men, and had too little education and too few means of escape when inevitably neglected or replaced by another favorite wife. Their plight was exacerbated by the practice of unilateral male divorce that allowed men to banish wives who failed to fall in line or who no longer offered children, labor, support, or sex. Women within the home were placed into competition with each other and the children for ever thinner resources, and reduced in effect to the status of slaves – bought and sold by wealthy and powerful men, hunted down and returned if they became fugitives, and put to hard work under unrelenting and unsupervised patriarchal discipline. Second, polygamy licensed and encouraged male lust for sex and power. It induced inevitable restlessness on the part of some males to add more women to their harems. It invited inevitable repression and ostracism of rival males eager to find a wife or lover among the shrinking supply of women who were left to them. It restricted marriage to the richest and most powerful, not necessarily the fittest and most virtuous males of the community. And third, polygamy created religious power structures that rivaled the legitimate power of the state. Church leaders slowly gained control of the property, economy, and work force. They compelled their congregants, workers, and family members to support their polygamous policies and to vote for new officials who would do the same. They colluded to create laws and policies favoring polygamy, and to suborn the perjury and contempt of those polygamists who were sought by the authorities. And when government officials sought to restore legal and moral order in the territory, these communities confronted them with boycotts, guns, riots, and violence. This simply could not be countenanced in a democratic land dedicated to the separation of church and state.[54]

Today, observers of polygamous communities scattered about the West point to similar problems of higher than average incidences of arranged, coerced, and underage marriages of young girls to older men; rape and statutory rape; wife and child abuse; social and educational deprivation of women and children in polygamous households; abuse and ostracism of young boys and poorer men who compete for fewer brides; rampant social welfare abuses; social isolation of polygamous communities; and dangerous conflations of religious and political authority. Outside of the West, most polygamous cultures are rural, poor, and uneducated, with low technology and labor-intensive economies that require many children to do the work and that feature low survival rates among these children. Or they are part of powerful political and religious families in Traditional tribal and/or Muslim settings. But regardless of "whether it is practiced in a Western democracy or sub-Saharan Africa, polygamy produces harmful effects that ripple throughout

---

[54] See discussion in Chapter 10, pp. 429–439.

a society," Brown University anthropologist Rose McDermott concludes after a thorough cross-cultural study of polygamy in 170 countries. All these polygamous communities "suffer from increased levels of physical and sexual abuse against women, increased rates of maternal mortality, shortened female life expectancy, lower levels of education for girls and boys, lower levels of equality for women, higher levels of discrimination against women, increased rates of female genital mutilation, increased rates of trafficking in women and decreased levels of civil and political liberties for all citizens."[55]

The Western legal tradition has thus long regarded polygamy as a *malum in se* offense – something "bad in itself." Other *malum in se* offenses today include slavery, sex trafficking, prostitution, indentured servitude, obscenity, bestiality, incest, sex with children, self-mutilation, organ-selling, cannibalism, and more. Polygamy is usually regarded as less egregious than some other offenses on this list. But, like other *malum in se* offenses, polygamy is too often the cause, consequence, or corollary of other wrongdoing. That someone wants to engage in these activities voluntarily for reasons of religion, bravery, custom, or autonomy makes no difference. That other cultures past and present allow such activities makes no difference. That these activities do not necessarily cause harm in every case also makes no difference. For nearly two millennia, the Western legal tradition has included polygamy among the crimes that are inherently wrong – because polygamy routinely routinizes patriarchy, deprecates women, jeopardizes consent, fractures fidelity, divides loyalty, dilutes devotion, fosters inequity, promotes rivalry, foments lust, condones adultery, harms children, and more. Not in every case, to be sure, but in enough cases to make the practice of polygamy too risky to condone as a viable legal option.

Furthermore, allowing religious polygamy as an exception to the rules is even more dangerous, the Western tradition has concluded, because it will make some churches, mosques, tribes, and temples a law unto themselves. It is notable that no religious communities in the West today regard polygamy as an absolute religious requirement. It is a custom, not a command, an option not an obligation for the faithful. It is also notable that some Western communities that once preached and practiced polygamy – namely, Jews and Mormons, and a number of Muslims, too – have now rejected the practice. But even if polygamy were religiously obligatory, modern Western constitutional laws still empower states to prohibit behavior that it considers harmful or dangerous. Again, some religious communities and their members might well thrive with the freedom to practice polygamy. But inevitably

---

[55] Rose McDermott and Jonathan Cowden, "Polygyny and its Effect on Violence Against Women, Children, and Within the State" (forthcoming). See also the detailed literature introduced in the expert opinion submitted by McDermott in the British Columbia case, referenced earlier in note 2 of this chapter, and further references in the Introduction to this book.

closed repressive and isolated regimes will also emerge – with under-aged girls duped or coerced into sex and marriages with older men, with women and children trapped in sectarian communities with no realistic access to help or protection from the state and no real legal recourse against a religious communities that is following its own rules. The West prizes liberty, equality, and consent too highly to court such a risk.

"So what?!" a modern skeptic might argue for the final time. Monogamous households are filled with many ugly harms, too: wife and child abuse, deprivation and abandonment of children, wastrel habits, welfare abuses, and, sadly, so much more. That has not led to the abolition of monogamy, but only to the closer policing and punishment of each harm as it occurs. Why not do the same here? If polygamy really does cause or correlate with various harms, why not just punish those harms when they occur? If polygamous wives or children really do suffer from increased levels of abuse, neglect, or deprivation, why not give them model contracts with strong built-in protections for the vulnerable that are scrupulously enforced? If religious leaders really do subvert due process, why not let polygamous parties just litigate their claims in state courts? If religious communities really do isolate their members at the risk of abuse, why not make polygamy more mainstream, transparent, and accountable? If "Big Love" and "Sister Wives" can make the polygamous family work, why can't everyone else be given a fair chance?

SYMBOLIC ARGUMENTS

"Bad cases make bad law," a familiar legal dictum has it, and so it is here. The compelling case for the lawfulness of polygamy is when three or more well-educated parties, similar in wealth, ability, and opportunity, eyes and doors wide open, choose to enter into a polygamous union. They can calculate and negotiate the costs and benefits, the advantages and disadvantages of their pending plural union. They can protect themselves through prenuptial and postnuptial contracts and through their own independent means. They can hire lawyers, accountants, private investigators, and security guards to help them if their partners betray or endanger them or their children. And they can hit the airwaves and social media to elicit sympathy and action if the state authorities do not respond quickly or fully enough. For these exceptional parties, the state criminal prohibition against polygamy hardly seems necessary.

But general criminal prohibitions against polygamy are not designed for the exceptional case, but for the typical case. And throughout Western history and still today, a typical case of polygamy too often involves vulnerable parties who do not have the knowledge, resources, or connections to engage in the kind of self-protection and self-help available to a "Big Love" or "Sister" wife. And although every Western state has general laws on the books against wife and child abuse, coerced marriage and statutory rape of young girls, deprivation of food, shelter, and education of children, welfare abuse, and more, the reality is that these laws in action have provided far too little support and protection for these vulnerable populations, especially as state administrative agencies face shrinking budgets, dwindling personnel, and political disincentives to prosecute. If the practice of polygamy is one root of these sundry domestic problems, why not enforce the criminal laws against this practice? If the legislatures have put and left polygamy laws on the books, by what right do state prosecutors or law enforcement officials simply ignore them?

But these traditional criminal laws against polygamy are more than just prudential prophylactics against harm. They also play an important symbolic and teaching function that the state and its family laws still play in our lives. Historically, in the West, the laws against polygamy were part of a broader set of family laws designed to support the classical Western ideal that the monogamous family was the most primal and essential institution of Western society and culture. Aristotle and the Roman Stoics called the union of husband and wife, and parent and child the "foundation of the republic" and "the private font of public virtue." The Church Fathers and medieval Catholics called the monogamous household "the seedbed of the city," "the force that welds society together," the sacrament that produces structural and symbolic stability. Early modern Protestants and Anglo-American common lawyers called the stable household a "little church," a "little state," the first school of love and justice, nurture and education, charity and citizenship. John Locke and the Enlightenment philosophers called monogamous marriage "the first society" to be formed as men and women moved from the state of nature to an organized society dedicated to the rule of law and the protection of rights. In all these traditional metaphors, what was being celebrated and taught was a certain vision of the good life and the good society, with monogamous marriage at its core.[56]

For all of the advances in our contemporary Western understandings of liberty, autonomy, and equality, and for all our current wariness about totalitarian state power, we still look to the Western state to teach and encourage activities or relationships that cater to private and public "health, safety, and welfare," and discourage activities and relationships that do not.[57] In the area of marriage and family life, we have shrunk the domestic ideals traditionally taught and symbolized by various sacramental or covenantal frameworks; the modern state now teaches

[56] See detailed sources in my *From Sacrament to Contract: Marriage, Religion, and Law in the Western Tradition*, 2nd ed. (Louisville, KY: Westminster John Knox Press, 2012).

[57] On the "teaching" function of law, see Cathleen Kaveny, *Law's Virtues: Fostering Autonomy and Solidarity in American Society* (Washington, DC: Georgetown University Press, 2012), esp. 97–110, 219–242; John Witte, Jr., *God's Joust, God's Justice: Law and Religion in the Western Tradition* (Grand Rapids, MI: Wm. B. Eerdmans, 2006), 263–294.

and allows for straight and same-sex relations, divorce and remarriage, marital and non-marital cohabitation, and more. And we have moved away from many of the absolute "thou shalt" and "thou shalt not" commands of the past, as well as the harsh and sometimes brutal measures used to enforce them. But still, in the "soft law" between these two apodictic poles, the modern state still does its teaching work, "nudging" its citizens in one direction or another.[58] The state encourages, exemplifies, supports, funds, facilitates, and licenses certain behavior that conduces to the public and private health, safety, and welfare of the community. It discourages and warns against the opposite types of behavior, and provides it with no funding, facilitation, licenses, or support.

The modern Western state does not require its citizens to get married, but it does "nudge" in that direction. It provides state marital licenses, tax and social security incentives, spousal evidentiary and health care privileges, and hundreds of additional federal and state benefits and incentives.[59] It models monogamous marriage in its political officials. Most Western nations still look askance on the single political candidate, or an elected official who commits adultery. In turn, the state now mostly nudges against polygamy, even if formal criminal prohibitions against polygamy remain on the books. De facto polygamy is now effectively allowed through much of the West. Constitutional norms of sexual liberty and domestic autonomy allow adults to live with multiple self-declared spouses so long as they all abide by the laws of adult consensual sex, and so long as they do not seek marital licenses or welfare benefits from the state based on marriage. The modern state also now provides the legal means to meet the traditional "necessity" arguments for polygamy. If a man wants more children than his wife can give him, he can adopt more, have them out of wedlock, or hire a surrogate. If a spouse is frustrated because his or her spouse cannot or will not have sex, unilateral divorce and remarriage options are now available. These steps are not costless or easy, but they largely meet the concerns that historically justified polygamy in cases of necessity.

In a democratic polity, the judgment of whether the state should nudge for or against certain behavior – let alone outright prescribe or proscribe it – rests ultimately with the people. And, at least in the West, the "people" have decided they still favor faithful monogamous marriage. "Two's company, three's a crowd," a common Western adage has it. That speaks to the reality that in certain long-term social contexts – especially in the intimacies of bed, board, and bath – there is something

---

[58] See Richard Thaler and Cass Sunstein, *Nudge: Improving Decisions About Health, Wealth, and Happiness* (New Haven, CT: Yale University Press, 2008); Carl Schneider, "The Channelling Function in Family Law," *Hofstra Law Review* 20 (1992): 495–532.

[59] See Nancy F. Cott, *Public Vows: A History of Marriage and the Nation* (Cambridge, MA: Harvard University Press, 2000); Anita Bernstein, "For and Against Marriage," *Michigan Law Review* 102 (2003): 129–212.

intuitively more attractive in being with one other person, not two or more. Yes, some say that dyadic attraction is a purely social construct, a routinization of habits that have gathered around an artificially privileged monogamous norm. They point to people who like living, sleeping, and bathing with several people at once; the commune, communal bath, and common bed are hardly anomalies among humans of various times and places. But these ample exceptions do not swallow the general preference for dyadic sexual pair bonding in the West – especially among Western women, who have rarely practiced or condoned polyamory historically or today. Let's face it: the Western case for polygamy is and always has been primarily about a small group of men seeking the social, moral, and legal imprimatur to have and to hold sundry females at once. But there is plenty of empirical evidence to show that most men and women alike are instinctively attracted to single partner intimacy for the long term and instinctively repulsed and angered if forced to shared their bed and partner with a third party. Despite our wide cultural acceptance of sexual liberty in the West, adultery still breaks marriage and longstanding intimate relationships more often than any other cause.[60]

Although some elite scholars and media now find polygamy acceptable, and even desirable, the vast majority of people in the United States still find polygamy to be deeply objectionable, even though many traditional sexual taboos no longer rankle them. According to a 2013 Gallup poll, solid majorities of the population now accept birth control (91 percent), divorce (68 percent), non-marital sex (63 percent), and having children outside of marriage (60 percent). Acceptance of abortion (at 42 percent) and gay and lesbian relations (at 42 percent) remains much lower, owing to sustained beliefs and campaigns against both, but even those numbers are four times higher than they were fifty years ago. By striking contrast, only 14 percent of American people accept polygamy; this is double the number of 7 percent that accepted polygamy in 2001, perhaps owing to the growing media campaign for it, but that number is still remarkably low. Only adultery (at 6 percent) ranks lower in social acceptability.[61]

This suggests that, at least in the United States, any change in traditional polygamy laws must come from below, not from on high, by gradual democratic adjustments in each state, not by judicial pronouncements from the federal courts. The constitutional case for polygamy is weak compared to the cases supporting the liberalization of other traditional sex, marriage, and family laws; there are just too

---

[60] For various perspectives on dyadic relationships, see, e.g., Frieder R. Lang and Karin L. Fingerman, eds., *Growing Together: Personal Relationship Across the Lifespan* (Cambridge: Cambridge University Press, 2004); Anita L. Vangelisti and Daniel Perlman, eds., *The Cambridge Handbook of Personal Relationships* (Cambridge: Cambridge University Press, 2006).

[61] http://www.gallup.com/poll/162689/record-high-say-gay-lesbian-relations-morally.aspx?version=print.

many serious concerns about harms and rights on the other side. Forcing the issue by constitutional brinkmanship might well trigger a strong democratic backlash if the fallout from *Roe v. Wade* is any indication. There may come a time that the West will more readily accept polygamy as a valid marital option that is licensed and regulated by the state. Polygamy may eventually move from Stonewall to *Windsor*. But that cultural and legal pilgrimage, to my mind, is still a long way off.

For the West to maintain its traditional stance against polygamy does not mean that it needs to trade in all the ugly rhetoric that sometimes historically attended this stance. We do not have to posit unilinear narratives of progress that brand polygamists as "barbarians" and "savages" lacking in virtue or value.[62] We do not have to say that the West is more "advanced" or "progressive" than the rest because of its monogamy. We do not have to repeat the haughty and xenophobic arguments used by Graeco-Roman writers against their imperial subjects, by early Christians against Jews and Muslims, by early modern Europeans against New World natives, by nineteenth-century Americans against emancipated slaves, Native Americans, Asian workers, or traditional Mormons who practiced polygamy.[63] The West can now simply and politely say to the polygamist who bangs on its door seeking admission or permission to practice polygamy: "No thank you; we don't do that here," and close the door firmly.

---

[62] See discussions in Chapter 2, pp. 85–93, and Chapter 4, pp. 159–161.

[63] See discussions in Chapter 2, pp. 104–105, Chapter 4, pp. 159–161, Chapter 7, pp. 285–290, and Chapter 10, pp. 421–439.

Bibliography

Abbot, George, *Vindicae Sabbathi* (London: n.p., 1641).

Abrams, Kerry, "Polygamy, Prostitution, and the Federalization of Immigration Law," *Columbia Law Review* 105 (2005): 641–716.

Acts and Laws of the English Colony of Rhode-Island and Providence-Plantations, in New England, in America (Newport, RI: Samuel Hall, 1767).

Adam of Bremen, *History of the Archbishops of Hamburg-Bremen*, F.J. Tschan, trans. (New York: Columbia University Press, 1959).

Agus, Irving S., *The Heroic Age of Franko-German Jewry* (New York: Yeshiva University Press, 1969).

Al-Hibri, Azizah Y. and Raja' M. El Habti, "Islam," in Don S. Browning, M. Christian Green, and John Witte, Jr., eds., *Sex, Marriage, and Family in World Religions* (New York: Columbia University Press, 2006), 150–225.

Al-Krenawi, Alean and Vered Slonim-Nevo, "Polygyny and Its Impact on the Psychosocial Well-Being of Husbands," *Journal of Comparative Law* 37 (2006): 174–189.

Alberigo, Giuseppe, ed., *Conciliorum Oecumenicorum Generaliumque Decreta Editio Critica* (Turnhout: Brepols Publishers, 2006).

Albertus Magnus, *Questions Concerning Aristotle's On Animals*, Irven M. Resnick and Kenneth F. Kitchell, Jr., trans. (Washington, DC: Catholic University of America Press, 2008).

Aldridge, Owen, "Polygamy in Early Fiction: Henry Neville and Denis Veiras," *Modern Language Association* 65 (1950): 464–472.

Alexander, Elizabeth Urban, *Notorious Woman: The Celebrated Case of Myra Clark Gaines* (Baton Rouge: Louisiana State University Press, 2001).

Alexander of Hales, *Glossa in quatuor libros sententiarum Petri Lombardi*, 4 vols. (Florence: Collegium S. Bonaventurae, 1951–1957).

Alexandre, Michel, "Big Love: Is Feminist Polygamy an Oxymoron or a True Possibility?" *Hastings Women's Law Journal* 18 (2007): 3–30.

Alfonsi, Peter, *Dialogue Against the Jews [1109]*, Irven M. Resnick, trans. (Washington, DC: Catholic University of America Press, 2006).

An Alphabetical Digest of the Public Statute Law of South-Carolina, 3 vols. (Charleston, SC: John Hoff, 1814).

Altman, Irwin and Joseph Ginat, *Polygamous Families in Contemporary Society* (Cambridge: Cambridge University Press, 1996).

Alvarus, Paul, *Indiculus luminosus* [c. 854], reprinted in *Corpus Scriptorum Muzarabicorum*, 1:270–315.

Ambrose, *On Abraham*, Theodosia Tomkinson, trans. (Etna: Traditionalist Orthodox Studies, 2000 [1919]).

Ambrosiaster, *Commentaries on Romans and 1–2 Corinthians*, Gerald L. Bray, trans. (Downers Grove, IL: InterVarsity Press Academic, 2009).

Ames, William, *The Marrow of Theology*, John D. Eusden, trans. (Durham, NC: The Labyrinth Press, 1968).

Amussen, Susan Dwyer, *An Ordered Society: Gender and Class in Early Modern England* (Oxford: Basil Blackwell, 1988).

An-Na'im, Abdullahi A., ed., *Islamic Family in a Changing World: A Global Resource Book* (London/New York: Zed Books, 2002).

Anderson, Scott, "The Polygamists," *National Geographic Magazine* (February 2010).

Andrea, Bernadette, *Women and Islam in Early Modern English Literature* (Cambridge: Cambridge University Press, 2000).

Anonymous, *An Heroic Epistle to the Rev. Martin M-d-n Author of a Late Treatise on Polygamy* (London: R. Faulder, 1780).

A *Letter to the Rev. Mr. Madan, Concerning the Chapter of Polygamy, in His Late Publication, Entitled Thelypthora* (London: Fielding and Walker, 1780).

Martin's Hobby Houghed and Pounded: Or, Letters on Thelyphthora, to a Friend, on the Subjects of Marriage and Polygamy (London: J. Buckland 1781).

Remedy for Uncleanness or Certain Queries Propounded to his Highness the Lord Protector (London: s.n., 1658).

The Virgins Complaint for the Losse of their Svveet-Harts by These Present Wars (London: Henry Wilson, 1642).

Aquinas, Thomas, *On Love and Charity: Readings from the Commentary on the Sentences of Peter Lombard*, Peter A. Kwasniewski, Thomas Bolin, and Joseph Bolin, trans. (Washington, DC: Catholic University Press of America, 2009).

Scriptum super Libros Sententiarum Petri Lombardiensis, in Thomas Aquinas, *Opera Omnia sancti Thomae Aquinatis Doctoris Angelici*, 13 vols. (Rome: C. de Propagandae Fidei, 1882), vol. 7, pt. 2.

Summa Contra Gentiles, 4 vols., Vernon J. Bourke, trans. (South Bend, IN: University of Notre Dame Press, 1975).

Summa Theologica: Complete English Edition in Five Volumes, Fathers of the English Dominican Province, trans., 5 vols. (New York: Benziger Bros., 1947–1948).

The Aramaic Bible – The Book of Ruth, D.R.G. Beattie, ed. (Collegeville, MN: The Liturgical Press, 1987).

Areen, Judith, "Uncovering the Reformation Roots of American Marriage and Divorce Law," *Yale Journal of Law and Feminism* 26 (2014): 29–85.

Aristotle, *The Ethics of Aristotle*, repr. ed., J.A.K. Thomson, trans. and ed. (New York: Penguin Books, 1965).

The Politics of Aristotle, Ernest Barker, trans. and ed. (New York: Oxford University Press, 1962).

Arnisaeus, Henning, *De Jure Connubiorum Commentarius* (Frankfurt am Main: Impensis Iohannis Thimij, typis Andreae Eichorn, 1613).

Arnobius, Against the Heathens, in *The Ante-Nicene Fathers: The Writings of the Fathers Down to A.D. 325*, 10 vols., repr. ed., Alexander Roberts, et al., trans. and eds. (Peabody, MA: Hendrickson Publishers, 1995), 6:432.

The Arraignment, Trial, and Conviction of Robert Fielding, Esq. for Felony in Marrying Her Grace, the Duchess of Cleavland His First Wife, Mrs. Mary Wadsworth Being Then Alive as the Session of the Old-Bailey (London: John Morphew, 1708).

Astolfi, Riccardo, *Studi sul matrimonio nel diritto romano postclassico e giustinianeo* (Naples: Jovene Editori, 2012).

Athanasius, History of the Arians, in Philip Schaff and Henry Wace, eds., *A Select Library of Nicene and Post-Nicene Fathers of the Christian Church*, Second Series, repr. ed. (Grand Rapids, MI: Eerdmans, 1952), 4:266–302.

Augustine, *City of God*, Gerald G. Walsh, et al., trans. Vernon J. Bourke, ed. (Garden City, NY: Image Books, 1958).

Contra Faustum, in *The Ante-Nicene Fathers: The Writings of the Fathers Down to A.D. 325*, Alexander Roberts, et al. trans. and eds., 10 vols., repr. ed. (Peabody, MA: Hendrickson Publishers, 1995), 4:155–345.

De bono coniugali, De sancta uirginitate, P.G. Walsh, ed. (Oxford: Clarendon Press, 2001).

De Doctrina Christiana, R.P.H. Green, ed. and trans. (Oxford: Clarendon Press, 1995).

De Genesi ad Litteram, in J.P. Migne, ed. *Patrologia Latina cursus completus* (Paris: 1844), 34:397–568.

On Marriage and Concupiscence, in *Early Church Fathers: Nicene and Post-Nicene Fathers*, First Series, Philip Schaff, trans. and ed., 14 vols. [1886–1889], repr. ed. (Peabody, MA: Hendrickson Publishers, 1994), 5:258–309.

On the Gospel of St. John, in *Early Church Fathers: Nicene and Post-Nicene Fathers*, First Series, Philip Schaff, trans. and ed., 14 vols. [1886–1889], repr. ed. (Peabody, MA: Hendrickson Publishers, 1994), 7:7–452.

On the Good of Marriage, in *St. Augustine: Treatises on Marriage and Other Subjects*, Charles T. Wilcox, trans., Roy J. Deferrari, ed. (Washington, DC: Catholic University of America Press, 1969), 9–54.

The Excellence of Widowhood, in Roy J. Deferrari, ed., M. Clement Eagan, trans., *Augustine, Treatises on Various Subjects* (Washington, DC: Catholic University of America Press, 1952), 279–322.

Two Books on Genesis Against the Manichees, in Ronald J. Teske, S.J., trans., *St. Augustine on Genesis* (Washington, DC: The Catholic University of America Press, 1991).

Baade, Hans W., "The Form of Marriage in Spanish North America," *Cornell Law Review* 61 (1975): 1–89.

Babie, Paul and Neville Rochow, eds., *Freedom of Religion Under Bills of Rights* (Adelaide: University of Adelaide Press, 2012).

Bache, Richard, *The Manual of a Pennsylvania Justice of the Peace*, 2 vols. (Philadelphia: W.P. Farrand, 1810–1814).

Bacon, Matthew, *The Abridgement of the Law*, ed. John Bouvier (Philadelphia: T. & J.W. Johnson, 1852).

Bacon, Nathaniel and John Selden, *A Historical and Political Discourse of the Lawes of England From the First Times to the End of Queen Elizabeth*, 2 vols. (London: John Starkey, 1689).

Bailey, Derrick S., *Homosexuality and the Western Christian Tradition*, repr. ed. (Hamden, CT: Archon Books, 1975).

Bailey, Joanne, *Unquiet Lives: Marriages and Marriage Breakdown in England, 1660–1800* (Cambridge: Cambridge University Press, 2001).

Bailey, Martha, "Polygamy and Unmarried Cohabitation," in Bill Atkin, ed., *The International Survey of Family Law*, 2011 ed. (Bristol: Jordan Publishing, 2011), 123–146.

Bailey, Martha and Amy J. Kaufman, *Polygamy in the Monogamous World: Multicultural Challenges for Western Law and Policy* (Santa Barbara, CA: Praeger, 2010).

Bainton, Roland, *Bernardino Ochino* (unpub. ms. 1965 included in the Library of Congress).

Baird, Henry Martin, *Theodore Beza: The Counsellor of the French Reformation, 1519–1605* (New York: G.P. Putnam's Sons, 1899).

Bala, Nicholas, "Why Canada's Prohibition of Polygamy is Constitutionally Valid and Sound Policy," *Canadian Journal of Family Law* 25 (2009): 165–221.

Baloyi, E.M., "Critical Reflections on Polygamy in the African Context," *Missionalia* (2014): 164–181.

Baltzly, Vaughn Bryan, "Same-Sex Marriage, Polygamy, and Disestablishment," *Social Theory and Practice* 38 (2012): 333–362.

Bamforth, Nicholas and David A.J. Richards, *Patriarchal Religion, Sexuality, and Gender: A Critique of New Natural Law* (Cambridge: Cambridge University Press, 2008).

Banner, Stuart, "When Christianity Was Part of the Common Law," *Law and History Review* 16 (1988): 27–62.

Bar, Ludwig von, *A History of Continental Criminal Law*, Thomas S. Bell, et al., trans. (Boston: Little Brown, 1916).

Barbour, Oliver L., *A Treatise on the Criminal Law of the State of New York*, 2nd ed. (Albany, NY: Gould, Banks, 1852).

Baron and Feme: A Treatise of the Common Law Concerning Husbands and Wives (London: Assigns of Richard and Edward Atkyns, Esq., 1700).

Bartholomew, G.W., "Origin and Development of the Law of Bigamy," *The Law Quarterly Review* 74 (1958): 259–271.

"Polygamous Marriages and English Criminal Law," *Modern Law Review* 17 (1954): 344–359.

Basch, Norma, *Forming American Divorce from the Revolutionary Generation to the Victorians* (Berkeley/Los Angeles: University of California Press, 1999).

Basil of Caesarea, The Canons of Basil of Caesarea (c. 370), in Philip Schaff and Henry Wace, eds., *A Select Library of Nicene and Post-Nicene Fathers of the Christian Church*, Second Series, repr. ed. (Grand Rapids, MI: Wm. B. Eerdmans, 1952), 14:604–609.

Saint Basil: The Letters, 4 vols., Roy J. Deferrari, trans. (New York: G.P. Putnam, 1930).

Baskin, Judith R., "Bolsters to Their Husbands: Women as Wives in Rabbinic Literature," *European Judaism* 37(2) (2004): 88–102.

Beaman, Lori G. and Gillian Calder, eds., *Polygamy's Rights and Wrongs: Perspectives on Harm, Family, and Law* (Vancouver, BC: University of British Columbia Press, 2013).

Beattie, J.M., *Crime and the Courts in England, 1660–1800* (Oxford: Clarendon Press, 1986).

Becher, Mathias, *Charlemagne*, David S. Bachrach, trans. (New Haven, CT: Yale University Press, 2003).

Becker, Carl L., *The Heavenly City of the Enlightenment Philosophers* (New Haven, CT: Yale University Press, 1932).

Becker, Gary S., *A Treatise on the Family*, rev. pbk. ed. (Cambridge, MA: Harvard University Press, 2003).

Becon, Thomas, *The Booke of Matrimonie both Profitable and Comfortable for all Them that Entende Quietly and Godly to lyue in the Holy State of Honorable Wedlocke* (c. 1560) (STC 1710).

The Catechism of Thomas Becon, S.T.P., John Ayre, ed. (London: The Parker Society, 1844).

Bedouelle, G. and P. LeGal, *Le Divorce du Roi Henry VIII: Études et Documents* (Geneva: Travaux d'Humanisme et Renaissance, 1987).

Beecher, Lyman, *A Plea for the West*, 2nd ed. (Cincinnati, OH: Truman and Smith, 1835).

Beger, Lorenz, *Kurze doch unpartheyisch und gewissenhaffte Betrachtung dess in dem Natur- und Göttlichen Recht gegründeten heiligen Eh[e]standes* (Heidelberg: n.p. 1679).

Belien, Paul, "First Trio 'Married' in the Netherlands," *Brussels Journal* (September 27, 2005), http://www.brusselsjournal.com/node/301.

Bell, Alfreda Evan, *Boadicea: The Mormon Wife* (Baltimore, MD: A.R. Orton, 1855).

Bellamy, John G., *Criminal Law and Society in Late Medieval and Tudor England* (New York: St. Martin's Press, 1984).

Benedict, Philip, *Christ's Churches Purely Reformed: A Social History of Calvinism* (New Haven, CT: Yale University Press, 2002).

Benko, Stephen, "The Libertine Gnostic Sect of the Phibonites According to Epiphanius," *Vigiliae Christianae* 21 (1967): 103–119.

Pagan Rome and Early Christians (Bloomington: Indiana University Press, 1984).

Bennett, Catherine, "It's One Sharia Law for Men and Quite Another for Women," *The Observer* (*The Guardian* [U.K.]), February 10, 2008, http://www.guardian.co.uk/commentisfree/2008/feb/10/religion.law.

Bennion, Janet, *Polygamy in Primetime: Media, Gender, and Politics in Modern Fundamentalism* (Waltham, MA: Brandeis University Press, 2012).

Benrath, Karl, *Bernardino Ochino von Siena: Ein Beitrag zur Geschichte der Reformation*, 3rd ed. (Nieuwkoop: B. de Graaf, 1968).

Bentham, Jeremy, *The Works of Jeremy Bentham*, 11 vols., John Bowring, ed. (Edinburgh: William Tait, 1843).

Bentley, D.R., ed., *Select Cases from the Twelve Judges' Notebooks* (London: John Rees, 1997).

Berger, Michael S., "Two Models of Medieval Jewish Marriage: A Preliminary Study," in Michael J. Broyde and Michael Ausubel, eds., *Marriage, Sex, and Family in Judaism* (Lanham, MD: Rowman & Littlefield, 2005), 116–148.

Berman, Harold J., *Law and Revolution: The Formation of the Western Legal Tradition* (Cambridge, MA: Harvard University Press, 1983).

Law and Revolution II: The Impact of the Protestant Reformations on the Western Legal Tradition (Cambridge, MA: Harvard University Press, 2003).

"Soviet Family Law in the Light of Russian History and Marxist Theory," *Yale Law Journal* 56 (1946): 26–57.

"The Religious Sources of General Contract," in John Witte, Jr. and Frank S. Alexander, eds., *Christianity and Law: An Introduction* (Cambridge: Cambridge University Press, 2008), 125–142.

Bernstein, Anita, "For and Against Marriage," *Michigan Law Review* 102 (2003): 129–212.

Bernstein, Nina, "In Secret: Polygamy Follows Africans to New York," *New York Times* (March 23, 2007) http://www.nytimes.com/2007/03/23/nyregion/23polygamy.html?th&emc=th.

Betzig, Laura L, *Despotism, Social Evolution, and Differential Reproduction* (Somerset, NJ: Aldine Transaction, 2008).

Betzig, Laura L., et al., eds., *Human Reproductive Behavior: A Darwinian Perspective* (Cambridge: Cambridge University Press, 1988).

Beza, Theodore, *A Briefe and Pithie Summe of the Christian Faith Made in the Form of a Confession*, R.F., trans. (London: Roger Ward, 1589).

De haereticis a civili Magistratu puniendis (Geneva: Vignon, 1554).

De repudiis et divortiis (Geneva: Vignon, 1569, 1573).

Du Droit des Magistrats, Robert M. Kingdon, eds. (Geneva: Droz, 1970), and in translation as *Concerning the Rights of Rulers Over Their Subjects and the Duties of Subjects Toward Their Rulers*, Henri-Louis Gonin, trans. (Cape Town/Pretoria: H.A.U.M., 1956).

Lex Dei moralis, ceremonialis et politica (Geneva: Apud Petrum Santandreanum, 1577).

Propositions and Principles of Divinity, Propounded and Disputed in the University of Geneva (Edinburgh: Robert Waldegrave, 1591).

Psalmorum Davidis et aliorum Prophetarum (London: Excudebat Thomas Vautrollerius, 1580).

Sermons sur les trois premiers chaptres du cantique des Cantiques, de Salomon (Geneva, 1586), translated as *Master Bezaes sermons upon the three first chapters of the Canticle of Canticles* (Oxford: Joseph Barnes, 1587).

The Judgment of a Most Reverend and Learned Man from Beyond the Seas, Concerning the Threefolde Order of Bishops: with a Declaration of Certaine Other Waightie Pointes, Concerning the Discipline and Government of the Church (London: Robert Walgrave, 1585).

The Psalmes of Dauid: truely opened and explaned by paraphrasis, according to the right sense of euery Psalme, Anthony Giblie, trans. (London: Iohn Harison and Henrie Middleton, 1580).

Tractatio de polygamia, in qua et Ochini apostatae pro polygamia, et Montanistarum ac aliorum adversus repetitas nuptias argumenta refutantur: addito veterum canonum et quarundam civilium legum ad normam verbi divini examine (Geneva: Apud Eustathium Vignon, 1573 [1568]).

Tractationum Theologicarum, 2nd ed., 3 vols. (Geneva: Excvdebat Evstathivs Vignon, 1582).

Biggs, J.M., *The Concept Of Matrimonial Cruelty* (London: University of London Press, 1962).

Biller, Peter, *The Measure of Multitude: Population in Medieval Thought* (Oxford: Oxford University Press, 2000).

Bishop, Joel, *Commentaries on the Law of Marriage and Divorce*, 4th ed., 2 vols. (Boston: Little Brown, 1864).

Commentaries on the Law of Statutory Crimes, 2nd ed. (Boston: Little Brown, 1883).

Bix, Brian "Private Ordering and Family Law," *Journal of the American Academy of Matrimonial Lawyers* 23 (2010): 249–285.

Black, Ann, "In the Shadow of our Legal System," in Rex Ahdar and Nicholas Aroney, eds., *Sharia in the West* (Oxford: Oxford University Press, 2010), 239–254.

Blackstone, William, *Commentaries on the Laws of England*, 4 vols. (Oxford: Oxford University Press, 1765).

Boehmer von, Johann S.F., *Meditationes in Constitutionem Criminalem Carolinam* (Halle/ Madeburg: Impensis Vidvae Gebaveri et Filii, 1774).

Boele-Woekli, Katharina, et al., *De Juridische Status van Polygame Huwelijken in Rechtsvergleichend Perpsectief* (The Hague: Boom Jurdische Uitgevers, 2010).

Bonaventura, *Breviloquium*, Erwin Esser Nemmers, trans. (St. Louis, MO: B. Herder, 1946).

Boniface, *Die Briefe des heiligen Bonifatius et Lullus*, 2nd ed., M. Tangl, ed. (Berlin: Weidmannsche Verlagsbuchhandlung, 1955).

Borok, Helmut, *Der Tugenbegriff des Wilhelm von Auvergne (1180–1249)* (Düsseldorf: Patmos Verlag, 1979).

Boswell, John, *Christianity, Social Tolerance, and Homosexuality: Gay People in Western Europe from the Beginning of the Christian Era to the Fourteenth Century* (Chicago: University of Chicago Press, 1980).

Boswell, John, *Same Sex Unions in Premodern Europe* (New York: Villard Books, 1994).

Botting, Eileen Hunt, *Wollstonecraft, Mill and Women's Human Rights* (New Haven, CT: Yale University Press, 2016).

Boyd, Marion, Office of Canadian Attorney General, "Dispute Resolution in Family Law, Protecting Choice, Promoting Inclusion" (2004), http://www.attorneygeneral.jus.gov .on.ca/english/about/pubs/body/fullreport.pdf.

Boyer, Richard, *Lives of the Bigamists: Marriage, Family, and Community in Colonial Mexico* (Albuquerque: University of New Mexico Press, 1995).

Bracton on the Law and Customs of England, 4 vols., Samuel E. Thorne, trans. and ed. (Cambridge, MA: Belknap Press, 1968–1977).

Bradley, Martha Sonntag, *Kidnapped From That Land: The Government Raids on the Short Creek Polygamists* (Salt Lake City: University of Utah Press, 1993).

Brandt, Lillian, *Five Hundred and Seventy-Four Deserters and their Families* (New York: The Charity Organization Society, 1905).

Breitenach, Edgar, "The Tree of Bigamy and the Veronica Image of St. Peter's," *Art Institute of Chicago Museum Studies* 9 (1978): 30–38.

Bretschneider, Peter, *Polygyny: A Cross Cultural Study* (Uppsala: Almquist and Wiksell International, 1995).

Brett, Annabel S., *Liberty, Right, and Nature: Individual Rights in Later Scholastic Thought* (Cambridge: Cambridge University Press, 1997).

Brewer, David Instone, "Jesus's Old Testament Basis for Monogamy," in Steve Moyise and J.L. North, eds., *The Old Testament in the New Testament* (Sheffield: Sheffield Academic Press, 2000), 75–105.

Brewer, J.S., J. Gairdner, and R.H. Brodie, eds., *Letters and Papers, Foreign and Domestic of the Reign of Henry VIII*, 21 vols., 2nd. ed. (London: Her Majesty's Stationery Office, 1862–1920).

Bristol, Elizabeth Chudleigh, *The Laws Respecting Women: As They Regard Their Natural Rights* (London: J. Johnson, 1776).

Brooke, Christopher L., *The Medieval Idea of Marriage* (Oxford: Oxford University Press, 1989).

Brooke, James, "Utah Struggles with a Revival of Polygamy," *New York Times* (August 23, 1998): sec.1, p. 12.

Brooks, Thom, "The Problem with Polygamy," *Philosophical Topics* 37 (2009): 109–122.

Brown, Elizabeth Gaspar and William W. Blume, *British Statutes in American Law, 1776–1836*, repr. ed. (New York: DeCapo Press, 1974).

Browne, Thomas, *Religio Medici & Other Writings of Sir Thomas Browne* (London: J.M. Dent & Co., 1906).

Browning, Don S., "A Natural Law Theory of Marriage," *Zygon* 46 (2011): 733–760.

"The Family and Christian Jurisprudence," in John Witte, Jr. and Frank S. Alexander, eds., *Christianity and Law: An Introduction* (Cambridge: Cambridge University Press, 2010), 163–184.

"A Natural Law Theory of Marriage," *Zygon* 46 (2011): 733–760.

Browning, Don S. and John Witte, Jr., *From Contract to Covenant: What Christianity Offers Modern Marriage Law* (forthcoming).

Broyde, Michael J., "Jewish Law and the Abandonment of Marriage: Diverse Models of Sexuality and Reproduction in the Jewish View, and the Return to Monogamy in the Modern Era," in Michael J. Broyde and Michael Ausubel, eds., *Marriage, Sex, and Family in Judaism* (Lanham, MD: Rowman & Littlefield, 2005), 88–115.

Broyde, Michael J. and Michael Ausubel, eds., *Marriage, Sex, and Family in Judaism* (Lanham, MD: Rowman & Littlefield, 2005).

Bruckner, Hieronymous, *Decisiones Iuris Matrimonialis Controversi* (Gotha: Sumptibus Jacobi Medivi, 1724).

Brundage, James A., "Implied Consent to Intercourse," in Angeliki E. Laiou, ed., *Consent and Coercion to Sex and Marriage in Ancient and Medieval Societies* (Washington, DC: Dumbarton Research Library and Collection, 1993), 245–256.

Law, Sex, and Christian Society in Medieval Europe (Chicago: University of Chicago Press, 1987).

"The Merry Widow's Serious Sister: Remarriage in Classical Canon Law," in Robert R. Edwards and Vickie Ziegler, eds., *Matrons and Marginal Women in Medieval Society* (Woodbridge, Suffolk: The Boydell Press, 1995), 33–48.

Brussman, Johannes, *Monogamia Victrix: a Criminationibus vindicata quibusvis* (Frankfurt am Main: n.p., 1679).

Brydall, John, *Lex Spuriorum or the Law Related to Bastardy Collected from the Common, Civil, and Ecclesiastical Laws* (London: Assigns of Richard and Edward Atkins, 1703).

Buck, Thomas H.W., "From Big Love to the Big House: Justifying Anti-Polygamy Laws in an Age of Expanding Rights," *Emory International Law Review* 26 (2012): 939–996.

Buckley, Thomas E., *The Great Catastrophe of My Life: Divorce in the Old Dominion* (Chapel Hill: University of North Carolina Press, 2002).

Buisson, Ludwig, "Die Entstehung des Kirchenrechts," *Zeitschrift der Savigny-Stiftung für Rechtsgeschichte (Kanonistische Abteilung)* 52 (1966): 1–175.

Burlamaqui, Jean Jacques, *The Principles of Natural and Politic Law*, Thomas Nugent, trans. (Indianapolis, IN: Liberty Fund, 2006 [1747]).

Bullard, V. and H. Chalmer Bell, eds., *Lyndwood's Provinciale: The Text of the Canons Therein Contained*, reprinted from the translation made in 1534 (London: The Faith Press, 1929).

Burn, Richard, *Ecclesiastical Law*, 8th ed., 4 vols. (London: A. Strahan, 1824).

Burnet, Gilbert, *Two Dissertations Written by the Late Bishop Burnet, viz., I. A Defence of Polygamy. Proving that it is not Contrary to the Law and Nature of Marriage and that an Express Prohibition of it is No where to be found in Scripture*, 3rd ed. (London: E. Curlll, 1731 [1670]).

Burns, Robert I., ed., *Las Siete partidas*, 5 vols., Samuel Parsons Scott, trans. (Philadelphia: University of Pennsylvania Press, 2001).

Burton, Francis J., *A Commentary on Canon 1125 Together with a History of the Legislation Contained in the Canon* (Washington, DC: Catholic University of America Press, 1940).

Bury, John B., *The Idea of Progress* (London: MacMillan and Company, 1921).

Butler, John, *The True State of the Case of John Butler . . . of a Lawful Concubinage in a Case of Necessity* (London: s.n., 1697).

Butler, Sara, "Runaway Wives: Husband Desertion in Medieval England," *Journal of Social History* 40 (2006): 337–359.

Bynum, Caroline Walker, *Jesus as Mother: Studies in the Spirituality of the High Middle Ages* (Berkeley/Los Angeles: University of California Press, 1982).

Cairncross, John, *After Polygamy was Made a Sin: A Social History of Christian Polygamy* (London: Kegan and Paul, 1974).

Cajetan, Tommaso de Vio, *Ad serenissimum Angliae regem fideique defensorem Henricum ius nominis octavum: de coniugio cum relicta fratis sententiae. De coniugio regis Angliae cum relicta fratis sui* (Rome: Anton. Bladi Asulani, 1535).

Cajetan Responds: A Reader in Reformation Controversy, Jared Wicks, ed. (Eugene: Wipf & Stock, 2011).

Omnia Opera Quotquot Sacrae Scripturae Expositionem Repuriuntur, 5 vols. (Hildesheim/ New York: Olms, 2005).

Caldwell, Christopher, *Reflections on the Revolution in Europe: Immigration, Islam, and the West* (New York: Doubleday, 2009).

Calhoun, Cheshire, "Who's Afraid of Polygamous Marriage? *San Diego Law Review* 42 (2005): 1023–1044.

Calvin, John, *Ioannis Calvini opera quae supersunt omnia*, G. Baum, et al., eds., 59 vols. (Brunswick: 1863–1900).

The Institutes of the Christian Religion [1559], John T. McNeill, trans., Ford Lewis Battles, ed., 2 vols. (Philadelphia: Westminster Press, 1960).

Sermons sur la Genèse, Max Engammarre, ed., 2 vols. (Neukirchen-Vluyn: Neukirchener Verlag, 2000).

Camparia, Giovanni and Olivia Salimbeni, *Marriage as Immigration Gate: The Situation of Female Marriage Migrants from Third Countries to EU Member States* (Berlin: Berlin Institute for Comparative Social Research, 2004).

Campbell, Angela, "Bountiful's Plural Marriages," *International Journal of Law in Context* 6 (2010): 343–361.

"Bountiful Voices," *Osgoode Hall Law Journal* 47 (2009): 183–234.

Sister Wives, Surrogates, and Sex Workers: Outlaws by Choice? (Farnham, Surrey: Ashgate, 2013).

Campbell, Angela, Katherine Duvall-Antonacopoulos, Leslie MacRae, Joanne J. Paetsch, Martha Bailey, Beverley Baines, Bita Amani, and Amy Kaufman, *Polygamy in Canada: Legal and Social Implications for Women and Children – A Collection of Policy Research Reports* (Ottawa: Status of Women Canada, 2005).

Capp, Bernard, "Bigamous Marriage in Early Modern England," *The History Journal* 52 (2009): 537–556.

England's Culture Wars: Puritan Reformation and its Enemies in the Interregnum, 1649–1660 (Oxford: Oxford University Press, 2012).

When Gossips Meet: Women, Family, and Neighborhood in Early Modern England (Oxford: Oxford University Press, 2003).

Cardwell, Edward, ed., *Synodalia: A Collection of Articles of Religion, Canons, and Proceedings of Convocations in the Province of Canterbury*, 2 vols. (Oxford: University Press, 1842).

Carlson, Eric Josef, *Marriage and the English Reformation* (Oxford: Blackwell, 1994).

Carter, Sara, *The Importance of Being Monogamous: Marriage and Nation Building in Western Canada to 1915* (Edmonton: University of Alberta Press, 2008).

Carvallo, Paulino Campbell, *El delito de bigamia ante la jurisprudencia de los tribunales chilenos* (Santiago: Universidad de Chile, 1948).

The Cases of Polygamy, Concubinage, Adultery, and Divorce (London: E. Curli, T. Payne, J. Chrichley, and J. Jackson, 1732).

Cassirer, Ernst, *The Philosophy of the Enlightenment*, Fritz C.A. Koelln and James P. Pettegrove, trans., repr. ed. (Princeton, NJ: Princeton University Press, 2009).

Cats, Jacob, et al., *Patriarcha bigamos* (Rudolphopoli: [s.n.], 1821).

Cassirer, Ernst, *The Problem of Knowledge: Philosophy, Science, and History Since Hegel*, William H. Woglom and Charles W. Hendel, trans. (New Haven, CT: Yale University Press, 1950).

Cere, Daniel, "Canada's Conjugal Mosaic: From Multiculturalism to Multi-Conjugalism?" in Joel A. Nichols, ed., *Marriage and Divorce in a Multicultural Context: Multi-Tiered Marriage and the Boundaries of Civil Law and Religion* (Cambridge/New York: Cambridge University Press, 2012), 284–308.

Chambers, David L., "Polygamy and Same-Sex Marriage," *Hofstra Law Review* 26 (1997): 53–83.

Chapais, Bernard, *Primeval Kinship: How Pair-Bonding Gave Birth to Human Society* (Cambridge, MA: Harvard University Press, 2008).

Charke, William, *A Treatise Against the Defense of the Censure* (Cambridge: Thomas Thomas, 1586).

Charlesworth, James H., et al., eds., *The Dead Sea Scrolls; Hebrew, Aramaic, and Greek Texts, with English Translations*, 4 vols. (Tübingen: Mohr Siebeck/Louisville, KY: Westminster John Knox Press, 1997).

Charlsley, Katharine and Anika Liversage, "Transforming Polygamy: Migration, Transnationalism and Multiple Marriages Among Muslim Minorities," *Global Networks* 13 (2013): 60–78.

Charron, Pierre, *Of Wisdom*, George Stanhope, trans. (London: J. Tonson, et al., 1729 [1608]).

Charter To William Penn, And Laws Of The Province Of Pennsylvania, Passed Between The Years 1682 and 1700 (Harrisburg, PA: Lane S. Hart, 1879).

Chitty, Joseph, *A Practical Treatise of the Criminal Law*, 5 vols., repr. edn. (New York: Garland Press, 1978 [1816]).

Choisy, Eugène, *L'État chrétien calviniste a Genève au temps de Théodore de Bèze* (Geneva: C. Eggimann & cie, 1902).

Chrysostom, John, *A Comparison between a King and a Monk/Against the Opponents of the Monastic Life: Two Treatises by John Chrysostom*, David G. Hunter, trans. (Lewiston, NY: Edwin Mellen Press, 1988)

  Homilies on Genesis, trans Robert C. Hill, 3 vols. (Washington, DC: The Catholic University of America Press, 1992).

  On Virginity. Against Remarriage, Sally R. Shore, trans. (Lewiston, NY: Edwin Mellen Press, 1982).

  St. John Chrysostom On Marriage and Family Life, Catherine P. Roth and David Anderson, trans. (Crestwood, NY: St. Vladimir's Seminary Press, 1986).

Chuchiak, John F. IV, ed., *The Inquisition in New Spain, 1536–1820: A Documentary History* (Baltimore, MD: John Hopkins University Press, 2012).

Chused, Richard H., *Private Acts in Public Places: A Social History of Divorce in the Formative Era of American Family Law* (Philadelphia: University of Pennsylvania Press, 1994).

Cicero, Marcus Tullius, *De Oratore*, 2nd ed., E.M.P. Moor, trans. (London, Methuen and Company, 1904).

Clark, G., "Human Monogamy," *Science* 282 (1998): 1047–1048.

Clarke, Franciscus, *Praxis Francisci Clarke omnibus qui in foro ecclesia* (Dublin: Nathanielem Thompson, 1666).

Cleaver, Robert, *A [G]odly Form of Householde Gouernment* (London: Thomas Creede, 1598).

Clement of Alexandria, Stromateis, Books One to Three, John Ferguson, trans. (Washington, DC: Catholic University of America Press, 1991).

Clignet, Remi, *Many Wives, Many Powers: Authority and Power in Polygynous Families* (Evanston, IL: Northwestern University Press, 1970).

Code of Laws for the District of Columbia, Prepared Under the Authority of the Congress of the
    29th of April, 1816 (Washington, DC: Davis & Force, 1819).
Codex Theodosianus, Paul Krüger, ed. 2 vols. (Berlin: Weidmann, 1923–1926).
Cohen, Jeremy, ed., Essential Papers on Judaism and Christianity in Conflict: From Late
    Antiquity to the Reformation (New York: New York University Press, 1991).
Cohn, Norman, The Pursuit of the Millennium (Oxford: Oxford University Press, 1970).
Coke, Sir Edward, The First Part of the Institutes of the Law of England, 1st American ed.
    (Philadelphia: Robert H. Small, 1853).
    The Second Part of the Institutes of the Lawes of England (London: Societie of
    Stationers, 1628).
    The Third Part of the Institutes of the Lawes of England (London: M., Flesher, 1644).
Colecci, Marino Aldo, Il delitto di bigamia (Naples: Jovene, 1958).
The Collection in Seventy-Four Titles: A Canon Law Manual of the Gregorian Reform
    (Toronto: Pontifical Institute of Medieval Studies, 1980).
Collins, John J., "Marriage, Divorce, and Family in Second Temple Judaism," in Leo G.
    Perdue, et al., Families in Ancient Israel (Louisville, KY: Westminster John Knox Press,
    1997), 104–162.
The Colonial Laws Of New York From The Year 1664 To The Revolution, 5 vols. (Albany,
    NY: James B. Lyon, 1896).
Colvin, John B., Magistrate's Guide and Citizen's Counsellor Being a Digest of those Laws of
    Maryland Most Necessary to Be Known (Fredericktown, MD: n.p., 1805).
Comyns, John, A Digest of the Laws of England, 5 vols. (London: H. Woodfall, 1762–1767).
Connolly, Hugo, The Irish Penitentials and Their Significance for the Sacrament of Penance
    Today (Dublin: Four Courts Press, 1995).
Cook, Alexandra Parma and Noble David Cook, Good Faith and Truthful Ignorance: A Case
    of Transatlantic Bigamy (Durham, NC: Duke University Press, 1991).
Cookson, James, Thoughts on Polygamy Suggested by the Dictates of Scripture, Nature,
    Reason, and Common-Sense (Winchester: J. Wilkes, 1782).
Cooley, Thomas M., A Treatise on the Constitutional Limitations which Rest Upon the
    Legislative Power of the States of the American Union, 3rd ed. (Boston: Little Brown, 1874).
Coons, John E. and Patrick M. Brennan, By Nature Equal: The Anatomy of a Western Insight
    (Princeton, NJ: Princeton University Press, 1999).
Coppe, Abiezer, A Second Fiery Flying Roule: To all the Inhabitants of the Earth, Specially
    the Rich Ones (London: s.n., 1649).
Corpus Iuris Civilis, Paul Krüger, ed. (Berlin: Weidmann, 1928–1929).
Cortest, Luis, The Disfigured Face: Traditional Natural Law and Its Encounter with Modernity
    (New York: Fordham University Press, 2008).
Cott, Nancy F., The Bonds of Womanhood: "Woman's Sphere" in New England, 1780–1835
    (New Haven, CT: Yale University Press, 1977).
    "Divorce and the Changing Status of Women in Eighteenth-Century Massachusetts,"
    William and Mary Quarterly, 3rd ser. 33 (1976): 586–614.
    "Eighteenth Century Family and Social Life Revealed in Massachusetts Divorce Records,"
    Journal of Social History 10 (1976): 20–43.
    Public Vows: A History of Marriage and the Nation (Cambridge, MA: Harvard University
    Press, 2000).
Cowley, Arthur E., ed., Aramaic Papyri of the Fifth Century, B.C. (Osnabruck: Otto
    Zeller, 1967).

Cranmer, Thomas, *Miscellaneous Writings and Letters of Thomas Cranmer*, John E. Cox, ed. (London: The Parker Society, 1843).

Cretney, Stephen, *Family Law in the Twentieth Century: A History* (Oxford: Oxford University Press, 2005).

Cristellon, Cecilia and Silvana Seidel Menchi, "Rituals Before Tribunals in Renaissance Italy: Continuity and Change, 1400–1600, in Mia Korpiola, ed., *Regional Variations in Matrimonial Law and Custom in Europe, 1150–1600* (Leiden/Boston: Brill, 2011), 275–287.

Crouzel, Henri, *L'eglise primitive face au divorce du premier au cinquieme siècles* (Paris: Beauchesne, 1971).

D'Avray, David L., *Medieval Marriage: Symbolism and Society* (Oxford: Oxford University Press, 2005).

  Medieval Religious Rationalities: A Weberian Analysis (Cambridge: Cambridge University Press, 2010).

D'Ewes, Simonds and Paul Bowles, *The Journals of all the Parliaments of the Reign of Queen Elizabeth*, rev. ed. (London: John Starkey, 1682).

Daly, James, *Sir Robert Filmer and English Political Thought* (Toronto: University of Toronto Press, 1979).

Damhouder, Jodocus, *Praxis rerum criminalium: Gründlicher Bericht und Anweisung, Welchermassen in Rechtfärtigung peinlicher sachen nach gemeynen beschribenen Rechten … zu behandeln* (Frankfurt am Main: Joh. Wolff, 1555).

Damiani, Peter, *Die Briefe des Petrus Damiani*, K. Reindel, ed., 2 vols. (Munich: Monumenta Germaniae Historica, 1983).

Dane, Nathan, *General Abridgement and Digest of American Law*, 8 vols. (Boston: Cummins, Hilliard, & Co., 1824).

Dasent, J.R., ed., *Acts of the Privy Council*, 32 vols. (London: Eyre and Spottiswoode, 1890–1907).

David, N., "Crusades and Propaganda," in K.M. Setton, ed. *A History of the Crusades*, 6 vols. (Madison: University of Wisconsin Press, 1989).

Davis, Adrienne D., "Regulating Polygamy: Intimacy, Default Rules, and Bargaining for Equality," *Columbia Law Review* 110 (2010): 1955–2046.

Davis, Peggy Cooper, *Neglected Stories: The Constitution and Family Values* (New York: Hill and Wang, 1998).

Dean, Trevor, "A Regional Cluster? Italian Secular Laws on Abduction, Forced, and Clandestine Marriage (Fourteenth and Fifteenth Centuries)," in Mia Korpiola, ed., *Regional Variations in Matrimonial Law and Custom in Europe, 1150–1600* (Leiden/Boston: Brill, 2011), 147–159.

Delaney, Patrick, pseud. *Phileleutherus Dubliniensis, Reflections Upon Polygamy and the Encouragement Given to that Practice in the Old Testament* (London: J. Roberts, 1734).

Demos, John, *A Little Commonwealth: Family Life in Plymouth County* (New York: Oxford University Press, 1970).

Den Otter, Ronald, "Is There Really Any Good Argument Against Plural Marriage?" (http://works.bepress.com/cgi/viewcontent.cgi?article=1000&context=ronald_den_otter).

Denike, Margaret, "The Racialization of White Man's Polygamy," *Hypatia* 25 (2010): 852–874.

Denzinger, Heinrich, *The Sources of Catholic Dogma*, 30th ed., Roy J. Deferrari, trans. (St. Louis, MO: B. Herder, 1957).

Desty, Robert, *A Compendium of American Criminal Law* (San Francisco, CA: S. Whitney, 1882).

Dibdin, Lewis, *English Church Law and Divorce* (London: J. Murray, 1912).

The Digest of Justinian, 4 vols., Theodor Mommsen and Paul Krueger, eds., Alan Watson, trans. (Philadelphia: University of Pennsylvania Press, 1985).

Digest of the Laws of the State of Georgia (Milledgeville, GA: Grantland & Orme, 1822).

Digges, Dudley, *The Unlawfulnesse of Subjects taking Up Armes Against Their Soveraigne* (s.l., s.n., 1644).

Divi Clementis Recognitionum Libri X (Basel: Bebel, 1526).

Dixon-Spears, Patricia, *We Want for Our Sisters What We Want for Ourselves: African-American Women Who Practice Polygyny by Consent* (Baltimore, MD: Imprint Editions, 2009).

Doddridge, John and Thomas Edgar, *The Lavves Resolutions of Womens Rights: or, The Lavves Prouision for Women* (London: John More Esq., 1632).

Doernberg, Erwin, *Luther and Henry VIII* (Palo Alto, CA: Stanford University Press, 1961).

Doherty, Dennis, *The Sexual Doctrine of Cardinal Cajetan* (Regensburg: F. Pustet, 1966).

Donahue, Charles, *Law, Marriage, and Society in the Later Middle Ages: Arguments About Marriage in Five Courts* (Cambridge: Cambridge University Press, 2007).

Dorff, Elliott A. and Arthur Rosett, *A Living Tree: The Roots and Growth of Jewish Law* (Albany: State University of New York Press, 1988).

Driggs, Ken, "After the Manifesto: Modern Polygamy and Fundamentalist Mormons," *Journal of Church and State* 32 (1990): 367–389.

Duncan, Emily J., "The Positive Effects of Legalizing Polygamy; 'Love is a Many Splendored Thing,'" *Duke Journal of Gender Law and Policy* 15 (2008): 315–337.

Durandus, Guillaume, *The Rationale Divinorum Officiorum of William Durand of Mende*, Timothy M. Thibodeau, ed. (New York: Columbia University Press, 2007).

Durham, W. Cole, Jr. and Brett G. Scharffs, *Law and Religion: National, International, and Comparative Perspectives* (New York: Aspen Publishers, 2010).

Dwight, S.E., *The Hebrew Wife: or The Law of Marriage Examined in Relation to The Lawfulness of Polygamy and ... Incest* (New York: Leavitt, Lord & Co., 1836).

Eastwood, C. Cyrill, *The Royal Priesthood of the Faithful: An Investigation of the Doctrine from Biblical Times to the Reformation* (Minneapolis, MN: Augsburg Press, 1963).

Eberle, Chris, *Religious Conviction in Liberal Politics* (Cambridge/New York: Cambridge University Press, 2002).

Eck, Ioannes, *Enchiridion Locorum Adversus Lutherium, et alios hostes Ecclesiae* (Louvain: Theobaldum Paganum, 1561).

Edwards, J.L.J., "Mens rea and Bigamy," *Current Legal Problems* 2 (1949): 47–67.

Eells, Hastings, *The Attitude of Martin Bucer Toward the Bigamy of Philip of Hesse* (New Haven, CT: Yale University Press, 1924).

Egan, Timothy, "The Persistence of Polygamy," *New York Times Magazine* (February 28, 1999): 51–55.

Ehler, Sidney Z. and John B. Morrall, *Church and State through the Centuries: A Collection of Historic Documents with Commentaries* (Westminster, MD: Newman Press, 1954).

Eisenman, Robert, *James the Brother of Jesus: The Key to Unlocking the Secrets of Early Christianity and the Dead Sea Scrolls* (New York: Viking Books, 1997).

Eldorado Investigation: A Report from the Texas Department of the Family and Protection Services (December 22, 2008), at http://www.dfps.state.tx.us/documents/about/pdf/2008-12-22_Eldorado.pdf.

Elon, Menachem, *Jewish Law: History, Sources, Principles*, trans. Bernard Auerbach and Melvin J. Skyes, 4 vols. (Philadelphia/Jerusalem: The Jewish Publication Society, 1994).

Emens, Elizabeth F., "Monogamy's Law: Compulsory Monogamy and Polyamorous Existence," *New York University Review of Law and Social Change* 29 (2004): 277–376.

Engel, Ludovici, *Universi juris canonici*, 4th ed. (Venice: Jacob Hertz, 1593).

Engels, Frederick, *The Origin of the Family, Private Property, and the State [1884]*, Ernest Untermann, trans. (Chicago: Charles H. Kerr and Co., 1902).

Epstein, Louis M., *Marriage Laws in the Bible and the Talmud* (Cambridge, MA: Harvard University Press, 1942).

Erasmus of Rotterdam, The Institution of Christian Matrimony (1526), in *Collected Works of Erasmus: Spiritualia and Pastoralia*, ed. John W. O'Malley and Louis A. Perraud (Toronto: University of Toronto Press, 1999).

Erdman, Walter, *Die Ehe im alten Griechenland*, repr. ed. (New York: Arno Press, 1979 [1934]).

Erickson, Arvel B. and Fr. John R. McCarthy, "The Yelverton Case: Civil Legislation and Marriage," *Victorian Studies* 14 (1971): 275–291.

Ertman, Marta, "Race Treason: The Untold Story of America's Ban on Polygamy," *Columbia Journal of Gender and Law* 19 (2010): 287–366.

Eskridge, William N., Jr., "Challenging the Apartheid of the Closet: Establishing Conditions for Lesbian and Gay Intimacy, Nomos, and Citizenship, 1961–1981," *Hofstra Law Review* 25 (1996-1997): 817–970.

Esmein, Adhemar, *Le mariage en droit canonique*, 2 vols., repr. ed. (New York: Burt Franklin, 1968).

Esposito, Anna, "Adulterio, concubinato, bigamia: testimonianze della normativa statuturia della Stato pontificio (secoli XIII-XVI)," in Silvana Seidel Menchi and Deigo Quaglioni, eds., *Trasgessioni: Seduzione, concubinato, adulterio, bigamia (XIV-XVIII secolo)* (Bologna: Il Mulino, 2004), 21–42.

Estin, Ann Lacquer, "Unofficial Family Law," in Joel A. Nichols, ed., *Marriage and Divorce in a Multicultural Context: Multi-Tiered Marriage and the Boundaries of Civil Law and Religion* (Cambridge/New York: Cambridge University Press, 2012), 92–119.

Evans, G.R. and Philipp W. Rosemann, eds., *Mediaeval Commentaries on the Sentences of Peter Lombard*, 2 vols. (Leiden: Brill, 2002, 2010).

The Extraordinary and Singular Law-Case of Joseph Parker who was Indicted as Thomas Hoag alias dictus Joseph Parker for Bigamy at the Court of Oyer and Terminer, held in the City of New York (Baltimore, MD: G. Keatinge's Bookstore, 1808).

Faces Augustae: sive poemeta (Dordrecht: Sumptibus Matthiae Havii & typis Henrici Essaie, 1643).

Fadel, Mohammed H., "Political Liberalism, Islamic Family Law, and Family Law Pluralism," in Joel A. Nichols, ed., *Marriage and Divorce in a Multicultural Context: Multi-Tiered Marriage and the Boundaries of Civil Law and Religion* (Cambridge/New York: Cambridge University Press, 2012), 164–199.

Falk, Ze'ev W., *Jewish Matrimonial Law in the Middle Ages* (Oxford: Oxford University Press, 1966).

Fasoli, Gina and Pietro Sella, *Statuti di Bologna dell'anno 1288*, 2 vols. (Vatican City: Biblioteca apostolica vaticana, 1937–1939).

Faulkner, John A., "Luther and the Bigamous Marriage of Philip of Hesse," *The American Journal of Theology* 17 (1913): 206–231.

Feldbrugge, F.J.M., "Criminal Law and Traditional Society: The Role of Soviet Law in the Integration of Non-Slavic Peoples," *Review of Socialist Law* 3 (1977): 3–51.

Feuerbach, Paul Johann Anselm von, *Lehrbuch des gemeinen in Deutschland geltenden peinlichen Rechts* (Giessen: G.F. Heyer, 1801).

Filmer, Robert, *Patriarcha and other Political Works*, Peter Laslett, ed. (Oxford: Oxford University Press, 1949).

Fineman, Martha A., "Beyond Identities: The Limits of an Antidiscrimination Approach to Equality," *Boston University Law Review* 92 (2012): 1713–1770.

"The Vulnerable Subject and the Responsive State," *Emory Law Journal* 60 (2010): 251–275.

Finkelstein, Louis, *Jewish Self-Government In the Middle Ages* (Westport, CT: Greenwood Press, 1972).

Firmage, Edwin Brown and R. Collin Mangrum, *Zion in the Courts: A Legal History of the Church of Jesus Christ of Latter-Day Saints*, pbk. ed. (Champaign/Urbana: University of Illinois Press, 2001).

Fletcher, Catherine, *The Divorce of Henry VIII: The Untold Story from Inside the Vatican* (New York: Palgrave MacMillan, 2012).

Foblets, Marie-Claire, et al., eds., *Islam & Europe: Crises are Challenges* (Leuven: UPL in Context, 2010).

Foner, Eric, *Free Soil, Free Labor, Free Men: The Ideology of the Republican Party Before the Civil War* (Oxford: Oxford University Press, 1995).

Foreman, Amanda, "Valentine's Revenge," *Smithsonian* (February, 2014): 29–31, 102.

Foster, Frances Smith, *Love & Marriage in Early African American* (Hanover, NH: University Press of New England, 2008).

"Til Death or Distance Do Us Part": Love and Marriage in African America (New York/Oxford: Oxford University Press, 2010).

Fouracre, Paul, "The Long Shadow of the Merovingians," in Joanna Story, ed., *Charlemagne: Empire and Society* (Manchester: Manchester University Press, 2003), 5–20.

Fowell, Frank and Frank Palmer, *Censorship in England* (New York: Barnes and Noble Digital Library, 2011).

Friedberg, Emil, ed., *Corpus Iuris Canonici* (Leipzig: Bernard Tauchnitz, 1879).

Friedl, Raimund, *Der Konkubinat im kaiserlichen Rom: von Augustus bis Septimus Severus* (Stuttgart: F. Steiner, 1996).

Friedman, Lawrence M., *Crime and Punishment in American History* (New York: Basic Books, 1993).

"Crimes of Mobility," *Stanford Law Review* 43 (1991): 637–658.

Friedman, Mordechai A., *Jewish Marriage in Palestine*, 2 vols. (New York: Jewish Theological Seminary, 1980).

"The Monogamy Clause in Jewish Marriage Contracts," *Perspectives in Jewish Learning* 4 (1972): 20–40.

"Polygyny in Jewish Tradition and Practice: New Sources from the Cairo Geniza," *Proceedings of the American Academy for Jewish Research* 49 (1982): 33–68.

Gaca, Kathy L., "The Pentateuch or Plato: Two Competing Paradigms of Christian Sexual Morality in the Second Century CE," in Amy J. Levine and Maria Mayo Robbins, eds., *A Feminist Companion to Patristic Literature* (Edinburgh: T & T Clark, 2008), 125–136.

Gamble, Richard C., ed., *Articles on Calvin and Calvinism*, 14 vols. (New York/London: Garland Publishing, 1992).

Gaudreault-Desbiens, Jean-François, "Religious Courts, Personal Federalism, and Legal Transplants," in Rex Ahdar and Nicholas Aroney, eds., *Sharia in the West* (Oxford: Oxford University Press, 2010), 59–70.

Gaustad, Edwin S., Philip L. Barlow, and Richard W. Dishno, *New Historical Atlas of Religion in America* (Oxford: Oxford University Press, 2001).

Gerhard, Johannes, *Loci Theologici … Tomus Septimus, De Conjugio* (Jena: Typis & Sumptibus Tobiae Steinmanni, 1657).

Geisendorf, Paul, *Théodore de Bèze* (Geneva: Droz, 1967).

Gellius, Aulus, *The Attic Nights of Aulus Gellius* (Cambridge, MA: Harvard University Press/ Loeb Classical Library, 1961).

George, Robert P., *In Defense of Natural Law* (Oxford: Oxford University Press, 1999).

Gereboff, J.D., *Rabbi Tarfon: The Tradition, the Man, and Early Judaism* (Missoula, MT: Scholars Press for Brown University, 1979).

Gher, Jaime M., "Polygamy and Same-Sex Marriage: Allies or Adversaries Within the Same-Sex Marriage Movement," *William and Mary Journal of Women and the Law* 14 (2008): 559–603.

Gil, Johannes, ed., *Corpus Scriptorum Muzarabicorum*, 2 vols. (Madrid: Consejo superior de investigaciones scientíficas, 1973).

Gilfoye, Timothy J., "The Hearts of Nineteenth-Century Men: Bigamy and Working-Class Marriage in New York City, 1800–1890," *Prospects* 19 (1994): 135–160.

Girgis, Sherif, Ryan T. Anderson, and Robert P. George, *What is Marriage? Man and Woman: A Defense* (New York: Encounter Books, 2012).

Godolphin, John, *Repertorium Canonicum*, 3rd ed. (London: Assigns of R. & E. Atkins, 1687).

Goldfeder, Mark A., "Chains of Love in Law: Revisiting Plural Marriage" (SJD Thesis, Emory University, 2013).

"The Story of Jewish Polygamy," *Columbia Journal of Law and Gender* 26 (2014): 234–315.

Gordley, James, *The Philosophical Origins of Modern Contract Doctrine* (Oxford: Oxford University Press, 1991).

Gordon, James, *A Treatise on the Unwritten Word of God, Commonly Called Traditions*, William Wright, trans. (Saint Omer: English College Press, 1614).

Gordon, Sarah Barringer, *The Mormon Question: Polygamy and Constitutional Conflict in Nineteenth-Century America* (Chapel Hill: University of North Carolina Press, 2002).

"'The Twin Relic of Barbarism' A Legal History of Anti-Polygamy in Nineteenth-Century America" (Ph.D. Diss., Princeton, 1995).

Gottlieb, Claire, "Varieties of Marriage in the Bible and Their Analogues in the Ancient World" (Ph.D. Diss. New York University, 1989).

Gouge, William, *Of Domesticall Duties: Eight Treatises* (London: John Haviland, 1622).

Gouge, William and Thomas Gouge, *A Learned and Very Useful Commentary on the Whole Epistles to the Hebrews* (London: Joshua Kirten, 1655).

Goyena, José Iureta, *Delitos de aborto, bigamia y abandon de niños y de ostras personas incapaces* (Montevideo: Casa A. Barreiro y Ramos, 1932).

Grabill, Stephen, *Rediscovering the Natural Law in Reformed Theological Ethics* (Grand Rapids, MI: Wm. B. Eerdmans, 2006).

Graham, Thomas, *A Marriage Sermon Called a Wife Mistaken* (London: s.n., 1710).

Gratian: The Treatise on Laws with the Ordinary Gloss, James Gordley and Augustine Thompson, O.P., trans. (Washington, DC: Catholic University of America Press, 1993).

Gray, P., "Ethnographic Atlas Codebook," *World Cultures* 10 (1998): 86–136.

Gray, Peter B. and Kermyt G. Anderson, *Fatherhood: Evolution and Human Paternal Behavior* (Cambridge, MA: Harvard University Press, 2010).

Graydon, William, *The Justices and Constables Assistant. Being a General Collection of Forms of Practice* (Harrisburg, PA: John Wyeth, 1805).

Grayzel, Solomon, *The Church and the Jews in the XIIIth Century*, 2 vols., repr. ed. (New York: Jewish Theological Seminary, 1989).

Great Britain, Law Commission, *Polygamous Marriages: Capacity to Contract a Polygamous Marriage and the Concept of the Potentially Polygamous Marriage* (London: Her Majesty's Secretery Office, 1982).

Greenidge, A.H.J., *Infamia in Roman Public and Private Law* (Oxford: Clarendon Press, 1894).

Gregory of Tours, *History of the Franks*, Louis Thorpe, trans. (Harmondsworth: Penguin, 1974).

Gresbeck, Heinrich and Carl Adolf Cornelius, *Berichte der Augenzeugen über das münsterische Wiedertäuferreich*, repr. ed. (Munster: Aschendorff, 1983 [1853]).

Griffith-Jones, Robin, ed., *Islam and English Law: Rights, Responsibilities and the Place of Shari'a* (Cambridge: Cambridge University Press, 2013).

Grimké, John F., *The South-Carolina Justice of Peace*, 3rd ed. (New York: T. & J. Swords, 1810).

Grisar, Hartmann, S.J., *Luther*, E. Lamond, trans., *Luigi Cappadelta*, ed., 6 vols. (London: Kegan Paul, 1913–1917).

Grossberg, Michael, *Governing the Hearth: Law and the Family in Nineteenth-Century America* (Chapel Hill: University of North Carolina Press, 1985).

Grossman, Avraham, "Ashkenazim to 1300," in N.S. Hecht, et al., eds., *An Introduction to the History and Sources of Jewish Law* (Oxford: Clarendon Press, 1996), 317–319.

"The Historical Background to the Ordinances on Family Affairs Attributed to Rabbenu Gershom Me'or ha-Golah ('The Light of the Exile')," in Ada Rapoport-Albert and Steven J. Zipperstein, eds., *Jewish History: Essays in Honour of Chimen Abramsky* (London: P. Halbam, 1988), 3–23.

Pious and Rebellious: Jewish Women in Medieval Europe, Jonathan Chipman, trans. (Waltham, MA: Brandeis University Press, 2004).

Grossman, Joanna and Lawrence M. Friedman, *Inside the Castle: Law and the Family in 20th Century America* (Princeton: Princeton University Press, 2011).

Grotius, Hugo, *Commentary on the Law of Prize and Booty*, Martine Julia van Ittersum, trans. and ed. (Indianapolis, IN: Liberty Fund, 2006).

De imperio summarum potestatum circa sacra, 4th ed. (The Hague: Adriani Vlacq., 1661).

De Jure Belli ac Pacis, Francis W. Kelsey, trans. (Oxford: Clarendon Press, 1925).

De veritate religionis Christianae (Oxford: William Hall, 1662).

Explicatio trium utilissimorum locurum N. Testamenti (Amsterdam: Joh. and Cornelium Blaev, 1640).

The Free Sea, Richard Hakluyt, trans., David Armitage, ed. (Indianapolis, IN: Liberty Fund, 2004).

Hugo Grotius on the Truth of Christianity, Spencer Madan, trans. (London: J. Dodsley, 1782).

Opera omnia theologica, 3 vols. (London: Mosem Pitt, 1679).

The Rights of War and Peace, Jean Barbeyrac, trans., Richard Tuck, ed. (Indianapolis, IN: Liberty Fund, 2005).

Grubbs, Judith Evans, "Christianization of Marriage? Christianity, Marriage, and Law in Late Antiquity," in Andreas Holzem and Ines Weber, eds., *Ehe-Familie-Verwandtschaft: Vergellschaftung in Religion und sozialer Lebeswelt* (Paderborn: Ferdinand Schönigh, 2008), 105–124.

Law and Family in Late Antiquity: The Emperor Constantine's Marriage Legislation (Oxford: Clarendon Press, 1995).

"Promoting Pietas in Roman Law," in Beryl Rawson, ed., *A Companion to Families in the Greek and Roman World* (Chicester: John Wiley & Sons, 2011), 377–392.

Women and the Law in the Roman Empire: A Sourcebook on Marriage, Divorce and Widowhood (London: Routledge, 2002).

Gunn, T. Jeremy and John Witte, Jr., eds., *No Establishment of Religion: America's Original Contribution to Religious Liberty* (Oxford: Oxford University Press, 2012).

Gutiérrez, Ramón, *When Jesus Came, The Corn Mothers Went Away: Marriage, Sexuality and Power in New Mexico, 1500–1846* (Stanford, CA: Stanford University Press, 1991).

Hagerty, Barbara Bradley, "Philly's Black Muslims Increasingly Turn to Polygamy, NPR (March 28, 2008), http://www.npr.org/templates/story/story.php?storyId=90886407.

Hale, Matthew, *Pleas of the Crown* (London: Richard Atkyns et al., 1678).

Hale, Matthew and Charles Runnington, *History of the Law*, 5th ed. (London: G.G. and J. Robinson, 1794).

Hale, William, *A Series of Precedents and Proceedings in Criminal Causes: Extending from the Year 1475 to 1640, Extracted from Act-Books of Ecclesiastical Courts in the Diocese of London* (London: F. & J. Rivington, 1847).

Hales, Brian G., *Joseph Smith's Polygamy*, 3 vols. (Salt Lake City, UT: Greg Kofford Books, 2013).

Hamilton, James Edward, *A Short Treatise on Polygamy, or, The Marrying and Cohabiting with more than one Woman at the Same Time, Proved from Scripture, to be Agreeable to the Will of God* (Dublin: n.p., 1786).

Hammond, Henry, *A Letter of Resolution to Six Quares of Present Use in the Church of England* (London: J. Flesher, 1653).

Hardy, Norman, "Papal Dispensations for Polygamy," *Dublin Review* 153 (1913): 266–274.

Harmer-Dionne, Elizabeth, "Once a Peculiar People: Cognitive Dissonance and the Suppression of Mormon Polygamy as a Case Study Negating the Belief-Action Distinction," *Stanford Law Review* 50 (1998): 1295–1347.

Harmon, Nolan B., *The Famous Case of Myra Clark Gaines* (Baton Rouge, LA: Louisiana State University Press, 1946).

Harrington, Joel, *Reordering Marriage and Society in Reformation Germany* (Cambridge: Cambridge University Press, 1995).

Hartley, T.E., ed., *Proceedings in the Parliaments of Elizabeth I*, 3 vols. (Wilmington, NC: M. Glazier, 1981–1995).

Hartog, Hendrik, *Man and Wife in America: A History* (Cambridge, MA: Harvard University Press, 2000).

"Marital Exits and Marital Expectations in Nineteenth-Century American," *Georgetown Law Journal* 80 (1991): 95–129.

Hatch, Nathan O., *The Democratization of American Christianity* (New Haven, CT: Yale University Press, 1989).

Hays, Richard, *The Moral Vision of the New Testament: A Contemporary Introduction to New Testament Ethics* (San Francisco, CA: HarperSanFrancisco, 1996).

H[eale], W[illiam], *An Apologie for Women, or Opposition to Mr. Dr. G. his Assertion . . . That it was Lawful for Husbands to Beate Their Wives* (Oxford: Joseph Barnes, 1609).

Hecht, N.S., et al., eds., *An Introduction to the History and Sources of Jewish Law* (Oxford: Clarendon Press, 1996).

Heeren, A.H.L., *Historical Researches in the Politics, Intercourse, and Trade of the Principal Nations of Antiquity*, 4 vols. (London: H.G. Bohn, 1846–1850).

Heering, J.P., *Hugo Grotius as Apologist for the Christian Religion* (Leiden: Brill, 2004).

Hefele, Karl Joseph von, *A History of the Councils of the Church, From the Original Documents*, 5 vols., repr. ed. (New York: AMS Press, 1972).

Heith-Stade, David, *Marriage as the Arena of Salvation: An Ecclesiological Study of the Marital Regulation in Canons of the Council of Trullo* (Rollinsford: Orthodox Research Institute, 2011).

"Marriage in the Canons of Trullo," *Studia Theologica* 64/2 (2010): 4–21.

Heidecker, Karl J., *The Divorce of Lothar II: Christian Marriage and Political Power in the Carolingian World* (Ithaca, NY: Cornell University Press, 2010).

Hellbach, Johann Christoph Theodor, *Selecta Criminalia eaque iam de Marito Hebraico Christiano, una uxore non contento* (Arnstadii: Schill, 1747).

Helmholz, R.H., "And Were There Children's Rights in Early Modern England? The Canon Law and 'Intra-family Violence' in England, 1400–1640," *International Journal of Children's Rights* 1 (1993): 23–32.

"Bastardy Litigation in Medieval England," *American Journal of Legal History* 13 (1969): 361–383.

"Children's Rights and the Canon Law: Law and Practice in Later Medieval England," *The Jurist* 67 (2007): 39–54.

"Human Rights in the Canon Law," in John Witte, Jr. and Frank S. Alexander, eds., *Christianity and Human Rights: An Introduction* (Cambridge: Cambridge University Press, 2010), 99–113.

"Marriage Contracts in Medieval England," in Philip L. Reynolds and John Witte, Jr., eds., *To Have and To Hold: Marrying and its Documentation in Western Christendom: 400–1600* (Cambridge: Cambridge University Press, 2007), 260–286.

Marriage Litigation in Medieval England (Cambridge: Cambridge University Press, 1974).

The Oxford History of the Laws of England: Volume 1, The Canon Law and Ecclesiastical Jurisdiction from 597 to the 1640s (Oxford: Oxford University Press, 2004).

The Spirit of the Classical Canon Law (Athens: University of Georgia Press, 1996).

"Western Canon Law," in John Witte, Jr. and Frank S. Alexander, eds., *Christianity and Law: An Introduction* (Cambridge: Cambridge University Press, 2008), 71–88.

Hening, W.W., ed., *The Statutes At Large Being A Collection Of All The Laws Of Virginia, From The First Session Of The Legislature, In The Year 1619*, 13 vols. (New York: R. &. W. & G. Bartow, 1823).

Henkin, Louis, et al., *Human Rights* (New York: Foundation Press, 1999).

Henning, W.W., *The New Virginia Justice*, 3rd ed. (Richmond, VA: J. & G. Cochran, 1820).

Heppe, Heinrich, "Urkundliche Beiträge zur Geschichte des Doppelehe des Landgrafen Philipp von Hessen," *Zeitschrift für historisches Theologie* 22 (1852): 263–283.

Herlihy, David, "The Family and Religious Ideologies in Medieval Europe," *Journal of Family History* 12 (1987): 3–17.

Medieval Households (Cambridge, MA: Harvard University Press, 1985).

Herman, Gerald, "The 'Sin Against Nature' and its Echoes in Medieval French Literature," *Annuale Mediaevale* 17 (1976): 70–87.

Hess, Hamilton, *The Early Development of Canon Law and the Council of Serdica* (Oxford: Oxford University Press, 2002).

Higgins, Tracey E., Jeanmarie Fenrich, and Ziona Tanzer, "Gender Equality and Customary Marriage: Bargaining in the Shadows of Post-Apartheid Legal Pluralism," *Fordham International Law Review* (2007): 1653–1708.

Hill, Christopher, *The World Turned Upside Down: Radical Ideas During the English Revolution* (New York: Viking Press, 1972).

Hill, Sir Richard, *The Blessings of Polygamy Displayed, in an Affectionate Address to the Rev. Martin Madan Occasioned by his Late Work, Entitled Thelyphthora or, A Treatise on Female Ruin* (London: J. Matthews, etc., 1781).

Hillerbrand, Hans J., *Landgrave Philipp of Hesse, 1504–1567: Religion and Politics in the Reformation* (St. Louis, MO: Foundation for Reformation Research, 1967).

Hillman, Eugene, "Polygamy and the Council of Trent," *The Jurist* 33 (1973): 358–376.

Polygamy Reconsidered: African Plural Marriage and the Christian Churches (Maryknoll, NY: Orbis Books, 1975).

Hittinger, Russell F., *The First Grace: Rediscovering the Natural Law in a Post-Christian World* (Wilmington, NC: ISI Publishers, 2003).

Holland, John, *The Smoke of the Bottomless Pit: A More True and Fuller Doctrine of those Men which call Themselves Ranters or the Mad Crew* (London: John Wright, 1651).

Holmes, Oliver Wendell, Jr., "Natural Law," *Harvard Law Review* 32 (1918): 40–44.

Holt, Andrew and James Muldoon, *Fighting Words: Competing Voices from the Crusades* (Westport, CT: Greenwood World Publishing, 2008).

Home, Henry, *Essays on the Principles of Morality and Natural Religion [1779]*, 3rd ed., Mary Catherine Moran, ed. (Indianapolis, IN: Liberty Fund, 2005).

Sketches of the History of Man, Considerably Enlarged by the Latest Additions and Corrections of the Author, James A. Harris, ed., 3 vols. (Indianapolis, IN: Liberty Fund, 2007).

Hooper, John, *The Ten Commandments* (Cambridge: Cambridge University Press, 1843).

Hopton, Andrew, ed., *Abiezer Coppe: Selected Writings* (London: Aporia Press, 1987).

Hostiensis, *Summa Aurea in titulos decretalium*, ed. and ann. Nicolas Superantii, repr. ed. (Aalen: Scientia Verlag, 1962).

Houlbrooke, Ralph, *Church and the People During the English Reformation 1520–1570* (Oxford: Oxford University Press, 1979).

Howard, George Elliott, *A History of Matrimonial Institutions*, 3 vols. (Chicago: University of Chicago Press, 1904).

Howell, T.B., ed., *A Complete Collection of State Trials and Proceedings for High Treason and Other Crimes and Misdemeanors from the Earliest Period to the Year 1783*, 42 vols. (London: T.C. Hansard et al., 1816).

Hruza, Ernst, *Polygamie und Pellikat nach Griechischem Rechte* (Erlangen/Leipzig: A. Deichert'sche Verlagsbuch, 1894).

Hughes, Paul L. and James F. Larkin, eds., *Tudor Royal Proclamations*, 3 vols. (New Haven, CT: Yale University Press, 1964–1969).

Hugo of St. Victor, *On the Sacraments of the Christian Faith*, Roy J. Deferrari, trans. (Cambridge, MA: The Medieval Academy of America, 1951).

Hull, N.E.H., *Female Felons: Women and Serious Crimes in Colonial Massachusetts* (Champaign-Urbana: University of Illinois Press, 1987).

Hulme, Peter and Tim Youngs, eds., *The Cambridge Companion to Travel Writing* (Cambridge: Cambridge University Press, 2002).

Hume, David, *Enquiries Concerning the Human Understanding and Concerning the Principles of Morals [1777]*, 2nd ed., L.A. Selby-Bigge, ed. (Oxford: Clarendon Pres, 1902, 2nd impr., 1963).

Essays Moral, Political, and Literary, rev. ed., Eugene F. Miller, ed. (Indianapolis, IN: Liberty Fund, 1987).

Hunter, David G., "Clerical Marriage East and West," in *Brill Companion to Priesthood in the Middle Ages* (forthcoming).

Marriage, Celibacy, and Heresy in Ancient Christianity: The Jovinianist Controversy (Oxford: Oxford University Press, 2007).

Marriage in the Early Church (Minneapolis, MN: Fortress Press, 1992).

"The Raven Replies: Ambrose, Letter to the Church at Vercelli (ep. ex. coll. 14) and the Criticisms of Jerome," in Andrew Cain and Josef Lössl, eds., *Jerome of Stridon: His Life, Writings and Legacy* (London: Ashgate, 2009), 175–189.

"Reclaiming Biblical Morality: Sex and Salvation History in Augustine's Treatment of the Hebrew Saints," in Paul M. Blowers et al., eds., *In Domino Eloquio/In Lordly Eloquence: Studies in Patristic Biblical Interpretation in Honor of Robert L. Wilken* (Grand Rapids, MI: William B. Eerdmans, 2002), 317–335.

Hunter, Ian, *The Secularization of the Confessional State: The Political Thought of Christian Thomasius* (Cambridge: Cambridge University Press, 2007).

Hürte, Norbert, *Jan Bockelson, gennant Johann von Leyden, die Wiedertäufliche-König im neuen Zion* (Reutlingen: Verlag von Fleischhauer und Spohn, 1854).

Hutcheson, Frances, *Logic, Metaphysics, and the Natural Sociability of Mankind*, James Moore and Michael Silverthorne, eds. (Indianapolis, IN: Liberty Fund, 2006).

Philosophiae Moralis Institutio Compendiaria, With a Short Introduction to Moral Philosophy, Luigi Turco, ed. (Indianapolis, IN: Liberty Fund, 2007).

Index Auctorum et Librorum (Rome: Ex officina Saluini, 1559), http://www.aloha.net/~mikesch/ILP-1559.htm#B.

Ingram, Martin, *Church Courts, Sex, and Marriage in England, 1570–1640* (New York/Cambridge: Cambridge University Press, 1987).

"Spousals Litigation in the English Ecclesiastical Courts, c. 1350–1640," in R.B. Outhwaite, ed., *Marriage and Society: Studies in the Social History of Marriage* (New York: St. Martin's Press, 1981), 35–57.

Innocent IV, *Commentaria: apparatus in V libros Decretalium (1570)*, repr. ed. (Frankfurt am Main: Minerva, 1968).

Institut Montaigne, "La polygamie en France: une fatalité"? (November 20, 2009), http://www.institutmontaigne.org/medias/documents/polygamie_en_france.pdf.

The Institutes of Gaius and Justinian: The Twelve Tables, and the CXVIIIth and CXXVIIth Novels, T. Lambert Mears, ed. (Clark, NJ: The Lawbook Exchange, 2004 [1882]).

Institutionum graeca paraphrasis Theophilo antecessori vulgo tributa ad fidem librorum manu, Cantadori Ferrini, ed. (Berolini: S. Calvary, 1884).

Iversen, Joan Smyth, *The Antipolygamy Controversy in U.S. Women's Movements, 1880–1925: A Debate on the American Home* (New York/London: Garland Publishing, 1997).

Jacobson, Cardell K. and Lara Burton, eds., *Modern Polygamy in the United States: Historical, Cultural, and Legal Issues* (Oxford/New York: Oxford University Press, 2011).

Jackson, Mark, *New-Born Child Murder: Women, Illegitimacy and the Courts in Eighteenth-Century England* (Manchester: Manchester University Press, 1996).

Jefferson, Thomas, *The Papers of Thomas Jefferson*, ed. Julian P. Boyd, 40 vols. (Princeton, NJ: Princeton University Press, 1950-1968).

The Works of Thomas Jefferson, P.L. Ford, ed., 12 vols. (New York: G.P. Putnam's Sons, 1904–1905).

Jerome, Against Jovinianus, in Philip Schaff and Henry Wace, eds., *A Select Library of Nicene and Post-Nicene Fathers of the Christian Church*, Second Series, repr. ed. (Grand Rapids, MI: William B. Eerdmans, 1952), 6:347–386.

Johnson, Luke Timothy, "Religious Rights and Christian Texts," in John Witte, Jr. and Johan D. van der Vyver, eds., *Religious Human Rights in Global Perspective: Religious Perspectives* (The Hague: Martinus Nijhoff, 1996), 65–96.

Johnson, William Stacy, *A Time To Embrace: Same-Gender Relationships in Religion, Law, and Politics* (Grand Rapids, MI: Wm. B. Eerdmans, 2007).

Jones, Timothy W., "The Missionaries' Position: Polygamy and Divorce in the Anglican Communion, 1888-1988," *Journal of Religious History* 35 (2011): 393–408.

Jordan, Mark D., ed., *Authorizing Marriage: Canon, Tradition, and Critique in the Blessing of Same-Sex Unions* (Princeton, NJ: Princeton University Press, 2006).

Blessing Same-Sex Unions: The Perils of Queer Romance and the Confusions of Christian Marriage (Chicago: University of Chicago Press, 2005).

The Invention of Sodomy in Christian Theology (Chicago: University of Chicago Press, 1997).

Josephus, Flavius, *Josephus in Nine Volumes*, Louis H. Feldman et al., trans. and eds. (Cambridge, MA: Harvard University Press, 1934–1965).

Joyce, G.H., SJ, *Christian Marriage: An Historical and Doctrinal Study*, 2nd ed. (London: Sheed and Ward, 1948).

A Justification of the Mad Crew in Their Waies and Principles (London: s.n., 1650).

Justin Martyr, "Dialogue with Typho," in *The Ante-Nicene Fathers: The Writings of the Fathers Down to A.D. 325*, Alexander Roberts, et al., trans. and eds., 10 vols., repr. ed. (Peabody, MA: Hendrickson Publishers, 1995), 1:194–270.

The Fathers of the Church: Saint Justin Martyr, Thomas B. Falls, trans. and ed. (Washington, DC: Catholic University Press of America, 1965).

"The First Apology," in *The Ante-Nicene Fathers: The Writings of the Fathers Down to A.D. 325*, Alexander Roberts, et al., trans. and eds., 10 vols., repr. ed. (Peabody: Hendrickson Publishers, 1995), 1: 159–187.

Justinian's Institutes, Paul Krüger, ed., Peter Birks and Grant McLeod, trans. (Ithaca, NY: Cornell University Press, 1987).

Kamen, Henry, *The Spanish Inquisition: An Historical Revision* (New Haven, CT/ London: Yale University Press, 1997).

Kanazawa, Satoshi and Mary C. Still, "Why Monogamy?" *Social Forces* 78 (1999): 25–50.

Kappeler, Peter M. and Joan B. Silk, *Mind the Gap: Tracing the Origins of Human Universals* (Berlin/New York: Springer, 2010).

Karras, Ruth Mazo, Joel Kaye, and E. Ann Matter, eds., *Law and the Illicit in Medieval Europe* (Philadelphia: University of Pennsylvania Press, 2008).

Katbamna, Maria, "Half a Good Man is Better than None," *The Guardian* (26 October 2009).

Kaufman, Brian W. and Christopher Huslak, "Polygamy State Law Case Analysis in the United States from 1860 to 1900" (unpublished report on file with the author).

Kaveny, Cathleen, *Law's Virtues: Fostering Autonomy and Solidarity in American Society* (Washington, DC: Georgetown University Press, 2012).

Kelly, Henry Ansgar, *The Matrimonial Trials of Henry VIII* (Palo Alto, CA: Stanford University Press, 1976).

Kelly, Lisa M., "Bringing International Human Rights Law Home: An Evaluation of Canada's Family Law Treatment of Polygamy," *University of Toronto Faculty of Law Review* 65 (2007): 1–38.

Kent, James, *Commentaries on American Law*, 4 vols. (New York: O. Halsted, 1826–1830).

Kern, Louis J., *An Ordered Love: Sex Roles and Sexuality in Victorian Utopias – The Shakers, the Mormons, and the Oneida Community* (Chapel Hill: University of North Carolina Press, 1995).

Kéry, Lotte, *Canonical Collections of the Early Middle Ages (ca. 400–1400)* (Washington, DC: Catholic University of America Press, 2000).

Kidd, Thomas S., *American Christians and Islam: Evangelical Culture and Muslims from the Colonial Period to the Age of Terrorism* (Princeton, NJ: Princeton University Press, 2009).

Kiesbye, Stefan, ed., *At Issue: Polygamy* (Detroit, MI: Greenhaven Press, 2013).

Kilbrie, Philip L. and Douglas R. Page, *Plural Marriage for our Times: A Reinvented Option?* 2nd ed. (Santa Barbara, CA: Praeger, 2012).

Kingdon, Robert M., *Adultery and Divorce in Calvin's Geneva* (Cambridge, MA: Harvard University Press, 1995).

    et al., eds., *Registres du Consistoire de Genève au Temps de Calvin*, 21 vols. (Geneva: Droz, 1996–).

Kinservik, Matthew J., *Sex, Scandal, and Celebrity in Late-Eighteenth-Century England* (New York: Palgrave, 2007).

Klaassen, Walter, *Anabaptism: Neither Catholic nor Protestant* (Waterloo, ON: Conrad Press, 1973).

    ed., *Anabaptism in Outline* (Scottdale, PA: Herald Press, 1981).

Knapp, Andrew and William Baldwin, *The New Newgate Calendar being Interesting Memories of Notorious Characters, Who Have been Convicted of Outrages on the Laws of England, During the Eighteenth Century*, 6 vols. (London: Albion Press, 1810).

Koch, Arnd, et al., eds., *Feuerbachs Bayerisches Strafgesetzbuch Die Geburt liberalen, modernen und rationalen Strafrechts* (Tübingen: Mohr Siebeck, 2014).

Kohler, Joseph and Willy Scheel, eds., *Die Peinliche Gerichtsordnung Kaiser Karls V: Constitutio Criminalis Carolina* (Halle: Buchhandlung des Waisenhauses, 1900).

Konner, Melvin A., *The Evolution of Childhood: Relations, Emotions, Mind* (Cambridge, MA: Harvard University Press, 2010).

    The Tangled Wing: Biological Constraints on the Human Spirit, rev. pbk. ed. (New York: Henry Holt, 2002).

Korpiola, Mia, *Between Betrothal and Bedding: Marriage Formation in Sweden 1200–1600* (Leiden/Boston: Brill, 2009).

    "Marriage Causes in Late Medieval Sweden: The Evidence of Bishop Hans Brask's Register (1522–27)," in Mia Korpiola, ed., *Regional Variations in Matrimonal Law and Custom in Europe, 1150–1600* (Brill Online: European History Culture, 2011), 212–247.

    "Rethinking Incest and Heinous Sexual Crime: Changing Boundaries of Secular and Ecclesiastical Jurisdiction in Late Medieval Sweden," in Anthony Musson, ed., *Boundaries of the Law: Geography, Gender, and Jurisdiction in Medieval and Early Modern Europe* (Aldershot: Ashgate, 2005), 102–117.

Korte, Barbara, *English Travel Writing*, Catherine Matthias, trans. (New York: Palgrave, 2000).

Krieger, Leonard, *The Politics of Discretion: Pufendorf and the Acceptance of Natural Law* (Chicago: University of Chicago Press, 1965).

Kritzeck, J., *Peter the Venerable and Islam* (Princeton, NJ: Princeton University Press, 1964).

Krusch, Bruno, "Liber Historiae Francorum," in Monumenta Germaniae historica: Scriptorum rerum Merovingicarum, vol. 2 (Hannover: Impensis Bibliopolii Hahniani, 1888).

Kuttner, Stefan, "Pope Lucius III and the Bigamous Archbishop of Palermo," in J.A. Watt, et al., eds., Medieval Studies: Presented to Aubrey Gwynn (Dublin: Colm o Lochlain, 1961), 409–451.

Kuttner, Stephan, Repertorium der Kanonistik (1140–1234) (Vatican City: Biblioteca apostolica vaticana, 1937).

Lactantius, Divine Institutes, in The Ante-Nicene Fathers: The Writings of the Fathers Down to A.D. 325, Alexander Roberts, et al., trans. and ed., 10 vols., repr. ed. (Peabody, MA: Hendrickson Publishers, 1995), 7:9–223.

Laeuchli, Samuel, Power and Sexuality: The Emergence of Canon Law at the Synod of Elvira (Philadelphia: Temple University Press, 1972).

Landau, Peter, Die Enstehung des kanonischen Infamiebegriffs von Gratian bis zur Glossa Ordinaria (Cologne: Böhlau, 1966).

Landes, Richard, The Varieties of the Millennial Experience (New York/Oxford: Oxford University Press, 2011).

Lang, Frieder R. and Karin L. Fingerman, eds., Growing Together: Personal Relationship Across the Lifespan (Cambridge: Cambridge University Press, 2004).

Langbein, John H., Prosecuting Crime in the Renaissance: England, Germany, France (Cambridge, MA: Harvard University Press, 1974).

Torture and the Law of Proof: Europe and England in the ancien régime (Chicago: University of Chicago Press, 1974).

Lape, Susan, "Solon and the Institution of the 'Democratic' Family Form," Classical Journal 98 (2002–2003): 117–139.

Latimer, Hugh, Sermons, George E. Corrie, ed. (Cambridge: Parker Society, 1844).

The Lawes Resolutions of Womens Rights, or, The Lawes Provision for Women (London: Assigns of John More, Esq., 1632).

Lawler, Michael G., Secular Marriage, Christian Sacrament (New York: Twenty-Third Publications, 1985).

Lawrence, William, Marriage by the Morall Law of God Vindicated [and] The Right of Primogeniture in Succession to the Kingdoms of England and Scotland (London: 1681).

Laws of the Commonwealth of Pennsylvania, 5 vols. (Philadelphia: John Bioren, 1810).

The Laws of Maryland, 3 vols. (Baltimore, MD: Philip H. Nicklin & Co., 1811).

Laws of the State of Maine, 2 vols. (Brunswick, ME: J. Griffin, 1821).

Laws of the State of Tennessee, Including those from North Carolina Now in force in this State, 2 vols. (Knoxville, TN: Heiskell & Brown, 1821).

The Laws Respecting Women as they Regard their Natural Rights (London: J. Johnson, 1777).

Lehmann, William C., Henry Home, Lord Kames, and the Scottish Enlightenment: A Study in National Character and in the History of Ideas (The Hague: Martinus Nijhoff, 1971).

Leigh, Edward, A Systeme or Body of Divinity, Consisting of Ten Books (London: A.M. for William Lee, 1654).

LeMahieu, D.L., William Paley: A Philosopher and His Age (Lincoln: University of Nebraska Press, 1976).

Leo, John, The History and Description, and of the Notable Things therein Contained, Robert Brown, ed., 3 vols. (Burlington, VT: Ashgate, 2010).

The History and Description of Africa, trans. John Pory (1600), in Andrew Hatfield, ed., *Amazons, Savages, and Machiavels: Travel and Colonial Writing in English, 1550–1630* (New York: Oxford University Press, 2001), 139–151.

Lesthaege, R.J., ed., *Reproduction and Social Organization in sub-Saharan Africa* (Berkeley: University of California Press, 1989).

Levine, Nancy E. and Walter H. Sangree, "Women With Many Husbands: Polyandrous Alliance and Marital Flexibility in Africa and Asia," *Journal of Comparative Family Studies* 11(3) (1980): 283–410.

Lewis, Ellis, *An Abridgement of the Criminal Law of the United States* (Philadelphia: Thomas, Cowperthwait, 1847).

Leyser, Johann, *Politischer Discursus zwischen Polygamo und Monogamo von der Polygamia oder Vielweiberey* (Freiburg: Apud Henricum Cunrath, 1676).

Leyser, Johann, pseud. Theophilo Aletheo, *Polygamia Triumphatrix* (Lund: n.p., 1682).

Lieber, Francis, *Essays on Property and Labor, as Connected with Natural Law and the Constitution of Society* (New York: Harper & Brothers, 1841).

Manual of Political Ethics, Designed Chiefly for the Use of Colleges and Students at Law, 2nd rev. ed., Theodore D. Woolsey, ed. (Philadelphia: J.B. Lippincott, 1890).

"The Mormons: Shall Utah be Admitted into the Union?" *Putnam's Monthly* 5 (March, 1855).

Lind, Göran, *Common Law Marriage: A Legal Institution for Cohabitation* (Oxford: Oxford University Press, 2008).

Lindsley, John Berrien, *On Prison Discipline and Penal Legislation: With Special Reference to the State of Tennessee* (Nashville, TN: Robertson Association, 1874).

Livingston, Edward, *A System of Penal Law for the State of Louisiana* (Philadelphia: James Kay, 1833).

Loader, William, *The New Testament on Sexuality* (Grand Rapids, MI: William B. Eerdmans, 2012).

Locke, John, *Essays on the Law of Nature*, W. von Leyden, ed. (Oxford: Clarendon Press, 1954).

A Letter Concerning Toleration and Other Writings, Mark Goldie, ed. (Indianapolis, IN: Liberty Fund, 2010).

Two Treatises on Government, Peter Laslett, ed. (Cambridge: Cambridge University Press, 1960).

The Works of John Locke, 10 vols. (London: Thomas Tegg, 1823).

Löffler, Klemens, *Die Wiedertäufer zu Münster, 1534–35: Berichte, Aussagung, und Aktenstücke von Augenzugen und Zeitgenossen* (Jena: Dietrichs, 1923).

Lombard, Peter, *The Sentences*, 4 vols. Giulio Silano, trans. (Toronto: Pontifical Institute of Medieval Studies, 2010).

Loughead, Lisa Shirley, *The Perception of Polygamy in Early Modern England* (Halifax, NS: Dalhousie University Press, 2008).

"The Perception of Polygamy in Early Modern England" (Ph.D. Diss., Dalhousie, 2008).

Lowy, S., "The Extent of Jewish Polygamy in Talmudic Times," *Journal of Jewish Studies* 9 (1958): 115–138.

Luscombe, Belinda, "I Do, I Do, I Do, I Do: Polygamy Raises its Profile in America, *Time: Health & Family* July 26, 2012, http://healthland.time.com/2012/07/26/i-do-i-do-i-do-i-do-polygamy-raises-its-profile-in-america.

Luther, Martin, *Martin Luther's Briefe, Sendschreiben und Bedenken*, Wilhelm Martin Leberecht de Wette, ed., 6 vols. (Berlin: G. Reimer, 1825–1828).

Luther: Letters of Spiritual Counsel, Theodore G. Tappert, ed. (Philadelphia: Westminster Press, 1955).

D. *Martin Luthers Werke: Briefwechsel*, 17 vols. (Weimar: Herman Böhlau, 1930–1983).

D. *Martin Luthers Werke: Kritische Gesamtausgabe*, 78 vols. (Weimar: Herman Böhlau, 1883–1987).

D. *Martin Luthers Sämtliche Werke, Briefweschsel*, Ernst L. Enders, ed., 19 vols. (Frankfurt am Main: Heyder und Zimmer, 1884–1932).

D. *Martin Luthers Werke: Tischreden*, 6 vols. (Weimar: Herman Böhlau, 1912–1921).

Luther's Works, 55 vols. Jaroslav Pelikan and Helmut T. Lehmann, trans. and eds. (St. Louis, MO: Concordia Publishing House, 1955–1968).

Lyon, Jonathan, *Islam Through Western Eyes: From the Crusades to the War on Terrorism* (New York: Columbia University Press, 2012).

MacCulloch, Diarmand, *Thomas Cranmer: A Life* (New Haven, CT: Yale University Press, 1996).

MacDonald, Kevin, "The Establishment and Maintenance of Socially Imposed Monogamy in Western Europe," *Politics and the Life Sciences* 14 (1995): 3–23.

Mackin, Theodore, *Marriage in the Catholic Church: Divorce and Remarriage* (New York: Paulist Press, 1984).

Marriage in the Catholic Church: The Marital Sacrament (New York: Paulist Press, 1989).

Marriage in the Catholic Church: What is Marriage? (New York: Paulist Press, 1982).

Madan, Martin, *Letters on Thelyphthora: With Occasional Prologue and Epilogue by the Author* (London: J. Dodsley, 1782).

Thelyphthora or, a Treatise on Female Ruin, in its Causes, Effects, Consequences, Prevent, and Remedy Considered on the Basis of the Divine Law, 2 vols. (London: J. Dodsley, 1781).

Maddern, Philippa, "Moving Households: Geographical Mobility and Serial Monogamy in England, 1350–1500," *Paregon* 24(2) (2007): 69–92.

Mahmood, Tahir, *Statute-Law Relating to Muslims in India* (New Delhi: Institute of Objective Studies, 1995).

Maitland, Frederic W., ed., *Select Passages From the Works of Bracton and Azo* (London: Barnard Quaritch, 1895).

Maimonides, Moses, *Mishne Torah Yad Hachzakah from The Book of Utterances, The Book of Agriculture, The Book of Purity, The Book of Damages, The Book of Acquisitions, The Book of Judgements, and The Book of Judges*, trans. Avraham Yaakov Finkel, 7 vols. (Scranton, PA: Yeshivath Beth Moshe, 2001).

Mäkinen, Virpi and Petter Korman, eds., *Transformations in Medieval and Early-Modern Rights Discourse* (Dordrecht: Springer, 2006).

Malthus, Thomas Robert, *An Essay on the Principles of Population* (London: John Murray, 1826).

Marasignhe, Laksham, "Conversion, Polygamy, and Bigamy: Some Comparative Perspectives," *Asia Pacific Law Journal* 4 (1995): 69–89.

March, Andrew F., "Is there a Right to Polygamy: Marriage, Equality, and Subsidizing Families in Liberal Public Justification," *Journal of Moral Philosophy* 8 (2011): 244–270.

Marchant, Ronald A., *The Church Under the Law: Justice, Administration, and Discipline in the Diocese of York 1560–1640* (Cambridge: Cambridge University Press, 1969).

Marchetto, Giuliano, "'Primus fuit Lamech': La bigamia tra irregolarità a delitto nella dottrina di diritto commune," in Silvana Seidel Menchi and Deigo Quaglioni, eds.,

Trasgessioni: Seduzione, concubinato, adulterio, bigamia (XIV-XVIII secolo) (Bologna: Il Mulino, 2004), 43–106.

Markel, Dan, Jennifer M. Collins, and Ethan J. Leib, *Privilege or Punish: Criminal Justice and the Challenge of Family Ties* (Oxford: Oxford University Press, 2009).

Maruyama, Tadataka, *The Ecclesiology of Theodore Beza: The Reform of the True Church* (Geneva: Droz, 1978).

Masnovo, Amato, *Da Gugliemo d'Auvergne a S. Tomasso d'Aquino*, 2nd ed., 3 vols. (Milan: Societa editrice Vita e Pensioro, 1945–1946).

Mason, Patrick Q., "Opposition to Polygamy in the Postbellum South," *Journal of Southern History* 76 (2010): 541–578.

Matthews, James M., *Digest of the Laws of Virginia of a Criminal Nature* (Richmond: West & Johnson, 1861).

May, Martha, "The 'Problem of Duty': Family Desertion in the Progressive Era," *Social Service Review* 62 (1988): 40–60.

Mayali, Laurent, "*'Duo erunt in carne una'*: and the Medieval Canonists," *in* Vincenzo Colli and Emanuele Conte, eds., *Iuris Historia: Liber Amicorum Gero Dolezalek* (Berkeley, CA: The Robbins Collection, 2008), 161–175.

McDermott, Rose and Jonathan Cowden, "Polygyny and its Effect on Violence Against Women, Children, and Within the State," in Lisa Fishbayn and Janet Bennion, eds., *The Polygamy Question* (Salt Lake City: University of Utah Press, 2015).

McDougall, Sara, *Bigamy and Christian Identity in Late Medieval Champagne* (Philadelphia: University of Pennsylvania Press, 2012).

"Bigamy: A Male Crime in Medieval Europe," *Gender and History* 22 (2010): 430–446.

"The Punishment of Bigamy in Late Medieval Troyes," *Medium Aevum* 3 (2009): 189–204.

McGlynn, Clare, *Families and the European Union: Law, Politics, and Pluralism* (Cambridge: Cambridge University Press, 2006).

McGoldrick, Dominic, "Accommodating Muslims in Europe: From Adopting Sharia Law to Religiously-Based Opt Outs from Generally Applicable Laws," *Human Rights Law Review* 9 (2009): 603–645.

McLaren, Anne, "Monogamy, Polygamy, and the True State: James I's Rhetoric of Empire," *History of Political Thought* 25 (2004): 446–480.

McNamara, Jo-Ann and Suzanne F. Wemple, "Marriage and Divorce in the Frankish Kingdom," in Susan Mosher Stuard, ed., *Women in Medieval Society* (Philadelphia: University of Pennsylvania Press, 1976), 95–124.

McNeill, John T., *The Celtic Penitentials and their Influence on Continental Christianity* (Paris: Librairie ancienne honoré champion, 1923).

McNeill, John T. and Helena M. Gamer, *Medieval Handbooks of Penance: A Translation of the Principal libri poenitentiales and Selections from Related Documents* (New York: Columbia University Press, 1990 [1938]).

McSheffrey, Shannon, *Marriage, Sex, and Civic Culture in Late Medieval London* (Philadelphia: University of Pennsylvania Press, 2006).

Meens, Rob, "The Frequency and Nature of Early Modern Penance," in Peter Biller and A.J. Minnis, eds., *Handling Sin: Confession in the Middle Ages* (York: The Medieval Press, 1998), 36–61.

Melanchthon, Philip, *Corpus Reformatorum: Melanchthons Werke*, 28 vols., Bretschneider, G., ed. (New York: Johnson Reprint Corp., 1963 [1864]).

Menander Rhetor, D.A. Russell and N.G. Wilson, trans. and eds. (Oxford: Oxford University Press, 1981).

Mendes, Isabel M. R., *Bigamia em Portugal na época moderna* (Libson: Hugin, 2003).

Menski, Werner, *Modern Indian Family Law* (Richmond, Surrey: Curzon Press, 2001).

Methodius, "The Banquet of the Ten Virgins," in *The Ante-Nicene Fathers: The Writings of the Fathers Down to A.D. 325*, Alexander Roberts, et al., trans. and eds., 10 vols., repr. ed. (Peabody, MA: Hendrickson Publishers, 1995), 6:309–355.

Meyendorff, John, "Christian Marriage in Byzantium," in *Dumbarton Oaks Papers* 44 (1990): 99–107.

Meyer, Paul, *Der römischen Konkubinat nach den Rechtsquellen und den Inschriften* (Leipzig: G.B. Teubner, 1895).

Mikat, Paul, *Die Polygamiefräge in der Neuzeit* (Opladen: Westdeutscher Verlag, 1988).

Miller, Leo, *John Milton Among the Polygamophiles* (New York: Loewenthal Press, 1974).

Milton, John, *Complete Prose Works of John Milton*, Don M. Wolfe, gen. ed., 7 vols. (New Haven, CT: Yale University Press, 1953–1980).

The Works of John Milton, 18 vols., Frank Allen Patterson, ed. (New York: Columbia University Press, 1931-1938).

Misztal-Konecka, Joanna, *Bigamia w prawie rzymskim* (Lublin: Wydawnictwo Kul, 2011).

Montagu, James, ed., *The Old Bailey Chronicle*, 4 vols. (London: S. Smith, 1788).

Montaigne, Ioannis, "Tractatus de utraque bigamia," in *Tractatus Universi Juris*, 16 vols. (Venice, 1584), vol. 9, folios 121v-132r.

Monter, E. William, "Crime and Punishment in Calvin's Geneva, 1562," in Richard C. Gamble, ed., *Calvin's Work in Geneva* (New York: Garland Publishing, 1992), 271–277.

Frontiers of Heresy: The Spanish Inquisition from the Basque Lands to Sicily (Cambridge: Cambridge University Press, 1990).

Montesquieu, *The Complete Works of Montesquieu*, 4 vols. (London: T. Evans, 1777).

Montorsi, William, ed., *Statuta Ferrari, Anno MCCLXXXVII* (Ferrara: Casa di risparmio di Ferrra, 1955).

Moore, Henry, *A Word to Mr. Madan or Free Thoughts on his Late Celebrated Defence of Polygamy* (Bristol: W. Pine, 1781).

Morgan, Edmund S., *The Puritan Family: Religion and Domestic Relations in Seventeenth Century New England*, rev. enl. ed. (New York: Harper & Row, 1966).

Morgan, Henry Lewis, *Ancient Society, Or Research in the Lines of Human Progress from Savagery Through Barbarism to Civilization* (New York: Henry Holt and Company, 1877).

Houses and House-Life of the American Aborigines (Chicago: University of Chicago Press, 1965 [1881]).

The Indian Journals, 1859–62, Leslie A. White, ed. (Ann Arbor: University of Michigan Press, 1959).

League of the Iroquois (New York: Corinth Books, 1851).

Systems of Consanguinity and Affinity of the Human Family (Washington, DC: Smithsonian Institution, 1868).

Morris, J.H.C., "The Recognition of Polygamous Marriages in English Law," *Harvard Law Review* 66 (1953): 961–1012.

Moryson, Fynes, "Fynes Moryson's Observations of the Ottoman Empire (1617)," in Andrew Hatfield, ed., *Amazons, Savages, and Machiavels* (Oxford: Oxford University Press, 2001) 166–178.

Motzki, Harald, "Marriage and Divorce," in Jane McAuliffe, ed., *Encyclopedia of the Qur'an* (Brill Online Reference Works: 2010).

Mruk, Antonius M., "Singularis opinion Gerardi Odonis, O.F.M., circa naturam divortii in casu adulterii," *Gregorianum* 14 (1960): 273–283.

Mühlegger, Florian, *Hugo Grotius, ein christlicher Humanist in politischer Verantwortung* (Berlin: de Gruyter, 2007).

Muldoon, James, *Popes, Lawyers, and Infidels: The Church and the Non-Christian World, 1250–1550* (Philadelphia: University of Pennsylvania Press, 1979).

The Americas in the Spanish World Order: The Justification for Conquest in the Seventeenth Century (Philadelphia: University of Pennsylvania Press, 1994).

ed., *The Spiritual Conversion of the Americas* (Gainesville: University Press of Florida, 2004).

Muncy, Raymond Lee, *Sex and Marriage in Utopian Communities: 19th-Century America* (Bloomington: Indiana University Press, 1973).

Murdock, George P., *Atlas of World Cultures* (Pittsburg, PA: University of Pittsburg Press, 1981).

Murray, Jacqueline, ed., *Love, Marriage, and Family in the Middle Ages: A Reader* (Toronto: Broadview Press, 2001).

Musonius Rufus: *The Roman Socrates*, Cora E. Lutz, trans. and ed. (New Haven, CT: Yale University Press, 1947).

Naphy, William G., *Calvin and the Consolidation of the Genevan Reformation* (Louisville, KY: Westminster John Knox Press, 1994).

Sex Crimes From Renaissance to Enlightenment (Stroud, Gloucestershire/Charleston, SC: Tempus Publishing, 2002).

Nedungatt, George and Michael Feathersone, eds., *The Council in Trullo Revisited* (Rome: Pontificio Istituto Orientale, 1995).

Neusner, Jacob and Bruce Chilton, ed., *The Golden Rule: The Ethics of Reciprocity in World Religions* (London: Continuum, 2008).

Neville, Henry, *The Isle of Pines* (London: T. Cadell, 1668).

Nichols, Joel A., ed., *Marriage and Divorce in a Multicultural Context: Multi-Tiered Marriage and the Boundaries of Civil Law and Religion* (Cambridge/New York: Cambridge University Press, 2012).

Noonan, John T., *Canons and Canonists in Context* (Goldbach: Keip, 1997).

"Who Was Rolandus?" in Kenneth Pennington and Robert Somerville, eds., *Law, Church, and Christian Society* (Philadelphia: University of Pennsylvania Press, 1977), 21–48.

Novak, David, *Natural Law in Judaism* (Cambridge: Cambridge University Press, 1998).

Oberholzer, Emil, *Delinquent Saints: Disciplinary Action in the Early Congregational Churches of Massachusetts* (New York: Columbia University Press, 1956).

Obermann, Heiko A., *The Roots of Anti-Semitism in the Age of Renaissance and Reformation* (Philadelphia: Fortress Press, 1984).

Ochino, Bernard, *A Dialogue on Polygamy, Written Originally in Italian* (London: John Garfield, 1657).

Senensis Dialogi XXX (Basel: P. Perna, 1563).

Oda, Hirishi, *Japanese Law*, 3rd ed. (Oxford: Oxford University Press, 2009).

Oden, Thomas, ed., *Ancient Christian Commentary on Scripture I: Genesis 1–11* (Downers Grove, IL: InterVarsity Press, 2002).

Ogden, Daniel, *Greek Bastardy in the Classical and Hellenistic Periods* (Oxford: Oxford University Press, 1996).

Polygamy, Prostitutes, and Death: The Hellenistic Dynasties (Swansea: Duckworth with the Classical Press of Wales, 1999).

"The Royal Families of Argead Macedon and the Hellenstic World," in Beryl Rawson, ed., *A Companion to the Families in the Greek and Roman World* (Oxford: Blackwell Publihsing, 2011), 92–107.

Origen, Commentary on Matthew, in *The Ante-Nicene Fathers: The Writings of the Fathers Down to A.D. 325*, Alexander Roberts, et al., trans. and eds., 10 vols., repr. ed. (Peabody, MA: Hendrickson Publishers, 1995), 10:412–512.

Homilies on Genesis and Exodus, Ronald E. Heine, trans. (Washington, DC: The Catholic University of America Press, 1982).

Osborne, Francis, *The Works of Francis Osborne*, 10th ed. (London: A. and J. Churchil, 1701).

Outhwaite, R.B., *Clandestine Marriage in England, 1500–1850* (London: Hambledon Press, 1995).

Pagden, Anthony, "Law, Colonization, Legitimation, and the European Background," in Michael Grossberg and Christopher Tomlin, eds., *The Cambridge History of Law in America*, 3 vols. (Cambridge: Cambridge University Press, 2008), 1:1–31.

Paley, William, *Principles of Moral and Political Philosophy [1785]*, D.L. LeMahieu, ed. (Indianapolis, IN: Liberty Fund, 2002).

Parish, Helen L., *Clerical Marriage and the English Reformation: Precedent, Policy, Practice* (Burlington, VT: Ashgate, 2000).

Parker, Stephen, *Informal Marriage, Cohabitation, and the Law 1750–1989* (New York: St. Martin's Press, 1990).

Parsons, Robert, S.J., *A Defence of the Censvre Gyven vpon Tvvo Bookes of William Charke and Meredith Hanmer, mynysters* (Rouen: Father Parsons Press, 1582).

Patterson, Cynthia B., *The Family in Greek History* (Cambridge, MA: Harvard University Press, 1998).

Paulus, N., "Cajetan und Luther über die Polygamie," *Historisches Politisches Blätter* 135 (1905): 95–100.

Payer, Pierre J., *Sex and the Penitentials: The Development of a Sexual Code 550–1150* (Toronto: University of Toronto Press, 1984).

Pearsall, Sarah, *Beyond One Man and One Woman: A History of Early American Polygamy* (forthcoming).

"'Having Many Wives' in Two American Rebellions: The Politics of Households and the Radically Conservative," *American Historical Review* 118 (October 2013): 1000–1028.

Pedersen, Frederik, "Marriage Contracts and the Church Courts of Fourteenth-Century England," in Philip L. Reynolds and John Witte, Jr., eds., *To Have and To Hold: Marrying and its Documentation in Western Christendom: 400–1600* (Cambridge: Cambridge University Press, 2007), 287–331.

Pelikan, Jaroslav, *Spirit versus Structure: Luther and the Institutions of the Church* (New York: Harper & Row, 1968).

Pennington, Kenneth, "The Growth of Church Law," in Augustine Casiday and Frederick W. Norris, eds., *The Cambridge History of Christianity, Vol. 2: Constantine to c. 600* (Cambridge: Cambridge University Press, 2008), 386–402.

Perdue, Leo G., et al., *Families in Ancient Israel* (Louisville, KY: Westminster John Knox Press, 1997).

Perkins, William, *The Works of that Famous and Worthy Minister of Christ in the University of Cambridge, M.W. Perkins* (London: John Legatt, 1613).

Perray, M. Michel du, *Traité des dispenses de mariage, de leur validité ou invalidité, et de l'état des personnes* (Paris: D. Beugnié, 1719).

Perry, John, *The Pretenses of Loyalty: Locke, Liberal Theory, and American Political Theology* (New York: Oxford University Press, 2011).

Perry, Marvin M. and Frederick M. Schweitzer, eds., *Jewish-Christian Encounters Over the Centuries* (New York: Peter Lang, 1984).

Perry, Michael J., *Constitutional Rights, Moral Controversy and the Supreme Court* (Cambridge: Cambridge University Press, 2009).

Human Rights in the Constitutional Law of the United States (Cambridge: Cambridge University Press, 2013).

Love and Power: The Role of Religion and Morality in American Politics (New York: Oxford University Press, 1991).

The Political Morality of Liberal Democracy (Cambridge: Cambridge University Press, 2010).

Peter, H.R.H. *Prince, A Study of Polyandry* (The Hague: Mouton & Co., 1963).

Phipps, Kelly Elizabeth, "Marriage and Redemption: Mormon Polygamy in the Congressional Imagination, 1662–1887," *Virginia Law Review* 95 (2009): 435–487.

Pike, Luke Owen, *A History of Crime in England*, 2 vols., repr. ed. (Montclair, NJ: Patterson Smith, 1968).

Pizarro, Claudia Ramirez, *Implicaciones civiles de la bigamia* (Bogota: Pontificia Universidad Javeriana, 1990).

Plane, Ann Marie, *Colonial Intimacies: Indian Marriage in Early New England* (Ithaca, NY: Cornell University Press, 2001).

Plato, *The Collected Dialogues of Plato, Including the Letters*, Edith Hamilton and Huntingdon Cairns, trans. and eds. (New York: Pantheon Books, 1961).

Symposium, Alexander Nehmans and Paul Woodruff, trans. (Indianapolis, IN: Hackett Publishers, 1989).

Plutarch, *Plutarch's Advice to the Bride and Groom and a Consolation to his Wife*, Sarah B. Pomeroy, ed. (New York: Oxford University Press, 1999).

Plutarch's Lives, Bernadotte Perrin, trans. (London: William Heinemann, 1928).

Plutarch's Moralia, L. Pearson, trans. (London: W. Heinemann, 1960).

Pocock, Nicholas, ed., *Records of the Reformation: The Divorce, 1527–1533*, 2 vols. (Oxford: Clarendon Press, 1870).

Pope, Stephen J., *Human Evolution and Christian Ethics* (Cambridge: Cambridge University Press, 2007).

Porter, Jean, *Ministers of the Law: A Natural Law Theory of Legal Authority* (Grand Rapids, MI: William B. Eerdmans, 2010).

Poska, Allyson M., "When Bigamy is the Charge: Gallegan Women and the Holy Office," in Mary E. Giles, ed., *Women and the Inquisition: Spain and the New World* (Baltimore, MD: The Johns Hopkins University Press, 1999), 189–207.

Posner, Richard A., *Sex and Reason* (Cambridge, MA: Harvard University Press, 1992).

Poudret, Jean François, *Coutumes et coutumieres: histoire comparative des droits des pays romands du XIIIe à la fin du XVIe siècle*, 5 vols. (Bern: Staempli Editions, 1998–2002).

Powell, Chilton L., *English Domestic Relations, 1487–1653* (New York: Russell & Russell, 1972 [1917]).

Pricke, Robert, *The Doctrine of Superioritie, and of Subjection, Contained in the Fifth Commandment of the Holy Law of Almightie God* (London: Ephraim Dawson & T. Downe, 1609).

Probert, Rebecca, *Family Law in England and Wales* (Alphen aan den Rijn: Kluwer Law International, 2012).

    Marriage Law and Practice in the Long Eighteenth Century: A Reassessment (Cambridge: Cambridge University Press, 2009).

Prompta, Lucius Ferrarius, *Bibliotheca canonica, juridica, morali, theologice*, 7 vols. (Venice: Gaspar Storti, 1782).

Pufendorf, Samuel von, *De Jure Naturae et Gentium libri octo*, C.H. Oldfather and W.A. Oldfather, trans. (Oxford: Clarendon Press, 1934).

    The Divine Feudal Law: Or, Covenants with Mankind Represented, Theophilus Dorrington, trans., Simone Zurbuchen, ed. (Indianapolis, IN: Liberty Fund, 2002).

    Elementorum Jurisprudentiae Universalis libri duo, W.A. Oldfather, trans., repr. ed. (New York: Oceana Publications, 1964).

    The Whole Duty of Man According to the Law of Nature, Andrew Tooke, trans., Ian Hunter and David Saunders, eds. (Indianapolis,IN: Liberty Fund, 2003).

Pulsipher, John David, "The Americanization of Monogamy: Mormons, Native Americans and the Nineteenth-Century Perception that Polygamy was a Threat to Democracy" (Ph.D. Diss., Minnesota, 1988).

Purchas, Samuel, *Pvrchas his Pilgrimes*, 4 vols. (London: William Stransby, 1625).

Quentin, Albrecht, *Naturkenntnisse und Naturanschauungen bei Wilhelm bei Auvergne* (Hildesheim: Gerstenberg, 1976).

Rankin, Hugh F., *Criminal Trial Proceedings in the General Court of Colonial Virginia* (Charlottesville: University Press of Virginia, 1965).

Raymond of Penyafort / S. Raimundus de Pennaforte, *Summa de iure canonico*, X. Ochoa and A. Diez, eds. (Rome: Commentarium pro religiosis, 1975).

Raymond of Penyafort, *Summa on Marriage*, Pierre J. Payer, trans. (Toronto: Pontifical Institute of Medieval Studies, 2005).

Reid, Charles J., Jr., *Power over the Body, Equality in the Family: Rights and Domestic Relations in Medieval Canon Law* (Grand Rapids, MI: William B. Eerdmans, 2004).

    "The Rights of Children in Medieval Canon Law," in Patrick M. Brennan, ed., *The Vocation of the Child* (Grand Rapids, MI: William B. Eerdmans, 2008), 243–265.

Reid, John Phillip, *The Law of Blood: The Primitive Law of the Cherokee Nation* (New York: New York University Press, 1970).

The Remarkable Trial of The Honourable James Stamp Sutton Cooke, Accused of Bigamy at the Old Bailey, on the 14th of April, 1812 (London: F. Marshall, 1823).

Reports of Cases at Law and in Chancery Argued and Determined in the Supreme Court of Illinois (Cambridge, MA: Harvard University Press, 1841).

Reports of the Prison Discipline Society, 3 vols. (Boston: T.R. Marvin, 1855).

Reynolds, Philip L., *Food and the Body: Some Peculiar Questions in High Medieval Theology* (Leiden/Boston: Brill Academic Press, 1999).

    Marriage in the Western Church (Leiden: Brill, 1994).

Reynolds, Philip L. and John Witte, Jr., eds. *To Have and to Hold: Marrying and its Documentation in Western Christendom, 400–1600* (Cambridge: Cambridge University Press, 2007).

Riccio, Stefano, *La Bigamia* (Naples: Dott. Eugenio Jovene, 1934).

Riedemann, Peter, *Account of our Religion, Doctrine, and Faith Given by Peter Riedemann of the Brothers Whom Men Call Hutterites*, Kathleen Hasenberg, trans., 2nd ed. (Rifton: Plough Publishing House, 1970).

Rinkens, Hubert, "Die Ehe und die Auffassung von der Natur des Menschen im Naturrecht bei Hugo Grotius (1583–1648), Samuel Pufendorf (1632–1694), und Christian Thomasius (1655–1728)" (Ph.D. Diss., Frankfurt am Main, 1971).

Rivoire, Emile and Victor van Berchem, eds., *Les sources du droit du canton de Genève*, 4 vols. (Aarau: H.R. Sauerlander 1927–1935).

Robertson, A.J., ed., *The Laws of the Kings of England from Edmund to Henry I* (Cambridge: Cambridge University Press, 1925).

Robinson, Hastings, ed., *Original Letters Relative to the English Reformation* (Cambridge: Cambridge University Press, 1846).

Rockwell, William W., *Die Doppelehe des Landgrafen Philipp von Hessen* (Marburg: N.G. Elwert'sche Verlagsbuchhandlung, 1904).

Rogers, Daniel, *Matrimoniall Honour* (London: Philip Nevil, 1642).

Rolker, Christof, *Canon Law and the Letters of Ivo of Chartres* (Cambridge: Cambridge University Press, 2010).

Roscoe, Henry, A *Digest of the Law of Evidence in Criminal Cases*, 3rd. Am. ed., T.C. Granger, ed. (Philadelphia: T. & J.W. Johnson, 1846).

Ross, Ian Simpson, *Lord Kames and the Scotland of his Day* (Oxford: Oxford University Press, 1972).

Rothman, Bernhardt, et al., *Bekenntnise von beyden Sacramenten, Dope und Nachtmaele der Predikanten tho Munster* (Münster: Rothman, 1533).

Rothman, Bernhard, *Die Schriften Bernhard Rothmanns*, Robert Stupperich, ed. (Münster: Aschendorff, 1970).

Rufinus, *Summa Decretorum*, Heinrich Singer, ed. (Aalen: Scientia Verlag, 1963).

Russell, William O., A *Treatise on Crimes and Misdemeanors*, 2 vols. (Boston: Wells and Lilly, 1824).

Saaed, Abdullah, "Reflections on the Establishment of Shari'a Courts in Australia," in Rex Ahdar and Nicholas Aroney, eds., *Sharia in the West* (Oxford: Oxford University Press, 2010), 223–239.

Sabatini, Rafael, *Torquemada and the Spanish Inquisition* (London: Stanley Paul, 1924), 168.

Saldaña, José Aguilar, *El delito de bigamia y su responsabilidad penal* (Mexico City: UNAM, Facultad de Derecho y Ciencias Sociales (Tesis de Licenciatura), 1955).

Salmon, Thomas, A *Critical Essay Concerning Marriage* (London: Charles Rivington, 1724).

Sánchez, Alberto Arteaga, *De los delitos contra las buenas costumbres y buen orden de la familias* (Caracas: Editorial Juridica Alva, 1989).

Sanchez, Thomas, *De sancto matrimonii sacramento disputationun tomi tres* (Antwerp: Heredes Martinii Nutii et Ioannem Meurisum, 1617).

Sandberg, Russell, et al., "Britain's Religious Tribunals: 'Joint Governance' in Practice," *Oxford Journal of Legal Studies* 33 (2013): 263–291.

Sandirocco, Luigi, "Binae Nupitae et Bina Sponsalia," *Studia et Documenta Historiae et Iuris* 70 (2004): 165–216.

Satlow, Michael L., *Jewish Marriage in Antiquity* (Princeton, NJ: Princeton University Press, 2001).

Saurez, Francisco, *Selections from Three Works*, 2 vols. (Buffalo, NY: William S. Hein, 1995).

Savage, Gail, "More than One Mrs. Mir Anwaruddin: Islamic Divorce and Christian Marriage in Early Twentieth-Century London," *Journal of British Studies* 47 (2008): 348–374.

Scaramella, Pierroberto, "Controllo e repression ecclesiastica della poligamia a Napoli in età moderna: dalle cause matrimoniali al crimine di fede (1514–1799), in Silvana Seidel

Menchi and Deigo Quaglioni, eds., *Trasgessioni: Seduzione, concubinato, adulterio, bigamia (XIV-XVIII secolo)* (Bologna: Il Mulino, 2004), 443–501.

Schachar, Ayelet, "Faith in Law? Diffusing Tensions Between Diversity and Equality," in Joel A. Nichols, ed., *Marriage and Divorce in a Multicultural Context: Multi-Tiered Marriage and the Boundaries of Civil Law and Religion* (Cambridge/New York: Cambridge University Press, 2012), 357–378.

Schadt, H. "Die Arbores Bigamiae als heilsgeschichtliche Schemata: Zum Verhältnis von Kanonistik und Kunstgeschichte," in *Kunst als Bedeutungsträger: Gedenkschrift für Günter Bandmann* (Berlin: Gebr. Mann, 1978), 129–147.

Scheidel, Walter, "A Peculiar Institution?: Greco-Roman Monogamy in Global Context," *The History of the Family* 14 (2009): 280–291.

"Monogamy and Polygyny," in Beryl Rawson, ed., *A Companion to Families in the Greek and Roman Worlds* (Malden, MA: Blackwell, 2011), 108–115.

Schlözer, August Ludwig von, *Die Wiedertäufer in Münster: Geschichte des Schneider- und Schwärmer-Königs Jan van Leyden Anno 1535* (Cologne: Kirchner, 1919).

Schmoeckel, Mathias, "Fall 6: Der lotharische Ehestreit: Seine Protaganisten und ihre Perspektiven," in U. Falk, M. Luminati, and M. Schmoeckel, eds., *Fälle aus der Rechtsgeschichte* (Munich: Beck, 2008), 77–95.

Schneegaas, Elias, pseud. *Antonius de Mara, Monogamia Triumphans* (Brunswick: n.p., 1696).

Schneider, Carl, "The Channelling Function in Family Law," *Hofstra Law Review* 20 (1992): 495–532.

Schnur Harry C., *Mystic Rebels: Apollonius Tyaneus – Jan van Leyden – Sabbatai – Zevi-Cagliostri* (New York: Beechhurst, 1949).

Schochet, G.J., *Patriarchalism in Political Thought: The Authoritarian Family and Political Speculation and Attitudes Especially in Seventeenth Century England* (New York: Basic Books, 1975).

Schremer, Adiel, "How Much Jewish Polygny in Roman Palestine?" *Proceedings of the American Academy for Jewish Research* 63 (1997–2001): 181–223.

Schroeder, H.J., *Councils and Decrees of the Council of Trent* (St. Louis, MO: B. Herder Book Co., 1941).

Disciplinary Decrees of the General Councils: Text, Translation, and Commentary (St. Louis, MO: B. Herder Book Co., 1937).

Schwartzberg, Beverly J., "Grass Widows, Barbarians, and Bigamists: Fluid Marriage in Late Nineteenth-Century America" (Ph.D. Diss. University of California, Santa Barbara, 2001).

Schwartzberg, Beverly, "'Lots of Them Did That': Desertion, Bigamy, and Marital Fluidity in Late-Nineteenth-Century America," *Journal of Social History* 37 (2004): 573–600.

Scott, James Brown, *The Spanish Origins of International Law: Volume 1, Francisco de Vitoria and his Law of Nations* (Oxford: Oxford University Press, 1934).

Scott, S.P., ed., *The Civil Law* 7 vols., repr. ed. (New York: AMS Press, 1973).

Scotus, John Duns, *On Bigamy, Ordinatio IV distinction 33, q. 1*, A. Vos, et al., trans. (Washington, DC: Research Group John Duns Scotus, 2010).

Searle, Mark and Kenneth W. Stevenson, *Documents of the Marriage Liturgy* (Collegeville, MN: The Liturgical Press, 1992).

Sears, Hal D., *The Sex Radicals: Free Love in High Victorian America* (Lawrence: The Regents Press of Kansas, 1977).

Seeger, Cornelia, *Nullité de mariage divorce et séparation de corps a Genève, au temps de Calvin: Fondements doctrinaux, loi et jurisprudence* (Lausanne: Société d'histoire de la Suisse romande, 1989).

Seibenhüner, Kim, *Bigamie und Inquisition in Italien 1600–1750* (Paderborn: Ferdinand Schöningh, 2006).

Selden, John, *Uxor Ebraica: seu, De nuptiis et divortiis ex jure civili, id est divino et Talumudico veterum ebraeorum libri tres* (Frankfurt an der Oder: Sumptibus Jeremiae Schreii, 1673).

Select Trials at the Session-House in the Old-Bailey for Murder, Robberies, Rapes, Sodomy, Coining, Frauds, Bigamy, and other Offences, 4 vols. (London: J. Applebee, 1742).

Semmes, Raphael, *Crime and Punishment in Early Maryland* (Baltimore, MD: Johns Hopkins University Press, 1938).

Seutonius Tranquillus, *The Lives of the Twelve Caesars*, Alexander Thomson, trans., T. Forester, rev. ed. (London: George and Sons, 1890).

The Seven Ecumenical Councils, Philip Schaff and Henry Wace, trans. and eds. (New York: Charles Scribner's Sons, 1900).

Serra, Antonio Truyol, ed., *The Principles of Political and International Law in the Work of Francisco de Vitoria* (Madrid: Ediciones Cultura Hispanica, 1946).

Sextus Pompeius Festus, *De verborum significatu quae supersunt cum Pauli epitome*, ed. Wallace Martin Lindsay (Leipzig: Teubner, 1913).

Shanley, Mary, "Marriage Contract and Social Contract in Seventeenth Century English Political Thought," *Western Political Quarterly* 32 (1979): 79–91.

Sharpe, J.A., *Crime in Seventeenth-Century England: A County Study* (Cambridge: Cambridge University Press, 1983).

Sharrock, Robert, *Judicia seu legume censurae de variis incontentiae, speciesbus adulterio, polygamia & concubinatu, fornication, stupor, raptu, peccatis contra naturam, incest & gradibus prohibitis* (Oxford: H. Hall, 1662).

Sheehan, Michael, "The Formation and Stability of Marriage in Fourteenth Century England: Evidence of an Ely Register," *Medieval Studies* 33 (1971): 228–263.

Marriage Family and Law in Medieval Europe: Collected Studies, J.K. Frage, ed. (Toronto: University of Toronto Press, 1996).

Shelford, Leonard, *A Practical Treatise on the Law of Marriage and Divorce* (London: S. Sweet, 1841).

Shepherd, L.D., "The Impact of Polygamy on Women's Mental Health: A Systematic Review," *Epidemiology and Psychiatric Sciences* 22 (2013): 47–62.

Sherwin, Oscar, "Madan's Cure-all," *The American Journal of Economics and Sociology* 22 (2006): 427–433.

Sigman, Shanya M., "Everything Lawyers Know About Polygamy is Wrong," *Cornell Journal of Law and Public Policy* 16 (2006): 101–185.

Simons, Menno, *The Complete Writings*, Leonard Verduin, trans., John C. Wenger, ed. (Scottdale, PA: Herald Press, 1956), 560.

Singular, Stephen, *When Men Became Gods: Mormon Polygamist Warren Jeffs, His Cult of Fear, and the Women Who Fought Back* (New York: St. Martin's Press, 2013).

Siricius, Michael, *Uxor Una: Ex Jure Naturae et Divino, Moribus Antiquis et Constitutionibus Imperatorum et Regnum. Eruta et Contra Insultus Impugnantium Defensa* (Giessen: Typis et sumptibus Josephi Dieterici Hampelii, 1669).

Skotnicki, Andrew, *Criminal Justice and the Catholic Church* (Lanham, MD: Rowman Littlefield, 2008).

Slatyer, William, *The Compleat Christian, and the Compleat Armour and Armoury of a Christian* (London: n.p., 1643).

Smearman, Claire A., "Second Wives' Club: Mapping the Impact of Polygamy in U.S. Immigration Law," *Berkeley Journal of International Law* 27 (2009): 382–447.

Smith, Adam, *Lectures on Jurisprudence*, R.L. Meek, D.D. Raphael, and P.G. Stein, eds. (Indianapolis, IN: Liberty Fund, 1978).

Smith, George D., *Nauvoo Polygamy* (Salt Lake City, UT: Signature Books, 2011).

Smith, John, *Polygamy Indefensible: Two sermons… Occasioned by a Late Publication, entitled "Thelyphthora"* (London: Alexander Hogg, 1780).

Smith, Linda F., "Child Protection Law and the FLDS Raid in Texas," in Cardell K. Jacobson and Lara Burton, eds., *Modern Polygamy in the United States: Historical, Cultural, and Legal Issues* (Oxford/New York: Oxford University Press, 2011), 301–330.

Smith, Preserved, "German Opinion of the Divorce of Henry VIII," *English Historical Review* 27 (1912): 671–681.

Smith, Stephen Eliot, "Barbarians within the Gates: Congressional Debates on Mormon Polygamy: 1850-1879," *Journal of Church and State* 51 (2009): 587–616.

Snyder, C. Arnold, *Anabaptist History and Theology* (Kitchener, ON: Pandora Press, 1995).

Song, Sara, *Justice, Gender, and the Politics of Multiculturalism* (Cambridge: Cambridge University Press, 2007).

Spalding, James C., ed., *The Reformation of the Ecclesiastical Laws of England, 1552* (Kirksville, MO: Sixteenth Century Journal Publishers, 1992).

Spanheim, Friedrich, *Dubia Evangelica in tres partes distributa* (Geneva: Sumptibus Petri Chouët, 1639).

Spurlock, John, *Free Love: Marriage and Middle-Class Radicalism in America, 1825–1860* (New York: New York University Press, 1988).

Socrates Scholasticus, *The Ecclesiastical History of Socrates, Surnamed Scholasticus or the Advocate* (London: George Bell and Sons, 1874).

Sokol, Mary, "Jeremy Bentham on Love and Marriage," *American Journal of Legal History* 30 (2009): 1–21.

Sommerville, J.P., ed., *King James VI and I: Political Writings* (Cambridge: Cambridge University Press, 1994).

Stegmüller, Frederic, *Repertoriorum commentarium in Sententias Petri Lombardi*, 2 vols. (Würzburg: Ferdinandum Schoningh Bibliopolam, 1947).

Stephen, James Fitzjames, *A History of the Criminal Law of England*, 3 vols. (London: MacMillan, 1883).

Stone, Lawrence, *Road to Divorce A History of the Making and Breaking of Marriage in England* (New York/Oxford: Oxford University Press, 1995).

Uncertain Unions (Oxford: Oxford University Press, 1992).

Story, Joseph, *Commentaries on the Conflict of the Laws, Foreign and Domestic, In Regards to Contracts, Rights, and Remedies, and Especially in Regard to Marriages* (Boston: Hilliard Gray, 1834).

Strassberg, Maura, "The Crime of Polygamy," *Temple Political and Civil Rights Law Review* 12 (2003): 353–431.

"Distinctions of Form or Substance: Monogamy, Polygamy, and Same-Sex Marriage," *North Carolina Law Review* 75 (1996–1997): 1501–1624.

"The Challenges of Post-Modern Polygamy: Considering Polyamory," *Capital Law Review* 31 (2003): 439–563.

Strauss, Gregg, "Is Polygamy Inherently Unequal?" *Ethics* 122 (2013): 516–544.

Strohm, Christoph, *Calvinismus und Recht* (Tübingen: Mohr Siebeck, 2008).

Strype, John, *The Life and Acts of John Whitgift* (London: T. Horne et al., 1718).

Memorials of Archbishop Cranmer, 3 vols. (Oxford: T. Combe, 1848).

Swinburne, Henry, *A Treatise of Spousals or Matrimonial Contracts* (London: S. Roycroft, 1686).

Talbot, C.H., ed. and trans.,*The Anglo-Saxon Missionaries in Germany* (London: Sheed and Ward, 1954).

Taylor, Charles, *A Secular Age* (Cambridge, MA: Belknap Press, 2007).

Tertilt, Michèle, "Polygny, Fertility, and Savings," *Journal of Political Economy* 113 (2005): 1341–1371.

Tertilt, Michèle, "Polygyny, Women's Rights, and Development," *Journal of the European Economic Association* 4 (2006): 523–530.

Tertullian, "An Exhortation to Chastity," in *The Ante-Nicene Fathers: The Writings of the Fathers Down to A.D. 325*, Alexander Roberts, et al., trans. and eds., 10 vols., repr. ed. (Peabody, MA: Hendrickson Publishers, 1995), 4:50–58.

"On Baptism," in *The Ante-Nicene Fathers: The Writings of the Fathers Down to A.D. 325*, Alexander Roberts, et al., trans. and eds., 10 vols., repr. ed. (Peabody, MA: Hendrickson Publishers, 1995), 3:669–679.

"On Monogamy," in *The Ante-Nicene Fathers: The Writings of the Fathers Down to A.D. 325*, Alexander Roberts, et al., trans. and eds., 10 vols., repr. ed. (Peabody, MA: Hendrickson Publishers, 1995), 3:59–73.

"To His Wife," in *The Ante-Nicene Fathers: The Writings of the Fathers Down to A.D. 325*, Alexander Roberts, et al., trans. and eds., 10 vols., repr. ed. (Peabody, MA: Hendrickson Publishers, 1995), 4:39–49.

Textor, Johann Wolfgang, *Synopsis of the Law of Nations*, John P. Bate, trans. (Washington, DC: Carnegie Institution, 1916).

Thaler, Richard and Cass Sunstein, *Nudge: Improving Decisions About Health, Wealth, and Happiness* (New Haven, CT: Yale University Press, 2008).

Thaner, Friedrich, ed., *Die Summa Magistri Rolandi nachmals Papst Alexander III* (Innsbruck: Verlag von Wagner'schen Universitäts-Buchhandlung, 1874).

Thomas, Donald, *A Long Time Burning: A History of Literary Censorship in England* (New York: Praeger, 1969).

Thomasius, Christian, *Institutes of Divine Jurisprudence With Selections from Foundations of the Law of Nature and Nations*, Thomas Ahert, trans. and ed. (Indianapolis, IN: Liberty Fund, 2011).

Institutiones jurisprudentiae divinae, in positiones succincte contractae in quibus hypotheses illustris Puffendorfi circa doctrina juris naturalis apodicti demonstrantur & corroborantur (Frankfurt and Leipzig: Sumptibus Mauritii Georgii Weidmanni, 1688).

Schediasma inaugurali juridicum de Concubinatu (Halle?: n.p., 1713).

Thomasius, Christian and Georg Beyer, *De Bigamie Praescriptione* (Leipzig: Johannis Georgi, 1685).

De Crimine Bigamiae: Vom Laster der zwiefachen Ehe (Leipzig: Johannis Georgi, 1715).

Thompson, John L., "Patriarchs, Polygamy, and Private Resistance: John Calvin and Others on Breaking God's Rules," *Sixteenth Century Journal* 25 (1994): 3–27.

Thorpe, Benjamin, ed., *Ancient Laws and Institutes of England*, repr. ed. (Clark, NJ: The Lawbook Exchange, 2003 [1840]).

Tierney, Brian, *The Idea of Natural Rights: Studies on Natural Rights, Natural Law, and Church Law, 1150–1625* (Grand Rapids, MI: William B. Eerdmans, 1997).

Liberty and Law: The Idea of Permissible Natural Law, 1100–1800 (Washington, DC: Catholic University Press of America, 2014).

"Sola Scriptura and the Canonists," *Studia Gratiana* 11 (1967): 347–366.

Tolan, John Victor, *Petrus Alfonsi and his Medieval Readers* (Gainesville: University Press of Florida, 2003).

Torres, Elvira Coralia Esparza, *El delito de bigamia* (Mexico City: n.p., 1961).

Torres, Juana, "De epístolas privadas a cánones privadas a cánones disciplinarios: las 'cartas canónicas' de Basilo de Cesarea," in *Lex et religio, Studia Ephemeridis Augustinianum* (Rome: Istituto Augustiniano, 2013), 437–446.

Towers, John, *Polygamy Unscriptural or Two Dialogues between Philalethes and Monogamus, in which the Principal Errors of the First and Second editions of the Revd. Mr. M-d-n's Thelyphthora are Detected*, 2nd ed. (London: Alex. Hogg, et al., 1781).

Trani, Gottofredo, *Summa super titulis decretalium (1519)*, repr. ed. (Aalen: Scientia Verlag, 1968).

Trapp, John, *A Commentary or Exposition upon the Four Evangelists* (London: A.M., 1647).

Trasmiera, Diego Garzia de, *De Polygamia et Polyviria libri tres* (Palermo: Apud Decium Cyrillum, 1638).

Treggiari, Susan, *Roman Marriage: Iusti coniuges From the Time of Cicero to the Time of Ulpian* (Oxford: Oxford University Press, 1991).

Tresniowski, Alex, "This is Home," *People Magazine* (March 23, 2009).

The Trial of Elizabeth Duchess Dowager of Kingston for Bigamy (London: Charles Bathurst, 1776).

The Trial of Robert Fielding, Esq. on Wednesday, December 4, 1706, in the Fifth Year of the Reign of Queen Anne (London: R. Snagg, Fleet Street, 1736).

The Trials of all the Felon Prisoners, Tried, Cast, and Condemned, This Session at the Old Bailey (London: n.p., 1798).

Tuller, Roger, "Bigamy in the Indian Territory, 1878–1890," *West Texas Historical Association Year Book* 68 (1992): 100–112.

Tyerman, Christopher, *God's War: A New History of the Crusades* (Cambridge, MA: Harvard University Press, 2006).

Valazza, Marie-Ange Tricarico, "L'officialité de Genève et quelque cas de bigamie à la fin du moyen âge: l'empêchement de lien," *Zeitschrift für schweizerische Kirchengeschichte* 89 (1995): 99–118.

Van der Vyver, Johan D., "Multi-Tiered Marriages in South Africa," in Joel A. Nichols, *Marriage and Divorce in a Multicultural Context: Multi-Tiered Marriage and the Boundaries of Civil Law and Religion* (Cambridge/New York: Cambridge University Press, 2012), 200–219.

Van Drunen, David, *Natural Law and the Two Kingdoms: A Study in the Development of Reformed Social Thought* (Grand Rapids, MI: William B. Eerdmans, 2010).

Vangelisti, Anita L. and Daniel Perlman, eds., *The Cambridge Handbook of Personal Relationships* (Cambridge: Cambridge University Press, 2006).

The Visigothic Code (Forum Iudicum), S.P. Scott, trans. (Boston: The Boston Book Company, 1910).

Vives, José, *Concilios visigóticus e hispano-romanos* (Barcelona: Consejo Superiod de Investigaciones Científicas, Instituto Enrique Flórez, 1963).

Vleeschouwers-van Melkebeek, Monique, "Marital Breakdown Before the Consistory Courts of Brussels, Cambrai, and Tournai: Judicial Separation a mensa et thoro," *Tijdschrift voor Rechtsgeschiedenis* 72 (2004): 81–89.

"Self-Divorce in Fifteenth-Century Flanders: The Consistory Court Accounts of the Diocese of Tournai," *Tijdschrift voor Rechtsgeschiedenis* 68 (2000): 83–98.

Wagoner, R.S. van, *Mormon Polygamy: A History*, 2nd ed. (Salt Lake City, UT: Signature Books, 1989).

Waldron, Jeremy, *"Nonsense Upon Stilts": Bentham, Burke, and Marx on the Rights of Man* (London/New York: Methuen, 1987).

Wall, John, et al., eds., *Marriage, Health and the Professions* (Grand Rapids, MI: William B. Eerdmans Publishing Co., 2002).

Walton, F.P., *Scot Marriages: Regular and Irregular* (Edinburgh: W. Green & Sons, 1893).

Watson, Alan, *The Law of Succession in the Later Roman Republic* (Oxford: Clarendon Press, 1991).

Weber, David J., *The Spanish Frontier in North America* (New Haven, CT: Yale University Press, 1992).

Weigand, Rudolf, *Die bedingte Eheschliessung im kanonischen Recht* (Munich: M. Hueber, 1963).

Die Naturrechtslehre die Legisten und Dekretisten von Irenaeus bis Johannes Teutonicus (Berlin: Hueber, 1967).

Weikart, Richard, "Marx, Engels, and the Abolition of the Family," *History of European Ideas* 18 (1994): 657–672.

Welchman, Lynn, ed., *Women's Rights and Islamic Family Law* (London/New York: Zed Books, 2004).

Weissman, Jennifer, "Killing Anti-Bigamy Laws Softly: Not to Prosecute Polygamy Must be Abandoned" (forthcoming).

Wemple, Suzanne Fonay, *Women in Frankish Society: Marriage and the Cloister 500–900* (Philadelphia: University of Pennsylvania Press, 1981).

Westerman, Claus, *Genesis 1–11: A Commentary*, trans. J.J. Scullion, S.J. (Minneapolis, MN: Augsburg Publishing House, 1984).

Westermarck, Edward, *The History of Human Marriage* (London/New York: MacMillan, 1891).

Wharton, Francis, *Treatise on the Criminal Law of the United States*, 4th ed. (Philadelphia: Kay and Bros., 1857).

A Treatise on the Criminal Law of the United States, 7th rev. ed., 3 vols. (Philadelphia: Kay and Bros., 1874).

Whitmore, William H., ed., *Colonial Laws of Massachusetts: Reprinted from the Edition of 1672* (Boston: Rockwell and Churchill, 1890).

The Widowes Lamentation for the Absence of their Deare Children and Suitors (London: s.n., 1642).

Willet, Andrew, *Hexapla* (London: n.p., 1611).

William of Auvergne, *Guilielmi Alverni Opera Omnia*, 2 vols. (Paris: 1674 repr. ed., Frankfurt am Main: G.m.b.H., 1963).

Williams, George Huntson, *The Radical Reformation*, 3rd ed. (Kirksville, MO: Sixteenth Century Journal Publishers, 1992).

Williams, Rowan, "Archbishop's Lecture – Civil and Religious Law in England: A Religious Perspective," (Feb. 7, 2008), http://www.archbishopofcanterbury.org/1575#.

Wills, Thomas, *Remarks on Polygamy &c. in Answer to the Rev. Mr. M-d-n's Thelypthora* (London: T. Hughes and F. Walsh R. Baldwin and W. Otridge, 1781).

Wilson, Robin Fretwell, ed., *Reconceiving the Family: Critique of the American Law Institute's "Principles of the Law of Family Dissolution"* (Cambridge: Cambridge University Press, 2006).

Wines, Frederick H., *Report of the Defective, Dependent, and Delinquent Classes of the Population of the United States as Returned at the Tenth Census, June 1, 1880*, repr. ed. (New York: Norman Ross Publishing, 1991).

Report on Crime, Pauperism and Benevolence in the United States at the Eleventh Census, repr. ed. (New York: Norman Ross Publishing, 1995).

Wing, Adrien Katherine, "Polygamy in Black America," in Adrien Katherine Wing, ed., *Critical Race Feminism: A Reader*, 2nd ed. (New York: New York University Press, 2003), 186–194.

Wing, John, *The Crown Conjugall or, The Spouse Royall* (London: John Beale for R. Mylbourne, 1632) (STC 25845).

Winroth, Anders, *The Making of Gratian's "Decretum"* (Cambridge: Cambridge University Press, 2000).

Winstanley, Gerrard, *The Law of Freedom in a Platform, or True Magistracy Restored*, R.W. Kenny, ed. (New York: Schocken Books, 1941).

Witte, John, Jr., *From Sacrament to Contract: Marriage, Religion, and Law in the Western Tradition*, 2nd ed. (Louisville, KY: Westminster John Knox Press, 2011).

God's Joust, God's Justice: Law and Religion in the Western Tradition (Grand Rapids, MI: William B. Eerdmans, 2006).

Law and Protestantism: The Legal Teachings of the Lutheran Reformation (Cambridge: Cambridge University Press, 2002).

"Law, Religion, and Metaphor Theory" (forthcoming).

The Reformation of Rights: Law, Religion, and Human Rights in Early Modern Calvinism (Cambridge: Cambridge University Press, 2007).

The Sins of the Fathers: The Law and Theology of Illegitimacy Reconsidered (Cambridge: Cambridge University Press, 2009).

Witte, John, Jr., and Frank S. Alexander, eds., *Christianity and Human Rights: An Introduction* (Cambridge: Cambridge University Press, 2010).

Witte, John, Jr., and M. Christian Green, eds., *Religion and Human Rights* (Oxford/ New York: Oxford University Press, 2012).

Witte, John, Jr., and Robert M. Kingdon, *Sex, Marriage and Family in John Calvin's Geneva*, 2 vols. (Grand Rapids, MI: William B. Eerdmans, 2005, 2015).

Witte, John, Jr. and Johan D. van der Vyver, eds., *Religious Human Rights in Global Perspective: Religious Perspectives* (The Hague: Martinus Nijhoff, 1996).

Wolf, Erik, *Grosse Rechtsdenker der deutschen Geistesgeschichte*, 4th ed. (Tubingen: J.C.B. Mohr, 1963).

Wollstonecraft, Mary, *A Vindication of the Rights of Woman* [1791], repr. ed. (Oxford: Oxford University Press, 2008).

Zeiten, Miriam Koktvedgaard, *Polygamy: A Cross-Cultural Analysis* (Oxford/ New York: Berg, 2008).

Zhishman, Jos., *Das Eherecht der orientalischen Recht* (Vienna: Wilhelm Braumüller, 1864).

Index of Biblical Citations

General Index

Aboriginal peoples, polygamy among, 10
abortion, penance for, 119
"Absalom and Achitopel" (Dryden), 329
Act in Restraint of Appeals of 1533 (England), 205
Act of 1753, Lord Hardwicke' (England)
    polygamy under, 317–318
    shotgun weddings under, 319
Act of Succession of 1533 (England), 205
Adam of Bremen, 125
Adams, Thomas, 312
adultery
    Beza on, 257–258
    under Christian canon law, 118
    Christian condemnation of, 70, 103
    Lactantius on, 84
    under Mosaic law, 63
    Paley on, 383–384
    penance for, 119, 124
    of Philip of Hesse, 214
    polygamy as, 273
    under Roman law, legal charges for, 110
    as sexual vice, 80
Advice to a Son (Osborne), 327
Africa, polygamy in, 282–283, 444n2
African Americans. *See also* miscegenation laws,
    in U.S.
    appellate court cases and, racism as factor in,
        413–414
    Bureau of Refugees, Freedman, and
        Abandoned Lands for, 426
    campaign against polygamy among, 426
    Marriage Covenant for, 426
    polygamy during slave era, 160
Albert the Great, 170
Alexander, Eva, 409
Alexander of Hales, 164

Alfasi (Rabbi), 59
Alfonso X, 157
alimony, 298n83
Ambrosiaster, 96, 136
Ames, William, 280
Ami (Rabbi), 57
Anabaptists
    Blood Friends and, 220
    Catholic Church and, 218–219
    Christerie for, 220
    Ochino defense of, 224–238
    polygamy among, 200, 218–223
    Protestant Reformation and, 224–225, 239
    Protestantism and, 218–219
    strict monogamy for, 219
ancient Greece. *See* Greece, ancient
ancient Israel. *See* Israel, ancient
Ancient Society (Morgan), 424
Anderson, Susan, 314
Anglican Church, 239
    Book of Common Prayer, 393, 397
    disestablishment of, 325
    in U.S., 393
Anglicus, Alanus, 151n25
Anglo-Saxons, polygamy for, 114
annulment, of marriages, 297–298, 395
Apostolic Canons, 134
appellate courts, U.S., polygamy charges in,
    407–416
    against African Americans, 413–414
    comity principle and, 414–415
    for foreign marriages, 414
    intrastate marriages and, 414–415
    racism as factor in, 413–414
    religious rights arguments for, 416
Aquinas, Thomas. *See* Thomas Aquinas

Polygamy Triumphant (Leyser), 337, 339
polygyny. *See also* Mormons
  adultery and, 63
  Aquinas on, 172–173
  children and, 453–454
  defined, 28–29
  Enlightenment liberalism and, 387
  for procreation, 452–453
  resource, 125–126
  women and, 453–454
porno-Utopian literature, 330
Potier, Denis, 267–269
power, polygamy for, 43–44
precontract cases, 291–293
Pricke, Robert, 287
"priesthood of all believers" doctrine, 76
priests, 49n73, 139
Probert, Rebecca, 305
procreation
  monogamous marriage for, 375–376
  natural law of, 165, 170–175
  natural pair-bonding strategies of, 170–175
  paternal certainty and, 171–172, 192–193
  polygamy for, 40–43, 166–168, 192
  polygyny as natural form of, 452–453
  through surrogacy, 211n33
prostitution
  as immoral, 68–69, 70
  penance for, 124
Protestant Reformation movement
  Anabaptists and, 224–225, 239
  Anglican Church after, 239
  Calvinists after, 239
  Catholic Church and, theoretical break
    from, 198
  clerical bigamy and, 198–199
  divorce after, 199
  immediate changes to church, 197
  Luther as influence on, 197–201
  marriage and, new norms for, 198, 239
  new civil laws as result of, 198
  polygamy during, 199–201
  remarriage after, 199
  sexuality and, new norms as part of, 198
Protestantism, 71. *See also* Beza, Theodore;
    Calvin, John; civil law
  Anabaptist's separation from, 218–219
  back-to-back engagements and, 264–266
  clerical bigamy within, 189
  engagement contracts and, 267–269
  engagements while married in, 266–267

rejection of clerical bigamy, 73
rejection of polygamy, 200–201
remarriage for, 72
successive polygamy rejected by, 71
in U.S., marriage models influenced by,
  392–394
Prussian Civil Code, 13
Purchas, Samuel, 284

quasi-polygamy, 30–31. *See also* constructive
  polygamy
Qumran community, 49
Qur'an, 19

Raba, 57
Rabbis. *See also specific rabbis*
  acceptance of polygamy by, 36, 52–55, 64
  on levirate marriage, 53–55
racism, in prosecution of polygamy, 413–414
Rapin, Pierre, 266
Raymond of Penyafort, 153, 179
real polygamy. *See* polygamy
Reancourt, Thomasse de, 267
Rebout, Antoine, 271
Redkison, Eliza, 314
Reformation of Ecclesiastical Law, 279, 296
religion. *See also* Catholic Church; Christianity;
    Judaism; Mormons; Protestantism;
    theological utilitarianism
  arguments against polygamy, 174–175, 278–285
  disestablishment of, 350, 351
  Second Great Awakening of, 429
remarriage. *See also* successive polygamy
  Aquinas on, 173–174, 185
  for Basil the Great, 121, 134–136
  Beza on, 254–255, 258
  Calvin on, 253
  in Catholicism, 72
  charivari after, 184, 194
  under Christian canon law, 117, 118, 121, 134–136
  Church Fathers on, 93–97
  clergy blessings for, restrictions on, 184
  after desertion, 122, 134–136, 141–142
  after divorce, 70–71, 76–77, 96–97, 121
  Locke on, 366
  during Medieval period, 182–186, 194–195
  negative social response to, 184
  in New Testament texts, 70–72, 121, 141, 142
  in Orthodox Christianity, 72, 136–137
  Paley on, 384–385
  papal dispensation for, 202, 203